VICTIMS, POLICY-MAKING AND CRIMINOLOGICAL THEORY

PIONEERS IN CONTEMPORARY CRIMINOLOGY

Series Editor: David Nelken

The titles in this series bring together the best published and unpublished work by the leading authorities in contemporary criminological theory. By drawing together articles from a wide range of journals, conference proceedings and books, each title makes readily available the authors' most important writings on specific themes. Each volume in this series includes a lengthy introduction, written by the editor and a significant piece of scholarship in its own right, which outlines the context of the work and comments on its significance and potential. The collected essays complement each other to give a retrospective view of the authors' achievements and a picture of the development of criminology as a whole.

Titles in the series

Working Out of Crime
David Downes

Criminological Forays and Skirmishes
David Greenberg

Victims, Policy-making and Criminological Theory
Paul Rock

Essays on Transnational Crime and Policing
James Sheptycki

Thinking about Punishment
Michael Tonry

Victims, Policy-making and Criminological Theory

Selected Essays

PAUL ROCK
London School of Economics and Political Science, UK

PIONEERS IN CONTEMPORARY CRIMINOLOGY SERIES

ASHGATE

Published by
Ashgate Publishing Limited
Wey Court East
Union Road
Farnham
Surrey GU9 7PT
England

Ashgate Publishing Company
Suite 420
101 Cherry Street
Burlington, VT 05401-4405
USA

Ashgate website: http://www.ashgate.com

ISBN 978-0-7546-2926-9

British Library Cataloguing in Publication Data
Rock, Paul Elliot.
Victims, policy-making and criminological theory : selected essays. – (Pioneers in contemporary criminology)
1. Criminology.
I. Title II. Series
364–dc22

US Library of Congress Control Number: 2009909619

Mixed Sources
Product group from well-managed forests and other controlled sources
www.fsc.org Cert no. SGS-COC-2482
© 1996 Forest Stewardship Council
FSC

Printed and bound in Great Britain by
TJ International Ltd, Padstow, Cornwall

Paul Rock

Contents

Acknowledgements

The chapters in this volume are taken from the sources listed below. The author and publishers wish to thank the original publishers or other copyright holders for permissions to use their material as follows:

Chapter 1: 'Observations on Debt Collection', *British Journal of Sociology*, **19**, 1968, pp. 176–90. Copyright © 1968 London School of Economics and Political Science.

Chapter 2: 'Some Problems of Interpretative Historiography', *British Journal of Sociology*, **27**, 1976, pp. 353–69. Copyright © 1976 London School of Economics and Political Science.

Chapter 3: 'Law, Order and Power in Late Seventeenth and Early Eighteenth Century England', *Annales Internationales de Criminologie*, **16**, 1977, pp. 233–65. Copyright © 1977 The International Society of Criminology.

Chapter 4: 'Governments, Victims and Policies in Two Countries', *British Journal of Criminology*, **28**, 1988, pp. 44–66. Copyright © 1988 Paul Rock. Published by Oxford University Press.

Chapter 5: 'The Present State of Criminology in Britain', *British Journal of Criminology*, **28**, 1988, pp. 58–69. Copyright © 1988 Paul Rock. Published by Oxford University Press.

Chapter 6: 'Witnesses and Space in a Crown Court', *British Journal of Criminology*, **31**, 1991, pp. 266–79. Copyright © 1991 Paul Rock. Published by Oxford University Press.

Chapter 7: 'Introduction: The Emergence of Criminological Theory', *History of Criminology*, Aldershot: Dartmouth, 1994, pp.xi–xxix.

Chapter 8: 'The Social Organization of a Home Office Initiative', *European Journal of Crime, Criminal Law and Criminal Justice*, **2**, 1994, pp. 141–67. With kind permission of Koninklijke Brill NW.

Chapter 9: 'The Opening Stages of Criminal Justice Policy Making', *British Journal of Criminology*, **35**, 1995, pp. 1–16. Copyright © 1995 Paul Rock. Published by Oxford University Press.

Chapter 10: 'Sociology and the Stereotype of the Police', *Law and Society*, **22**, 1995, pp. 17–25. Copyright © 1995 Wiley/Blackwell.

Chapter 11: 'Murderers, Victims and "Survivors": The Social Construction of Deviance', *British Journal of Criminology*, **38**, 1998, pp. 185–200. Copyright © 1998 Paul Rock. Published by Oxford University Press.

Chapter 12: 'Victims, Prosecutors and the State in Nineteenth Century England and Wales', *Criminal Justice*, **4**, 2004, pp. 331–54. Copyright © 2004 Sage Publications.

Chapter 13: 'Chronocentrism and British Criminology', *British Journal of Sociology*, **56**, 2005, pp. 473–91. Copyright © 2005 London School of Economics and Political Science.

Chapter 14: 'Aspects of the Social Construction of Victims in Australia', *Victims and Offenders*, **1**, 2006, pp. 289–321. Copyright © 2006 Taylor & Francis Group.

Chapter 15: (With Tim Newburn) 'Urban Homelessness, Crime and Victimisation in England', *International Review of Victimology*, **13**, 2006, pp. 121–56. Copyright © 2006 A B Academic Publishers.

Chapter 16: 'The Treatment of Victims in England and Wales', *Policing*, **2**, 2008, pp. 1–10. Copyright © 2008 Paul Rock. Published by Oxford University Press.

Every effort has been made to trace all the copyright holders, but if any have been inadvertently overlooked the publishers will be pleased to make the necessary arrangement at the first opportunity.

Introduction

I came to criminology, as so many of my contemporaries did, as a matter of chance and contingency rather than through clear-sighted, long-nursed and well-informed ambition (see Holdaway and Rock, 1998). I had intended to enrol on a course in demography (it was a rather tenuous interest in that field that had impelled me to apply to read for a degree in sociology at the London School of Economics between 1961 and 1964) but, when I discovered more about its substance and methods, I baulked at the statistics and elected, *faut de mieux*, to study criminology instead, knowing next to nothing about what it might be.

Criminology had been introduced to the School by Hermann Mannheim, a member of the Law Department since 1935,[1] a major *emigré* scholar who had produced incisive and sociologically informed analyses of the social organization and contexts of crime (and, in particular, his *Social Aspects of Crime in England between the Wars*, 1940). But his conception of criminology as a general enterprise followed what had been established almost from the outset in Britain (see Garland, 1988). It was a *rendez-vous* discipline (in David Downes' phrase) that stemmed variously from law, philosophy, penal and legal reform, psychiatry, criminal anthropology, sociology, political economy and administration, and its character was manifest in the very diverse men he took to stand as its pioneers.[2] His teaching mirrored that eclecticism. Criminology was, he said, 'far from secure' (Mannheim, 1960, p. 1). It was an *entrepôt* of intellectual languages and methodologies; 'multi-factorial' and 'multi-causal' in its stance; rooted in medicine, physiology and biology; informed both by simple intellectual curiosity and a practical drive to ameliorate, correct and reform; defined principally by its attention to a substantive entity rather than by a unifying body of theory (see Rafter, 2009 and Rock, Chapter 7, this volume), and sometimes appearing to drift towards what C. Wright Mills (1959) once described as abstracted empiricism. In 1938–39, his 'Principles of Criminology' course at the LSE was a *potpourri* that consisted of:

> I. The meaning, methods and tasks of Criminology. The use of Criminal Statistics. History and present character of crime in England and abroad. II. The criminal types and the causes of crime: (1) Physical factors: the anthropological theory (Lombroso).

---

[1] Hermann Mannheim, 1889–1974, was the subject of an obituary by Leon Radzinowicz in *The Dictionary of National Biography*, which was reprinted in Rock (1988, pp. 18–19). He was appointed an honorary part-time lecturer at the LSE in 1935, and became a full-time lecturer in 1944 and a reader in 1945. He retired in 1955. See, too, Roger Hood's article on Mannheim's role at the LSE (2004).

[2] In his introduction to *Pioneers in Criminology* (1960, p. 1) he reflected, '… many of those included may not have regarded themselves as criminologists at all, but rather as lawyers, psychiatrists, sociologists, administrators or architects, who happened to be interested in crime and criminals. ... With some slight over-simplification it might well be said that most criminologists are still inclined to think of themselves in terms of the discipline in which they took their first university examinations …'

> The biological theory. The significance of physical defects. (2) Psychological and pathological factors: the intelligence of the criminal. Insanity and mental deficiency. The psychoanalytical explanation … (3) Alcoholism. Climate. Race and Religion. (4) The age factor … (5) The sex factor: Female delinquency and prostitution. (6) Social and economic factors: Family, broken homes, housing, delinquency areas … The gang. Profession and Unemployment. Poverty. Economic and political crisis.

In 1962 the programme of criminology through which I was led by Eryl Hall Williams, also of the Law Department, was an echo of that scheme, although it did also accommodate his special interest in penology and penal reform (see Hall Williams, 1970, 1975, 1978, 1982):

> Conception of crime. Functions and methods of criminology. Criminal types and causal factors in crime: physical, psychological, social and economic factors. Special problems; juvenile and female delinquency. Penal philosophy and psychology, especially meaning and objects of punishment. Penal history. The modern English penal system and the criminal courts. Problems of crime prevention.

To be sure, Terence Morris, a member of the Sociology Department and one of its graduates,[3] also taught at the School, and he was opening up a dedicated sociological criminology, inspired in part by his apprenticeship as one of Mannheim's last graduate students and by his acquaintance with Henry McKay of the University of Chicago and Donald Cressey of the University of California. Morris's work was embedded in functionalist anomie theory (Morris and Morris, 1963), the ecological studies of the 'Chicago School' (Morris, 1957) and a strong reformist instinct, Fabian in character and modulated by religious sentiment that drove him to play a part in the campaigns for the abolition of capital punishment (Morris and Blom-Cooper, 1964) and the alleviation of prison conditions. Morris was to exercise an intellectual influence on me (he personified my first proper acquaintance with criminology as sociologically defined) as well as acting as a patron and sponsor at an important turning point, propelling me to Nuffield College, Oxford, where I was to study for a D.Phil under Nigel Walker.[4] But it was at Hall Williams's knee that my learning was formally acquired, and it was for his seminar that I read a succession of prescribed writings: Taft's *Criminology*; Reckless's *The Crime Problem*; the Gluecks's *Unravelling Juvenile Delinquency*; Tappan's *Juvenile Delinquency*; Healy and Bronner's *New Light on Delinquency and its Treatment*; Wootton's *Social Science and Social Pathology*; Cloward and Ohlin's *Delinquency and Opportunity* and much else.

---

[3] Morris graduated in sociology with a major option in social anthropology in 1953 and taught at the LSE from 1955 to 1995. He was for a time a vice-president of the Howard League for Penal Reform and served as a member of the Longford Committee, which advised Harold Wilson, later prime minister, on penal and legal reform immediately before the return of the first Wilson administration.

[4] At the time, Reader in Criminology at the University of Oxford. Subsequently he became the Wolfson Professor of Criminology at the University of Cambridge. He was the author of a number of works, including major textbooks (1965, 1987). His autobiography, *A Man Without Loyalties*, was published in 2003.

At the same time, and in parallel, I was being fired by a more private, almost clandestine, independent and rather random reading of works on crime and criminology lodged in the British Library of Political and Economic Science – the LSE library. I read about *thuggi*, pirates, New York fighting gangs, Chicago police officers, medieval bandits and the Bow Street Runners. I read the autobiographies of police officers and criminals (for example, Hill, 1955, Sharpe, 1929; Wildeblood, 1955). I read Henry Mayhew and Henry Fielding. And I read the works of the sociologists who had worked in and around the University of Chicago at the beginning of the twentieth century: Burgess, Cressey, Goffman, Hughes, Landesco, Lindesmith, McKay, Park, Shaw, Sutherland, Wirth and Foote Whyte.

I was not alone. Outside the formal confines of the lecture and seminar, a hedge school had begun to emerge amongst sociology students, including Frances Heidensohn[5] (then Doherty), Phil Hughes[6] and Jock Young.[7] We were effectively autodidacts, piecing together for ourselves what seemed to be the beginnings of a more vibrant and immediate sociology of the here-and-now, a sociology coursing out of a social anthropology of the city that focused on what, to a little-travelled student, appeared to be the fascinating life-worlds of criminals, delinquents and police officers, largely in an American setting. It worked through irony, paradox and what Gouldner once called 'perspective through incongruity' – the use of familiar perspectives to examine unfamiliar settings, and of unfamiliar perspectives to examine the familiar (Everett Hughes once remarked that 'the comparative student of man's work learns about doctors by studying plumbers, and prostitutes by studying psychiatrists' (1971, p. 342)). It was an approach that at times contrasted markedly with the official curriculum of LSE Sociology in the early 1960s.

That department was loosely bifurcated into the proponents of a high theory that was infused on occasion by the moral or political passion of a Bottomore (see 1965), Gellner (see 1959) or Ginsberg (see 1944, 1968); and of a Fabian social democratic project that dwelled, sometimes a little too closely and attentively, on social, policy and political problems of class inequality, education and social mobility (see Dahrendorf, 1995; Glass, 1954; Halsey, 2004; Westergaard and Resler, 1975). John Martin reflected that 'the department was split between the theoreticians led by Ginsberg and the empiricists led by Glass. Most of the latter were involved in the classic studies of social mobility then under way' (1988, p. 38).

The maverick sociological criminology that we, as students, discussed (and were perhaps forging) thus came to represent to me a possible third way:[8] an escape, on the one hand, from

[5] Heidensohn was to take a teaching appointment at the London School of Economics, and then at Goldsmiths College, University of London, where she became Professor of Social Policy. She pioneered feminist criminology, particularly in her article on 'The Deviance of Women' (1968) and enlarged in her book *Women and Crime* (1985), and the sociology of the police (1992).

[6] Phil Hughes left England to read for a PhD at the University of New Mexico. He was an avid reader, revelling in his own Homeric phrases (he would talk frequently about 'Mr Urmson on grading', for example), who spoke sociology, and symbolic interactionism especially, as a second language.

[7] Jock Young was to become an innovative criminologist, variously a 'new' criminologist, 'critical' criminologist, 'left realist' and 'cultural' criminologist. He taught initially at Enfield Polytechnic (later Middlesex University), then at the University of Kent at Canterbury and subsequently at John Jay College, New York.

[8] I exaggerate. There were, of course, major exceptions, and Ron Dore's lectures on 'The Social Structure of Modern Japan' were a thrilling example.

the tedium and phenomenological sterility of the grand abstractions purveyed by the works of those whom Jason Ditton once called 'some dead Victorian gentlemen' – the holy trinity of Marx, Weber and Durkheim, and by the lesser theorists, Hobhouse, Wheeler, Ginsberg, Westermarck, Wittfogel, Pareto and Parsons; and, on the other hand, an escape from the Blue Book sociology of Bowley, Beales, Carr-Saunders, McGregor, Glass, Floud, Halsey and others.

Criminology became a priest-hole or refuge: it seemed slightly *risqué*,[9] colourful, accessible, a celebration of what, in some instances, would become labelled a sociology of the absurd (Lyman and Scott, 1970) – a respite from the earnestness, loftiness, overly schematic abstraction, preaching and bookishness of sociology proper.[10] Criminology, as the ethnography of everyday life, was absorbing and fun; it was inductive rather than deductive; simply and accessibly written rather than opaque and portentous;[11] exploratory rather than declaratory; it had a phenomenological authenticity and humility lacking elsewhere; and it did not condescend to its subjects or talk *de haut en bas* of people's false consciousness, rationalizations and ideology or of society's latent functions.[12] I was moved to persevere and entered Nuffield College, Oxford, where I began to work for a D.Phil degree.

I have described elsewhere the state of criminology at the University of Oxford in the mid-1960s (Rock, 2007). Academic criminology was no more than a fledgling discipline nationally,[13] and there were but three research students, Kit Carson,[14] Dogan Akman[15] and

9 A little unfairly, perhaps, Gouldner wrote at the time of the emergent sociology of deviance that: 'This group of Chicagoans finds itself at home in the world of hip, Norman Mailer, drug addicts, jazz musicians, cab drivers, prostitutes, night people, drifters, grifters and skidders, the cool cats and their kicks. To be fully appreciated this stream of work cannot be seen solely in terms of the categories conventionally employed in sociological analysis. It has also to be seen from the viewpoint of the literary critic as a style or genre and particularly as a species of naturalistic romanticism' (Gouldner 1962, p. 209).

10 In their turn, it was not always well regarded by those who taught us (see Gellner, 1975, for example).

11 See Howard Becker's admirable strictures on how to write sociology (1986).

12 William James was moved to reflect that: 'It is the personal experience of those best qualified in our circle of knowledge to *have* experience, to tell us *what is*. Now what does *thinking about* the experience of those persons come to, compared to directly and personally feeling it as they feel it? The philosophers are dealing in shades, while those who live and feel know truth.' (James,1949, p. 30).

13 There were minute outcrops in Bedford, Birkbeck and University Colleges at the University of London and in the Universities of Glasgow, Leicester, Liverpool, Manchester and Nottingham, and larger but still small enough numbers of criminologists at the London School of Economics and the Universities of Oxford and Cambridge.

14 W.G.O. Carson ('Kit') moved first to Bedford College, then to the Universities of Exeter and Edinburgh, before emigrating, first to Australia, where he was to become Professor of Legal Studies, Dean of Social Sciences and then Deputy Vice-Chancellor of La Trobe University, and New Zealand, where he was to be Vice-Chancellor of the University of Auckland. He pioneered historical and sociological studies of crime and regulation.

15 Dogan Akman returned to North America where he undertook criminological research, collaborating with Normandeau, Sellin and Wolfgang, for example, on the measurement of crime and crime seriousness (see Ackman and Normandeau, 1967; Ackman *et al.*, 1968), and then turned to the law, becoming a Crown Counsel.

me, in the discipline at Oxford when I entered in 1964. There were too few of us to form a critical mass, although there *was* a regular seminar, founded by Max Grünhut[16] and labelled 'Crime: A Challenge', to which outside speakers were invited.

As graduate students, we were again obliged to be autodidacts, independently assembling homespun theoretical syntheses to give meaning, purpose and order to research, and our resources were threefold. As novices in what was regarded as a marginal and somewhat *declassé* discipline (Professor Max Beloff of All Souls College insisted on my slowly, repetitively and clearly spelling its name when I presented myself before him to 'upgrade' from probationer B.Litt to D.Phil status), we were necessarily driven centrifugally towards Oxford's better-established and better-organized intellectual worlds – towards philosophy, politics and the new social history that was beginning to flower in the History Workshop and the journal, *Past and Present*, under the suzerainty, at Oxford, of Raphael Samuel and, beyond, of Eric Hobsbawm and Edward Thompson.[17] Some of my more interesting and consequential conversations were to be with fellow-students from that burgeoning world of social history: Pat Hollis,[18] Gareth Stedman-Jones[19] and Gill Sutherland.[20] It was there that I came to acquire an abiding interest in history, although I lacked the professional competence to pursue it thoroughly (see Rock, Chapters 3 and 12, this volume). For a discussion of some of the analytic tangles I encountered in attempting to write history as a would-be phenomenologist, see my essay reprinted as Chapter 2 of this volume).

The second resource was the beginnings of a modest network, an invisible college (De Solla Price, Derek and Beaver, 1966) of research students in Oxford and beyond, and I shall touch on it again. And a third resource was the books and journals that were stumbled upon, sometimes haphazardly in bookshops, sometimes in conversation with members of that network. Kit Carson recommended that I should read the works of Edwin Lemert (especially 1951), and Lemert's conception of primary and secondary deviation was revelatory. I stumbled across Becker's year-old *Outsiders* (1963) in Blackwell's bookshop and Stan Cohen,[21] then a research student at the London School of Economics, and I celebrated it together.

Some part of *Outsiders* had originally appeared in *The American Journal of Sociology* and *Social Problems,* the official journal of the Society for the Study of Social Problems, of which Howard Becker was to become president. In 1965 I opened a subscription to *Social Problems,*

---

16 Max Grünhut, 1893–1964, was one of the three *emigrés* who established criminology in England and Wales (see Hood, 2004). He was the first Reader in Criminology at the University of Oxford

17 Kit Carson, himself a history graduate, was drawn there to develop a distinctive voice as a social historian of crime and regulation lodged in an analysis of class conflict and class accommodation (see Carson, 1974, 1980, 1985).

18 Later Baroness Hollis. She was to become a teacher at the University of East Anglia in Norwich from 1967 until 1990, and has written extensively on women's history and labour history.

19 Stedman-Jones's research topic was the casual labour problem in London, later published as *Outcast London* (1971). He was appointed Professor of Political Science at the University of Cambridge in 1997.

20 Sutherland researched the social history of education and, subsequently, nineteenth- and twentieth-century British history. Now retired, she was to become Director of Studies in History at Newnham College, University of Cambridge.

21 Stan Cohen came to the London School of Economics in 1963 where he took his PhD. He returned to the LSE in 1994, to become Professor of Sociology in 1996.

whose editorial board included Stanton Wheeler, Sheldon Messinger, Howard Becker, Eliot Freidson, Blanche Geer, Thomas Scheff and Edwin Schur – men and women linked at first or second hand to the University of Chicago and loosely associated with what David Matza (1969) was later to call an 'appreciative' sociology that gave emphasis to the part played by meaning in the unfolding of action between embedded selves in 'natural settings'.

The journal was then the principal conduit for the dissemination of an emerging, 'new' sociology of deviance rooted in symbolic interactionism and its constituent traditions of pragmatism, formalism and ethnography. Consider the tone and substance of some of the articles housed in the first two issues of that 1965 volume: Mercer's 'Perspectives for Understanding the Mentally Retarded'; Briar and Piliavin's 'Situational Inducements to Delinquency'; Hughes's 'A Note on Georg Simmel'; a reprinting of Simmel's 'The Poor'; Gagnon's 'Female Child Victims of Sex Offenses'; and Simmons's 'Public Stereotypes of Deviants'. *Social Problems* perfectly refracted and objectified my dawning interests, and it was more than fortunate that it entered my life at that point.

Stan Cohen also led me to the ideas of Leslie Wilkins (1964), particularly that of deviance amplification, and together we tried our arm at writing about the rise and fall of Teddy Boys (Cohen and Rock, 1970), a piece that acted, in effect, as a pilot and precursor for ideas that he would later elaborate, following Wilkins and Becker, and presented in his PhD dissertation, as 'folk devils' and 'moral panics' (Cohen, 1972).

Searching for a topic for my own D.Phil, interested in the social anthropology of prisons and total institutions as yet another instance of the ethnography of strange places (see Rock, 2002), aware that no study had then been undertaken of the social world of a women's prison – although a couple of American studies of women's prisons *were* to be published within the next few months (Ward and Kassebaum, 1965; Giallombardo, 1966) – I initially floated the idea of studying the social organization of Holloway Prison for women in London.

Nigel Walker advised me that, rather like the Jews in James Joyce's *Dubliners*, they would never let me in.[22] He suggested instead that I look at civil prisoners, debt defaulters housed chiefly in Brixton Prison in London,[23] who had been committed under the 1869 Debtors Act (c 62). The long title of the Act was *An Act for the Abolition of Imprisonment for Debt, for the punishment of fraudulent debtors, and for other purposes* but, through an artful technicality, imprisonment remained as a final sanction for contempt of court committed by those who had disobeyed a legal judgement to repay money. In the event, the subsequent thesis ('The System of Debt Collection in England and Wales and its Social Consequences') touched rather little on imprisonment. Its themes were twofold, and they flowed out of the preoccupations of an emerging interactionist sociology of deviance, on the one hand, and, on the other, the impressions I formed inductively as I interviewed debtors, solicitors, county court judges and registrars, and observed county court proceedings and bailiffs at work, becoming briefly an unpaid bailiff myself at Lambeth County Court.

The ensuing book, *Making People Pay*, published in 1973, centred on the mass collection of small consumer debts, a system that, for reasons of scale, economy and the geographical

---

22 However, I did undertake just such a study many years later (Rock, 1996).

23 He almost certainly did so because an acquaintance, Paul de Berker, a psychologist based at Brixton Prison, was working on the area at the time (see de Berker, 1965).

dispersal of borrowers and defaulters, could rarely entail face-to-face encounters, relying instead on the mechanical and routine manipulation of an escalating series of threats by telephone and mail. Where controls were weak and expensive to implement, it was not prudent to alienate the debtor and encourage him or her to become intransigent in his or her refusal to pay – creditors could not afford to manage the consequences of that form of recalcitrant secondary deviation. Neither, it appeared, where public, politicians or officials were not wholly condemnatory of defaulters or wholly supportive of creditors and debt-collectors, could enforcement be allowed to appear unduly oppressive (see Payne, 1969). Occupying an ill-defined moral standing, to be cajoled rather than coerced, debtors were coddled through a succession of stages contrived by the paper machinery of enforcement itself: letters would be sent by the creditor, increasingly urgent and menacing in style; they would be succeeded by a second cascade of letters from a debt-collector who was often no more than the creditor sporting a new letter-heading; *in extremis*, those letters would be followed by yet a third stream from a solicitor, specializing in the role, who would issue threats of court proceedings; and, exceptionally, those threats would lead to proceedings in the county court, mass litigation and a number of visits by bailiffs, the court's officers. The whole was an elaborate and protracted exercise in the manipulation of ambiguously constructed threats that raised the possibility, first, that the defaulter was at bottom taken to be a man or woman who had suffered misfortune, forgetfulness or poverty,[24] one who really intended to pay and would certainly do so in due course; and, second, that there would be dire and often unspecified penalties – but not just yet. Defaulters were almost never to be punished or confronted personally because that would be costly and oppressive. And, for reasons that largely eluded creditors and debt-collectors, many defaulters did eventually pay their debts, sometimes after their case had been abandoned and enforcement had ceased.

Creditors and collectors, working at a distance, could know very little about their prey. They knew something about what they had purchased, their credit history, their address, age and gender. They knew that some replied to letters immediately, some after a while and some never. They knew that some people paid immediately they were approached, some after the application of pressure, and some not at all. They knew that some paid in full, some in part and some not at all. Out of this sparse feedback they constructed the typifications upon which they worked: the collection routine created the honest, feckless and professional debtor. For their part, defaulters were reassured repeatedly that they were honest people, no more so than by the bailiffs who told them that the sanctions of seizing goods or imprisoning debtors would not be implemented, and reports would be returned to the court that the debtor was not at home or could not be seen, if only some composition were made. At the very end, when all had been exhausted, the bailiffs smoothed the transition to prison with the persuasive argument that incarceration would expunge the debt (an argument that made enforcement less onerous but which had no standing in law).

In short, debt collection was a progression, engineered through the transmission of letters and infrequent visits, which systematically generated, step-by-step, accounts, situated selves and justifications for the appearance of action. It lent itself remarkably well to analysis

[24] Thus representing a mildly unconventional form of secondary deviation, where the work of formal social control is to attempt to confirm the identity of the deviant as conforming and compliant.

couched in the new and inviting symbolic interactionist language of deviance: becoming, control, meaning, identity and the moral career (see Goffman, 1959; Roth, 1963). Anticipating the thesis, and as my first journal article, I published 'Observations on Debt Collection' (see Chapter 1, this volume).

The only other piece I completed while at Nuffield College was a review of David Downes's *The Delinquent Solution* (1966) in the *British Journal of Sociology* of December 1966. I did not then know David Downes,[25] but it was as well that the review was benign because, on returning to the LSE as an assistant lecturer in January 1967, we were to be friends, colleagues and collaborators for the next 30 years.[26] Our world-views melded in many things,[27] and we were both tolerably eclectic and accommodating, but I remained the micro-sociologist firmly wedded to symbolic interactionism, and he was the LSE man – a Fabian, preoccupied with structures of inequality, the pains of imprisonment and with what Alvin Gouldner once called 'the master institutions of society'. In this there was a perfect complementarity: when we taught together in MSc and PhD seminars, and when we wrote together (as we were to do, for instance, in successive editions of *Understanding Deviance* (first published in 1982)), he would deal with the big questions of political economy and policy, and I the smaller questions of interpretative sociology. I used to say that we were the Tweedledum and Tweedledee of criminology, but our conversations would have been tedious indeed if we really had been identical academic twins.

The invisible college, grounded initially in a web of research students, bolstered when they took academic posts, and ever growing, was to become institutionalized in the National Deviancy Conference after a cabal met at a criminology conference in Cambridge in July 1968 and elected to strike out on its own,[28] meeting regularly at the University of York, the home university of Laurie Taylor, one of its members and an associate of Stan Cohen.[29]

[25] David Downes read history at Oxford and then studied for a PhD under Eryl Hall Williams and Terence Morris at the London School of Economics (published in 1966). He began teaching in the Department of Social Policy and Administration in 1963, becoming a professor until his retirement in 2003. He was to be the author of a number of significant books, including *Contrasts in Tolerance* (1988), a comparative study of British and Dutch penal policy.

[26] I remained so long in the LSE because I always regarded myself as especially fortunate in being amongst such bright, congenial students; having within reach a magnificent library; and, above all, being blessed with such congenial colleagues. The criminologists at the School form a warm, collaborative and supportive group – institutionalized as a virtual institution, the Mannheim Centre – which could not be rivalled. I cannot be grateful enough to Stan Cohen, Dick Hobbs, Janet Foster, Frances Heidensohn, Nicky Lacey, Mike Shiner, Tim Newburn, Coretta Phillips, Jill Peay, Robert Reiner, Paul Wiles and Lucia Zedner who, at different times, proved to be invaluable colleagues. Outside the LSE, I was fortunate to have links with many criminologists, and with Richard Ericson, Elaine Player, Maurice Punch and Tank Waddington, in particular.

[27] See, for instance, our joint article, 'Social Reactions to Deviance', published in 1971 and our dual *riposte*, based on rather different arguments, to the claims of the apparently dominant radical criminology of the early 1970s (Downes and Rock, 1979).

[28] Its core members were Stan Cohen, David Downes, Mike Hepworth, Mary McIntosh, Ian Taylor, Laurie Taylor, Jock Young, Paul Walton and me.

[29] Taylor wrote a number of books, especially in collaboration with Stan Cohen (see Cohen and Taylor, 1972, 1976, 1978), becoming Professor of Sociology at the University of York, and then quitting the academy to enter the BBC as a presenter.

The Conference at first celebrated the 'new' deviancy theory, conceiving it to represent a radical break from a past and present somewhat demonized as overly positivistic, overly ensnared by the state and lacking engagement with sociology proper. In his introduction to an edited collection of a number of its early papers, Stan Cohen pointed to what he conceived to be its key sources of differentiation: it was, he said, dedicated to 'connecting with the public' – being more accessible than criminology conventionally practised; 'looking at the others' – treating the classification of people as deviant as subjectively problematic in its procedures and consequences; treating 'deviance as process' – by focusing on the stages and mechanisms of 'becoming'; emphasizing 'the defence of meaning' by treating deviation as significant activity; taking deviance to be 'continuous and permeating', not to be set apart as distinct socially and symbolically from other forms of activity; and appreciating 'the political implications of studying deviance', because such study bears with it an array of 'evaluative, moral and practical implications' (Cohen, 1971, pp. 9–24).

There was a core ambiguity in that stress on radical departure, difference and politics. It seemed to some that the reintroduction of an understanding that deviation was meaningful, willed activity, shaped by informal and formal control, and regulated by the state and its institutions, suggested the need for a combative political economy of crime and control that could reinforce and seek nurture from the wider radicalism of the students' and prisoners' movements, the protests against the war in Vietnam, the politics of experience which revolved around a new libertarianism of drugs and sex and, more generally, the questioning of deference and authority marked by what Haug and Sussman called 'the revolt of the client' (1969). A short time later, three of those attending the Conference issued a manifesto for a 'new criminology', which was positioned as much in a newly vaunted 'soft' Marxism as in symbolic interactionism (Taylor, Walton and Young, 1973.) Taylor, Walton and Young championed a 'socialist diversity' which would supersede capitalism and allow a new culture of difference, culture and civility to bloom. They attempted 'to erect the elements of a criminology that was concerned, above all else, to act in defence of working-class interests' (1975, p. 3). They were schismatics whose move was subject to little open debate at the time, although it appeared to me to encourage a political editing of what could and should be said, and a return to the arid abstractions of high theory. It took time before a response was mobilized, partly because the Left commanded the political and moral high ground, many doubters were timorous and criticism could be construed as reactionary. But, eventually, there *was* a breaking of the ranks, and a number of us wrote dissenting essays in a book which David Downes and I edited. *Deviant Interpretations* appeared in 1979: Ken Plummer issued there a masterly defence of symbolic interactionism; Stan Cohen talked of his 'aversion to the apocalyptic' – 'socialist legality', he mused, tends to mean 'a model of social control in which offenders wearing sandwich boards listing their crimes before a crowd which shouts, "Down with the counter-revolutionaries!" are then led away to be publicly shot' (Downes and Rock, 1979, p. 44); and David Downes talked about the dangers of placing faith in the benevolence of an unanalysed and unanalysable future revolutionary society, about making a revolutionary leap without considering what might lie on the other side. And I queried the utility and verisimilitude of a triumphalist criminology that once again returned to dismiss as false consciousness the practical preoccupations, meanings and motives of people in everyday life.[30]

It was propitious that I came to know three American sociologists, all visitors to the University of London, at the beginning of the 1970s. Aaron Cicourel, Peter Manning and Bob Scott were legates, as it were, from the heartland of the new qualitative sociologies which I was attempting to grasp from afar. Aaron Cicourel[31] was a pioneering and inventive ethnomethodologist, chiefly interested in matters of method (see Cicourel, 1964), who fizzed with ideas that sometimes touched on crime and delinquency. In *The Social Organization of Juvenile Justice* (1968), above all, he put probing questions to the very constitution of social life, exploring the bureaucratic generation of facts and statistics by asking how it was that deviant identity was assembled retrospectively and prospectively in the routine practices and conversations of families, probation officers, psychiatrists and police officers (see also Kitsuse and Cicourel, 1963). In 1972 he invited me to visit the United States for the very first time, to teach at the embryonic University of California at San Diego, and it was there that I not only observed the America which I had only read about – an America at its most showy in southern California, where identities seemed to be donned and discarded at will in a ceaseless masquerade – but also met what must have been at the time one of the most interesting groupings of 'new' sociologists assembled in any one department: Randy Collins,[32] Fred Davis, Jack Douglas, Joe Gusfield and Aaron Cicourel himself.

The second American was Peter Manning,[33] a sociologist of the police, visiting Goldsmiths College from Michigan State University in 1972, who was something of an intellectual dandy, continually toying with the possibilities of new words[34] and ideas – interactionism, phenomenology, ethnomethodology, hermeneutics, semiotics and on and on in a dizzy parade. He, too, could dazzle, had a wide range of acquaintance and was exceptionally well read, and he taught me much.

30 It is interesting that there was, in time, to be a modest recantation by Jock Young. First, in response to the first British Crime Survey of 1981, he and John Lea reflected how they had once believed that 'property offences are directed solely against the bourgeoisie and that violence against the person is carried out by amateur Robin Hoods in the course of their righteous attempts to redistribute wealth. All of this is, alas, untrue' (Lea and Young, 1984, p. 262). Second, with Jones and MacLean, he conceded, in response to feminist criticism about the victimization of women, that there had been 'a general tendency in radical thought to idealize [its] historical subject (in this case the working class) and to play down intra-group conflict, blemishes and social disorganization. But the power of the feminist case resulted in a sort of cognitive schizophrenia amongst radicals …' (Jones, MacLean and Young, 1986, pp. 2–3).

31 Aaron Cicourel graduated from the University of California at Los Angeles and received a PhD from Cornell University. He was to become Professor of Sociology at the University of California at Santa Barbara, and then Professor of Sociology in the School of Medicine and the Department of Sociology at the University of California at San Diego.

32 I resumed my acquaintance with Randy Collins when I became Visiting Professor at the University of Pennsylvania. His work on interaction ritual chains (2004) and violence (2008) was to prove more than useful when I worked on the incomplete success of a pilot project to introduce impact statements in homicide trials in England and Wales (Rock 2010 and in this volume).

33 Peter Manning was to occupy the Elmer V.H. and Eileen M. Brooks Chair in the College of Criminal Justice at Northeastern University, Boston, MA. He was the author of some outstanding books, and especially *Police Work* (1977), *The Narcs' Game* (1980) and *Symbolic Communication* (1988).

34 The term 'interdigitation' was a neologism that gave him especial pleasure at one point.

The third American was Bob Scott, then of Princeton University, who became a lifelong, wise and witty friend. His *Making of Blind Men* (1969) was a masterly interactionist study of the manner in which a 'real' or apparent physical disability could be understood as a learned social role contingent on institutional processes. I was attracted by his flirtation with structuralist anthropology and phenomenology (Scott, 1972), and particularly with Mary Douglas's ideas of the taboo and Berger and Luckmann's work on the social construction of reality (Douglas, 1966; Berger and Luckmann, 1967). Scott invited me to teach at Princeton in 1974–75, where I fielded the Guggenheim Seminar, choosing and chairing visiting speakers, and it was through that seminar that I again met Howard Becker and encountered Irving Louis Horowitz for the first time. Little by little, the names on the spines of books and the pages of articles were attaining flesh.[35]

One other world into which I was inducted was the Oxford Centre for Socio-Legal Studies, founded in 1972, whose management committee I eventually joined in 1983. Under the inspired direction of Don Harris, members of the Centre, and Robert Baldwin,[36] Keith Hawkins[37] and Bridget Hutter[38] in particular, fostered the development of a sociology of compliance-based regulation which demanded a reinterpretation of the social and institutional dimensions of crime, deviance and control. It had been all too easy to think of criminology, in Irvin Waller's alliterative phrase, as 'cops, crime and corrections', but the Centre forced a recognition that most formal control is practised by agents other than the police, is pre-emptive rather than responsive, and consists of cajolery and persuasion rather than coercion. The typifications of deviance and rule-breakers centrally in place were often, if not always and permanently, those of otherwise rule-observant men and women who could eventually be coaxed into compliance. My own thesis had been just such a report about compliance-based regulation *avant la lettre*, and the Centre reinforced the contention that the conventional criminological repertoire of acts and actors simply could not stand unreformed (see Rock, Chapter 9, this volume; for a discussion of some of the controversy that that approach excited, see Rock, 2007).

The late 1960s and early 1970s were a time when universities and student numbers were expanding in the wake of the Robbins Report on higher education (1963). Up until 1950 there had only been 29 British universities; eight were then founded in the 1950s and 14 in the 1960s – eight in 1966 and 1967 alone. The total number of 'home acceptance' students doubled between 1963 and 1969 and were then to increase by another 40 per cent by 1980. Staff were recruited in proportion: there were 13 per cent more staff in universities in the second half of the 1970s than in the first. Publishers commissioned and accepted books to

---

35 Howard Becker, for example, gave me a number of very helpful comments on the typescript of my *Making of Symbolic Interactionism* (1979), which I wrote while at Princeton.

36 Robert Baldwin was to become Professor of Law at the LSE. His books include *Regulating the Airlines* (1985) and (with Martin Cave) *Understanding Regulation* (1999).

37 Keith Hawkins was to become Professor of Law and Society at the University of Oxford, retiring in 2005. His publications include *Environment and Enforcement* (1983) and *Law as Last Resort* (2002).

38 Bridget Hutter was to become Professor of Risk Regulation and Director, Centre for Analysis of Risk and Regulation, at the LSE. Her publications include *The Reasonable Arm of the Law?* (1988), *Compliance, Regulation and Environment* (1997) and *Regulation and Risk* (2001).

feed a swelling readership, and writing moved smoothly and as if on a conveyor belt into print (the saying about academics then was that they 'never had an unpublished thought'). I, too, serviced that conveyor belt, publishing my dissertation as *Making People Pay* (1973a), followed by two complementary books – one commissioned and one independently conceived – that were intended to investigate, formulate and consolidate quite what it meant to be a symbolic interactionist sociologist of deviance.

Deviant Behaviour (1973b) and *The Making of Symbolic Interactionism* (1979) were in effect acts of self-education, an attempt to move beyond a rough nodding acquaintance with theories that had become important to my work, to ascertain more rigorously what the roots, composition and claims of those twin fields might be. *Deviant Behaviour* was a precocious book, conceived prematurely and before I had been long enough into the field; but *The Making of Symbolic Interactionism* proved to be more than useful in mapping the terrain I hoped to occupy. The books set a pattern, dictated partly by the need periodically to take stock of theoretical developments for the purposes of teaching[39] and partly to reflect beyond the confines of what was to become a programme of empirically grounded research. A commitment to fieldwork has its justifications and rewards, but reading primary and secondary documents, observing social settings and interviewing people has its costs, and principal amongst them is time foregone in reading and thinking about theory. It is easy enough to slip from the empirical into the empiricist, and I did attempt continually to distance myself from the worlds I studied, treat them as anthropologically and analytically problematic, and stimulate and fortify arguments with some rudiments of theory more abstractly conceived.[40]

Having undertaken a *tour d'horizon*, and having established the outlines of an intellectual position by affirmation and by negation, I was ready to move on to a project, although I had no clear conception of what it might be. At first, I toyed with the idea of looking at auditing as a form of regulation,[41] and I did manage to gain access to a firm of accountants through a friend and neighbour. But chance again played a part and took me elsewhere.

Chris Nuttall, on secondment from the Home Office as Assistant Deputy Minister in charge of the Programs Branch of the Ministry of the Solicitor General of Canada, invited me to become a Visiting Scholar attached to the Branch in 1981–82. I was the first occupant of a post which was still undefined, and none of us knew quite what to do with me. I had, however, long harboured a curiosity about policy-making processes, about how knowledge about crime, criminal justice and criminology is identified, shaped and put administratively to work. There had certainly been ample academic speculation about the politics of crime, largely reflecting the political and theoretical presuppositions of its authors, but it had been phenomenologically distant for the most part, few having peered inside the black box of the state. Further, much of that speculation was based on *ex post facto* accounts that had been carefully constructed for public and political purposes, when outcomes were known and a

[39] See, for example, 'The Present State of Criminology in Britain' (Chapter 5, this volume).

[40] Over the years, I was to write about the social organization of British criminology (1988); broad developments in theory (1997); the links between symbolic interactionism and the sociology of deviance (1991); symbolic interactionism and ethnography (2001, 2007); and the neophiliac capacity of criminologists and sociologists to forget their intellectual past (Chapter 13, this volume).

[41] Although it is perhaps for the best that I did not persist because I could never have matched Michael Power's own later work on the subject (Power, 1997).

neat, persuasive and coherent narrative could be supplied.

Officials proposed that I should study the Ministry itself, and, ensconced in one of its offices in the Wilfred Laurier Building, I was allowed to attend meetings, read papers and interview ministers and officials. What was then in progress was the gestation of a small federal–provincial initiative for victims, and I was allowed to follow how it unfolded stage-by-stage until the production of a task force report in 1983.

What was recorded (Rock, 1986) was refracted through the twin lenses of my own intellectual expectancies and of the accounts, actions and papers punctuating the processes that unfolded before me. No doubt other sociologists with other eyes and ears would have described matters differently, but policy-making did seem to have some bold and incontestable features: it was emergent, absorbing events and changing in ways that could never have been evident at the outset; it was indeterminate, those involved in its making having no clear idea of where exactly, if anywhere, it would lead (see Rock, Chapter 9, this volume); it was contingent, responding to other political, financial and social events that arose and could not have been foreseen at the beginning; it was the subject of what Becker once called sequential causation, the 'same' events at each successive stage working in quite different and sometimes contrary ways; it was a rhetorical artefact, a thing of words and argument that created facts artfully, sometimes out of very thin material; it spun webs of motives, meanings, relations and identities that fed back on itself and changed it; and it relied on its authors, in Karl Weick's words (1979), enacting an environment of demands and events to which they and others (and especially ministers) had to respond.

But not all was uncertain or contingent: policy-making was also lodged firmly inside an architecture of committee meetings, legislative and fiscal cycles, stock-taking exercises, planning reviews and administrative plans which lent it a predictable structure, timetable and teleology. Submissions had to be presented to a chain of prescribed groups in prescribed order for comment and endorsement; they would recite tried political and administrative arguments to win consent; and they had to mesh – sometimes uncomfortably – with other policies and politics then in train. In short, they were all forced into the same Procrustean bed and, whatever their content, they tended inevitably to acquire much the same form and style.

When I returned to England in the mid-1980s, I was able to conduct what was in effect a comparative study of the opening stages of criminal justice policy-making in the government of that country, focusing heavily on the birth and growth of Victim Support, a voluntary organization, and its eventual acceptance and adoption by the Home Office. Its themes were roughly isomorphic with those of *A View from the Shadows*, but there were important contrasts (see Rock, Chapter 4, this volume). England and Wales was not a federal state: the Home Office, the criminal justice ministry then charged with administrative responsibility for victims of crime, tended to be *dirigiste*, not obliged to win over powerful states or provinces and needing no support from civil society in its negotiations in Whitehall, Westminster and beyond.

Victim Support was born at a time of a radical municipal politics, awash with police monitoring groups bent on discrediting the police and state, and it was at first treated with suspicion. Much of *Helping Victims of Crime* (1990) thus focused on how a new organization, launched into a wary world, advanced square-by-square, as if in a game of chess, winning the sponsorship of suspicious criminal justice agencies one after another, until, like a successful pawn, it was awarded permanent government funding and crowned a queen.

The comparative analysis of victim movements has intrigued me. In 2005, as a Visiting Fellow at RegNet (the Regulatory Institutions Network) at the Australian National University, I was able once more to contrast how the politics of victims had arisen and unwound in Australia with the history of Victim Support in England and Wales. The one had its anchorage in groups supporting and campaigning for the families of murder victims, the other in an organization emanating broadly from NACRO (the National Association for the Care and Resettlement of Offenders) and the world of penal reform; the one could be vociferous and was rights-based, the other was deliberately subdued and service-based;[42] the one talked about trauma and the permanent scars of victimization, the other about helping victims cope with crime and move rapidly out of victim status; the one catered expensively only for a small population of seriously distressed victims, the other for the generality of victims, including the victims of 'volume crime' (see Chapter 14, this volume).

It seemed that, as a would-be ethnographer, I had acquired two conjoint tribes – victims and policy officials, and a territory in the form of government departments – and it was to those tribes and that territory that I would repeatedly return. I did so again when I chronicled the conception and growth of witness support in the crown courts of England and Wales, concentrating heavily, it must be said, on the social organization and procedures of the courthouse and courtroom (Rock, 1993). I did so when I tracked the emergence of another cluster of victims' organizations in England and Wales, those campaigning for, and supporting, the families of homicide victims (Rock, 1998). And I did so once more when I followed from the outset the development of policies for victims in the first years of the New Labour government (Rock, 2004). It was apparent in that last book that victims and their organizations still lacked the political power and authority to impress their demands on the state, but that the state and its agencies constructed victims in their own image, invoking them rhetorically as a prop and ornament in policy-making. Victims' organizations were more defined than defining, and it was other political processes, then on the march, which were awarded greater urgency and consequence in constructing what they were and what they needed. It was not what victims themselves *said* or *did*, it was not what victims themselves *were* (confused, ill-defined and variegated as any such statistical aggregate might be), but human rights legislation, the emergence of the new managerialism, restorative justice and the politics of race and gender which impressed their stamp and furnished a succession of pragmatically driven, locally framed and idiosyncratic stereotypes, programmes and policies.

It was perhaps inevitable that, having worked so long in the area, I acquired a concern about the lot of victims which went beyond mere intellectual curiosity. Victims had been progressively marginalized by the growing power of the state, becoming little more in criminal law and procedure than complainants, witnesses and possible claimants to compensation. Blackstone had argued in an early definitive statement that it was not the personal victim but 'the sovereign, in whom centres the majesty of the whole community, [who] is supposed by the law to be the person injured by every infraction of the public rights belonging to that community …' (1769, p. 12). That conception has remained intact. It was the sovereign

[42] For a more general discussion of the theme, see Van Dijk (1986).

against whom crimes were committed, not the individual. It was the sovereign who had an interest in justice, not the individual, who might well be regarded as venal, mendacious or vindictive (see Rock, Chapter 12, this volume). It was the sovereign in whose name trials were conducted, whilst it was the individual as a trial witness whose creditability and credibility were systematically challenged. In short, as Garland remarked, 'individuals and victims featured hardly at all, other than as members of the public, whose complaints triggered state action. Their interests were subsumed under the general public interest ...' (2000, p. 357). Victims were all too readily vilified or anathematized in law, journalism and criminology (see Rock, Chapter 16, this volume) and I took it that I had a duty to do something to restore balance and redeem them from a largely undeserved neglect and calumny.[43] It was partly for that reason that I looked sympathetically at the experimental introduction of family impact statements in trials for murder and manslaughter, noting how families wished to restore proportion, context, history and character in what was effectively a doomed mourning ritual (see Rock, forthcoming b).

Each piece of research seemed eventually to unearth a distinctive pattern that explained how processes evolved, and discovering that pattern, that key, finding what it was that lent form and momentum to an area of social life, was something of an aesthetic experience (see Poincaré, 1929), always joyful and always the prime object of analysis. In the case of my study of the groups set up by the families of homicide victims, it was clear that a chaos of confused and percussive emotions, typically described as anger, drove people on in an urgent attempt to restore moral order, meaning, comfort and purpose in a universe turned upside-down. It tends to engender stark binary oppositions between the good victim and the bad offender; the life lost and the life still yawning ahead for the offender; the legal support available to the defendant and its denial to the family; the rights bestowed on the defendant and their denial to the family and the victim. It can lead to campaigning and memorialization. It can impart a sense of social solidarity in the face of an indifferent and uncomprehending world, but it is also divisive and incommunicable, and the linked antinomies which infuse it usually seek a target against which to muster – police racism, the improper care of mental patients in the community, the coroners' treatment of the bereaved, leniency of sentencing, the rules attached to forensic procedures and the like.

People supporting and campaigning for the bereaved would come together in highly effervescent and cohesive groups, but would split and split again along the fault-lines and oppositions that separate one grief and one faction from another. Parents of Murdered Children, later SAMM (Support After Murder and Manslaughter), was a group that formed within Compassionate Friends, a self-help organization for those who had lost children. In time, they splintered because it became their claim that those whose children had died from natural causes simply could not understand the anguish of one whose child had been murdered. Justice for Victims then formed within SAMM because its members castigated SAMM for its failure vigorously to campaign – for its suppression of the wells of anger

---

43 Perhaps most acute where the victim was multiply stigmatized and vulnerable. Tim Newburn and I conducted a survey of the victimization of homeless people in London, a group effectively exiled from civil society, and the portrait that emerged was quite harrowing (see Rock and Newburn, Chapter 15, this volume).

which they felt.[44] In all this there was a visible dialectic of fusion and fission, of coalescence and conflict, which underpinned the continual formation and re-formation of groups over a decade or more (Rock, 1998).

What was of some interest was the growing proliferation of claims to victim status: the families called themselves victims (although 'survivors', 'co-victims' and 'secondary victims' were also being floated as possible ways of capturing those whose victimization was experienced at second hand). It is evident that crime ripples out to encompass a multitude of people who may come to regard themselves as victims: victims proper, the families of victims, witnesses and bystanders, court staff, criminal justice personnel and even, in one contested case, the families of serious offenders (see Rock, Chapter 12, this volume).

In other work, I became interested in the interplay between the social, symbolic and physical dimensions of space. It was an interplay evident in the geopolitics of English crime and law enforcement at the beginning of the eighteenth century (see Chapter 3, this volume). There was a central state but it was weak, there were local pockets of power concentrated in garrison towns, but, in the main, movement was difficult and enforcement was arduous. The greater the distance from the centre, the greater was the ambiguity and negotiability of deviance and control, so that, at the fringes, poachers could become gamekeepers, pirates privateers, and smugglers excise men. Punishments might appear draconian in law, but much enforcement was actually a practical matter of bargaining over bounties, rewards, pardons and pleas. Organized criminals, such as Jonathan Wild, could then represent themselves in the multiple identities of gang leaders, managers of lost property offices and bounty-hunting thief-takers.

Another instance was a study of a small initiative that had been launched by Chris Nuttall on his return from Canada. Nuttall surmised that the Home Office had been overly directive and centralizing in its formulation of crime prevention policies. It could learn from, and support, some of the many locally based, vernacular projects that were then welling up in community groups. As I explored how that initiative unfurled, it became apparent that the meanings of crime and policy intervention altered appreciably, tier by tier, with distance from the hub of policy-making in England and Wales (see Chapter 8, this volume). At the core, in Whitehall, there was talk of crime prevention; at the periphery, in the 'community', it was of 'empowerment'.

Again, in studying the rebuilding of the courthouse at Wood Green (Rock, 1993), I spoke with architects, court users and members of the public, and compared behaviour in an old, temporary building (known to counsel as 'the bunker') with conduct in the new and rather splendid crown court centre, known as the *Palais de Justice*, which was to replace it. Courthouses were artfully designed as a nest of segregated 'circulation systems' which kept key groups physically and symbolically apart until they confronted one another in the courtroom itself. The criminal trial revolves critically around a structured conflict that feeds on allegation and counterallegation; it can have explosive repercussions, and the arrangement of physical space does much to control who meets whom and in what circumstances, who can

[44] One of its leaflets proclaimed 'We have tried being polite, we have tried to be logical. We have tried to let justice take its course! We have held our anger, our emotions in check .... We have tried above all to be the reasonable, tolerant, honest people we once were, we have tried so very hard to hold on to this. We have been tried too much!!!!!!'

overhear whom and what information can safely be disclosed to whom (see Chapter 6, this volume). Architecture carefully and discreetly regulates conduct, and it did so to effect in the new Wood Green courthouse.

It was otherwise in the rebuilding of Holloway Prison for women (Rock, 1996). There, the design of built space multiplied confusion, anomie and deregulation. The original prison, opened in 1852, had followed Joshua Jebb's radial design which permitted prison officers, clustered in and around 'the centre', to stare down the long lines of the wings at prisoners themselves clustered in small groupings, to exercise surveillance from a distance, and allowed prisoners and staff to keep safely apart. Eventually deemed anachronistic, too capacious, too severe and formal, too ill-suited to the proper treatment of women defined as 'inadequate', the old prison was razed and replaced by a building intended to resemble a conventional municipal institution – more hospital than penitentiary – that would treat inmates as though they were as much victims as perpetrators. It was laid out as a serpentine chain of therapeutic spaces through which prisoners would progress stage-by-stage from reception and diagnosis to discharge.

The new Holloway Prison was erected on the same site as the old, the one being demolished as the other arose. Construction was beset by multiple difficulties: subsidence that came with the discovery that Holloway Prison was indeed built over a hollow way; changes from imperial to metric measurement that led to a lack of materials and changes in specification; strikes and shortages of labour; the realization that, far from inadequate, some women could be violent and required secure conditions;[45] economic crises and a continual nibbling-away at the costs and physical dimensions of the project; and a rise in the numbers of women prisoners and an increase in the lengths of their sentences. As important, there was to be a sea-change in penal ideology that seeped in almost unnoticed during the long process of rebuilding. The therapeutic became discredited, all its original champions had died, retired or moved on, and the new Holloway Prison was required to serve purposes for which it had never been designed. When it opened in 1977 it was seen by inmates and staff to be a frightening labyrinth, a mass of small, confrontational spaces, mean vistas and dog-leg turns threatening ambush. There was a riot on the very first day, and the history of the prison was to be peppered thereafter with scandal and crisis turning on conflicts between different coalitions of staff, managers and inmates wrestling over the control of contested and disconcerting space. A reprieve was won briefly by an inspirational governor, Colin Allen, who returned the prison in 1988 to some semblance of the regime for which it had been designed, despite (and perhaps because of) a strike by prison officers which left the institution to the inmates and a skeleton staff of administrators. For that one short time, and almost as if in an anarchist's dream, Holloway Prison was run with the virtual consent of the incarcerated.

The Holloway book had been prompted by the long-suppressed desire to look at a women's prison, by the wish to demonstrate that I could actually write about a phenomenon other than policy-making for victims, and, once again, by serendipity. In chance conversation I discovered that a friend, the architectural photographer John Donat, had been commissioned

[45] Not least among them was Leila Khaled who had assisted in the hijacking of an aeroplane, and Dolores and Marion Price, members of the Irish Republican Army, who had placed bombs outside the Central Criminal Court and Pentonville Prison.

to create a record of the last year of the life of the old prison, and it was out of the possibilities of using that archive that the project grew.

Now, finally, and reverting to type, in conjunction with David Downes and Tim Newburn, I have begun working on an official history of criminal justice, commissioned by the Cabinet Office. If that can be pulled off, it should prove to be a satisfying way of ending a career by reflecting upon, summing up and taking stock of major developments in crime, criminology, criminal justice and policy-making in the last decades of the twentieth century. I shall undertake some major part of that writing at the University of Pennsylvania, where I serve as Visiting Professor through the intercession of Larry Sherman, a fourth American friend and colleague with an extraordinary knowledge of the field and its hinterland. Larry and his partner, Heather Strang – an Australian academic versed in restorative justice and the politics of victims – have shown great kindness in enriching my professional and social life beyond my formal retirement from the LSE in 2008.

References

Akman, D. and Normandeau, A. (1967), 'The Measurement of Crime and Delinquency in Canada', *British Journal of Criminology*, **7**, pp. 129–49.

Akman, D., Normandeau, A., Sellin, T. and Wolfgang, M. (1968), 'Towards the Measurement of Criminality in Canada: A Replication Study', *Acta Criminologica*, **1**(1), pp. 135–260.

Baldwin, R. (1985), *Regulating the Airlines: Administrative Justice and Agency Discretion*, Oxford: Clarendon Press.

Baldwin, R. and Cave, M. (1999), *Understanding Regulation: Theory, Strategy, and Practice*, Oxford: Oxford University Press.

Becker, H. (1963), *Outsiders: Studies in the Sociology of Deviance*, New York: The Free Press.

Becker, H. (1986), *Writing for Social Scientists: How to Start and Finish Your Thesis, Book or Article*, Chicago: University of Chicago Press.

Berger, P. and Luckmann, T. (1967), *The Social Construction of Reality: A Treatise in the Sociology of Knowledge*, Harmondsworth: Penguin.

Blackstone, W. (1769), *Commentaries on the Laws of England*, Book 4, Oxford: Clarendon Press.

Bottomore, T. (1965), *Classes in Modern Society*, London: Allen & Unwin.

Canadian Federal–Provincial Task Force on Justice for Victims of Crime (1983), *Report*, Ottawa: Ministry of Supply and Services, Canada.

Carson, W. (1974), 'Symbolic and Instrumental Dimensions of Early Factory Legislation', in R. Hood (ed.), *Crime, Criminology and Public Policy*, London: Heinemann.

Carson, W. (1980), 'Early Factory Inspectors and the Viable Class Society – A Rejoinder', *International Journal for the Sociology of Law*, **8**, pp. 187–92.

Carson, W. (1985), 'Hostages to History: Some Aspects of the Occupational Health and Safety Debate in Historical Perspective', in B. Creighton and N. Gunningham (eds), *The Industrial Relations of Occupational Health and Safety*, Sydney: Croom Helm Australia.

Cicourel, A. (1964), *Method and Measurement in Sociology*, New York: Free Press of Glencoe.

Cicourel, A. (1968), *The Social Organization of Juvenile Justice*, New York: Wiley.
Cohen, S. (ed.) (1971), *Images of Deviance*, Harmondsworth: Penguin.
Cohen, S. (1972), *Folk Devils and Moral Panics*, Oxford: Martin Robertson.
Cohen, S. (1979), 'Guilt, Justice and Tolerance', in D. Downes and P. Rock (eds), *Deviant Interpretations*, Oxford: Martin Robertson.
Cohen, S. and Rock, P. (1970), 'The Teddy Boy', in V. Bogdanor and R. Skidelsky (eds), *The Age of Affluence*, London: Macmillan.
Cohen, S. and Taylor, L. (1972), *Psychological Survival: The Experience of Long-Term Imprisonment*, Harmondsworth: Penguin.
Cohen, S. and Taylor, L. (1976), *Prison Secrets*, London, NCCL.
Cohen, S. and Taylor, L. (1978), *Escape Attempts: The Theory and Practice of Resistance to Everyday Life*, Harmondsworth: Penguin.
Collins, R. (2004), *Interaction Ritual Chains*, Princeton, NJ: Princeton University Press.
Collins, R. (2008), *Violence: A Micro-Sociological Theory*, Princeton, NJ: Princeton University Press.
Dahrendorf, R. (1995), *LSE: A History of the London School of Economics and Political Science, 1895–1995*, Oxford: Oxford University Press.
de Berker, P. (1965), 'Research and Methodology: Impressions of Civil Debtors in Prison', *British Journal of Criminology*, **5**, pp. 310–14.
De Solla Price, D., Derek, J. and Beaver, D. (1966), 'Collaboration in an Invisible College', *American Psychologist*, **21**(11), November, pp. 1011–18.
Douglas, M. (1966), *Purity and Danger: An Analysis of the Concepts of Pollution and Taboo*, London: Routledge and Kegan Paul.
Downes, D. (1966), *The Delinquent Solution*, London: Routledge and Kegan Paul.
Downes, D. (1988), *Contrasts in Tolerance: Post-War Penal Policy in the Netherlands and England and Wales*, Oxford: Oxford University Press.
Downes, D. and Rock, P. (1971), 'Social Reactions to Deviance and its Effects on Crime and Criminal Careers', *British Journal of Sociology*, **22**(4), pp. 351–64.
Downes, D. and Rock, P. (eds) (1979), *Deviant Interpretations*, Oxford: Martin Robertson; New York: Barnes & Noble.
Downes, D. and Rock, P. (1982), *Understanding Deviance*, Oxford: Oxford University Press. Fifth edn, 2007; Canadian edn (with C. McCormick), 2009.
Garland, D. (1988), 'British Criminology before 1935', in P. Rock (ed.), *A History of British Criminology*, Oxford: Oxford University Press.
Garland, D. (2000), 'The Culture of High Crime Societies', *British Journal of Criminology*, **40**(3), pp. 347–75.
Gellner, E. (1959), *Words and Things: A Critical Account of Linguistic Philosophy and a Study of Ideology*, London: Gollancz.
Gellner, E. (1975), 'Ethnomethodology: The Re-Enchantment Industry or the Californian Way of Subjectivity', *Philosophy of the Social Sciences*, **5**, pp. 431–50.
Giallombardo, R. (1966), *Society of Women: A Study of a Women's Prison*, London: Weidenfeld & Nicolson.
Ginsberg, M. (1944), *Moral Progress*, Glasgow: Glasgow University Press.

Ginsberg, M. (1968), *Essays in Sociology and Social Philosophy: Selections*, London: Penguin.

Glass, D. (ed.) (1954), *Social Mobility in Britain*, London: Routledge and Kegan Paul.

Goffman, E. (1959), 'The Moral Career of the Mental Patient', *Psychiatry*, **22**(2), pp. 123–42.

Gouldner, A. (1962), 'Anti-Minotaur: The Myth of a Value-Free Sociology', *Social Problems*, **9**(3), pp. 199–213.

Hall Williams, E. (1970), *The English Penal System in Transition*, London: Butterworths.

Hall Williams, E. (1975), *Changing Prisons*, London: P. Owen.

Hall Williams, E. (1978), *Ten Years of Parole: Retrospect and Prospect*, Croydon: ISTD.

Hall Williams, E. (1982), *Criminology and Criminal Justice*, London: Butterworths.

Halsey, A. (2004), *A History of Sociology in Britain: Science, Literature and Society*, Oxford: Oxford University Press.

Haug, M. and Sussman, M. (1969), 'Professional Autonomy and the Revolt of the Client', *Social Problems*, **17**(2), pp. 153–61.

Hawkins, K. (1983), *Environment and Enforcement: Regulation and the Social Definition of Pollution*, Oxford: Clarendon Press.

Hawkins, K. (2002), *Law as Last Resort: Prosecution Decision-Making in a Regulatory Agency*, Oxford: Oxford University Press.

Heidensohn, F. (1968), 'The Deviance of Women: A Critique and an Enquiry', *British Journal of Sociology*, **19**(2), pp. 160–75.

Heidensohn, F. (1985), *Women and Crime*, Basingstoke: Macmillan.

Heidensohn, F. (1992), *Women in Control? The Role of Women in Law Enforcement*, Oxford: Clarendon Press.

Hill, B. (1955), *Boss of Britain's Underworld*, London: Nalldrett Press.

Holdaway, S. and Rock. P. (eds) (1998), *Thinking about Criminology*, London: UCL Press.

Hood, R. (2004), 'Hermann Mannheim and Max Grünhut: Criminological Pioneers in London and Oxford', *British Journal of Criminology*, **44**, pp. 469–95.

Hughes, E. (1971), 'Mistakes at Work', in *The Sociological Eye: Selected Papers*, Chicago: Aldine-Atherton.

Hutter, B. (1988), *The Reasonable Arm of the Law?: The Law Enforcement Procedures of Environmental Health Officers*, Oxford: Clarendon Press.

Hutter, B. (1997), *Compliance, Regulation and Environment*, Oxford: Clarendon Press.

Hutter, B. (2001), *Regulation and Risk: Occupational Health and Safety on the Railways*, New York: Oxford University Press.

James, W. (1949), *Pragmatism*, New York: Longmans.

Jones, T., MacLean, B. and Young, J. (1986), *The Islington Crime Survey: Victimization and Policing in Inner-City London*, Aldershot: Gower.

Kitsuse, J. and Cicourel, A. (1963), 'A Note on the Uses of Official Statistics', *Social Problems*, **11**, pp. 131–39.

Lea, J. and Young, J. (1984), *What is to be Done about Law and Order?*, London: Penguin.

Lemert, E. (1951), *Social Pathology: A Systematic Approach to the Theory of Sociopathic Behavior*, New York: McGraw-Hill.

Lyman, S. and Scott, M. (1970), *A Sociology of the Absurd*, New York: Appleton-Century-Crofts.
Mannheim, H. (1940), *Social Aspects of Crime in England between the Wars*, London: Allen & Unwin.
Mannheim, H. (1960), 'Introduction' in *Pioneers in Criminology*, London: Stevens.
Manning, P. (1977), *Police Work: The Social Organization of Policing*, Cambridge, MA: MIT Press.
Manning, P. (1980), *The Narcs' Game: Organizational and Informational Limits on Drug Law Enforcement*, Cambridge, MA: MIT Press.
Manning, P. (1988), *Symbolic Communication: Signifying Calls and the Police Response*, Cambridge, MA: MIT Press.
Martin, J. (1988), 'The Development of Criminology in Britain 1948–60', in P. Rock (ed.), *A History of British Criminology*, Oxford: Clarendon Press.
Matza, D. (1969), *Becoming Deviant*, Englewood Cliffs, NJ: Prentice-Hall.
Mills, C. Wright (1959), *The Sociological Imagination*, New York: Oxford University Press.
Morris, T. (1957), *The Criminal Area: A Study in Social Ecology*, London: Routledge and Kegan Paul.
Morris, T. and Blom-Cooper, L. (1964), *A Calendar of Murder: Criminal Homicide in England since 1957*, London: M. Joseph.
Morris, T. and Morris, P. (1963), *Pentonville: A Sociological Study of an English Prison*, London: Routledge and Kegan Paul.
Payne, Mr Justice (1969), *Report of the Committee on the Enforcement of Judgement Debts*, Cm. 3909, London: HMSO.
Poincaré, H. (1929), *The Foundations of Science*, New York: Science Press.
Power, M. (1997), *The Audit Society: Rituals of Verification*, Oxford: Clarendon Press.
Rafter, N. (ed.) (2009), *The Origins of Criminology: A Reader*, Abingdon: Routledge.
Robbins, L. (1963), *Higher Education: Report of the Committee Appointed by the Prime Minister under the Chairmanship of Lord Robbins*, London: HMSO.
Rock, P. (1973a), *Making People Pay*, London: Routledge and Kegan Paul.
Rock, P. (1973b), *Deviant Behaviour*, London: Hutchinson.
Rock, P. (1979), *The Making of Symbolic Interactionism*, London: Macmillan; New York: Rowman and Littlefield.
Rock, P. (1986), *A View from the Shadows: The Ministry of the Solicitor General of Canada and the Justice for Victims of Crime Initiative*, Oxford: Clarendon Press.
Rock. P. (ed.) (1988), *A History of British Criminology*, Oxford: Oxford University Press.
Rock, P. (1990), *Helping Victims of Crime: The Home Office and the Rise of Victim Support in England and Wales*, Oxford: Clarendon Press.
Rock, P. (1991), 'Symbolic Interactionism and Labelling Theory', in K. Plummer (ed.), *Symbolic Interactionism*, Aldershot: Edward Elgar.
Rock, P. (1993), *The Social World of an English Crown Court: Witness and Professionals in the Crown Court Centre at Wood Green*, Oxford: Clarendon Press.
Rock, P. (1996), *Reconstructing a Women's Prison: The Holloway Redevelopment Project, 1968–88*, Oxford: Clarendon Press.

Rock, P. (1997 and successive editions), 'Sociological Theories of Crime', in M. Maguire *et al.* (eds), *The Oxford Handbook of Criminology*, Oxford: Oxford University Press.

Rock, P. (1998), *After Homicide: Practical and Political Responses to Bereavement*, Oxford: Clarendon Press.

Rock, P. (2001/2007), 'Symbolic Interactionism and Ethnography', in P. Atkinson *et al.* (eds), *The Handbook of Qualitative Methods*, London: Sage.

Rock, P. (2002), 'The Sociology of Prison Life', in N. Smelser and P. Baltes (eds), *International Encyclopedia of the Social and Behavioral Sciences*, Amsterdam: Elsevier Science.

Rock, P. (2004), *Constructing Victims' Rights: The Home Office, New Labour and Victims*, Oxford: Clarendon Press.

Rock, P. (2007), 'The Sociology of Compliance-Based Regulation: An Intellectual History', in A. Brannigan and G. Pavlitch (eds), *Adventures in the Sociology of Law: Essays in Honour of W.G. Carson*, Abingdon: Routledge-Cavendish.

Rock, P. (2010), '"Hearing Victims of Crime": The Delivery of Impact Statements as Ritual Behaviour in Four London Trials for Murder and Manslaughter', in A. Bottoms and J. Roberts (eds), *Hearing the Victim: Adversarial Justice, Crime Victims and the State*, Cullompton: Willan.

Rock, P. (forthcoming), 'Approaches to Victims and Victimisation', in T. Newburn (ed.), *The Sage Handbook of Criminological Theory*, London: Sage.

Roth, J. (1963), *Timetables: Structuring the Passage of Time in Hospital Treatment and Other Careers*, Indianapolis: Bobbs-Merrill.

Scott, R. (1969), *The Making of Blind Men; A Study of Adult Socialization*, New York: Russell Sage Foundation.

Scott, R. (1972), 'A Proposed Framework for Analyzing Deviance as a Property of Social Order', in R. Scott and J. Douglas (eds), *Theoretical Perspectives on Deviance*, New York: Basic Books.

Sharpe, M. (1929), *Chicago May: Her Story*, London: Sampson, Low and Co.

Stedman-Jones, G. (1971), *Outcast London*, Oxford: Oxford University Press.

Taylor, I., Walton, P. and Young, J. (1973), *The New Criminology*, London: Routledge and Kegan Paul.

Taylor, I., Walton, P. and Young, J. (eds), (1975), *Critical Criminology*, London: Routledge and Kegan Paul.

Van Dijk, J. (1986), 'Victim Rights: A Right to Better Services or a Right to Active Participation', in *Criminal Law in Action*, Amsterdam: Kluwer.

Walker, N. (1965), *Crime and Punishment In Britain: An Analysis of the Penal System in Theory, Law, and Practice*, Edinburgh: Edinburgh University Press.

Walker, N. (1987), *Crime and Criminology: A Critical Introduction*, Oxford: Oxford University Press.

Walker, N. (2003), *A Man Without Loyalties: A Penologist's Afterthoughts*, Chichester: Barry Rose Publishers.

Ward, D. and Kassebaum, G. (1965), *Women's Prison: Sex and Social Structure*, London: Weidenfeld and Nicolson.

Weick, K. (1979), *The Social Psychology of Organizing*, Reading, MA: Addison-Wesley.

Westergaard, J. and Resler, H. (1975), *Class in a Capitalist Society: A Study of Contemporary Britain*, London: Heinemann Educational.

Wildeblood, P. (1955), *Against the Law*, London: Weidenfeld and Nicolson.

Wilkins, L. (1964), *Social Deviance: Social Policy, Action, and Research*, London: Tavistock.

Published Writings

Books

Making People Pay (Routledge and Kegan Paul, 1973).
Deviant Behaviour (Hutchinson, 1973).
The Making of Symbolic Interactionism (Macmillan and Rowman and Littlefield, 1979).
Understanding Deviance (Oxford University Press, 1982, 2nd edn 1988, 2nd rev. edn 1995, 3rd edn 1998, 4th edn 2003, 5th edn 2007; Canadian edn June 2009, 6th edn currently in preparation); with David Downes.
A View from the Shadows: The Ministry of the Solicitor General of Canada and the Justice for Victims of Crime Initiative (Clarendon Press, 1986).
Helping Victims of Crime: The Home Office and the Rise of Victim Support in England and Wales (Clarendon Press, 1990).
The Social World of an English Crown Court: Witness and Professionals in the Crown Court Centre at Wood Green (Clarendon Press, 1993).
Reconstructing a Women's Prison: The Holloway Redevelopment Project, 1968–88, (Clarendon Press, 1996).
After Homicide: Practical and Political Responses to Bereavement (Clarendon Press, 1998).
Constructing Victims' Rights: The Home Office, New Labour and Victims (Clarendon Press, 2004).

Edited Books

Deviance and Social Control (Tavistock, 1974); with M. McIntosh.
Drugs and Politics (Transaction, 1977).
Deviant Interpretations (Martin Robertson and Barnes & Noble, 1979); with D. Downes.
Practice and Progress (George Allen & Unwin, 1981); with P. Abrams *et al.*
The British Journal of Criminology, special issue reprinted as *A History of British Criminology* (Oxford University Press, 1988).
Victimology (Dartmouth Press, 1994).
The History of Criminology (Dartmouth Press, 1994).
Thinking About Criminology (UCL Press and University of Toronto Press, 1998); with Simon Holdaway.
The Politics of Crime Control: Essays in Honour of David Downes (Clarendon Press, 2007); with Tim Newburn.
Crime, Social Control and Human Rights: From Moral Panics to States of Denial. Essays in Honour of Stanley Cohen (Willan, 2007); with D. Downes and others.

Articles and Chapters

'Observations on Debt Collection', *British Journal of Sociology*, **19**(2), June 1968, pp. 176–90.

'New Reflections on Violence', in D. Martin (ed.), *Anarchy and Culture* (Routledge and Kegan Paul, 1969); with F. Heidensohn.

'The Teddy Boy', in V. Bogdanor and R. Skidelsky (eds), *The Age of Affluence* (Macmillan, 1970); with S. Cohen.

'Social Reaction to Deviance and its Effects on Crime and Criminal Careers', *British Journal of Sociology*, **22**(4), 1971, pp. 351–64; with David Downes.

'Phenomenalism and Essentialism in the Sociology of Deviance', *Sociology*, **7**(1), January 1973, pp. 17–29.

'News as Eternal Recurrence', in S. Cohen and J. Young (eds), *The Manufacture of News* (Constable, 1973).

'The Sociology of Deviance and Conceptions of Moral Order', *British Journal of Criminology*, **14**(2), 1974, pp. 139–49.

'Some Problems of Interpretative Historiography', *British Journal of Sociology*, **27**(3), September 1976, pp. 353–69.

'Law, Order and Power in Late Seventeenth and Early Eighteenth Century England', *Annales Internationales de Criminologie*, **16**(1/2), 1977, pp. 233–65.

'Another Common-Sense Conception of Deviancy', *Sociology*, **13**(1), January 1979, pp. 75–88.

'Public Opinion and Criminal Legislation', in European Committee on Crime Problems, *Collected Studies in Criminological Research. Volume 17: Public Opinion on Crime and Criminal Justice* (Strasbourg, 1979).

'The Sociology of Crime, Symbolic Interactionism and Some Problematic Qualities of Radical Interactionism', in D. Downes and P. Rock (eds), *Deviant Interpretations* (Martin Robertson, 1979).

'Has Deviance a Future?', in H. Blalock (ed.), *Sociological Theory and Research* (Collier Macmillan, 1981).

'Rioting', *London Review of Books*, September 1981.

'The Bureaucratic Collection of Small Consumer Debts', in P. Hollowell (ed.), *Property and Social Relations* (Heinemann, 1982).

'Symbolic Interaction', in R. Smith and P. Manning (eds), *Handbook of Social Science Methods. Volume 2: Qualitative Methods* (Ballinger, 1982).

'Society's Attitude to the Victim', in E. Fattah (ed.), *Reorienting the Justice System: From Crime Policy to Victim Policy* (Macmillan, 1986).

'Victims and Policy in Canada: The Emergence of the Justice for Victims of Crime Initiative', in E. Fattah (ed.), *Reorienting the Justice System: From Crime Policy to Victim Policy* (Macmillan, 1986).

'A Natural History of Research on Policy-Making', in N. Fielding (ed.), *Actions and Structures* (Sage, 1988).

'Crime Reduction Initiatives on Problem Estates', in T. Hope and M. Shaw (eds), *Communities and Crime Reduction* (HMSO, 1988).

'Governments, Victims and Policies in Two Countries', *British Journal of Criminology*, **28**(1), 1988, pp. 44–66.

'The Present State of Criminology in Britain', *British Journal of Criminology*, **28**(2), 1988, pp. 58–69.

'On the Birth of Organizations', *LSE Quarterly*, **2**(2), Spring 1988, pp. 123–53 and *The Canadian Journal of Sociology*, **13**(4), 1988, pp. 359–84.

'Criminology, Research and the Making of Policy in a Canadian Setting', in K. Hawkins and J. Thomas (eds), *Making Regulatory Policy* (University of Pittsburgh Press, 1989).

'Symbolic Interactionism and Labelling Theory', in K. Plummer (ed.), *Symbolic Interactionism* (Edward Elgar, 1991).

'The Victim in Court Project at the Crown Court at Wood Green', *Howard Journal of Criminal Justice*, **30**(4), November 1991, pp. 301–10.

'Witnesses and Space in a Crown Court', *British Journal of Criminology*, **31**(3), Summer 1991, pp. 266–79.

'The Social Organization of British Criminology', in M. Maguire *et al.* (eds), *The Oxford Handbook of Criminology* (Clarendon Press, 1994).

'The Social Organization of a Home Office Initiative', *European Journal of Crime, Criminal Law and Criminal Justice*, **2**(2), 1994, pp. 141–67.

'Sociology and the Stereotype of the Police', *Law and Society*, **22**(1), March 1995, pp. 17–25, and in D. Galigan (ed.), *Socio-Legal Studies in Context* (Blackwell, 1995).

'The Opening Stages of Criminal Justice Policy-Making', *British Journal of Criminology*, **35**(1), Winter 1995, pp. 1–16.

'The Inquiry and Victims' Families', in J. Peay (ed.), *Inquiries after Homicide* (Duckworth, 1996).

'Sociological Theories of Crime', in M. Maguire *et al.* (eds), *The Oxford Handbook of Criminology* (2nd edn, Oxford, 1997).

'Murderers, Victims and "Survivors": The Social Construction of Deviance', *British Journal of Criminology*, **38**(2), Spring 1998, pp. 185–200.

'Rules, Boundaries and the Courts; Some Problems in the Neo-Durkheimian Sociology of Deviance', *British Journal of Sociology*, **49**(4), December 1998, pp. 586–601.

'Acknowledging Victims' Needs and Rights', *Criminal Justice Matters*, **35**(1), Spring 1999, pp. 4–6.

'Aftermath and the Construction of Victimisation: "The Other Victims of Crime"', *Howard Journal of Criminal Justice*, **39**(1), February 2000, pp. 58–77.

'Homicide, Voluntary Organizations and the State', *Homicide Studies*, **4**(1), February 2000, pp. 37–62.

'Symbolic Interactionism and Ethnography', in P. Atkinson *et al.* (eds), *The Handbook of Qualitative Methods* (Sage, 2001, 2007).

'The Sociology of Prison Life', in N. Smelser and P. Baltes (eds), the *International Encyclopedia of the Social and Behavioral Sciences* (Elsevier Science, 2002).

'Sociological Theories of Crime' in M. Maguire, R. Morgan and R. Reiner (eds), *Oxford Handbook of Criminology* (3rd edn, Oxford University Press, 2002).

'On Becoming a Victim', in C. Hoyle and R. Wilson (eds), *New Visions of Crime Victims* (Hart Publishing, 2002).

Entry on John Stanley Gittins for *The New National Dictionary of Biography* (Oxford University Press, 2004).

'Victims, Prosecutors and the State in Nineteenth Century England and Wales', *Criminal Justice*, **4**(4), November 2004, pp. 331–54.

'Victims' Rights in England and Wales at the Beginning of the 21st Century', in A. Heath *et al.* (eds), *Understanding Social Change* (British Academy and Oxford University Press, 2005).

'Victims' Policies as Contingent Accomplishments', in E. Vetere and D. Pedro (eds), *Victims of Crime and Abuse of Power: Festschrift in Honour of Irene Melup* (United Nations, 2005).

A Survey of the Victimisation of Homeless People (Crisis, 2005); with T. Newburn.

'Chronocentrism and British Criminology', *British Journal of Sociology*, **56**(3), 2005, pp. 331–54.

'The Politics of Victimhood', *Safer Society* (29), Summer 2006, pp. 11–13.

'Aspects of the Social Construction of Victims in Australia', *Victims and Offenders*, **1**(3), 2006, pp. 289–321.

'Urban Homelessness, Crime and Victimisation in England', *International Review of Victimology*, **13**(2), 2006, pp. 121–56; with Tim Newburn.

'Caesare Lombroso as a Signal Criminologist', *Criminology and Criminal Justice*, 7(2), 2007, pp. 117–33.

'Sociological Theories of Crime', in M. Maguire, R. Morgan and R. Reiner (eds), *Oxford Handbook of Criminology* (4th edn, Oxford University Press, 2007), pp. 3–42.

'New Labour Policies for Victims', *Criminal Justice Matters*, **67**(1), Spring 2007, pp. 38–39.

'The Sociology of Compliance-Based Regulation: An Intellectual History', in A. Brannigan and G. Pavlitch (eds), *Adventures in the Sociology of Law: Essays in Honour of W.G. Carson* (Routledge-Cavendish, 2007).

'Theories of Victimisation', in S. Walklate (ed.), *A Handbook of Victimology* (Willan, 2007).

'The Treatment of Victims in England and Wales', *Policing*, **2**, 2008, pp. 1–10.

'Victims', *The New Oxford Companion to Law* (Oxford University Press, 2008).

Forthcoming Publications

'Crime and Deviance' in *Blackwell's Dictionary of Twenty First Century Social Thought* (Blackwell).

'"Hearing Victims of Crime": The Delivery of Impact Statements as Ritual Behaviour in Four London Trials for Murder and Manslaughter', in A. Bottoms and J. Roberts (eds), *Victims in the Criminal Justice System* (Willan).

'Approaches to Victims and Victimisation', in T. Newburn (ed.), *The Sage Handbook of Criminological Theory* (Sage).

Other

Preface to I. Paulus, *The Search for Pure Food* (Martin Robertson, 1975).
Subject editor and contributor to *Macmillan Encyclopedia of Sociology* (Macmillan, 1983).
Contributor to *The Social Science Encyclopedia* (Routledge and Kegan Paul, 1985).
Foreword to T. Marshall, *Alternatives to Criminal Courts* (Gower, 1985).
Contributions to *The Blackwell Dictionary of Twentieth Century Social Thought* (Blackwell, 1993).
Foreword to J. Lowman and B. MacLean (eds), *Realist Criminology in the 1990s* (University of Toronto Press, 1993).
Foreword to E. Fattah, *Criminology Past, Present and Future* (Macmillan, 1997).
'Holloway', in N. Hahn *et al.* (eds), *Encyclopedia of Women and Crime* (Oryx, 2000).
Module 4: Final Reports on Bulgaria, Czech Republic, Hungary, Poland, Slovak Republic and Slovenia, *Reinforcement of the Rule of Law: Final Report of the First Part of the Project*, Phare Horizontal Programme on Justice and Home Affairs, European Commission (Centre for International Legal Cooperation, 2002), pp. 517–34, 543–48, 569–78, 587–605.
'Deviance: Theories of' in G. Ritzer (ed.), *The Blackwell Encyclopedia of Sociology* (Blackwell Publishing, 2007), Vol. 3, pp. 1135–40; with David Downes.
Evaluation of the Victims' Advocate Scheme Pilots (Ministry of Justice, 30 October 2008); with Anna Sweeting, Rachael Owen and Caroline Turley, British Market Research Bureau; and Miguel Garcia-Sanche, Laura Wilson and Usman Khan, Matrix Knowledge Group.

[1]
Observations on Debt Collection

The sociological study of deviance seems to be most rewarding when it examines the deviant as part of a system which generates and enforces definitions. *Deviance* is simply a label which has been successfully applied by one group to another, and those who label are just as significant to the process of deviance as those who receive the label. Becker argues that one consequence of this approach is that 'We become much more interested in the process by which deviants are defined by the rest of society. We do not take for granted, as has sometimes naively been done, that a given action is deviant because it is commonly regarded so. Instead, we look to the process by which the common definition arises.'[1]

Many types of deviance are 'unambiguously' outside the boundaries of 'acceptable' activity. Murder, theft and heroin addiction are so obviously social problems that little of the behaviour organized to contain them is occupied with definition and selection. The labels do not require elucidation. There are, however, other groups whose deviance is less immediately apparent. These groups lie in the frontier areas between 'normality' and 'abnormality' where the criteria for labelling have to be most articulate. Those required to cope with such frontier deviance must evolve rules for deciding who does, or does not, belong to the problem group, or whether, in fact, the group justifies the application of social control at all. It is here that L.S.D., abortion and obscenity illuminate what it is about social phenomena that acquires the label of deviance.

Default on debts does not appear to be either fully deviant or fully normal behaviour. There are millions of cases of default each year in England but, of these, only a small proportion will be thought pathological enough to merit intensive manipulation and coercion. Debt-collectors have constantly to choose which defaulters they are going to treat as deviant. Their behaviour may lead to a better understanding of the definitional process generally.

Creditors justify some of their actions by the claim that a significant number of their debtors are deviant, but this definition does not seem to be widespread and it has not entered into the academic writing on

* P. E. Rock B.SC.(SOC.) Assistant Lecturer in Sociology, London School of Economics

deviants. If a group is faced with outsiders who present a problem, such as default, the manner in which the problem is defined is useful for understanding how it is tackled. If the concept of deviance is to mean anything more than this, the defining group's ideas must be reinforced by other conditions.

There are two main criteria for establishing whether certain debtors *are* deviant. Social deviance occurs when people class a number of acts together as a group and label it a problem. They must be able to establish the boundaries of that group so that they are able to distinguish between behaviour which is odd or unusual and similar behaviour which is, in addition, wrong and intolerable. Above all, they must be able to enforce their opinions of the group; that is, they must be able to 'do something about it'.

It is perfectly possible to have a single deviant episode, but if a phenomenon is to represent an enduring problem, about which behaviour is organized, it should persist over time and have more than one instance. To the extent that people can recognize that an incident is an example of a class of deviance, the more readily will that incident become identified as deviant itself. Creditors place certain actions under the heading of default and organize a response to deal with it. Furthermore, they allege that some of those who commit these actions cannot be understood as normal or reasonable beings and that they require extraordinary handling.

Most people have been in default at one time. They cannot all be effectively thought of as deviant. If action is to be taken against the deviant debtor, a boundary has to be drawn between him and his fellows. Debt-collectors appear to have certain standards by which they judge what a 'normal' person would do in a situation and compare the debtor with this norm. Debtors who do not conform are deviant. Bailiffs, solicitors and creditors argue that they adopt a punitive stance because no normal person would behave as the people they deal with behave. There are, in addition, a number of assumptions which are arbitrarily built into the process—it is argued that no reasonable debtor would ever arrive at one of the later stages in an enforcement career, for example.

Simmons has suggested that it is unlikely that any social group can evade being labelled deviant by at least a few others.[2] What distinguishes disapprobation from the creation of deviance is an ability to counteract the defined group. Opinions must become realizable in effective action. Debt-collectors are provided with an elaborate system of courts, prisons and so on with which they can coerce debtors. Their definitions receive authoritative approval from the state.

If default is deviant, it assumes a peculiar form of deviance. It is, for example, one of the few types of deviance which is known in its entirety to the enforcers. Civil law dictates that those who are offended against are also responsible for tackling the offender. There is no 'iceberg' of bad debt. Thus there are no problems of detection, only ones of selection.

This selection takes place within the context of an unusual interaction. Debt-collection involves the very minimum of face-to-face contact between its participants. The enforcers may see their defaulters on only one or two occasions during an exchange lasting for years. This has a profound effect on the shape taken by the system, and I will examine its consequences below.

Debt-collection is a gigantic exercise in deterrence. Most creditors budget for bad debt and they can claim allowances in taxation. They can also adjust their prices by gearing them to their expectation of default. Their primary concern, therefore, is to keep losses within 'manageable' proportions. What they fear is an escalation of the numbers of their 'bad' accounts. If they do not collect debts, their losses may grow to a bankrupting size. The money they do lose is regretted, but usually accounted for. Debtors are pursued, often as conspicuously as possible, in order to deter others. Certain areas may be subject to strenuous enforcement in an attempt to demonstrate that a company's reputation for 'softness' there is unfounded. Similarly, flagrant default may be uneconomically punished. On the whole, however, the enforcement of debts is unique in that it is controlled by considerations of how economically advantageous each step is likely to be.

The whole process conforms to a blueprint and is machine-like. It is structured as a career—that is, it is made up of deliberately phased stages. Each stage has its own personnel, and each is designed to be more punitive. The timing of the career is minutely ordered by the enforcers—after one month a letter is sent out, after six months debt-collectors are resorted to, after nine months court action is taken, and so on. Debt-collection is a consciously conceived series of actions, and the result is a far more articulate system than that which obtains with any other mode of enforcement. The system has to cope with a vast number of cases, and procedures have to be routinized and simplified. This leads to a relative inflexibility and to the use of very general assumptions about causes and effects. It also leads to an automatic increasing of the pressure put upon the defaulter, coupled with an assumption of his increasing guilt and deviance. If the debtor does not intervene, he will routinely become identified as a deviant.

Finally, a great many types of deviance involve the illegal exchange of desired objects, such that the offended and the offender both seek its perpetuation. Indeed, Schur refers to examples of deviance as 'crimes without victims'. Debt has victims, creditors do not encourage it, and it is no crime.

Default is near the frontier where there are difficulties in deciding whether behaviour is 'normal' or 'pathological'. There is thus an absence of consensus about the population to be dealt with. Solicitors seem to be split between those who define debtors as deviant and those who do not, and this schism permeates the whole structure. The decision will be the prime determinant of how the system works itself out at any given point.

If a debtor persistently remains in default, he will pass through an enforcement career which is built on five general stages. Payment in any of these stages will lead to an immediate cessation of coercion. As a result, a debtor's evil is rarely dramatized. He is unlikely to be told that he is irrevocably deviant. Such labelling might result in the assumption of a deviant role-style which forbade any payment or negotiation. The debtor is informed that he will be subjected to increasingly unpleasant sanctions, but that these sanctions do not mean that he is becoming correspondingly more wicked. The definitions which govern the operation of the system are kept as covert as possible.

In the following description of a 'typical' case of debt-collection, I will assume that the creditor is a large institution and that the debt is small and legally recoverable.

The bulk of debts in Britain are owed to such large bureaucratic creditors as mail-order firms and hire-purchase companies. These organizations receive applications for credit at a great rate and in vast numbers. A creditor of this type has to decide whether to extend credit to an unknown and probably unseen population. Moreover, the decision-making is usually located at a fairly low level in the organization and must be governed by uncomplicated rules laid down from above. Judgments of applications must therefore be routine, mechanical and simple.

Creditors tend to impose a structure on their uncertainty by attributing great significance to the limited information which they receive. An applicant may well be stigmatized if he lives in a particular street or works in a particular occupation. Cues are endowed with a significance derived from the creditor's past experience of default and they are used to predict future losses. They are often given idiosyncratic meanings; one firm may believe that a policeman represents a 'good' risk, another that he is an appalling risk and a third that his occupation has no predictive value at all.

Creditors tend to build models of types of candidate: the 'good', the 'bad' and the 'marginal'. All seek the ideal applicant who is the 'stable man'; a person who is middle-aged, middle-class, a householder and so on, but some are unable to attract him. The debtors rejected by a bank may be happily received by a moneylender. The models are thus all phrased within the realm of the possible, not in terms of absolute qualities. The smaller the amounts of credit which a firm advances, the less it can devote to investigating applications. Such a firm will have to type applications on very crude data and its models will be correspondingly crude and rigid. It may well deal with no marginal cases at all. Other firms, with more complete information, may debate a marginal candidate and, if they approve him, will take steps to make him better. They may insist on a guarantor or a larger deposit.[3]

If a debtor who has obtained credit defaults, his creditor will invariably send him the first of a sequence of letters. There are three main objects sought by the firm in the initiating of this sequence. It seeks to regain its money—this is primary; it seeks to open negotiations with the debtor; and it seeks to place him. The whole enforcement process is directed towards the recouping of debts, but there are subsidiary goals pursued to further this end.

The most important factor in debt-collection is the nature of the communication between debtor and creditor. Few creditors are punitive or unsympathetic—they cannot afford to be. The whole course of the process is altered if there is some feedback from the debtor. Creditors tend to think of their defaulters in terms of three stereotypes—the Feckless, the Unfortunate and the Professional. Throughout enforcement they attempt to place a debtor in one of these categories. A debtor will probably be treated leniently if he is considered feckless or unfortunate. If he is a professional debtor—a person who intentionally lives on credit which is never repaid—the creditor will possibly be uneconomically severe towards him.

A debtor who does not reply to letters will be assumed to be one of three persons; a dishonest debtor, a stupid debtor or an evasive debtor. The creditor's letter stream therefore becomes more and more threatening. The first two letters were controlled by an apprehensiveness that threats might alienate a debtor who was merely forgetful, or whose money had not been sent because of absence or postal delay or clerical inefficiency. As each successive letter is sent, the sum defaulted on increases, and the debtor's deviance swells proportionately.

If the debtor *does* reply, pleads illness or unemployment, and suggests smaller payments, his offer will almost invariably be accepted. A creditor considers it far more worthwhile to accept smaller sums than to estrange a debtor by expensive pursuit. Some creditors attempt to evaluate the 'sincerity' of these letters, others may seek documentary proof of the debtor's statement; but all monitor the new repayments closely. If there is further default, the debtor is doubly harassed—he is both a defaulter and a dangerous betrayer of trust.

When the letter sequence fails, the creditor redefines the debtor.

The defaulter is labelled a dishonest and unreasonable person for whom more severe sanctions are appropriate. He is thus automatically made more deviant. The creditor's organization may include personnel who make face-to-face calls or use the telephone to pursue the defaulter. Even if these attempts do not recover the debt, they may furnish information which can direct the future tactics of the enforcer. An unsuccessful creditor is presented with four choices at this stage.

He may write the debt off as part of a standard policy for all debts, or for all small debts. He considers that the sums involved are too small to warrant any further expense and he has budgeted for default. If losses do rise beyond the limits which he has set as tolerable, he may take action other than the writing of letters.

He may sell the debt. This is triply useful to him: he has minimized his losses (and may have worked the relative costs of using the courts and selling debts); he can cut down on staff needed to cope with elaborate collection; and he has performed a book-keeping task —accounts are neatly ended.

He may pass the debt on to one of three kinds of debt-collector. The large urban collectors are institutions whose primary function is to act as a credit reference bureau or as a trade protection society— and they are not especially concerned with the collection of debts. They regard such collection as a service which they are required to perform by their members. They will send out a further stream of letters and, if these are unsuccessful, will either return the debt to the creditor or initiate legal action for him.

The smaller urban or suburban collectors employ a mixture of letters and calls. They define themselves as the performers of a professional service. The third type of collector tends to rely heavily on the use of guile and threats. It takes very little capital to establish a debt-collecting firm and many are born and die annually. The business of these firms comes from three sources. There are large creditors who dissociate themselves from the behaviour of their collectors. They believe that a rigorous approach is the most appropriate for the recalcitrant. There are local firms who do not become involved in a large enough volume of bad debt to warrant membership of a trade protection society. Finally, these debt-collectors may act as agents for the larger firms of collectors whose resources are inadequate to cover the whole of the country. All types of collector believe that their usefulness lies in the important symbolic value of the change of heading on the dunning letters to that of the stigmatizing name of a firm of debt-collectors. They attempt to maximize the unpleasant meanings associated with their occupation. Indeed, some creditors fabricate their own bogus firm of debt-collectors whose notepaper they use in their letter sequences.

He may pass the debt on to his solicitor. The solicitor will write further letters threatening court action. Solicitors, like their predecessors in the process, have faith in the efficacy of a change of heading on notepaper. Indeed, they may be employed solely because the creditor wishes to flourish the threat implied by a solicitor's warning. The mooted court proceedings may never, in fact, take place.

It is perhaps here that definitions of deviance first come to be applied. It is sometimes argued that the debtors who are prepared to be taken to court must be so insouciant that they must also be deviant. Some creditors pursue this further by suggesting that these debtors will also be unaffected by the sanctions made available by the county court. It is at this stage that the first major filtering of debtors takes place. Although some firms mechanically feed all defaulters into the courts, others discard those cases which they feel will meet with little success.

There are two sorts of solicitor. Those who spurn debt-collection tend to be geographically distant from the county courts. They see county court work as unremunerative and uninteresting. They are, however, blackmailed into undertaking it for they fear losing clients who offer them profitable work as well. A valuable index of whether a solicitor does or does not fall into the debt-collecting class is his conception of the minimum debt worth pursuing in the courts. The county court solicitor will quote two pounds and ten shillings as a minimum sum, the 'blackmailed' solicitor will cite between ten and twenty pounds. The debt-collecting solicitors will tend to act as agents for their reluctant colleagues. They will transform themselves into another part of the enforcement machine, routinely coping with a great number and variety of actions. One such solicitor may appear in very nearly all the actions of his local county court. He will develop an acute sensitivity to the idiosyncrasies of 'his' Registrar and judges, and interaction will often be nonverbal. He will know what orders are acceptable, will understand esoteric cues, and will acquire the ability to make his behaviour completely complementary to that of the judge. There is an innocuous Freemasonry about this which excludes the reluctant solicitor.

County court proceedings are usually initiated in the debtor's local court. The debtor is issued with a default summons, and is given eight days in which he may enter a defence. If he loses in his defence, 'judgment' is entered that the debt is one legally owing. Most often, no defence is offered, and judgment is automatic. Non-communication by the debtor remains the key factor. The creditor, now become the 'judgment creditor', is entitled to use a number of different sanctions. Debt-collection is difficult. It is by no means certain that a creditor will be successful, and many small creditors retire defeated. The sanctions which are available are weak, and often do not disturb the inveterate and experienced debtor.

County court sanctions are all ostensibly oriented towards one goal, the repayment of debts. Once a debt has been paid, the enforcers lose interest in the offender. Debt is one of the rare forms of deviance that may be purged simply and totally at any stage in the enforcement process. If a debtor restores the lent money, he is no longer an object of concern. I cannot think of any other type of deviance which has this property. Secondly, the sanctions exist in order that they should not be used. There is an explicit assumption in debt-collection that once the sanctions have been wielded, the collectors have lost. What the creditors employ, therefore, is an extensive manipulation of threats. That is why quite humane judges are happy about routinely giving orders backed with the threat of committal to prison. The enforcers and the defaulters are largely sparring. In most other forms of deviance sanctions are applied to the detected offender. Finally, the available sanctions are weak and will become weaker. The strategy is one of attempting to maximize the threat value of the sanctions, not one of using them. Debt-collection has something of the confidence-trick about it. The chief strength of the enforcers lies in their threats of action, not in action itself.

Very few of the sanctions offered the creditors by the courts are used in practice. There are seven procedures of collection in the county courts; garnishee proceedings, charging orders on property, bankruptcy, administration orders, execution on goods, 'part-execution' on goods, and committal proceedings. The last three are the only numerically significant ones. This is due largely to the simplified approach which most creditors and solicitors adopt. The flood of summonses which they issue militates against a sensitivity to the individual case. Some creditors place faith in the efficacy of one method and adhere to it in all actions.

When a judgment has been entered against a debtor, he receives an order to repay the debt either by instalments, by a certain date, or immediately. If default is made on this order, the creditor is entitled to execute on the debtor's goods. Goods are seized by a bailiff and auctioned off. This tends to be unsuccessful because (*a*) the debtor only occasionally has enough property to satisfy the whole debt; (*b*) certain goods, such as bedding and 'tools of trade', are exempt; (*c*) goods often belong, or are alleged to belong, to the spouse of the debtor or (*d*) are subject to a hire-purchase agreement and cannot be taken. The sums which the goods realize also tend to be low, for they are typically of small resale value and there are no minimum prices below which they cannot be sold. 'Full execution' is, however, extremely useful to the creditor. The threat of the loss of one's possessions is a frightening one. 'An . . . instinctual impulse drives us to collect property; and the collections thus made become, with different degrees of intimacy, parts of our empirical selves,' the loss of these collections induces 'a sense of the shrinkage of our personality, a partial conversion of ourselves to nothingness, which is a psychological phenomenon by itself'.[4] In addition, execution proceedings may have the effect of producing a kind of 'reality-shock' in the debtor. A defaulter, whose goods have been levied on will have had a direct confrontation with the brutality social control. In 1962, for example, there were one million and two hundred thousand judgments entered in the county courts of England and Wales. There were 1,607,585 executions issued against goods, but only 7,314 sales were made. There were thus more executions issued than there were judgments. It is apparent that the monies acquired through the actual sale of goods are statistically unimportant. Although there were a substantial number of 'abortive' executions, cases of debtors leaving their addresses and so on, it was the threat of action, not the action itself, which was significant.

These figures also cover 'part-executions'. A 'part-execution' takes place when a portion of the debt is repaid by execution on goods. Where there is, for example, a fifty pound debt, a creditor may order part-execution for five pounds. This method tends to be more successful than demands for larger sums. The chances of a sale being actually made are still remote, but the bailiff is allowed to progress further in the ritual. He is more likely to find enough goods to satisfy the warrant, remove the goods from the debtor's home and allow the debtor to pay for his property and retrieve it.

If execution is abortive or disliked, the creditor may issue a judgment summons. It is at this point that the labelling process becomes paramount. When a judge decides that the debtor did have the means to pay the court order, but had refused to do so in flagrant default, the debtor will be proclaimed to be in contempt of court and there exists a penal sanction for this. If the debtor has relatively substantial means, he may be ordered to pay the debt immediately; if limited means, to pay it by instalments. In both cases, the order may be backed by a suspended prison sentence. The sentence was designed to be used against deviants. 'An order for committal to prison can only be made where there is a contumacious debtor.'[5]

At almost any stage, two modifying influences may operate. If the bailiff defines the debtor as a sympathetic person, and not a deviant, he may couple exhortion to the defaulter with reports to the court that he could not execute the warrant because he was 'unable to see' the debtor. A debtor may also make an application to the court for a further suspension of the warrant. Debts tend to be gradually recovered through this control over the debtor. Orders are usually made on small instalments—with an implicit felicific calculus underlying the threat. Threatening warrants bring about a small stream of payments. A warrant is no longer regarded as an effective sanction if it *is* used. Although imprisonment is for contempt of court and does not expunge a debt, it effectively extinguishes the debt. The defaulter assumes that he has been punished for his default and the creditor considers that any further action is useless if the toughest sanction fails.

It is apparent that an absence of communication is again crucial at this stage. Over half a million judgment summonses were issued in 1962. Seventy per cent of these were heard—the rest were not served, or abandoned or paid. One hundred and eighty thousand orders of commitment were issued, but only four and a half per cent of these resulted in the imprisonment of debtors. Prisons are not used to punish debtors, but to deter them. An imprisoned debtor is a victorious debtor.

CONCLUSION

Debt-collection is a process split up into stages. Each stage is the basis of intensive interaction between debtors and various groups concerned to coerce them into paying their debts. This process may most usefully be conceptualized as a career—a career with status-forcing, bench-marks and the idea of development. The debtor is serially an applicant, a debtor, a defaulter, a defendant and a prisoner. His role-others are creditors, solicitors, debt-collectors, plaintiffs, bailiffs, registrars, judges and prison officers. Each change of name symbolizes a forced change of status and a new pattern of action directed against the debtor. 'By a series of common-sense constructs [human beings] have preselected and pre-interpreted this world which they experience as the reality of their daily lives. It is these thought objects of theirs which determine their behaviour by motivating it.'[6]

When a debtor changes his status, he also changes the way in which he will be treated by the 'world'. Each change of status is presaged by warnings. 'Dear Sir, Unless . . .' The debtor is told that he will no longer be labelled a defaulter, but will now become a defendant. Each milestone is made significant, for each presents the debtor with a choice. He may continue in the career or he may leave it. His role-others desire that he should leave it. Debt-collection is therefore ritualized as much as possible.

The career is institutionalized and precise. It runs parallel to another important sequence of events—the commercial ordering of time. Creditors live in a world dominated by the financial year, by monthly agreements, and by working weeks. Debt-collection is, after all, concerned with money. It is therefore constructed to mesh with the creditor's other world. When debt-collection reaches the courts it becomes structured by judicial time. There are judicial terms and vacations. More especially, there are legal conceptions of what are reasonable lengths of time which may intervene between two stages. Finally, the career is affected by expediency. Most debtors are paid weekly, but instalment orders are made on a monthly basis, for example, 'Long stretches of time may be made more "psychologically manageable" by being broken up into smaller segments. When the markers used to divide periods of time into segments are also sign-posts of progress in a given direction, we have the foundation of a career timetable.'[7] There is no reason to assume that deviance can be measured on a strict monthly basis. A foreign time-scale estimates the extent of a debtor's deviance. Imposed on the career are a number of arbitrarily placed 'bench-marks' which evaluates the defaulter's progress. A debtor who has reached the judgment summons 'must' be a greater deviant than one who has not. The career is seen as a sequence into greater and greater deviance. In a sense, therefore, it manufactures deviance itself—it does not contain or control it. An experienced registrar told me that 'I have yet to meet a recalcitrant debtor'. Nevertheless, debt-collection imposes the label of 'recalcitrance' on the defaulters.

Each set of role-others operate one stage of the process. There is therefore the possibility of friction between their conceptions of what the debtors are like and how they should be treated. The creditor who passes a debtor on to a court has found him too deviant to handle without the aid of legal coercion. The court staff, however, grant the debtor a probationary period before applying their own definitions. They can only judge cases on the basis of the information with which they are provided. Registrars and judges talk of the 'stage army' of defendants who regularly appear before them. They do not readily comprehend how firms can be so liberal with their credit to such notorious defaulters. Yet the creditors see this selfsame stage army as their toughest opponents. Again, when debtors come to court, the roles which they play are often the reverse of those which they played before the creditor. The debtor who attempted to demonstrate that he was more than capable of paying instalments now pleads poverty. The debtor who was evasive and uncommunicative now presents himself as unemployed or ill. The two groups, the creditors and the court officials are, in fact, tackling different people. Finally, one of the chief sources of friction between solicitors and courts lies in the area of instalment orders. The solicitors are under pressure from their clients to effect a rapid recovery of the debt. They see the debtors as deviants who warrant firm action. The courts reason that an order which is payable is better than a large order which is not;

that a debtor who defaults on an excessively large instalment order is a debtor whose co-operation is lost; and that enforcement procedures are the same whatever the size of the instalment order.

The debtor's progress through the career is thus not carried out at a uniform speed. The career's blueprint does not conform to what actually does take place. One stage is not immediately more severe than its predecessor. Each stage is potentially more severe, but the debtor has to be labelled anew before he experiences this greater severity.

Erikson argues that 'deviance is not a property *inherent in* certain forms of behaviour; it is a property *conferred upon* these forms by the audiences which directly or indirectly witness them. The critical variable in the study of deviance, then, is the social audience rather than the individual actor, since it is the audience which eventually determines whether or not any episode of behaviour or any class of episodes is labelled deviant.'[8] The dynamics of debt-collection are peculiarly susceptible to such analysis. It is probably easier to understand the decision-making of this particular audience than that of any other.

The primary goal of the creditor is to make good his losses. He is provided with organizations, both private and public, to assist him; and his defaulters are automatically subjected to a variety of pressures. His methods of enforcement are standardized to make for the least complexity. Hence one solicitor, who acts for some of the largest creditors, makes a flat demand for court orders of one pound a month for all defendants. If these orders are defaulted on, he will demand a part-execution to the value of two pounds ten shillings. By asking for enforcement procedures which are applicable even to the poorest defendant, he can deal with thousands of cases a week in the most expedient manner. If this were all that there is to debt-collection, it would be of little interest. Most creditors, however, seem to have three additional pressures working upon them. Firstly, they fear that they may alienate a 'good' customer by tactless handling. Even until quite late in the career, it is always possible that there is a 'reasonable' excuse for a customer's default. There is a rich mythology in the creditor's world. It abounds with cautionary tales. A certain firm, for example, was in disorder with its accounts. This firm was unable to send out threatening letters to defaulters who were quite seriously in arrears. Despite the absence of these letters, money still came in erratically. The firm, and the creditors who tell the story, conclude that most of their customers are basically honest and that the letter stream is not necessarily responsible for repayments. It is this kind of incident which makes creditors reluctant to label defaulters deviant at any early stage in the process.

Secondly, there is a considerable sensitivity to press accounts of debt-collection. The county courts seem to feature very little in the press, but there have been cases of small children or eighty-year-old widows being brought to court and selected as objects of press sympathy. The details of one Scottish case were recited to me by the representatives of three separate companies. When the newspapers decry the activities of the large firms, these firms suffer. They lay great stress upon the importance of good public relations and remember humiliating incidents for a long time. Creditors will therefore exert much effort to avoid bad publicity. Some firms will even abandon every defended court action.

Finally, the professional debtor haunts every credit manager. Each firm is able to recite how it 'was taken for a ride' by such a person. Professional debtors, they argue, broadcast a firm's reputation for vulnerability. They advertise the methods by which a creditor may be cheated. The losses which one professional debtor may cause will be much larger than those created by one unfortunate or feckless debtor. The professional debtor is, I am told, rare. The creditor will fear him in the manner in which the prison officer fears the escaping prisoner. Creditors cannot, then, apportion exactly equal amounts of energy to each type of debtor. There is still some selection.

There are debtors who do not have enough money to promptly repay a debt. A large proportion of them may be gradually coerced to make good the default. This may take a long time, but the debt will be repaid. Such poor people may flout a creditor, and incur debts they will not, or cannot, repay. They may be unco-operative and uncommunicative. A number of these will become labelled deviant. There are others who are so patently poor that even lengthy and patient enforcement is abandoned. There is a third group of people who appear to have enough means to repay a debt but do not do so. This group bewilders the creditor. It must be unreasonable. There must be further selection.

Such decision-making is difficult. The creditor has little information upon which to act and the whole onus of collecting it rests upon him. The creditor must pay for the tracing of debtors or for the gathering of facts about them. He must either employ his own personnel or private firms. In most cases, the debts are so small that it is uneconomic to learn details about those who owe them. The creditor falls back on those clues which he has at his disposal. These are few and only tangentially related to orienting policy. A few creditors (the giant mail-order firms, for example) seem to know what are the objective correlates of default. The rest rely upon 'hunch' and 'experience'. The really well-known debtors are the inveterate defaulters, but the creditor should not have allowed them credit at all.

The information available to a creditor covers the type of goods financed; the type of credit; the address of the debtor; the dealer or agent through whom credit was obtained; the stage in the agreement when default was made; and what responses the debtor has made. There are, in addition to these, a number of 'status' characteristics which are recorded on the debtor's application form. This is almost all the creditor has to act on. He must extract as much as he can from each item. He argues, for example, that certain goods are more prone than others to serious default. Easily marketable goods and goods which cannot be resold are both defaulted on. The professional debtor, he claims, will deal in profitable and popular objects. Other debtors may know that certain goods are not worth repossessing. Enforcement is rendered more difficult in such a situation, and the debtor may become more secure in his default. Where a debtor defaults on, say, a bedroom suite or on a tape-recorder, he may well arouse suspicion.

Every little piece of information becomes pregnant with meaning. There are 'good' dealers and 'bad' dealers. A 'bad' debtor from a 'good' dealer will probably be treated more gently than a 'good' debtor from a 'bad' dealer. A debtor who defaults immediately is taken to be a professional debtor who has no intention of paying; one who defaults halfway through an agreement is a feckless debtor who is not able to manage his affairs; and the unfortunate debtor defaults towards the end of the period. No creditor will know whether this reasoning is correct, but he must make an unknown world familiar.

The most comprehensive information which an enforcer has before him concerns the debtor's status attributes. He will know the debtor's occupation, where the debtor was born, how old he is and so on. Secondary status characteristics will precipitate the stereotyping of a debtor. 'Among those who are known to have committed a deviant act, those who seem to possess additional qualities concurring with the stereotypic image of that kind of deviance are far more likely to be labelled and processed a deviant.'[9] People living in certain streets, performing certain jobs and possessing a certain nationality will undergo strenuous enforcement. It is improbable, for example, that a Negro living in Ladbroke Grove will be accorded the same treatment as a Cheam headmaster.

It is apparent, then, that an enforcement apparatus of this kind tends to create deviants through self-fulfilling prophecies. When the processing is in operation, a great variety of data assumes increasingly sinister meanings. The meanings lend momentum to the process and the process colours the meanings. Only a debtor's intervention will cause this interaction to cease.

Notes

1. H. S. Becker (ed.), *The Other Side: Perspectives on Deviance,* Free Press of Glencoe, 1964, pp. 2–3.

2. J. L. Simmons, 'Public Stereotypes of Deviants', *Social Problems,* vol. 13, no. 2 (Fall 1965), pp. 223–32.

3. This seems to be an excellent example of the resolution of 'cognitive dissonance'. Cf. Festinger, Riecken and Schachter, *When Prophecy Fails,* New York, Harper Torchbooks, 1964, p. 26.

4. W. James, *Psychology—the Briefer Course,* New York, Harper Torchbooks, 1961, p. 45.

5. Lord Justice Vaughan Williams, *Credit,* vol. 1, no. 4 (London, October 1960), p. 5.

6. A. Schutz, 'Concept and Theory Formation in the Social Sciences', *J. Phil.,* vol. 51 (April 1954), pp. 266–7.

7. J. A. Roth, *Timetables,* New York, Bobbs-Merrill, 1963, p. 115.

8. K. T. Erikson, 'Notes on the Sociology of Deviance', in H. S. Becker (ed.), op. cit., p. 11.

9. J. L. Simmons, op. cit., p. 231.

[2]
Some Problems of Interpretative Historiography

'We all know that social science is, in principle, impossible. If it were possible, we would not do it anyway.'[1]

INTRODUCTION

Much of the German philosophy of history revolved around the problems that flowed from Kant's epistemology. A number of grand strategies were proposed to gain access to the elusive objects of historical and social life. Dilthey's *Erlebnis*, Lukács' dialectic and Simmel's formalism served as models for transcending the seemingly unbridgeable gulf between observer and observed. Such problems are likely to be resurrected in a modified and humble guise as certain minor versions of contemporary sociology are employed to explore the past. For instance some sociologists of deviance are attempting to unearth the early developmental forms of asylums, prisons, police forces and the like. To a marked extent, their perspectives are derived from the American phrasing of sociological phenomenology and rest upon the works of Alfred Schutz, Aaron Cicourel, Jack Douglas and Edward Tiryakian. In turn, those works stem almost directly from the earlier writings of Simmel, Weber and Husserl.

Efforts to transform a modest social phenomenology of the present into a strategy for confronting the past are likely to become riddled with familiar difficulties. That phenomenology stresses the embeddedness of meaning, the ineffability of much experience, and the impermissibility of substantial generalization. Although many of these themes are paradoxical or self-contradictory, they have been fruitfully applied to contemporary worlds. If a history acknowledging those themes is to be possible, some resolution of their accompanying problems must be accomplished. This paper offers a few ideas about how that resolution might be framed. My concern will be with only one rather special conception of history, a conception which is tied to a particular sociological tradition. It will address the peculiar problems of a single intellectual approach. In that sense, it may contribute to a division of labour. Its focus should complement the arguments of other papers in this *Journal*, concentrating on one interesting and relatively contained style of reasoning. I shall proceed by reviewing the typical arguments that might be advanced by bearers of the tradition. Those arguments raise considerable objections to the possibility of a tenable historiography, but they also present some resources for a limited defence. That defence will be far from sure. It will accept with Samuel Butler, that 'there can be no doubt about faith and not reason being the *ultima ratio*'. Yet a defence is required if history is to become a legitimate territory for the interactionist and phenomenologist.

THE PROBLEM STATED

Whatever its level of abstraction or magnification may be, historical analysis must finally be construed as an attempt to capture the everyday reality of men. Any treatment of massive historical changes or minor occurrences is no more than an imploded discussion of that reality. It receives its animation and intelligibility from its accounts of typical motives and courses of action. Without those accounts, it has no discernible anchorage. It becomes, instead, devoid of any demonstrable connection with the social life it purports to describe. A construct such as class conflict, mercantilism, war or crisis may have an analytic usefulness for the historian and, in many circumstances, for the people whose behaviour it describes. Yet it cannot be taken to have an autonomous existence outside its realization in men's experience.[2]

As mediator and creator of order, the historian produces a particular kind of description whose coherence and plausibility flow from his techniques of reconstructing that everyday reality. He can 'know' the past, but the content and form of any knowledge he acquires are finally shaped by his existential relationship with the dead.[3] The dead are not available to him as his contemporaries are; he cannot bodily enter their environment; he cannot converse with them; and he can know them only through fragmented and problematic records. He cannot survey them as he would a contemporary, observing the detail of gesture, tone, expression and position. He cannot question them. He cannot assume any community of context or experience to unite him with the dead. He shares no intersubjective world which transcends his existence and theirs. He cannot properly probe his own past for stocks of knowledge which he might possess in common with them. In short, a reconstituted past is phenomenologically impoverished and unsure. It is also transformed by the apprehension that it is closed and determinate: the world of one's predecessors 'is a definitively past world; *it has no open future*. . . . my predecessors *cannot be experienced as free*'.[4] The dead are thus known mediately, by means of typifications which are derivative, inferential and speculative. They are re-assembled without any assurance that they or the worlds which they populated conform to anything which the historian has himself directly experienced. He cannot take his own existentially-based sense of adequacy as a firm guide but must, instead, turn to more anonymous and abstract typifications of conduct. His phenomenological distance from the described events is often acute, his knowledge being an organization of ideas which he has synthesized out of others' syntheses. He regroups and reformulates typifications of typifications, unable to obtain any immediate access to the settings which he explores. Such an ordering of mediated knowledge has been defined by Schutz as a 'personal ideal type': 'the unity of the Other is originally built up in the unity of *my* experience, more precisely, in the synthesis of *my* interpretations of the Other's experiences'.[5] The historical personal ideal type is possibly the most complex of all. It raises possibilities of solipsistic imputations. It is a compound of many interlocking interpretations which must be sifted in a fashion that answers purposes of intellectual demonstration.

Such an ideal type must be based on the signs and records that collectively make up the knowable past. Those traces must be read as meaningful productions which stem from stated and unstated contexts of meaning. They cannot be usefully employed until those contexts are reassembled. It is necessary to provide a 'theory which accounts for the common-sense meanings used by the actor and by the social structure within which the material was produced'.[6] Until that theory is furnished, historical traces must be regarded as tantamount to meaningless. Although they may appear to have some intelligibility, it is a conjectural and problematic intelligibility that may be held to proceed from the historian's own common-sense understanding and not from any appreciation of the actor's world. That appreciation is both the means and end of historical analysis. One who has attained it can undertake descriptive work, but it cannot be attained without an extraordinary feat of the imagination. It is in this sense that history becomes a virtually impossible object of enquiry. If signs cannot be assessed until their larger meaning and mode of production are first established, they must remain closed systems of significance. There is no totally defensible strategy for entering them.

The traces which are clustered to form historical 'events' must be assumed to have some facticity which is independent of the historian's imagination, but they can be interpreted and situated only by the exercise of that imagination. As personal ideal types, they acquire their unity and coherence chiefly from the historian's ability to order and synthesize ideas. 'Historians are aware that their own minds are the spheres in which the past comes alive again and that the data of their researches are converted into "histories" by a process involving personal qualities of insight, sympathy and imagination'.[7] Indeed, the 'past' has no existence at all outside its reconstitution by the historian; it appears only when it has been creatively disinterred, and its appearance can never be the same as that which the dead themselves experienced. It is simply an artifact, a contrivance, and not a resurrection.[8]

Historical projects thus revolve around the ability of the historian to capture and know what are probably alien existential worlds. His attempts to do so are necessarily riddled with difficulties. Knowing some person, group or event inevitably entails a degree of subjective chance. The motives and meanings which infuse another's conduct are always problematic. Yet attributions are not all equally suspect, and Schutz has suggested that they may be arrayed in a spectum of interpretative uncertainties. At one pole, the 'We-relation' of the face-to-face encounter exists in a collaboratively constructed, intersubjective world that presumably transcends the personal environment of each individual participant.[9] There is an ostensible community and simultaneity of experience which permit reasonable inferences about the other's sense of his world. Those inferences can feed upon the wealth and immediacy of expressions that unfold before people thus linked. Verbal and non-verbal interrogation and scrutiny are quite possible.

At the other pole, there is massive doubt. The typifying scheme that is employed to define the dead cannot rest on the assumption that they share 'with me a rather vaguely defined core segment of common knowledge'.[10] There is no participation in joint experience or joint schemes of interpretation. There can be no reciprocal monitoring or questioning. The meanings of acts and gestures are therefore framed by different existential contexts; they simply cannot be taken to represent the 'same' phenomena. 'What cannot be decided with certainty . . . is the degree of congruity between the scheme of expression which determined my predecessor's communicative acts and my scheme of interpretation.'[11]

Congruity can be gauged only by matching the tacit inner world of a past event with the modes of being and knowing that are employed by the historian and are believed to be typical of his contemporaries. It is apparent that such a review has many disturbing qualities because the historian's own sense of what passes for plausible social description must be used to judge the very worlds which he has reconstructed. Whatever the grasp that is obtained on those worlds, it is likely to be infirm.

If recorded materials are resistant to ready decoding, those which must be inferred are even more obdurate. The historian must inspect traces that bear with them very little of the environments that produced and maintained them. Much that constitutes the experienced context of meaning is simply ineffable. The content and form of such sentiments as love, fear, pleasure, pain and anxiety lend a vital significance to communications although they defy translation into words. Indeed, as Douglas argues, they 'are almost completely outside of verbal language, which often disrupts them more than it builds in these realms'.[12] Paralinguistic modes of appropriating the world can contextualize, complement and replace words, and words cannot be fully appreciated without them. But they cannot be cast into words without losing some of their meaning. It may only be the cerebral or the deracinated which the historian can discuss.

Most of our immediate experience is then pre-predicative, organized into speech or writing only occasionally and always retrospectively.

Other experience can never be predicated. Because no system of typifications is exhaustive, there must always be areas of life which lie outside a society's stock of categories and are consequently free and 'unregulated'. Such areas permanently escape documentation and publicly-available reflection, but they nevertheless fuse the core of the interpretations which have to be made.

Much, too, is taboo, secret or private. Individuals, groups and organizations often house guilty knowledge. They devote some effort to the task of constructing publicly-respectable faces.[13] The discreditable is guarded and suppressed. The shameful and intimate facets of our conduct rarely receive expression in documents intended for promiscuous public consumption. They may nevertheless represent a vital explanation of behaviour:

> So much of what really 'counts' to people in our society goes on in secret. . . . Anyone who approaches our society as an outsider . . . will miss most of the important things and have a completely wrong understanding. It is vital that he have his own experience of these matters to draw upon in trying to understand our society. If he does not, he may never 'discover' them and may . . . mistake the most simple myths for realities . . .'[14]

Some secrets may not be kept and others may be inferred. Yet the historian cannot reassure himself that he knows all that there was to be known about a society. Neither can he be sure that documents and utterances were not intended to deceive; that they were not left as a form of joke, decoy or disguise.[15] Further, the problematic character of the historical imagination does tend to limit the scope of interpretation, induction and questioning. Not knowing what he does not know, the historian is armed only with partial perspectives and uncertainly defined fragments. In a sense, then, he is forced to contend with husks of language which he can never properly understand. That language resists satisfactory deciphering because it derives its significance from uncommunicated experience, experience which preceded it and existed independently of it: 'the meanings which are given expression in speech arise mostly in other zones of our existence'.[16] It is clear that the only strategies available to the historian are ones offered by his own existential knowledge, a knowledge which is itself largely pre-predicative, situational and unscrutinized. He cannot but assume that the expressed, the unexpressed and the unexpressible are all locked together in a closed system of meaning. Even if he did manage in some fashion to break into that system and learn its constitution, he could never be certain that he had acquired meretricious rather than adequate knowledge.[17]

If these arguments have any substance at all, they reveal the precarious nature of historical knowledge. Indeed, unless some qualification is possible, they render the pursuit of that knowledge absurd. One of the prime difficulties that accompany the marshalling of such doubts is presented by the lack of any effective critical canons by which they may be assessed. Sociological arguments may permit the recognition of anomaly, contradiction and paradox, but they offer little guidance about how their significance should be weighted. There are no procedures whereby such objections may be regarded as slight or grave in their consequences for a particular theoretical scheme. In the case of historical description, it is utterly unclear whether reflections flowing from the sociology of knowledge completely undermine historical analysis, or whether they merely emphasize the need to employ especially fastidious and delicate tactics.

Critiques and defences of interpretative sociology are incapable of furnishing remedies for doubt. They provide no criteria for measuring the gravity of sceptical assertions. It is not apparent whether the phenomenological gulf which separates the historian from his objects is massive or narrow, whether it is thoroughly disabling or simply an inconvenient obstruction. The scale and nature of the gulf certainly make history problematic because they are problematic themselves. Yet they provide no basis for despair or confidence. Indeed, many of the arguments which constrain the historian also hamper the sociologist of strange, contemporary worlds. The present is recalcitrant too, and it is evident that the sociologist who would study it does not occupy an entirely privileged position.[18]

In sum, certain sociologists would deny the claims made by those who have sought to explore the past. They would maintain that adequate understanding hinges on a proper interpretation of the subjective worlds that were once occupied by people who are now dead. Those subjective worlds are irrevocably inaccessible to the historian. Any attempt to reconstitute them must make use of procedures which are anachronistic and untenably speculative. Even if a reconstruction were successfully accomplished, there are no recognized practices which allow the historian to demonstrate that his is a faithful rather than a spurious explanation. The materials for such a demonstration cannot be discovered by any of the methods which are available to him. On the contrary, some independent vantage point is required to assess the fit between a description and what is described. Historiography cannot provide that external perspective on itself, and it cannot underwrite any of its interpretations.

Some limited reservations may be made about the forcefulness of this argument about historical analysis. They can be best advanced by examining that argument more fully. I shall consider three principal obstructions to the development of an interpretative historical sociology. My discussion will centre on the parts played by the tolerable invariance of common-sense schemes of understanding; the co-existence of past and present in some phenomenologically-apprehended 'now'; and the relative emancipation of certain cultural items from a complete absorption in their contexts.

THE OBJECTIVITY OF CULTURAL ITEMS

Cicourel has argued that there are hazards attached to 'viewing indexical expressions as if they could be repaired and thus transformed into context-free objective statements'.[19] He would assert that any utterance must be interpreted as a collapsed shorthand account whose proper significance cannot be appreciated until it has been once more lodged in the environment of meaning which first engendered it. That environment represents the unstated and stated semantic background which forms the production of an expression. The disentangling of meanings will always be incomplete unless their manner of assembly can also be understood. Sociology lacks principles of extraction which would enable the interpreter of an expression to assess how it may be discussed independently of its originating context.[20] Without those principles, analytic strategies must ground themselves in an intimate reproduction of the situations which generate action. Douglas, too, claims:

> All experience is . . . rooted, grounded, situated. . . . Given this necessarily situated nature of human experience, all truthful understanding of that experience must be based upon a *grasping* of that experience in its natural situation. Like most experience in its initial stages, this *grasping* is a highly situated experience . . .[21]

The indexicality of historical records threatens to remove them permanently from the reach of adequate retrospective interpretation. The closure and incalculable alienness of past events makes the encoding practices that furnished the records irrecoverable. Yet it does not follow that all records are equally indexical or that they are all indecipherable. Speech and writing may give rise to some linguistic productions which are relatively autonomous. Any discussion of that autonomy must be most circumspect because it cannot be controlled by rules for ordering doubt, but it would be unprofitable to assume *a priori* that every cultural item is equally embedded.

Kwant has suggested that 'there are two dangers to avoid when we consider the relationship between language and existence. The first of these is that of isolating speech from the whole of our existence as giver of meaning. The second . . . is to emphasize the bond between language and existence so much that the proper character of speech is denied'.[22] That proper character resides in the peculiar capacity of speech to acquire a limited phenomenological decontextualization. All existence is immediately and initially apprehended through 'lived meaning'; it is grasped without any knowing detachment from the flow of experience. Lived meaning is not reflexively organized by typifications, but any attempt to make sense of it—retrospectively or prospectively—must be symbolically mediated. When we reflect upon what we have done and what has happened to us, we no longer inhabit a pure realm of lived meaning. The mediations which are consciously employed to bestow form upon experience may be personal and incommunicable, or they may enjoy a public currency. The chief public form is speech, the ordering of meaning by and into words. Speech is dialectically fused with experience: existence is transformed by words which are themselves lent content and context by existence.

When phenomena are spoken about, the speaker translates them in a fourfold fashion. Speech places the observer at a distance from an object. He becomes simultaneously detached and knowledgeable. The object is no longer grasped; it is, instead, pointed at. Pointing enforces a separation between subject and object. The object itself becomes prised out of its context. It is given a definition which distinguishes it from its environment. All speaking therefore imposes some shedding of context although, paradoxically, it also creates the object-context distinction. Thirdly, speech rests on generic forms. It translates meaning into signification, casting the unique and rooted into transcendental categories. All words can give rise to experience which is general and 'trans-situational'. They arrange and abstract meanings so that they are applicable across the boundaries of events and times. When an item is described in language it becomes practically dislocated. Finally, speaking can organize a separate mode of experience which is not simply a transmutation or decipherment of prepredicative thought. It has its own distinct phenomenological properties which exceed those of the prereflexive world.[23]

Words are available to any man. The special contexts of their production are not recapitulated every time they are used. Merleau-Ponty has distinguished between *parole parlée* and *parole parlante.*[24] *Parole parlée* is the creative word which arises immediately out of lived meaning. Once formed, however, it can be repeated by others who have never experienced the same lived meaning. It can become *parole parlante*, part of the general stock of significations that are conventionally employed within a community. Members of that community can retrieve some generalized and typified meaning for *paroles parlantes*, and indexicality is not completely lost. But they cannot revive all the texture and detail of the experience which first gave birth to such words.

Environments of meaning are largely preformed by spoken words. They provide competent people with promiscuous access to knowledge about the world. In the main, that knowledge is a common-sense understanding which serves everyday purposes. It is generalized, stylized and compressed. The spoken word, *parole parlante*, is itself a formalizing, generalizing and condensing medium of typification. It is a highly conventional symbolic form which may be carelessly used because of its frequent lack of a close connection with the contents of existence. Many words are abused or misused by strict lexicographical criteria. Most are spoken without much reflection: they are available 'as a matter of course' without attention being given to their precise meaning or connotations. They form a taken-for-granted and, in a sense, existentially-neutral means of appropriating the world. Their origins and combinations are often obscure even to those who speak them.[25]

Lived meaning and spoken meaning thus share a most problematic relation with one another. Indexicality is not uniform and may occasionally cease to be analytically central. The world of speech cannot be reduced down to the world of unmediated meaning; what is said can be experienced as unfaithful to what is felt; and what is felt may be inexpressible. Words tend to be used so rapidly and so conventionally that they frequently fail to conjure up any parallel stream of experienced meaning which slavishly mirrors them. Even highly evocative and dramatic speech can emanate from a person who is bored or disengaged. Indeed, the practice of speaking can become a form of play which is cultivated for its own sake. It can become a pure form which is relatively barren of consequential meaning. Thus indexicality is often stereotyped and abstract. Many words are situated in contexts of what 'everyone knows', bearing only the slightest reference to localized and grounded knowledge.

The problematic connections between speech and lived meaning are further complicated by the capacity of speakers to combine words and sentences in novel ways, by the ability of language to 'produce' its own meaning. Words may describe fantastic events that have been encountered by no-one. They may award a plausible semblance of reality to phenomena that have no counterparts in lived meaning. They can thereby acquire a certain independence which isolates them from other styles of grasping the world. It is in this fashion that they can become a sealed context for one another. Linguistic traditions can foster the development of 'autonomous' cultures of the word. Language's 'opaqueness, its obstinate reference to itself, and its turning and folding back on itself are precisely what make it a mental power; for it in turn becomes something like a universe, and it is capable of lodging things in this universe—after it has transformed them into their meaning'.[26]

Indexicality is most diffuse when it is associated with words and documents intended for a wide public, that is, for the catholic community of people who participate in what 'everybody knows'. Of course, they are given their fullest meaning when the identity and world of their authors are known, but such an identity and world can be actually or effectively anonymous. The words are usually interpreted as having the most general and abstract anchorage. They are supposed to reach and be intelligible within all the different settings that compose a society. For practical purposes, then, they attain objectivity within a community. They may well take on constructions which were never envisaged by their authors, and an author's control is always lost when publication takes place.

THE PRESENCE OF THE PAST IN THE HERE-AND-NOW

The allegation that some public documents may be somehow intelligible to outsiders is, of course, ultimately indefensible. There are no practices by which interpretations of past writings can be shown to correspond with the intended and unintended meanings of their authors. Indeed, it has been argued that these productions are sealed in closed systems of understanding which are irrevocably alien to the historian.[27]

The critical question turns on whether what 'everybody knows' can eventually become what 'nobody can know'. The phrasing of an answer depends on whether the present is construed as a moving synthesis of the past or as one of a number of staggered and discontinuous episodes. If it is taken to be the former, the past may still be recreated only by unravelling and passing back through a series of transformations which have reworked its significance. Yet that reworking is not inevitably profound. What everybody knew rarely disappears in its entirety. It may be re-organized or vestigial, but phenomenological distance need not be commensurate with temporal distance. The present should not be regarded as utterly novel.

Any person enters an environment of words, representations and institutions which is already prestructured. He must deal with symbolic materials whose origins are distributed back through time. The Here-and-Now is a complex amalgam of contemporary and historical realities whose exact composition can never be known. The past is continually celebrated in the present, although it is a reconstituted past which would not be wholly familiar to the dead:

> A society that could be completely molded by its immediately preceding period would have to have a structure so malleable as to be virtually invertebrate. It would also have to be a society in which communication between generations was conducted, so to speak, in 'Indian file'—the children having contact with their ancestors only through the mediation of their parents. Now, this is not true. It is not true even when the communication is purely oral. . . . Still more strongly, between even widely scattered generations, the written word vastly facilitates those transfers of thought which supply the true continuity of a civilization.[28]

What is phenomenologically immediate may be more ancient than the phenomenologically distant. Our understandings are completely contemporary only in the sense that they occupy a point of time which is 'now'. Any other attribution of the contemporary ignores the manner in which historically diverse materials are synthesized by consciousness. It also neglects the unity of social reality over the generations, a unity which is sometimes attenuated but very rarely fractured.[29] The young consort with the old, and the old themselves consorted with the old when they were young.[30] As Schutz has observed, 'a continuous We-relation exists from the dawn of mankind to this day'.[31] Whatever a communal sense of the past may be, the everyday world of one's predecessors is probably more durable and influential than is ordinarily supposed. We live in a world which is still fed by ideas flowing directly from the dead. The past permeates the present.

Lived meaning and some paralinguistic forms of experience cannot be translated into standardized and stabilized systems of signification. They are consequently fluid and changeable. They are silent languages which do not lend themselves to communication across the boundaries of subjective worlds, and they may alter in ways that no outsider can appreciate. Written language, however, has some superficial structural rigidity. Documents produced in the seventeenth or eighteenth centuries, for instance, relied on most of the expressions, words and syntax that are in use now. They may have shifted their meanings over time, but they are based on a skeleton of unchanging forms. The slight stylistic modifications that have taken place are not unintelligible. Language can contribute to the objectivation and stabilization of meanings so that they persist longer than their originating contexts. Symbols, metaphors and expressions can pass from generation to generation. Some dominant constellations of symbolism may replace others, but the others are rarely so completely suppressed that they attain meaninglessness.[32] Ever since the printing press imposed some relative uniformity on written language, there has been a formal unity of symbolic mediations which may well have impressed itself upon experience. Moreover, the preservation of writing made possible by mass production has led to the literate being exposed to the ideas (however misconstrued) of several hundred years.

All these arguments find a condensed expression in Husserl's idea of *Stiftung* or foundation. Almost any practice represents a compacted tradition, an opportunity to enter into the forms and contents of life prepared by the dead. The seizing of such an opportunity renews that life so that it becomes a phenomenological reality grounded in the present. The nature of the 'present' is thus far from clear: it cannot simply be reduced to a complete existential break with an opaque past. What has been lost, and what has been transformed, cannot be ascertained. Neither is it possible to know how past and present intersect. There still remains considerable uncertainty about the adequacy of any reconstruction. Yet it does not follow that the world of our predecessors is totally closed or that all reconstruction is quixotic.

THE TOLERABLE INVARIANCE OF COMMON-SENSE UNDERSTANDING

Cicourel has asserted 'the researcher needs a theory which will seek to establish what invariant relationships exist over time as well as the particular and variable features of a given era. The problem of meaning is a central issue again.'[33] At bottom, variance and invariance can never be definitively demonstrated. If the meanings of conduct cannot be confidently grasped, then the manner in which they change or resist change cannot itself be described. The 'mob' of the early eighteenth century may or may not have signified much the same as the 'mob' of the twentieth century. Its significance cannot be taken as invariant without a prior understanding of the contexts of its generation and use. In turn, that prior understanding depends upon the establishment of invariance. It appears to be impossible to build a base for the judgments which Cicourel has prescribed.

Outside propositional logic, nothing can be 'proved' once and for all. Indeed, propositional logic is not itself completely secure. Sociology, and especially interpretative sociology, can never be satisfactorily defended against a rigorously sceptical attack. It cannot even manage the problems presented by an elementary solipsism. I take it that it was in this sense that Becker argued 'social science is, in principle, impossible'. All sociology must represent a massive act of faith, an attempt to make sense of what must finally defy sense. Its analytic assaults upon the social world must be supported by pragmatic criteria which partially suspend issues of truthfulness and fidelity.

Pragmatically, the historian and the sociologist are forced to assume some invariance of meaning over time. Weber contended, for instance, that all historical sociology is impossible unless it can be believed that *danger* in the past meant something equivalent to *danger* now. Without that belief, there would be no language to depict history. The transcendental properties of meaning would become deceits. A faith in the immutability of social forms thus underpins all social explanation. When Erikson stated 'every event has properties that can be assumed under a more general heading: if this were not so, we would be unable to identify the event in the first place',[34] it would seem that his argument proceeds less from ontological assurance than from pragmatic trust.

Phenomena can be captured only by an extensive use of familiar metaphors which impose invariance on the world. Metaphors can be employed with some confidence when they are applied to the world of our contemporaries, but with markedly less confidence when transferred to the past. Yet metaphorical reconstitution is the sole strategy available to the historian. Without such borrowing from contemporary forms of life, the analyst would become a mute.[35] Historiography is therefore again dependent on the practices whereby personal ideal types are formed out of current existential knowledge. It may be checked by the past, but it is given an initial definition and availability by metaphor which flows out of the present. History may be interpreted only if it is held to be largely analogous to the present.

The case for that invariance has been framed by need and by the *prima facie* intelligibility of many records that survive from the past. It has been alleged that documents do not read, in the main, as if they were the products of an alien intelligence. Rather, they 'make sense'. It is moot how much sense they actually still contain, and how it can be adequately resurrected. Yet their authors *appear* to be understandable, and the reader is capable of entering a state of 'pseudo-contemporaneity' with them. That state may be fallacious, but it affords a common-sense response of identification and fellow-sympathy.[36]

Such an argument perhaps represents the last ditch of the phenomenological defence, the ultimate act of faith. The appeal to the common-sense response of sympathy is weak, but it undoubtedly supports the whole sociological edifice. Used historically, it may be partially buttressed by Husserl's idea of *Stiftung*, and by the argument that social understandings and practices display a certain inertia,[37] that they rarely become profoundly or erratically discontinuous over time. The argument hinging on invariance must thus finally rest on the belief that the ranges of human experience are so constrained that they do not radically separate men of different eras and situations. As Schutz asserts, 'I can say . . . that my predecessor's experience was human experience: I can interpret it in the context of my knowledge of human experience as meaningful experience in general'.[38]

Of course, a resort to the invocation of such a wide community of sentiment and knowledge does little to clarify the particular and detailed problems which confront any historical analysis. It does not permit fine interpretation because its claims are so vague and broad. More importantly, it does not distinguish between the variant and the invariant. The relegation of all experience to some universe of shared humanity hampers the recognition of what is peculiar to an event. The past cannot be intelligently reduced to a flow of unchanging understanding, as a mere accumulation and series of displacements of common knowledge. Variance in activity, the range of social forms, and the evident diversity of social reality would then become simply inexplicable. If historical work serves any purpose, it is to document the numerous structures of experience and existence, not to transform them into an imprecise and homogeneous totality. After all, the particular courses which action takes must be explained by variations in constellations of meaning, not by some nebulous sameness of meaning.

Were invariance too great, it would render some documents either wholly unintelligible or else only deceptively intelligible. I have argued that most documents appear to be *prima facie* comprehensible and that, on pragmatic grounds, they must be construed as tolerably uniform in meaning. No variance would make historiography absurd. Excessive variance would make it impossible. Within the limits of manageable comprehension, some procedures must be introduced to enable the historian to discriminate between the claims of competing ideal types. He must be able to identify the historically-plausible actor and dismiss the homunculus which arises solely from his deployment of an anachronistic common sense.

In *Die Probleme der Geschichtsphilosophie*, Simmel proffers a modest answer to this issue of discrimination. Upon its cogency may depend the success of the historiographical enterprise. Simmel accepted a Kantian epistemology: his position has been described by Mandelbaum as one which holds that 'the mind creates . . . knowledge through its own activity, forming by means of its own categories the material which is presented to it . . . history as we know it is a product of our mind's activity. . . .'[39] The business of reconstructing history must then be judged by examining the constitutive properties of mind. The workings of consciousness may be scrutinized in order to discover whether the historian has created a puppet which apes him or an ideal type which has some authentic 'otherness'. *Verstehen* is the necessary first phase of analysis, but *Verstehen* may deceive:

> . . . Simmel contends that the only way in which we can know that a contemplated psychical manifold is not merely a part of our own experience, but also belongs to another, is to see that the elements comprising it fit together in a fashion which is not explicable on the basis of the partiality and accidental conditions of our own subjective psychical life . . .[40]

Simmel was quite aware of the difficulties posed by his solution. He also recognized the impossibility of a complete escape from the historian's own common-sense world. Yet he may have achieved some limited resolution of the dilemmas that can bedevil the historian. Personal ideal types must be continually monitored. If they have any authenticity, it is likely to stem from their capacity to surprise, inform and change the historian. They must be experienced as moderately recalcitrant and as part of a world which is itself resistant and external. They must take on appearances which are novel and unfamiliar enough to reassure their producer that he is not simply engaged in a form of solipsistic introspection. They must, moreover, convey the impression that they are descriptions of 'independent' yet possible persons and events. They must share a common but separate humanity. In this sense, they have to participate in a mode of common-sense experience, but not in a mere mirroring of the historian's own experience. As Merleau-Ponty states, the philosopher of history 'must see himself within the dialogue of minds, situated as they all are, and grant them the dignity of self-constituting beings at the very moment that he claims that dignity for himself'.[41]

Additionally, the historian is obliged to reflexively examine his own thinking in order to gain some knowledge of its processes. It is from the absence of a complete fit between those processes and the processes which he has attributed to his ideal type that plausibility emerges. The historian is constrained to attend to himself as a problematic figure whose work is to be dismembered and compared with its productions. The ineluctable regression of the sociology of knowledge may appear, but some self-distancing is required to allow the historian to explore the strangeness of his own creations.

It is in the pursuit of Simmel's method that history can become disciplined and defensible. It permits the historian to assume that the past may be cautiously discovered in documents which take on a certain objectivity; that it is, in some ways, co-extensive with the present; and that its events were not sited in totally foreign worlds. More importantly, it also permits him to exercise some kind of critical distance from his own works so that their authority may be judged. None of this justifies much confidence. Indeed, it may be argued that Simmel's solution is both markedly contrived and open to distortion.[42] There are no impressive *a priori* reasons for assuming that dead worlds and dead people *must* be so unfamiliar that they provoke a sense of alienation. (Conversely, novelists sometimes claim that their fictitious characters appear to acquire independent life. It is clear that Simmel's recipe is misleading in this context too.) It could well be the case that the past is occasionally wholly familiar. On those occasions, it might be mistakenly dismissed as an imaginative projection. Were one to defer to this argument in its entirety, the business of writing history would be again completely impossible. It is thus pragmatically inconvenient to accord it too much deference.

What is most apparent is that there are great regions of experience and happenings that can never be recovered. Only a skeletal portrait of the past is possible. Anything else would entail an excessive imputation of existential knowledge which can never be checked against the past. Personal ideal types must always be given sufficient substance to make them recognizably human. But must also take the form of phenomenologically denuded and parsimonious constructions. Their composition and use cannot be the same as those which characterize descriptions of the present. There is no legitimate warrant to flesh them out so completely. In addition to being sparse, they cannot but be phrased in the most general metaphor. Historical analysis is necessarily reified because it invokes metaphors to prise out classes and conditions of events. It lacks any semblance of the detailed and sure knowledge which might dispel reification. Only the language of simple structural forms is available to the historian. Explanation and description must perhaps be even more circumspect in history than in sociology because all the understanding of penumbral issues is foggier in historiography. When firm understanding is impossible, grand generalization becomes hazardous. Wholesale reification is as subversive to historical interpretation as it is to sociology. It is also clear that no thoroughgoing phenomenological microsociology of the past is feasible. If history is to be written, it must forfeit many of the qualities of work performed on contemporary social worlds. Yet sociology is enhanced when vanished social forms are re-assembled. Without history, it would merely be the pursuit of a fleeting and elusive 'present' which affords access to only a most restricted spectrum of human possibilities. Sociology cannot revolve around the assumption that the 'present' contains sufficient matter for a reasonable understanding of social life. Neither can it be dominated by the assumption that the 'present' mysteriously appeared without a past.

Paul Rock,
London School of Economics

* I am extremely grateful to Patricia Thane for her comments on an earlier draft of this paper.

Notes

1. H. Becker in R. Hill and K. Crittenden (eds.), *Proceedings of the Purdue Symposium on Ethnomethodology*, Purdue, Indiana, Institute for the Study of Social Change, Purdue University, 1968, p. 200.

2. Cf. R. Collingwood, *The Idea of History*, London, Oxford University Press, 1946, p. 215.

3. This, and the argument that follows is heavily dependent on the thesis proposed by Alfred Schutz in 'The Dimensions of the Social World', *Collected Papers*, Martinus Nijhoff, The Hague, 1964, Vol. 2.

4. Ibid., pp. 57–58.

5. Ibid., p. 44.

6. A. Cicourel, *Method and Measurement in Sociology*, New York, The Free Press, 1964, p. 154.

7. K. Erikson; 'Sociology and the Historical Perspective', in W. Bell and J. Mau (eds.), *The Sociology of the Future*, New York, Russell Sage Foundation, 1971, p. 71.

8. Cf. R. Collingwood; *Essays in the Philosophy of History*, Austin, Texas, Texas University Press, 1965, p. 101.

9. A. Schutz, op. cit., p. 31.

10. Ibid., p. 60.

11. Ibid., pp. 60–61.

12. J. Douglas; 'Existential Sociology', unpublished paper, 1973, p. 45.

13. Cf. A. Cicourel, op. cit., p. 147.

14. J. Douglas, op. cit., p. 37.

15. Cf. H. Garfinkel in R. Hill and K. Crittenden, op. cit., pp. 153–4.

16. R. Kwant, *Phenomenology of Language*, Pittsburgh, Pennsylvania, Duquesne University Press, 1965, p. 18.

17. Cf. J. Douglas, op. cit., p. 40n.

18. Cf. K. Erikson, 'Sociology and the Historical Perspective', op. cit., p. 70, and P. Manning, 'History and Sociology: The Logic of Socio-Historical Explanation', unpublished paper, May 1973, p. 6.

19. A. Cicourel, quoted in M. Phillipson and M. Roche, 'Phenomenology, Sociology, and the Study of Deviance', in P. Rock and M. McIntosh (eds.), *Deviance and Social Control*, London, Tavistock, 1974, p. 157.

20. Cf. H. Sacks in R. Hill and K. Crittenden (eds.), op. cit., pp. 187–8.

21. J. Douglas, op. cit., pp. 38–9.

22. R. Kwant, op. cit., p. 32.

23. M. Merleau-Ponty, *Signs*, Evanston, Illinois, Northwestern University Press, 1964, Chs. 1 and 2.

24. M. Merleau-Ponty, *Phénoménologie de la Perception*, Paris, 1945, p. 229.

25. Cf. R. Kwant, op. cit., pp. 143–4.

26. M. Merleau-Ponty, *Signs*, op. cit., p. 43.

27. Cf. O. Spengler, *Decline of the West*, London, Allen and Unwin, 1926.

28. M. Bloch, *The Historian's Craft*, Manchester, Manchester University Press, 1954, pp. 40–41.

29. Fractures of a kind do, of course, occur. Cf. K. Polanyi, *Origins of Our Time*, London, Victor Gollancz, 1945; and P. Laslett, *The World We Have Lost*, London, Methuen, 1965.

30. For an attempt to exploit this

chain of experience, see W. Hudson, *A Shepherds Life*, London, Methuen, 1948. First published in 1910, it recaptured the rural England of the 1830s through the interviewing of the very old.

31. A. Schutz, op. cit., p. 62.

32. Cf. K. Burke, *Attitudes Towards History*, Los Altos, California, Hermes, 1959, p. xiii.

33. A. Cicourel, *Method and Measurement in Sociology*, op. cit., p. 145.

34. K. Erikson, op. cit., p. 64.

35. Cf. P. Manning, op. cit., p. 13.

36. Cf. R. Stover, *The Nature of Historical Thinking*, Chapel Hill, North Carolina, University of North Carolina Press, 1967, p. 154.

37. Cf. M. Bloch, op. cit., p. 39.

38. A. Schutz, op. cit., p. 61.

39. M. Mandelbaum, *The Problem of Historical Knowledge*, New York, Liveright Publishing Corporation, 1938, p. 102.

40. Ibid., pp. 106–7.

41. M. Merleau-Ponty, *Signs*, op. cit., pp. 106–7.

42. I am indebted to Patricia Thane for this point.

[3]
Law, Order and Power in Late Seventeenth and Early Eighteenth Century England

«Money ... is the true Fuller's Earth for Reputations, there is not a Spot or a Stain but what it can take out. A rich Rogue now-a-days is fit Company for any Gentleman ; and the World ... hath not such a Contempt for Roguery as you imagine». (Peachum [Jonathan Wild], *The Beggar's Opera*, Act. 1, Scene IX).

Introduction.

This paper will offer a highly schematic and focused explanation of a few features of communal and organised crime at the beginning of the eighteenth century. It will largely concentrate on the negotiated character of criminal and social order. I intend my argument to illuminate the effects of rudimentary policing (1) and some special properties of moral status. That argument has been made possible by a deliberate arrangement of structural metaphors, an arrangement which can be justified only by principles of utility and parsimony (2). It does not pretend to be comprehensive. Neither is it designed to capture any essential truths about criminal phenomena. Raher, it has knowingly neglected much that would prove interesting. For instance, there is no full discussion of the ordering of moral beliefs, although those beliefs furnished vitally important recipes for political action.. There is no attempt at developmental analysis recipes despite the enlightenment which would undoubtedly flow from an examination of the evolution of criminal processes. Mine will be a comparatively simple exercise in social statics, dwelling on the relationships between social distance, crime and the coercive capacity of the state. Such an exercise cannot assign logical or « causal » primacy to the individual phenomena which it describes. It must merely insist on the analytic interdependence of its parts.

Decentralisation and Formal Social Control.

The quality of formal social control in England at the end of the seventeenth century stemmed chiefly from the peculiar geometry of its relations. The aggregations and concentrations of the English people gave rise to an irregular and uneven policing. They imposed and refracted markedly varying constraints on possibilites of central direction. Indeed, the very idea of *policing* is probably anachronistic because there was then no counterpart to any contemporary agency. Certain areas were unpatrolled or unpatrollable, and they enjoyed an autonomy of state control. They developed about the external and internal frontiers of the country, transforming it into a landscape of regulated and deregulated regions. Some parts achieved a political consequence which translated the moral status of their inhabitants into a matter which demanded negotiation rather than simple control.

Gregory King's estimates suggested that England and Wales possessed a population of over five millions which was spread most unevenly over their terrain (3). Whilst half a million people were congregated in London, eight hundred and eighty thousand lived in the other cities and towns, and four millions lived in villages and hamlets. Substantial tracts of England were an unpoliced wilderness without a system of established roads (4). Such wild areas were inhabited by «squatters» and «heathers)» who formed communities lying outside official management and constituting no recognised part of the political body.

Travel was hazardous, even inside London itself (5), and roads were frequently impassable. There was no uniform or effective system of maintenance, and floods, ruts, quisksands, holes, subsidence and defective drainage so affected routes that they sometimes could be no used for long periods. In Sussex, for instance, travel was virtually abandoned during the winter months. Rogers states « in 1700 the roads [were] scarcely less dirty, dangerous and unreliable than they were in the Middle Ages (6) ». Riders could be thrown, carriages upset and heavy carts rendered useless. Journeys of even a few miles might take a considerable length of time and their success was always problematic. Places adjoining London were taken to be relatively inaccessible (7) and Rogers describes Glasgow as having been « unimaginably remote from southern England (8) ».

The social significance of distance and the practical reach or action were thus radically modified by the sheer physical difficulty of movement. Major relations were structured by the effort which was required to sustain them. But effective access was not only influenced by physical contingencies. It was also circumscribed by the illiteracy of many Englishmen (9). In a society which was heavily dependent on oral communication and personal confrontation, the social world of most was confined and local.

It is therefore appropriate to portray England as a web of tenuously connected and necessarily self-supporting groupings. It was an array of separate areas which were distinguished by such marks of isolation as the possession of peculiar dialects and economic interests. So remote were some communities that local currencies had to be improvised when the central money supply failed (10). Problems of central co-ordination were such that each county tended to display an appreciable political autonomy, an autonomy which was itself nurtured and defended by local elites (11). The English counties were dominated by their own governments in miniature :

> « the county was, not inappropriately, referred to as the « country », for it was a microcosm of the nation, having its armed force, the militia ; its judiciary, the justices in petty or quarter sessions ; its local parliaments, such as the meetings of the lord lieutenant with the deputy lieutenants ... » (12).

At all levels a fluid exchange of support and information between sectors of the country was obstructed. Not only was there an enforced immobility (13), but there were few institutions devoted to the business of political co-ordination and the compilation of reports. For many practical purposes, a large number of communities were virtually self-policing. Whilst the movement of groups regarded as deviant may have been hindered (14), so also was that of agents of control. As Thompson observed, « the provincial magistracy was often in extreme isolation. Troops, if they were sent for, might take two, three or more days to arrive, and the crowd knew this very well (15) ». Poor transport and communications reduce the radius of efficient military action (16), and it was impossible for comparatively secluded populations to rely on useful relief from outside. Unless the members of a community armed themselves to form a surrogate militia, as the population of Goudhurst did to meet a group of smugglers (17), the maintenance of a legally-defined order could become most problematic. Throughout the late seventeenth and early eighteenth centuries, there were instances of areas being forcibly seized and held against control agencies. Thus, in 1670, the country about Kempsey was governed by a « band of marauders » (18) and, in 1692, a highwayman named Whitney offered to police the roads in exchange for a fee and a patron. He claimed effective control over a sizeable portion of the country (19).

The Coercive Institutions.

The magnification of distances was probably less significant than the inability of the state to muster an appreciable institutional response to law-breaking. The state lacked the force to exact uniform compliance. Indeed, the Hammonds claimed that central government was in abeyance in the first decades of the eighteenth century (20). The rudimentary formal control that did exist was exerted by four major organisations each offering a set of opportunities for the shaping of crime.

The Army.

Any substantial congregation of vagrants, smugglers, poachers or robbers a grouping which could not be mastered by routine policing agencies. It constituted a mobilisation of force which was overwhelming (21) Henry Fielding remarked that constables were frequently reluctant to act, and « they could not be blamed for not exposing themselves to sure destruction ; for it is a melancholy truth that, at this very day, a rogue no sooner gives the alarm, within certain purlieus, than twenty or thirty armed villains are found ready to come to his assistance » (22). Constables were, moreover, rooted to their own small policing districts and could not properly act outside them. Anyone who was mobile could fairly readily place himself outside the aegis of the constable's authority (23). The contable's work was further complicated by his local links. He was nominally the occupant of an unpaid and voluntary position, returning to an unofficial place in the community after a period of duty. His implication in a network of relations inevitably constrained his ability to serve as an anonymous and authoritative agent of control. In consequence, "the army was the only police force that stood between authority and anarchy, and the only preventive service that could enforce the revenue laws ... It was impossible to put down even a formidable gang of poachers without the help of the military" (24). The radical decentralisation and enforced self-reliance of communal control thus made all but the most routine tasks onerous and uncertain. The army was the chief organisation that could muster adequate force, numbers and institutional competence to manage particular problems of law enforcement. But it was an organisation of last resort and it was itself weak.

Partly because Britain lacked land frontiers, the role of a standing army became increasingly subordinated to that of the navy (25). There was a steady decline in funds allotted for military purposes during the first decades of the eighteenth century (26), and troops had to be scattered amongst small towns for their maintenance (27). That shift in strategic emphasis was sponsored by those who resisted the establishment of a national, centralised army. Such a concentration of force could threaten local accumulations of power, accumulations which dispersed political control and strengthened oligarchy (28). The bulk of defensive work became transferred to a militia which was under local rather than state supervision (29). There was, in particular, a sustained opposition to the use of the army as a policing institution. The organisational base for a French system of *gendarmerie* was not only eroded, but there were gross political impediments to its emergence (30). The Commonwealth had provided an earlier model of superintendence by an army acting as a police force, and it was a model that was effectively rejected by consequential groups.

The army could only be an instrument for the resolution of extraordinary crises. It was organisationally ill-equipped to perform work other than the suppression of riots, and even that work was held in disfavour by military authorities (31). It was most generally summoned to handle specific episodes of social unrest and its role was circumscribed functionally and temporally. The presence of troops appeared to generate friction (32), and "troops billeted in a town quickly became unpopular, even with those who had first called them in. With uncanny regularity requests for the aid of troops are followed ... after an interval of five or six weeks, by petitions for their removal" (33). The army could thus be a repressive implement, but it was incapable of engaging in the commonplace business of monitoring and detecting crime (34). It represented a crude and insensitive solution to social problems, and individual or sporadic crimes were beyond its powers of management. Its control work can have had only the most oblique impact on the constitution of everyday criminality.

The Militia.

The second major coercive institution was composed of the militia and train bands. They were the armed forces of a decentralised and oligarchical authority, being locally recruited and based, and symbolising opposition to a national system of social control (35). But they, too, were ill-financed and often represented no more than a nominal force. Musters were infrequently held, armaments were defective and there was no standardised supervision of their activity (36). The militia proved an uncertain support for legal order. Whilst it provided a rudimentary reserve against foreign invasion, it was held by some to be less sure in the settlement of domestic disputes (37). On occasion, its embeddedness in local communities led it to become markedly partisan in its management of law-breaking. It was sometimes partial to those who attempted to resist the collection of taxes and revenues. It did little to restrain rioting in 1675, and troops had to be called in to replace its reluctant members (38). Moreover, like the army, it was unable to undertake routine peace-keeping and detection work (39). It was, again, chiefly employed as an agent of riot-control, and it was inept at patrolling mundane criminal events. It formed one of the buttresses against political disorder, but its general influence seemed slight and it declined steadily throughout the eighteenth century.

The Constables.

In the formal division of control work, the minute supervision of local populations was exercised by the constables and watch. They were required to regulate the activities of a community, enforcing an order upon all the detailed life of their social worlds. The crossing of parish boundaries was patrolled. In London, nightly checks were made on lodgers who had entered a district and watchmen were enjoined to arrest strangers. They were required to apprehend "Nightwalkers, or any other persons whatsoever that are uncivil, or cannot give a good account of themselves, and the Reason for their being abroad ..." (40). The migrations of gipsies, labourers, fortune-tellers and peddlers were surveyed and directed. Those who wandered without a legitimate purpose could be handed from one constable to another across the parishes until they were returned to their last place of settlement. Within the boundaries, there was supposed to be a coerced hierarchy, decorum and order. Servants who had left employment without leave were controlled. Ale-houses were inspected, violations of the Sabbath suppressed, and gambling curtailed (41). Constables could punish mothers bearing bastards, whip vagabonds, force the unwilling to work, uphold apprenticeship statutes, confine begging to the licenced, restrain lunatics and detain the suspicious. They also had to embark on fine detective and crime-control work. They were formally responsible for raising the hue and cry, apprehending criminals and housing them until they were charged.

The maintenance of control in local areas was often precarious. Constables were organised by procedures laid down by the Statute of Winchester, a statute that had been devised to manage a dispersed, settled and weak population (42). They were based on a division of territory into policing districts that had been appropriate to medieval England. They fell under the supervision of numerous and competing authorities ; were governed by diverse structures of rules ; and could not engage in any concerted action. They were able to exercise only the most limited powers of arrest and did not have to act outside their own, often Lilliputian, areas. In the City of London alone, or instance, there were six hundred and seventy six precincts (44). They could not search or forcibly enter property. Their work had virtually no bureaucratic support, no system of records, and no effective mobilisation of aid when they were confronted by numbers of antagonists. Generally serving for short terms, they achieved little professional competence and could not accumulate or transmit developed skills. So structurally-orphaned were they that they were rendered no legal assistance for guidance or defence. If they were sued or tried, they were without institutional funds to pay fines or underwrite the costs of legal representation. They formed an amateur and often reluctant force. As largely unpaid officials, their commitment to the occupation tended to be slight.

The constabulary system was prone to break down whenever it confronted a substancial concentration of crime (45). Although the constables may have been able to control the more visible activity of individuals or small groups, they could be defied by almost any organised or sizeable grouping (46). Thus the mobile populations of vagrants represented a segment of society which fell outside effective management (47). Again, the suppression of riots, as in Kendal in 1696 and in Coventry in 1705, was beyond the capacities of conventional policing (48). There was therefore a token policing which appeared efficient only when the members of a community were geographically static, scattered and peaceable.

The Practical Diffusion of Violence.

The weakness of public agencies was accompanied by a spread of corrective violence into private or semi-private control. England became transformed into a mosaic of petty organisations which grew up around the practical possibilities of aggression and defence. Force became a matter of opportunity rather than legal right. The distribution of private violence exerted a critical influence on the shaping of crime, the recruitment of victims and the experience of immunity. It rested on the power which flowed from wealth and social organisation. Men were armed and those who commanded resources could equip themselves with their own police forces (49). Houses and estates were sometimes turned into fortified units that were designed to provide some security (50).

Immuniy in some areas could simply be grasped by force or organisation. The boundaries between areas of private licence and public regulation were highly fluid during the late seventeenth and early eighteenth century. They were responsive to the application of violence, and the private area could be enlarged by those who possessed adequate coercive power (51). Resistance enabled men to carve out regions of liberty for themselves.

In part, the capacity of groups to appropriate social space rested on a shift in the nature of violence that could be offered. In the middle of the sixteenth century were the beginnings of technical innovations in arms that subverted the basis of a feudal control scheme. The statute of Winchester had established a policing organisation that depended on a special distribution of the means of violence. Authority and power could be decentralised because representatives of the state and sovereign possessed military skills and equipment which were denied the rest of the population. A combination of fortifications, the horse, armour and the stirrup were too formidable to be resisted by an ill-armed people fighting on foot (52). Centrifugal political tendencies can emerge when groups are radically differentiated in their ability to procure weapons and training in combat (53). Such superiority enables those charged with control work to be widely dispersed. It led to a style of devolution which continued to underpin police methods at the beginning of the eighteenth century.

Yet the spread and improvement of firearms had brought about a minor revolution in relations between state and populace. The development of cheap, efficient and portable guns threw the prevailing balance of power out of joint. In particular, the invention of the flint-lock gave individuals a new range and a new power to intimidate (54). First introduced in about 1635, it came into widespread use by the end of the century (55). It led to a democratisation of violence. In Europe, the appearance of such handguns was partially responsible for the growth of standing armies under the command of a central authority. It prepared the way for an implosion of power. Those armies could be put to the work of organising domestic social control. But in England, as I have argued, the army played a much more modest part and was relatively incapable of counteracting the effects of the new distribution of violence. There arose a corresponding uncertainty in policing. Smugglers, poachers and footpads were more nearly equal to those charged with their suppression (56). There were, moreover, new forms of crime attendant upon the dispersal of force. Thus it is possible that the evolution of the highwayman may be attributed to the spread of light arms (57).

England was fissured to form an agglomerate of largely independent groupings which were capable of wielding impressive force in their own right. Their allegiance to royal and state institutions was occasionally problematic. The revolts of 1640, 1688, 1715 and 1745 illustrate how militarily and politically autonomous some significant segments could become. In 1715, for example, the outcome of the Jacobite rebellion hinged chiefly on the ability of oligarchs loyal to the Hanoverians to defeat those allied to the Pretender. One of the most critical phases of the rebellion was resolved by the capacity of the army of tenants mustered by the Earl of Sunderland to overwhelm the forces of the Earl of Seaforth and the Marquis of Huntley. In that encounter, they underscored the extent to which private groups could detach themselves and become the possessors of formidable power. Such groups could uphold a practical and *de facto* order which was only tangentially related to legally-constituted government. The state held no monopoly over the exercise of violence :

> "The power of the seventeenth century gentry was sanctioned by violence : riding out against their enemies, hamstringing their neighbour's dogs, beating their farmers' sons, or shooting down their riotous labourers. They played ducks and drakes with the law when it suited them, breaking with impunity what they were supposed to maintain" (58).

When the state could guarantee neither physical security nor legal control, effective government passed in large measure over to those who were independently powerful. Political order was mediated by webs and hierarchies which developed around local centres of influence. Those networks were structured by access to the Court and by the possibilities that were afforded by command over territory and people (59). Patronage bestowed order on the otherwise rudimentary structures created by a weak government and a weak system of communal control. Relations with a patron knit the client into a fluid system of power which substantially replaced formal state government. Positions within that system were personally awarded and personally exploited. Offices, prerogatives and franchises became items of property that were practically removed from external supervision (60).

Patronage, in turn, was crystallised by one of the most pervasive models of political organisation, the transformation of society into a collection of domain managed by a small number of powerful families (61). Membership of a central family, or its contractual equivalent in the form of a connection with a patrimonial bureaucracy, defined a person's substantial worth and privilege. It produced a population which possessed an effective immunity against the exercise of almost all legal regulation (62). Significantly, the moral status of the patron or the well-patronised could neutralise virtually every form of deviancy but treason, itself a fundamental attack on the moral basis of hierarchy. Thus, although a number of peers were tried for murder by the House of Lords between 1660 and 1702, no penalties were inflicted on them (63). Such trials may have had some limited symbolic effect, but it appears that they were never intended to inflict significant stigma or pain. Indeed, Hay has argued "the private manipulation of the law by the wealthy and powerful was in truth a ruling class conspiracy, in the most exact meaning of the word" (64). Similarly, Defoe observed "the Gentry and Magistrates of the Kingdom, while they execute ... Laws upon us the poor Commons, and themselves practising the same Crimes, in defiance of the Laws both of God and Man, go unpunished" (65).

The Transformation of Community and Population.

Officially, the practice of shedding responsibility forced communities to assume corporate liability for crime. A parish formed one of the few identifiable and permanent structures which could be administratively absorbed into the formal control system. It was required to pay indemnities to those who were robbed whilst travelling in its area, although that obligation was waived at night and on Sundays. It was also supposed to constitute itself into a collective police force, the hue and cry, and those who did not respond to a muster could be punished. Hue and cry transformed the community into a group of vigilantes, the *posse cornitatus,* who were expected to hunt the criminal in periods of crisis. The poverty of formal patrolling and policing was ostensibly remedied by casting the entire adult male population into the role of constable.

In the eighteenth century, the hue and cry seemed to be principally successful against isolated and unarmed people who were conspicuous strangers. Its effectiveness depended, too, on a quarry being comparatively incapable of travelling with any speed to a refuge which might confer anonymity. Urbanisation was tending to render the *posse* somewhat anachronistic. It might have countered one who fled on foot to unpopulated territory but, around London for instance, it was difficult to single him out from anyone else. John Fielding argued :

> "at a [great] distance from London ... it would be absolutely impossible for any villain in the country to escape justice ; but near London I apprehend [the hue and cry] would lose its affect, not only from the vast variety of passengers on the road, mounted and dressed alike ; but if they should not succeed before the rogue reaches London, seeking him there, by means of the hue and cry, would be fruitless indeed" (66).

The hue and cry was not able to produce any substantial concerted activity or prolonged pursuit. It was a local response which was spatially confined because of the difficulties of movement. It was also cumbersome to organise, and the responsibility for its mobilisation seemed undefined until quite late. Before 1735, it appears that its raising was supposed to proceed almost spontaneously (67). Moreover, like the army and the militia, it did not form a skilled policing response, able to pursue regular detective or patrolling work. It presented no more than a sporadic and weak restraint in those areas where crime was at all common.

Partly as a ready for detective policing (68), and partly as its cause (69), social control was formally delegated to the entire population. The inhabitants of England were turned policemen on themselves. Throughout the eighteenth century, the state depended on private self-interest as its cardinal means of exerting control (70). People were methodically bribed, exhorted and coerced to transform themselves into agents of the state. The management of deviance was forced to become a matter of personal enterprise. Since 1691, legislation routinely offered considerable rewards for the successful prosecution of certain offenses. The scope of crimes covered by such rewards was steadily enlarged until it embraced burglary, housebreaking, horse-stealing, highway robbery and the like. State rewards became systematically supplemented by other sums offered by insurance companies, the excise and voluntary associations. Neighbours, friends and associates of the victim might also contribute to particular rewards. It eventually became a matter of course for the victim himself to promise a reward, often by public advertisement. So commonplace did this practice become that a failure to follow it could be construed as a tacit condoning of an offence (71). The business of crime control became entrepreneurial, an area to be exploited for gain by small organisations devoted to thieftaking (72).

Coercion was supplied by a major strategy that was designed to make deviants accessible to enforcement work. In the absence of any official procedures for accomplishing the business of detection, criminals were sealed against much formal control. For some purposes, they had to be treated as the population of a virtually independent region. It is significant that the epithet "thieves' republic" was to become common, indicating an appreciation of the independence of deviant worlds. When they could not be adequately surveyed from without, techniques had to be deployed to make them visible. Those techniques rested on the standard diplomatic devices of subversion and disruption (73). An internal disunity was fostered to throw up information that could never have been otherwise obtained. As Winslow observed, "the greatest threat to the individual smuggler ... appears to have been neither the revenue officers nor the Army and Fleet, but rather the informer" (74). People were encouraged to inform on others in order to gain their own pardon. In some cases, the statutes stipulated that the informer should not himself be in custody if he sought a pardon. In others, it was laid down in a utilitarian fashion that he must bring about the conviction of a certain number of offenders or a conviction for a crime that was more heinous than his own. Arrested suspects were urged to turn evidence in an effort to win their freedom.

Impeachment might have granted the informer a limited or major immunity against prosecution, and much legal process was designed to promote the defection of criminals. Such a systematic use of the pardon made possible the acquisition of what was tantamount to a licence to commit crime. For instance, under an Act of William and Mary, a person who was not in custody and who brought about the conviction of two or more persons guilty of highway robbery could earn a free pardon for all similar crimes which he may have committed before he had impeached his associates (75).

Accomplices were enjoined to turn on one another. Thieves were set against receivers. It was intended to introduce a fundamentally divisive element into criminal organisation, and that intention would seem to have been partially realised. The tactic of flourishing pardons engendered suspicion and disarray. For instance, one of the participants in a mail robbery revealed how the threat of competitive impeachments could undermine solidarity. That participant, Wilson, recalled how he had been shown a letter by a Post-Officer :

> « Sir, I am one of the Persons who robbed the Mails, which I am sorry for ; and to make Amends, I'll secure my two Companions as soon as may be : He whose Hand this shall appear to be, I hope will be entitled to the Reward and his pardon". As soon as I read it, I knew it to be *Sympson's* Letter, so that without any more Words I made a Discovery and I am of Opinion that any Man in *England* would have done the same. That League of Friendship which was between us was certainly dissolved by this Design against me. As for those who talk of Solemn Oaths and Protestations, I can assure them never were any such amongst us ; and if there had, no Oath is binding ... » (76).

The fear of impeachment often led associates to scramble amongst themselves for the privileged status of informer. One arrest could produce long chains of prosecutions. The state came to rely progressively on such machinations. As Thompson observed, « in the state papers we seem to meet a society of creeps and informers» (77). Government accordingly was involved in the generation of two distinct planes of regulation. On one plane, law and policing agencies tried to manufacture a moral universe whose contours and consequences were clear. There was a lucid dramatisation of the properties of social order. A great number of offenses were made capital. Gallows confessions, sermons, legal statutes, jurisprudence and judicial pronouncements emphasized the magnitude of the divide which separated the wicked from the good. The criminal and the deviant were thrust out beyond the margins of propriety, and order was ritually affirmed. On the other plane, however, everyday control practices systematically made those margins ambiguous and murky. The consequences of law were eminently negotiable. Legal penalties and inducements combined to create an equivocal, malleable and complex scheme which could be exploited by the knowing. In the case of hanging, for instance, the death sentence was attached to numerous offenses but comparatively few people were actually executed. Hall argued, « in the early part of the eighteenth century the persons, lay and official, who administered the criminal law, invented and indulged in practices which almost nullified the capital penalty in most non-clergable offenses (78). Law was open to ample bargaining and collusion. Deviant populations could not be immediately controlled, and command over information conferred a power which could affect most court proceedings. Justice came to resemble a market place in which an elaborate trading economy developed. The moral and the immoral, the regulated and the regulators, came to be utterly entangled in one another.

The Possibilities of Autonomy.

I have argued that policing was most irregular. It was shaped by power and influence ; it was distorted by geographical contingencies ; it revolved around the distribution of population ; and it made available different opportunities for negotiation and accommodation. Such variable control reflected and encouraged the emergence of multiple relations with the political centre. The country's communities and regions were presented with diverse possibilities of establishing a place within the legal and moral order. Some were wholly subordinate to the centre, some evolved modes of compromise with it, and others were relatively free of its influence. When central direction was precarious, the nature and significance of illegality were substantially defined by its social location. Indeed, even so small an area as London was popularly mapped out into districts which carried radically contrasting moral connotations. Rogers remarks that in The Dunciad, for example, « a topographic identity becomes a moral equivalence » (79).

A number of areas were virtually autonomous of formal social control. Powerful figures and communities became detached from the centre for the purpose of undertaking criminal enterprises. Social regions could become independent on occasion because those held responsible for administering justice were themselves implicated in law-breaking. In a division of labour based on geographical segregation, entire communities could pursue wrecking, smuggling or poaching as collective projects. Just as the southern border towns of the United States are now sometimes given to wholesale participation in smuggling, so coastal towns in England had widely-ramifying communal involvements in crime. Thus Romney in Kent was so taken up with smuggling that revenue officers were unable to safely consign those whom they had arrested to the town's gaol. Even the mayor supported smuggling. Similarly, in 1708, the magistrates of Wigtown were involved with the smugglers who attacked the revenue officers ; « Robert Walpole, a J.P. of Norfolk, had smugglers call regularly at his back door at Houghton and even used an Admiralty barge to run his wine up the Thames » (81) ; and a justice of the peace led a group of smugglers who assailed the salt-officer at Conway in 1712 (82). In the instance of wrecking, too, Rule observes « it shows how strong was the local strength of tradition if such a form of criminal action could be persistently employed by the whole community » (83).

As important was the preservation of urban areas which retained much of the character of the medieval sanctuaries. Some, like the liberties of the Fleet, Marshalsea and King's Bench Prisons, were protected by statute (84). Within their bounds, prisoners could purchase an immunity from the enforcement of much legislation (85). They represented rich farms to be managed by prison administrators for profit. Other areas held on to an immunity long after the formal abolition of their privileges. The sanctuaries had originally been districts which fell under a lay or ecclesiastical jurisdiction that was independent of royal control. One form was the temporary refuge offered by all churches and churchyards. Fugitives could enjoy a limited safety there if they submitted to a discipline and agreed to abjure the realm within forty days (86). Such a practice was effectively banned by the middle of the sixteenth century, but another kind of sanctuary persisted in law and then in fact for several hundred years more. This more significant form, perpetual sanctuary, constituted an extreme instance of franchise (87). Its legal status was tantamount to that of a foreign territory, not dissimular to the contemporary embassy. Representing the domain of some powerful authority, it fell outside the reach of royal justice. Its inhabitants « took a new oath of allegiance and obeyed a new sovereign and a new law, which could protect them against any other ... » (88).

The independence of the original perpetual sanctuaries was progressively eroded from the fifteenth century onwards. The early legislation of Henry VIII was supplemented by Acts of 1604, 1606, 1623, 1693, 1722 and 1727. Yet a few of the sanctuaries survived because the state lacked the power to eradicate them all. A marriage between geographical advantage and organisational strength allowed the Mint, the Savoy, Whitefriars, St Giles and other districts to retain their autonomy. Like the rural communities of smugglers and wreckers, the thieves' districts of London enjoyed considerable stability. As Pike remarks :

> « Sanctuaries ... were for many generations stronger than a medieval police or ambitious law-givers. In the reign of William III not only were there sanctuaries in England, but they existed in places not even mentioned in the statute of Henry VIII ... In London and its neighbourhood they abounded » (89).

The sanctuaries were spaces appropriated from central and local government. They were held by law, by tradition or by force. They concentrated populations, established styles of collective life, and set up frontiers between centrally-dominated and privately-governed space. Growing up around an area of religious or lay power, a particularly stigmatised district (such as a leper hospital or an insane asylum), or a geographically propitious region, they became organised and relatively permanent. Those sanctuaries which could not claim a direct charter were often supported in their claims by forged documents (90). Others simily formed places which were maintained against law enforcement agents, places that could not be easily gained or regained. In a sense, they were functionally and historically akin to the *seigneuries collectives* which the gilds of Europe had attempted to found. Such collective lordships were able to act as appreciable rivals to the barony and the king. They were endowed with privileges, the right to jurisdiction, and a region which was their own. In some instances, they offered protection to criminal fugitives (91). The London gilds sometimes managed to acquire these lordships, either by open charter or by surreptitious means (92). London in the fifteenth and sixteenth centuries contained a number of areas of semi-private jurisdiction.

It is plausible that the latterday bastard sanctuaries of the seventeenth and early eighteenth centuries preserved something of the nature of the districts once controlled by the *seigneuries collectives.* It is certainly the case that English professional crime took on many of the trappings of the fraternity or mystery, that it resembled the gild in its purpose and structure. First emerging at some time in the fourteenth century (93), it revolved around a division of labour, an apprenticeship system, patterns of mutual support, the exclusion of outsiders, and the construction of a community of colleagues (94). Cenral problems and practices were celebrated in a special language which often assumed an arcane and intricate form. For instance, the business of picking pockets or engaging in confidence games was lent structure by a highly developed vocabulary which described all the salient roles and procedures of the craft (95). Such crime was typically the work of small, intimate groups who collaborated together over long stretches of time. Through apprenticeship and closure, the world of many professional criminals became stabilised and isolated. There are, for example, revealing continuities between the work styles and terminology of the sixteenth century pickpocket and his heir in contemporary England and America (96).

Unwin has argued that gilds and their unofficial surrogates, the adulterine gilds, represented the predominant organisational style of almost all groups at the time when professional crime acquired its initial form. The gild, in turn, hinged on the fraternity :

> « ... there can be no manner of doubt that society in the 14th and 15th centuries was literally honeycombed with fraternities in every direction ... That of this great mass of social activity we should know so little is simply due to the secretive nature of the facts » (97).

Secrecy was grossly enhanced when the activity that was organised was itself unambiguously deviant. Yet, a *priori,* it seems reasonable to suppose that the fraternity served as a model for criminals and outlaws as well as for those following legal pursuits. In a society displaying a poverty of organisational metaphors, where the typical social unit was small and the craft monopolised occupational structures, the choices available to those managing problems of social co-operation were most restricted. Many pariah and dispossessed groups *did* adopt the fraternal form as a matter of course (98). For example, the highly stigmatised occupation of coal- heaving was made up of men who, when some amelioration of their conditions was proposed, « *naturally* sought to organise themselves into a fraternity, such as that of the Billingsgate porters who were "free" of the city (99). Indeed, the fraternity suggested a most useful pattern for any clandestine group which affected secrecy and rested on solidarity. Contemporary descriptions of criminal groups may simply have borrowed from readily available simile. Yet there tended to be a routine dependence on the language of the craft or mystery. Vagrants, vagabonds, confidence tricksters, thieves, prostitutes, and cheats were regularly portrayed as if they constituted some version of the adulterine gilds.

The sanctuaries may then be regarded as the domain *of de facto* collective lordships which seized regions and held them. They formed natural areas governed by a specific, illegitimate segment of society. The originating charters of the sanctuaries might have proved useful to those who sought immunity (100) but, in practice, they had been superseded by claims based on force, special calling and custom. Just as there was a goldsmiths' or a banker' quarter in a London that was occupationally segregated into different districts, so there were a number of criminal quarters under the dominion of those who practiced illegal mysteries. One such area was described by Ward in 1709, and his account strongly conveys an impression of the sheer density of the deviant populations of certain districts :

> « We steer'd our course up *Salisbury-court* where every two or three steps we met some Old Figure or another, that look'd as if the *Devil* had Rob'd em of their *Natural Beauty* ... *Theft, Whoredom, Homicide* and *Blasphemy*, peep'd out at the very Windows of their *Soul*; *Lying Perjury, Fraud, Impudence,* and *Misery,* were the only *Graces* of their *Countenance* ... All this part, quite up to the Square, is a *Corporation* of *Whores, Coiners, Highway-Men, Pick-Pockets*, and *House-Breakers*; who, like *Bats* and *Owls*, Sculk in Obscure Holes by Day-Light, but Wander in the Night in Search of Opportunities wherein to Exercise their Villainy » (101).

Indeed, despite its relatively small size, London was most heterogeneous (102). The localism and decentralisation of the country were reflected in microscosm in its capital city. London was divided up into diverse areas which were highly distinctive. Its growth had been so rapid and ill-planned that its various parts lacked cohesion and organisation. Districts and villages had been absorbed and fused to become a collection of areas without a recognisable centre. The disparities between the parts were reinforced by the absence of a network of roads providing ready access from one area to another. What roads there were tended to be badly maintained and often dangerous (103), and it was physically difficult to move about the metropolis. Such hindrances were further aggravated by the proliferation of "dangerous districts" and unpatrolled spaces into which it was thought perilous to wander (104). Travel at night was especially hazardous because of the until, narrow and pitted nature of the streets.

People usually lived in or near their workplace, grouped together with others who followed a similar trade (105). Most areas were thus relatively homogeneous : distinguished by a separate mode of occupation ; following a district timetable ; differentiated from one another by the wealth of their inhabitants ; and forming largely self-contained words which emphasized particular styles of life. The populations of neighbouring districts were often kept apart by a great social distance. London constituted a mosaic of discrete and bounded areas. Addison remarked, for example :

> « When I consider this great city in its several quarters and divisions, I look upon it as an aggregate of various nations, distinguished from each other by their respective customs and interests ... In short, the inhabitants of St Jame's, notwithstanding they live under the same laws, and speak the same language, are a distinct people from those of Cheapside, who are likewise removed from those of the Temple on the one side, and those of Smithfield on the other, by several climates and degrees in their ways of thinking and conversing together » (106).

The congregations of criminals in the bastard sanctuaries did not only reflect the radical diversity of London, and they were not simply an ecological counterpart of the areas in which weavers or chandlers gathered. They also represented the internal marches of the city (107). The policing, administration and jurisdiction of London were splintered and stratified in an extraordinarily complex fashion. The various parts that came to form the greater metropolis retained most of their original institutions of control, and the resulting whole contained abundant anomalies and conflicts. London was governed by a number of distinct and autonomous authorities who « had little to do with each other and, as far as they were concerned, ruled separate kingdoms » (108). Burgesses' courts, manorial courts, magistrates courts, the courts of the City Companies, sheriffs' courts and aldermanic courts vied with one another. Separate police agencies patrolled their several districts and precincts. Beadles, javelin men, constables, watchmen, sheriffs' officers, the train bands, City Marshals, magistrates' assistants an King's Messengers attempted to impose some order, but their work was not co-ordinated. It lacked central direction or even a precise demarcation of task. Different organisations maintained their own goals and prisons, and Defoe observed « there are in London ... more public and private prisons, and houses of confinement, than any city in Europe, perhaps as many as in all the capital cities put together » (109).

The city was thus carved up into a welter of sectors of control. The principal administrative regions fell under the Cities of London and Westminster and the counties of Surrey and Middlesex. Within these regions there was a mass of individual districts. Political and geographical areas did not necessarily coincide, and the divisions often appeared most arbitrary. The areas themselves were frequently characterised by jurisdictional uncertainty, particularly at their boundaries. Indeed, Rude states that Westminster's government was «for many years a jungle of rival jurisdictions » (110).

Between and within such regions there were abundant zones that were marked by ambiguity. On the frontiers between different jurisdictions were to be discovered places that were not clearly regulated by any single authority or by any authority at all. « The activities of constable and watchman were for the most part limited to his own parish, precinct or liberty, and where the authorities of city and county marched there was every opportunity for the development of little Alsatias (111) 112) ». Bastard sanctuaries were threaded along these borders. St Giles's for example, was officially sited in neither Westminster nor the City but abutted on both (113).

The strength of the sanctuaries was even further supported by their internal design (114). Since 1580, there had been a series of attempts to prevent the physical growth of London. Coupled with restrictions aimed at controlling the spread of plague, these proscriptions made it illegal to erect buildings on new foundations. For about a century, any construction work had to take place covertly in areas that were already built up. New buildings became ever more dense because a substantial proportion of the rapidly increasing population were denied work in the City of London. Since few were freemen, they were debarred from pursuing trades there. More and more buildings were consequently piled into a belt fringing on the City's liberties. Effective authority to restrain development was at its weakest in that inerstitial zone, the zone which formed the ring of debatable jurisdictions. Building regulations were systematically evaded by making new structures as unobtrusive as possible. Areas that conferred invisibility on construction were fully exploited. Behind walls and at a distance from public space, courts and yards were built up, alleys were narrowed, cellars extended and garrets put to use. There thus arose a great maze of intricate passages and huddled buildings that were compressed into the interstices of official power. One area was actually named the «

Caribee Islands » because of its topographical complexity. Deteriorated and adapted by the beginning of the eighteenth century, those mazes proved almost impossible for enforcement agents to penetrate (115).

Ecology, stigma, organisation and custom conspired together to preserve the sanctuaries. Some of their last legal privileges were lost in 1727, but they continued as if no law had been passed. For instance, mid-nineteenth century descriptions of the Mint and St Giles's reveal little change in the areas (116). Thus Binney discussed the Mint of the late 1840s as « a well-known harbour of low-characters, [containing] knots of thieves at the corners of the different streets » (117), and Beames remarked « rookeries still survive by their very isolation, by their retention of past anomalies » (118).

The Mediations of Power.

The criminal areas of the country and town are examples of structures which defied direct formal control. Their regulation had often to be mediated and tortuous, involving processes of suborning and the brokerage of power. Attempts to impose order were sometimes more redolent of conciliation and diplomatic manoeuvre than straightforward command. Those attempts illustrate how criminality was negotiated rather than awarded, entailing a practical recognition of political necessity.

Internally, English society was arranged into a series of groupings which enjoyed vastly discrepant privileges. The least powerful were in no position to barter for the significance of their actions or their selves. They were the objects of an uncomplicated repression, governing their movement employment and behaviour. The meanings of that group were defined by a particular vision of the social order. It was a vision infused with organic imagery, an imagery which depicted the state as a corporate being with distinct outlines and an inner differentiation of unlike parts. The social organism excluded many. It was constituted by groups which performed fixed and identifiable functions. Those groups represented the only authentic components of society, the only members entitled to recognition as the morally substantial : « the freeholder on the land and the freeman in the town were, each in his own sphere, the accredited elements in a society, in comparison with which other men appeared, not as rival classes, but as adjuncts or excrescences, or even social dangers » (119). Indeed, in an organic language, the politically marginal were a disordering agent akin to disease, parasite or pathology. Much of the writing on crime alluded to the emergence of epidemics and disorders which plagued the body politic. The outsider was not a natural feature of social organisation. Thus Nourse condemned the hiring of an excessive number of servants, arguing "tho"they seem the best Juice to themselves, whilst the genuine Parts languish to be Part of the Body, and to add to the Bulk, [they] do in Truth sucit the best Juice to themselves, whilst the Parts languish and decay» (120).

Groups lying outside the approved contours of society were not awarded the same worth as those firmly embedded within them. They were taken to be less than fully human, a qualitatively different breed of men who required special treatment. All their actions were necessarily tinged with their twin qualities of dangerousness and devalued social status. When regulation rested on the maintenance of an uncertain correspondence between private interest and a special conception of the corporate good, those without a manifest commitment to the political order were alien and threatening. As strangers, they did not merit the same concern as those who were secure. The significance of what they did and who they were was thus quite different from that of the morally-grounded population. Large segments of the penumbral group were expected to be hanged as a matter of course. The wandering and the rootless, the gipsy and the unpropertied, the follower of a disreputable trade were assumed to be preordained for execution (121). It was the offender, not the offence, which fixed the meaning of law-breaking : « the privileged might often commit great crimes with impunity ; for petty offences the unprivileged were hanged » (122)

By contrast, some groupings were not only served as the principal dispensers of justice but were themselves too powerful to be wholly exposed to it. The holders of wealth and authority were able to translate their activities into areas free of almost all interference. Indeed, « liberty » was defined as the right to an independence of external control. Those who enjoyed such liberty occupied a place which neutralised many of the more conventional connotations of their acts. Peers could do murder with considerable impunity, and Ogg states that their trials in the House of Lords « usually had an element of farce » (123). A systematic resort to patronage afforded some groups the opportunity to acquire an unofficial licence to break the law. Highwaymen, for example, were at one time heavily recruited from the ranks of the powerful (124), and they were buttressed by protective associations which reduced their chances of being executed. Although pardon did not mechanically follow conviction, and many highwaymen were hanged, a substantial measure of immunity could be achieved by such men (125).

That shaping of invulnerability and freedom was also to be discovered in the formal organisation of the state. Offices in a patrimonial bureaucracy were generally held to be proper sources of private profit. Those who secured posts as governors, prison administrators, city marshals, government ministers and the like were led to treat their positions as something like personal property (126). Many offices were purchased, sometimes in competitive auction. The expenses that were laid out had to be offset by the money that could be earned by the official (127). Offices in agencies of social control were almost invariably bought, and their incumbents were tacitly allowed to reimburse themselves by means of bribery and extortion (128). When some scandal occurred, the business of official extortion was usually defined as tolerable providing certain implicit limits had been respected. Thus the Earl of Macclesfield, whilst Lord Chancellor, was found guilty of embezzling some £100,000 of chancery funds. He defended himself by asserting that such appropriations had « long been practiced without blame)) ; was fined £30,000 ; and received a promise from the king that the fine would be repaid to him from the privy purse (129). The powerful were therefore occasionally encouraged to describe criminality as a normal and largely uncontrolled feature of their work. Offices represented protected areas of law-breaking even within the confines of law-enforcing bodies.

Legitimate concentrations of power accordingly constituted structures which were granted an impressive autonomy. They deflected most regulation. Concentrations of illegitimate power also presented obstacles to regulation. They had a political consequence in their own terrain which sometimes rivalled that of government. They could be managed either by subversion or by co-optation. That policy of co-optation, in turn, conferred some stability and *de facto* legitimacy on areas of criminal enterprise. An orderly institutionalisation and incorporation of criminal sectors was one strategy of a weak government, and it rendered the very meaning of criminality uncertain. Piracy offers an important illustration of that form of translation of legality.

Until the end of the eighteenth century, the seas around Britain were never completely controlled by the navy. Although the volume of piracy fluctuated, the state was rarely able to suppress it (130). Acts might have been passed to order its elimination, but there was no policing agency to implement them fully. Instead, the state was sometimes constrained to recruit pirates themselves to patrol the seas (131). Pirates were co-opted to serve as privateers or, indeed, as adjuncts to the navy during wartime. In this fashion, the management of piracy turned as much on bribery and alliance as on simple conflict. Pirates could not be easily suppressed because they were the major possessors of force. Possessing the means of violence, they were useful as privateers ; they could be supported by foreign states ; or they could take virtual command over territories, a command which bestowed a tenuous legality on their activities. Madagascar and the West Indies formed such bases at one time. The governors of the American colonies, too, were quite frequently prepared to grant letters of marque to pirates. It appears that they were tacitly supposed to supplement their incomes with the profits of raids. Piracy was often an entrepreneurial exercise funded by the wealthy and the powerful. Some expeditions even gained royal patronage. The seas were thus politically and legally ambiguous areas which were open to complicated processes of compromise and exploitation. The status of pirates was quite indefinite :

> « In international affairs ... the distinction between enemy and criminal is a nice one ...[the difference between pirate and privateer] relates more to power and to claims to legitimacy than to the actual activities of the pirates or their protectors » (132).

Those with influence in the criminal regions were sometimes of too great a moment to be treated with any stance but deference, a deference which might be generalised. One highwayman, for example, was able to become Attorney-general (133). Pirates could be knighted (134). Indeed, there was some mobility between the legal and illegal centres of power. Just as pirates might become respectable, so the respectable could turn pirate or highwayman. There was an occasional equivalence of authority and command which eased a transition in the ambiguous area of the independently powerful. There were real structural affinities between the organisations which incorporated legitimate and illegitimate enterprises. Officers in patrimonial bureaucracy were prone to profiteering, blurring the moral character of their undertaking. Members of criminal corporations sometimes turned to apparently benevolent activity, blurring the immorality of their projects. Viewed naively, the difference between the acts of a City Marshal like Charles Hitchen and a receiver and theiftaker like Jonathan Wild is very slight. Both people were able to accuse the other of criminality and corruption. Each claimed a public usefulness for his own role. Whilst Hitchen was dismissed for corrupt practices and then reinstated, Wild believed himself entitled to petition for the honour of the freedom of the City of London. It was perhaps only a nominal distinction which fixed what and who were criminal. Indeed, Wild was to serve as a symbolic archetype for satires on Hanoverian government, the affinities being emphasized in criticisms of Walpole and his ministers (135). Wild became Walpole and Walpole Wild. As Thompson argued :

> « ... an examination of the practices of the administration in these years reveals the same use of informers and evidences, employment of blood-money, the same casual sacrifice of colleagues who had outlived their utility, and a similar parasitism upon the public ... The "subculture" of the Hanoverian Whig and the "subculture" of Jonathan Wild were mirror-images of one another » (136).

On a more modest scale, the contingencies of social control forced the state to recruit the deviant as its own agent. Diffusely, such recruitment took the guise of the specific and temporary contracts which marked the employment of the reward and pardon system. Accused men became temporary instruments of government. More particularly, that tendency to recruitment led official institutions to hire pirates as pirate-catchers, smugglers as revenue-officers (137), thieves as thieftakers and poachers as game-keepers. In France, one of the most celebrated of all policeman, Vidocq, was himself rescued from the world of deviants and sent back to control it (138). Few but those personally schooled in deviant practices were able to acquire the expertise of a competent enforcement agent. Such men, in turn, often played equivocal roles, acting as the middlemen of crime (139). Serving as factors, they mediated the operation of law. They defined the immunities and vulnerabilities of criminal and allegedly criminal populations.

The most significant development of that role of middleman was realised in the eighteenth century thieftaker. Thieftakers were not original to that time, but they came to a special prominence in the economy of rewards and pardons created by the state (140). Thieftakers could not borrow from any body of knowledge or practice produced by formal agencies of control. Theirs could also be a dangerous undertaking because it lacked effective support in a situation where violence was common. Since it was not eased by any considerable exchange of information and aid, it became practised by those who merged imperceptly with the world which they were supposed to regulate. It became the special province of those who exercised some initial command in that world. Those who were best positioned structurally were the receivers, and receivers either became thieftakers or were displaced by them (141). The thieftaker-receiver existed on the interface between the reputable and the disreputable. He was armed with the ability to impeach the older receiver and to control competition. He had some capacity to restrict the potential treachery of clients and informers. Further, his domination of routine policing enabled him to work outside official scrutiny. Enjoying a practical immunity, which was strengthened by the collusive aid of official enforcement agents, he could retain his organisational integrity at a time when other groups were in some disarray. He held one another major advantage. Because he was one of the few people who were properly and professionally engaged in trafficking between criminals and noncriminals, he was provided with a useful front. His dealings could be explained as part of a legitimate calling. His clients were dependent on him, but it was not necessarily a reciprocal dependence. Receivers have often informed, but their clients tend to protect them (142).

The thief takers relied on an intimate acquaintance with deviance and, because their stake in it was principally financial, they often husbanded and encouraged crime in order to develop a flow of useful and manageable cases (143). Thus Mandeville alluded to the « Damage the Public sustains from the Trade that is drove by the Thiefcatchers, and the various ways now in vogue of compounding Felonies, by which the Safety as well as Maintenance of Thieves and Pilferers are industriously taken care of, and the Laws that enforce prosecution altogether eluded ». Thieftakers might support thieves, afford them protection and ensure their immunity. In many instances, they monopolised police work and enjoyed total discretion over the selection of those who would be arraigned. Howson has remarked that the manipulation of rewards and pardons gave thieftakers « virtual power of life and death over thieves » (145). They appeared to engage in the business of wholesale crime farming, carefully reaping profits from cultivated areas of rule-breaking. Their mediating role led to elaborate patterns of cooptation, collusion and conflict. As herdsmen of deviance, they culled as well as protected, delivering to the courts people who were refractory or strangers within their territories. They tended to penalise those who were incapable of offering much resistance or retaliation when arrested. There was thus a major process of discrimination against the marginal, the novice, and the unorganised, the main structures of criminal activity being largely unaffected providing they submitted to a new discipline (146). Despite their predatory and conservative role, they constituted the only active agency of control which was able to superintend the behaviour of criminals. They were the real predecessors of the contemporary police, being employed as a necessary albeit unfortunate model for the founding of the Bow Street Runners (147).

The principal thieftaker of the eighteenth century, Jonathan Wild, established an almost total monopoly over theif-catching, receiving and thieving in southern England (148). His subordinates stole on commission, and surrendered what they had taken to Wild who then returned the goods to their erstwhile owners. As a major broker in stolen goods, Wild was able to ascertain what thefts had taken place and was armed with material to control his dependants. He employed his power as thieftaker to suppress rivals and to maintain an internal discipline. His organisation was consequently a political accomplishment, a significant instance of the brokerage of crime and power. He described himself as a « factor » journeying between different worlds (149). His command over criminal worlds represented an *imperium in imperio*, an accumulation of power which required at least temporary acknowledgement by the state. At his trial, Wild protested « I have brought many bold and daring malefactors to just punishment, even at the hazard of my own life ... I have done merit, because at the time the things were done, they were esteemed meritorious by the government ... » (150). Similarly, Hall observed « during Wild's career as a thieftaker he was rendering valuable services to the police for which he received the usual reward from these officials, a compensation still paid to criminals. He was not prosecuted, and he was permitted to operate » (151). Wild managed to acquire the status of expert and consultant on matters of crime control. His advice was sought by the Privy Council in 1720 (152), and there were rumours of his assuming a clandestine role for the state (153). Calling himself « Thieftaker-General of Britain and Ireland », he surrounded himself with the trappings of authority. In short, Wild came near to assuming an official place as policeman and broker:

> « [Governments] not only receive and accept of Informations of the worst of Crimes, from the worst of Criminals, and take Knowledge of the Offence from the Offenders themselves, but encourage such Criminals to come in and confess the Offence, and Discover their Accomplices, Promising as well Pardon for the Crimes, as a Reward for the Discovery, even to those who are Guilty. Now this willingness of the Government to detect Thieves, seem'd to be a kind of authority, for *Jonathan* in his vigorous pursuit of those he thought fit to have Punish'd ... » (154).

It was that authority, recognised by magistrates and the government (155), which lent force to the argument that criminality was negotiable and fluid. What distinguished Wild's organisation in the first decades of the eighteenth century was also to characterise the Sicilian *mafiosi* (156) : the capacity to serve as an acknowledged and necessary intermediary between weak community and weak government. That capacity was sufficient to ensure, however briefly, the assumption of political stature and immune status.

Conclusion.

I have argued in a somewhat simplistic fashion that legal domination in the late 1600s and early 1700s was uncertain. A forced communal self-sufficiency and relatively uninfluential enforcement agencies combined to permit the emergence of much variation in the subordination of different groups. Some groups were allowed to attain a comparative autonomy and were shielded against formal social control. In turn, those who were in effective command over those groups were able to negotiate the character of criminality and criminals. At its extreme, such variation had the consequence of confusing the borders between morality and immorality, between legality and illegality :

> « Such were the blessings of that state ;
> Their crimes conspir'd to make them great :
> And virtue, who from politics
> Has learn'd a thousand cunning tricks,

Was, by their happy influence,
Made friends with vice :
And ever since,
The worst of all the multitude
Did something for the common good » (157).

Paul Rock

REFERENCES

1. Radical criminologists have been urging a return to what are basically eighteenth century forms policing. It seems useful to examine some of the implications of such a system in its original guise. For one instance of that radical plea, see Young (J.), «Working Class Criminology », IN Taylor (I.) and al. (eds.) ; *Critical Criminology*, London, Routledge and Kegan Paul, 1975,

2. I have tried to defend such an approach in «Some Problems of Interpretative Historiography», *British Journal of Sociology*, 1976, September.

3. Quoted in Ogg (D.), *England in the Reigns of James II and William III*, Oxford, Clarendon Press, 1955, p. 30.

4. C. f. Parkes (J.), *Travel in England in the Seventeenth Century*, London, Oxford University Press, 1925, p. 1.

5. Ibid., pp. 18-20.

6. Rogers (P.), introduction to Defoe (D.), *A Tour Through the Whole Island of Great Britain*, Harmandsworth, Penguin, 1971, p. 24.

7. C. f. Rogers (P.), *Grub Street*, London, Methuen, 1972, p. 4.

8. Rogers (P.), introduction to Defoe (D.), *A Tour Through the Whole Island of Great Britain*, op. cit., p. 24.

9. C. f. Laslett (P.), *The World We Have Lost, London*, Methuen, 1965, pp. 19, 66.

10. 10. C. f. Parkes (J.), *Travel in England in the Seventeenth Century*, op. cit., p. 283.

11. C. f. Scott (J.), *Comparative Political Corruption*, New Jersey, Prentice Hall 1972, p, 38.

12. Ogg (D.), *England in the Reigns of James II and William III*, op. cit., p. 122.

13. C. f. Zirker, *Fielding's Social Pamphlets*, Berkeley, University of California Press, 1966, p. 17.

14. C. f. Beloff (M.), *Public Order and Popular Disturbances*, London, Oxford University Press, 1938, pp. 22-23.

15. Thompson (E.), «The Moral Economy of the English Crowd in the Eighteeenth Century», *Past and Present*, 1971, February, N° 50, pp. 120-121.

16. C. f. Andreski (S.), *Military Organization and Society*, London, Routledge and Kegan Paul, 1954, p. 79.

17. C. f. pringle (P.), *Honest Thieves*, London, Robert Hale, 1938, p. 35.

18. C. f. Beloff (M.), *Public Order and Popular Disturbances*, op. cit., p. 23.

19. C. f. Clark (G.) Sir, *The Later Stuarts*, Oxford, Clarendon Press, 1955, p. 259.

20. Hammond (J.) and Hammond (B.), «Proverty, Crime and Philosophy» IN Turberville (A.) (ed.), *Johnson's England*, Oxford, Clarendon Press, 1933, p, 301.

21. C. f. Knapp (A.) and Baldwing (W.), *The New Newgate Calendar*, London, J. Robins, 1824, Vol. I., p, 226.

22. Quoted in Pringle (P.), *Hue and Cry*, London, Museum Press, 1955, p. 52.
23. C. f. Howson (G.), *Thief-Taker General*, London, Hutchinson, 1970, p. 25.
24. Fortescue (J.) Sir, «The Army» IN Turberville (A.) (ed.), *Johnson's England*, op. cit., pp. 69-70.
25. C. f. Hill (C.), *The Century of Revolution*, Edinburgh, Thomas Nelson, 1961, p. 15.
26. C.f. Fortescue (J.) Sir, «The Army», op. cit., p. 68.
27. Ibid., p. 68.
28. C. f. Western (J.), *The English Militia in the Eighteenth Century*, London, Routledge and Kegan Paul, 1965, p. 3.
29. C. f. Barnett (C.), *Britain and her Army*, London, Allen Lane, 1970, pp. 107-110.
30. Ibid., p, 107.
31. C. f. Thompson (E.), «The Moral Economy of the English Crowd in the Eighteenth Century », op, cit., p. 121.
32. C. f. Winslow (C.), «Sussex Smugglers» (« Hay (D.) and al. (eds), *Albion's Fatal Tree : Crime and Society in Eighteenth-Century England*, London, Allen Lane, 1975, p. 144.
33. Thompson (E.), «The Moral Economy of the English Crowd in the Eighteenth Century », op. cit., p. 121.
34. C. f. Clark (G.) Sir, *The Later Stuarts*, op. cit., p, 259.
35. C. f. Plumb, (J.), *The Growth of Political Stability in England*, London, Macmillan, 1967, p. 20.
36. C. f. Western (J.), *The English Militia in the Eighteenth Century*, op. cit., p, 27.
37. Ibid, pp. 72-73.
38. Ibid, p, 72.
39. C. f. Clark (G.) Sir, *The Later Stuarts*, op. cit., p. 259.
40. De laune (T.), *The Present State of London*, London, George Larkin, 1 681, p. 288.
41. C. f. Ogg (D.), *England in the Reign of Charles II*, Oxford, Clarendon Press, 1934,, Vol. 2, p. 493.
42. C. f. Pike (L.), *A History of Crime in England*, London, Smith Elder and Co., 1876, Vol. II, p. 369.
43. C. f. Radzinowicz (L.), *A History of the English Criminal Law and its Administration*, London, Stevens and Sons, 1956, Vol. II, p. 27.
44. Shaw (J.), *Paris Law*, London, Lintot, 1753, p. 344.
45. C. f. Beloff (M.), *Public Order and Popular Disturbances*, op. cit., p. 26.
46. C. f. Parkes (J.), *Travel in England in the Seventeenth Century*, op. cit., p. 45.
47. Ibid., p. 152.
48. C. f. Beloff (M.), *Public Order and Popular Disturbances*, op. cit., p. 24.

49. C. f. Ibid., p. 133.
50. C. f. Howson (G.), *Thief-Taker General*, op, cit., p. 4.
51. C. f. Winslow (C.), «Sussex Smugglers », op. cit., p. 128.
52. C. f. White (L.), *Medieval Technology and Social Change*, Oxford, Oxford University Press, 1962, p. 38.
53. C. f. Andreski (S.), *Military Organization and Society*, op. cit., p; 81.
54. C. f. Fuller (J.), *Armament and History*, London, Eyre and Spottiswoode, 1946, p. 99.
55. Ibid.
56. C. f. Thompson (E.), *Whigs and Hunters: The Origins of the Black Act*, London, Allen Lane, 1975, p. 64.
57. C. f. Pringle (P.), *Stand and Deliver*, London, Museum Press, 1951, p, 63.
58. Plumb (J.), *The Growth of Political Stability in England*, op, cit., p.21.
59. C. f. Scott (J.), *Comparative Political Corruption*, op. cit., p. 40.
60. C. f. Swart (K.), *Sale of offices in the seventeenth Century*, The Hague, Martinus Nijhoff, 1949.
61. C. f. Laslett (P.), *The World We Have Lost*, op. cit., p. 19.
62. C. f. Hay (D.), «Property, Authority and the Criminal Law», IN Hay (D.) and al. (eds.), *Albion's Fatal Tree*, op. cit.
63. C. f. Ogg (D.), *England in the Reigns of James II and William III*, op. cit., p. 107.
64. Hay (D.), « Property, Authority and the Criminal Law», op. cit., p. 52.
65. Defoe (D.), *The Poor Man's Plea*, London, No named publisher, 1968, pp.7-8.
66. Fielding (J.), *A Plan for Preventing Robberies Within Twenty Miles of London*, London, A. Millar, 1755, pp. 22-23.
67. C. f. 8 Geo. 2, c. 16, s. 11, 1735.
68. C. f. Pringle (P.), *Hue and Cry*, op. cit., p. 48.
69. C. f. Holdsworth (W.) Sir, *A History of English Law*, London, Methuen, 1938, Vol. XI, p. 585.
70. C. f. Radzinowicz (L.), *A History of the English Criminal Law and its Administration*, op. cit., Vol. 2, p, 33.
71. Ibid.
72. C. f. Howson (G.), *Thief-Taker General*, op. cit., for an excellent account of thieftaking.
73. For a more recent example, see Marx (G.), «Thoughts on a Neglected Category of Social Movement Participant : The Agent Provocateur and the Informant », IN Halleck (S.) and al. (eds), *The Aldine Crime and Justice Annual* 1974, Chicago, Aldine, 1975. See also the report in *The New York Times*, 1975, 2nd, April.

74. Winslow (C,), «Sussex Smugglers », op. cit., p. 144.
75. 4 W. and M., c. 8, s. 7.
76. Wilson (R.), *A full and Impartial Account of all the Robberies Committed by John Hawkins, George Sympson ... and their Companion ... by Ralph Wilson, late one of their Confederates*, London, J. Peele, 1722, p. 24.
77. Thompson (E.), «The Crime of Anonymity», IN Hay (D.) and al. (eds.), Albion's Fatal Tree, op. cit., p. 272.
78. Hall (1.), *Theft, Law and Society*, Boston, Little Brown, 1935, p. 87.
79. Rogers, (P .), *Grub Street*, op. cit., p. 12.
80. C. f. Pringle (P.), *Honest Thieves*, op. cit., p. 18.
81. C f. Plumb (J.), *The Growth of Political Stability in England*, op. cit., P. 21.
82. Beloff (M.), *Public Order and Popular Disturbances*, op. cit., P. 95.
83. Rule (J .), «Wrecking and Coastal Plunder », IN Hay (D.) and al. (eds.), *Albion's Fatal Tree*, op, cit., p. 186.
84. C. f. Defoe (D.), *A Tour through the Whole Island* ... op, cit., p. 295.
85. C. f. Rock (P.), *Making People Pay*, London, Routledge and Kegan Paul, 1973, Ch. 12.
86. C. f. Jusserand (J.) *English Wayfaring Life in the Middle Ages*, London, T. Fischer Unwin, n° date, p. 165.
87. C. f. Ogg (D.), *England in the Reigns of James II and William III*, op. cit., p. 66.
88. Thornley (I.), «The Destruction of Sanctuary», IN Seton-Watson (R.) (ed.), *Tudor Studies*, London, Longmans, Green and Co., 1924, p. 184.
89. Pike (L.), *A History of Crime in England*, op. cit., p. 253.
90. C. f. Thornley (I.), «The Destruction of Sanctuary », op. cit, p. 202.
91. In the case of the Sicilian gilds, see Hess (H.), *Mafia and Mafiosi*, Hants, Saxon House, 1973, p. 17.
92. C. f. Unwin (G.), *The Gilds and Companies of London*, London, Frank Cass, 1908, p. 42.
93. C. f. Judges (A.), *The Elizabethan Underwood*, London, George Routledge and Sons, 1930, XXVII.
94. See Sutherland's standard definition of professional crime : Sutherland (K), *The Professional Thief*, Chicago, University of Chicago Press, 1956.
95. C. f. Maurer (D.), *Whiz Mob*, New Haven, College and University Press, 1964, and Maurer (D.), *The Big Con*, New York, Signet, 1962.
96. C, f. Maurer (D.), *Whiz Mob*, op. cit., p. 52.
97. Unwin (G.), *The Gilds and Companies of London*, op. cit., p. 98.
98. C. f. Thompson (K), *Whigs and Hunters*, op. cit., p. 81.
99. Ogg (D.), *England in the Reigns of James II and William III*, op. cit., p. 84, (emphasis added).

100. Thus, the inhabitants of the Mint in London continued to claim their privileges in 1708. C. f. Thornbury (W.), *Old and New London*, London, Cassell, Petter and Galpin, undated, Vol. VI, p. 61.

101. Ward (E.), *The London-Spy*, London. J. How, 1709, pp. 155. 156.

102. C. f. George (M.), «London and the life of the town », IN Turberville (A.) (ed.), *Johnson's England*, op. cit., p. 163.

103. C. f. Ward (E.), *The London-Spy*, op, cit., p. 151.

104. C. f. George (M.), *London Life in the Eighteenth Century*, London, Kegan Paul, Trubner and Co., 1925, p. 68.

105. C. f. Laslett (P.), *The World We have Lost*, op. cit., p. 14.

106. Quoted in George (M.), «London and the Life of the Town », op. cit., p. 163.

107. C. f. Weir (W.), «St. Gile's, Past and Present », IN Knight (C.) (ed.), London, *London Bohn*, 1851, Vol. III, p. 262.

108. Howson (G.), *Thief-Taker General*, op. cit., p. 22.

109. Defoe (D.), *A Tour through the Whole Island ...*, op. cit., p. 321.

110. Rude (G.), *Hanoverian London*. London, Seeker and Warburg, 1971,p. 128.

111. "Alsatia" was named after the disputed frontier region between France and Germany, itself being a disputed territory.

112. George (M.), *London Life in the Eighteenth Century*, op. cit., p. 82.

113. C. f. Weir (W.), «St. Gile's Past and Present », op. cit., p. 262.

114. C. f. Lyons (F.), *Jonathan Wild : Prince of Robbers*, London, Michael Joseph, 1936, pp. 101-102.

115. C. f. Fielding (H.), *An enquiry into the Causes of the Late Increase of Robbers*, London, 1751.

116. C. f. Tobias 0.), «A Statistical Study of a Nineteenth-Century Criminal Area », IN Halleck (S.), and al.· (eds.), *Aldine Crime and Justice Annual 1974*, op, cit.

117. Binney, (J .), «Thieves and Swindlers », IN Mayhew (R.), *London Labour and the London Poor*, London, Griffin, Bohn and Co, 1862, Vol. IV, p. 301.

118. Beames (T.), *The Rookeries of London*, London, Thomas Bosworth, 1850, p. 41.

119. Ogg (D.), *England in the Reigns of James II and William III*, op. cit., pp. 56-57.

120. Nourse (T.), *Campania Foelix*, London, Bennet, 1700, p. 17.

121. C. f. Ogg (D.), *England in the Reigns of James II and William III*, op. cit., p. 102.

122. Ibid., p. 57.

123. Ibid., p. 107.

124. C. f. Pringle (P.), *Stand and Deliver*, op, cit., p. 28.

125. C. f. Parkes (J.), *Travel in England in the Seventeenth Century*, op. cit., pp. 162-164.

126. C. f. Swart (K.), *Sale of Offices in the Seventeenth Century*, op. cit.,

127. C. f. Plumb (J.), *The Growth of Political Stability in England*, op. cit., p. 77.

128. C. f. Howson (G.), *Thief-Taker General*, op. oit., p. '28.

129. C. f. Pringle (P.), *Hue and Cry*, op. cit., p. 46.

130. C. f. Pringle (P.), *Jolly Roger*, London, Museum Press, 1953, passim.

131. C. f. ibid., p. 47.

132. McIntosh (M.), *The organisation of Crime*, London, MacMillan, 1975, p. 19.

133. C. f. Pringle (P.), *Stand and Deliver*, op. cit., p. 25.

134. C. f. Pringle (P.), *Jolly Roger*, op. cit., p. 47.

135. C. f. Irwin (W.), *The Making of Jonathan Wild*, New York, Columbia University Press, 1941, p. 3.

136. Thompson (E.), *Whigs and Hunters*, op.-cit., p. 218.

137. C. f. Pringle (P.), *Honest Thieves*, op. cit., p. 71.

138. C. f. Stead (P.), *Vidocq* : A Biography, London, Staples Press, 1953,

139. This was, indeed, part of a larger efflorescence of middlemen discussed by Thompson (E.), «The Moral Economy of the English Crowd in the Eighteenth Century», op. cit., and Westerfield (R,), *Middlemen in English Business*, Transactions of the Connecticut Academy of Arts and Sciences, New Haven, Yale University, Press, 1915.

140. For a description of an earlier, Elizabethan' thieftaker, c. f. Hutton (L.), *The Black Dogge of Newgate*, London, G. Simson. and W. White, 1596.

141. C. f. Howson (G.), *Thief-Taker General*, op, cit., pp. 37-38.

142. For more recent examples, c. f. Mack (J,), '*The Crime Industry*, Hants, Saxon House, 1975, esp. pp. 126-127.'

143. C. f. Marx (G.), « Thoughts on a Neglected Category of Social Movement Participant », op. cit.

144. Mandeville (B.), *An Enquiry into the Causes of the Frequent Executions at Tyburn*, London, J. Roberts, 1725, part 'of unnumbered' preface.

145. Howson (G.), *Thief-Taker General*, op. cit., p. 37.

146. C. f. Pringle (P.), *Hue and Cry*, op. cit., p. 36.

147. C. f. Pringle (P.), Ibid , p. 35.

148. C. f. Howson (G.), *Thief-Taker General*, op. cit.,p. 5.

149. C. f. Lyons (p.), Jonathan Wild, op, cit.

150. Quoted in Hayward (A.), Lives of the Most Remarkable Criminals ..., London, George Routledge and Son, 1927, p. 266.

151. Hall (J.), *Theft, Law and Society*, op, cit., p, 136.

152. C. f. Howson (G.), *Thief-Taker General*, op. cit., p. 125.

153. C. f. Benson (L.), *The Book of Remarkable Trials and Notorious Characters*, London, Reeves and Turner, undated, p. 89. This charge is also put in a most fanciful form by Ainsworth CW. H.), *Jack Sheppard*, London, Richard Bentley, 1839.

154. Defoe (D.), *The True and Genuine Account of the Lite and Actions of the Late Jonathan Wild*, London, John Applebee, 1725, p. 17.

155. C. f. Smith (A.), *Memoirs of the Life and Times of the Famous Jonathan Wild*, London, Sam. Briscoe, 1726, p. x.

156. C. f. Ianni (Fi), *A Family Business*, London, Routledge and Kegan Paul, 1972, p. 40.

157. Mandeville (B.), *The Fable of the Bees*, New York Capricorn, 1962, p. 31.

[4]
Governments, Victims and Policies in Two Countries

Policies and programmes for the victims of crime are beginning to emerge in Canada, the United Kingdom and elsewhere. In Canada, the federal Government launched its Justice for Victims of Crime Initiative and spent money trying to prompt a relatively inert "private sector" into organising itself. In England and Wales, a rapidly expanding National Association of Victims Support Schemes repeatedly petitioned an apparently unresponsive Government for funding. When it was offered appreciable support, its character and methods were set. Federal and central Governments display important differences in their style, rate and structure of policy-making, and it is those differences which explain some of the contrasts in the social organisation of relief for victims of crime.

Introduction

In the Summer of 1981, whilst a Visiting Scholar at the Programs Branch of the Ministry of the Solicitor General of Canada, I began what was to become a four year research project on policy-making in the Canadian criminal justice system. The project examined the early development of the Justice for Victims of Crime Initiative (Rock, 1986a). On the completion of that book, I decided to explore the emergence of policies and schemes for the victims of crime in this country. There were the makings of a fairly major interest in services for victims: the National Association of Victims Support Schemes is a highly successful voluntary movement with just over 300 schemes; the Criminal Injuries Compensation Scheme was under review; there was talk in Home Office circles about possible policy initiatives, talk that resulted very recently in the announcement at the 1986 Conservative Party Conference of a massive increase in Home Office funding for victims support schemes from an average annual payment of £150,000 to £3,000,000; the treatment of rape victims had become contentious; two national victim surveys had been conducted by the Home Office; and reparation and mediation projects were in the course of being established. It seemed that there was an opportunity to produce a history that not only deserved to be recorded in its own right but also lent itself to comparative analysis. Accordingly, in the Spring of 1984 I began to compile materials, conduct interviews and attend meetings in the area of victims support, projects for assaulted women, criminal injuries compensation and victim–offender reconciliation projects. The ultimate intention is to produce a book minutely examining developments and contrasts. This paper is a sketch of its possibilities.

* Professor of Sociology, London School of Economics. I am grateful to David Faulkner, Tony Marshall, Helen Reeves, Jayne Seagrave, Joanna Shapland and Mary Tuck for their advice in the writing of this paper.

I shall proceed by exploring contrasts between the early stages of Canadian and British policy formation, concentrating on a number of clear themes which have arisen, some peculiar to the evolution of policies for victims, others of more general application. Throughout, I shall view policy-making through the lenses provided by two special histories which may not have been at all "typical". It is more than possible that other histories would have given other foci.

I shall concentrate on how it came about that, in Canada, a government made policies for victims in an unprepared world, whilst, in England and Wales, a prepared world waited for its government to respond. Maguire and Corbett have observed:

> In Canada, following very effective pressure by a small "victims lobby" upon and within the Ministry of the Solicitor General, the federal government was persuaded to set up an expensive package of research and experimental programmes of services to victims.... In Great Britain, by contrast, despite the pioneering in the sixties of a state compensation scheme for victims of violent crime, the notion of "victims' rights" has not been widely discussed, and there has been until recently little government interest in funding special services for victims (Maguire and Corbett, 1987, p. 1).

It is that apparent contrast which I shall attempt to explain.

Governments, Victims and Policies

In Canada, criminal justice policy-making seems to be inordinately difficult. The country is geographically vast, the second largest in the world, and it is beyond the reach of a single Ministry in Ottawa to monitor and manage everything that happens in Vancouver, Moose Jaw or the Yukon. There is a necessary reliance on the "private sector" for the implementation of policy, and matters cannot often proceed very far without that sector's consent. Formal decision-making itself is apportioned between two, and occasionally more federal departments and the governments of the provinces. There is an ensuing concern about the impact which decisions, programmes and initiatives might have upon what are often fragile and wary interdepartmental and federal–provincial relations. Very frequently, the importance of a reform in criminal justice must be balanced against gains and losses in intergovernmental politics.

Federal policy-making is a cautious and diplomatic process, and it has two principal consequences for the character of the materials that pass through it. Canadian officials find themselves engaged in a continuous round of structured negotiations and talks. It is imperative to signal visibly to others that full consultations take place from the first. As a result, decision-making is organised by a long and predictable chain of meetings, and it engenders numerous supporting policy papers. There are federal–provincial committees, task forces and working parties, meetings of Deputy Ministers and meetings of Ministers, the Joint Justice Committee and many others, each with an agenda and a place in the official timetable. Each is significant not only because of the substantive work that is done but also because of the very fact that work is being seen to be done in an effective, solicitous and harmonious way. It is a signal of the unity of the Canadian state.

The Home Office, by comparison, appears to have many fewer organisations with which it must deal in the early phases of decision-making, confronts less opposition, and occupies a simpler environment. To be sure, its staff do define their task as complicated, and there is a vast array of organisations and people that *might* be consulted, but few outsiders have the stature of provincial ministers or officials. The Home Office consequently tends towards a greater intellectual and structural self-sufficiency. It has simplified its environment. It does not respond as readily as the Ministry of the Solicitor General to external bodies such as the United Nations. In Canada, resolutions of the United Nations Congresses on Prevention of Crime and the Treatment of Offenders are automatically fed into the agendas of meetings between the federal criminal justice ministries. They do so, in part, because the Canadian delegations to those Congresses are usually very large, being composed of all the different segments and constituencies of the Canadian criminal justice system, and their conclusions have significance for the internal politics of the Canadian state. The Home Office will send a small delegation which tends not to be as catholic in its membership. The Department will not automatically incorporate the congresses' resolutions in its decision-making. Lobbies play a very important role in Canadian federal politics, being used to signal the presence of popular demand for federal action before provincial and private audiences. The Home Office sometimes appears to define lobbies as bodies that block a clear view of the general will. In 1986, for example, the Home Secretary argued, "Members of Parliament and ministers both in my view need to shake themselves free to some extent from the embrace of pressure groups and interest groups"(*The Times*, 20th September, 1986). The Home Office engages in proportionately fewer formal deliberations. It incorporates the wishes of its constituencies at a distance, surmising their probable responses in its assessment of the "political environment".

There are a number of important consequences:

i. Decisions and planning in the Ministry of the Solicitor General may be relatively onerous but they are also much more structured, deliberate and considered. The first major effect of federalism then is that there is much talk in official Canada, much conscious deliberation and reflection, and a clear articulation of policies. From quite an early stage, proposals are subject to fairly elaborate scrutiny and efforts are made to examine their implications for other institutions and practices. In particular, there is a succession of internal departmental workshops which seem to give rise to thoughtful reviews of what the Ministry is doing and what it might do in the future. They afford a distinct opportunity to "stop and think". The process introduces coherence and purpose in a fashion that is not readily detected throughout the Home Office. To be sure, senior British officials confer frequently and informally but, until quite late in the policy-making process, their decisions may strike the outsider as rather tacit and piecemeal. It will only be when a Minister acts that bureaucracy moves with any visibly great purpose. And that is how it is supposed to be.

ii. The long train of committees and discussions in Canada gives a marked timetable and order to processes, demanding that agendas be constructed, papers written and policies formulated. It quite clearly increases the rate of innovation and activity: ideas and plans must be conceived to occupy all those meetings. To be sure, the role of a federal Ministry charged with a leadership role is necessarily vigorous, but it does receive some of its animation from the sheer number of occasions on which officials are required to be present and purposeful.

From time to time, by contrast, the Home Office can seem relatively inert, managerial rather than innovative, responsive rather than active. The opening stages of policy-making are conducted in informal encounters in corridors, conferences and rooms. In particular, they are mediated by "putting papers up". Written proposals circulate in homemade networks, gaining gravity and clarity in the process. It is only when it appears that the proposals will have to emerge into the external world that outsiders are brought in. There is no visible and permanent process of definition. Neither is there an obvious driving momentum comparable to that of a federal system. Things may be left unformed for very much longer. To be sure, officials do have ambitions for schemes and they are business-like enough when the time comes, but the beginnings lack the pace and organisation of Canada. They are not required to advertise their business to outsiders. Contradictions and ambiguities in policy-making can remain for a considerable while, and it will often take the action of an enterprising and innovative senior official or a Minister to dispel them and initiate the work that will lend clarity and structure to proposals. Moreover, such an innovative official cannot rely, as his Canadian counterparts can, on such a quantity of linked routine processes to take his or her ideas forward. Most typically, then, it is the Ministers who initiate the actions which their civil servants execute.

iii. Intricate interdepartmental and intergovernmental negotiations in Canada give a conciliatory and diplomatic appearance to proposals. Work is rarely undertaken without contemplating its likely effects upon significant constituencies. It may be presumed that the Canadian criminal justice system achieves an added measure of authority as a result. Simultaneously, however, policy-making does undergo systematic reshaping. The framing of policy has become a pre-eminently political process, political questions superseding other questions. Thus, the willed or inadvertent absence of particular groups from consultations in Canada brought about the neglect of their respective victims. Politically unpopular or marginal victims like homosexuals and the victims of motoring offences were somewhat overlooked (Rock, 1986b). Other, more powerful or favoured groups were over-represented. There were good reasons to give special attention to the elderly, for instance; the elderly are particularly fearful of crime and they suffer more grievously when they *are* victimised. But it was not wholly for those reasons that the elderly victim was given priority. There was not always an adequate foundation of research or expressed need for such a decision, and the result was something of a twisting of the direction of effort.

Policy proposals then acquire a distinct character in Canada. As they are steered from committee to committee and from government to government, they are constructed quite deliberately to convey two impressions. They are often indistinct, possessing enough vagueness not to appear final, allowing new groups to modify them by making a recognisable mark of their own. Their indecisiveness may be read as a visible sign of the federal government's readiness to comply with the wishes of important people and organisations. Further, they are devised as bundles of significant gestures, placatory obeisances, which signal that the wishes and clients of central organisations have been given their proper respect. Moving before federal–provincial committees, they will defer to provincial sensibilities; before women's organisations they will talk of women; and before the Department of Indian and Northern Affairs they will recognise natives. Policy proposals are mirrors of their readers' concerns. They will become moving reflections of the settings through which they will pass. In the Home Office, there are also sensitivities to respect, but a relatively dominating department without provinces or states about it will not produce proposals that refract its political environment in quite the same fashion.

iv. Elaborate networks of consultation and dependencies have other effects on the policy-making process in Canada. Chief amongst them is the greater vulnerability of negotiations that can always become snarled in the intricacies of interdepartmental and intergovernmental politics. In a federal state, especially, what is done between governments or Ministries can take on an added weight of meaning, being interpreted as evidence of federal or provincial intentions and attitudes towards rights, the constitution and the division of labour. Especially when there are wider anxieties or conflicts within the State, many of the more minor and seemingly innocent efforts to make policy can become embroiled. Initiatives for victims, for example, were affected by disputes between Quebec and Ottawa about the constitution. In the later 1980s, they became cramped by territorial debates between different federal departments. Abundant, regular and ritualised meetings can give order and movement to policies, but they also prepare many more hazards for them. Policy-making in Canada is a relatively eventful and dramatic business, pregnant with crises and excitements.

v. And a second effect is that the propulsive mechanisms of the Canadian criminal justice ministries can quite easily produce ideas at a greater rate than the environment of agencies and volunteers surrounding them. The cosmopolitanism of officials in continuous contact with foreign ideas, the intensity and frequency of talk about criminal justice issues, and the frequent movement from one policy concern to another, can combine to bring about a kind of culture lag between the Ministry of the Solicitor General and its clients. By the time officials had solved to their own satisfaction many of the practical and political problems of working for victims, their audience was in a state of evident unreadiness. Thus, in 1981, Canadian officials sought to create a victims lobby, and they were persuaded of its indispensability, but victims organisations were not prepared. There is a perennial problem of dislocation.

vi. There is another major feature that must be marked. In Canada, a division of mandates and responsibilities between governments has brought it about that the Ministry of the Solicitor General of Canada has quite limited powers of intervention in what are often provincial or disputed areas. What it starts will usually have to be finished by the provinces, sometimes involving them in sizeable expenditure. The Ministry has followed the practice of funding demonstration or exemplary projects for no more than three years, allowing their eventual success to be determined by the provinces, municipalities and private sector.

The Secretariat of the Ministry of the Solicitor General accordingly regards itself as relatively constrained, being confined to "policy development" and "policy support" rather than to "program delivery". It is fairly tentative in its approach to new ventures in criminal justice, being anxious not to be read as a source of threat to provincial and private interests. Initiatives are not supposed to lead to the permanent addition of new and substantial federal institutions. They are generally presented to the provinces as short-lived enterprises for which they might care to assume eventual responsibility. Project will then follow project in a long chain. A result has been that outsiders are prone frequently to comment on one characteristic of the Ministry of the Solicitor General. Indeed, some of the Ministry's own liaison officials were inclined to refer to this characteristic themselves, becoming outsiders for practical purposes.

The Ministry was defined repeatedly as "faddish". It was suggested that the Secretariat was responsible for a long succession of little undertakings which were attended with some initial enthusiasm and then forgotten and displaced. People in provincial and private reaches of the criminal justice system were tempted to devalue the importance of the Secretariat's work, adopting something of a cynical stance towards what was done. It was argued that, whatever might currently be in vogue, it would pass soon enough. Outsiders professed their detachment from the Secretariat's efforts. They doubted the commitment of the Ministry and, one may assume, feared seeming foolish in their excessive attachment to a fashion that was bound to disappear in a short while. (Indeed, talk within the Secretariat itself provided a foundation for that fear. There was some little contempt for people who were thought to be bound up in old and discredited enterprises like diversion.) The Ministry suffers from its reputation for faddishness. What is at stake, in part, is the social organisation of appearances, of presentational strategies. There are many officials who can and do offer a perfectly convincing case for the coherence and persistence of the Ministry's initiatives over time. Crime prevention, victims assistance, diversion, police efficiency and so on may be represented as reasonably harmonious with one another. But external audiences sometimes find themselves more persuaded by the appearance of discontinuity and whimsicality.

The Home Office, by contrast, is lodged in a much more fateful policy environment. What it starts, it will often have to maintain and finish. Only occasionally will other bodies (like the Cadbury Trust, Sainsburys or local authorities) assume responsibility for funding and administering projects. Any

Home Office venture can entail indefinite commitments, limit future freedoms, and give a fixed definition to the criminal justice system. Of course, it is always possible to describe what is being done as "experimental" or move to a small, atypical enclave of the criminal justice system which is unlikely to set disturbing precedents. Some schemes like the "wet shelters" and Community Development Programmes have been aborted. But a Home Office policy decision is almost always more momentous than a decision of the Solicitor General of Canada. There are major incentives to be cautious about rushing towards innovation. Things will be monitored and appraised rather more circumspectly, particularly when there are very broad Government constraints on public sector expenditure in a country that is relatively poorer than Canada. In this case, the private sector can sometimes race ahead of government. (Nevertheless, it is interesting that, when the time came, funding for victims schemes in England and Wales will be more generous than in Canada. All that may be said eventually is that the decision to spend took longer to make.)

vii. There is one other minor contrast between patterns of social organisation in the Ministry of the Solicitor General and the Home Office. There are radical differences in the social geography of decision-making. The patterns are possibly not intentional but they do embody unlike styles of organising people, and the consequences are interesting.

Since 1981, the Secretariat of the Ministry of the Solicitor General has been crammed into somewhat limited accommodation in the Wilfrid Laurier Building in Ottawa. There has been a partial move towards "open-plan" offices in which the barriers surrounding officials' work stations are often more than a little token. Even when offices are enclosed by walls, it seems to be a convention to leave doors open. Staff are able to monitor one another's doings, overhear conversations and track movements. There is a constant traffic of people along the spaces between the work areas, and many meetings take place in lavatories, near elevators, coffee machines and photocopiers. In short, staff are generally visible and accessible to one another.

The older Home Office buildings in Whitehall were also small and crowded, fondly remembered by some of their former occupants as a site of a friendly, chatty *Gemeinschaft*. But the Home Office moved to vast new buildings designed by Basil Spence and its internal design is now quite different. The new building is much bigger and there is a more generous provision of space. Photocopiers are manned by specialised staff and are not directly available to officials as they are in the Ministry of the Solicitor General. There is little encouragement to huddle in the photocopying rooms and gossip. The inner geography of the new Home Office is made memorable by a maze of relatively empty corridors of uniform colour, by dozens of closed doors concealing whatever activities take place behind them, and by a large number of enclosed offices containing officials working in relative isolation. Communication is very typically conducted on paper or over the telephone, and to be "good on paper" is the mark of an official bound for success. Very often, deliberations will take the form of a long chain of letters circulating between staff who only infrequently meet face-to-face.

This impersonal, distant and mediated style of communication is superimposed upon a relatively undeveloped structure of meetings. As I have argued, the Home Office does not quite possess the conspicuous framework of conferences, agendas, working parties and committees characteristic of the Ministry of the Solicitor General. Staff working in Canada tended rather to resent their lack of privacy, but it did seem to engender a marked co-operativeness, involvement and busyness. It is certainly the case that officials there are comparatively knowledgeable about one another's doings, transacted much of their work in little chance encounters, found it easy to confer in a spontaneous and casual manner, and built up rather an active working world in consequence.

The Home Office, however, appears to be fragmented, its staff not as often meeting and consulting about matters of common interest. Formal communication between colleagues is supposed to move vertically, not horizontally, within specialist divisions devoted to particular portions of the Home Office task. When matters (such as victims) occupy the staff of more than one division, strategic individuals in one area may find themselves intentionally or unintentionally excluded from the deliberations of another, sometimes to the detriment of planning. Patchiness and fragmentation are thereby reinforced. In many, although not all, the levels of the Home Office, there was little of the obvious engrossment, communality and enthusiasm that can be so visible in the Ministry of the Solicitor General. Enthusiasm was at its most apparent in the most senior grades, perhaps reflecting how the most powerful officials were able to synthesise, study and manoeuvre clumps of activity and knowledge in a manner impossible to their subordinates. Not only did the world make sense to them but they could impart sense to it.

viii. The Canadian Justice for Victims of Crime Initiative was conceived, defined and animated by the Policy and Expenditure Management System which was introduced in 1981 and abandoned a few years later. One of the components of the System was to require departments to submit annual forward looks in which they would detail, cost and justify new initiatives. It was only in the internal discussions which accompanied the drafting of the Strategic Overviews that the Ministry's Branches came to appreciate the scale and character of their own and others' investment in work on victims. It was a reasonably orderly and searching process, and it injected an organisation, purpose and direction into what was done. Above all, it took officials away from their preoccupation with small, local and immediate problems and forced them to confront the long-term, overall movement of the Secretariat. Without the Policy and Expenditure Management System, planning would probably have been *ad hoc,* patchwork and prone to drift. The new process of strategic planning in the Home Office may be the beginnings of just such organisation. In the main, however, Home Office decision-making lacks some of the purposiveness and co-ordination of work in Canada.

ix. In the Home Office, it is customary for the younger, able, ambitious and aspiring officials in the policy divisions to change post every two or three years. It is unusual for British officials to superintend a policy initiative for any great portion of its life. Typically, only the very senior civil servant will be immobile, and he or she tends to manage great areas of policy from a distance. Such a one may participate personally in forwarding schemes, but there are many schemes to superintend and others exercise close control. More junior colleagues have the task of actively steering events and, characteristically, if they conceive a policy, they will not see its implementation; if they implement policy, it will not have been of their own making. There seems to be a companion lack of personal investment in the substance of what is done. Stress is placed on procedure.

By contrast, Canadian civil servants appear to be relatively stable and immobile by the standards of Whitehall. Canadian officials working on what was to become the Justice for Victims of Crime Initiative were able to devote some considerable length of time to the problems of victims. They developed expertise, experience and commitments in the process. In the instance of the Victims Initiative at least, it was sometimes a little difficult to distinguish between the organisational objectives of the Ministry and the personal ambitions of its staff. The effect has been to introduce a very high level of personal identification, some officials giving themselves in unstinting fashion to policy-making. The effects are transparent. Unlike the dispassionate and somewhat distant style admired in the British civil service, the officials of the Ministry of the Solicitor General felt implicated personally in the success of the Justice for Victims of Crime Initiative. They gave more and did so more eagerly. The very effectiveness of the Initiative in its early days may be attributed to their dedication. (Although I must also remark that differences in style between the two Ministries concealed similar passions on occasion. There appears to be a greater economy of enthusiasm in the British civil service, and it appears to be less seemly to put enthusiasm on display when it is felt.)

Yet it is also transparent that a number of complications stem from the identification shown by Canadian civil servants. In the first instance, within the small world of the Ministry of the Solicitor General there is something of an inclination for policy initiatives to become closely associated with those who are thought to be its authors. What is done to and for an initiative can become, by extension, a response to the person most nearly linked to it. Although that personalisation of policy processes can help to promote the success of a Government's work, it can also impede or divert what is done. The work of the Home Office seems to be dispatched with an apparent impersonality and impartiality. In the Ministry of the Solicitor General, there is a risk that important and useful ventures will be hampered by the play of personal rivalries and tensions.

There is a second problem. A high level of personal identification can be attended by possessive or territorial sentiments that keep outsiders at bay. From time to time, the Canadian victims initiative was administered rather proprietorially, slowing its progress, limiting co-operation and restricting the sharing of knowledge and experience. The advance of the initiative was hindered most conspicuously when it was supposed to pass from the personnel manning one stage to those of another.

The Development of Schemes in Canada

I do not propose to linger with the history of Canadian schemes. That story has been told at length in *A View from the Shadows*. What is notable is that the Canadian victims support programmes were rather markedly the creatures of officials working in government and criminal justice agencies. They were one of many innovations that flowed out of an interventionist Ministry of the Solicitor General of Canada, they were inspired by the example of projects and associations developed in the United States, and they were responses to local exigencies. They were established almost wholly by professionals who were members of a larger international network of criminal justice professionals. They were the product, initially, of enthusiasms and motives acquired in meetings of the American National Organisation for Victim Assistance, and they represented developed solutions to problems of victims' trauma, alienation and pain. From the first, programmes were considered, orderly, visible and balanced. They had been constructed artfully in a complex chain of meetings within and between governments. They were supposed to be part of a modest short-term policy initiative. Their entry into the world was carefully managed, being designed neither to excite expectations until provincial funding intentions were clear, nor to represent too great an incursion into provincial and private domains.

Government ambitions became well-formulated before the private sector was organised. They grew in some large measure independently of substantial popular demand from the victims of mundane crime (who only rarely constitute an organised group) or from voluntary associations helping victims. They were constructed by governments and criminal justice agencies whose politics and programmes had tended to race ahead of the "private sector". Indeed, when governments confronted the private sector at a meeting of the National Organisation for Victim Assistance held in Toronto in 1981, there was a want of understanding between them. The Governments of Canada and Ontario had articulate plans in train, and they needed a lobby to voice an external demand for their development. Private groups centred on victims, however, were as yet only beginning to evolve: they did not recognise an affinity amongst themselves, were wary of the possibilities of aid for victims, were wary of one another and governments, lacked a grand vision of their own future, and refused to coalesce. They were not then ready.

Policies for victims, by extension, were draped around organisations which were open to the influence of government. Federally, they moved chiefly to police forces because the Ministry of the Solicitor General has responsibility for the premier police force of Canada, the Royal Canadian Mounted Police, and it has assumed a "leadership role" in initiating reforms of police work. It was to be police-based "victim service units" that the Solicitor General sponsored. Provincially, they moved to the spheres that were controlled by the Departments which had acquired an interest in victims. In Ontario, for example, they were set within an environment of decarceration and Victim-Offender Reconciliation Programs by the Ministry of Correctional Services. Canadian projects were moulded by bureaucratic mandates.

The prosperity and robustness of Canadian schemes depended substantially on continuing government support. Their fates centred on the success of Departments in making joint applications to Cabinet committees for funding, on the fortunes of provincial economies, and on state policies of expansion or contraction. Financially and organisationally, victims support in Canada reflects bureaucratic enterprise.

The Development of Schemes in England and Wales

By contrast, the politics of victims in England and Wales has had no distinct identity and boundaries until very recently. Neither has there been an obvious and stable co-ordination of policies, projects and schemes. There has instead been a tenuous system whose loosely-coupled parts evolved independently. Members of the various groups and organisations involved often confessed to being mystified about the motives and plans of other significant figures. There has been much talk about poor communication and about lack of consultation. Invitations have not been issued to attend conferences when people thought they should have gone. Much has developed in a fog, bodies and movements being barely discernible to different participants, understated and difficult to decipher. Groups have groped for an understanding of what others have been doing and the character of their intentions.

As I shall argue, some of that understated quality may be attributed to the plans of the people who have moved different parts forward. Some may be attributed to the absence of a single grand designer at the centre. The Canadian initiative was almost wholly sponsored and developed by one Government Department that conceives itself to have a reforming and co-ordinating role in the management of the criminal justice system. Processes have occurred without much direction or harmonisation in England and Wales. In a sense, the Canadian initiative was an artefact of the organising intelligence of a Government Department. The British history has been the shapeless artefact of many minds.

Until very recently, outsiders would have maintained that there has been no articulate and visible Home Office policy on victims. The Home Office seemed to react rather than act, and its approach has been piecemeal and fragmented. There has only just come about a straightforward Ministerial commitment to action, and officials, in their turn, have not been able to be very obviously forceful in the presence of external audiences, finding themselves constrained to do little more than gently encourage the desirable and discourage the undesirable. They maintained a holding pattern, unable to move but signalling some vague preparedness to do so when it became timely. Indeed, their gestures were so mild, unaccompanied by substantial action or expenditure, that, until the end of 1986 when the Home Secretary committed his department to appreciable expenditure on victims support schemes, outsiders have been a little bewildered by their ambiguity. The Home Office has been quite Delphic. There was, until now, little incentive not to be Delphic.

Until now, therefore, the Home Office has tended to have what might be described as a loose posture or an attitude rather than a clear policy. Running through its approach have been a number of themes lacking complete consistency or organisation: (a) an extolling of the unpaid volunteer and hostility towards the bureaucratisation of otherwise spontaneous community initiative; (b) the desire not to spend new money; (c) a recognition of the need to make some response to the prodigious growth in the numbers of victims support schemes in England and Wales; (d) a wariness about lobbies and organisations promoting new criminal justice policies before they were agreed by Government; (e) a wish to ensure the survival of what is regarded as a commendable National Association of Victims Support Schemes (N.A.V.S.S.) and check its less attractive rivals; (f) an interest in monitoring how things would evolve before commitments were given; (g) a recognition of the need to place criminal injuries compensation on a statutory basis, coupled with (h) alarm about the "demand-led" and rising costs of criminal injuries compensation, currently about £42,000,000 a year (Criminal Injuries Compensation Board, 1986); and (i) a strong sentiment in some central areas that the proper business of a criminal justice ministry is to concentrate effort on deterrence, detection and punishment, and that succour to victims is a rather marginal, weak and defeated response. Inevitably, and in the absence of an effective and purposive political thrust from within the Department, policies for victims were identified simply as the sum of what the Home Office had done for and with victims in the past. Internally, different divisions were responsible for compensation, reparation and victims support and separations were preserved. Externally, however, the result has often appeared to be an administrative aggregation of measures touching on criminal bankruptcy, compensation by the offender, restitution, victim surveys, victims support schemes and criminal injuries compensation. It has not been an aggregate with much unity apart from its empirical theme of victims, but it has been defined by mandates and history, and it tended to influence the drafting of proposals and arguments.

The Home Office assumes control of all those activities and they possess an implied bureaucratic coherence on occasion. The outcome has been a rudimentary attempt to marry reparation, mediation and criminal injuries compensation with support services to victims. It is a somewhat fragile marriage which threatens not to survive very long. Relative inactivity has not led to its being tested, extended or strained in practice. But coherence has been bestowed. The dominance of the Home Office mandate in the criminal justice system has led to the identification of a particular clump of activities as the politics of victims. Administration has imposed definition. Thus the report of the Parliamentary All-Party Penal Affairs Group entitled *A New Deal for Victims* (P.A.P.P.A.G., 1984) treated criminal injuries compensation, reparation and victims support as a single issue. So did the Home Affairs Select Committee (Home Affairs Select Committee, 1984). So did a Kent Probation Service Working Party (Kent Probation Service, 1985). Most importantly, so did the Home Office's own statement of its strategic objectives, *Criminal Justice: A Working Paper* (Home Office, 1986), which grouped police reforms, financial compensation by offenders, criminal injuries compensation and victims support schemes under the single heading of "Helping the Victim".

Those developing victims support schemes have been doubly constrained. As I shall argue, they have made themselves quite deliberately unforceful. They have also found themselves aligned with other initiatives with which they may not have an immediate affinity. In turn, they have been obliged to take a position towards those other initiatives, becoming implicated in them, and the alignments have been strengthened. Thus, for some considerable time, the National Association of Victims Support Schemes received inquiries about mediation and victim–offender reconciliation projects. Its own stance towards those projects was equivocal, calling them "a new distraction" (NAVSS, 1984), but it felt obliged to answer queries, organise conferences and become the Godfather of a new organisation, the Forum for Initiatives in Reparation and Mediation, a body that was later to become autonomous in its own right.

The Beginnings

Services to victims were shaped by their beginnings. For a long while, they were regarded by significant groups as being virtually identical to the provision of criminal injuries compensation. Compensation actually exhausted remedies for a time. It was initiated in the late 1950s and early 1960s by two separate groups largely unknown to one another. One group was composed of people active in the politics of criminal justice who used it as a device to forestall the anger of victims cheated of their right to punishment in an increasingly rehabilitative age. Actual proofs of anger were few but there was a predominant assumption that the public would not stomach too much reform. Compensation represented an attempt to outflank a latent vigilantism. Indeed, the politics of criminal justice have always been girded by a fear, particularly on the left, of the irrational and punitive sentiments of the public: "if the popular press is to be believed, the thirst for punishment among the public is very great" (Stern, 1987, p. 148). Reformers have been a little scared of the British and their anxiety has made its mark in a number of phases of the history of policies for victims.

The other group was made up of outsiders who regarded compensation as a simple extension of welfare insurance. That was certainly the view of the Conservative Political Centre report, *Victims of Violence* (Conservative Political Centre, 1962), that was to have a major influence on the evolution of compensation. It was also the view of a Member of Parliament, Reg Prentice, who had made several attempts to have passed a Private Member's Bill on compensation. Prentice had worked on workmen's compensation and industrial injuries compensation as an official of the Transport and General Workers Union and criminal injuries compensation seemed a plausible application of an accepted principle.

At the time of the debates about compensation, victims did not form a corporate entity and they were never consulted about their demand for compensation. The compensation scheme was done in what were imagined to be their best interests. Indeed, in a sense, it was done against victims rather than with them. Victims were conceived as dormant adversaries, potential vigilantes and reactionaries who would obstruct progress. They had to be appeased. Although the scheme has had considerable success, there has never been any evidence that victims of violence wanted large sums of monetary compensation from the State (see Shapland, 1985). Such inattention to victims as a significant participant in the policy-making process has been marked elsewhere. Elias, for example, remarked of the United States, "we must examine why so many victim programs have emerged without having asked victims their own preferences and needs" (Elias, 1986, p. 188). Nevertheless, despite the lack of an external demand and a vocal consumer, criminal injuries compensation has for a long time been seen by politicians, officials and reformers as an answer to the problems of victims. It is regarded as demand-led and expensive, a worrying precedent for reforms aimed at victims, and it has sometimes obscured and displaced consideration of other programmes for victims. It could always be said by some that much was already being done.

As important, when compensation was secured, reformers tended to move on. It was as if they operated with an agenda of discrete objectives, and they imagined that the attaining of one freed them to proceed to the next. They were not supported by, or in touch with a group of victims that sustained their interest. The movement for criminal injuries compensation was a creature of lawyers, penologists and criminologists, not victims. The campaign which centred on victims died when the reformers lost interest. There was a silence for some ten years. It was a solipsistic enterprise.

The Sexual Neutrality of the Victim in England and Wales

When the time came, in the 1970s, the victims of crime who re-appeared before British policy-makers were to take a very special guise. Elsewhere, in Canada, Australia and the United States, the archetypal victim was a raped and battered woman, championed by feminist campaigns about patriarchal violence. In England and Wales, the archetype is a burglary or robbery victim of no distinctive gender. The emergence of programmes and policies for women who have suffered from criminal violence has been a separate, insulated process in Britain and it has had very little impact on the wider politics of victims.

In part, the gender of victims is a creature of the organised watchfulness of Government: in Canada, the response to the United Nations Decade for Women was to be the establishment of a Cabinet post with special responsibility for women, and all social policies, including criminal justice policies, must be perused for their bearing on women. In Britain, the response was the Equal Opportunities Commission which has never busied itself with criminal justice matters or, indeed, with the issue of violence to women. In Canada, there is an appreciable body of women civil servants who conceive it to be their role to promote the interests of women. In Britain, the attentive feminist official does not exist. There has been no special bureaucratic sponsorship of assaulted women.

In part, the gender of victims has been influenced by what was presented to Government. The style and politics of British feminism seemed to have diminished the influence of rape and battering on policies for victims. There has been an emphasis on collective decision-making, a hostility to leadership and leaders and a propensity to treat politics as theatre. The result has either been a want of national or regional organisation or else spectacular and sometimes short-lived activist groups, such as Women Against Rape and Women Against Violence Against Women, which have no direct commerce with Government. Feminist women have been reluctant to use the terminology of victims, talk of victim-blaming, and tend often to a radical separatism that makes transactions with men difficult. Men are not allowed to enter the headquarters of the Women's Aid Federation of England. Central figures engaged in making policies for victims have been almost entirely shunned by the women's movement. Feminism has been unseen, unheard and impotent in the bureaucratic circles where victims have been discussed. When rape and battering received Government attention in England and Wales, it was chiefly as a result of the intervention of men and women who did not call themselves radical separatists or feminists. The treatment of rape is being transformed, in part, as police (mediated by senior officers such as Ian Blair and Thelma Wagstaff) respond to the scandal of a television programme's revelations about the Thames Valley force and its treatment of rape victims, and to the pronouncements of judges about contributory negligence and the need to protect otherwise praiseworthy men (Adler, 1987). Government has not joined rape and domestic violence to other policy concerns. Rape crisis centres and refuges for battered women have not been the beneficiaries of new Government spending on victims.

The National Association of Victims Support Schemes

My own focus has been on the history and environment of the National Association of Victims Support Schemes. The identification of beginnings is always arbitrary, but a clear line of development can be traced back to the ideas of an American criminologist, Richard Korn, who organised seminars for judges, inmates and prison staff in the United States. Korn engineered confrontations between all the central participants in the criminal justice system so that they could be exposed to their own and others' beliefs, experiences and expectations (see Korn, undated, *c.*1968). He maintained that many of the mystifications and abuses of the system would evaporate in such spontaneous encounters. He even suggested that victims could be participants although none seems actually to have been invited.

Korn's writings were to be read by an English criminal justice reformer, a former probation officer, Philip Priestley, who was at that time a Regional Organiser of the National Association for the Care and Resettlement of Offenders (N.A.C.R.O.), a large private sector organisation devoted to rehabilitation and crime prevention. Priestley toyed with the idea of a relatively open-ended "victim–offender discussion group" but he had no clear conception of how it would proceed or what it might achieve. He himself did not know any victims solely in their status as victims and, indeed, he experienced some difficulty in recruiting them to his scheme. He proceeded, in part, by following up stories in the press. The group was to be established in February 1969 and, within it, he gathered police officers, magistrates, a psychiatrist and offenders, some of whom he had known as a probation officer working in Shepton Mallet Prison. The group laid bare how traumatic victimisation could be, even for the victims of non-violent offences. It revealed, too, the unmet needs of victims, a population who seemed to lack support or understanding. Priestley himself observed, "a collusion of silence, deliberate ignorance and indifference has prevailed in relation to victims for many centuries now ... [In criminology,] balanced against a wealth of work on offenders as individuals or as products of social forces is a scanty literature on cash restitution and the role of some victims in precipitating certain kinds of offence. A rich and potentially fruitful area of investigation has until now lain practically fallow" (Priestley, 1970, p. 1). The group promoted an encounter between an offencer and his victim which was to be televised in February 1975, forming one of the forerunners of victim–offender reconciliation schemes in Britain. It was itself to evolve and then fissure. One fraction became the National Victims Association under the chairmanship of Charles Irving, then Mayor of Cheltenham, and with Philip Priestley, now no longer in NACRO, as Secretary.

Irving is a flamboyant, prosperous, energetic Member of Parliament, at that time Chairman of South West Region of NACRO (where he met Priestley), a founder of the Stonham hostels for discharged prisoners and a conspicuous campaigner. The National Victims Association was established in January 1973 and it moved with speed. Its principal work was agitation. It was never wealthy or numerous in its membership. What it did do was issue copious press releases and engage in voluminous correspondence with Ministers. There is a pronounced affinity between Irving's personal and political styles. It was his doctrine that politics must be active, making an audible and visible mark on the world, and that, without badgering and publicity, it is nothing. His agitation centred on the speed and size of payments made under the criminal injuries compensation scheme, the restoration of supplies and problems of liability when fuel meters are broken into, and the general neglect of the victim. Irving and Priestley also established a victims' advisory centre in Bristol, a walk-in office, staffed by a social worker. It was not the result of lengthy planning and it did not thrive. Victims seemed unwilling to define themselves as victims or seek help themselves with any vigour. Yet what should be noted is that, although Irving and Priestley together mounted a campaign that was unusually active and noisy for such a small organisation, they had had their roots in NACRO and probation and were anxious not to attack offenders or stir what was again thought to be a dormant vigilantism in Britain. The National Victims Association lasted only a few years, to be absorbed by the National Association of Victims Support Schemes when that came into its own, Irving becoming the first President.

The other fraction, remaining within NACRO, included Christopher Holtom of NACRO and Bristol University Social Administration Department, Martin Gay, a psychiatrist, and Susan Thomas, a doctor. It took a little longer to make plans. It was to found the first Victims Support Scheme in

Bristol in January 1974 (see Gay, Holtom and Thomas, 1975). The model drafted then remains substantially in force now, a formula for nearly 300 other schemes.

Victims support was conceived to have a number of defining characteristics: its roots in NACRO made it antipathetic to a politics hostile to offenders; its roots in probation emphasised practical assistance to victims; and its roots in psychiatry, and in Gay's psychiatry in particular, led to the practice of "crisis intervention", the short-term, immediate provision of support to those afflicted by crime.

The Bristol Scheme was to become a prototype for other work, but the spread of victims support was accelerated by a BBC Television Programme, *One Every Twenty Seconds,* advertising the work in Bristol and broadcast in February 1975. Phenomenologically, what is of interest about that programme and its aftermath was that NACRO received numerous enquiries about victims support, acquainted members of the Bristol scheme with other projects elsewhere, and then brought all those concerned together where they could directly observe the practical possibilities of work for victims. The programme about the Bristol Scheme produced an environment for itself and its heirs, and parts of that environment were regarded as distinctly uncongenial.

In particular, there were present a number of individuals and groups whose politics were not those of NACRO, the probation service and criminal justice reformers. Some seemed to have separate objectives which had little to do with the commonly identified needs of victims and some were considered disreputable by those who followed the pattern of Bristol. There were representatives of rape crisis centres who showed a marked animosity to the police and followed a private separatist politics of feminism. Worryingly, others seemed to incarnate the latent retributivism so feared by the professionals. They were a powerful display of all that should be avoided: they addressed victims as victims; they celebrated and fossilised that status, instead of easing victims away from it; they advertised the plight of victims individually and generally, seeming to exploit the misery of the vulnerable; they showed no countervailing concern about the offender; and they threatened to become a minor political force in their own right. In short, they symbolically compressed reformers' fears about vigilantism, and they emerged just as the reformers were questioning themselves about who they were and what they were about to do.

Those pariah groups played a role in a dialectical encounter unwittingly engineered by the Bristol Scheme: they entered the environment of victims support and they worked to amplify anxieties about retributive justice, abrasive politics and the exciting of moral panics. The meeting was eventually to give rise to the formation of a national association which set standards of entry and performance that attempted to control undesirable traits. The Association also came quite deliberately to eschew publicity and political agitation (and there was some consequent friction with the first President of the National Association, Charles Irving). It understated itself and its achievements, refusing to discuss with the press the names or histories of particular victims, inflame public alarm or mobilise political campaigns. It declares that it "does not make statements about the causes of crime or the treatment of offenders, except where issues such as compensation to victims are involved" (NAVSS, 1986). Its National Director, Helen Reeves, shuns the very phrase "victims movement".

Understatement became even more deeply etched into the National Association's public identity. When the Association was registered as a charity in August 1979, it became bound by the condition that no charity should engage in political agitation. When the Association moved to win the approval of other bodies in criminal justice, it sought to demonstrate its clear and calm professionalism. The National Association of Victims Support Schemes was not turned outwards to the public (the public was, after all, an uncertain entity and there would be many different costs in approaching it). There were no visible campaigns or flag days. Instead, the Association tried to secure resources, referrals and support from the police, probation service and magistracy, and it performed something of a "balancing act" in consequence. Such an ill-defined, quiet and possibly dangerous newcomer in the social circles of criminal justice did not attain ready definition or acceptance. There was anxiety about "which way we were going to jump": significant members of the probation service intimated that victims support might be part of a retributivist movement; some police officers were believed to think that victims support might be embedded in the new, activist strain towards "police-monitoring groups"; and magistrates did not wish to be joined publicly with a group that could be antagonistic to the offender. Victims support was to be about a new alignment of those agencies: it would depend on good working relations and a reassuring presence: "a low profile was very conscious."

Because it has not propelled itself roughly into the politics of criminal justice, the National Association of Victims Support Schemes has been exposed to the interpretations of others more forceful than itself. Bodies like probation services, parliamentary groups and officials have not been the makers of victims support policies, they have often been structurally distant from their evolution, and they have tended to define the National Association and its member groups rather freely. Until very recently, public descriptions of victims support have not been established by its own authors. They have been set within contexts favoured or feared by the forceful. In particular, victims support has been associated with the politics of offenders and punishment which it has quite deliberately eschewed. Some have seen it in part of the drift towards reparative justice, and that is not its mission. Others have seen in it the vigilantism and evangelism of the more vocal American victims movement.

The Association has been prodigiously successful, described as the fastest growing voluntary movement in England and Wales, but it has also lacked visibility. As Maguire and Corbett have argued:

> Unlike many of the victim initiatives in the United States ... these ... Victims Support Schemes ... had no political aims or "hidden agendas". They took little interest in the offender, the court process, or the sentences passed. Their primary objective was very simple: to act as a "good neighbour", or perhaps a "good

Samaritan", to people who had suffered at the hands of a thief or an assailant. (Maguire and Corbett, 1987, p. 2).

It was that understatement and that objective which commended the National Association to critical Home Office officials. But it was that understatement which sometimes obscured the character and motives of victims support to others, making it relatively indistinct and inhibiting a political impact for a time. There has been a willingness to profess political support for the Association from all four political parties, but it was not a support that culminated in rapid action. Victims support was not conspicuous or contentious enough to become the centre of party political agitation. Further, it is interesting that the National Association of Victims Support Schemes should have had, until now, little prominence internationally despite the palpable effectiveness of its methods. Indeed, its own Newsletter contained a rather forlorn review of a collection of papers from a Canadian conference on victims support, "victims support schemes of the British type are hardly mentioned; even allowing for the three year delay in publication this seems a surprising omission" (Raynor, 1986, p. 15).

The National Association's very independence of the planning of government and criminal justice agencies has made it somewhat anomalous within conventional political frameworks. Victims support schemes were not designed primarily to rehabilitate offenders or ease the work of the police but to help victims cope with crime. In that sense, they represent a new constituency and new conception of criminal justice, not a simple reform of the old. British victims support is not directly and solely the extension of any one government agency. It does not exist to supply services to the courts as American victim–witness programmes do. It does not relieve the police or support penal decarceration as Canadian projects do. Indeed, there has been a vigorous refusal to become affiliated with any single portion of the criminal justice system. Thus the National Association was most reluctant to accept the Home Affairs Select Committee's recommendation that the co-ordinators of victims support schemes should be housed within probation departments.

One of the Association's first acts was to appoint a senior probation officer, Helen Reeves, as a full-time, salaried organiser, and her appointment further amplified those trends already present in the movement towards victims support services. She is commonly recognised as a person of presence and charm, capable of unobtrusively promoting the ends of NAVSS to great effect. She takes her post to be a job not a mission, part of a professional career quite compatible with her earlier work in probation. To be sure, she does fully applaud the ends of victims support, but she has imported none of the personal and evangelical fervour of her American counterparts. More, her experience in probation has underscored the demand that the needs of victims should not obliterate the rights of offenders.

Almost the first venture undertaken by the newly appointed Helen Reeves was to go on a grand tour of the fledgling victims support schemes. She was to discover that there were two principal models in use: one was devoted to the provision of practical assistance, mending the doors, locks and windows of burglary victims, and helping with the completion of claims for compensation and insurance. The other addressed the trauma of victimisation, and it supplied "crisis intervention" support. Helen Reeves concluded that neither was sufficient without the other, and insisted that schemes should amalgamate the two. The other conclusion she drew was that the principal task of victims support should be to aid victims to *cope* with crime (see Reeves, 1984). Coping entailed an early abandonment of a stigmatised and disabling victim status, practical attention to damage, and symbolic reparation by a community whose neglect could cause or exacerbate loss. The Management Committees of Support Schemes were supposed to stand for the community in microcosm, containing representatives of lay, voluntary and statutory organisations. In particular, they contained police officers because the unsuccessful National Victims Association's advisory centre had demonstrated the necessity of securing police referrals. Victims do not necessarily define themselves as victims and they are not prone to seek succour themselves.

Victims support schemes are a working demonstration of the new community policing strategies of such chiefs of police as Sir Kenneth Newman. They have advanced without the rancour of the victims movement in North America which has been bitterly critical of the indifference displayed to victims by police and courts. (Indeed, a new cliché of the North American victims movement is that victims are doubly victimised by crime and by agents of social control.) Such talk may be heard in marginal areas in England and Wales but not within the National Association. A quiet and necessary accommodation with the police, the source of referrals, has further reinforced the dim appearance of victims support.

NACRO had fostered NAVSS from the beginning. It supplied a member of staff to deal with queries and to draft a model constitution for victims support schemes. But, when the National Association was registered as a charity, it began to achieve its independence from NACRO. For a while it remained housed in NACRO's London headquarters, and it was serviced by people with NACRO affiliations, but it had been recognised, as soon as Philip Priestley's group gave organisation to the issue, that victims support was politically and practically separate from work with offenders. Helen Reeves herself has never been a member of NACRO. By the time she was appointed, NACRO had receded.

The birth of NAVSS was fissiparous, and it betrayed its parentage in its application of the institutional idiom of NACRO, doing, as John Van Maanen put it, new things in old ways (Van Maanen, undated). That was the second dialectic of victims support. It grew up inside the fabric of an environment from which in time it had to part symbolically, constitutionally, functionally and physically. Members of NACRO claim that NAVSS had a distinct identity from the first. But the two organisations share common mannerisms, personnel and preoccupations.

In time, NAVSS was to give its own fissiparous birth to FIRM, the Forum for Initiatives in Reparation and Mediation, and that birth was to reproduce its own. Demands and queries about mediation and conflict-resolution had come to NAVSS as a body occupied with victims. There was no other. Almost despite itself, NAVSS discovered that it was bringing to life a new organisation devoted to reparative justice. It hosted conferences and lent accommodation. Its memberships overlapped. In time, too, a process of symbolic differentiation occurred as NAVSS and FIRM declared that their ends were not the same, that victims might have interests apart from and irreconcilable with offenders. A splitting took place. But the continuities remained. Helen Reeves and Christopher Holtom were members of the executive committees of both organisations. They lent practical advice about the formation of new charities and campaigns. They too offered recipe knowledge about accomplishing new things. And then the dialectic of individuation superseded.

Indeed, it does appear as if the orchestration of criminal justice policy-making has been entrusted to a very small, intimate social world with few people and multiple affiliations. The same persons may be encountered in very different settings, settings that may seem functionally or ideologically incompatible with one another. They are present precisely because they have stocks of practical knowledge. (The Cadbury Trust, for example does not actively solicit funding applications. Its representative moves about a network of familiar and trusted people.) They know one another. They know how to do things. And the result is that they knit the criminal justice system together. More important, they knit the experiences and working assumptions of criminal justice policy-making together. Work revolving around victims has been transacted by a medley of people with similar biographies and groupings who are called different names as organisations and campaigns dictate. They have fused and parted and fused again as the flow of action moved them. They have given a history, legitimacy, character, and connections to the National Association, integrating it with other parts of the criminal justice "system".

It took seven years before NAVSS received full official patronage. To be sure, it was funded modestly, and thus given legitimacy, by the Home Office and the Department of Health and Social Security from the first. Ministers publicly approved what was happening. And the money given to the headquarters organisation was to increase little by little. But the National Association petitioned repeatedly for funds for regional organisation and for paid co-ordinators in schemes where volunteer co-ordinators were not forthcoming.

For some while, Ministers seemed not very eager to underwrite victims support services. There has been a period of austerity in which it has been difficult to do anything for the first time. Reticence was signified and justified by an official commendation of the unpaid volunteer and wariness about State encroachment on the private domain. Ministers, and Leon Brittan in particular, voiced their reluctance to bureaucratise the spontaneous, professionalise the voluntary and nationalise local initiative.

There were influential Conservatives who held that a victims initiative would be a defeated diversion from the main business of a criminal justice Ministry, the war against crime. And much was happening without any Government intervention. As one Home Office official observed, "perhaps the 'preparedness' of voluntary organisations in this country *allowed* the government to stand back and avoid formulating a clear policy." Yet, in retrospect, it is possible to discern the steady movements by which the National Association came to acquire a political and organisational presence in the criminal justice system. The National Association collaborated in the preparation of Home Office research projects (Williams, 1983; Hough and Mayhew, 1985; Marshall, 1984; Maguire and Corbett, 1987). Home Office funding and collaboration may be read as a symbolic expression of intent. The Association's members and organisers met in the conferences and seminars that give order to the social world of criminal justice. Victims support was commended by major bodies such as the Association of Chief Police Officers and the Association of Chiefs of Probation. It attracted the attention of senior officials who also feared vigilantism. It attracted the special attention of the Head of the Home Office Research and Planning Unit and the Under Secretary in charge of criminal policy. From about 1983 onwards, substantial funding for the Association was commended in briefing documents, statements and speeches coming before Ministers. It was subject to circumspect praise in conferences. Occasions were sought to promote it.

And then Douglas Hurd replaced Leon Brittan as Secretary of State. Leon Brittan had held the major subsidy of victims support to be obviously marginal to a criminal justice strategy. Douglas Hurd held it to be obviously sensible. Both had been briefed by senior officials persuaded of the wisdom of funding. By the time the National Association was massed as an organisation with some 300 schemes, it was thought to have proved its worth by a new Home Secretary who approved an expenditure of £9,000,000, over three years. Nine million pounds is a large sum. People are as yet a little confused about its likely consequences and portents: the future scale, organisation and role of victims support are uncertain, but schemes do appear to have become an established feature of the criminal justice system.

Conclusion

When the time came, and Ministers awarded them substantial funding, the victims support schemes of England and Wales were developed. In a sense, Ministers had waited for organisation to emerge before they passed judgement, and they were presented with rather little scope for articulate and detailed political direction of their own. The British response has been simple: Ministers have merely approved what has been done and seek to maintain it. In the main, victims support schemes were robust and independent before the Government was moved to act, and they constitute a new organisation with its own vision. To be sure, the Government is interested in increasing the professionalism and cost-effectiveness of the service. It is likely to respond to Maguire and Corbett's recommendations about the restructuring of schemes. But the character of victims support *has* been set. In Canada and the United States, by contrast, victims support evolved under the careful management of officials. Victims support is a complement to established organisations, changing them as it evolves. There, the future of victims support work in the short and medium term will rest on State subvention: it will thrive or fail as Governments will.

References

ADLER, Z. (1987). *Rape on Trial*. London: Routledge and Kegan Paul.

CONSERVATIVE POLITICAL CENTRE (1962). *Victims of Violence*. London: Conservative Political Centre.

CRIMINAL INJURIES COMPENSATION BOARD (1986). *Twenty-Second Report. Accounts for the year ended 31 March 1986*. London: HMSO.

ELIAS, R. (1986). *The Politics of Victimization*. New York: Oxford University Press.

GAY, M., HOLTOM, C. and THOMAS, S. (1975). "Helping the victim". *International Journal of Offender Therapy and Comparative Criminology*, **19**, 263–68.

HOME AFFAIRS SELECT COMMITTEE (1984). *Compensation and Support for Victims of Crime*. London: HMSO.

HOME OFFICE (1986). *Criminal Justice: A Working Paper*. London: HMSO.

HOUGH, M. and MAYHEW, P. (1985). *Taking Account of Crime*. London: HMSO.

KENT PROBATION SERVICE (1985). *Report of the Working Party on Linking of Victims and Offenders*.

KORN, R. *et al.* (undated). *Consumers, Practitioners and Citizens as Colleagues: A Manual in the Application of the Agency Self-Study Principle as an Instrument for Institutional Change*. Berkeley. *A Positive State Program: Crime and Corrections Workshop:* Nevada.

MAGUIRE, M. and CORBETT, C. (1987). *The Effects of Crime and the Work of Victims Support Schemes*. Aldershot: Gower.

MARSHALL, T. (1984). *Reparation, Conciliation and Mediation*. London: HMSO.

N.A.V.S.S. (1984). *Fourth Annual Report 1983/4*. London: NAVSS

N.A.V.S.S. (1986). *Sixth Annual Report 1985/86*. London: NAVSS.

P.A.P.P.A.G. (1984). *A New Deal for Victims*. London: NACRO.

PRIESTLEY, P. (1970). "What about the victim?" Reprinted by National Victims Association, Cheltenham.

RAYNOR, P. (1986). Review of *From Crime Policy to Victim Policy*. *Victims Support, Newsletter of the National Association of Victims Support Schemes*. **26**.

REEVES, H. (1984). "Coping with crime: victim support." *Christian Action Journal*. Summer, 26–29.

ROCK, P. (1986a). *A View from the Shadows: The Ministry of the Solicitor General of Canada and the Justice for Victims of Crime Initiative*. Oxford: Oxford University Press.

ROCK, P. (1986b). "Society's attitude to the victim". In E. Fattah (ed.): *From Crime Policy to Victim Policy*. London: Macmillan.

SHAPLAND, J., WILLMORE, J. and DUFF, P. (1985). *Victims in the Criminal Justice System*. Aldershot: Gower.

STERN, V. (1987). *Bricks of Shame*. Harmondsworth: Penguin.

VAN MAANEN, J. (Undated). "Doing new things in old ways: the chains of socialization." Unpublished paper.

WILLIAMS, K. (1983). *Community Resources for Victims of Crime*. London: HMSO.

[5]

The Present State of Criminology in Britain

There has been no adequate survey of contemporary criminology in Britain. The discipline has evolved quickly and erratically, appearing sometimes to advance in opposing directions, and it has been more than a little difficult to make sense of its progress. There are only a few criminologists in post who might have wished to report its development, and they have at best reconstructed criminology in their own image. Indeed, any attempt to interpret current movements must refract the preoccupations of the observer. My own description will be just such a special organization of perspectives. It could not be otherwise. I shall focus on a small number of themes that I regard as important although I am aware that others might well have reviewed the field quite differently. In a short article, there cannot be a proper discussion of many things. For instance, I must neglect analysis of the important but vastly intricate exchanges that have occurred between British and foreign ideas about crime and control. British criminology has evolved in an intellectual environment constituted by others' thought, just as it has attained a modest presence elsewhere, but I shall not pay attention to that history. I shall concentrate instead upon the development of British criminology *in* Britain. In particular, I shall describe the negotiated order which has begun to emerge amongst the core members of a generation of criminologists who have worked together and known each other for some two decades.

In the autumn of 1986, for the purposes of this article, I conducted a census of all the 160 British university departments and institutes in which criminologists might be found. I also approached the Home Office Research and Planning Unit with questions about its staff and funding. I did, of course, appreciate that criminologists were to be found elsewhere, particularly in the polytechnics, but I could not undertake more than a sample survey of academic institutions in the United Kingdom. It is uncertain what effect the addition of polytechnics and colleges of further education might have had on my argument.

Excluding the Research and Planning Unit, 92 departments replied, and their replies produced some elementary demographic information about 118 specialist criminologists. Thirty-seven criminologists worked in law departments, eight in psychology departments, thirty-three in sociology

*I would like to thank A. Armstrong of the Association of University Teachers; David Downes and Margaret Savage of the London School of Economics; Don Harris of the Oxford Centre for Socio-Legal Studies; P. Oakley, General Secretary of the Universities Central Council on Admissions; the Law and the Social Sciences Committee of the ESRC; and Mary Tuck of the Home Office Research and Planning Unit for their help in the writing of this article. I am particularly grateful to David Garland and Peter Young of the University of Edinburgh, Pat Mayhew of the Home Office Research and Planning Unit and to Tony Bottoms of the Institute of Criminology, Cambridge, for their detailed comments on earlier drafts.

departments, twenty-seven in social administration departments, and thirteen in centres of criminology. It is not possible to establish how unusual those responding departments might be. My impression is that they contained the bulk of working criminologists and that the departments which did not reply refrained from doing so because they had no criminologists to report. I certainly knew of no criminologists in those departments. (There was also one "spoilt paper" from an ethnomethodologist representing a large department. I was accused of reifying the division of labour within sociology.)

The demography of British criminologists was moulded by a brief period of rapid university growth. Until 1950, there were only twenty-nine British universities. Thereafter came increase: eight universities were founded in the 1950s and fourteen in the 1960s, eight in 1966 and 1967 alone. 27 per cent of Britain's universities were chartered in that one decade of the 1960s. And the older universities were also enlarged. Student populations mushroomed: the total numbers of "home acceptance" undergraduates more than doubled between 1963 and 1969, and then increased by another two-fifths by 1980. As they became established, so in time the burgeoning universities began to acquire new staff, recruiting most energetically in the 1970s: there were 13 per cent more staff in universities in the second half of the decade than in the first. After that time, new universities ceased to be built. None was founded in the 1970s and only one, in Ulster, was established in the early 1980s.

Criminology and criminologists were part of that bounded phase of expansion. Bottoms observed that, twenty-five years ago, "at the beginning, despite the existence of several major theories and some significant empirical research, there was really very little that could properly be classed as established criminological knowledge" (Bottoms, 1987). He may have been a little too emphatic. After all, there was a rudimentary framework in place, the framework established by Radzinowicz and Mannheim and others, and it was against that framework that criminology reacted, but it was really in the 1970s that criminology took off. Few (2·5 per cent) of the staff in my sample had been hired in the 1950s, and only 19 per cent had been hired in the 1960s. 58 per cent had been recruited in the 1970s, 30 per cent in the years between 1973 and 1976 alone. Recruitment in the 1980s then declined: two people were reported to have been hired in 1981, none in 1982 and only a few each year thereafter. 20 per cent of practising criminologists were hired this decade.

In effect, the social organisation of criminology has been bifurcated. The bulk of contemporary teachers and researchers moved into place in the late 1960s and 1970s, and it was they who manufactured the intellectual framework that continued to be used into the 1980s. A second and smaller wave of younger criminologists then entered in their wake, inhabiting the environment which their predecessors had created. As I shall argue, appointments made in the 1980s were different in kind: the younger criminologists find it difficult to be paradigm changers: they are not *virtuosi* but professional scholars. Importantly, too, they do not appear to constitute a distinctive intellectual generation in their own eyes. They are not organised. They have not met collectively as their predecessors had done in the National Deviancy Symposium. For example, one significant member of the second wave, David

Garland of Edinburgh, confers principally with older criminologists: "one reason why my generation seems to lack cohesion or an invisible college is that there has been no central forum to bind it together" (Garland, 1987). It is with the earlier prime group that I shall remain for a while.

The recent history of criminology in Britain has been largely, if not wholly, the work of a fortunate generation appointed in and around the single decade of the 1970s. Although that generation never enjoyed a monopoly of teaching and research, it did represent a substantial force that was moved into position within a very short space of time. Its attempt to provide an intellectual habitat and identity for itself was accompanied by a corresponding proliferation of argument. Publishing also exploded during the 1970s. Firms recognised an expanding market and fed it with books. The catalogues of publications received for review by the journal *Sociology* between May 1973 and November 1986 reveal a great swelling of works in criminology and the sociology of deviance in the later 1970s. Of the 342 criminological books that were mentioned throughout that total period, 164 (or 48 per cent) were listed between 1976 and 1979. The 1970s were evidently turbulent and factious. There was a polemical time before the new criminologists began to settle down. In their search for intellectual definition and territory, they tended to bind themselves together and set themselves apart in an intricate dialectic of attraction and repulsion. They sought to discover what they *were* by proclaiming what they were *not*, working on what Gouldner once called a "conflictual validation of the self". Thus the York Deviancy Symposium was established in 1968 by embryo criminologists in their last months of graduate research or in the very first months of teaching. When they published their first anthology of papers in 1971, members of the Symposium allowed themselves to be described as entertaining:

> feelings towards official criminology [which] ranged from distrust at its orientation towards administrative needs and impatience with its highly empirical, anti-theoretical bias, to simply a mild lack of interest in the sort of studies that were being conducted... So, as our own theory might put it—we found ourselves with a common identity problem... (Cohen, 1971).

In a conference held in 1971 by the British Sociological Association, a conference which seemed to mark the "coming out" of the new sociology of deviance, Cohen was to talk of the neglect of meaning by orthodox criminologists (Cohen, 1974), and the phenomenologists, Phillipson and Roche, of reification (Phillipson and Roche, 1974). A year later, the Marxism of the Birmingham Centre for Contemporary Cultural Studies was turned on

> mainstream sociology [which] is dominated by official or authoritarian perspectives in the service of the present organisation of interest and privilege ... many radical students of society and culture have themselves moved into a closer alliance with the deprived and stigmatised groups (Jones, 1972).

In 1973, the Marxist exegetists, Taylor, Walton and Young, pointed to the hidden politics of bourgeois criminology (Taylor, Walton and Young, 1973). In 1977, the feminist Carol Smart listed the patriarchal attitudes which buttressed criminology (Smart, 1977). And almost everybody professed to recoil from positivism (Platt, 1981). In effect, the new generation were refracting and amplifying wider debates, bringing into criminology the definitional quarrels and developments of sociology. Within that rather tumultuous jostling for space, encouraged and displayed in the books of the 1970s, there may well have been a purposeful exaggeration of conflict. In retrospect, many of the differences seem to have resided more in style and vocabulary than in substance (Cohen, 1980). (Bottoms has talked of how "political challenges to mainstream criminology... [were] a mixture of truth and exaggeration" (Bottoms, 1987).) Yet, at the time, they were thought to be substantial enough. They gave a useful order to an emerging field.

I have written elsewhere about the principal features of the sociology of crime as it appeared in the late 1970s (Rock, 1981). I described the administrative criminologists who had a practical bent; the systemic analysts who, seeking to develop global theories, turned to deviance from time to time as a source of material; and the phenomenalists who subordinated theory to a mapping of the substantive world. Some were indissolubly committed to the discipline. Administrative criminologists in centres of criminology and the Home Office had an occupational and organizational stake in the preservation of applied research. Interactionist, ethnographic and other phenomenalist sociologists typically did not work with an abstractness or scale of thought that threatened to remove them from the prolonged study of a single empirical area. But the systematic sociologists were ill-prepared to linger in one small portion of the social world: their interest lay in form and not in substance, in wholes and not in parts. It seemed as if the sociology of deviance was fated to become the intellectual property of administrative researchers, phenomenalists and renegades from systemic analysis.

Some of the systematic theorists who had marked the discipline in the 1970s did indeed veer off to pursue other concerns. Thus, Phillipson, Hirst, Hall and Douglas no longer write extensively about crime and deviation. In large measure, it has been the other members of the fortunate generation of the 1970s who have stayed to superintend the progress of the sociology of deviance into the 1980s. The loss of the more abstract thinkers has transformed the character of debate. The sociological criminology of the 1980s is no longer quite as metaphysical, abstract and argumentative. If it has retained any ambitions to advance a wider social theory, they are to be found in such areas as Garland and Young's sociology of control and punishment (Garland, 1985), a sociology which began with labelling theory, passed through an examination of social control and moved on to a discussion of state structures and their workings. But those areas are few.

The rump remain in universities that have suffered contraction. The numbers of graduate students in sociology departments rose from 2480 in 1974–5 to 2514 in 1979–80 and then declined to 2122 in 1983–4. The population of undergraduates decreased from 4355 in 1979–80 to 3533 in 1983–4.

The total teaching and research staff of British universities shrunk by 11 per cent from 1979–1980 to 1984–85 (Universities Statistical Record, 1986). Contraction has affected criminology itself. An older cohort of criminologists, including Eryl Hall Williams, Nigel Walker, Donald West and Leon Radzinowicz, has begun to enter retirement. A few critical members of the prime generation have emigrated: Stanley Cohen to Israel, Kit Carson to Australia, Ron Clarke and Stuart Henry to the United States, and Ian Taylor to Canada. Fifteen criminologists were reported in my census to have left teaching and research in the last five years but there was small prospect of replacing them. Forty-five of the departments had no plans to recruit new staff in the field. Only nine departments did have such intentions, and six of them were law departments. The stock of sociologists of deviance is not being fully replenished and it is ageing. In late 1986, the average age of a criminologist in a law department was 40, in a sociology department 42, and in a department of social administration 43.

Since that Golden Age of the 1970s, no comparable body of young criminologists has been allowed to rise up to make their own mark on the world of theory. Graduate research training has declined. The chief patron of graduate students, the ESRC, has been awarded a budget which contracted steadily from the *annus mirabilis* of 1978 until it became lower in real terms in 1986 than it had been in 1974. A smaller proportion of that smaller budget has been allocated to postgraduate training, shrinking from two-thirds in 1978 to two-fifths in 1986 (*Network*, 1987). Indeed, the Director of the London School of Economics wrote rather wistfully, "one gathers the impression that there is a tendency in some influential quarters to question the very usefulness of Ph.D. degrees as a vehicle for research in social sciences" (Patel, 1986).

The fortunate generation remains the major executor of the British tradition. And there appears to have been a consequent fall in the rate of intellectual innovation. Theoretical revolution no longer follows theoretical revolution in a dizzy procession. Instead, sociologists of deviance seem still to be investigating the ramifications of the ideas which were introduced in the 1960s: they have become the normal scientists of ethnography, interactionism, feminism (Heidensohn, 1985) and Marxism. To be sure, the bearers of each of those separate traditions might phrase that intellectual history differently, discovering a greater consistency of purpose and a more solid achievement. Garland has certainly written to me arguing that there "*is* a continuous legacy" of a "self-conscious movement towards both the theory and politics of Marxism", a movement which has been disrupted by recent political change. Others would probably point to other strains which have also been preserved and advanced. But revolution-making is in palpable decline.

It is the emergence of a routine competence which distinguishes criminological work from the first giddy phase of sociological criminology. The earlier books of the 1970s were usually bravura pieces, published versions of doctorates produced by graduates who had worked in some intellectual isolation. They were the bold creations of lone autodidacts who forged new, venturesome, eccentric and sometimes precarious syntheses between Marxism and interactionism, or interactionism and cybernetics (Young, 1971; Cohen,

1972). Many were influential but they were also too individual to permit simple replication.

The period of disputation set the character of the field and it has gone. Later publications have become professional studies produced in a matter of fact manner. The second generation of the 1980s consists chiefly of a smaller and younger group of professional scholars. It is a group that missed the period of major recruitment to teaching posts, having to turn instead to research contracts in applied criminology. Their work has necessarily been empirical and policy-oriented, and it has disclosed much. Thus the Oxford Centre for Socio-Legal Studies was founded in 1972 with four part-time staff and it began to flourish two years later. It set people to work on long-term, empirical and co-operative projects that would be beyond the scope of solitary criminologists in teaching posts. It has emitted a steady flow of elegant ethnographic studies of law and law enforcement, attending above all to the compliance based strategies of such organisations as offices of fair trading, environmental health departments and water boards (Cranston 1979; Hawkins, 1984). The Centre has its own distinctive and communicable intellectual idiom. Similarly, the Oxford Centre for Criminological Research acquired a presence in 1976 and its staff, Shapland, Maguire, Corbett, Player, Vagg and others, write professionally as a matter of course. The Institute of Criminology at Cambridge has Trevor Bennett on research contract, and he has begun to reveal some of the situated rationality of criminal decision-making. Proficient scholarship is no longer an extraordinary or virtuoso accomplishment. It has become uneventful, transmitted routinely and competently in Cambridge, Edinburgh, Hull, Keele, London, Oxford and Sheffield. (Sadly too, it is now also somewhat insecure, threatened by precarious funding in a country which has begun to devalue scholarship and research (see Martin and Irvine, 1986).)

The era of manifestos passed largely because an ageing group of scholars in the prime generation had no need repeatedly to fight the battles of its youth. The generation has not been effectively challenged from behind. (Perhaps, as Garland has suggested to me, it is so heterodox that it does not *need* to be challenged from behind. Too many identities are on offer to warrant opposition.) It has attained a satisfactory respectability and influence. It has as much power as any to command resources. To be sure, there are always a few who lose none of their combativeness: Sumner and Brogden are instances. But the fortunate generation has come into its own and there is apparent agreement that many of the earlier problems of theoretical definition and identity have grown stale or have been resolved for most practical purposes. Differences remain but there is decreasing profit in stressing them. A law of the diminishing marginal utility of academic criticism would hold that less and less will be gained by continual, repetitious attacks on others. After a point, much that could be said without moving on will have been said. The central terrain of the sociology of deviance is no longer subject to bellicose dispute, most criminologists having become more conciliatory and catholic, engaging in a reasonably civil trade in one another's ideas. It is about the margins that skirmishes are now being fought. There are battles where criminologists explore regions abutting the preserves of others: the sociology of the police has begun to encroach on analyses and polemic about the State, industrial disputes and civil order (Reiner, 1985); and the sociology of crime in the inner city has collided with the politics and study of race (Lea and Young, 1984).

Indeed, those politics have jolted almost all criminologists. The civil disorders of 1981 and 1985 and the Miners' Strike of 1984–85 stirred disparate and sometimes conflicting reflections about Saturnalia, collective bargaining by riot, criminal areas, the dangerous classes, the politicisation of policing and the oppressiveness of life in the inner city. Criminologists have had to think anew about crime as a collective process formed in the politics and geography of race and class. In the work of Alice Coleman, Anne Power, Frances Reynolds, the Priority Estates Projects, the Safe Neighbourhoods Unit, the Home Office Research and Planning Unit and the Middlesex Centre for Criminology, there has been a resurrection of interest in the difficulties of policing crime-ridden communities. Indeed, according to Bottoms, those communities may be something new, special and disturbing in the social and criminal ecology of Britain, a resurrection of the rookeries: there may be a "major qualitative difference between such areas—or some pockets of such areas—and the remainder of the country" (Bottoms, 1987).

An ageing, shrinking generation that has come into its own has tended also to find itself surrounded by a new, interesting and increasingly diverse environment of sponsorship. It has become, as it were, the established group, virtually the sole repository of expertise and authority. There is no other for outside funding agencies to support.

It is difficult to ascertain patterns of movement in research grants. One strategic sponsor has been the Education and Science Research Council (ESRC), the patron of the Oxford Centre for Socio-Legal Studies. The only records available to the ESRC about its own research funding touch on the awards made to criminology by its Social Sciences and the Law Committee between 1972 and 1984 (ESRC, 1984). Those records disclose rather modest numbers and sizes of awards until the mid–1970s: £334 was shared between two projects in 1972 for instance. One award was made annually between 1972 and 1976. Funding did become more substantial by 1978: £63,450 was given to three projects in that year. Thereafter, the ESRC made yearly awards totalling tens of thousands and, in two years, over a hundred thousand pounds. Most recently, its "Crime and Criminal Justice Initiative" has allocated £750,000 to research over several years.

Another strategic sponsor has been the Home Office, the patron of the Cambridge Institute of Criminology and the Oxford Centre for Criminological Research. In the era of collective contention, a different Home Office was much criticised by younger and rather more belligerent members of the fortunate generation (see Cohen and Taylor, 1976). But people and stances have changed. The Home Office's research history has been something of a mirror of wider academic work, moving from essays in abstracted empiricism to small, clever artisanal studies in applied theory. There was the need to formulate a policy response to the fragility of race relations and the unrest of the 1980s. There was a loss of faith in the "medico-psychological model" and the rehabilitative powers of the penal system. Together, they combined to bring about movement from abstracted empiricism and a seemingly obsessive penology to a much wider analysis of situational crime prevention, civil disorder, police-community relations and victimisation (Clarke and Cornish, 1983). In so doing, they grew closer to other criminologists working on the outside. And their influence has been considerable. With a staff of just over 45 in 1986, the Research and Planning Unit is the Goliath of the British criminological world.

One special decision was taken in the new phase. In 1981, the Home Office elected to follow the pattern of the United States Department of Justice and conduct victim surveys. Two sweeps have taken place in England and Wales in 1982 and 1984 (Hough and Mayhew, 1983; 1985) and a third is planned. A parallel sweep took place in Scotland in 1982. The surveys were intended chiefly to illuminate the "dark figure" of unreported crime, although there has been an additional baggage of questions about the fear of crime, attitudes to the police and "dealing with risk" (Home Office, 1981). Crime surveys have redefined policing, victimisation and the politics of crime. And they have engendered a spate of satellite projects bearing the mark of the new concerns about uncertain policing and public disquiet. There have been reports centred on the fear of crime (Maxfield, 1984), the victimisation of women (Worrall and Pease, 1986) and the social geography of offending (Smith, 1986). Significant segments of radical criminology have also responded to a new vision of crime as another intolerable affliction of the already vulnerable and suffering. Where once there were only offenders, working class victims have appeared to prompt analysis:

> There was a schizophrenia about crime on the left where crimes against women and immigrant groups were quite rightly an object of concern, but other types of crime were regarded of being of little interest or somehow excusable. Part of this mistake. . . stems from the belief that property offences are directly solely against the bourgeoisie and that violence against the person is carried out by amateur Robin Hoods in the course of their righteous attempts to redistribute wealth. All of this is, alas, untrue (Lea and Young, 1984).

The research staff of the Home Office Research and Planning Unit are now of much the same age and background as the academic sociologists of deviance. They passed through a similar cycle of growth and decline: their numbers also increased during the 1970s, rising from a total of 56 in 1973 to 61 in 1975. They also underwent a steady contraction between 1981 to 1985, when only 37 staff were in post. (The process of decline has been reversed of late, the complement at the end of 1986 being 45·5). They also seem to be members of the fortunate generation: only 24 per cent of the research staff being in their twenties and 7 per cent being older than fifty. The rest were in their thirties and forties in the winter of 1986 (Mayhew, 1986).

Staff of the Research and Planning Unit and the universities and polytechnics share a rough community of experience. There has been some considerable effort made by the Department to narrow the social, organisational and intellectual gulf between itself and the universities and polytechnics. Its

Research Programme for 1986–87 talks of the Research and Planning Unit's valuing "links with academic researchers, many of whom help the Unit in its day-to-day activities, for example in consultancies and seminars" (Home Office Research and Planning Unit, 1986). Academic criminologists have been invited to participate in the Unit's research planning process. They have been given novel access to research materials within the Unit, it becoming the practice to encourage outsiders to work on the British Crime Surveys and other data bases. Participants in such projects have included radical or critical criminologists who would not once have been invited and would probably have refused if they had been. Jock Young, Geoffrey Pearson and John Lea attended a Home Office Workshop on community initiatives in crime reduction in 1986. Jock Young took part in the public review of the Research and Planning Unit's research programme.

Home Office external funding has been steadily enlarged. External expenditure for law services by the Research and Planning Unit grew progressively from £185,000 in 1976–77 to £648,000 in 1985–86 (Mayhew, 1986), and an extra £500,000 has been added in 1986–87 to form a development fund for action projects and the like. However, the politics of research sponsorship have intervened to establish a rhetoric of relevance and utility. The Home Office has declared that "in the past it was possible to fund university studies whose relevance to current policy was somewhat limited. Now that resources are more constrained, more stringent criteria of relevance must be applied to the funding of research for the Home Office" (Home Office, 1985). The emergence of a more pronounced demand for "policy relevance" in externally funded research may well further accelerate the universities' movement away from the theoretical and contemplative.

A third sponsor is new and important. There has arisen in the United Kingdom a proliferation of radical local authorities staffed by people who had themselves passed through the universities of the 1960s and 1970s. They have constructed the new municipal populism of urban Britain, attempting to galvanise the more marginalised portions of society: organised groups of Blacks and Asians, homosexuals and Lesbians, women, trades councils and trades unions, unilateral disarmers, the more militant tenants' groups, travellers and squatters. As Campbell has argued, "the alliance around radical labourism has changed the contours of local and national politics, it set the new left agenda of the 1980s. For the first time, movements which lived their life outside the state and political parties found themselves moving in the same orbit" (Campbell, 1987). The dialectics of the new populism have tended to revolve around conflict with the police: the police being held to represent the central State to which the politicians of local councils are opposed; the police having given some practical definition to the marginalised groups (Holdaway, 1983); the police tending to focus much of their attention on the regulation of those groups; and, in David Downes' phrase, the police tending to over-control and under-protect the inner city. There is new money for research and a new response to radical criminological argument in the Police Committees and Monitoring Groups and Community Relations Councils and Women's Committees. Radical criminology has acquired powerful patrons.

In the wake of the British Crime Surveys, left-wing criminologists have mounted their own focused surveys of victims, examining sexual and racial assault, domestic violence and mundane working class crime in Merseyside, Islington (Jones, Maclean and Young, 1986) and Haringey. They have acquired a practical importance in the politics of the radical councils. Their words are taken seriously. They have become the new administrative criminologists of the left, and they have experienced every incentive to address problems of policy. Pragmatic questions that had once been the sole preserve of others began to interest such radicals as Geoffrey Pearson, Jock Young, Richard Kinsey and John Lea. John Lea himself reflected, "the research techniques at our disposal in the development of crime prevention policy have progressed in leaps and bounds during the last decade. The importation of the victim survey gave us a qualitatively new type of data on which to base policy formation" (Lea, 1986). Some important radicals thus became applied criminologists at a time when applied criminologists turned towards the situated analyses of communal behaviour. And both seem able to work with the social anthropologists of deviance and control.

In all this movement there are the beginnings of an interesting convergence. It would be surprising if something of the sort had not taken place. Britain is geographically small and many of its universities are located in the South East. British criminology itself is the work of only two hundred or so scholars. It revolves around the doings of one pivotal generation and a smaller second generation who were trained principally in Cambridge and London and then in Sheffield and at much the same time. British criminologists know one another, they educate one another, they sometimes marry one another, they read each other's works and they gossip about each other. Criminologists must meet repeatedly in conferences, committees, seminars, pressure groups and in boards of examiners and editors. For practical purposes at least, it has become increasingly difficult to maintain a substantial distance between them. They form a social world. Politically, too, theorists and administrative criminologists collide with increasing frequency. As Hood remarked:

> There is a natural tendency (or so it seems) to draw criminologists, or rather criminological "experts" as practical advisers—or even as decision-makers—into the realm of policy-making or implementation. . . .Furthermore, there is an equally strong tendency for those concerned with penal policy and practice to look to criminology for solutions to the many problems posed by crime and the operation of the agencies which exist to deal with it (Hood, 1987).

To be sure, the criminological world is composed of structures of activity which may never overlap: Merseyside Marxists and Exeter empiricists can bypass one another for long periods, and there are always some sociologists who will refuse to talk to one another. But quite strenuous efforts have been made to suppress the acrimony which once marked British criminology and, indeed, an unstable pattern of agreement has started to emerge. A common interest is not a consensus, and critical argument passes backwards and forwards, yet there is a central commitment to exploring a landscape defined by a few salient features: the new politics of victims, a recognition of the limitations of mundane policing and the problematics of social control, and agreement about the centrality of informal social control.

Conclusion

An intellectual and political generation in their late thirties and early forties dominates the sociology of crime and deviance. Its agenda was set largely in the 1960s and 1970s, focusing on problems of interactionism, feminism and Marxism but bent a little towards the investigation of matters touching on social policy. It has been joined by a younger generation of professional criminologists with empirical leanings. Together, they find themselves surrounded by a new and complicated web of dependencies and connections made possible by their own rise to maturity, the persistence of conventional sponsorship and the emergence of novel, somewhat unorthodox patrons with money and power. The work that is being done is marked by a decelerating rate of innovation, a drift towards normal science and a new pragmatism which addresses, above all else, the problems of victims, social control, the police, women and ethnic minorities in the communities of the inner cities.

References

Bottoms, A. (1987). "Reflections on the Criminological Enterprise". Unpublished inaugural lecture.

Campbell, B. (1987). "Charge of the Light Brigade". *Marxism Today*. February 1987.

Clarke, R. and Cornish, D. (1983). *Crime Control in Britain*. Albany, State University of New York Press.

Cohen, S. (1971). Introduction to *Images of Deviance*. Harmondsworth, Penguin.

Cohen, S. (1974). "Criminology and the Sociology of Deviance in Britain". In P. Rock and M. McIntosh (eds.) *Deviance and Social Control*. London, Tavistock.

Cohen, S. (1972). *Folk Devils and Moral Panics*. London, Paladin.

Cohen, S. (1980). Preface to second edition of *Folk Devils and Moral Panics*. London, Paladin.

Cohen, S. and Taylor, L. (1976). *Prison Secrets*. London, National Council for Civil Liberties.

Cranston, R. (1979). *Regulating Business*. London, Macmillan.

ESRC (1984). "Research Grants: The Social Sciences and the Law Committee". Appendix I. November 1984.

Garland, D. (1985). *Punishment and Welfare*. Aldershot, Gower Publishing Company.

Garland, D. (1987). Private communication.

Hawkins, K. (1984). *Environment and Enforcement*. Oxford, The Clarendon Press.

Heidensohn, F. (1985) *Women and Crime*. London, Macmillan.

Holdaway, S. (1983). *Inside the British Police*. Oxford, Blackwell.

Home Office (1981). *Public Surveys of Crime: Report of a Workshop.* London, Home Office.

Home Office Research and Planning Unit (1985). *Research Programme.* London, Home Office.

Home Office Research and Planning Unit (1986). *Research Programme.* London, Home Office.

Hood, R. (1987). "Some Reflections on the Role of Criminology in Public Policy", Address to the British Society of Criminology, 28th January 1987.

Hough, M. and Mayhew, P. (1983). *The British Crime Survey: first report.* London, HMSO.

Hough, M. and Mayhew, P. (1985). *Taking Account of Crime: Key Findings from the 1984 British Crime Survey.* London, HMSO.

Jones, B. (1972). "Perspective". *Working Papers in Cultural Studies.* Spring 1972. 2.

Jones, T., Maclean, B. and Young, J. (1986). *The Islington Crime Survey.* Aldershot, Gower.

Lea, J. (1986). "Towards Social Prevention". *Middlesex Polytechnic Centre for Criminology Working Paper.* November 1986.

Lea, J. and Young, J. (1984). *What is to be Done About Law and Order?* London, Penguin.

Martin, B. and Irvine, J. (1986). *An International Comparison of Government Funding of Academic and Academically Related Research. ABRC Science Policy Studies No 2.* Falmer, Science Policy Research Unit.

Maxfield, M. (1984). *Fear of Crime in England and Wales.* London, HMSO.

Mayhew, P. (1986). Private communication.

Network (1987) Newsletter of the British Sociological Association, January 1987.

Patel, I. (1986). *Report by the Director 1985–86.* London, London School of Economics.

Phillipson, M. and Roche, M. (1974). "Phenomenology, Sociology and the Study of Deviance". In P. Rock and M. McIntosh (eds.) *Deviance and Social Control.* London, Tavistock.

Platt, J. (1981). "The Social Construction of 'Positivism' and its Significance in British Sociology, 1950–1980". In P. Abrams *et al.* (eds.) *Practice and Progress.* London, George Allen and Unwin.

Reiner, R. (1985). *The Politics of the Police.* Brighton, Wheatsheaf.

Rock, P. (1981). "Has Deviance a Future?" in H. Blalock (ed.) *Sociological Theory and Research.* New York, Collier Macmillan.

Smart, C. (1977). *Women, Crime and Criminology.* London, Routledge and Kegan Paul.

Smith, S. (1986). *Crime, Space and Society.* Cambridge, Cambridge University Press.

Taylor, I., Walton, P. and Young, J. (1973). *The New Criminology.* London, Routledge and Kegan Paul.

Universities' Statistical Record (1986). *University Statistics 1984–1985, Volume One, Students and Staff.* Cheltenham, Universities' Statistical Record.

Worrall, A. and Pease, K. (1986). "Personal Crime Against Women: Evidence from the 1982 British Crime Survey". *The Howard Journal of Criminal Justice.* **25,** 2.

Young, J. (1971). *The Drugtakers.* London, MacGibbon and Kee.

[6]
Witnesses and Space in a Crown Court

The social world of a Crown Court is differentiated into groups segregated practically, symbolically, and physically. Prosecution witnesses, in particular, are kept apart from professional 'court users'. They are expected to behave in ways that present problems of control, and the special architecture and organization of the Court are a response. Their segregation may explain some of the pariah status of victims at large.

Introduction

I propose to discuss some first ideas stemming from a period of observation, interviewing, and documentary research in the Crown Court at Wood Green in north London.[1] My point of entry was secured through a study of one of Victim Support's seven trial 'victim in court' projects, which encouraged an examination of the court through the experiences of the victims who attend it. A working title for the project has been 'Time, Space, and Victims in a Crown Court', the social organization of time and space being among the most important influences that shape the experience of witnesses in court. It is aspects of space that I shall touch on here, and in doing so I shall illuminate the more general character of victims themselves.

The Crown Court

The Crown Court at Wood Green is not large. It is what administrators call a third-tier, ten-court centre, comprising six criminal courts, three county courts, and a patent court, the criminal courts receiving cases graded predominantly third and fourth class. It tries no murders and only the occasional rape transferred from another court. Its staple cases are burglaries, assaults, robberies, and thefts. Trials, judges, defendants, and counsel are affected correspondingly. The typical trial is a short affair of one or two days and only very rarely is a case conducted by senior counsel or by more than one prosecutor. The court is thronged by an ever-changing crowd of younger and relatively junior barristers, defendants, witnesses, police officers, and victims.

The court itself is an imposing building set in an unprepossessing street and its doings attract little public attention. There are, to be sure, two elderly spectators who flit daily from trial to trial in a search for diversion. There is a succession of agency journalists, typically too young and impermanent to be taken fully inside the informal social world of the court, who circle the courtrooms in a quest for local cases. Rarely will they stay

* Department of Sociology, London School of Economics and Political Science. I am indebted to Geoff Spain and Michael McMullan, respectively Senior Probation Officer and Resident Judge at the Wood Green Crown Court, for their comments on an earlier draft of this paper.

[1] Intensive, uninterrupted observation and interviewing took place in the one Crown Court between September 1989 and June 1990. I was the sole researcher and I spoke to some forty prosecution witnesses, six judges, thirty counsel, and numerous members of the court staff, including the Chief Clerk, ushers, clerks, security staff, resident police officers, shorthand writers, receptionists, secretaries, and others.

for any length of time to hear one whole case: their aim is the production of simple lists of names, addresses, indictments, and sentences to report in local newspapers. On occasion, there are bands of what security staff and police call followers or supporters, groups of friends and family attending trials. That is all. The public work of the Crown Court only infrequently attracts a public. It is composed of a sequence of formal, repeated—indeed, ritualized—processes administered and serviced by familiars in a state of near-privacy.

Trials and Conflicts

Two features of the court's work emerge as of preliminary interest to an understanding of the relations between witnesses and space in a Crown Court. One is the excitation of intense feeling. Truth in the English criminal justice system is won dialectically and agonistically. Trials involve adversaries and adversity, defeats and victories, winners and losers. They pivot around serious allegations presented by their champions as wholly true and by their opponents as almost wholly false. At stake are very grave matters of liberty and confinement, accusation and vindication, reputation and veracity, matters which passionately concern defendants and defence witnesses, victims and prosecution witnesses. The prosecution in a contested trial must persuade members of a jury so that they become sure that a particular crime was committed by a particular person or persons, and witnesses will be called to give evidence to that effect. It is the business of the defence to cast doubt on those allegations and discredit prosecution witnesses and their evidence. They may call witnesses whom the prosecution will wish to discredit in their turn. In this sense, a trial is a succession of systematic attempts to expose testimony and testifiers.

Some time ago, Garfinkel described trials as degradation ceremonies, and talked about the degradation of the defendant (Garfinkel 1956). The defendant's objective character will be re-cast and abased, he said. It may be a little extravagant to call all trials degrading (after all, some defendants are acquitted). And it must also be noted that such re-casting is directed not only at defendants but at prosecution witnesses and victims as well: efforts will be made methodically to transform *their* characters. The work of defence counsel in cross-examination is substantively the same as that of the prosecution. It is to make witnesses appear so inconsistent, forgetful, muddled, spiteful, or greedy that their word cannot safely be believed. Victims and defendants, prosecution and defence witnesses alike face accusations of mendacity, impropriety, and malice. Victims who come to court supposing that a trial will be an assertion of their wrongs will discover that it is *their* probity that is at issue as well. In a contested trial, they will almost certainly be exposed to a bruising interrogation in which there is no presumption that they are the injured party. At best, they will be the *alleged* victims. A judge reflected: 'a close investigation of people's motives and actions may be very uncomfortable for those investigated.' Witnesses frequently leave the box angrily and in tears. They may well become angry with one another, mouthing or shouting imprecations across the court. Their supporters can supply a Greek chorus, commenting on the performance and character of those in the dock and the box. The outcome is that trials are among the most charged of all secular rituals. They are infused with feelings which threaten continually to erupt.

Emotionality is built into the very construction of witnesses. Indeed, it is *demanded* by the professionals who have dealings with them. Trials are grounded in lawyers' repeated appeals to the jury's common-sense knowledge of the social world. Jurors are invited to judge the reasonableness of the different stories that are paraded before them and compare them with what they themselves know of typical motives and courses of action (Bennett and Feldman 1981). Such appeals hold that reasonable people *should* display anger, grief, frustration, and astonishment when their reputation and liberty are in jeopardy. Credibility will depend, in turn, on lay witnesses making the appropriately emotional response at the appropriate time, and juries will be tacitly invited to scrutinize just how they conduct themselves under examination (Saward 1990). Implicitly or explicitly, by word or act, counsel will draw a jury's attention to the bearing, self-discipline, and demeanour of witnesses. What they actually emphasize will take its significance from the theme that they seek currently to develop, and it may not always be consistent over time or between cases.

On occasion, for instance, it may be useful to point to the fact of a witness's self-control. This can be taken as a sign of a person's command over his or her behaviour, a command which may then be represented as quite incompatible with allegations made by prosecution or defence. Conversely, that very self-control can become translated into evidence of guilt and complicity in wrongdoing. Counsel can argue that the facts of victimization or false accusation are so manifestly distressing that apparent indifference cannot but signify a want of conviction and truthfulness.[2] An animated expression will then be required of the sincere witness who calls painful incidents back to life: impassivity lacks persuasive power. Counsel hold that police officers, in particular, make poor witnesses because their delivery is frequently leaden through rehearsal.

Counsel may directly or indirectly indicate the *inadequate* self-control of those in the box. Indeed, misbehaviour is sometimes quite deliberately fomented to uncloak what may then be conveniently represented as the witness's real, underlying character. Almost every cross-examination will contain a passage in which counsel puts on a mocking or stern face and presses the witness hard as if trying to drive him or her to anger. Goading accomplishes many ends. It is a routine, practical demonstration to client and jury that a counsel has worked hard and remorselessly to present a case; it is considered a vicarious catharsis for the client; it may prompt candid answers from witnesses disarmed by fury or distress; and it may conjure up the violent or provocative person claimed by counsel to exist behind a mask of calm reasonableness. 'See?' counsel will seem to say: 'see the kind of man this is. See how he reacts merely to questions? Could he not have done what I say?' Lay witnesses will then be coaxed and incited to show themselves as if naked. Their faces, gestures, and utterances will become part of a performance to be elicited and analysed. As a matter of course, counsel expect judges to invite juries to consider how witnesses acquitted themselves in the box.

In effect, then, a typical trial conducted in the Crown Court consists of advocates calling one another's witnesses liars, 'blackguarding them' as one judge put it. Counsel conduct their cross-examinations on the routine and pragmatically necessary assumption that an opponent's witnesses must be either misguided or mendacious and, so defined, such people cannot be entitled to much protection. On the contrary, it may be argued, they should be exposed. Hard attacks will be cleverly made on the probity,

[2] Journalists, too, will point to the impassivity of those being sentenced as if it indicated merely callousness, instead of the numbness that can accompany the final stages of a trial.

veracity, and character of almost all but the expert witness, and the expert witness is not usually required to enter the witness box in commonplace cases in the Crown Court.

There are rules of evidence and cross-examination, but these are not designed to protect the feelings of those who are interrogated. In practice, judges do intercede from time to time, correcting counsel for the use of disagreeable language and displays of gratuitous rudeness. They may offer a witness tissues, water, or a seat.[3] But their interventions are designed as much to preserve the general decorum of the courtroom as to protect witnesses. Judges hold that cross-examination cannot be a soft activity, they cannot prevent questions that should be put,[4] and above all they cannot appear to shield any one witness or group of witnesses. What *does* effectively protect the witness is the sensitivity of the jury, as perceived by lawyers. Counsel are reluctant to seem too hectoring or cruel lest they 'alienate the jury'. Even the smallest trial can become bitter and antagonistic and many people retire from it in tears. Professionals show little surprise if they do so.

Yet conflict is also a form of association: 'one *unites* in order to fight, and one fights under the mutually recognized control of norms and rules' (Simmel, in Coser 1968: 121). Trials are highly regulated, disciplined, and controlled. They have their conventions and limits. They are despatched efficiently, frequently, without fuss, and with a pervasive good humour by teams of counsel, judges, administrators, and staff. What is for some a matter of great emotion and uncertainty, indeed of personal crisis, is the everyday, repetitive work of others. That is the stuff of a profession and a professional institution. It distinguishes doctors and hospitals as well as lawyers and courts. I shall pursue that contrast in a while, for it helps to define the situated meanings of populations and spaces in court.

Trials and Knowledge

The second pertinent feature of trials rests on the nature and deployment of what may be called warranted knowledge, and it involves a number of subordinate issues. One such issue is that, in any conflict, strategic advantage will turn on knowledge of the other side. What counsel know about opponents and their intentions will shape the management of a case. The ideal is to predict witnesses' responses clearly and accurately. Counsel have a maxim that one should never ask a question to which one does not know the answer. Examinations in chief, in particular, are supposed to bring one's own witnesses 'up to proof', to reproduce orally and in court matters already known through written statements and transcribed interviews. They are not supposed to furnish new information which will disconcert the questioner.

Many trials proceed uneventfully and without major surprise. They are intended to do so. Much is open within the rules of combat; but trials also revolve around the protection of special caches of knowledge. Thus, defence counsel do not have a duty to the prosecution to disclose the names of their witnesses until a very late stage. Not all their evidence will be revealed in advance. It is within the power of the defence to spring what are called 'ambushes', and ambushes depend on secrecy. Again, jurors are

[3] Witnesses normally stand when giving evidence.

[4] Indeed, as Joanna Shapland pointed out, 'the rules of evidence require defence counsel to call a prosecution witness a liar.'

the final arbiters of the 'facts of a case', and care is taken about the facts to which they can be exposed. Certain pieces of knowledge will be hidden from them. Jurors should not learn about a defendant's previous criminal convictions unless by design in open court. Professionals have privy knowledge of antecedents, but juries do not. Juries should not hear or learn about excluded evidence whose admissibility may have been decided in a 'voir dire', a trial within a trial conducted by a judge in the jury's absence. Juries are often required to leave the courtroom when counsel make legal submissions.

Most protected of all stocks of knowledge are the instructions given to counsel by their clients, the Crown Prosecution Service or the instructing solicitor and the defendant as professional and lay clients respectively (General Council of the Bar 1989: 16.4). Instructions vary. Some, indeed, are curt to the point of invisibility. But others are such a candid review of a case that their contents cannot be divulged without prejudice. They are hedged about with secrecy. They do not enter the court's own papers. Judges, court staff, and opponents will not see them. Their sole readers should be the counsel for whom they have been drafted. Even the express subjects of defence instructions, defendants, the defence counsel's own lay clients, do not read the instructions prepared about them by solicitors serving as the counsel's professional clients.

There is another relevant issue affecting the character of knowledge in the trial process. It centres on evidence. Evidence has distinct properties in the theory and practice of law. It is knowledge about knowledge, being 'any matter of fact, the effect, tendency or design of which is, to produce in the mind a persuasion, affirmative or disaffirmative, of the existence of some other matter of fact' (Best 1922: 6). Its principal form is oral testimony delivered on oath and subject to cross-examination. Lawyers ask juries to infer what may have happened by 'calling witnesses who have perceived the facts in question' (Cross 1980: 1) and inviting them to evaluate what they say and how they say it. I have already asserted that the statements and demeanour of witnesses *now* are read as clues to what they allege happened in debated circumstances *then*. In that sense, evidence acquires another twist, becoming knowledge about knowledge about knowledge. Inferences have to be made about past happenings on a hearing of present testimony, and the character of the testifier's mind and memory becomes a matter of some consequence.

Trial lawyers maintain that what is said in evidence should be the witness's own naïve recollection, 'refreshed' perhaps by reference to written statements taken nearer the time. It should be innocent of others' knowledge and ends, a mirror reflecting an experience of the past as faithfully as possible. To be sure, people will talk with others before the trial (and such talk can endanger subsequent testimony) but, in and about the courtroom, recollection is supposed to remain as free from contamination as possible. It must not be 'coached', in the lawyers' word, because it would then no longer be the witness's own artless impression but that of some other who may have special purposes in mind. Above all, it must not be coached by lawyers, because they have very special purposes indeed. Counsel do not 'discuss the case with or in the presence of potential witnesses of a non-expert character . . . save in exceptional circumstances, which require the careful exercise of . . . judgment and discretion' (General Council of the Bar 1989: 23.4).

Apprehension about the dangers of contamination leads to the segregation and management of participants in a trial. Legal tradition, says Twining, holds that 'evidence which is both relevant and reliable [should be] presented (in a form designed to bring out truth and discover untruth) to a supposedly competent and impartial decision-maker with adequate safeguards against corruption and mistake and adequate provision for review and appeal' (Twining 1985: 16). Nothing can be considered unless it has been appropriately edited, introduced in a proper form, delivered orally, and recorded in public before the affected parties, who are kept apart and allowed to scrutinize and interrogate one another only under the control of a presiding judge who should intervene if certain rules are breached. There must be no unsupervised communication between prosecution and defence witnesses, jurors, defendants, and victims.

I have argued that Crown Court trials are accompanied by special displays of emotion and stocks of knowledge which require cautious administration. I shall now turn to the social and physical organization which supplies that administration, and I shall begin by describing something of the moral order of the court.

Professionals and Civilians

The court itself is serviced by staff who associate with one another day after day, closely and in conditions of considerable interdependence. Security staff talk approvingly of the resident police officers who support them when there are signs of trouble, although it is not strictly those officers' duty to do so. Probation officers used to find themselves looking after prosecution witnesses' children[5] (there is no crèche or nursery, although the Salvation Army, at some distance from the court, sometimes cares for children). Staff tend to liken themselves to a family, pointing affectionately to an implied distinction between the relatively small, co-operative, and intimate domain of their court and what lies outside. Of course, the court has its own clearly signalled inner divisions, distances, disciplines, and hierarchies. Language is characteristically formal and deferential. There are groups and people who meet only rarely and then awkwardly. But there is also a pervading sense of the court as a unity. Even the judges are 'our judges' and are sometimes known by fond or not-so-fond nicknames.

The staff's universe contains three principal groups: 'civilians', the staff of the Crown Court itself, and professionals who are not taken to belong to the familial world of the court. The greatest divide is between professionals and civilians, and it emphasizes the pragmatically dominant issues of danger, emotionality, and confidentiality. There is a vital difference between those who are paid to work in the criminal justice system and those who are not; between lawyers, police officers, probation officers, and court staff on the one hand and the laity on the other; between those who can be expected to know something of the rules and respect confidence and trust and those who cannot; between those who engage continually in a lattice of friendly exchanges and those who are distant; between those who are known and those who are strangers; between those who preserve a civilized equanimity and those who cannot be expected to do any such thing.

Consider the significance of that gap. On the one hand, professionals are supposed to be relatively calm and dependable. They are liable to be sanctioned if they are not, the object of rebuke in court and gossip in the corridors. The names of individual counsel who lose their composure and are rude become widely known. Even addressing a judge

[5] The practice was discontinued when it was discovered that staff were not properly insured for this purpose.

with a hand in one's pocket can attract reproof. Barristers will remain rooted and immobile in their positions on the counsels' row. They are rarely florid. They are not encouraged to flounce. They will say they do not wish to distract the jury from the witness. Prosecuting counsel, in particular, have no licence to be demonstrative. They are supposed to act as the disinterested and calmly reasonable representatives of the Crown. It is only defence counsel who are allowed to appear to lose their composure and they can do so only in a controlled staging of advocacy. Their part is to be the skilled mouthpiece of their client and they may sometimes choose to simulate a defendant's indignation and incredulity at the nonsense which is supposed to be uttered. It is as if they were delegated the task of projecting emotions felt in the dock. When that happens, and it happens as a matter of routine, signals will be given to other professionals to show how very distant defence counsel actually wish to seem from the impressions they are required to make. It is as if such questions do not emanate from them at all but from the client who instructs them. In such displays of 'role-distance', they will say 'I must put it to you' or 'I am obliged to suggest' before proceeding further. Were their indignation to appear less cultivated and managed, it could be open to judicial correction.

The professional cannot take civilians to be regulated in the same manner. Some civilians are present in court precisely because they have been held to defy regulation in the past. In court, they will be expected spontaneously to give vent to anger, contempt, indignation or amazement, and it is hoped only that such outpourings will be managed enough to occur at the proper time and in the proper place. There is a taxing and perhaps impracticable demand that spontaneity should be under control.[6] It cannot be presumed that civilians know the *mores* or rules of the court. They seem often to have no firm anchorage, no stake in institutional conformity, no local reputation to defend. They may well be anonymous. They are quite unpredictable and uncertain. To be sure, the Crown Court at Wood Green is peaceable enough most of the time, its civilians tending to congregate in anxious, undemonstrative huddles. But there is a continuous professional apprehension about the *possibility* of disorder, amplified by salutary stories and gossip which report all the unusual and disquieting happenings of the day. Security guards and police officers regularly and discreetly survey the building, monitoring the more fissile trials, the affrays and sexual assaults which can attract angry followers. Their activity is noted by staff and it reinforces an impression of ever-present danger. It is as if organization could always collapse. Even in the absence of overt threat, there can never be time or competence enough for staff to be confident about the behaviour of all the strangers who flock in and out of the court every day.

In this sense, there is thought to be a division of moral labour. Civilians manifest feelings and professionals do not (after all, it is the *civilians'* problems which are paraded in court, not those of the professionals). Professionals are disciplined and dependable. Civilians are not.[7] And it is precisely because they are not that they are also a source of

[6] Managed spontaneity seems to be a common enough phenomenon. For example, not all the congregation of pentecostal churches or Quaker meetings will be allowed to be moved to speak at any time. There is an order of precedence and timing even to the most unbidden visitations.

[7] Both groups have their anomalies. The laity includes expert witnesses such as doctors who are taken to be professionals of a sort. They may have appeared in court before. They are not taken to have an emotional investment in what happens. By extension, they may be expected to remain on the right side of the emotional divide. And professionals include people on the margins, solicitors' clerks, for instance, who are para-legals and do not always enter fully into the social world of the court.

some little risk to the trial and the court. They can explode, indeed, they are regularly induced to explode, and trials will be disrupted. They can threaten or inflict violence. They can be disorderly. They can angrily challenge the authority of lawyers to put questions. (A frequent retort made by witnesses cornered under cross-examination is 'How do you know? You weren't there,' and counsel will as frequently reply 'I am here to put questions, not to answer them.') They can storm out of the courtroom to talk or shout to witnesses waiting outside, placing *their* evidence at risk. Professionals stand for organization, civilians for potential disorganization.

Professionals themselves are split between insiders and outsiders. Insiders are the resident probation, security, and police staff, the clerks and the ushers, the judges and administrators. They are those whose everyday life is absorbed by the court and its doings, who are privy to its gossip and history, understand how things are 'really done', know colleagues by sight and name, and enter into those myriad, intertwining relations which transcend and blur the formal boundaries of groups and roles to engender idiomatic and often discreet patterns of organization. Outsiders may not come to the court at all frequently and they play little or no part in its informal life. They will not necessarily know much about the court's special style, working instead with a standard recipe knowledge as if Wood Green Crown Court were merely another Crown Court, its judges, juries, and clerks much the same as others anywhere else, to be treated in very much the same way.[8]

If the court is a family, it is an odd family, composed of different septs, housed in the one building but occupying distinct, private enclosures and marked always by the effects of the central, dramatic, absorbing, ramifying conflict of the trial process. Conflict is carefully administered. It persists day after day without too much evident hurt being done to professionals and to members of the family. It can persist safely because it is neutralized by the very organization and fabric of the court.

Organizationally, control centres on a formality and gravity of process which force charged contents into a disciplining frame. Even a case of petty shoplifting will become the subject of a measured performance in a theatrical arena, a performance in which all the professional participants are gowned or uniformed, language is restrained, and action contained. It will follow known and enforced rules of procedure and evidence, what lawyers call 'tramlines', that carry events firmly from stage to stage. It will centre on a multitude of little techniques which maintain a symbolic distance between actor and drama, protagonist and battle: counsel banter gently with one another and with the court staff before and after trials as if to demonstrate they are not *really* antagonistic. When they adopt an unpleasant style, they will generally signal that they are obliged professionally to do so and that their rancour is all contrived. Control will stem from the intimacy of a professional world whose members know much of one another at first or second hand but relatively little of defendants and victims and *their* troubles. Civilians hurry across the scene. They cannot become the subject of permanent attachments. Indeed, I have observed that counsel do not talk to their witnesses. There is an emotional chasm between the peaceable world of professionals and the charged domain of civilians, a chasm which will be bridged only very occasionally in an

[8] Even so, again there are anomalies. A number of police officers, barristers, and solicitors' clerks can become well enough known, acquire reputations, chat with staff, know their first names and get called by their first names or nicknames in return. They may also talk about the court as a family. More especially, there are Assistant Recorders and Recorders who sometimes come as outsiders to appear as counsel and sometimes as insiders to sit as judges.

exceptionally poignant or protracted case or when counsel adopt a radical politics of gender, party, or race and make a client's cause their own.

Physical Control

Moral and social control have been built into the physical structure of the court itself.[9] Architecture mediates conflict. A Crown Court houses a conglomerate of different, sometimes competing agencies, known as 'users', who share the space of the building but are answerable formally to organizations outside the court, co-exist in a kind of working condominium, and entertain relations which may best be described as loosely coupled. Within the court and given their own quarters are: the Crown Prosecution Service, which services the bringing of prosecutions; the probation service, which attends to the defendant after trial; the police, who are responsible for the production of oral, documentary, and physical evidence against and about defendants; security guards, concerned with the social and physical fabric of the building; administrative staff, accountable to the Lord Chancellor's Department and responsible for servicing trials and courtrooms; judges, who preside over trials; custody staff, answering to the Prison Department, who produce and guard remanded and incarcerated defendants and return them to prison on conviction; private caterers, who feed those who attend trials; and shorthand writers, who report what is said. Each of those users has been given a distinct enclosure inside the Crown Court, a set of offices, a space. An enclosure represents, in effect, the user's designated home territory, a protected place of business where files are kept and people work and confer about what are sometimes confidential matters. Equally important, it also represents a place of comparative informality within a formal institution. In chambers, for example, counsel do not call a judge 'your honour' but simply 'judge'. The enclosures are what Goffman called 'back regions' (Goffman 1959). They are places where people are no longer on display but can shed some of the disciplines of their official role. Kettles, coffee machines, plants, photographs, and pictures are kept there. It is in such spaces that people can gossip safely about themselves, their colleagues, their families, and their holidays. They will be literally and figuratively unbuttoned.

Architects have arranged those enclosures so that potentially antagonistic septs are kept clearly apart. Embarrassing encounters between their members are inhibited. So it is that Crown Prosecution law clerks are unlikely to wander into the probation offices in error; and prosecuting counsel will not find themselves in the custody area by chance. But professionals tend to know and observe the moral order governing the use of space. It is improbable that they will be found in a wrong area by mistake or design and they do not require tight architectural control. More important are civilians and their movements, because no such presumption can be made about them.

Public and Private Space

The moral and pragmatic gulf between professional and civilian has been built into the very physical fabric of the court. Private enclosures are carefully separated from the

[9] Not all courts contain such rigorous controls, and the controls of other courts are actually quite recent, a feature of changes in physical design introduced in the nineteenth century. A judge has pointed out to me that 'the courts in Westminster Hall had, at first, no physical demarcation, later quite low fences at the sides only, the fronts open, no ceiling, leaving the courts exposed to the general traffic and uproar in the Hall, the pedlars, hawkers, professional witnesses plying for hire, etc., and the proceedings in the neighbouring courts.'

public spaces where civilians cluster. Some, indeed, can be entered only through doors marked unambiguously 'private'. Around others it has been conventional to plan a kind of no-man's-land, an identifiable interstitial space, which notifies strangers that they are beginning to leave a common area to encroach on that of another. The Crown Prosecution Service, the barristers, and the shorthand writers may all be discovered at the end of short and very obvious culs-de-sac. It is as if the architecture of a court announces that no one could wander down those corridors without a very good purpose. They are structurally forbidding.

Professionals themselves judge the quality of their home territory by its accessibility to the public. Characteristically, the more open it is, the less will it be favoured. Security staff in the Crown Court at Wood Green, for example, inhabit a small, glass-partitioned, guardroom-like chamber adjoining the main entrance. A glass wall allows them to observe the comings and goings of civilians but, *pari passu*, they are themselves visible to civilians who wander in to make enquiries. Civilians are treated courteously enough but the permeability of the guards' enclosure is a matter of complaint. The police, by contrast, have a ground floor office sealed from the public by an opaque door, and that office *is* liked. Seclusion becomes desirable when enclosures are surrounded by public territory housing the volatile civilian.

A judge remarked that 'Wood Green (and similar courts of its generation) might turn out to be China-clippers of court building, taking one particular line of evolution, insulation of the court-room, as far as it can usefully go.' The courtrooms are insulated indeed. Around them there are double sets of ceremonial doors advertising the scale of the transition that must be made when people quit public space for an area reserved for a set of very special activities, when they leave the smoky, sometimes bustling world of the waiting areas for the decorum of the court. The doors mark a frontier between a private, sober inside and a wilder outside, between the orderliness of the trial and the disorderliness of the lobbies, between the sphere of the civilian and that of the professional. Judges will occasionally set ushers to police the lobbies, silencing those whose noise has irrupted into their courtroom, bringing outer disorder into their preserves.

The most emphatic physical segregation is between those groups and users whose collision would present the greatest danger. A Crown Court is a Chinese box of what architects call 'circulation areas'. Juries, remanded and committed defendants, judges, civilians, and administrative staff are sealed inside their own discrete spaces. They will arrive at the Crown Court through special doorways and then enter a series of parallel universes composed entirely of separate rooms, corridors, stairways, and lifts. They will be able to move unmolested, unwatched by others who may occasion them harm, contaminate their minds, or embarrass their performance, progressing back and forth between their private enclosures in cells, jury waiting areas, or chambers and their appointed entrances in the dock, jury box, or bench. The symbolic, moral, and functional divisions of the court are there mirrored perfectly by its material structure.

The most charged spaces of all are those available to civilians. However elaborate the architecture of a Crown Court may be, however many hidden passages and lifts and stairways may have been installed, not all professionals can remain shielded forever. Professionals must often move through public space, either because no other route is available to them or because an assignation with outside professionals or civilians is the express object of their journey. Probation officers meet with defendants, counsel with clients, solicitors' and Crown Prosecution Service clerks with counsel, solicitors' clerks with defendants, ushers with witnesses. Professionals moving in space will not see one single universe of events and people at all. On the contrary, theirs is a pragmatically motivated vision. Probation officers will scout waiting areas for young black defendants to divert from custody and for trials and pleas requiring social inquiry reports. Security staff patrol for potentially unruly supporters. Crown Prosecution Service clerks look for prosecution counsel, detectives for prosecution witnesses, defence counsel for defendants, the list officer for cases 'going short', and the jury bailiff for courtrooms where juries are about to be empanelled. Ushers look for counsel. Spectators look for entertainment. They simply do not see the same world. Tasks plot areas and modes of engagement, shaping which civilians will be seen and recognized, how they are defined, and how they will be approached.

Unless civilians are absent, professionals tend to be somewhat wary when they are loose and working in public space. Consider the risks. At first hand, there is a danger of embarrassment and confrontation. Professionals wish to avoid the civilians who can do them damage: defence counsel, prosecution counsel, and probation officers shun victims and prosecution witnesses; police officers shun defendants and defence witnesses; and all are worried about jurors and 'followers'. At second hand, there are threats to the confidentiality of knowledge: conferences about strategy, criminal history, witnesses, and evidence are all regularly exposed to eavesdropping by outsiders in the public areas of a court.

Public space is dangerous because the clear oppositions of a trial leak out to affect every relationship contracted in and about the courtroom. Court and judicial staff, counsel, and others may all become embroiled in the partisanship of a process grounded in an immediate and intense conflict. Any prolonged physical or symbolic proximity to lay protagonists can impugn their own appearance of neutrality. And the outcome is that they work strenuously to advertise their disinterestedness, their moral distance from an all-too-close contention and contenders. Ushers and clerks are loath to be seen lingering in the company of civilians lest it be thought that they and their court have grown partial. They are wary, anxious about the identities of strangers around them, guarded about the overtures they may receive and the responses that will have to be made in return. Strangers' questions cannot be answered too fulsomely. There will be caution about discussing anything but the barest bones of a trial, its likely duration and timing. Little else will be volunteered until the stranger has been established as safe, a fellow-professional, a noncombatant, or an expert witness, a person who cannot damage the standing of the staff or allow the staff to damage the innocence of the civilian. There must be no semblance of coaching, of partisanship, or of a seepage of significant knowledge from the protected world of the courtroom to the outer world of witnesses in waiting.

During the time of my study, in April 1990, the court moved from what the architects knew as a 'crash building' and barristers as 'the bunker' to a new piece of monumental architecture called by some counsel the *Palais de Justice*. One of the most widely and frequently criticized features of the old building had been the canteen. The bunker had contained no separate jurors' dining room or barristers' mess. Witnesses, jurors, defendants, police officers, court staff, and counsel were obliged to eat and drink together promiscuously and in close association. No one knew who their neighbour might be. There was an ever-present possibility of conversations being overheard.

Worse, there might be confrontation, intimidation, or violence. Contamination is one of the principal preoccupations of court staff and the canteen exacerbated its risks to such a pitch that those who ate and drank did so nervously and circumspectly.

Professionals may be recognized in public space. Counsel are usually robed and wigged; ushers and clerks are gowned; police officers are commonly to be seen carrying bundles of evidence and blue cardboard files; Crown Prosecution Service and solicitors' clerks walk about with great armfuls of paper. Professionals as a group appear familiar enough even without their distinctive symbols of office. Their deportment will signify that they are in court to do a job, that they have been in such situations before, and it is not *their* personal problems which are about to be exposed. Civilians do not bear any such insignia, although stereotypy provides the professional with a rough, working guide to their identities. In public encounters, one can never be sure of the other, and the professional's response is to be suspicious. Those, like secretaries and administrators, who need have no personal dealings with the public, will walk briskly through common space, eyes fixed firmly in front of them, signalling their reluctance to become involved in transactions with strangers. They will be invisible, incurious, and purposeless, 'nonpersons' not wishing to see or be seen. Others, like counsel and police officers, who *do* have business in public space, will none the less attempt to construct what might be called a personal exclusion zone around themselves, keeping strangers at bay, staring before them or at their papers, showing little curiosity about the affairs of their neighbours, visibly not eavesdropping themselves, engrossed in their own small activities, speaking defensively when they have to and never about the substance of cases. Very typically, they will keep physically apart from the anonymous public of witnesses, jurors, victims, and defendants about them.

Nevertheless, there are a number of particularly difficult times for professionals stationed in public space. During the prelude to a trial especially, the distancing techniques which I have described cannot be deployed with complete rigour. At the very beginning of a trial, civilian identities are especially unclear: yet it is precisely then that professionals will have to approach strangers to construct the teams that will be set to work in the courtroom. Police officers will have to establish that their witnesses are present (although those witnesses should be known to them through previous encounters). Defence counsel will have to meet their clients and solicitors' clerks. Crown Prosecution Service clerks have to search for prosecution witnesses. In the early part of the day, then, professionals may be seen treading gingerly through public space, trying to find the strangers they need without exposing themselves to any of the dangers that strangers can offer. Counsel will promenade the concourse areas, avoiding eye contact but yet calling out names to the world at large. Rough typifications will be applied to fix probable identities before closer contact is made. A civilian wearing a suit *might* be a doctor, an expert witness. Another *might* be a solicitor's clerk or probation officer. But counsel cannot be sure and they make their approaches with visible trepidation. One intermediate solution is to summon a civilian or fellow professional by tannoy, but problems of identification remain. The stranger who approaches the reception desk need not be the person whom the professional is actually seeking, he or she could well be another, and anxious overtures will still have to be made.

That is a most taxing portion of the day, when professionals have to make forays into the crowd, unable to maintain the physical, moral, and symbolic distance which usually insulates them from bruising connections. But it is a period that does not last long. Those who throng public space in a Crown Court will eventually resolve themselves quite neatly into functional huddles centred on recognizable professionals, and it is the identity of the professional which labels that of the civilian participants. Defendants and their supporters are those who may be seen in the company of solicitors' clerks and defence counsel (defence counsel themselves bear distinctive white briefs tied with a pink ribbon). Prosecution witnesses will often be attended by police officers.

Some professionals, counsel and police officers above all, have to spend considerable lengths of time waiting outside courtrooms to be called or for trials to begin. But it will be at that point, when civilians have lost their anonymity and the crowd has broken up into an archipelago of little groupings, that public space will have lost some of its risks. Professionals-in-waiting are able to map the territory around them and position themselves appropriately and safely. The identity of the professional forming the nucleus of each group will enable others to know how to place themselves. Defence counsel will avoid the clusters formed by prosecution counsel, police officers, and Crown Prosecution Service clerks. Prosecution counsel will remove themselves from huddles of solicitors' clerks, defendants, and defence counsel. In short, the behaviour of professionals-in-waiting reinforces a social geography which is produced daily by the pragmatic demands and abiding conflicts of the trial.

There is a second time of danger, at the other pole of the trial, and that is when courtrooms empty into the small public spaces that adjoin them. When trials adjourn or end, all the different participants in an antagonistic process are at risk of spilling out together and in a state of agitation. Victims and their followers may be aggrieved at acquittals, mild sentences, or what is said in mitigation speeches. Defendants and *their* followers may resent convictions and sentences and what has been said by the prosecution and prosecution witnesses. There may be anger at questions put by counsel in opening, closing, or cross-examination. In short, civilians and professionals will be only too readily identifiable at an excitable time, and it is then that outbursts are likely to occur. Remedies are simple. Evacuations will be staggered by command or informal understanding: defendants or victims are sometimes instructed to delay leaving the court until opposing witnesses have had time to depart. More simply still, counsel will either linger until others have dispersed or else make a dash for the doors themselves, shaking off those who attempt to detain them, quitting the hazards of public space rapidly and somewhat unceremoniously, gaxing fixedly ahead all the while.

Some Implications

Some time ago, David Downes remarked that victims are an admixture of pariah and saint. Voluntary associations devoted to victims have certainly complained how uncommonly difficult it has been to raise money in their support (Rock 1990). The stigma of victimization seems to be real enough but its origins are obscure. Feminists would argue that the very word 'victim' conjures up an imagery of defeat, defilement, and passivity (Chambers and Millar 1983: 5). But something more may be involved. Knowledge about victims is affected by its phenomenology. Being a victim of burglary, assault, or theft is often a comparatively private matter, an isolated, unframed, disordered, and passing experience lacking in visibility or collective organization. Few will see or know the victim *as* a victim. One of the very few roles in which victims *are* seen publicly is as a witness in a criminal trial. It is then that they come openly before outsiders and professionals in the criminal justice system.

It is probable that the formal identity of victims is entwined with that of prosecution witnesses. And victims themselves experience their attendance at court chiefly as a succession of lengthy and lonely periods of waiting in public space, periods which culminate in the pain of cross-examination. Instead of vindication and redress, they may find themselves treated as unclean and untruthful. Prosecution counsel turn out not to be 'their' champions at all: indeed, they are enjoined not to speak to them lest they be accused of coaching witnesses. Others will shun them. Their sole companion might be a guardian police officer, and any conversation they have will almost certainly be intermittent and sparse.[10] In short, the English criminal justice system prepares a formal role for victims which is somewhat isolated and volatile, a source of difficulty for the professional, best kept morally and physically apart. If that is indeed the case, the pariah status of victims may be a little less puzzling.

References

Bennett, W., and Feldman, M. (1981), *Reconstructing Reality in the Courtroom*. London: Tavistock.

Best, W. (1922), *The Principles of the Law of Evidence*, 12th edn., ed. S. Phipson. London: Sweet and Maxwell.

Chambers, G. and Millar, A. (1983), *Investigating Sexual Assault*. Edinburgh: Scottish Office Central Research Unit, HMSO.

Coser, L., ed. (1968), *The Functions of Social Conflict*. London: Routledge & Kegan Paul.

Cross, R. (1980), *An Outline of the Law of Evidence*. London: Butterworth.

Garfinkel, H. (1956), 'Conditions of Successful Degradation Ceremonies', *American Journal of Sociology*, 61.

General Council of the Bar (1989), *Code of Conduct for the Bar of England and Wales*. London: Bar Council.

Goffman, E. (1959), *The Presentation of Self in Everyday Life*. New York: Doubleday–Anchor.

Rock, P. (1990), *Helping Victims of Crime: The Home Office and the Rise of Victim Support in England and Wales*. Oxford: Oxford University Press.

Saward, J. (1990), *Rape: My Story*. London: Bloomsbury.

Twining, W. (1985), *Theories of Evidence: Bentham and Wigmore*. London: Weidenfeld & Nicolson.

[10] All that is beginning to change with the introduction of 'victim in court projects' in a number of Crown Courts, including the court at Wood Green itself. Prosecution witnesses report that the very offer of support by volunteers has a significance that extends beyond the provision of practical assistance. It dispels some of the experience of isolation, confusion, and estrangement that can accompany attendance at court.

[7]
Introduction: The Emergence of Criminological Theory

> ... the turning to activity for the sake of form is a historical event, taking place at different times for each form. The progress of a preliminary form is gradual; at some point, perhaps never precisely specifiable, the form is 'ready' to become the object, rather than the instrument, of human activity.[2]

In 1968, Sellin argued that 'no adequate history of criminology exists and the textbooks give scanty information'.[3] What he argued then tends to hold now. There is no adequate history and there certainly never will be a *definitive* history of criminology. The discipline is an accumulation of theories, each with its own protagonists; each with its special environment of politics, methods and preoccupations; and each offering a different vantage point from which to tell a story about its evolution and the evolution of the other theories that are its complements and rivals. That, in part, is what theorists and theories are supposed to *do*: they supply a way of seeing the world and the ideas and scholarship that exist within it. Above all, they furnish the criteria by which argument should be judged. Thus the highest form of criminology was held by the positivist, Hermann Mannheim, to be positivism;[4] by the phenomenologists, Jack Douglas (see Chapter 25) and David Matza,[5] to be existentialism;[6] by the quantitative criminologists Cohn and Farrington to be quantitative criminology;[7] by the radicals Taylor, Walton and Young (see Chapter 30)[8] to be socialist criminology (thinking having passed through 'classical' and 'positivist' phases *en route*[9]); by the feminist Carol Smart[10] to be a 'gendered theory';[11] by the post-modernist Alison Young to be post-modernist criminology;[12] and by yet other criminologists professing no theoretical allegiance to be a dogged practicality.[13] Amidst such diversity, there is unlikely to be accord about the substance, structure and significance of any imaginable intellectual history.[14]

All that discord has been magnified by the unscholarly emotions that crime and its analysis can engender. Many criminologists have seen crime as an urgent moral, political, theological or social problem that demands redress, and they have been apt to display a passion and an impatience with one another for failing to agree on what was so evidently wrong and on what must be done to put it right. Nuances and differences can become exaggerated all the while as scholars struggle to make sense of a confused world, seize on a few variables as the key to knowledge, engage in what Douglas called 'simplificationism',[15] and dismiss as knaves or fools those who do not share their appreciation of the overriding importance of race, gender, control, victims, age, space, inequality, the State or censure.

There is then a problem of multiplying stories which is compounded because theories interweave and thinkers themselves are not consistent over time. Criminologists have their own changing lives, and they can always reinterpret what they praised or neglected in the past[16] (Karl Mannheim observed that 'we become aware that we are observing the world from a moving staircase, from a dynamic platform ... ').[17] Being observed from a moving platform, being reconstructed with each telling, intellectual history changes every time it is written. There can be no timeless, neutral, atheoretical point from which criminology can be seen as it really is, once and for all, beyond contradiction. Quite the reverse.

Academic criminology will always be confused, and that is probably its greatest strength: a single, bold theory could never match the complexity, flux and ambiguity of the social world. Criminology is centred on a terrain defined *empirically* by the presence of crime and criminals; the State and the criminal law; the police, courts and prisons; victims and bystanders; reform, deterrence, treatment and punishment. Its character has been fixed chiefly by its *substance* rather than by any coherence or unity of analytic approach. It is what David Downes once called a '*rendez-vous* subject' – a subject where people from different theoretical backgrounds and with very different purposes meet and sometimes fail to understand one another.

A Pragmatic Framework

Any proposal to give order to the history of such a discipline will always be seen by some as a little arbitrary. Yet there are a number of perfectly sensible ways of representing the development of theory: one would be to focus on the political evolution of criminology (which is what Smart and Taylor, Walton and Young did); another might focus on its interaction with internal and external intellectual movements (a history of ideas). A third would attend to its response to problems and events in the world about it (and to riots, scandals and crime waves in particular); a fourth would examine the effects of changing financial and political sponsorship; a fifth could turn to the emergence of new facts and new kinds of facts (the impact of crime surveys and self-report studies has been especially momentous),[18] and a sixth would translate criminology into an artifact of institutions and controlling activities (the approach taken by those working in the tradition of Michel Foucault). I shall take yet another course and treat thought as a concomitant of practical activity.

People cannot readily develop ideas without social organization, and social organization itself flows from and refracts ideas. In this sense, criminology could be described as a form of reasoning that shapes and is shaped by the institutions in which it is set. Presenting it as the emerging outcome of social relations seems as helpful a way as any of framing a collection of papers on the history of criminology.[19]

Some time ago, Hermann Mannheim observed that:

> By and large, criminological research has hitherto usually been done in one of the following ways:
>
> (a) by private individuals working alone: for example John Howard, Jeremy Bentham, Henry Mayhew;
> (b) by public officials having access to official material, but working in a private capacity, for example A.M. Guerry, Cesare Lombroso ... ;
> (c) by public officials working in an official capacity, e.g. Charles Goring, Norwood East;
> (d) by university departments or individual teachers, which is the largest capacity;
> (e) by Government departments or special research units. ...[20]

Mannheim may not have explicitly intended it, but his apparently static classification is also a way of presenting a *history* of criminological theory. It is in effect an evolutionary morphology, a series of steps laid out in time. Defined in this manner, criminology becomes a succession of phases in which ideas, institutions and people have been clustered together in configurations that are both distinct and intertwined. Characteristically, the beginnings of each phase are attended by great intellectual activity and the energetic building of social worlds, activity that subsides only to be superseded by a comparable excitement heralding the emergence of a new phase. It is something of that pattern of succession that I shall trace in the rest of this Introduction, and I shall do so by concentrating on the emergence of criminology in one illustrative country, Britain. To attempt more would be to adopt an impossibly large canvas; however, it is reasonable to suppose that, appropriately modified, the argument should hold elsewhere.[21]

The First Phase: Ur-Criminology (1500–1750)

Like many another social science, the study of crime and criminals[22] first appeared some 200 years ago out of a great unorganized mass of allegation, speculation and observation that may be described variously as ur-criminology, proto-criminology or shadow criminology, a mass composed of the writings of dramatists;[23] clergymen (and prison chaplains in particular); pamphleteers and essayists; journalists and doctors; lawyers[24] and magistrates;[25] reformers and would-be reformers; and anyone else who could claim an expertise on prisons and prisoners, the thieves' republics and the beggars' guilds. It was supposed to fascinate, inform, amuse, appal and instruct by turns (although its tone was sometimes little more than mock-serious). It relied on anecdote, reminiscence and the authority of social position; indeed, scholars now quarrel about the exact importance of what was said and written.[26]

Ur-criminology was the offspring of those who professed principally to have a practical or experiential stake in the problems of crime, criminals and prisoners (there was almost no other legitimate source of expertise to be invoked); having such a stake, its public posture was principally that of the man (rarely the woman) of affairs, the administrator, the reformer and the moralizer. It came to air most of the common-sense explanations of crime available then and now, anticipating the axioms of a later academic criminology, and propounding what may be recognized as primitive versions of functionalism,[27] *anomie* theory,[28] social ecology,[29] 'labelling theory', control theory, eugenics, 'crime prevention through environmental design' and much else. But its most prevalent mode of argument, as Faller shows in this volume (see Chapter 3) was to insist on the simple depravity of the criminal.[30] Crime was a moral matter. Ur-criminology itself was characteristically idiosyncratic; it was part of no cultivated tradition and lacked obvious cumulative development.

Ur-criminologists did not profess to be academic teachers or researchers of knowledge about crime. There were no such roles for them to take. Seen retrospectively through the lens offered by academic criminology, their work often looks crude; not written in a professional language; informed by no common store of knowledge; underwritten by no sound methodology; checked by no ordered process of criticism; unorchestrated, and lacking apprentices willing to learn and transmit its ideas. It was a succession of starts that appeared to tail off into inconsequentiality. In short, it was not 'institutionalized'. It could not evolve or reproduce itself as a specific discourse (although it did persist at the margins for a very long while and was part of what Garland called 'wider cultural traditions and understandings'). It did not resemble the familiar and conventional forms of contemporary criminology and is now largely forgotten as a particular way of describing the world,[31] its achievements no longer valued and its authors omitted from the lists of criminology's 'heroic' ancestors.[32] At best, as David Garland reminded me, it represents a form of common sense about crime and morals with which academic criminology is in competition.

The Second Phase: Philanthropy and the Emergence of Criminology (1750–1830)

It was not until the end of the 18th century that the first makings of a recognizably scientific criminology began to emerge. These crystallized little by little out of ur-criminology, doing so as part of a larger process of institution-building. This was, in effect, the kind of knowledge that arose when people gathered together and organized themselves to plan the construction of what would later be called the criminal justice systems[33] of Europe and North America.

A scholarly discipline requires an identity, a sense of its past and place in the world, a recognizable membership and regular meetings, orderly methods of communication, and a common language and reservoir of ideas. It requires a collective life.[34]

Criminology was first given that life by groups promoting reform of the law, prisons, asylums and courts. Penal reform was one of the big ideas of the industrializing world, an ingredient of the political assault on what were held to be the brutalities, corruption and inefficiencies of the *ancien régime*. In Britain, it was associated particularly with the national[35] and international[36] networks of radical Whigs, Nonconformists and Utilitarians who championed a more rational, effective and just machinery of control, surveillance and rehabilitation. Theirs was a practical, religious and philosophical inspiration that later writers would describe as 'moral'. They conceived wrong-doing to be a matter of choices badly formulated, of wills poorly disciplined, of spirituality undernourished, of populations under-controlled and of consciences underdeveloped. Their answer was to adopt what Barnes and Teeters once called 'the civilized attitude toward crime'.[37] They planned a system of policing that was supposed to lead inexorably to the detection and capture of malefactors; a system of fair trials that did away with trading justice; and a system of correctional institutions that classified and segregated different categories of prisoners before subjecting them to carefully calibrated inducements and punishments that would be neither gratuitously lenient nor excessively severe. The whole amounted to a machine, as Bentham put it, to 'grind rogues honest', a machine that would instil habits of sobriety, respect and discipline.[38]

The civilized attitude was espoused by reformers who banded themselves together into literary, philanthropic and scientific societies, into the Prison Discipline Society, the Society for the Suppression of Vice and the Society for Bettering the Condition of the Poor. They analysed, compared and planned. They conducted surveys, toured prisons and institutions in Europe and the US, and discovered new facts. They experimented with models of reform and with a novel social engineering whose most significant blueprints were Colquhoun's *A Treatise on the Police of the Metropolis*,[39] Bentham's *Panopticon or Inspection House* (see Chapter 5),[40] Romilly's *Observations on the Criminal Law of England* (see Chapter 4),[41] Beccaria's *On Crimes and Punishments*[42] and Howard's *The State of the Prisons in England and Wales*.[43] Although not uniform, in combination, theirs was a moral philosophy of action and a political economy of control that enjoined the State to play a greater and more effective role in the regulation of its subjects.

Some of the certainties of that new knowledge disappeared soon enough, and the reforming associations themselves were often insubstantial bases for organized enquiry (their most prominent members tended to be independent men and women of means who had no need or wish to fashion enduring careers for themselves as reformers).[44] The second phase did not last long (its very success brought about its own end), but it *had* generated the prospect of thinking about crime in a novel way:[45] theirs was a practical, enquiring, comparative methodology that rested on frequent communication between men and women embarked on the same work.

By 1830, Philips argued, the reformers' project had been largely accomplished: 'the recognizably "modern" model of administration and enforcement of the law had arrived in England – with a paid, bureaucratic police force, stipendiary magistrates, and a system of prosecution designed to encourage prosecution whenever an offence was committed'.[46] He could well have added the workhouses, the prisons, the factories and the asylums to the new model State that the reformers had constructed.[47]

The Third Phase: Criminology and the Administered State (1830–1890)

Officials of that new State had a new confidence in their ability to govern,[48] a confidence resting in part on a growing foundation of knowledge supplied by new groups of experts. The beginnings of an efficient, administered State were accompanied by the collection of reports, accounts and numerical information. The legitimating rationality of the new politics required that it should do so. The scale of the economic, political and social transformations it was undergoing (changes in what were known collectively as 'moral' conditions) was too momentous to warrant neglect. Although it would not do to exaggerate the scale of the new administration (the Home Office, for instance, was only a very small institution at first),[49] there was an appetite for, and a rhetoric about, information that was quite distinctive of early Victorian government.

The first consequence was that the State acquired its own administrative science – the tellingly-named statistics – a science that dealt with 'the collation, classification, and discussion of facts bearing on the condition of a state or community'.[50] The term 'statistics' first came into use in 1787[51] and 'statistician' in 1825. Their emergence is significant, signalling the coming of fact (and numerical facts especially) as a constitutive feature of government in Gradgrind's world. Chevalier remarked of that period in France that there was a 'determination to obtain figures for everything, to measure everything, to know everything, but to know it by numbers, [it was an] encyclopedic hunger. ... '[52]

The first national census was conducted in England and Wales in 1801, and the new police, judicial and penal authorities began to produce their own annual statistical returns after the 1830s. The Metropolitan Police Criminal Returns were published first in 1831,[53] and the Prison Inspectors, established in 1835, issued annual 'published reports [that] exercised a growing influence on official and parliamentary opinion. ... '[54] Knowledge about the incidence and distribution of moral conditions became increasingly quantified in the first half of the 19th century,[55] recorded rates becoming accepted as a superior (perhaps the only really authoritative) source of evidence.[56] Rates had the appearance of being suprahuman, impersonal, reliable and *objective*.[57]

The relations between those recorded rates lent themselves to a new science of social physics that could work with all the rigour of the newly ascendant positive sciences of nature. Quetelet, Guerry and Fletcher (see Chapter 8)[58] above all represented society as a massive field of forces amenable to precise measurement and prediction. Crime itself was conceived to be marked by regularities that co-varied with other regularities in determinate fashion. The Frenchman, Guerry, could argue in 1833 that 'there are no reasonable grounds to deny that moral as well as physical events are subject to invariable laws', while the Belgian, Quetelet, claimed in 1846 that 'we can count in advance how many individuals will soil their hands with the blood of their fellows, how many will be swindlers, how many poisoners, almost as we can number in advance the births and deaths that will take place. ... '[59] Criminology (and British criminology in particular) took shape in that third phase as a distinctive, specialist study with its own subject matter. It became a handmaiden of a State that was useful to management and numerate in its methods. Garland described the tradition so formed as 'institutionally-based [and] administratively-oriented'.[60]

The second consequence of the rise of the administered State was the flowering of professions whose job was to staff and legitimate the proliferating institutions of the new criminal justice system. If the reformed courts, prisons and mental hospitals were part of a new and purportedly efficient machinery of social regulation, if they were based on the application of a new rationality, their very claim to authority was grounded in the assertion of an expert *knowledge* of social problems. It was the professional, not the laity, who knew what was *really* wrong with the patient, the defendant and the inmate, and it was the professional who had the right to diagnose and cure;[61] for, as Freidson observed, 'any profession bases its claim for its position on the possession of a skill so esoteric or complex that non-members of the profession cannot perform the work safely or satisfactorily and cannot even evaluate the work properly'.[62]

The professions and quasi-professions of social control increasingly came into their own after the 1830s. Scull has written of 'the remarkable expansion and reconstitution of the traditional professions ... '[63] during that period. The British Medical Association had its origins in a professional body, the Provincial, Medical and Surgical Association, founded in 1832.[64] The Law Society had its direct antecedent in a body established in 1825. The Council of Legal Education was established in 1852,[65] and the Association of Medical Officers of Asylums and Hospitals for the Insane in 1841.[66] It was in 1848 that the word 'professional' first took its contemporary meaning of one who engages in a skilled or learned profession, and it was in 1856 that the word 'professionalism' came first to be used.

Control over problematic populations became vested more and more heavily in the professions who had charge of the legal system, the prisons and asylums. Convict management itself became a cadet science[67] – *la science pénitentiare* – canvassed energetically by prison congresses and International Commissions.[68]

In the framing of legitimacy, the moral was to be joined by the scientific,[69] and it was medicine that came to be regarded as the archetypal science of social conditions in the 19th century. What other comparable profession was on hand to apply science to wrongdoers?[70] What better metaphor could there be for the scientific rehabilitation of the criminal than the prevention of ills and the diagnosis and cure of the sick (particularly in a nation where society was still occasionally likened to a body and its limbs)? Sim claimed that 'the prison became a laboratory in which the advice and expertise of the medical profession, both physicians and psychiatrists, was geared to reintegrating the confined back to normality'.[71] Criminology became, in major measure, applied medicine. Indeed, Drapkin chose to capture the whole of what he called the 'pre-Lombrosian' phase of the criminological search for causes (all that took place before 1875) as the work of 'physiognomists, phrenologists, early psychiatrists, and prison physicians'.[72] So powerful did medicine become that even now it is still a little difficult to avoid using its terminology in talking about crime and its treatment. It was believed that criminology

> ... would replace the ineffectual niceties of legal punishment by practical technologies involving diagnostic, prevention and curative instruments and institutions. Criminality was now a knowable positive entity which, with the aid of scientific investigation and appropriate technique, could be removed from the social body.[73]

Some of the very first men to call themselves 'criminologists' were doctors and psychiatrists. In and about the prisons, asylums and the medical schools, they classified, measured, compared, examined and treated pathological individuals and their conditions.[74] Deviance was transformed into a property of the individual, akin to physical disorder and defined, with the coming of genetics, as a transmitted pathology. Garland wrote that there

> ... existed in Britain, from the 1860s onward, a distinctive, indigenous tradition of applied medico-legal science which was sponsored by the penal and psychiatric establishments, and it was this tradition which formed the theoretical and professional space within which 'criminological science' was first developed in this country.[75]

The Fourth Phase: Criminology as an Academic Pursuit (1880–1960)

By the end of the 19th century, enough had been accomplished to persuade people to view the infant criminology as a special way of looking at the world, somewhat distinct from its parent disciplines, and amenable to detachment from the practical and immediate pursuits of the prison and asylum.[76] It could be taught and analysed as if it were an increasingly independent application of sociology, law, statistics or medicine. In this beginning of separation, it followed the more general pattern of increasing specialization of disciplines that characterized the universities of the time.[77]

The very word 'criminology' seems to have been first used in the 1850s and come into more general use in the 1890s when the subject began to be taught in the universities of western Europe, at Marburg, Bordeaux, Lyons, Naples, Vienna and Pavia.[78] Under the spell of Cesare Lombroso,[79] in particular, criminology busied itself with measuring, comparing and classifying types of deviant.[80] Criminology was to be a positive science, wedded to the goal of changing crime and criminals, captured by David Matza's title of 'correctionalism'.[81] It was reformist, practical, interventionist and implicated in policy-making, moved, Stan Cohen remarked, 'by a sense of faith: that the business of crime and delinquency control could be made not only more efficient but also more human'.[82]

Having a foundation in moral philosophy,[83] criminology's new step-parents themselves invariably claimed a mandate to correct. Thus the new science of sociology was designed principally to put the world right.[84] One of the original and most eminent of the sociologists of crime, Émile Durkheim, saw himself as a healer of social ills, as one who could diagnose and prescribe, incorporating and reconciling in a positive science the descriptive and the normative.[85] The early Marxist criminologists – Willem Bonger[86] and Rusche and Kirchheimer – anticipated the revolution when social pathologies would disappear. It was perhaps only in an occasional study conducted in the US that the correctionalist and political impulses of criminology were restrained,[87] and even there they were strong.[88] Cavan observed of the sociology department at the University of Chicago, the country's pre-eminent early department (indeed the country's only department of substance until the early 1930s), that 'sociology had to find its way out of the general social reform temper of the times and separate itself from the religious slant of the university itself'.[89]

According to Garland, criminology was first taught in a British university, the University of Birmingham, in the early 1920s by M. Hamblin Smith, the first man to call himself a criminologist in Britain[90] (it was perhaps unremarkable that Hamblin Smith had previously been a psychiatrically-trained prison medical officer). But it was to be some time before criminology became established in British universities, and it did so as a consequence of the flight of intellectuals from fascism in Europe in the 1930s. Three criminologists, Hermann Mannheim, Max Grünhut and Leon Radzinowicz, fled to found and then control criminology in the Universities of London, Oxford and Cambridge respectively, [91] carrying with them the emerging European criminological synthesis. Enrico Ferri's former student, Radzinowicz, established a Department of Criminal Science at Cambridge in 1941.[92] Mannheim, a Prussian judge and former student of law and political science at the Universities of Munich, Freiburg, Strasburg and Königsberg,[93] was to teach courses on crime and punishment under the aegis of the Sociology Department of the London School of Economics. In the academic session 1938–39, for instance, he delivered ten lectures on the 'Aims and History of Punishment'[94] with the professed purpose of 'giving an insight into the philosophical basis of punishment and into the historical development of the various penal methods'. He recommended the reading of English works, principally the Webbs's *English Prisons under Local Government*, John Howard's *The State of the Prisons*, Page's *Crime and the Community* and Fox's *The Modern English Prison*. His 'Principles of Criminology' course addressed the following:

> I. The meaning, methods and tasks of Criminology. The use of Criminal Statistics. History and present character of crime in England and abroad. II. The criminal types and the causes of crime: (1) Physical factors: The anthropological theory (Lombroso). The biological theory. The significance of physical defects. (2) Psychological and pathological factors: The intelligence of the criminal. Insanity and mental deficiency. The psychoanalytical explanation ... (3) Alcoholism. Climate. Race and Religion. (4) The age factor ... (5) The sex factor: Female delinquency and prostitution. (6) Social and economic factors: Family, broken homes, housing, delinquency areas ... The gang. Profession and Unemployment. Poverty. Economic and political crises.

Mannheim advised his students to read Bonger's *Introduction to Criminology*, Burt's *The Young Delinquent* (see Chapter 17), Calvert's *The Lawbreaker* and Hamblin Smith's *The Psychology of the Criminal* (see Chapter 16). It may be seen that his criminology was substantively defined, problem-driven and theoretically eclectic, a blend of the sociological, psychological, legal, historical and statistical.

British criminology in the 1940s and 1950s remained largely in that vein. It was to be fused with the activities of reforming organizations such as the Howard League, above all with the League's campaigns against corporal and capital punishment. It was periodically to import theoretical inspiration from its parent disciplines, from psychoanalysis, and from the sociology of Harvard, Columbia and Chicago Universities especially. The more adventurous criminologists toyed variously with (1) Merton's *anomie* theory[95] (Terence Morris did so in *Pentonville*[96] and, a little later, David Downes was to do so in *The Delinquent Solution*);[97] (2) with the social ecology of the 'Chicago School'[98] (it was Terence Morris who did so again in *The Criminal Area*)[99] and (3) with subcultural theory (John Mays did so in *Growing Up in the City*[100] (see Chapters 18, 21 and 22). But criminology remained the obvious progeny of medicine, psychology, the law and statistics, a progeny that served the State and the agencies and organizations of the criminal justice system. Consider the manifesto for the new *British Journal of Delinquency* that was published first in July 1950 under the editorship of Hermann Mannheim, a lawyer, Emmanuel Miller, a psychiatrist, and Edward Glover, a psychoanalyst. Its first editorial proclaimed that:

> ... the *British Journal of Delinquency* is not in the customary sense a clinical journal. Clinical contributions will of course receive special consideration, but it is hoped to publish articles, both theoretical and practical, from trained workers in the various departments of criminology; namely, medical psychology, psychiatry, psychoanalysis, organic medicine, educational psychology, sociology, economics, anthropology, psycho-biology and statistics; also from social workers, probation officers, prison and other institutional personnel, and from forensic specialists whose work brings them into intimate contact with the problem of delinquency.[101]

The Fifth Phase: The Institutionalization of Criminology

What brought an end to that phase was a triple reflex, stirred in large measure by the rise and subsequent decline in the rate of expansion of the British university. Halsey observes that 'the expansion of higher education in Britain started from a tiny base at the beginning of the century, with an accelerated growth in the 1960s and 1970s'.[102] The number of British universities grew from 30 in the early 1960s to 52 by the end of the 1980s. The number of academic staff rose from 19,000 to 46,000, and the number of full-time students in higher education from 130,000 to 600,000 (with an additional 350,000 part-time students attending higher education).

Criminology was part of that wave. A large group, 58 per cent, of a 1986 survey of criminologists teaching in universities had been appointed in the 1970s, and 30 per cent in the years between 1973 and 1976 alone.[103] The criminologists of the new wave began to write vigorously: about half the books published in the field between 1973 and 1986 appeared in the years between 1976 and 1979. Criminology became expansive, argumentative, exuberant, factious and open: in all that explosiveness, its history resembled a perfectly familiar pattern in the more general evolution of scientific knowledge.[104]

Criminology attained a critical mass of ambitious and energetic young scholars who looked to each other rather than to their elders for intellectual stimulation, formed an 'invisible college', and achieved a temporary social and intellectual independence.[105] It was what an influential criminologist working in the Home Office Research Unit was later to call 'glitzy'. For a while, indeed, criminology seemed to be free and imaginative; those visiting Britain would sometimes observe that the most promising work was being accomplished here.

In November 1968, the younger 'sociologists of deviance' broke away to found their own National Deviancy Symposium at the University of York.[106] In its first year, members heard papers by Jock Young on 'The Police as Negotiators of Reality, Translators of Phantasy and Amplifiers of Deviancy', Ian Taylor on 'Football Mad: A Speculative Sociology of Football "Hooliganism"', and Stan Cohen on 'Middle Class Violence'.[107] The Young Turks turned away from a past defined as positivistic, jostling one another to give new definition to their discipline. They flirted with the phenomenological and interactionist (largely under the influence of the Americans Edwin Lemert[108] and Howard Becker;[109] Chapters 23 and 24), with the radical (under the influence principally of the American, Alvin Gouldner)[110] and, later, with the feminist (first under the influence of Frances Heidensohn[111] – see Chapter 27 – and then, decisively, under that of Carol Smart). It was a time marked by what Gouldner once called the 'conflictual validation of the self', a validation wrought by pitting oneself against what was held to be an old and obfuscating atheoretical orthodoxy. So eager were the Young Turks to shed tradition that they eschewed the very title of criminology for a while, preferring instead to call themselves sociologists of deviance.

Stan Cohen reflected that what marked the new sociology of deviance was its insistence on a 'continuity with sociology' (the study of deviance was to move away from the statistical, the medical and the legal); its identification of 'the significance of social control' in the delineation of a field (deviance resided as much in the interaction between definers, definitions and defined as in any properties of the defined themselves); 'appreciation' (deviance was taken to be a symbolic, meaningful activity), and 'the political implications of studying deviance' (the study of deviance was itself conceived to be a politically-charged process).[112]

The new was deemed to be radical, a word which held irresoluble ambiguity. For some, radicalism signified an intellectual regeneration of criminology, a return to roots, back to Marx, to Schutz and to the Chicago School: it was a celebration of the theoretical as an independent pursuit that bowed to no questions of politics or policy. Those radicals sought to affiliate themselves intellectually with the new sociologies of North America, and with the early work and aspirations of the Society for the Study of Social Problems in particular. For others, radicalism meant a veering to the politics of the left and a realignment of criminology with the deviant, the dispossessed and the dissident (it was a time described by Haug and Sussman as the end of professional autonomy and the revolt of the client).[113] The latter sought to join with the Claimants' Union, the Mental Patients' Union and PROP (Preservation of the Rights of Prisoners), the prisoners' union.[114]

The sociology of deviance bifurcated, one part to pursue a more austerely scholarly conception of the discipline, the other to politicize scholarship (the massively influential *The New Criminology* being its fruit). Both wings sought to distance themselves from Government, one to practise a new disinterestedness and the other a partisanship.[115] Those, then, were the first two tines of the triple-pronged reflex: a rejection of criminology conceived chiefly to be a medico-legal practice and a redefinition of the relation between criminology and the State.

The third reflex came a little later, although it was presaged in the founding of the Home Office Research Unit in 1956, of the Cambridge Institute of Criminology in 1959 and the Oxford Centre for Criminological Research in 1976. Criminology was to become institutionalized. In part, the combination of a critical mass of scholars and a Government willing to fund research on social problems (Barbara Wootton once defined a social problem as something on which Governments are prepared to spend money) encouraged a growing number of criminologists to consider themselves a somewhat separate community, severing themselves from their parent departments of sociology, psychology, law and social administration.

Criminologists had become more numerous, interconnected and mature, more confident in themselves, and more professional in their work. They had settled down, no longer so quarrelsome or vexed about the collective purpose and identity of their discipline. In settling down, they allowed earlier disputes to fragment criminology into what Garland calls 'lively sub-specialisms', areas kept apart by a consensual avoidance of confrontation and an abandonment of the attempt to create one master paradigm for the entire discipline. People may not have agreed, but they agreed not to disagree too rancorously. In that, too, their history was quite characteristic of the scientific community at large.[116]

Moreover and most importantly, after the early 1980s criminologists were responding to new facts and new events, and to crime surveys in particular. Crime surveys had been initiated in the 1970s and 1980s[117] chiefly, as the phrase went, to 'improve the criminal justice data base'. Instead of relying on figures of crimes reported to the police, those conducting surveys questioned members of households directly about their experience of criminal incidents. One of the two authors of the *British Crime Survey* argued that 'the main rationale of victim surveys ... has been to get a better estimate of the number of certain crimes actually occurring than is available from offences recorded by the police'.[118] Surveys were supposed to aid computations of the extent and distribution of crime, but they did much more as well. Their main effect on criminological theory was to transform conceptions of the character, incidence and impact of crime in everyday life. Crime appeared to be more extensive, more frequent and more debilitating than had been supposed.

Theorists were obliged, as the authors of the *Islington Crime Survey* reveal in this volume (see Chapter 33), to come to terms with the implications of a new portrait of their subject. So overwhelming and indisputable did the new facts appear to many, that a change occurred in the working consensus concerning the nature of the social world and the science that should address it. It was no longer possible for radical, libertarian and phenomenological criminologists to deny the social reality of crime as a significant crisis in the lives of ordinary men and women (especially women). Perhaps, they conceded, the correctionalists had not been so wrong after all. Perhaps they *did* have some understanding of the way the world worked. Crime ceased to be treated merely as a figment of an absolutist morality or as an ideological conceit devised to distract the proletariat from real problems of oppression and exploitation. The sociology of deviance and the new criminology became solicitous, where once they had dismissed the false consciousness of the unenlightened. There was less certainty about the grand metaphysics of the 1970s, a new humility about 'who knows best',[119] and a new deference to the empirical. Radicals and non-radicals alike began to interest themselves in quite mundane questions that some of them would never have considered before. They explored the effects of police strategy, housing design, street planning and street lighting on crime prevention.

In effect, the criminology of the 1980s and 1990s was renewed by that combination of empiricism and the withering away of big theory,[120] but it was to be renewal in a cold climate. Criminology was more purposeful, but it was also necessarily more defensive. It faced the urgent problem of determining how it could compete for funds and students in a world made newly uncertain by Government policy. From about 1978 especially, it seemed as if the environment of British higher education had turned inhospitable. Universities contracted. The number of teaching staff shrank by 11 per cent between 1979–80 and 1984–85.[121] The postgraduate training budget of the Economic and Social Research Council declined, so that it was lower in real terms in 1986 than it had been in 1974. The very name of the Economic and Social Research Council was changed from the Social Science Research Council because Keith Joseph, the then Minister of Education, had declared that 'there was no social science'. Strong (although ultimately inaccurate) rumours circulated that the Home Office Research Unit was about to be disbanded. Financial cuts seemed to be ubiquitous and threatening although, in the case of criminology, the cuts were more fictitious than real, part of a prudent official rhetoric of parsimony rather than any loss of funding in real terms.[122] However, British universities and polytechnics could no longer be so sure of themselves and their place in the world. They certainly could no longer depend on stable State funding over the quinquennia. They had to *compete* for resources under a new Manchester liberalism that made market imperatives seem ever more imperious.

Towards the end of the 1980s and the beginning of the 1990s, then, criminologists took on another incarnation. They became entrepreneurs, bringing about the emergence of what one elder criminological statesman has been wont to call the 'Jock Young PLC phenomenon'. Criminologists became entrepreneurial *fauts de mieux*, founding courses for practitioners, chasing research grants and contracts, responding to what were hoped might become new student markets.[123]

What had once been distinctive of North America[124] was to be emulated in the UK.[125] Centres of criminology and criminal justice sprang up at the universities of Edinburgh in 1974, Sheffield in 1979, Bristol in 1986, Exeter in 1987, Loughborough (the Midlands Centre) in 1990, Manchester in 1988, Brunel in 1990, London in 1991, Wales in 1992–93, and elsewhere. And the consequence has been that criminological theorizing in Britain has entered a newly quiescent phase: it is less strident, less acrimonious, less argumentative, more middle-aged and more preoccupied with the empirical than the abstract, with the 'policy-relevant' than the scientifically revolutionary, directed at the practitioner as much as at the intellectual.[126] Criminologists are not all now in some simple happy state of accord with one another but, instead of entering into rank confrontation and public debate, they seem tacitly to have agreed to pull in their horns and resort to a more conventional strategy of mutual neglect. It is as if many opposing criminologists have elected not to meet each other, engage in each other's projects, criticize each other's work or, in effect, even acknowledge each other's presence. They have embarked on what Becher called 'the systematic avoidance of controversy'.[127] Theoretical debate has lapsed for want of angry champions. For a while, at least, criminology has become a 'normal science' in an institutional *laager*.

Implications

In reading what is to come, it would be best to recall how turbulent has been the making of criminology, a turbulence that has affected what people have had to say. Intellectual history is a special pursuit, exploring ideas about the history of ideas, and it can tease itself in disconcerting ways, being at once subject and object, looping back on itself as it becomes the very thing it discusses. In such a setting, commentary is often far from innocent. On the contrary, it may be motivated, designed to achieve particular ends, turning its audience towards certain conclusions. The timing of arguments and the location and relations of authors need to be heeded.

What follows is a collection of examples of argument and of argument about argument from the different phases of criminology's history. It is difficult to be comprehensive in a single volume, and readers will be able to point to other papers that could very well have been included. But the book should convey not only how criminological theory defines and arranges its themes, but also how it can change over time (and yet remain very much the same too), and that is more than valid in an introduction to a difficult field of enquiry.

The Organization of this Book

The essays reproduced in this collection illustrate the principal phases of the evolution of criminology. Part I begins with two specimen pieces of ur-criminology: a characteristic description of the cheating underworld of Elizabethan London that hints at possibilities of subcultural analysis, and a pamphlet from Daniel Defoe (see Chapter 2) that attempts to lodge the causes of crime and criminality in the moral workings of an hierarchical society. They are complemented by a contemporary commentary on the causal themes underpinning the writing of early criminal biography, themes that illuminate the *moral* and the individual in criminal behaviour, themes that were to be taken forward into the next phase, the phase of social engineering.

Examples of such engineering are reproduced in Part II. They include Bentham's concrete proposals for a new house of correction (that were never actually to be executed), Colquhoun's tally of the indigent and criminal classes of Great Britain, and Sir Samuel Romilly's plans to reform the penal law (see Chapter 4). Bentham and Colquhoun were concerned principally with strategies of *control* (see Chapters 5 and 6), Romilly with justice, but all three were highly influential in their day. They contributed to a new criminal justice system embedded in a new State, though contemporary historians and criminologists interpret them in a variety of ways. The construction of a new system of formal control at a time of political, economic and social change is no small matter, and commentators have read into it a great span of meanings, from the benign to the malign, from altruism to a conspiracy of class interests, from the spiritual to the material. Michael Ignatieff's 'State, Civil Society, and Total Institutions' (see Chapter 7) usefully reviews some of those debates about the motives and significance of the philanthropic reforms of the late 18th and early 19th century.

In Part III the new administered State, its statistics and its new statistical science are represented by Joseph Fletcher (see Chapter 8), a barrister, an Inspector of Schools and Honorary Secretary of the Statistical Society of London, whose *Summary of the Moral Statistics of England and Wales* represents an impressive attempt to apply Guerry's and Quetelet's methods to the moral conditions of the UK. At a greater distance, the excerpt from Gatrell's and Hadden's 'Criminal Statistics and their Interpretation' (see Chapter 9) offers an overview of the emergence and character of 19th-century criminal statistics.

The other stream of administrative criminology, the medical, is championed with fervour and some adulation by a prison chaplain of 15 years' standing in his introduction to the English edition of Lombroso's and Ferrero's *The Female Offender* (see Chapter 10). It is as fervently criticized (and for many decisively) by Charles Goring, the man who brought criminal anthropology before the bar of statistics and found it wanting. Lucia Zedner and David Garland pronounce on these and other debates in the middle and later parts of the 19th century, tracing the transition from the moral to the scientific, the rise of medicine and the lingering importance of Lombroso in the administrative response to crime.

Mayhew's observations on the pickpockets of mid-19th century London (see Chapter 14) mark the resilience of shadow criminology, a criminology that could well have prefigured the later subcultural, ecological and ethnographic work of the Chicago School and the symbolic interactionists (it was perhaps only a want of institutional continuity that prevented the earlier emergence of a social anthropology of crime). Levin and Lindesmith (himself no mean interactionist) were evidently impressed by the subterranean criminology of the 19th century, their laudatory piece on Fletcher and Mayhew being moderately successful in its attempt to sustain an otherwise neglected criminology (see Chapter 15).

Part IV on criminology as an academic pursuit records the 20th-century blossoming of the medical model of crime and criminology in the work of Hamblin Smith and Burt (see Chapters 16 and 17), but it also includes a selection of some of the significant criminological ideas that were beginning to spread from America. Subcultural analysis, social ecology and *anomie* theory were *the* paradigmatic theories of the 1930s, 1940s and 1950s. These were subject to repeated and fruitful adaptation by the 'normal' scientists of crime.

The final section narrates the rise and partial demise of theoretical criminology, a wave that began in the heady early days of the sociology of deviance (with Edwin Lemert playing John the Baptist to Howard Becker); a wave that engendered the Society for the Study of Social Problems and the National Deviancy Conference; that bifurcated into the political and the scholarly; was reproached by feminism; and finally turned against itself under the weight of a new practicality hostile to any thought seeming to lack utility. There is a new impatience with the speculative and the disinterested, and some would oblige criminology to pay every inch and centimetre of its way. No doubt the utilitarian will itself be displaced in time as a younger generation, not yet heard, takes stock and moves theory on again.

Notes

1 I am most grateful to Roger Hood and Elaine Player for their advice in the preparation of this book. I am especially grateful to David Garland, Robert Reiner and Lucia Zedner who read earlier drafts of the Introduction and made numerous perceptive and helpful comments.
2 R. Weingartner, 'Form and Content in Simmel's Philosophy of Life' in K. Wolff (ed.) (1959), *Essays on Sociology, Philosophy and Aesthetics*, New York: Harper Torchbooks, p. 48.
3 T. Sellin (1968), 'Criminology', *International Encyclopedia of the Social Sciences*, New York: Macmillan and the Free Press, Vol. 3, p. 508.
4 H. Mannheim (1960), *Pioneers in Criminology*, London: Stevens and Sons.
5 D. Matza (1969), *Becoming Deviant*, Englewood Cliffs, New Jersey: Prentice-Hall.
6 See J. Douglas (ed.) (1972), *Research on Deviance*, New York: Random House (Chapter 25).
7 See E. Cohn and D. Farrington (1990), 'Differences between British and American Criminology: An Analysis of Citations', *The British Journal of Criminology*, **30** (4), Autumn.
8 I. Taylor, P. Walton and J. Young (1973), *The New Criminology*, London: Routledge and Kegan Paul.
9 Ibid.
10 C. Smart (1977), *Women, Crime and Criminology*, London: Routledge and Kegan Paul.
11 Ibid.
12 A. Young (1991), 'Feminism and the Body of Criminology', paper delivered at the British Criminology Conference, York.
13 See J. Wilson (1975), *Thinking About Crime*, New York: Basic Books.
14 There are, to be sure, limits on the scope and character of discord. The world 'can answer back'.

As David Garland remarked, 'the historical record may not bear any and every interpretation' (personal comunication).

15 J. Douglas (1977), *The Nude Beach*, Beverly Hills: Sage, p. 51.

16 A prime example is Jock Young who was eventually to dismiss the criminology of his own *The New Criminology* as 'left idealism'. See J. Lea and J. Young (1984), *What is to be Done about Law and Order?*, Harmondsworth: Penguin.

17 From a letter to K. Wolff in K. Wolff, 'The Sociology of Knowledge and Sociological Theory' in L. Gross (ed.) (1959), *Symposium on Sociological Theory*, New York: Harper and Row, p. 571.

18 See J. Lowman and B. MacLean (1992) (eds), *Realist Criminology in the 1990s*, Toronto: University of Toronto Press.

19 Consider Geertz's observation about how the social anthropologists of knowledge conceive 'ideation'. Ideation, he says, 'subtle or otherwise, is a cultural artifact ... it is something to be characterized by construing its expressions in terms of the activities that sustain them'; C. Geertz (1983), 'The Way we Think Now' in *Local Knowledge*, New York: Basic Books, p. 152.

20 H. Mannheim (1965), *Comparative Criminology*, London: Routledge and Kegan Paul, Vol. 1, p. 79.

21 It should, of course, be remembered that the world never lays itself out very neatly, and that there are always problems of overlap and confusion at the boundaries of the phases I shall describe. Phases were never as simple or as homogeneous as a brief introduction might suggest. What I offer is simply a way of thinking about the growth of criminology, not an iron pattern into which everything *must* fit.

22 I take it that the sciences of punishment and control – penology and criminal justice – are separate, sister disciplines.

23 See, for example, the collections represented by A. Judges (1930), *The Elizabethan Underworld*, London: Routledge and Sons.

24 A prime instance of the genre is A. Knapp and W. Baldwin (1824), *The New Newgate Calendar: being Interesting Memoirs of Notorious Characters, Who have been convicted of Outrages on THE LAWS OF ENGLAND, During the Seventeenth century, brought forward to the Present Time, Chronologically Arranged ... with occasional Essays on Crimes and Punishments, Original Anecdotes, and Observations on Particular Cases: Explanations of the Criminal Laws, the Speeches, Confessions, and LAST EXCLAMATIONS OF SUFFERERS, to which is added A correct Account of the Various Modes of Punishment of Criminals in different Parts of the World*, London: J. Robins and Co., in numerous volumes.

25 See H. Fielding (1751), *An Enquiry into the Causes of the Late Increase of Robbers*, London: no named publisher; and H. Fielding (1755), *A Plan for Preventing Robberies within Twenty Miles of London*, London: A. Millar.

26 See, for instance, J. Samaha (1974), *Law and Order in Historical Perspective: The Case of Elizabethan Essex*, London: Academic Press.

27 See B. Mandeville (1714), *The Fable of the Bees*, reprinted in 1962 by Capricorn, New York.

28 See T. Nourse (1700), *Compania Foelix*, London: Bennet.

29 T. Beames (1850), *The Rookeries of London*, London: Thomas Bosworth.

30 L. Faller (1987), *Turned to Account: The Forms and Functions of Criminal Biography in Late Seventeenth- and Early Eighteenth-Century England*, Cambridge: Cambridge University Press (Chapter 3).

31 Some forms of ur-criminology persisted. Most notable was the work of Henry Mayhew in the 1860s (see Chapter 15, Levin and Lindesmith in this volume). A kind of shadow criminology still remains in popular accounts of heinous crimes and criminals (see, for instance, J. Paisnel (1972), *The Beast of Jersey*, London: New English Library; F. Schreiber (1983), *The Shoemaker*, Harmondsworth: Penguin; J. Ritchie (1988), *Myra Hindley: Inside the Mind of a Murderess*, London: Angus and Robertson; A. Rule (1980), *The Stranger Beside Me*, New York: New American Library, and D. Yallop (1981), *Deliver Us from Evil*, London: MacDonald Futura); in picture books of crime; coffee-table criminology and the like (see *The Boys' Book of Scotland Yard*, London: Burke, 1951; C. Wilson and D. Seaman (1983), *Encyclopedia of Modern Murder*, London: Pan; and H. Keating (1982), *Great Crimes* London: Artus). Shadow criminology itself is not at all uniform in its seriousness, aspirations or impact. Whilst much is knowingly sensationalist, at its best (in

the work of Roger Graeff, Norman Mailer and Tony Parker especially), it is an important and useful complement to academic criminology proper. 'They are,' observed Robert Reiner, Private Communication, 'doing outside academe what we're trying to do inside. It's only the lack of an institutional base which makes them different.'

32 See D. Crane (1972), *Invisible Colleges: Diffusion of Knowledge in Scientific Communities*, Chicago: University of Chicago Press, esp. p. 74.

33 The term would never have been in use at the time. Then and now the word 'system' conveys too great an impression of coherence, interrelatedness and formal structure. The term 'loose-coupling' captures the relations between institutions far better than 'system'. See K. Weick (1976), 'Educational Organizations as Loosely Coupled Systems', *Administrative Science Quarterly*, **21** (1), March.

34 See R. King and J. Brownell (1966), *The Curriculum and the Disciplines of Knowledge*, New York: John Wiley.

35 See J. Rose (1980), *Elizabeth Fry*, London: Macmillan, p. 111.

36 Members of the Society for the Improvement of Prison Discipline corresponded regularly with such bodies as the Boston Prison Discipline Association and the Philadelphia Association, for instance.

37 H. Barnes and N. Teeters (1943), *New Horizons in Criminology*, New York: Prentice-Hall, p. 11.

38 See, for example, M. Ignatieff (1978), *A Just Measure of Pain*, New York: Pantheon Books.

39 P. Colquhoun (1806), *A Treatise on the Police of the Metropolis*, London: C. Dilly.

40 J. Bentham (1791), *Panopticon or Inspection House*, London: T. Payne (Chapter 5).

41 Sir S. Romilly (1810), *Observations on the Criminal Law of England*, London: T. Cadell and W. Davies (Chapter 4).

42 C. Beccaria (1764), *On Crimes and Punishments*; reprinted by Bobbs-Merrill, Indianapolis, 1963.

43 J. Howard (1784), *The State of the Prisons in England and Wales*, Warrington: William Eyres, 3rd edition.

44 Frouxides described them as a 'few philanthropically-minded individuals with humane and often strong religious convictions'. He noted that members of the Society for the Improvement of Prison Discipline included two Dukes, a Marquis, ten Earls, three Lord Bishops, 11 Lords, and 19 Members of Parliament. S. Frouxides (1983), *The English Prison Inspectorate 1835–1877*, Ph.D. dissertation, London School of Economics, pp. 24–25, 97.

45 See R. Reiner, 'British Criminology and the State' in P. Rock (ed.) (1988), *A History of British Criminology*, Oxford: Clarendon Press.

46 D. Philips, 'A New Engine of Power and Authority' in V. Gatrell, B. Lenman and G. Parker (eds) (1980), *Crime and the Law: The Social History of Crime in Western Europe since 1500*, London: Europa Publications, p. 188.

47 To be sure, there was, as Lucia Zedner has reminded me, a 'marked gap between the rhetoric of reform and its achievement'. Much continued as before. It was to be some while before the prisons were uniformly brought under the State, for instance. But the emergence of a new rhetoric was to be very important for the charting of new forms of knowledge about moral conditions.

48 A confidence built, in part, on experience acquired in managing large groups of men and resources in the Napoleonic wars.

49 See R. Nelson (1969), *The Home Office, 1782–1801*, Durham NC: Duke University Press.

50 *The Shorter Oxford English Dictionary*.

51 Jeremy Bentham had been an early advocate of the orderly collection of data on convictions for crime. In *A View of the Hard-Labour Bill* published in 1778, he described statistical returns as a kind of political barometer that would assist the legislator.

52 L. Chevalier (1973), *Labouring Classes and Dangerous Classes in Paris During the First Half of the Nineteenth Century*, London: Routledge and Kegan Paul, p. 43.

53 See D. Jones (1982), *Crime, Protest, Community and Police in Nineteenth Century Britain*, London: Routledge and Kegan Paul, p. 117.

54 L. Fox (1934), *The Modern English Prison*, London: George Routledge and Sons, p. 17.

55 The establishment of an adequate system of data collection and analysis was a lengthy process that met with occasional resistance. It was perhaps not until 1857 that criminal statistics were prepared with any efficiency. See L. Radzinowicz and R. Hood, *The Emergence of Penal Policy*, *op. cit.*, Ch. 4.

56 Indeed, it was a long while before their authority was challenged. See, for example, J. Douglas (1967), *The Social Meanings of Suicide*, Princeton: Princeton University Press.
57 See É. Durkheim (1892), *Le Suicide*; reprinted by Routledge and Kegan Paul in 1952.
58 See J. Fletcher (1849), 'Moral and Educational Statistics of England and Wales', *Journal of the Statistical Society*, **12**, pp. 151–76 (Chapter 8).
59 In L. Radzinowicz and R. Hood (1990), *The Emergence of Penal Policy in Victorian and Edwardian England*, Oxford: Clarendon Press, p. 51.
60 D. Garland, 'British Criminology before 1935' in P. Rock (ed.), *A History of British Criminology, op cit.*, p. 7.
61 See T. Caplow (1964), *The Sociology of Work*, New York: McGraw-Hill, pp. 139–40.
62 E. Freidson (1970), *Profession of Medicine*, New York: Dodd, Mead, p. 45.
63 A. Scull (1991), *The Asylum as Utopia: W.A.F. Browne and the Mid-Nineteenth Century Consolidation of Psychiatry*, London: Tavistock/Routledge, p. x.
64 See P. Elliott (1972), *The Sociology of the Professions*, London: Macmillan, p. 38.
65 See A. Carr-Saunders and P. Wilson (1933), *The Professions*, London: Frank Cass, p. 8.
66 See A. Scull (1979), *Museums of Madness: The Social Organization of Insanity in Nineteenth-Century England*, Harmondsworth, Middlesex: Allen Lane, p. 164.
67 See J. Barry, 'A. Maconochie' in H. Mannheim (ed.) (1960), *Pioneers in Criminology*, London: Stevens.
68 See Sir E. Ruggles-Brise (1921), *The English Prison System*, London: Macmillan, p. XIII.
69 Vinogradoff talked about a 'craving for a scientific treatment of the problems of social life' (P. Vinogradoff (1904), *The Teaching of Sir Henry Maine*, quoted in L. Radzinowicz and R. Hood, *The Emergence of Penal Policy, op. cit.*, p. 30). It must however be noted that prison chaplains at first retained great power and prison chapels were the most imposing single buildings in the new penitentiaries. Perhaps the turning point was the publication of Darwin's *The Origin of Species* in 1859. See M. Wiener (1990), *Reconstructing the Criminal*, Cambridge: Cambridge University Press.
70 Eight of the 'pioneers of criminology' nominated by Hermann Mannheim were lawyers, five were members of the medical profession, two were sociologists, one was a naval officer and geographer, and one was an architect. See *Pioneers in Criminology, op. cit.*, p. 2.
71 J. Sim (1990), *Medical Power in Prisons: The Prison Medical Service in England 1774–1989*, Milton Keynes: Open University Press, p. 9.
72 I. Drapkin, 'Criminology: Intellectual History' in S. Kadish (ed.) (1983), *Encylopedia of Crime and Justice*, New York: The Free Press, p. 551.
73 D. Garland (1985), *Punishment and Welfare: A History of Penal Strategies*, Aldershot: Gower, p. 106.
74 See H. Ellis (1890), *The Criminal*, London: Walter Scott.
75 D. Garland, 'British Criminology before 1935' in P. Rock, *A History of British Criminology, op. cit.*, p. 2.
76 Garland writes of the process that 'criminology's entry into the universities and colleges has produced some small degree of independence and critical distance from the institutions of crime control ... ' (D. Garland, 'Criminological Knowledge and its Relation to Power', unpublished paper, p. 8). It was partly in that sense that it became an activity for the 'sake of form', as identified by Weingartner and Simmel.
77 See T. Caplow and R. McGee (1958), *The Academic Marketplace*, New York: Basic Books, pp. 14–15.
78 The second edition of the *Oxford English Dictionary* records the earliest reference to the word 'criminologist' in the *Saturday Review* of 1857. It took time for the new terminology to become established. The French word '*criminologie*' *was* claimed variously to have been used first in 1888 (*Lexis: Dictionnaire de la langue française*, Paris: Librairie Larousse, 1975) and 1890 (*Dictionnaire alphabétique et analogique de la langue française*, Paris: Presses Universitaires de France, 1953). Until quite a late date, some dictionaries and encyclopaedias contain no reference to criminology (see, for example, the *Dictionnaire Général de la Langue Française*, Paris: Librairie Delagrave, 1932).

79 As Garland, Zedner and others have indicated, Lombroso's influence was *relatively* weak in the UK despite attempts by his disciples to evangelize his work. Lombroso does nevertheless represent the zenith of criminal anthropology and he was much discussed (as excerpts in this volume illustrate).
80 A spell that was never universal in its effects and certainly weakened by the onslaught of Charles Goring (Chapter 11 from Goring's *The English Convict* in this volume). London: HMSO.
81 D. Matza (1969), *Becoming Deviant*, Englewood Cliffs, New Jersey: Prentice-Hall.
82 S. Cohen, 'Criminology' in A. Kuper and J. Kuper (eds) (1985), *The Social Science Encyclopedia*, London: Routledge, p. 174.
83 Indeed, Burton Clark called moral philosophy the 'mother subject' of political science, a science that in its turn gave birth to economics and then to sociology. See B. Clark (1987), *The Academic Life: Small Worlds, Different Worlds*, Princeton, NJ: Carnegie Foundation, p. 28.
84 See, for instance, G. Hawthorne (1976), *Enlightenment and Despair: A History of Sociology*, Cambridge: Cambridge University Press.
85 See É. Durkheim (1895), *The Rules of Sociological Method*; republished by the Free Press in 1958.
86 See W. Bonger (1916), *Criminology and Economic Conditions*, Boston: Little, Brown & Co.
87 See, for example, J. Landesco (1923), *Organized Crime in Chicago*, Chicago: University of Chicago Press, and F. Thrasher (1927), *The Gang*, Chicago: University of Chicago Press.
88 See J. Carey (1975), *Sociology and Public Affairs: The Chicago School*, Beverley Hills: Sage.
89 R. Cavan (1983), 'The Chicago School of Sociology: 1918–1933', *Urban Life*, **11** (4), January, p. 409.
90 D. Garland, 'British Criminology before 1935', *op cit.*, p. 8. London: Methuen & Co Ltd., (Chapter 16).
91 See J.P. Martin, 'The Development of Criminology in Britain 1948–60' in P. Rock (ed.), *A History of British Criminology*, *op. cit.*, p. 36.
92 See L. Radzinowicz (1988), *The Cambridge Institute of Criminology: Its Background and Scope*, London: HMSO.
93 See L. Radzinowicz; 'Hermann Mannheim (1889–1974)' in Lord Blake and C. Nicholls (1986), *The Dictionary of National Biography 1971–80*, Oxford: Oxford University Press.
94 *The Calendar of the London School of Economics and Political Science for the Forty-Fourth Session 1938–39*, The London School of Economics, 1938, p. 243.
95 R.K. Merton (1938), 'Social Structure and Anomie', *American Sociological Review*, **3** (Chapter 18).
96 T.P. and P. Morris (1963), *Pentonville*, London: Routledge and Kegan Paul.
97 D. Downes (1966), *The Delinquent Solution*, London: Routledge and Kegan Paul (Chapter 22).
98 See, for example, R. Park and E. Burgess (eds) (1925), *The City*, Chicago: University of Chicago Press.
99 T. Morris (1957), *The Criminal Area*, London: Routledge and Kegan Paul (Chapter 21).
100 J. Mays (1954), *Growing Up in the City*, Liverpool: Liverpool University Press.
101 *The British Journal of Delinquency*, 1950, **1** (1), July.
102 A. Halsey (1992), *Decline of Donnish Dominion*, Oxford: Clarendon Press, p. 4.
103 See P. Rock, 'The Present State of British Criminology' in P. Rock (ed.), *A History of British Criminology*, *op. cit*, p. 59.
104 See D. Crane (1972), *Invisible Colleges: Diffusion of Knowledge in Scientific Communities*, Chicago: University of Chicago Press, p. 2.
105 In all this, their evolution closely followed the model described by Griffith and Mullins who also talk about the emergence of networks out of an initial surge of interest in new ways of looking at the world, the growth of external boundaries and the eventual institutionalization of an approach. See B. Griffith and N. Mullins (1972), 'Coherent Groups in Scientific Change', *Science*, No. 177.
106 A collection of the National Deviance Conference papers published in 1971 under the editorship of Stan Cohen as *Images of Deviance*, Harmondsworth: Penguin Books.
107 *Register of Abstracts 1968–1972*, Sheffield: National Deviancy Conference, 1973.
108 See E.M. Lemert (1951), *Social Pathology*, New York: McGraw-Hill. (Chapter 23).
109 In particular, see H.S. Becker (1963), *Outsiders*, The Free Press, A Division of Macmillan Inc. (Chapter 24).

110 See A. Gouldner (1968), *The Coming Crisis of Western Sociology*, London: Heinemann.
111 See F. Heidensohn (1968), 'The Deviance of Women: A Critique and an Enquiry', *British Journal of Sociology*, **19**; London: Routledge and Kegan Paul (Chapter 27).
112 See S. Cohen, 'Criminology and the Sociology of Deviance in Britain' in P. Rock and M. McIntosh (eds) (1974), *Deviance and Social Control*, London: Tavistock Publications Limited (Chapter 26).
113 See M. Haug and M. Sussman (1969), 'Professional Autonomy and the Revolt of the Client', *Social Problems*, **17** (2), Fall.
114 See M. Fitzgerald (1971), *Prisoners in Revolt*, Harmondsworth: Penguin.
115 All that would change in time, as I narrate in 'The Present State of British Criminology', *op. cit.* There was, in any event, not much evidence that the State was very interested in the Young Turks during the late 1960s and early 1970s.
116 See D. Crane, *Invisible Colleges*, *op. cit.*, p. 37.
117 The large, originating survey was the American National Crime Survey, conducted first in 1966 and consolidated in 1972 (see C. Kalish *et al.* (1974), *Crimes and Victims*, Washington DC: US Department of Justice). It was followed by comparable (although smaller) surveys in England and Wales in 1982, in Canada in 1983 and elsewhere. One of the pioneering British crime surveys was R. Sparks, H. Genn and D. Dodd (1977), *Surveying Victims*, London: Wiley and Sons.
118 P. Mayhew (1984), 'The Effects of Crime: Victims and the Public', 16th Criminological Research Conference, Council of Europe, Strasbourg, p. 2.
119 For a prescient attack on the doctrine of 'we know best', see S. Cohen, 'It's All Right For You to Talk' in R. Bailey and M. Brake (eds) (1975), *Radical Social Work*, London: Edward Arnold.
120 It is probably true that, under the influence of Foucault and Habermas, penology continues to explore the influence of 'penality' on the social world, but criminology proper now tends to hover around theories of the middle range.
121 *University Statistics 1984–85, Volume One: Students and Staff*, Cheltenham: Universities Statistical Record, 1986.
122 I give precise detail in my 'Present State of British Criminology', *op. cit.*
123 The Midlands Centre for Criminology and Criminal Justice described itself as a response to 'increasing demands for courses in criminology and criminal justice. They have come from two main groups. First, and by far the largest, from professionals working in these fields. ... The second group, new graduates seeking pre-qualifying courses, are usually looking for something to give that edge in a competitive field.'
124 North American centres of criminology were created some 20 to 30 years before their British counterparts: thus the mean year in which 11 major North American centres were founded was 1968; see P. Dresser and K. Hill (eds) (1990), *Research Centers Directory*, Detroit: Gale Research, Vol. 2.
125 Thus the University of Exeter Centre for Police and Criminal Justice Studies asserts that it is intended to 'develop one of the few University postgraduate courses for policemen and people working the broad field of Criminal Justice [and] to create an interface between academics and practitioners on the US model for the study of problems in the Police and Criminal Justice Fields.'
126 In settling down in this manner, if only for a while, it seems to have followed the pattern of other disciplines whose members tend increasingly to avoid controversy. See T. Becher (1989), *Academic Tribes and Territories*, Milton Keynes: Open University Press, p. 99.
127 T. Becher (1989), *Academic Tribes and Territories*, p. 100.

[8]
The Social Organization of a Home Office Initiative

'[The] social world is by no means homogeneous but exhibits a multiform structure. Each of its spheres or regions is both a way of perceiving and a way of understanding the subjective experiences of others.'[2]

1. INTRODUCTION

For a long time, the Home Office could quite reasonably be portrayed as a rather cautious institution that sat at the still centre of the criminal justice system. In an earlier description, I certainly presented it as a relatively inert Department whose officials preferred to manage rather than to innovate, responding to problems and crises as they arose.[3] The few officials with the greatest influence or the greatest expectation of influence, the men and women in the 'fast stream', moved from post to post with such frequency that they formed very few attachments to particular developments in train. The working ideal was to despatch business efficiently but without obvious personal engrossment.[4] All officials were hedged about with legal and quasi-legal precedents restricting new ventures; were apprehensive about displaying undue enthusiasm in an institution where evangelism was considered unseemly; were anxious

---

[1] The research for this paper was commissioned by the Home Office Programme Development Unit, and I am most grateful to Christopher Nuttall for inviting me to work in such an interesting area. Christine Lehman, the head of the Unit, was most helpful throughout and I would like to thank her too. I am indebted to John Carrier, Christine Lehman, Jane Lewis, Shula Ramon, Sally Sainsbury for their help in the preparation of this paper. I am also grateful once again to Seeta Persaud for her work on the thankless task of transcription. David Farrington and David Faulkner read the paper in draft and I would like to thank them for their comments. I am grateful to Kate Harris who undertook the bulk of the statistical data entry and to Audrey Stephenson who heroically completed that task and then moved on to tabular analysis.

[2] A. Schutz, *The Phenomenology of the Social World* (Evanston 1967) p. 139.

[3] See my *Helping Victims of Crime. The Home Office and the Rise of Victim Support in England and Wales* (Oxford 1990).

[4] One of Andrew Rutherford's subjects, described as a senior Home Office official, reported of the 1960s that 'we still thought of ourselves as performing functions and carrying out procedures – we did not, as we do now, see ourselves as personally responsible for achieving results.' Quoted in A. Rutherford, Criminal Justice and the Pursuit of Decency (Oxford 1993) p. 57.

to guard their ministers against embarrassment in a volatile world where embarrassments abound; were enjoined not to encroach unnecessarily on the freedom of the individual; and, as agents of the major paymaster of the criminal justice system, were concerned not to become entangled in new and expensive projects.

All that was to change a little in the 1980s. Innovation and intervention began to be encouraged because it was becoming increasingly apparent to officials and research officers that the conventional repertoire of the criminal justice system was less than effective. Recorded crime was rising inexorably (growing from some half a million offences a year in the 1950s to a million in the mid-1960s, two million in the mid-1970s and three million in the early 1980s) and the old answers seemed to be failing. I reported in *Helping Victims of Crime* how the Permanent Secretary had told a Department seminar in 1980 that, 'on a gloomy view, we seem to be locked into negative forces and negative results. The police and prison service require more and more men and more and more money. But crime increases steadily and becomes nastier, and the prison population rises.'

The decline of faith in stock recipes has been chronicled elsewhere.[5] It was founded on a swelling pessimism about the obstinate growth of crime, a pessimism that was fed, *inter alia*, by Martinson's verdict that 'nothing works' in treatment;[6] by Cohen's philippics about the paradoxes of 'net-widening';[7] and by the Home Office Research Unit's own published conclusions that variations in sentencing[8] and police strategy[9] achieved no apparent impact. What the Canadian criminologist Waller was wont to call the 'three C's of criminal justice, cops, courts and corrections' were found wanting, and officials began to turn elsewhere, to the 'community', to voluntary organizations, alternative sanctions and crime prevention strategies.[10] There was what Hope and Shaw, then of the Home Office Research and Planning Unit, defined as a 'policy drift towards a `community orientation'.'[11]

---

5 *See*, for example, the introduction and first chapter of D. Downes, ed., *Unravelling Criminal Justice* (London 1992), and E. Stockdale and S. Casale, eds., *Criminal Justice Under Stress* (London 1992).

6 *See* R. Martinson, 'What Works? Questions and Answers about penal Reform', The Public Interest (1974) p. 35. D. Lipton, R. Martinson and J. Wilks, *The Effectiveness of Correctional Treatment. A Summary of Treatment Evaluation Studies* (New York 1975).

7 S. Cohen, *Visions of Social Control, Crime, Punishment and Classification* (Cambridge 1985).

8 *See* S. Brody, *The Effectiveness of Sentencing. A Review of the Literature* (London 1976).

9 *See* R. Clarke and M. Hough, *Crime and Police Effectiveness* (London 1984).

10 One clear statement of that new formulation of policy was John Graham's review of crime prevention measures conducted under the aegis of the United Nations. Graham, a member of the Home Office Research and Planning Unit, wrote of 'how the formal processes of criminal justice – apprehending, prosecuting, sentencing, punishing and rehabilitating offenders - have been shown to have only a limited effect on controlling crime... . As a result, criminal policy in many countries has turned towards developing proactive measures to prevent and reduce crime, which are much cheaper than the costs of providing police forces, courts and prisons and would appear to hold out more promise of success in combating the problem of crime. Responsibility for crime prevention has consequently broadened to include agencies and individuals *outside* the criminal justice system.' J. Graham, *Crime Prevention Strategies in Europe and North America* (Helsinki 1990) pp. 6–7.

11 T. Hope and M. Shaw, eds., *Communities and Crime Reduction* (London 1988) p. 203.

The case for greater innovation and intervention had to be constructed. Home Secretaries from Leon Brittan onwards were undoubtedly becoming more active and activist, questioning established practice and talking about the need for demonstrable efficiency, effectiveness and value for money. The Permanent Secretary of the 1980s, Sir Brian Cubbon, was disposed to change. But, above all, the case for experimentation was to be interpreted and enacted by an exceptional man, the Deputy Under-Secretary who assumed control of the Criminal Department in late 1982.[12] That man, David Faulkner, was exceptional in part because he remained responsible for criminal policy for nine years, a long period in a single position for a senior person and one that allowed him to become knowledgeable and engaged. Over that period, he came to shed some of the anonymity and distance of his predecessors, not only initiating ventures but bringing them to a conclusion, and assuming (and being seen by outsiders to assume) a clear personal authorship of specific policies. He was, in short, a highly placed and powerful man who was bolder than most, more open and more candid, one who played an adventurous role within the rules. When he observed that the 'successful Home Office civil servant of the 1990s ... [is] likely to be ... open to new ideas, accessible to the world outside the office, [and] able to communicate effectively with it ... ' he could well have been describing himself as he was in the 1980s.[13] Joined for a while by Ron Clarke and then by Mary Tuck as Heads of the Research and Planning Unit, the Criminal Department of the Home Office became markedly more exploratory in its approach to the world.[14]

One sign of that dawning propensity to innovate and intervene was the adoption of new methods of responding to crime, methods that stressed 'proactivity,[15] prevention[16] and a new collaboration with external bodies, and it was marked by a long chain of events: the establishment of the Crime Prevention Unit in 1983 to 'promote preventative action against crime;' the reconstitution of the Home Office Standing Conference on Crime Prevention in 1983;[17] the interdepartmental injunction to promote 'multi-agency initiatives' that was issued in 1984;[18] the interdepartmental Ministerial Group on Crime Prevention that was set up in 1986; and the Safer Cities Programme and Crime Concern that were announced in March

---

[12] He was to say a year after his appointment as head of the Criminal Department, in 1983, that 'we may be seeing the beginning of a change. This may have been brought about as a reaction to the continuing increase in reported crime and through frustration over the apparent lack of success or lack of resources in meeting it.' 'Crime and the Criminal Justice System', unpublished Howard League Lecture, 19 April 1983

[13] D. Faulkner, 'Continuity and Change in the Home Office' (London 1991) p. 15.

[14] Mary Tuck was to remark in 1988 that 'I believe we are just beginning to emerge from [the] historic period ... which placed control and custody as the central response to crime ... 'Is Criminology Any Use?', paper given at the British Society of Criminology, 18 May 1988.

[15] Some of what was done had its precursors in the United States. *See* D. Rosenbaum, 'The Problem of Crime Control', in D. Rosenbaum, ed., *Community Crime Prevention: Does it Work?* (Beverly Hills, California 1986) esp. p. 11.

[16] *See* N. Tilley, 'Crime Prevention and the Safer Cities Story', 32 *The Howard Journal of Criminal Justice* (1993) no. 1.

[17] *See* K. Heal, 'Crime Prevention in the United Kingdom: From Start to Go', *Home Office Research and Planning Unit Research Bulletin* (1987) p. 10.

[18] *See* 'Crime Prevention', Circular HO 8/84, Home Office, London, 1984.

1988.[19] It was marked too by the acquisition in 1986 of a special annual budget of some half a million pounds within the Research and Planning Unit for demonstration projects in crime prevention. David Faulkner recalled that that budget was not:

> 'Tied down to specific projects agreed in advance with the Treasury or subject to restrictive or artificial evaluative criteria. Nor was it subject to the kind of customer-contractor relationship which can only operate in a setting where the policy and the intended outcomes are rigidly determined in advance. We wanted to be able to put money into encouraging people to do practical things, of an imaginative and innovative kind, to see what worked and what didn't and why. The budget was still to be properly managed and the results properly evaluated, but a project or a scheme was not to be seen as a failure or as an improper use of 'funds just because it did not produce results which had been precisely determined for it in advance, or because it was not of a kind where the results could be precisely determined in advance. It needed a different methodology from the more academic research which the Research and Planning Unit had previously been used to.'[20]

The money enabled the Home Office to:

> 'go out and find out and do things about crime problems in different places, to do something about them or see what could be done about them, to move a team into a location to look at drugs or the situation in a particular housing estate, to set up a project – often with a voluntary organization – and see what it would produce. Work of that kind was being done by others, for example by the NACRO Safe Neighbourhoods Project, but more of it needed to be done and the Home Office needed to give it more specific direction and encouragement.'

Examples of what could be done lay before the Home Office in the work of other governments,[21] for example France (on crime prevention), the Netherlands and the United States (on the role of the prosecution), and Germany (on sentencing and relations between the judiciary and the executive). On programme development, David Faulkner looked to Canada and his former colleague, Christopher Nuttall, who had left the Home Office Research Unit in 1975 for the Ministry of the Solicitor General of Canada, eventually to become Assistant Deputy Solicitor General between 1982 and 1989.[22] In Canada, Nuttall had administered and developed the Ministry's Programs Branch, a Branch which housed a number of divisions and a Consultation Centre that possessed a 'mandate to act as an agent for change ... by ... initiating, assisting and supporting experimental and innovative programs with particular attention to the development of new concepts in criminal justice ... '[23]

During 1989, with the retirement in that year of Rita Maurice as Head of the Home Office Statistical Department and of Mary Tuck as Head of the Research and Planning Unit, the opportunity was taken to create a new post as Head of a combined Research and Statistics

---

19 *See* N. Tilley, *Safer Cities and Community Safety Strategies* (London 1992).

20 Interview. All quotations without footnotes should henceforth be taken to stem from interviews.

21 David Faulkner encouraged the compilation and dissemination of information about initiatives world-wide on the growth of crime prevention. *See* the introduction to J. Graham *op. cit.*, p. 3 (n. 10).

22 I touch on Nuttall's career and working style in Canada in my *A View from the Shadows: The Ministry of the Solicitor General of Canada and the Justice for Victims of Crime Initiative* (Oxford 1986).

23 Solicitor General Canada, *Annual Report 1980–1981* (Ottawa 1981) p. 7.

Department and to advertise it for open competition. Christopher Nuttall applied and was appointed. There were a number of qualities it was hoped he would bring with him, and an imaginative deployment of the development fund was but one, yet he did offer a clear opportunity to channel North American practices directly into the Home Office.[24] That was certainly part of his own reading of why he had been appointed:

> 'I think that one of the reasons why I was actually given the job here was because of that experience in Canada. I think that was one of the things that Faulkner wanted to import from Canada, the notion of programme development.'

And David Faulkner concurred:

> 'the fact that he might try and do some of the things that he did in the Programs Branch at the Solicitor General had crossed my mind.'

On returning to London, Nuttall set about organizing his new department ('I came back with ... the Canadian [idea that] the role of an organization like this was to innovate.') He was in charge of an array of divisions that included a Research and Planning Unit, a Statistics Division and a Crime Prevention Unit. He had also inherited the development budget of £600,000 'in the Research Unit [that] was being used for some sorts of innovative projects but not in the way the Consultation Centre was.' In June 1991, that budget was also to be subjected to the larger process of re-structuring, being given an independent location outside the Research and Planning Unit, a separate identity and administration, a more ambitious purpose and a new name. It was perhaps not surprising that that reborn entity, now known as the Programme Development Unit, should have come more closely to resemble the Consultation Centre in Ottawa. Just as the Consultation Centre had been intended to innovate, experiment and disseminate information, so an internal paper defined programme development as:

> 'A technique which generates information, knowledge and insights by setting up and evaluating experimental and demonstration projects and programmes. Its primary method is to test out innovative ideas (for us, concerned with criminal justice improvement), related to identified needs, in the real world, and then to evaluate and disseminate the results.'[25]

Just as the Programs Branch had not assumed permanent responsibility for new ventures, so the Home Office was not prepared to fund projects indefinitely ('the whole point of this is that this is not something which is ongoing. The whole point is that you try something out and see

[24] Nuttall recalled that programme development was something 'we discussed right from the word go, and I think we even discussed it in my interview for the job'. Yet, he reflected, it was relatively a side issue. There was no reference to programme development in the specifications of Nuttall's new post. After all, supervising an expenditure of half a million pounds on development was not a major responsibility: the Government spent a little less than £7bn on the criminal justice system and the Home Office just under £11,550,000 on crime prevention matters alone in 1989-1990 (*A Digest of Information on the Criminal Justice System*, Home Office, London 1991).

[25] In another paper, the purpose of the Programme Development Unit was described as 'to set up and develop innovative local programmes in the criminal justice field, to ensure that they are properly monitored and evaluated, to disseminate the results and to help with the replication of similar programmes where appropriate.'

whether it works, you evaluate it and then you disseminate the information,' said Christopher Nuttall). Just as the Consultation Centre had appointed national consultants in substantive areas of criminal justice policy, so the new Programme Development Unit was to be staffed by a woman who would 'play exactly the same role' in one of the areas eventually selected for cultivation in the first wave of projects.

There was to be a second direct injection of North American methodology when Christine Lehman was appointed Head of the embryonic Programme Development Unit, charged first with 'setting up' the new organization and then with administering it. In 1986, some six years before that appointment, Christine Lehman had come back to the Home Office from the post of assistant director of a voluntary action centre in Syracuse, New York: 'the thing that was relevant about it was that after a year or two we started to apply for federal funding from the Law Enforcement Assistance Administration, which in the great days of Carter was distributing money out left, right and centre. So we had quite a lot of experience of starting up criminal justice innovative projects, and we did start some quite good ones ... ' During those intervening six years in the Home Office, she had been an official in the Criminal and Prison Departments, and she represented in her working personality a practical synthesis of the different styles of organization and thought prevailing in the criminal justice ministries of the United States and England and Wales, the 'two agendas' as she called them:[26]

> '[It is] not exactly that there were two agendas, but I think Chris [Nuttall] has one very clear agenda for the Programme Development Unit, and that's a very innovative one, based very much on the kind of thing that goes on a lot more in North America generally. But I think the rest of the Office, and thinking at the time of the ... Criminal Department, they are very interested in its policy implications as much as the [in] the innovativeness. So they wanted it very firmly embedded really in the structure of the Office. Which doesn't mean that they wanted to control it, because they obviously don't, but they are very interested in having it be an integrated part of policy as well as Research and Statistics.'

The genealogy of programme development was thus quite transparent. It was mediated by the doings of some four or five people who had come to constitute a small 'policy community'.[27] It married the old policy emphases and the new activism of the Home Office to the innovatory work of the Canadian Ministry of the Solicitor General[28] and some of the practical methods of the United States Law Enforcement Assistance Administration.[29] It was a hybrid, a product of the deliberate blending of organizational styles – of what Strauss once called 'interorganizational negotiation,'[30] and its hybrid qualities showed quite starkly from time to

---

[26] And that made her, Christopher Nuttall remarked, 'unbeatable when it came down to it'.

[27] See D. Marsh and R. Rhodes, *Policy Networks in British Government* (Oxford 1992) p. 22. Nuttall said 'we certainly thought we should be innovative and that was the whole point. Christine had done it in Syracuse. I'd done it in Ottawa. Faulkner was that way inclined. Patten was perfectly willing to innovate.'

[28] Christopher Nuttall reflected that 'it is much more of a Canadian implant than an American one.'

[29] To be sure, as I shall argue, most of the methods employed by the unit were domestic in origin but the American influence was also pronounced.

[30] Anselm Strauss remarked that 'elements in [the] environment [are] literally inside [an] organization itself, in the form of workers carrying the outside into the work of the organization.' *See* his

time. For instance, a number of the applicants for the new development grants were eventually to voice some puzzlement about the terminology of the application form and especially about the phrase 'programme narrative' that headed one section (one successful applicant observed that 'programme narrative' was very strange. I wasn't certain about that,' and another, an experienced employee of NACRO, said of 'programme narrative', 'it seems to be a bit of jargon, really.') The form had borrowed some of its terminology from the National Institute of Justice's *Manual for Evaluation Grants*, a manual familiar to Lehman,[31] and 'programme narrative' was actually part of the language of the funding procedures employed by the United States federal government.[32]

2. PROGRAMME DEVELOPMENT AS A LOOSELY-COUPLED ACTIVITY

The words most frequently employed to describe programme development were 'innovative', 'practical', 'action-based', 'flexible' and 'local'. Programme development was to be innovative in that it would seek out, apply and test new ideas that did not always flow directly from the existing patterns, demands and preoccupations of policy-making within the Office.[33] It should 'enhance' those patterns if possible (indeed, it was supposed to emerge out of them), it should be 'relevant', but room should also be left 'at the margin for other interesting initiatives'.

Innovation would come about if funding were for no more than three years and if it were given to a quantity of small experiments rather than to a few large projects.[34] Experiments limited in size and duration could always be terminated or fostered out to others: their chief object was to supply knowledge. But large projects were at risk of becoming enduring government commitments, expensive 'main programmes', for which there were no committed resources. The Programme Development Unit did not intend to become the author of major policy initiatives itself. That was not supposed to be its function at all.

Programme development was to be local in that it would be based on projects that were themselves rooted in 'real-life situations, frequently in conjunction with the public, voluntary or private service providers'.[35] Its very success was held to depend on the local generation

'Interorganizational Negotiation', 11 *Urban Life* (1 982) p. 352.

[31] She was to say that she had drafted 'an application form and some programme criteria ... having [had] a look at the NIJ guidelines and also ... at forms that other people in the Office used, like C6 and F10 ...'

[32] *Application for Federal Assistance, Standard Form 424 REV 4.88*, was filed amongst the Programme Development Unit's papers. A 'program narrative' was defined on page 13 of the National Institute of Justice's Manual as 'the technical portion of the proposal [which] should consist of [a] clear concise statement of the problem, goals, and objectives of the project ... '

[33] When a Home Office minister announced the first group of projects to be funded, he proclaimed them 'extremely innovative.' 'Michael Jack Announces Funding for Family Violence and Crime Reduction Projects', Home Office Press Release, 26 June 1992.

[34] It had originally been envisaged that funding should be restricted to a mere *two* years. Such limits can create difficulties, particularly in times of economic restraint. One senior probation officer in the Midlands found that his superiors were not prepared to sponsor an application because they had no wish to accept a commitment for funding beyond the three year period.

[35] In the margin of the Unit's copy of a speech by the Home Secretary, a speech that talked of the need for projects to reduce criminality and of how 'success requires good local strategies,' a member of

and ownership of new ideas that were *seen* to be local. A prerequisite for the approval of any new project would be the applicant's capacity to demonstrate local need and local support.[36] After all, it was argued, local bodies knew local needs best and, in the long run, they might well have to assume financial responsibility for projects when Home Office funding came to an end.

Programme development was to be more informal and pragmatic than conventional Home Office practice. Although it should be monitored and evaluated, although the knowledge it produced had to be disseminated (too many projects disappear without trace, it was claimed), it was also to be the offspring of the 'voluntary sector' and the 'community' and it would not do to insist on an undue objectivity, tight procedures and the disciplines of orthodox research. The style of programme development was to be practical, active and colloquial. The phrase used internally to describe its character was 'semi-independent'. Weick would have called it 'loose-coupled', '[loose-]coupled events [being] responsive, *but* ... each event also preserves its own identity and some evidence of its physical or logical separateness ...'[37]

Figuratively, the Programme Development Unit was to be set near the margin between the Home Office and the wider world beyond. Being experimental, innovative and local, retaining a 'discretion to look at new ideas', representing more than a simple reflex to established departmental thinking, it had to be semi-independent of the individual policy divisions. It certainly could not observe conventional 'customer-contractor requirements' which dictated that new ventures must win the explicit approval of particular divisions. *Its* customer was conceived to be the Department as a whole, and it should be broadly acceptable to all parts of the Office, 'cutting out the contractor principle'. Neither should it always be the subject of competitive tendering because that could stifle what was distinctively local, interesting and new.

The Unit would be semi-independent of politicians. Ministers would certainly be asked to consider submissions about broad questions at every important stage, but the usefully innovative and local had to embody more than the current preoccupations of central government. Neither could they be a 'quick fix'.

It had to be semi-independent of its original home, the Research and Planning Unit, because it was inevitable that it would have a 'different view of the world,' a view which would be more experimental and pragmatic, justifying knowledge principally by its utility rather than by the application of strict research canons (programme development, it was argued, 'is closely related to research, but it is not the same. It is less rigorous, more flexible, less objective and more pragmatic.'[38]) Its style would be that of 'action research' that monitored and modified practices as they evolved rather than studied them as if from an impeccable scientific distance. One applicant said later of a meeting with members of the Unit, 'they want something that is

the Unit had inserted a large asterisk and the word 'locality'.

36 Michael Jack's statement of 26 June 1992 talked of 'innovative new *local* responses to crime problems' (emphasis added).

37 K. Weick, 'Educational Organizations as Loosely Coupled Systems', 21 *Administrative Science Quarterly* (1976) p. 3.

38 'What is Programme Development?', Research and Statistics Department Conference, Cambridge, 18-20 July 1991.

contributing to its success, and that is working with the projects, and the shortcomings that it observes are actually changed then and there rather than to sit and watch it fail.'

In a sense, too, the Unit would also have to be semi-independent of the projects. It would not simply react to requests for funding stemming from bodies in the outside world. Rather, it would lay down the broad programme areas within which the new projects would be located as well as something of their structure and functioning. Projects would be both innovative and local, on the one hand, and guided from the centre, on the other; programme development itself being at once centrifugal and centripetal. Christine Lehman remarked:

> 'Something we toyed with before we started the programme was asking people to tender for a particular kind of project. We decided against that because one message that had come through very clearly was that, although this was government money, what [people] did like was someone coming round and saying what did they think the solution was, instead of saying 'we're giving you money to develop an X'. So we didn't want to do that. We wanted to encourage things in the field. Equally, what we did want to encourage were things that were new, and that was the most difficult thing to put across. So we tried to say 'it has got to be new and innovative and it's got to address these, and here are some possible ways'.'

Thus formulated, the logic of programme development edged the Unit away from a submission to strong centralised control in the Office. What came inevitably to temper that logic was the need to subject proposals about the Unit's priorities and procedures to the scrutiny of officials working in other parts of the Office. All files pass between officials considered to be affected or likely to be affected by an issue, leading to the construction of paper debates, the taking of soundings, and the creation of working models of opinion that are intended to grow more coherent and cohesive over time. So it was with proposals about the Unit itself. The Unit's character had, in effect, to be approved by some of the very bodies from whom it sought a semi-independent relation. In 1991, the year when programme development was being formed, arguments accumulating in those circulating files made the officials planning the Unit aware of the dangers of duplicating existing work in, say, the Safer Cities Programme; of the need to confer inside and outside the Office; and of the importance of transforming the Unit into a 'wide resource' within the Office. It was agreed that the Unit's 'priority-setting' should be responsive to the needs of the entire Home Office and that it should entail very general consultations with divisions before proposals were submitted to Ministers.

What preserved the Unit's semi-independence, allowing it to remain near the margin, was the growing familiarity of officials in other divisions with the idea of fostering local innovation ('I think possibly it's not been seen as startling or radical or potentially difficult – so much as a potential resource,' said Joan McNaughton, one policy official); a recognition of the insignificance of any actions likely to flow from such a modest budget ('£600,000 does not make much of a splash, you can't do anything very wrong' said Christine Lehman), a budget that had indeed already been approved ('it wasn't *new* money'); and an initial uncertainty about what this small, new entity might actually be ('I would guess that if there has not been a response to this officially it may be because people are not quite sure what it is there to *do*' said Lorraine Rogerson, a policy official).

3. 'PRIORITY-SETTING'

The new Unit was founded formally in June 1991 and was introduced to the Research and Statistics Department at their conference in Cambridge in July.[39] The broad 'programme areas' that would be addressed in its first year were to be selected in consultation with Home Office divisions, the Research and Planning Unit and outside bodies such as NACRO (the National Association for the Care and Resettlement of Offenders) and ACOP (the Association of Chiefs of Probation) before being submitted to ministers in the autumn.

The Unit's own 'shopping list' of policy initiatives, drafted in November, contained a number of headings that were general, vague and novel by design but which were, in addition, not too ambitious for projects that were supposed to be short-lived, relatively inexpensive and local. (Vagueness and choice are features of policy proposals internationally: they work against an unwelcome appearance of issues having been foreclosed, of arguments having been pre-empted, and of those consulted having been denied an effective voice.) Suggested were 'criminality reduction', domestic violence, the 'criminal justice process', 'offenders and the community', ethnic minorities, and the dissemination of information and good practice.

3.1. Criminality prevention

The first item, 'criminality prevention', was a neologism unlikely to have been in very general circulation towards the end of 1991: its parentage was complicated; its meaning not quite firmly established or stable.[40] It was 'multi-vocal', signifying rather different things to different audiences (and I shall list some of those differences below). Yet it was also evident that the idea was beginning to take independent life and shape and proposals touching it were in time reported to have been well received by people inside and outside the Office.

To one audience, the senior members of the Programme Development Unit, steeped in the language of applied criminology, the origins of criminality prevention lay in metaphors borrowed from health care and from control and anomie theory. Just as primary public health care was supposed to be devoted to the prevention of disease (and criminologists and social control experts have long been fond of medical analogies) so, it was argued, there should be primary intervention to modify the physical and social conditions propitious to crime.[41] The idea was attractive to the Unit. It was being usefully championed by a group of criminologists and by one British criminologist, David Farrington, especially, who were confident that delinquency could not only be predicted but that measures were actually available to control it. It seemed that something might indeed actually work after all. It was asserted that there

[39] Members of the Department were told that 'programme development builds on existing knowledge, tests assumptions and generates new information by setting up and evaluating innovative programmes. Where *research* is directed primarily at generating knowledge through processes of inquiry, investigation and analysis, *programme development* is aimed at testing the success of the application of knowledge in achieving practical objectives. It bridges the gap between research and policy.' 'What is Programme Development?'

[40] There was not even an agreed terminology at first. Some called it 'criminality prevention' and others 'criminality reduction' and 'criminal prevention'.

[41] *See* P. Brantingham and F. Faust, 'A Conceptual Model of Crime Prevention', 22 *Crime and Delinquency* (1976) pp. 284–296.

was strong empirical evidence that a few, simple variables in early life were linked with later criminality. Of cardinal importance were the firmness and consistency of social bonds attaching the young to family and school, and policy-makers and politicians were advised to attend to the social integration of those particular institutions.[42] Such ideas, said Lorraine Rogerson, were 'readily to hand.' There was one article in particular that circulated about the Office at just that time, an article that had again made out the case for using longitudinal studies to predict and control delinquency, and for 'social prevention experiments ... to prevent the development of crime and antisocial behaviour. These could begin by targeting three important predictors of offending that may be both causal and modifiable: economic deprivation, school failure and poor parental child-rearing behaviour.'[43] An official remarked of Farrington's influence:

> 'There is a theory for a particular time and maybe what he is saying is just one of the things that particularly suit at the moment. There are things that ministers don't want to hear about. They don't want to hear too much about poverty or unemployment and crime. They don't want to hear about the failure of society to do things. They want to hear about the failure of people who aren't doing it themselves the right way.'

Moreover, criminality prevention was attractive precisely because it was so *new*. It was a break from the 'secondary' crime prevention of target-hardening and opportunity reduction whose experimental and political half-life was deemed to have expired,[44] whose demise had followed the emigration of its principal author, Ron Clarke, to the United States, and which had begun to appear a little impolitic in its tendency tacitly to 'blame' victims for their own suffering.[45] It was just the kind of innovation that programme development had been planned to pursue. Christine Lehman remarked:

> 'In the Home Office, the genesis ... partly came from a realisation that crime prevention, in terms of old-fashioned situational crime prevention, wasn't doing the trick ... It is no good just tinkering with the street lighting. You have to look at what's making people do this. [Secondary crime prevention] was a busted flush in terms of political advantage... '

Members of the Research and Statistics Department phrased criminality prevention in the language of social engineering. It was their diagnosis that families and schools were failing, that social bonds had become attenuated, and that the young had been set free to drift into conflict and delinquency. The job of criminality prevention would be to restore control by helping vulnerable young people make the transition from isolation and alienation to membership of

---

42 *See* the collection edited by J. Burchard and S. Burchard, *Prevention of Delinquent Behavior* (Newbury Park 1987).

43 D. Farrington and D. West, 'The Cambridge Study in Delinquent Development: A Long-Term Follow-Up of 411 London Males', in H.J. Kerner and G. Kaiser, eds., *Kriminalität* (Berlin 1990) p. 132.

44 *See* the statement by the then Home Office Minister, John Patten, reported in *The Guardian*, 12 July 1989: 'the language of five years ago about crime prevention, of 'target hardening' or the 'external enemy', now has an archaic ring to it.'

45 *See*, for example, his 'Situational Crime Prevention: Theory and Practice', 20 *British Journal of Criminology* (1980).

a stable social group. It could become the focus, for instance, of projects to assist children leaving care, families in need of support, and schools with problems of truancy.

Ministers had been developing their own nuanced conception of criminality prevention (indeed a member of the Research and Statistics Department claimed that it was a minister, John Patten, who had introduced the term to the Home Office.) Home Office ministers are responsible for the politics of difficult moral problems, and their task is to lead and define, to prescribe and exhort.[46] They are the visible and audible face of the Office and their public utterances are designed to be noticed. When *they* talked about criminality prevention, they centred it in an evolving Conservative politics of the family that emphasized the importance of responsibility,[47] discipline, and right conduct.[48] They described the family as a *moral* institution whose members should not only become more strongly self-reliant and self-regulating,[49] but also more obviously accountable for one another's delicts. The proper business of the State was to interfere in cases of manifest failure, when the family had broken down, but at other times the family should be publicly liable for its own actions. The development of that political theme within the Home Office was to culminate powerfully and publicly in a speech by the Home Secretary to the annual conference of the Association of Chiefs of Probation in early 1992:

---

46 The left are conventionally thought to seek explanations for crime and deviance in structural causes, the right in individual wrongdoing, but left politicians can talk about moral matters too. So it was that, in the wake of the outcry about the murder of James Bulger in Liverpool in February 1993, left and right wing front bench politicians spoke in identical terms. Just as John Patten, then Secretary of State for Education, argued about 'moral chaos', so Tony Blair, shadow home secretary was reported to have said 'if we do not learn and then teach the value of what is right and what is wrong, the result is simply moral chaos which engulfs us all' (reported in *The Times*, 22 February 1993).

47 *See*, for example, the observations of John Patten, then Minister of State for Home Affairs, in his letter to the Chairman of the Conservative Party Social Affairs Forum, 5 March 1990: 'To say that the erosion of social responsibility which characterized much of the 60s and 70s failed is not in any sense to be other than an accurate observer; it failed in the same fashion as industrial corporatism failed. The message that the family had to be worked at, and that the consequences of its collapse were severe, was all too easily forgotten then.... the 1990s have opened with a bang as far as family policy is concerned. The Home Secretary has announced Government proposals to make more parents more responsible for the criminal acts of their children. Thought to be a deeply daring idea a couple of years ago when first discussed, this has now been warmly welcomed.' On the importance of moral responsibility for the young, see John Patten's statement reported in *The Times* of 11 I July 1987 and his article in *The Spectator* of 18 April 1992 in which he argued that 'the very young are the problem, though looking for the good and stopping the bad can seem a Sisyphean task... . Delinquent parents need to feel the contemporary lash if they won't persuade their children to behave ... .'

48 *See* J. Lewis, *Women in Britain since 1945. Women, Family, Work and the State in the Post-War Years* (Oxford 1992) esp. Ch. 1; and N. Dennis and G. Erdos, *Families without Fatherhood* (London 1992).

49 *See*, for example, the speech by Angela Rumbold, then Minister of State at the Home Office, at the Conservative Party Conference, 9 October 1990: 'I am distressed when I see the family undermined. It is not good enough to read about youngsters who leave home because they felt unwanted.... It is just not good enough for us to accept that the family cannot meet the challenge of setting a high standard of behaviour for their children. Theses things are the core of family responsibility.'

> 'Crime prevention begins in the home. There is evidence that children's experience of family life, and their relationship with their parents, play a significant role in whether or not they offend. Strong relationships between parents and children, with good communication, the use of firm, affectionate and consistent discipline, an interest in children's activities and schooling, and effective supervision, can all increase the chance that the child will grow up to respect other people and the law, and able to withstand the temptations of crime. In this, research confirms what most people already believe – in a recent survey, the majority of people questioned thought that parents and the family should take main responsibility for reducing crime – much more than the police, the Government, or the courts.'[50]

John Patten, the minister responsible for criminal policy at the time the Programme Development Unit was created, himself believed in strong moral imperatives, talking later about 'moral chaos' and holding that 'you do have to face up to the fact people sometimes behave very badly .... I do think we have to recognize that bad means bad.[51] He too was an advocate of criminality prevention pursued within the family and school, arguing that the 'seeds of crime are planted at an early age'[52] and that violence 'breeds in youth from an early age'[53] and he and the Home Secretary had also been encouraged by the work of David Farrington.[54]

The new applied criminology displayed an affinity with the new Conservative politics of the family, coaxing moral arguments to embrace techniques of early intervention.[55] It articulated what had not yet been formalised. Lorraine Rogerson observed that 'criminality prevention was easy because that was something that ministers were concerned about without enough knowledge to say exactly what should be done.'

Policy officials in the buffer zone between the politicians and researchers had also heeded the developing emphasis on the family, crime and primary prevention. They too were aware of reports about research that were filtered at second hand, from a distance and somewhat namelessly through the files. They advised ministers and devised and implemented policy in the confidence that there were facts or pieces of evidence or good research somewhere in the background that *could* be employed to sustain a case in need. Unlike members of the Research and Planning Unit, they are not specialists but generalists, not researchers but the masters of

---

[50] Home Secretary's Speech to ACOP Annual Conference: 26 February 1992.

[51] John Patten, speaking as Secretary of State for Education, BBC radio interview, 22 February 1993.

[52] John Patten, reported in *The Times*, 7 March 1988.

[53] John Patten in *The Times* 12 April 1988

[54] The then Home Secretary, Kenneth Baker, had organized a series of luncheons at which matters of criminal justice policy were discussed. Farrington had himself been a guest at one such luncheon in the summer of 1991, and the Home Secretary was said to have become fired by what he had heard of the Cambridge cohort study.

[55] In 1989, Patten was reported to have stated of the latest phase of the Cambridge study, 'this important study has been influential both in this country and in the United States. It bears out much of the Home Office's current thinking about juvenile crime. It is an excellent example of how academic work funded by government, can help in policy-making... . This work is evidence of the importance of responsible parenting in preventing future crime. Its findings bear out the idea that the family is the first and most appropriate line of defence against delinquency. I will be examining Dr. Farrington's conclusions, and their pointers towards future action, very carefully indeed.' News Release: Delinquent Development Research; Home Office, 19 July 1989.

a more general, formal process of reasoning. Good official argument relies on a display of reasonableness, even-handedness and consistency, on choices put clearly and without passion by officials who have no necessary scholarly expertise or personal stake in what is advocated.[56] They were supposed to be considered and rational in the service of politicians, their stance having something of the character described by Gellner: 'when dealing with serious matters, when human lives and welfare are at stake, when major resources are being committed, the only kind of knowledge which may legitimately be used and invoked is that which satisfies the criteria of Enlightenment philosophy ... '[57]

Officials had noticed and fed the new political thinking about criminality prevention. *Their* cues were politicians' and others' reactions to the briefing papers and speeches which they had themselves written: 'the policy on reducing criminality had been worked up and put to ministers, ministers were very much in favour of this area being explored. So our work, whether it be the writing-up of speeches or the projects ... is actually to give effect to what we perceive to be ministers' wishes, and that's what we're here for' said Joan MacNaughton. Their knowledge was of political responses, of the paper arguments amassing in files and briefings, and of the spoken arguments of meetings.

It was evident to members of the policy divisions that a new idea was unfolding in the Office, an idea that was beginning to acquire a name and a presence, although it was difficult to award it an exact history and provenance. Ideas tend to have no need of such a clear intellectual pedigree in the world of policy-making. Policy officials possess instead a very general phenomenological sense of the timeliness, appropriateness and political patterning of argument: 'what we tend to find in the policy area is that an idea emerges whose time has come and suddenly everybody is saying the same thing ... ' It was just so with criminality reduction. That idea, heading at one stage towards the creation of a task force on criminality that might have led, in its turn, to the classification, identification and differential treatment of 'pre-delinquents'[58] as young as six or seven years old (a politically 'difficult and dangerous' question best avoided,[59] some thought), was instead channelled into programme development

56 For a discussion of bureaucratic rationality, *see* M. Weber, *Economy and Society* (New York 1968).

57 E. Gellner, *Postmodernism, Reason and Religion* (New York 1992) p. 92.

58 *See*, for instance, the report in *The Times*, 13 February 1991. John Patten was claimed to have said that 'the new concept of criminal prevention concentrates on trying to identify those among the sometimes very young who are likely to end up as they get older committing a disproportionate number of the crimes in this country ... To deal with this problem we need more participation ... to pinpoint those sad children from sometimes sad families who need help when very young to stop them getting punishment when they are teenagers. I believe it is possible to identify those children, on the face of it, that are at risk of turning into tomorrow's criminals.' Mr Patten added: 'The association between unhappy homes, health problems, failure to thrive, under-performance at school and truancy with later offending are all too clear'.'

59 David Farrington himself remarked that there was a wish 'to identify individual children, children who were at risk of becoming delinquent in the future, and I think that's quite possible to do. But I think, politically, if you want to sell something, it would be wiser not to do it. I think there was a lot of sense in it, logically and scientifically, but in terms of getting something off the ground, a new policy, then I think it is better to say we are going to target certain deprived housing estates where a lot of the people would fulfill the criteria for 'likely to become delinquent'.'

with the establishment of the Unit and the search for new initiatives in 1991–1992.[60] Indeed, the Home Secretary's speech of February 1992, the speech that had talked so centrally about delinquency and the family, proceeded to recite how Mr Baker believed that 'there is scope for action to reduce criminality, and to learn about 'what works' so as to be able to distil and disseminate what produces results in practice.'[61] It was evident that he was pointing straight towards the Unit. 'Preventing criminality has come to us' said Christopher Nuttall.[62]

3.2. Domestic Violence

Domestic violence was a somewhat less obvious candidate at first. To be sure, it had become established as a policy issue for the police, one of the criminal justice agencies for which the Home Office has broad responsibility.[63] Police officers had been urged to be more sympathetic in their response to assaulted women; to record reported offences more frequently; to caution, arrest and charge more often; and to establish 'multi-agency' programmes and 'domestic violence units'. The Home Office had encouraged its client organization, Victim Support, to aid battered women. But domestic violence had certainly not been the subject of one of the new initiatives in secondary crime prevention in the 1980s.[64] It had not been considered for exploration when the development budget was first approved and there were obstacles to its acceptance when, later, the Programme Development Unit was established.

Domestic violence is conventionally regarded as a difficult subject for policy-making. There are problems of effective enforcement and prosecution, it being said that junior police officers are loath to intervene because they view such violence as a messy, private, dangerous business lacking certain structure, unambiguous victims and independent witnesses.[65] There

---

60 Its history nevertheless created some inevitable confusion. Some of those who received the application forms from the Programme Development Unit read into 'criminality prevention' the older meanings of the term. One said, for instance, 'it was associated in my mind with various initiatives that never got off the ground in any formal sense, but relating to rather younger children - John Patten's stuff about targeting five or six-year olds.'

61 Home Secretary's speech to ACOP Annual Conference, 26 February 1992.

62 That movement was confirmed after the general election of April 1992 when the two Home Office ministers most closely identified with criminality prevention, Kenneth Baker and John Patten, moved elsewhere. For a brief account of this episode *see* D. Downes and R. Morgan, 'Hostages to Fortune?: The Politics of Law and Order in Post-War Britain', in M. Maguire et al., eds., *The Oxford Handbook of Criminology* (Oxford 1994) pp. 183-232.

63 In West Yorkshire, for instance, the police committed themselves to take 'major steps to place the problem of domestic violence in the forefront of its priorities... ' *Domestic Violence Survey* 1991, West Yorkshire Police, no date, no place of publication, p. 1.

64 *See* H. Blagg *et al.*, 'Inter-agency co-ordination: rhetoric and reality', in T. Hope and M. Shaw, eds., *op. cit.*, p. 204 (n. 11).

65 *See* M. Chatterton, 'Police Work and Assault Charges' in M. Punch, ed., *Control in the Police Organization* (Boston 1983). A recent National Inter-Agency Working Party, based at Victim Support and chaired by Mary Tuck, reported that 'the police tend to be a male-dominated, action-oriented organization who like decisions to be clear cut and problems to have a solution. Constables ... tend to see dealing with domestic violence as a low-grade activity unlikely to attract either prestige or excitement, and all too likely to raise insoluble problems.' *Report of a National Inter-Agency Working Party on Domestic Violence* (London 1992) p. 11.

are problems of winning the acquiescence of the policed: perpetrators may not view themselves as criminals and victims as victims.[66] There are problems of territory, violence against women being a social problem falling within the mandates of a number of departments of State, and 'no one department wanted to be in the forefront, no one wanted to bite the bullet.' There are problems of ideology, domestic violence having become associated symbolically with the women's aid movement, a movement that has had its difficulties in dealing with Govemment.[67] Indeed, the very categorization of domestic violence as a crime requiring a response from the criminal justice system and its ministries has sometimes been resisted by those who would rather speak of patriarchy and oppression than of victims and offenders.[68]

In the careful language of the Home Office, domestic violence was not yet 'on the agenda' but it *was* a 'subject of growing concern' in late 1991. Domestic violence was undergoing the stock natural history of deviance amplification, action having bestowed a luminosity that prompted new action. Seen from within the policy divisions, the problem seemed to have grown in scale and importance as the new police recording practices generated more and more reports of violent criminal incidents,[69] and, said Lorraine Rogerson, 'when you get a significant increase, you begin to appreciate the extent of the problem. Then you begin to ask naturally the next question which is 'are we doing enough about working to try to prevent this particular type of crime?', and I think the answer is that we haven't really addressed that one. So that is why domestic violence came up, on its merits as it were.'

Seen from the vicinity of the Programme Development Unit, the transformation of domestic violence into an issue seemed primarily to have been accelerated by an impetus stemming from within the Unit itself. If domestic violence was not 'on the agenda' in England and Wales, it certainly was so in Canada. Violence against women had acquired a political presence in Ottawa, if only because the federal government had organized itself to see and hear it. One institution acting as the eyes and ears of government was Status of Women Canada, a department founded in 1976 with special powers to monitor cabinet proposals (including proposals on criminal justice matters) as they affected women.[70] There was no such special body in England and Wales. In Canada, a number of women officials (including women in the criminal justice ministries) had taken it upon themselves to promote feminist policies from within the federal government. In England and Wales, women officials appear by contrast to be 'gender neutral' and disinterested in their work, eschewing overt evangelism and special causes (although it should be noted that, by the mid-1980s, there had evolved a core group of women in the Home Office who were interested in the problem of domestic violence and 'wished strongly to keep things going.') In Canada, a miscellany of women's organizations (including those concerned with rape and domestic violence) had formed themselves into a

---

66 In the United States, it was observed that 'a large proportion of family violence is committed by people who do not see their acts as crimes against victims who do not know they are victims,' *Report, Attorney General's Task - Force on Family Violence*, Washington, DC, 1984, p. 5.

67 I discuss some of these matters in *Helping Victims of Crime*, *op. cit*., pp. 178-185 (n. 3).

68 *See*, for example, 'Battered Women, Refuges, and Women's Aid', a report from the National Women's Aid Federation, London, n.d.

69 *See* L. Davidoff and L. Dowds; 'Recent trends in crimes of violence against the person in England and Wales', *Home Office Research and Planning Unit Research Bulletin* (1 989) p. 14.

70 *See* my *A View from the Shadows*, *op. cit*., Ch. 8 (n. 22).

national body, the National Action Committee on the Status of Women, that worked creatively and pragmatically with allies in Status of Women Canada and government departments (including the criminal justice ministries). There was no such pragmatism or coalition in England and Wales. The victimized woman had a special significance in the official politics of criminal justice in Canada. She did not in England and Wales.

What made the politics of Canadian women salient to the politics of women in England and Wales was the direct importation of Canadian ideas by Christopher Nuttall, the former senior Canadian civil servant who had fostered experiments in the policing of domestic violence in Canada, the man who had now become a senior Home Office official with responsibility for research, statistics and programme development:[71]

> 'It was an area which I had been very much involved with in the Solicitor General in the late 70s, early 80s, in the [work of the projects] in London, Ontario.... I was interested when I came back from Canada ... [how] in fourteen years [Canada had become] way past what was going on here.... Status of Women Canada, all the politics which you know about, took a leap ahead of what was going on here ... [So the emphasis on] domestic violence, I think that came more from us. I think we thought, I thought, that it was an area which was not getting the priority that it ought to get.'

And, when it did become an issue, when, in December 1991, domestic violence was proposed as an area for exploration,[72] 'there wasn't a great deal of a problem ... we knew we were pushing on an open door.' There was an existing political mandate to intervene should anyone care to use it: the Ministerial Group on Women's Issues had flagged the response to family violence as a priority; the Research and Planning unit had just published a literature review illuminating the issue;[73] there was growing and recognisable political interest within the Office;[74] the protection of women, the prevention of crime and the apprehension of offenders were the department's clear responsibilities. Programme development afforded officials the opportunity they had sought to move matters forward: 'things needed to be more innovative through project work.' And above all, it must be recalled, domestic violence could be regarded as eligible precisely *because* it was new.

Timeliness counts in the official world: policies are most likely to prosper if they are being formulated at the very moment that money becomes available and thought begins to turn to the making of choices. It is then that current policies are at their most prominent in the official

---

[71] He was to confer with Sandra Horley, herself a former Canadian and importer of Canadian ideas, the director of Chiswick Family Rescue, the pioneering 'independent' refuge that was unattached to the National Women's Aid Federation. Horley has been massively influential in spreading the influence of policing and voluntary initiatives developed first in London, Ontario. She is taken particularly seriously by the Metropolitan Police, the largest police force in Britain.

[72] It was envisaged that initiatives might focus on working with the children of violent families, the training of young males in their duties as husbands and fathers, or the expansion of the joint police-community reaction to violence against women.

[73] *See* L. Smith, *Domestic Violence* (London 1989).

[74] *See*, for instance, the report in *The Times* of 19 April 1991 of an announcement by John Patten that the police should automatically make an arrest in cases of domestic violence. The policy had been influenced by Sandra Horley's work in spreading knowledge about the practices of the police in London, Ontario.

mind, most malleable and most open to the forging of symbolic links (two things considered at the same time could well be thought to have an immanent unity).[75]

John Patten and the Home Secretary approved the selection of criminality prevention and domestic violence towards the end of December, observing that those two issues would be enough for the Unit at that stage. The next step was to advertise the initiative and solicit proposals.

4. THE 200 AND THE 732

It was thought that there would be money sufficient for some dozen projects in the first funding round.[76] To become eligible for funding, any applicant would have to comply with standard Home Office criteria (identical to those applied to the funding of Safer Cities projects and probation projects for young offenders, for instance) and, in smaller measure, criteria once current in Washington. It was, said Christine Lehman, 'very prescriptive and structured. [Applicants] knew what they had to do.'[77] Each project would have to be an innovative and practicable answer to a clearly defined problem, capable of yielding discernible results in the form of 'output measures' and 'performance indicators', supported by firm plans for evaluation and monitoring, backed by 'a statement of local need', demonstrating 'value for money' and involving a 'multi-agency approach'.

Notes sent to would-be applicants explained that two themes would be promoted in the coming year. Projects submitted under the one heading should 'explore and address possible causes of and contributors to criminality, rather than crime prevention or treatment of offenders.'[78] There could be applications to fund projects concentrating on 'social integration' and targeted at young homeless people, young people leaving care, ex-offenders and 'at-risk adolescents;' role model projects; pre-school projects; 'parenting projects'; projects for children with problems at school; and projects to 'support young people and parents in families at risk of disintegration.' Projects under the other heading should be 'new and thoughtful' ways of avoiding and preventing family violence, and they might include educational projects for boys and young men, projects 'working with children in violent families' and projects developing 'the police, prosecution and community response' to family violence.'

Information about the initiative was to be broadcast widely to 'statutory and nonstatutory organizations'[79] although it was understood that there could well be a number of other interested groups beyond the practical reach or knowledge of the Unit. There being no list of

75 *See* E. Husserl, *The Phenomenology of Internal Time Consciousness* (The Hague 1964).

76 It was announced that funding for any one project could not normally exceed £100,000 in a year. Programme Development Unit letter of 6 January 1992.

77 One successful applicant recalled that the 'priorities were monitoring and evaluation, very well structured timetables, priorities about - you knew that it had to be a new initiative, an innovative project in order for it to be successful. You knew that it had to bring in a number of agencies and develop a kind of inter-agency work.'

78 'Home Office Programme Development Unit Grants: Notes for Guidance for Applicants'.

79 An internal mailing list was used, letters being sent to all local authorities 'except the tiny district councils, where they went to county councils,' to the London boroughs and the probation services, to agencies in criminal justice (but not to the police), to 'quite a lot of voluntary groups through the

such candidate organizations, and no realistic prospect of compiling one, the Unit was in effect obliged to trust to the workings of the 'two-step' flow of communication.[80] Known national organizations, the 'cosmopolitans', would be used to relay intelligence to the unknown 'locals' within their neighbourhood through the networks of the criminal justice system.[81] So it was that the initial recipients of letters and application forms were asked to pass copies on 'to other groups, particularly smaller local voluntary organizations ... '[82] 'In the end,' said Christine Lehman, 'I'd say that we had about two hundred [names]... And then we waited to see what would happen.'

News spread. News about money spreads fast in hard times. One successful applicant reflected afterwards 'I still think why, in these times of recession, did this happen? It's just unbelievable!' Some groups learned about the Unit and its plans long *before* the two hundred public letters and application forms were sent out on 6 January 1992. For example, a Professor of Criminology, well known to the Home Office, informed a municipal social services department about what was to come ('this helped us because I think we were in fairly early because of that fact – a bit of fortune really'). The director of an independent women's refuge, also well known to the Home Office, informed the staff of a Safer Cities programme ('we knew through a grapevine that this thing called PDU was going to be set up with some money.')

The networks relayed knowledge *after* the public letter was sent. For instance, the Community Affairs Department (now the Community Development Department) of Lewisham Council, passed copies of the forms to groups in its area and then convened a meeting to discuss the organization of responses to the programme. Cosmopolitans aided locals in the two-step flow of communication, just as it had been hoped they would. Christopher Nuttall recalled that one cosmopolitan, a senior member of Crime Concern, telephoned him and asked 'are you expecting a lot of replies?', and I said 'well, they are very slow at the moment,' and he said, 'well, take it from me, there are going to be *hundreds!* ... There have been people writing to us, 'phoning me up, and saying 'how do we fill this in? Can you give us some help?'' Sometimes the flow of traffic through the networks was almost over-determined. It certainly appeared so when it began to converge on the 'obvious' people and groups in central organizations. Members of one social services department received four separate copies of the same letter of 6 January (one directly from the Home Office, one from the director of social services, one from the NSPCC (the National Society for the Prevention of Cruelty to Children), and one from the local probation service). A senior probation officer in the West Midlands received three copies.

'The word got around quite well,' said Christine Lehman. But it took time to do so. The letters and application forms could travel quite slowly and fitfully as they were passed from person to person. One applicant remembered, 'there wasn't anything that came through the mail to us and we didn't read about it. It was only another colleague in another organization

Voluntary Agencies Directory.' A number of bodies, such as NACRO, were consulted about the names of other bodies to approach.

80 *See* E. Katz and P. Lazarsfeld, *Personal Influence* (New York 1955) and E. Rogers, *Diffusion of Innovations* (New York 1962).

81 *See* D. Marsh and R. Rhodes, eds, *op cit*., p. 7(n.27).

82 Programme Development Unit, letter of 6 January 1992.

who knows us who rang us up ... She gave us the materials [and by then] we only had about two weeks left to get the application in.' Those who received copies at second-or third-hand (often the most 'local' and the least experienced) claimed that they had had very little time to consult or devote to drafting (one complained that 'we were a bit upset ... I think we had about nine days to write the thing, which is plainly nonsense.')

The forms required attention and sometimes their language needed deciphering. They required scrutiny and endorsement from colleagues and superiors, from the bodies who might be used to demonstrate 'local support' and the groups that could come together as multi-agency teams, and that could not always be hurried. The applications were returned slowly at first (only a fifth, 22%, had arrived by the penultimate week before the expiry of the deadline), and there was some attendant nervousness at the Unit. But then they came back in what was called an avalanche, 68% arriving in the final week alone. The two hundred forms had spawned seven hundred and thirty two applications by the closing date at the end of February 1992.[83] Had they all been funded, it was estimated, the cost would have been some £50,000,000.[84]

The two-step flow had worked well in feeding news of the initiative to local organizations:[85] 134 (or 18%) of those applications whose parent organization could be identified were from national bodies and 592 (or 82%) were from local bodies. The great bulk of applications were submitted by local voluntary organizations (39%) and by local authority departments (31%). Criminal justice agencies, chiefly the probation service, submitted another 10% and women's aid organizations 7%. There were 25 bids (or 4%) from church-based and 7 (or 1 %) from university-based bodies. There were applications flowing from every single one of the counties of England and Wales although they were inevitably more numerous from the more densely populated regions, a quarter (26%) emanating from London, and 7% each from the West Midlands and from Tyne and Wear.

5. THE PROPOSALS

Following the central prescriptions of the initiative, it is not surprising that over half of what was proposed (55% of the applications) lay in the area of criminality reduction and about a quarter (23%) in that of domestic violence. There were other proposals on a range of problems (such as the 2% on what was called the after-care of offenders), but most of those other bids would later be ruled irrelevant and ineligible for funding. There was no clear division of labour between institutions. Thus, women's aid organizations offered bids to work on domestic violence and on no other area (representing a third of the total of such applications),

---

83 Information about all those proposals was tabulated by Audrey Stephenson and some of the principal results are employed to support the analysis that follows.

84 Also moving around the network was the apprehension that the chances of any one project receiving funding were small. An applicant from NACRO reflected 'it was generally felt amongst voluntary organizations that there were going to be vast numbers of applications for a relatively small [sum] – which was the case, and therefore the chances of [a single application] bearing fruit were slim.'

85 I had planned to compare the dates by which different types of organization submitted their applications, but it was clear that they all tended to leave their submissions until just before the closing date and no inferences about the working of networks could be drawn.

but voluntary organizations (27% of the total) and local authority departments (22%) also made applications in that area. Again, whilst voluntary organizations submitted 40% of the applications to reduce criminality, local authority departments submitted 33%.

Most of the applications were imprecise as to the detail of diagnosis and remedy. There had been rather little time and not much space on the application to supply such detail. For instance, the vast majority of the proposed schemes were seemingly indifferent to the race of offenders: only 12 applications referred to race, half of them targeting African-Caribbeans, and 6 of those applications stemmed from voluntary organizations. The vast majority were similarly indifferent to the gender of offenders (presumably because the criminal is stereotypically male) or to the character of the offence to be prevented (93% of the applications did not name the offences that would be prevented or reduced – of those few specifying an offence, over a third pointed to the single crime of 'autotheft', the largest single officially recorded offence (forming 28% of all recorded crime in 1989) and a topical and frequently-committed crime of young people deemed to be 'at risk' at the time). Of the 117 proposals to reduce criminality which also specified a target population, it was the young homeless (in 47 instances), persons in care (19 cases), the drug and alcohol dependant (13 cases) and school truants (10 cases) who were to receive attention, and, in that specification, they tended largely to echo the words of the Programme Development Unit's own explanatory notes. Victims were rarely specified (in only 15% of the applications) and they were defined only in the context of domestic violence, it being women (in 76% of named instances) and children (22%) who were singled out.

5.1. The Local Reception of the Initiative

Foucault once described the criminal event as an 'intersection of discourses.'[86] Discourses can never be completely distinct, discrete or sealed: they seep into one another; they mimic one another; and members of one group sometimes speak the language of another, particularly when they wish to win favour or patronage. Yet differences remain, reflecting the diversity of practices, audiences and purposes in the world of criminal justice. Programme development, criminality prevention and domestic violence were at just such an intersection, and they were given yet another interpretation when they touched the local groups invited to apply for funds.

If the logic-in-use of politicians was prescriptive and exhortatory, and that of officials rational and managerial, there was a third mode of reasoning employed by many of those who submitted applications.[87] Those who actually drafted the application form appeared to be 'middle managers': senior probation officers, social service managers, the 'coordinators' and 'assistant coordinators' of projects and programmes, and the like. Their understanding of the criminal justice system was characteristically embedded, parochial, vivid and practical. It was not of systems and generalities but of local phenomena and issues known intensely

---

[86] M. Foucault, *I, Pierre Rivière, having slaughtered my mother, my sister and my brother ... A Case of Parricide in the 19th Century* (Harmondsworth 1978) p. x.

[87] What follows is based on my 10 interviews with applicants. It certainly applies to those people, but I cannot be confident about its larger scope. *A priori* I can see no good reason why it should not be generalized to the larger population of applicants.

and at first hand. The special mandate which *they* invoked was underwritten by a personal experience of the 'real world.'[88] Whilst others might write or argue about matters abstractly, they could assure themselves that they had actually seen and heard what they talked about. To be sure, from time to time and in moderate measure, they *did* refer to things read or to things heard at conferences and seminars, but theirs was not a predominantly bookish, reflective or methodical knowledge. It could not easily have been so. They were busy people who lacked ready access to seminars or research libraries. One applicant talked about his 'lack of preparation' and the problems of 'inaccessible and unreadable, hardly-ever-there-anyway material.' And a man working in a youth services department remarked that 'one of the problems with the youth service is we don't damn well write things down ... [we have only] very ad hoc, very piecemeal means of communicating ... '

The applicants' reasoning was comparatively practical, atheoretical, immediate, messy, complicated and indexical,[89] based on the insider's profound but often unexplicated knowledge of the unique case[90] rather than on the outsider's analytic and structured but more distant knowledge of many cases (an applicant remarked that 'I don't think there is a simple theory of crime.[91] I've got ideas about crime. I just can't think what the ideas are!') Practitioners and middle managers tended to argue from experience, from a history of practical acquaintance with local projects and initiatives, from what had been witnessed in their own area of work, and from what trusted confederates had said to them. In short, theirs was what could be described as a vernacular understanding of social problems (just as the core knowledge of programme development was *supposed* to be).[92] Thus one woman recited that her proposals on domestic violence had:

> ' ... just came through the work that I was developing ... they came through knowing, I suppose, that there are certain situations that, there are certain options for help and support that are closed to women. And any women's aid group or any group that has been involved in working with women will

[88] Tony Marshall was one who had occupied the two worlds of the Home Office and the practitioner, and it is interesting that he should have traced just such a divide between their styles of reasoning in his preface to *Community Disorders and Policing* (London 1992) p. xi: 'The informing belief behind this book is that progress in social policies will only come from a free interchange between theoretical development and practical experience. The former needs to remain open to the complexity and 'messiness' of the real world, not retreating to ivory towers for the sake of an academic 'purity' that may be aesthetically neat but is ultimately sterile.'

[89] *See* J. Rumgay, Alcohol, *Crime and Judgements of Responsibility* (Ph.D. dissertation London School of Economics 1992) pp. 60-61.

[90] And, *pari passu*, it was typical that they also took their proposals for funding to be equally unique.

[91] *See* C. Ragin, 'Cases of 'What is a case?', in C. Ragin and H. Becker, eds., *What is a Case? Exploring the Foundations of Social Inquiry* (Cambridge 1992) esp. p. 3; and K. Hawkins, 'On Legal Decision-Making', 43 *Washington and Lee Law Review* (1986) no. 4.

[92] It was often sound enough for all that. There are epistemologists who would argue that such grounded knowledge is the more solid form of reasoning. Take James who once asserted that 'it is the personal experience of those best qualified in our circle of knowledge to *have* experience, to tell us *what is*. Now what does *thinking about* the experience of these people come to, compared to directly and personally feeling it as . they feel it? The philosophers are dealing in shades, while those who live and feel know truth.' W. James, *Pragmatism* (New York 1949) p. 30.

give you the same stuff. It is actually very well known within women's groups...'

Another applicant reflected that his proposal had not 'been based on any kind of theoretical research or any empirical research ... I think it was more a question that ... we thought we were quite good as an organization [at] promoting change within other organizations ... ' And yet another remarked that her application on domestic violence had been based on a 'daily contact with staff and practitioners' and her 'discussion with other people ... in the [local] group that we had together, but no, we weren't looking at other schemes anywhere in the country.' She had not looked at published arguments or consulted 'experts'. And hers was a characteristic enough response.

Middle managers are often too fully occupied, too intimately involved with clients and their problems, too engrossed in the particulars of the here-and-now, to stand back and theorize[93] (one said 'it's not like I have actually got the time to sit and read books and have academic discussions.') Their distinctive knowledge centred on clients and cases and it contained at its heart what Buber once called the 'personal making present', that close awareness of the other appearing before one 'as a whole and yet at the same time [as an entity] without reduction or abstraction, in all its concreteness.' It was a form of awareness that could be contrasted with the 'analytical, reductive, and deriving look between man and man' that transforms knowledge of the other into 'schematically surveyable and recurrent structures.'[94] Buber claimed that it is a special property of 'making present' that it is able to confirm the other as 'different ... in the definite, unique way which is peculiar to him.'[95] From time to time, practitioners would have had just such an intimation, treating a client as thou rather than as *you*, as *Du* rather than *Sie*, as an unmediated presence rather than as a type. And, it may be supposed, even if the work of some practitioners had taken them away from frequent, face-to-face contacts with clients, their world did still turn around such awareness at its centre. Schutz called it the 'Thou-orientation', a pure, prepredicative mode of awareness which contains no judgments.[96] At first or second-hand, remembered or immediate, it was the practitioners' special form of knowledge and it would have continued to exercise influence.

What remedy for criminality prevention and domestic violence did that special, embedded, 'life-worldly' reasoning of the practitioner supply? It was not abstract or donnish. Neither was it organized around the precept that people should be administered sensibly or reconstituted morally. It was instead a blend of elements of Buber's 'making present' with something else, a dim (perhaps altogether forgotten) radical past that was preserved as a vestigial, subterranean tradition.

---

[93] Their knowledge resembled that described by Schutz and Luckmann as a 'sedimentation of subjective experiences of the life-world [rather than a series of] clear and contradictionless propositions which are systematically ordered into a hierarchy of universality.' A. Schutz and T. Luckmann, *The Structures of the Life-World* (London 1974) pp. 123,122.

[94] M. Buber; 'Elements of the Interhuman', in *The Knowledge of Man* (London 1965) pp. 80, 81.

[95] *Ibid*, p. 79.

[96] A. Schutz, *op. cit*., pp. 163–164 (n. 2).

5.2. Empowerment

'Empowerment' is a fairly venerable term with multiple ambiguities[97] and meanings.[98] *The Oxford English Dictionary* gives the earliest date of the usage of 'empower' as 1654 and of 'empowerment' itself as 1849. But it was in the 1960s that the word came fully into vogue as part of the vocabulary of the libertarian Left and liberation movements. Fanon,[99] Freire and others built on the Marxism of Gramsci and Marcuse and the radical psycho-analysis of Fromm to talk of the self-estrangement of people under capitalism and imperialism.[100] The poor, exploited and weak had been subjugated by the State and its ideology, it was argued. They had lost their will, their self-consciousness and their voice. The imperative was to restore autonomy, control, responsibility and self-direction to the oppressed under the guidance, if necessary, of theorist-politician-teachers who had already transcended their own alienation.[101] The argument was extended and generalized very widely to encompass the disabled,[102] blacks,[103] women,[104] clients, students, psychiatric patients and patients at large – in short, to almost any group defined[105] as subordinate[106] and exploited. It was the stuff of university and polytechnic teaching in the 1960s and 1970s,[107] and the stuff of radical social

---

[97] T. Brandon called it an 'emotive term which is often left unspecified in regard to process and outcome.' Unpublished literature review, 1992, p. 1.

[98] Paul, for instance, described empowerment variously as an active process in which beneficiaries influence the direction and execution of what is done for them; as a growth of political awareness and strength; as a struggle for control; as the provision of a voice for its beneficiaries; and as an equitable sharing of power in projects and programmes. S. Paul; 'Community Participation in Development Projects: The World Bank Experience', Workshop on Community Participation, Economic Development Institute, Washington, D.C., 1986.

[99] F. Fanon; *The Wretched of the Earth* (London 1965).

[100] Thus it was Fromm who remarked that 'freedom, though it has brought [man] independence and rationality, has made him isolated and, thereby, anxious and powerless. This isolation is unbearable and the alternatives he is confronted with are either to escape from the burden of this freedom into new dependencies and submission, or to advance to the full realization of positive freedom... ' E. Fromm, *The Fear of Freedom* (London 1960) p. x.

[101] *See* P. Freire, *Pedagogy of the Oppressed* (London 1972).

[102] *See* M. Oliver, 'Speaking Out: Disabled People and State Welfare', in G. Dalley, ed., *Disability and Social Policy* (London 1991).

[103] *See* W. Ellis, *White Ethics and Black Power* (Chicago 1969) p. x., and the Black Panther Party Platform and Program, October 1966, reprinted in B. Seale, *Seize the Time* (London 1968).

[104] *See* S. Rees, *Achieving Power: Practice and policy in social welfare* (London 1991) p. 8.

[105] Indeed, definitions themselves were to become politically contested. *See* M. Oliver, *The Politics of Disablement* (London 1990) p. 3.

[106] *See* M. Haug and M. Sussman, 'Professional Autonomy and the Revolt of the Client', 17 *Social Problems* (1969) no. 2.

[107] Although it was never to be part of sociology proper. It was not mentioned in any of the standard sociology textbooks, encyclopedias and dictionaries I consulted.

work[108] and probation.[109] In time, it also became part of the working common sense of many voluntary and professional organizations, of politicians of the Left'[110] and Right (after all, the Right also profess a dislike of the State and its tendency allegedly to pauperise and demoralize the poor[111]) and, indeed, of some of those working for the Home Office's own Research and Policy Planning Unit.[112] It became so ingrained and familiar that some have already begun to dismiss it as debased and threadbare, as a 'catchword,' a 'buzzword', or a *cliché*.[113] *One of the applicants to the Programme Development Unit grant observed, for example, that '[our] model that people either before [a] crisis or after the crisis would seek help that would help themselves is actually an* empowerment *model, but we didn't talk about it in those terms. But it is.... For my part you start to feel a bit cynical about [the term] ... it's a buzzword.'*

The word 'empowerment' was sometimes written formally into the applications submitted to the Home Office (it appeared 5 times in the 16 successful applications[114] and 6 times in a random, comparative sample of 12 unsuccessful applications). Its traces could also be discerned in a language that spoke of 'breaking cycles of poverty, criminality and disadvantage' (in a successful criminality prevention proposal); 'enabling young people to make informed choices and positive decisions about their drug use' (in an unsuccessful detached streetworker proposal); the 'finding of appropriate options' (in a successful proposal to aid battered women); 'confronting feelings of self-hatred and self-blame by building positive self-images' (in another proposal to help battered women); and the 'building of self-esteem' (in a successful criminality prevention proposal).

Of the 116 applications made to prevent crime by dealing with offenders, 35 (or 30%), the largest group, would have made resort to 'counselling'; 16 (or 14%) 'education'; 14 (or 12%) 'early intervention'; and 12 (or 10%) 'motor schemes', reflecting the preoccupation with crimes related to motorcars. Of the 416 applications to deal with 'people at risk', the largest group of 70 (or 17%) talked about 'activity programmes'; 56 (or 14%) of enhancing the social skills of those who were vulnerable and at risk of offending; 57 (or 14%) of 'counselling' and a like number of the vague 'early intervention'; 47 (or 11 %) of community projects and 22 (or 5%) or motor projects. Of the 136 projects to aid victims, almost all, 70%, proposed support and counselling; 9% 'self-help' and 9% 'agency-training'. In short, it seems that the projects were not centred on conventional methods of control, treatment or punishment but were designed largely to strengthen and support actual and embryonic offenders and victims, to 'empower' them.

---

108 *See* M. Loney, *Community Against Government* (London 1983); R. Bailey and M. Brake, eds., *Radical Social Work* (London 1975).

109 *See* H. Walker and B. Beaumont, *Probation Work.* Critical Theory and Socialist Practice (Oxford 1981).

110 Thus, John Smith, Leader of the Labour Party, was to emphasize the importance of empowerment in his vision for Britain in 1993. *See The Times*, 12 February 1993.

111 *See* J. Lewis, *op. cit.*, esp. p. 26 (n. 48).

112 *See*, for instance, the many references to empowerment in J. Foster and T. Hope, *Housing, Community and Crime. The Impact of the Priority Estates Project* (London 1993).

113 *See* S. Ramon, 'Principles and Conceptual Knowledge', in S. Ramon, ed., *Beyond Community Care* (London 1991) p. 17.

114 16 applications were eventually to be grouped together as a portfolio of 12 projects, a cluster of Leeds bids on domestic violence being treated as one.

'Empowerment' was even more emphatically a part of applicants' explanatory talk in interview and conversation. Over and over again and quite spontaneously, the word was invoked to describe what the practitioners did and thought. Thus one woman, part of a large project concerned with domestic violence, said simply that 'the models of support for women that we are talking about are models of empowerment ... if agencies can give women information about what they can do, then that gives women access to women, that means they are in a better position to make decisions for themselves. It can empower them to create change.' A man working in youth services declared that 'our primary function is to work with young people as members of the community and look at how they can be empowered to take very real decisions.' A man employed in a Safer Cities Programme said 'it's not my job to make a [battered woman's] life decisions for her, but to see that she is in the best position to make those decisions, and to know what they are, and to know what the consequences are.' And a member of the staff of another Safer Cities programme said:

> 'Empowerment is a word that is used in so many circles and it is an official word in City Challenge language. It's an official word if you go to any local [projects], and look at American management textbooks. It's there all the time. It's about people's understanding of the situation they are in and recognizing that they have skills themselves to make decisions themselves or to acquire the skills themselves to better their situation or to change their circumstances. Self-determination as I see it.'

The precise meanings of empowerment were not much elaborated by the middle managers who had drafted the applications. Its origins and intellectual history were largely obscure. Why should it have been otherwise? Practitioners are not historians of ideas. Empowerment was simply assumed to be an ingredient of good practice, part of what Husserl would have called *Stiftung*, the taken-for-granted foundations of work and thought (a man employed by NACRO said empowerment 'was before my time, because I think it is something that [has always] run through the philosophy that NACRO tries to espouse in a range of work ... ' and another applicant said 'it had been one of the cornerstones for quite a long time, and ... when one is involved in that feeling, the process, we've never actually stood up and said ... 'what do we mean by empowerment?' People say that's obviously been the one that's been very difficult to explain ... ') Although their mark could still be traced, Freire, Gramsci, Fromm, Fanon and the Black Panthers must have seemed quite anonymous and remote at times.

In sum, proposals made to the Programme Development Unit welled up out of the practitioner's relatively concrete, subjective knowledge of face-to-face meetings with people in trouble. Those people, the young men with criminal records; battered women; adolescents with no qualifications and insecure futures; tenants living on hard-to-let estates (1 of the 12 successful projects and 1 of a comparative sample of unsuccessful bids for projects would have been set on housing estates); truants (2 of the unsuccessful sample would have been set in schools), drug-users and others, were defined as clients with difficulties, as dependents, as people in need or as seekers for help. They were taken to be plagued by psychological and social problems, problems of powerlessness and poverty, alienation and meagre choice, dependency and insufficient freedom. They were trapped into a helplessness that presented no apparent solutions.[115] The practitioners' solution was to aid clients to regain power,

[115] And some practitioners feared that the very title of 'criminality prevention' in a project might serve only to exacerbate that helplessness. As part of their 'making present knowledge', the members

assertiveness and choice in their lives and so break free from helplessness. It was based on the old radical theory of 'empowerment,' and it was championed as the one universal nostrum for criminality and domestic violence.

Take two specimen cases perfectly illustrative of the rest. One was a bid described *formally* as a proposal to construct and 'implement programmes that address the links between social learning, schools, the family and the development of delinquency.' The education system, it was said, would be brought 'alongside criminal justice agencies' to focus on the 'frustration, low self-esteem and 'proving yourself' [that] have all been identified to feature amongst the influential factors for promoting 'delinquent careers'. We aim to restore the balance in favour of young people, – by developing and actively promoting new programmes to build self-esteem, deal effectively with peer pressure, avoid 'opportunities to offend' and also enable successful conflict resolution.' But the applicant who had drafted that proposal said *informally* in an interview:

> 'a lot of what they are trying to do is to come to terms with the word 'empowerment'. I know that's a very trendy word and I thinks it probably gets misused but I think [that is] what they'd like to do is generally – they try to give people some control over parents and children and teachers – saying you don't need us to do it – even given the kind of structural problems, even given the economic problems, you can do a bit more than you think can perhaps.'

The second was a bid directed at domestic violence that proposed *formally* to recruit advocates who would work with the police to 'provide crisis counselling, information on options and the legal process, information on, and where appropriate, initiate, referrals to other agencies.... The fundamental principle informing the model is that early intervention increases the likelihood of positive action being taken by victims and of referrals to other agencies being followed through.' But, *informally*, one of the two applicants formulating the bid said 'it's going to empower. Well, what I think it is going to do, ... with the degree of sensitivity necessary, it's going to empower the woman to make some choice or another, even if the choice is that she's not making the choice this time round ... '

6. CONCLUSION

In the late 1980s and early 1990s, North American methods were imported into a Home Office that was moving towards a greater engagement with innovation in the wake of a growing disillusionment with the conventional armaments of the criminal justice system. The Programme Development Unit was established on the metaphorical boundary of the Home Office, facing out towards the 'community' and its activist, statutory and voluntary groups,

---

of a number of voluntary organizations believed that the world 'crime' would stigmatise their clients. A woman working with young black men said that 'the whole idea of the criminal label is one that didn't sit very easily with me – the whole idea that crime can be an agenda when young black men are spoken about is quite a difficult one to swallow.' Another said that 'we were very careful when we wrote the submission to bring out ... the problem of labelling young children, we knew that was an issue and we were careful to write that issue into the , submission.' Their resistance seemed to be part of a wider distaste for the stigmatisation of the client. *See* D. Brandon *et al.*, *The Survivors. A Study of Homeless Young Newcomers to London and the Responses Made to Them* (London 1980) p. 31.

free-standing and separate from policy divisions. It sought to explore an experimental, vernacular social engineering that built on the ideas of those outside Whitehall. In its first year, it was to mediate, in a fashion, the politician's moral economy of the family and the official's administrative rationality as it encouraged applications for projects to reduce or prevent criminality and domestic violence, two of the policy issues that were beginning to emerge just at the time when funding procedures were being addressed.[116] Further out, in the community itself, ideas about innovation were interpreted squarely in a context of knowledge that was concrete and intersubjective, on the one hand, and residually radical on the other. They revolved around empowerment as the answer to the problems of the powerless, alienated and troubled, but they were not always expressed explicitly in a vocabulary of empowerment. And the ideas that actually returned to the Home Office, partially refracted by the official discourse of the department, talked about supporting, counselling and educating target populations of victims or of people at risk of victimizing others.

[116] Christine Lehman said 'I think there's one line of thinking that goes on in the office and then there's another line of thinking that goes on with ministers, obviously in some way you try to build a bridge between them. There's the criminality, the various papers on the preventing criminality initiative showed they are not always I going in the same direction but sometimes you end up at the same place.'

[9]
The Opening Stages of Criminal Justice Policy Making

This article describes how commonplace policy making is organized by a series of dialectical processes that transform the first, tentative ideas of officials and researchers into objective, anonymous policies dispersed throughout the criminal justice system.

A number of small structures and processes animate the very core of the routine politics of criminal justice. They have such a marked effect on the formulation of policy in its opening stages, the stages before legislation and implementation, that they explain much of its character. They deserve attention.

Those structures almost certainly permeate other areas of policy development as well, but I propose to confine myself to the workings of the world with which I am most familiar, the criminal justice system. More particularly, I shall base my description on a succession of linked empirical studies of 'bottom-up' policy making in government departments in Canada and England and Wales between the late 1960s and the early 1990s, drawing on published research on policies for victims (Rock 1986, 1990) and prosecution witnesses (Rock 1993) initiated in the 1980s, on the origins and development of the Home Office Programme Development Unit's first initiative in the early 1990s (Rock 1994), and on the decision taken by the Prison Department in the late 1960s to transform Holloway Prison for women into a secure hospital.

It would be best to define the precise focus and limits of this article. My objectives are circumscribed. I shall not deal much with the *content* of policy making: the history and empirical detail of four of the five initiatives are described at length in books and an article elsewhere. In the comparatively abstract argument of a short paper, I propose merely to stand back to examine a few of their more formal properties. And, in doing so, I shall concentrate on the everyday policy making that is stirred less by big events in the outside world than by the commonplace internal processes of bureaucracy itself.

This will be an analysis of routine policies that rise slowly, inconspicuously and methodically through 'the system' (although all prolonged episodes of policy making have their dramas and the history of the rebuilding of Holloway Prison was undoubtedly punctuated by grave crises). This is not an article about the social organization of Royal Commissions and the grander public committees, and it does not discuss the responses of politicians to sudden public disasters such as riots, murders and prison escapes. Neither, should it be stressed, can it be an article about some of the very newest and as yet largely unanalysed modes of policy making.

The organization and politics of criminal justice policy making are currently in flux. One source of change has been a partial turning away from the once standard processes of internal consultation, from committee meetings, briefings and circulating files, towards procedures that are more fragmentary, centrifugal and loosely bounded. Portions of criminal justice policy making have become somewhat less cohesive, coherent, controlled, and centralized as they come under the sway of devolution, 'contracting out', Next Steps Agencies and external consultants. Although the consequences and dimensions of that shift are uncertain and deserve close scrutiny, the new procedures were not at present in any of the initiatives I studied and they cannot be the subject of informed discussion here. At most, it may be said that they co-exist with the older methods in ambiguous relation, those older methods still remaining, if only for a while, as the officials' core recipe knowledge of how to do things.

The newest modes of policy making are themselves the fruits of a new politics of populism, moralism, and the market. Attempting to reform such matters as the organization of the police and prisons, the incarceration of young offenders, and the 'right to silence', a number of Home Office ministers appear recently to have been impelled by a strong sense of the political, by personal volition, a doughty common sense, and appeals to what are thought to be popular sentiment. They have consulted and conferred less often with the experts, distrusting the professionals, the criminologists, officials, and practitioners, who used to define much of the character of crime and criminal justice policy. One cabinet minister, John Redwood, was reported to have remarked in April 1994 that 'there were few in the universities ready to ask the new questions. Where was the criminologist who could explain the crime rate and tell us what to do about it?' (*The Times*, 25 April 1994). Ministers seem now to act more quickly and impulsively. Theirs has become the politics of the general will idiosyncratically conceived and it, too, co-exists uneasily with the standard forms of policy making that are the focus of this article.

Such departures from conventional conduct have occasioned dismay amongst many of the senior officials and baronial powers of the criminal justice system. They are a clear flouting of stock bureaucratic judgements about how things should be done, of what Bittner once called 'the [official] sensibility of esthetic appreciation [which] is summoned for direction, information and control in various concrete situations' (Bittner 1965: 252–3). And it has been an outcome that things *have* begun to go quite manifestly wrong in criminal justice policy making. There has been audible and often effective opposition to the new style inside and outside Parliament (even from the Lord Chief Justice and from former Conservative Home Secretaries such as Lord Whitelaw), visible retreats in policy (particularly in the case of the 1991 Criminal Justice Act) and a frequent loss of face. The reverses of Home Office policy have been politically embarrassing, representing just that public discomfiture of ministers and senior officials that civil servants sought traditionally to avoid,[1] a proof perhaps of the wisdom of the older methods. It is possible to suppose that they will eventually be superseded by a greater reliance on the cautious, safe, and orthodox pattern that I analyse in this article.

The Beginnings of Routine Policy Making

Let me describe the ingredients of that pattern. Even within a substantial government department such as the Home Office or the Ministry of the Solicitor General of Canada, proliferating tasks and the division of labour bring it about that only a small number of officials can devote themselves to a specific area of policy, especially at first when the area may not have received much in the way of departmental recognition and resources. The very newest areas are unlikely to be treated as a part of the established division of labour at all, but as an additional task to be allotted to officials already occupied with other matters. To be sure, the numbers of officials in attendance will swell as a piece of policy making becomes more urgent, complex, and immediate in its demands, as political alliances are sought and new boundaries are explored, but the formative early life of a policy can rarely be nurtured by more than a few people. Many policies, and certainly those policies whose trajectory is described as 'bottom-up', advancing from officials to ministers, begin by acquiring their identity in the aspirations, imaginations, relations, and activities of perhaps three or four individuals.

Those small policy-making worlds tend to lack permanence and stability. Quite by design, 'high-flying' Home Office officials are moved from post to post about every three or four years to prevent them 'going native' and to afford them a panoptic vision of ever-wider reaches of government. The officials of other governments (of Canada, for example) may not be shuffled about so methodically, but it is inevitable that they will also change position as they fall ill, become pregnant, pursue their careers, receive promotion and secondment, and retire.

A stable group may well be intellectually fertile, and it can certainly foster commitments and loyalties, but it is the instability of the small group that seems to provide the stronger immediate catalyst for the innovation and diffusion of ideas. People on the move take their histories, expertise, and experience with them, carrying knowledge from site to site. They are prone to transfer, contrast, mix, and refashion the larger common sense and practices of the organizations in which they have worked. It is often the newly-arrived official, seeing parts of the world with a questioning eye, who proposes change. So it was that Irvin Waller, Director of Research in the Ministry of the Solicitor General of Canada, imported the evangelism of the National Organization for Victims Assistance, the American victims movement, in the 1970s; Christopher Nuttall, the new Director of Research and Statistics at the Home Office, and his colleague, Christine Lehman, carried the idea of programme development from Canada and the United States into the Home Office in the late 1980s; and Joanna Kelley, a former governor seconded to the Prison Department as Assistant Commissioner at the end of the 1960s, took her ambition to remodel Holloway Prison into the

[1] One senior official involved in the Holloway Redevelopment Project informed a meeting in June 1975 that he was 'responsible to the public to ensure that public money was well spent. Put more defensively, [I have] a duty to protect the Prisons Board and the Permanent Under-Secretary from the possibility of public and Parliamentary criticism'.

heart of penal policy making. They injected old ideas and procedures into new settings where they no longer seemed to be quite so old.

In the small world of the policy maker, personal character, influence, and reputation count. Policies will not and cannot be anonymous there. Rather, they will be the acknowledged offspring of particular people. Thus, the rebuilding of Holloway Prison was linked inextricably with the person of Kelley, Programme Development with Nuttall, and the Justice for Victims of Crime Initiative with Waller, the man once called Mr Victims by his colleagues in the Ministry of the Solicitor General of Canada (see Rock 1986: ch. 4).

A new venture is then liable to become regarded as the symbolic property or adjunct of a named individual or small group of individuals, part of their material self, and *its* worth and prospects will rest in part on *their* social and professional standing, the one colouring the other. What is done for and to a proposal at first may also stand as a response to its proponent, the seemingly impersonal work of policy making actually being transacted quite personally, a set of transfigured social relationships being affected, as are all relationships, by feelings of admiration, friendship, animosity, jealousy, and obligation. The progress of policies themselves will be blocked, diverted, or accelerated in the play of social interaction, the one being a mirror of the other.

Of obvious importance in those early phases is the structural position of the innovating individual or individuals. The more powerful and senior they are, the more unambiguously their formal responsibilities seem to bear on a new proposal, the smoother will be the path of the initiatives they promote. But such a marriage between projector, role, and project is rarely complete. Whilst officials are liable to be most knowledgeable and enthusiastic about matters directly salient to their work, bringing about a convenient coupling of inspiration and duty, bright ideas also have a way of arising unplanned in chance meetings, casual conversations and unexpected juxtapositions that confound the neat boundaries of the division of labour. Indeed, many proposals will be so new that they fail to find a ready home at all (in the mid-1980s, for instance, no government department in England and Wales had formal responsibility for assisting prosecution witnesses who appeared in court). It is inevitable that new ideas will often have to enter an environment which is not formally prepared for them, an environment that consists of activities approved, funded, and targeted at other things altogether. It is also inevitable that the officials who would promote those ideas, just as commonly seem to be stuck in the wrong place or in the not-quite-right place for the task at hand.

Something can always be achieved by rhetoric. Policy making occupies a world of paper and words, of argument and efforts to persuade. The highest praise one Home Office official can give another is to say that he or she is 'good on paper'. Confronted by a misalignment between formal responsibility and aspiration, between the new idea and its environment, officials can improvise, stretching arguments about the limits and terms of mandates and precedents to accommodate the new, discovering and enhancing useful consistencies, differences, and continuities. At the very germination of the Canadian Justice for Victims Initiative, for instance, before the Solicitor General had given any formal commitment to help victims, it was politically inconceivable for policies for victims to advance under their own name. They had instead to be smuggled in under the cloak of the older, established policies of crime prevention and the promotion and dissemination of good police practice.

The first appearance of any new policy may then be more than a little odd, forced, as it were, to parade in disguise. And that disguise will be real enough in its consequences, being quite capable of constraining and moulding what can be done politically and practically. In Canada, it was to be a while before measures could be proposed for victims that were not seen manifestly to address the ends of crime prevention and the enhancement of police practice.

There are other deformations. Appearing to serve older ends, new policy issues will have in effect to fill the crevices offered by approved mandates, tasks, and duties. They may be diffracted and scattered as they enter an existing pattern of work and thought. In the Home Office, for example, policies for victims surfaced simultaneously in crime surveys as a means of 'improving the criminal justice database'; as an instrument of a reparative justice that was supposed to replace the fine as a sanction against the poor and unemployed defendant; and as the recipients of criminal injuries compensation that had been intended to buy off the angry victim of violence. That was how expertise about victims was officially organized and approved: it was piecemeal and incoherent, and it proved difficult indeed to reformulate and synthesize so that radically newer and larger images of victims and their needs could be considered.

I have argued that new ideas must often remain somewhat cloaked, incoherent, unfocused, and undeveloped until they have been allowed to become an explicit object of attention. Matters cannot be taken far without formal sanction. They cannot come properly into their own, and little money will be spent in their name, until they have been confirmed in the proper manner by a high official or, more effectively still, by a minister. Indeed, it is part of the bureaucratic art of persuasion that new ideas appear unfocused and unformed at first: they are *supposed* to be so until they receive political authority (it is, after all, the politician who must present the decision, become publicly identified with it and then answer for it to the wider world). Were it to seem otherwise, it might be thought that there had been an act of *lèse majesté*, a pre-empting of the senior's right to judge, govern, and make changes. Decisions must always seem to flow down from those who are accountable, not rise fully formed from obscure officials below.

Mandates

Political approval translates an idea into a political mandate, an internal notion into an external action, and 'going to ministers' is a transition for which there has to be considerable preparation.

In instances of bottom-up policy making, the setting where new ideas were engendered may well be structurally distant from the settings in which they will be inspected and approved by senior officials or politicians. They may stem at first or second hand from research or from what Canadians call 'program delivery', from the activities of those whose chief duty is not to write policy papers at all. Theirs will be the language of research and practice, a language ill suited to the drafting of policy papers, and it is a characteristic complaint of policy officials and politicians that researchers do not know how to speak or write for purposes of political action.

Policy proposals have their own idiom. They must be transformed into a semblance of the reasonable, consistent, solid, and coherent, transformed, indeed, into something rather more coherent and solid than those who draft them might privately concede them to be. Drafting is a delicate skill. On the one hand, proposals must be given a history, a teleology, and secure links with established policies. They must seem reasonable, safe, and sensible, something worth pursuing, a plausible 'next step' that follows from mandates and manifestos, a step, moreover, that is unlikely to embarrass ministers or expose them to untoward criticism. Yet, on the other hand, they must also seem new and important enough to warrant exciting ministerial interest and perhaps even ministerial patronage, sufficiently distinctive to permit politicians to win 'some ink' as Canadian officials would put it. And all the while, as I have observed, proposals cannot be allowed to seem *too* solid, closed, or well argued because ministers would then think that they have been denied their right to decide and influence policy. Proposals must thus be at once convincing and open, new and not-so-new, clear and ambiguous, coherent and loose.

Above all, policy proposals must be phrased politically. That is, they must be designed to win approval from the powerful individuals and organizations that can impede or accelerate their progress, from other politicians and from 'practitioners' in the criminal justice system in particular. Those 'practitioners'—'private sector' organizations and police forces, probation services, prisons, judges and magistrates, prosecutors and lawyers, and all their representative organizations—compose a wary array of loose-coupled bodies that continually eye and treat with one another and with government at their centre. They are, in effect, a loose mass of significant others that retain what one former Home Secretary, Douglas Hurd, described as an 'independent interdependence'. They are neither autonomous nor subservient. They cannot be controlled by government, they do not control government themselves, but they do mediate the decisions of government, sometimes translating them beyond recognition; they are usually taken to be authorities about matters of government policy; they can reverse and transform what government does (the fate of the 1991 Criminal Justice Act being a prime instance), and ministers neglect them at their peril. Placating them is the first political imperative.

The second imperative is to allow ministers to appear consistent, reasonable, and plausible in the presentation and defence of their policies. The work of Canadian Solicitors General and British Home Secretaries is fraught. It is the dirty work of society (see Hughes 1971), the work from which others choose usually to draw back. It centres on the exercise of violence and coercion, the restraining of those who do not wish to be restrained, the investigation of guilty knowledge, and the routine management of pain, anger, distress, and injury. Allegations of brutality towards demonstrators, immigrants, prisoners and offenders, of negligence in the handling of cases, and of indifference to the victim and public abound. Dirty work is marked by a potential for criticism and scandal (another Home Secretary, James Callaghan, recalled how he used to 'switch on the radio news at seven o'clock in the morning mainly to find out what examples of alleged unfair treatment had cropped up during the night as a result of a Home Office decision' (Callaghan 1983: 15)).

Further, the dirty work of criminal justice is not only flawed by its inability to do much that is demonstrably effective, but it also gives rise to a proliferation of unintended consequences when things *are* attempted: recall that the suspended sentences designed to reduce the prison population merely enlarged it; that the unit fines supposed to restore fairness in sentencing were represented publicly and forcefully as most unfair; and that the short, sharp shock of penal reform was reported actually to be liked by its recipients. New proposals must be offered gingerly because it is often safer to do very little or nothing at all for fear of things appearing to go wrong.

The third imperative is to hasten other objects sought by government. The politics of criminal justice are but part of a wider pattern of commitments and objectives. In Canada, for instance, federal criminal justice policies were pursued as much for their capacity to strengthen the integrity of the federal system as for any impact they might have on lesser problems of crime and justice. Indeed, federal–provincial relations (for which there was a separate Cabinet office) superseded much else. So it was that a policy emanating from the Ministry of the Solicitor General or the Ministry of Justice in Ottawa could not be allowed to estrange politicians from the provinces, and from Quebec or the western provinces above all, by seeming to encroach on their rights and sensibilities. In England and Wales, there has been for a long while an overriding political imperative to curtail public expenditure and enhance 'efficiency', and criminal justice policy cannot be seen to run markedly counter to it. At the very least, public rhetoric must contain some ostentatious reference to parsimony.

In all this, it may be seen that the argument of policy making does not necessarily model itself on the reasoning of criminology and the social sciences. That reasoning is of lesser importance. It is politically immaterial. Of course, politicians and senior officials do generally tend to want the tacit reassurance that what they are asked to endorse will not run foul of the good sense of criminologists and junior criminal justice practitioners. They would like to assume that they are supported at critical points by a largely invisible body of experts and expertise. They do not wish to appear foolish. But political argument has its own style which does not defer to social science (political speeches and briefing papers are not punctuated by scholarly citations but by references to political endorsements and the possible reactions of powerful institutions and constituencies). It may even be a little casuistical on occasion. In the Prison Department of the 1960s, for example, policies for women were frequently represented as *sui generis*, having no bearing on policies for men and establishing no precedents, because women offenders were themselves *sui generis*. In April 1969, Lord Stonham argued in a speech 'women are a special case requiring forms of treatment which are not necessarily suitable for men. They are special not because they are women but because the woman who risks a custodial penalty is a comparative rarity and thus justifies consideration as a special case'. It probably mattered little whether such an argument was always put with full conviction, whether officials did really imagine that women offenders were significantly different. What mattered was that an argument based on a difference between the sexes could sometimes help to take policies forward within the Home Office of the time.

If criminological reasoning is not always paramount, neither is criminological reasonableness. The discourse of politicians about criminal justice is sometimes less rational and utilitarian ('causative' is Christie Davies's word (Davies 1990)) than moralising, and the two forms of argument do not necessarily converge. Ministers act from moral conviction, political need, and personal opportunism. Their response to much scholarly research, and especially to contradictory research undertaken by their own staff, will be to ignore it, or to wish that it had never been conducted, and, if it *had* been conducted, never published. At a press conference held on 6 January 1994, for instance, the Prime Minister championed the superiority of common sense to 'fashionable theories' about moral conduct. The following day, again exhorting common sense, he was reported by the BBC to have talked about 'airy-fairy theories for dealing with criminals'. Criminology may be as much a political hazard or nuisance as a guide in the politician's world.

Committees as Modes and Models of Action

Seminars, surveys, literature reviews, and fieldwork supply the criminologist's knowledge, but it is the committee that chiefly supplies the knowledge and methodology of policy makers and politicians. Committees are the stock instrument of government: they put flesh on the first, deliberately vague arguments of submissions to senior officials or ministers; they develop, protect, and shepherd ideas through successive stages of the political process; they enlarge the number of organizations seen to have a manifest interest in an issue; they may ultimately be responsible for the implementation of policy; and, in all this, they have their own detailed phenomenology.

The very composition of a new committee is usually intended to convey political meaning to a knowing audience. In the distrustful world of criminal justice, a world built on conflict and competition, the members of a committee tend to be appointed expressly to reassure powerful onlookers that they and their stance have been recognized and incorporated, that a balance has been struck between jarring interests, that the committee will not be the creature of any faction. There are stock configurations: in England and Wales, the probation service is used conventionally to play the part of the offender's champion, the symbolic counterweight to the police, and probation officers will often be found facing police officers in committee meetings; in Canada, a geographically gargantuan federal state riddled with complicated political jealousies, federal officials will be matched by provincial officials, state representatives by representatives of the 'private sector', the eastern provinces by western provinces, and men by women (and Canadian committees are much more substantial, abundant, and prolix than those to be found in England and Wales. Indeed, the Canadian delegations to United Nations congresses on matters of crime and control are amongst the very largest of all.)

Thus recruited and so aligned, the members of a committee act in part to embody the policy maker's expectation of how a new issue might make its political mark on the world. They are an anticipation of who will receive and define the issue; of who will implement it or impede its implementation; of who, in short, must be won before it can succeed. They display a careful political iconography, an encoded statement of the kind of thing the policy must become. It matters less that they do not always contain those who consider themselves the wisest and most experienced men and women in criminal justice, the criminologists and professors of criminal law perhaps, than that they represent a conspicuous obeisance to the institutions that could do their fledgling issue harm.

Forming a committee confirms an important transfer of ownership and it is not without its existential costs for the original small group of officials who engendered a policy. In Canada especially, where it is not considered unseemly to display personal commitment to the ends of policy making, officials sometimes found it difficult to relinquish 'their' issue to others (and especially to others who appeared to have no great regard for the task); to share information, materials, and sources; in short, to lose control over their creation. At various critical opening phases of the history of the

Canadian Justice for Victims of Crime Initiative, for example, some officials chose to cling to what they had themselves set in motion, impeding its movement to the next stages of what, in Ottawa, is always an elaborately figured sequence of policy development. It was as if they claimed to know and care much more about victims than could any of their successors, the officials and politicians who had shared none of the early investments, experiences, and relations that had infused the beginnings of a new and enthralling area of policy development. Of course, in doing so, they were behaving a little perversely, but they did find it hard to forego what had become symbolically a piece of themselves. Transitions are always difficult.

I have argued that by convention government committees contain the formal representatives of institutionally-embedded interests and practices thought likely to bear significantly on a new policy. They are devised to draw outsiders in, to anticipate and accommodate their views, to implicate them practically and symbolically, perhaps even to transform them into agents who will turn to work on their own parent institutions, and to present them as reassuring tokens of the kind of policy that is considered to be in the making.

Outsiders may do much to promote an issue, they may enlarge the number of its supporters, they will bring fresh knowledge, methods, and ideas to bear, but they will always be included at a price. Those who invite them in will be obliged to surrender some of their ability to define an issue and control how it is treated (and they will be obliged to do so gracefully). The very logic and content of policy making can begin to acquire what seem to be alien forms as the new members work on the original, core idea and transform it into their own property.

Who is invited to draft shapes what will be said. In this sense, policy proposals may be read as transcriptions of the social structure of the committee that considered them. For instance, Status of Women Canada was a federal government organization entrusted with vetting relevant policy papers submitted to Cabinet in the late 1970s and early 1980s, and its representatives were invited as a matter of course to become members of policy-making committees within the Ministry of the Solicitor General. As routinely, almost all criminal justice policy proposals emanating from that Ministry would make conspicuous reference to the interests of women. The Home Office has no commerce with an English counterpart of Status of Women Canada and it does not make such visible genuflections to women. The papers of the Canadian Justice for Victims of Crime Initiative, an initiative addressed to all Canadian victims, were heavily laden with images of crimes against women and with allusions to the special needs of women. Home Office proposals on victims at large were not thus 'gendered' (although, to be sure, there have been other, discrete Home Office initiatives on rape and domestic violence). It was just so with federal–provincial relations, relations between the state and private sector, links between the eastern and western reaches of the nation, and the like. Canadian policy proposals tend to be vastly more ornate and lengthy than their British counterparts, and they make many more detailed references to political mandates and obligations. In so doing, they are a mirror of the greater complexity of relations within that divided, cumbersome federal state. Canadian officials themselves seem to be significantly more conscious of the art and artfulness of policy making. They treat their work as a mystery which demands the greatest attention. They talk incessantly about themselves and their activities as 'process persons'. The British official is, by contrast, less visibly prone to self-examination.

Over time, a committee can become rather more than a simple aggregation of diverse interests. It can become a social group with a sense of joint purpose, a history and a distinctiveness that sets it apart from the larger world (including the institutions from which its members were themselves recruited). The experience of working together for a period of time on a single project under a common name recognized by others can lead members to share an identity and the beginnings of a subculture. So it was that the chairman of the Holloway Redevelopment Project Group recorded in his first, unpublished progress report in March 1969 that 'I regard continuity of membership . . . as important in contributing to the development of a loyalty to the group and the project as such. In such a major enterprise it is necessary that the key contributors should feel personally identified with its success'.

What is one chairman's process of personal identification is another's 'going native', and it is just that risk of their representatives 'going native' which can occasion anxiety amongst staff working in other institutions, leading to the periodic replacement of personnel and the deliberate disruption of continuity.

A committee is a way of seeing, and it is a way of seeing, moreover, that is quite purposefully cultivated as members set to work constructing narratives to strengthen and elucidate themselves and their project (a task especially valuable for those who are newcomers to the policy area and who require rapid briefing). One such narrative will centre on an issue's place in the larger history of criminal justice policies. I have argued that issues are often forced to begin their life in strange clothing, being represented as attempts to promote other goals already approved. I have also argued that they will have been deliberately phrased in an underdeveloped and ambiguous form. At the outset, they can seem more than a little confused and ill defined to the naive eye.

It is the job of early committee papers to undo some of that vagueness, to give workable concreteness and definition to an issue and its resolution. In giving them greater solidity, a committee will begin to acquire what is, in effect, the political equivalent of its navigational bearings. Like most elaborate projects in everyday life, policy making is experienced *in situ* as an emergent, indeterminate, anxious, and uncertain process, buttressed by no guarantees of success. At the very beginning, not much will be known about an issue and the problems that will be encountered, it is difficult to predict outcomes, and the manufacture of a semblance of structure and direction is an indispensable first step. From time to time thereafter, there are likely to be further reinterpretations of structure and direction as key officials leave and their successors take stock of their new position. In early 1974, for example, the security advisor to the Holloway Redevelopment Project changed and, with his leaving, there came a significant revision of the new prison's security provisions.

If briefings confer structure and direction, it can never be forgotten that the committee's political mandate was underdeveloped, and that the committee has no licence to change its fundamental import. Re-drafting cannot be free. It must, instead, build carefully on what was originally approved, retaining the statement's sense and, indeed, much of its phrasing, returning pointedly to its principal themes, piling detail on a narrow base. It will begin by locating itself in time, giving itself what McHugh called a retrospective-prospective reading (McHugh 1968).

Retrospectively, it will search for a past, for the precedents and early stirrings that explain how it was that a policy issue arose and the committee came to be formed at all. I remarked how, before they are approved, issues tend to be cultivated as instances of other policies altogether, and I gave the instance of Canadian victims who were first helped in the name of improving police efficiency. There will be no need to resort to such flags of convenience once a firm political mandate has been secured. To the contrary, such a mandate will enable policy makers to look back and claim other policies and near-policies as part of their own legitimating history. What had been disguised will then be revealed as the clear forebear of policies now in the making. It is as if policies must begin their lives with a false identity imposed by others, but that they will come in time to force others to become part of *their* solipsism, histories switching back and forth in sympathy with changes of political fortune.

The reconstruction of the past can become quite bold on occasion, particularly when it is conducted by a bureaucrat fired with zeal for a cause. Things that might have been thought quite peripheral will then be retrieved and claimed historically, being awarded a teleology in which they become the ancestors and antecedents of a present politics. For instance, papers advancing the growth of policies for victims and reparative justice refer quite routinely to Moses and Hamurabi, to Solon and the Anglo-Saxon moot.

Prospectively, a committee must plot a course based on bureaucratic and political schedules so that patterns of work can be planned and difficulties forestalled. Any piece of policy making requires that its papers will be presented to a succession of meetings and its decisions co-ordinated with those of parallel bodies. Politicians and civil servants work to lesser and greater timetables. There is the round of the parliamentary year and the Public Expenditure Survey and, within it, the smaller rounds of departmental and interdepartmental meetings. Such schedules present a strong teleology for any policy making, laying out an exact sequence of actions that must be undertaken if a committee is to succeed in its task. They reduce uncertainty by preparing a future. They impart a clear, formal logic to policy making: *this* paper must be ready for *that* meeting with *this* argument. They specify much of the content of policy making: a paper must contain recommendations consonant with other recommendations, declarations, and manifestos already agreed by ministers and government. They give a pulse and a rhythm to policy making; *this* meeting on a particular date will be succeeded by *that* meeting of another date and then by yet another meeting thereafter. They give an unambiguous goal for the opening stages of most policy making; most probably a successful submission to Cabinet and Treasury. They give a political audience for policy making; laying out what is, in effect, a chain of significant others who must be addressed effectively if matters are to go forward and prosper. They give duration to policy making. In short, they furnish a strong grammar and choreography which will impress themselves on what must be done.

It is a consequence that policies are fairly homologous within states. They follow set forms of argument that carefully refract the contours and history of the political world through which they are steered. The more complex that world, the more complex must policies and policy documents themselves be. I have already observed that Canadian federal policies deferred to the rights of women and natives; to the private sector; and to the provinces. They were taken before Status of Women Canada, interdepartmental and federal–provincial meetings, and conferences with voluntary organizations. The working year of Canadian officials could be described as a great, orderly spate of meetings, and the wordy policy documents that emerged at its end were replete with bows and curtsies to all the bodies that had been so fulsomely consulted. The Home Office official, by contrast, tends traditionally to reckon with fewer outside powers, attend fewer meetings, communicate chiefly through internal files, and produce fewer, shorter, and more simply-structured briefing papers.

An accompanying step is neither prospective nor retrospective but synchronic. Policy officials may search about them publicly for information about the character of the issue that has newly to come into view, to establish what others are doing in its name. Such a quest also leads to the creation of a narrative about what the issue now amounts to as a practical problem. It would have been compromising to have conducted it before, in advance of formal permission to proceed, because a premature public display of interest might have been misinterpreted by outsiders as a political willingness to act. Besides, policy officials, busy as they often are, have little enough time to interest themselves in affairs to no profit. They tend to present themselves as officially deaf to problems not officially recognized (although unofficially, of course, things may be otherwise, and research staff, entrusted with a different role, are expected to have a reasonably broad knowledge of what is afoot in criminology and criminal justice).

When a policy matter lies wholly within the government's domain, when those liable to be affected are all state employees and state dependants, it may well be the case that officials take it that they know enough to proceed without much visible enquiry. Deafness will prevail. In the instance of the rebuilding of Holloway, for example, consultations were made rather late in the life of the initiative. Plans were quite far advanced when the shape of the new prison was finally disclosed to the public in 1971, three years after the decision was announced in Parliament. And consultations about the new prison were described by those involved as perfunctory indeed. (Even in the instance of rebuilding Holloway, an institution in an urban area, government officials were not quite sovereign: local authorities, Members of Parliament, and residents' groups protested vehemently about the use of scarce land for a prison, and they had to be appeased a little).

In other cases, the political endorsement of a new issue ends indifference. Officials who had formerly been inattentive can become very attentive indeed as they move rapidly to accumulate stocks of knowledge about an area. Government departments have routine techniques for the purpose: research officers or consultants will be set to work compiling 'literature reviews'; money will be allocated to found 'resource centres'; old files and speeches will be trawled; and conferences will be organized. In all this, it is apparent that officials seek to amass, list, and categorize information to furnish a pragmatically useful description of what is being done in and around an issue. But, in such a public amassing of data, they will always accomplish more than mere description. Theirs is a world pregnant with meaning. It will be scanned by politicians, practitioners, and critics and, with a peculiar intensity, by research, voluntary, and statutory organizations continually hungry for money. Officials have to proceed in the full understanding that their every act will be read as a possible sign of shifting government intentions. Indeed, they will knowingly act to signify.

Formal public enquiry stirs up multiple meanings. It is a practical method of advertising that a government or department is considering whether to move in on a social problem (and it may be initiated precisely to invite pressure to move). It will be interpreted as a running indication of the kinds of plan that government has in mind for that problem. It brings into official view those who are the target of enquiry, laying them out within a framework supplied by the state, emphasizing certain facets and suppressing others. It encourages those target organizations to examine themselves, to ask whether they are, in fact, inhabitants of the world supposed to centre on that problem and in that manner, whether, indeed, they recognize the problem as an entity that should be so defined at all.

Take one instance: the manner in which the composition of a conference will define a problem. Inclusions, exclusions, timings, and orders of appearance count. When, for example, the mounting of a crime survey was first mooted at a conference organized by the Home Office in early 1981, no invitation to attend was issued to members of the fledgling National Association of Victim Support Schemes, the body responsible for aiding victims of crime. It was thereby made abundantly clear that crime surveys were not supposed to illuminate the character of victims or the experience of crime. They were instead taken to be a method of improving what was called the 'criminal justice data base'.

Conferences have their own manifest phenomenology. They signify that a problem has been acknowledged by government; they define its ingredients and its social constituents; they bring those constituents together and present them to one another, perhaps for the first time, and under a common name, in the hope, perhaps, that they will come to recognize a common identity and purpose; and they act as an audience, response, and catalyst for the decisions that officials will prepare (the teleology of an approaching speech is a powerful means of eliciting public commitments from ministers and senior civil servants, and conferences are frequently organized precisely for that end).

In this search for information and convening of meetings, officials can stretch out quite far to encompass organizations and people who may not have considered themselves parts of the emerging policy issue, and who may indeed resent the belated attempt of central government to determine who and what they really are. After all, such official definitions tend to arise late in the careers of those organizations, usually after they have become established under their own chosen names. One example is given by the Home Office Programme Development Unit that set about funding community-based projects in 1991 by inviting the submission of original proposals to reduce criminality and domestic violence. Its chief object was to discover and foster something of the vernacular criminology currently being practised by local groups. It was fired by a broad Conservative ministerial interest in revitalizing the moral fabric of the family and by the civil servant's interest in the social engineering of 'headstart' and other programmes devised to compensate for social disadvantage. What it *did* meet was a wholesale lay interest in the 'empowerment' of the young, an interest that echoed the Big Bang of the radical liberation movements of the 1960s.

Similarly, when the governments of Canada and of England and Wales set about formulating policies for victims, they encountered groups and individuals who had made little use of the word 'victim', who did not at first conceive themselves to be part of the politics of crime and criminal justice, and who resisted efforts to become incorporated into what appeared powerfully to be another's reality. Those who worked with abused children, assaulted women, and incest and rape survivors, did not enter willingly into the politics of *victims*. Victims, crime, and criminal justice were not central to their vocabulary. They had their own rival political history which was not to be shed lightly.

Such encounters take place on uneven ground because the state has the greater ability to define and reward, especially when those on the boundaries of its newly-proclaimed policies are ill organized, poor, and lacking in substantial authority within the criminal justice system. Yet organizations can and do answer back. It would be most undiplomatic of officials and politicians to rebuff their conceptual challenges too roundly, particularly when they hope to enlist members of the organizations to support them, to give them legitimacy and to do some of the work that the implementation of a policy will require.

Policy Making as a Dialectical Process

At every successive stage of the policy-making process, then, issues will be dressed and proffered to a larger group for inspection, collaboration, and the possibility of symbolic co-ownership, and, at every stage, officials cannot be certain about what that larger group might do. The process is emergent; not quite within the official grasp. If the group's response is not a simple repulse, policy proposals must receive at least some token imprint to register that officials have deferred to the group and heeded what it has said. The whole amounts to a dialectic in which policies enter the public domain step by step, being sent out to ever-wider social circles and presented for possible acquisition, and returning each time transformed. In Canada, a country so vast it must depend on a major decentralization of the criminal justice system, those social circles extend out into the provinces, municipalities, and the private domain, and they are wooed quite assiduously. In England and Wales, the array of circles is smaller, tighter, and more nearly confined to the state, but there must conventionally be consultation with ACPO and ACOP, the Lord Chancellor's Department and the Lord Chief Justice, the Magistrates' Association and perhaps, very tentatively, with friendly bodies in the private sector defined by the Home Office as 'house-trained'. There is a British dialectic too and, if it is ignored, ACPO, ACOP, the Magistrates Association and the others can round on government. They did so quite fiercely in the aftermath of the 1991 Criminal Justice Act.

Policy Making as Reflective Action

The dialectic and its forms are familiar to officials, being the very stuff of statecraft. They deploy presentation and signification to propel subjects through the sequence of phases that will transform them into entities fit for political action. Policies are the effect of an accumulation of stimuli.

Officials cannot always wait patiently for the right stimulus to arise and do its work precisely at the appropriate time. They intervene continually, nursing the dialectic, and they do so by standing back to reflect on the pace, direction, appearance, and impact of their own actions. In what the Canadians call a 'paper world', they use the medium proper to policy making: the manipulation of argument and rhetoric. They objectify themselves, their work, their artefacts and their environment, transforming them all into materials for symbolic management. The world of policy making is then itself reflexive, becoming a thing to be embellished and arranged, goaded into action by stimuli which it has itself created and planted. In Weick's phrase (Weick 1982), officials work to enact their own environment: they engender the apparently objective conditions to which they themselves must respond, and, in responding, carry matters forward. I described how ministers would be asked to speak on particular themes, committing them to make the public utterances and perhaps even the commitments that officials would draft for them. Entire conferences will be organized to elicit just such a speech. More obvious still is the 'planted' parliamentary question to which there will be a prepared answer, and officials speak with occasional pride and amusement about the replies they drafted for their own questions. Policy making thus turns round on itself, and officials in those states where such a process is especially elaborate may be heard talking about themselves talking, referring to themselves quite impersonally as a third party.

It must be noted that timetables do not always unfold smoothly and officials cannot always be in command of events which they have themselves engineered. Criminal justice policy making is so extensive, unpredictable, and fragmented that they cannot foresee just what may happen about them. In this sense, policies are set in an intricate and volatile environment of other initiatives and events that are also on the move, and their fate will be shaped by the manner in which officials can use that environment to political effect. Theirs must be an opportunistic world that rewards the alert and the persuasive. They are strategists preoccupied always with what they call the 'windows of opportunity' that come and go before them, strategists who try to employ ingenious arguments to manoeuvre their candidate policies into place when the time is right.

So it is that fledgling policies are often obliged to ride to success in the wake of other, more mature political movements and rhetoric will be devoted to the effort of harnessing them together. In *A View from the Shadows* (1986), for instance, I showed how the Canadian Justice for Victims of Crime Initiative, designed for all victims, men and women, acquired its political momentum from the women's movement and its campaigns against rape and battering. A bundle of policies for Canadian victims was advanced within the Trojan horse of a proposed federal initiative to help assaulted women, and, being thus transported, it had to take its timing from another initiative altogether.

So it is, too, that policies must often be hurried for promotion when the propitious occasion presents itself, however unexpected that occasion may be. The National Association of Victim Support Schemes received major government support in 1986 in response to a sudden funding crisis induced by that same government's imminent abolition of a number of the Association's prime patrons, the metropolitan authorities. And the Canadian Justice for Victims of Crime Initiative was assembled rapidly in 1981 because it could be represented as a new, inexpensive venture that could be funded at the very moment when a sum of Treasury money needed to be spent on a cheap policy innovation. Ottawa officials held that the timing was actually not quite 'right', that they were not really prepared at that stage to emerge into the public domain, but financial austerity was looming and money was unlikely to be available when the policies themselves were in a state of greater readiness.

In this and other instances, the intention might well have been to engage in the careful designing, orchestration, and execution of plans, but the practice is as likely to be expedient and improvisatory, and policy itself can become transformed into something makeshift. Many policies have to enter the world premature and incomplete, lacking fine detail and content. It is only after they have been announced that officials can set themselves the task of discovering or inventing quite what has been approved.

Conclusion

Policy making is the instrument through which the original, subjective inspiration of a few individuals closeted within a bureaucracy can move out to become a public, anonymous, and objective component of the criminal justice system at large. It proceeds typically by preparing and submitting ideas to an ever greater mass of significant others for judgement and investment, and it turns, first, on the physical and symbolic incorporation of outsiders and secondly, on spinning webs of causality about itself and its projects. It is, in this sense, both its own object, a creature of parthenogenesis, and an object proffered to others for fostering. It would be an otherwise smooth metamorphosis were it not for the sudden lurches and opportunities imposed by uncontrolled problems of timing and context.

References

Bittner, E. (1965), 'The Concept of Organization', *Social Research*, 32.

Callaghan, J. (1983), 'Cumber and Variableness', in *The Home Office: Perspectives on Policy and Administration*. London: Royal Institute of Public Administration.

Davies, C. (1990), *From the Sacred Hierarchies to Flatland*. Reading: University of Reading.

Hughes, E. (1971), 'Good People and Dirty Work', in *The Sociological Eye*, Chicago: Aldine-Atherton.

McHugh, P. (1968), *Defining the Situation*. Indianapolis: Bobbs-Merrill.

Rock, P. (1986), *A View from the Shadows*. Oxford: Clarendon Press.

—— (1990), *Helping Victims of Crime*. Oxford: Clarendon Press.

—— (1993), *The Social World of the English Crown Court*. Oxford: Clarendon Press.

—— (1994), 'The Social Organization of a Home Office Initiative', *European Journal of Crime, Criminal Law and Criminal Justice*, 2.

Weick, K. (1982), 'Enactment Processes in Organizations', in B. Staw and G. Salancik (eds.), *New Directions in Organizational Behavior*. Malabar: Robert E. Krieger.

[10]
Sociology and the Stereotype of the Police

INTRODUCTION

I was asked to contribute to a 'review [of] the work of the Oxford centre within the context of socio-legal studies over the last 21 years . . . [and to] provide an opportunity to explore the current nature and scope of the discipline . . . '. And that is what I shall do.

I have a recollection of attending the inaugural conference of the centre twenty-one years ago. My memory is hazy, but I seem to recall discussion of matters that were of little immediate appeal to one who was then, and still is, a sociologist of crime and deviance, wedded to qualitative methods, to ethnography, and to 'thick description'. There was a propensity to cast the study of law as part of a pre-eminently bookish activity, as a discourse of scholarly ideas about scholarly ideas that floated freely in libraries and seminar rooms. It would have been very easy to continue that drift. After all, it was the authoritative, approved way of talking about law in universities. It sounded impressive. It smacked of philosophy and the history of ideas to which the social sciences in Oxford (and elsewhere) have always been pulled. But that drift was *not* sustained. In its place, some useful and original lines of work appeared, and they appeared, it seemed, almost out of nowhere.

I shall settle on only one or two of those lines of development although others were and are equally important. What is significant, I would argue, is that sociology and socio-legal studies at the centre came to treat the enforcement of law, and of regulatory law in particular, as a complicated, situated, evolving, and interpretive practice whose character could not be divined simply from reading books or from pure reason alone.[1] It was to be treated as empirically problematic, grounded in meaning, negotiated, and emergent, and that was to be illuminating indeed.

* *Professor, Department of Sociology, and Director of the Mannheim Centre, London School of Economics and Political Science, Houghton Street, London WC2A 2AE, England*

I am grateful to Bridget Hutter and Keith Hawkins for their help in commenting on an earlier draft of this chapter.

Of course, there were precursors to such an approach. There were the United States legal pragmatists and the first sociologists of the police.[2] There were the United States sociologists of deviance who had presented rule-making, rule-breaking, and rule-enforcement as intertwined symbolic processes.[3] In the United Kingdom, there was Kit Carson who had promised in the early 1970s to direct interpretive sociology towards the work of the factory inspectors.[4] But Carson was virtually alone and he faltered, in part, perhaps, because there was not much of a language or group to sustain him. Instead, it was the centre, founded in 1972 and directed by Don Harris, that promoted research that was not only co-operative but sustained over long periods of time[5] by scholars from different intellectual backgrounds, and the outcome was something of a new intellectual fusion. In Hutter's words, 'the multidisciplinary atmosphere of the centre . . . moved the focus away from something closely related to an enlightened lawyer's approach, to a distinctive subject/discipline, from which some useful and original lines of work emerged . . .'.

THE CENTRE'S REDEFINITION OF THE FIELD

In effect, members of the centre undertook and sustained a classic analytic manoeuvre that is almost always likely to be attended by success. They transposed familiar, established thought to an unfamiliar terrain in which it appeared new and daring. Just as in the 1950s and 1960s, Lemert, Becker, Cicourel, and others had galvanized criminology by transplanting relatively commonplace interactionist ideas about careers, identities, and relations from the conventional realm of medicine, work, and education to the unconventional realm of crime, deviation, and control, disclosing how very conventional the unconventional can be, so, in the 1970s, the centre ferried very similar interactionist and phenomenological theories to yet another territory in which they would again attain a strange character. The centre was dedicated to the new field of socio-legal studies, not to criminology, and it applied the emerging logic of the sociology of deviance, of what some call 'social constructionism', to phenomena in areas of law hitherto neglected, the areas that fell outside what Keith Hawkins called the 'traditional criminological boundaries'.

That emerging logic of interactionism was not quite an orthodoxy in British universities at that time (and is probably not so even now[6]), and it was not taught formally in many places. It was more than a little homespun, the product of younger scholars working sometimes idiosyncratically to fashion their own understanding of what was being said and written in the United States of America. Just as those first British sociologists of deviance, the sociologists of the 1960s, had had to be autodidacts, so the new socio-legal scholars were obliged to teach themselves much of what was to become important. Keith Hawkins, for instance, had been a graduate student at the

University of Cambridge Institute of Criminology and he had had to 'struggle to a version of interactionism on my own'. He had been, he said, 'painfully re-inventing the wheel'. The new socio-legal scholars individually and sometimes jointly discovered, extrapolated, and then reformulated a sociology of social control in the work of Peter Manning,[7] Jonathan Rubinstein,[8] Jerry Skolnick, James Wilson,[9] and others. They then proceeded to apply what they had found to what a member of the centre called the 'banal everyday routines' of regulation. In 1989, Hawkins and Thomas were to observe:

> As a theoretical framework having certain methodological implications, the social constructionist perspective is part of the broad tradition of interpretive sociology of deviance, and in many areas of the sociology of deviance, scholars have given much less attention to its potential for furthering our understanding of public policymaking in general and of regulatory policymaking in particular.[10]

It is useful to recall some of the imagery embodied in that 'broad tradition', an imagery whose features I shall exaggerate for purposes of effect, an imagery that was Janus-faced. The sociologists of deviance of the 1960s and 1970s had worked simultaneously to negate an older criminology and to affirm a new. As agents of negation, they been stirred into being by a reaction against an iconography described variously as positivist, correctionalist or administrative. Dennis Chapman remarked at that time how conventional sociology had been bedeviled by a particular stereotype of the criminal (and it is his argument that I have adapted for the title of this paper):

> much of the work done by social scientists in the field of Criminology [he argued] has been unprofitable because it has begun with definitions – stereotypes [of the criminal] – which have determined the course of the inquiry and the conclusions that have emerged.[11]

He argued that such stereotypes depicted criminals as young working-class men 'lacking education, influence and resources', and they removed the crimes of the middle and upper classes from purview. And, it was said (although not by Chapman), those stereotypes also failed to consider motive and meaning and subverted the very possibility of adequate understanding. The interactionists' and radical criminologists' resulting attempt to put matters right led to what Stan Cohen called a 'very radical break from traditional perspectives'.[12]

As agents of affirmation, the new sociologists were preoccupied with the interplay between deviance and regulation and, in particular, with the symbolic and practical incorporation of formal social control into the unfolding deviant gesture. They necessarily dwelt on the doings of people who were visibly at hand; those whom they could effectively study as graduate students and young teachers; the denizens of their own and adjoining social worlds; people who could be found most frequently in public space; the deviants, very often, who engaged in symbolic displays; the people described by Gouldner as 'drug addicts, jazz musicians, cab drivers, prostitutes, night people, drifters, grifters, and skidders, the cool cats . . . '.[13]

One such American sociologist mused in 1971, 'after all, we were only talking about ourselves'. Many of the deviants populating the arguments of the new sociology were, in short, those whom Americans would call 'street people'.

When 'social constructionist' sociologists took the next step and explored proscriptions and proscribers as constituents of deviant acts and identities, they had little enough of a research or literary tradition with which to work, they had few economic and social resources to mobilize, and they were committed to the use of direct, ethnographic methods. In the main, they had started with the study of street people, and it was behaviour on the streets that they were inclined to study when they turned to examine rule enforcement in the guise of policing and police officers.

The first anthropological reports of policing typically described how uniformed beat officers strove to maintain order over working-class males in urban space.[14] They were, in essence, accounts of comparatively fleeting, anonymous, and isolated meetings between groups of young men abroad in public: one group, the police officers, being authoritative and powerful, and the other, the working class, possessing very little formal authority at all. Those groups met after rules had been broken, when situations seemed to be running out of control[15] or when there was a contest over the domination of territory.[16] And, when they did meet, their encounters had inevitably to be based on rapidly-formed judgements; on stereotype and pragmatics; on the constraints exercised in public by audiences of strangers;[17] on the use or threatened use of force; and on the ever-present prospect of punishment.

To be sure, the standard portrait of policing was never simple or monochrome. It was qualified by sociologists who insisted always on the situated, nuanced, negotiable, and ambiguous character of social life. Police officers mediated conflict as well as making quick, punitive interventions.[18] They handled much outside the sphere of crime and the criminal law.[19] But there was undoubtedly a clear thesis that much policing should be understood as simple practical activity taking place in a world of oppositions between us and them, the moral and the immoral, the powerful and the powerless, the trustworthy and the untrustworthy, the insider and the stranger, the few and the many, the known and the unknown, the orderly and the chaotic.[20] The police, it was claimed, over-categorized deviants. Deviants were essentialized, reified and depersonalized, quickly reduced to a few core traits for purposes of management.

So vivid and plausible was that picture, so strengthened by the representations of film, news reporting, and drama was it (it is no accident that a number of sociologists of the police are avid watchers of movies), that the uniformed officer patrolling the streets became something of an icon of policing at large, a very personification of the state and its power to coerce, of Matza's Leviathan.[21] The activities of the male, urban beat constable have continued to loom large in the sociology of formal social control. Until very recently, it could be said that there have been very few complementary studies of senior ranks, of women officers,[22] of specialist policing, of rural policing[23] or of police policy-making.[24] It could also be said that there have very few studies of other agents of control, of tax inspectors and customs officers, of the NSPCC and the RSPCA, private police and security staff, bailiffs and tipstaffs. In effect, the gallery of agents of formal social control has been virtually exhausted by the police officer. The interactionist sociology of deviance harboured its own problematic stereotype, and, in turning against it, Hawkins, Hutter, Baldwin, Cranston, and others at the Oxford Centre have done just what the once new criminologists and sociologists of deviance did before them.

They found that, beyond the borders of criminology, in the centre's own special terrain where codes no longer seemed sacred but secular, not moral but technical and instrumental, the older analysis and stereotypy did not work very well. Problems touching on matters of pollution, consumer protection and environmental health, the safety of airlines, railways and nuclear power plants, were certainly controlled and patrolled. They were policed. But they were not policed in quite the same way as that presented by the stock studies of the sociology of deviance.

I remember confronting precisely those problems of fit when, in the 1960s, I was writing my own homespun interactionist thesis on the activities of debt collectors and county court bailiffs. I had to modify and trim analysis to accommodate the special character of a cheap, staggered enforcement system intent on coaxing deviants not conventionally regarded as deviant to co-operate with agents who, for the most part, lacked significant power and legitimacy.[25]

At the centre itself, Hawkins argued:

> What is known about enforcement behaviour has been garnered almost entirely from work on the police, to the neglect of those countless numbers of individuals whose job it is to enforce regulations punishable by the criminal law.[26]

And Hutter has written about people whose:

> presence often goes unnoticed . . . Their work is typically undramatic and largely hidden from the public eye. Yet, these officials are daily making decisions which may be crucial to our general well-being and which, unknown to many, comprise part of our legal system.[27]

Those substantially unnoticed officials may be less dramatic and conspicuous in their actions, they may be less vivid in their symbolization of the state's power to repress (and have not been noticed for that very reason), but they actually control huge swathes of social and economic life. They attend to the collection of debts, taxes, rents, and revenues; the auditing of accounts; the execution of civil writs; the inspection of shops, offices, installations, services, and factories; the work of coroners' courts; and, with increasing effect, the patrolling of private and semi-private space. No accurate census has or possibly could be taken of how many they are and what it is they do (although it has been estimated that the private police alone may outnumber those employed by the state).[28] Were such a census to be taken, it would probably become evident that the citizen's characteristic experience of formal control is not supplied by the uniformed police at all. Rather, it would take the form of a dunning letter or a visit from a government inspector.

COMPLIANCE-BASED ENFORCEMENT

That form differs from the standard model of policing. It is affected, as all enforcement is affected, by the organization of relations and knowledge between controller and controlled. Contrast an ideal-typical police officer, say a constable patrolling an inner-city street, with an ideal-typical regulatory agent, say a factory inspector, county court bailiff or environmental health officer (I shall again exaggerate for purposes of effect): the one enforces rules conceived to carry a clear moral burden, the other does not; the one is confronted by matters of moral culpability, the other is not (or at least not in the first instance);[29] the one often deals with matters after the event, the other with matters that may not yet have occurred at all or are open-ended, continuing, episodic or infrequent; the one has a relatively limited range of enforcement strategies, the other must balance competing strategies, administering an admixture of retribution, prevention, deterrence, exhortation, and mediation over time;[30] the one deals with people who are physically mobile and perhaps even evasive, the other does not necessarily do so; the one's relations can be ephemeral, requiring the quick and authoritative mastery of problematic situations; the other's relations may well be prolonged and require no such instant command; the one deals with people about whom almost nothing may be known, to whom the routine 'cook-book knowledge' of policing will have to be applied;[31] the other is usually somewhat better placed to observe, judge, and learn; the one tends to deal with those held to be morally discredited, the other cannot make any such immediate judgement about credit or discredit; the one may be obliged to rely on a show of force, the other can, in the first instance, frequently assume that it may be possible to rely on appeals to good sense. It is those and other differences, amplified to be sure, that supply the materials for a model of what some members of the centre have called 'compliance-based' enforcement and others 'accomodative enforcement',[32] enforcement that 'follows a serial pattern, a loosely structured but none the less organized process relying heavily upon negotiated conformity, with a gradual increase in pressure being applied to the uncooperative.'[33]

Such enforcement is set in a social, moral, and economic environment, and its structure often has to reflect the resolution of complex, pragmatic, and political questions about what can be done to people whose offending could be construed as a routine part of life in substantial organizations; whose offending could indeed be regarded as a problem of institutions rather than of persons (recall Sutherland's heavily ironic questions about the psychopathology of corporations); who may not so much have done or omitted to do some definitive thing in a past now closed as failed merely to perform an act so far (although any such future performance *could* well put matters right and overturn the significance of acts and actors); whose behaviour, in other words, is phenomenologically open, uncertain as to its precise intention, meaning, and consequence.

Such enforcement has its own internal, recursive forms, its structure unfolding over time; intention, meaning, and consequence becoming revealed chiefly in the evolving pattern of an offender's replies to enforcement, a matter of his or her apparent co-operativeness, respectfulness, and honesty;[34] deviance and conformity being translated, in effect, into forms of contumacy and deference. Attributions of morality and immorality thus become even more emphatically contingent and embedded properties of enforcement careers, responses to responses, the meanings given to patterns of activity elicited in large measure by social control itself.

Compliance-based enforcement tends usually to be discreet and unobserved, confined by circumstance or choice to private or near-private space, waged by people without uniforms or distinctive insignia, who are unrecognizable to most outsiders. Yet it also attains much of its character from the fact that it is permeated by the shared knowledge that, rarely and as a last resort, when the agents' blandishments and threats have ultimately failed, when the offender is indeed defined as beyond the reach of reasonable appeal, the issues in dispute can be rendered formal and public,[35] the courts can be invoked, and the offender can become liable to exposure and punishment.

In all this, compliance-based enforcement seems to work as much informal control works. It resembles, and is probably rooted in, the workings of a more extensive, intricately-figured, as yet little understood but almost certainly highly effective, network of natural surveillance, inspection, and definition,[36] a network of exhortation, mediation, conciliation, and signification that also turns to formal threats of punishment only when other measures fail,[37] a network composed of mundane activity. Much of its success, one may imagine, revolves around the mobilization of informal strategies, and shaming strategies in particular, that are the currency of discipline in everyday life.[38] One may imagine too that it is by exploiting those complementarities, affinities, and connections with mundane methods that compliance-based enforcement produces its chief effects. Whether and how that is so has not yet been investigated with any thoroughness, although such inquiry would be a logical next step for the Oxford Centre.

CONCLUSION

Despite objections from those who still cling tenaciously to the more obvious, punitive model,[39] compliance-based enforcement probably deserves to be taken as the major pattern or archetype of formal social control in Western society. We are certainly told by JUSTICE[40] that it is the most prevalent style of enforcement. However important and interesting it may be, the work of the conventional police officer is actually relatively infrequent and atypical (although it, too, is often, and perhaps most frequently, also 'compliance-based'), one of the last resorts that bring unresolved disputes and problems to view, and, if that is so, we are obliged to take the work of the centre seriously indeed. Although British sociologists of crime and social control do not seem yet to have properly heeded that work, being beguiled still by the strong, theatrical stereotype of the police, the centre's analysis of the criminal sanction demands attention. With Durkheim, it should be asserted that it is restitutive, not retributive, justice that is the representative form of control in industrial society.[41] What now remains to be resolved is not only a more general and schematic analysis of the implications of that work, but also more extensive empirical enquiry into the linkages between compliance-based enforcement and wider nets of informal social relations.

NOTES AND REFERENCES

1 To be sure, as Hawkins and others would concede, some of those arguments may require the qualifying balance offered by Doreen McBarnet, another member of the centre, who reflected that what is written in legal codes does markedly constrain and order practical action. See her 'False Dichotomies in Criminal Justice Research' in *Criminal Justice: Selected Readings*, ed. A.K. Bottomley (1978). The issue is complicated because, as Hawkins argues, 'one of the characteristics of regulatory codes is that they are frequently designed (for all sorts of interesting reasons) in a very vague and spare fashion, thereby granting regulatory officials correspondingly more formal discretion than their counterparts in the police enjoy . . . It seems to me that one of the major empirical tasks for socio-legal studies is to understand the conditions under which legal rules guide and constrain practical action' (letter).

2 Of acknowledged influence were such works as R. Emerson, *Judging Delinquents* (1969); A. Reiss, *The Police and the Public* (1971); J. Skolnick, *Justice Without Trial* (1966); and W. Westley, 'Violence and the Police' (1953) 59 *Am. J. of Sociology* 59.

3 See H. Becker, *Outsiders* (1963), and A. Cicourel, *The Social Organization of Juvenile Justice* (1968).

4 See W.G. Carson, 'Symbolic and Instrumental Dimensions of Early Factory Legislation' in *Crime, Criminology and Public Policy*, ed. R. Hood (1974).

5 Hawkins remarked that 'one of the original rationales for a Centre was that people should be able to engage in empirical research that it might be difficult or impossible to undertake under a conventional university regime. This has been an important feature in enabling a number of us to do quite extensive ethnographic fieldwork.'

6 Although interactionism has a remarkable following amongst criminologists and sociologists of deviance, being the single largest intellectual school to which scholars professed loyalty in a survey of the profession I conducted in mid-1992. See my 'The Social Organization of British Criminology' in *The Oxford Handbook of Criminology*, eds. M. Maguiere et al. (1994).

7 See P. Manning, *Police Work* (1977). The influence of Manning grew as he became involved with the work of the centre, becoming a visiting fellow at Balliol College in 1981 and then a Senior Associate Researcher at the centre itself, working on the regulation of occupational health and safety between 1984 and 1986.

8 See J. Rubinstein, *City Police* (1973).
9 See J. Wilson, *Varieties of Police Behavior* (1968).
10 K. Hawkins and J. Thomas, 'Making Policy in Regulatory Bureaucracies' in *Making Regulatory Policy*, eds. K. Hawkins and J. Thomas (1989) 10–11.
11 D. Chapman, *Sociology and the Stereotype of the Criminal* (1968) ix.
12 S. Cohen, introduction to *Images of Deviance* (1971) 19.
13 A. Gouldner, 'Anti-Minotaur: The Myth of a Value-Free Sociology' (1962) 10 *Social Problems* 209.
14 See A. Stinchcombe, 'Institutions of Privacy in the Determination of Police Administrative Practice' (1963) 69 *Am. J. of Sociology*.
15 See E. Bittner; *The Functions of the Police in Modern Society* (1970).
16 See C. Werthman and I. Piliavin, 'Gang Members and the Police' in *The Police: Six Sociological Essays*, ed. D. Bordua (1967).
17 See A. Reiss, *The Police and the Public* (1971).
18 See E. Bittner, 'The Police on Skid Row' (1963) 28 *Am. Sociological Rev.* 699–715.
19 See E. Cumming et al., 'Policeman as Philosopher, Friend and Guide' (1965) 12 *Social Problems* 276–86.
20 See S. Holdaway, *Inside the British Police* (1983).
21 See D. Matza, *Becoming Deviant* (1969).
22 But see F. Heidensohn, *Women in Control* (1992).
23 To be sure, there was the early study by M. Cain, *Society and the Policeman's Role* (1974).
24 Of course, that has begun to change. See, for instance, R. Reiner, *Chief Constables* (1991).
25 See P. Rock, *Making People Pay* (1973).
26 K. Hawkins, *Environment and Enforcement* (1984) xiii.
27 B. Hutter, *The Reasonable Arm of the Law?* (1988) 3.
28 See C. Shearing and P. Stenning (eds.), *Private Policing* (1987).
29 Hawkins observes that 'the issue of moral culpability is interesting and very significant in law enforcement work generally. One of the key distinctions in the regulatory field, however, is that much of the behaviour which is theoretically criminal does not violate moral expectations . . . What happens in regulatory enforcement . . . is that an act is morally screened in the first place and enforcement behaviour (if any) organised accordingly (i.e. a moral frame is applied). If the actor is blameless (a discharge is defined as an accident , a technical problem etc.) the event is framed accordingly, and legal consequences will almost certainly be regarded as inappropriate. Otherwise, the actor becomes a "polluter" and the law is maintained as an option.'
30 See W.G. Carson; 'White Collar Crime and the Enforcement of Factory Legislation' (1970) 10 *Brit. J. of Criminology* 393.
31 See M. Chatterton; 'Police Work and Assault Charges' in *Control in the Police Organization*, ed. M. Punch (1983).
32 Hutter, for instance, regards the word 'compliance' as too broad.
33 Hawkins, op. cit., n. 26, p. 7.
34 See R. Cranston, *Regulating Business* (1979) 169.
35 See L. Mather and B. Yngvesson, 'Language, Audience, and the Transformation of Disputes' (1981) 15 *Law and Society Rev.* 775–821.
36 See, for example, J. Shapland and J. Vagg, *Policing by the Public* (1988).
37 See S. Merry, *Getting Justice and Getting Even* (1990).
38 See J. Braithwaite, *Crime, Shame and Reintegration* (1989).
39 See F. Pearce and S. Tombs, 'Ideology, Hegemony, and Empiricism: Compliance Theories of Regulation' (1990) 30 *Brit. J. of Criminology* 423-43.
40 JUSTICE, *Breaking the Rules* (1980).
41 E. Durkheim, *The Division of Labour in Society* (1964 ed., originally published 1893).

[11]

Murderers, Victims and 'Survivors': The Social Construction of Deviance

Two visions of homicide, murderers and victims are contrasted. One, conventional in criminology, has it that murders are the culmination of drawn-out, acrimonious transactions occurring within demographically homogeneous sectors of the population. It leads to a blurring of moral identities and causal relations. The other is championed by homicide 'survivors' organizations, and it claims an existentially validated authority. Homicide is experienced by 'survivors' as a chaotic episode which gives way to strong, antagonistic archetypes of victim and offender. The two visions are examined, in part, to promote an appreciation of the analytic complexities of the phenomenon of murder; in part, to point to the fraught politics that are beginning to emerge around resolving the character of murder.

Symbolic interactionist, phenomenological and other, allied criminological approaches established in the 1960s and 1970s pointed to the usefulness of analysing phenomena as socially embedded, dialectical events that turn on the reflective capacity of people to make sense of the processes and identities that unfolded before them. 'The central demand of socially situated conduct,' argued Katz, 'is that one makes collaborative sense of who one is and what one is doing . . .' (Katz 1996: 574). In the

* Written at the Center for the Advanced Study of the Behavioral Sciences, Stanford, California. I am grateful for financial support provided by the National Science Foundation Grant SBR-9022192. I am also grateful to Carol Delaney, David Downes, Bridget Hutter, Gary Marx and Joanna Shapland for their comments on earlier drafts of this paper.

earliest formulations of Becker, Cicourel, Matza and others, crime was held to be not one invariant thing but many, an artifact with as many faces as there were principals to bestow meaning upon it. Its significance resided, in part, on the pragmatic purposes which people pursued: different objectives would lead an offender, a police officer, a politician, a fence, a judge, a defence lawyer, a prosecutor or a probation officer to construct burglary or theft in different ways. It resided in practical experience and in the manner in which that experience could be progressively modified with use. It resided in the organization and distribution of stocks of knowledge, and there was a strong interest not only in how typifications of crime were manufactured and disseminated by such bodies as the press and television, but also in how they became enacted in the routine work of courts, police stations and prisons. Attention was given to the social stratification of knowledge: people did not speak with equal authority, power or effect, and it was necessary to lodge the study of criminal transactions in political context. And those transactions were themselves studied as transformative processes that folded back on their participants in ways that could not always be anticipated at the outset, which became social objects in their own standing, and which supplied the selves and situations that affected further conduct. The meanings of crime and criminals were thus conceived to be emergent, contingent and synthetic, incorporating chains of responses, and of responses to responses, that coalesced around developing lines of action. A failure to understand those meanings, it was said, would prevent the observer from comprehending how crime took form.

The possibilities of those arguments still await full exploration. Crime may have been treated as a symbolic construction, but its analysis has tended to focus on only a few of the many representations that could shape its course. Partly because the paradigmatic texts were written before a number of critical substantive changes had occurred within criminology itself, inquiry was overwhelmingly restricted to an examination of relations within a relatively simple and underpopulated world: Howard Becker's *Outsiders* was published in 1963, Aaron Cicourel's *Social Organization of Juvenile Justice* in 1968, and David Matza's *Becoming Deviant* in 1969, that is, before the work of Al Reiss (1972) had underscored the reactive role of the police and the significance of the lay witness and bystander; and feminism (Brownmiller 1975; Griffin 1986) and the first national crime surveys in America had begun to establish the importance of the victim for criminology (Bureau of Justice Statistics 1981).

All too often, situated descriptions of crime elided issues of harm and suffering, and descriptions of formal control proceeded as if it had no proper object but a kind of aimless self-aggrandisement. Yet the discipline is clearly incomplete without an appreciation of how crime is experienced by those it injures and by those who observe that injury, that is, of how victims and witnesses construct and are constructed by the processes in which they are anchored. How people suffer, perceive and respond to crime shapes its trajectory and its political and practical environments. A start has certainly been made. Morgan and Zedner (1992), for instance, described the impact of burglary and other crimes on a hitherto largely unnoticed group, young children. Manning (1992) and Waddington (1993) have written about the encoding and decoding practices of witnesses, despatchers and police officers as reports of crime pass through a series of organizational settings. I hope to take that stance yet a little further.

What is reported here is part of a larger project, based on interview, observation and reading in England and Wales and North America,[1] on the social organization of practical and political responses to the aftermath of homicide. In this paper, I propose to contrast facets of just two, quite discrepant sets of pragmatic typifications of victims and murderers. It is a contrast that throws into strong relief the different kinds of knowledge that can shape criminal transactions.

The first set is grounded in and around the scholarly work of criminology and victimology, and it affects how experts talk about homicide to themselves and, directly and indirectly to policy officials, politicians and others. The second is grounded in the experiences of 'secondary victims' or 'survivors'[2] of homicide, the families of the victim, and it affects the framing of their demands. The divergence between the two is marked. On one level, it illustrates the origins, workings and consequences of very different forms of symbolic representation, and it may invite reflection on the all too often neglected proposition that the data of criminology are furnished by diverse hermeneutic schemes that do not always permit recognition of one another. It is not difficult, McCall and Wittner observe, for some truths to get lost in criminology and sociology: 'The experiential knowledge of subordinate people . . . is kept submerged by positivist methodologies which assume that social scientists know enough to ask the questions that yield meaningful explanations of society and social life' (1990: 47). It could well be argued that the secondary victims of homicide survivors, rape victims[3] and others have in the past been just such 'subordinate people'. A failure to heed them impairs a proper analysis of the social organization and meanings of criminality.

On another level, the divergence has had practical consequences, complicating the development of reasoned exchanges between those who resort to the criminologists' and practitioners' expertise and those who are members of organized groups of 'survivors', and it has led to occasional accusations of unreasonableness and 'stridency' (Casey 1995: 25), on the one hand, and of a lack of comprehension and compassion, on the other. At issue are a number of political questions, not least of which is the appropriate way to interpret homicide and the right of the 'secondary victim' to be recognized as a 'proper' victim at all, that is, as one who has property in crime and its

[1] Fieldwork started in January 1995 and still continues in 1997. It has consisted, first, of some 95 formal and informal interviews with the principals responsible for founding and developing homicide survivors' organizations and with members of those organizations in England and Wales (The Compassionate Friends; Parents of Murdered Children; Support After Murder and Manslaughter; RoadPeace; Justice for Victims; the Zito Trust; the Suzy Lamplugh Trust and Victim's Voice), Canada (CAVEAT) and the United States (Parents of Murdered Children; Families and Friends of Murder Victims and Citizens Against Homicide); and with those with whom the principals have had dealings in the Home Office; Bar Council; Victim Support; Crown Court Witness Service; Parliament; Liberty; newspapers; funding organizations and the like. It has consisted, second, of attending and observing local and national meetings of survivors' organizations in America and England and Wales; attending memorial services; and participating in marches. Third, it has consisted of a perusal of primary and secondary written materials, including the relevant files of SAMM, Victim Support, Justice for Victims and the Home Office; newspaper libraries; videos and tapes of television and radio programmes; and the personal files of individual survivors.

[2] So new are the groups formulating those responses that there is no agreed word to describe their members. 'Survivor' is a term that was fostered in the politics of rape, incest and child abuse to promote images of strength and endurance rather than the implied passivity of 'victim'. However awkward it may sound and read, on occasion, 'homicide survivor' is actually how many secondary victims' organizations choose to describe their own members.

[3] What I have to say about the divergent beliefs of experts and homicide survivors has its parallels. The expert criminology of rape, for instance, made very similar points to the criminology of homicide. For examples, see Amir (1971) and Miller (1976). I am grateful to Paula Fass for showing me the typescript of of her forthcoming *Kidnapped: Stories of Child Kidnapping in American History*, which cites the reference to Miller. The Amir book had an intellectual pedigree which stretches back to, and is subsumed by, Wolfgang (1958).

aftermath, and who can, in consequence, make legal, administrative and moral claims on government and its agencies. The matter is important because definitions of the boundaries and substance of the criminal act are being actively contested.[4] The content and urgency of those current demands for recognition, respect, control and information—that is for the symbolic incorporation of secondary victims into the criminal justice system—would be quite unintelligible without an informed understanding of their world-view.

Those survivors' groups are quite new in England and Wales. For instance, the largest organization, POMC, Parents of Murdered Children, was founded in 1984, and was later re-established as SAMM, Support After Murder and Manslaughter, ten years later;[5] the Zito Trust was founded in 1994; NEVA, the North of England Victims Association, in 1993; and RoadPeace in 1993; and there are other associations with comparable histories. Little is known about how people come to join them, although many appear to learn about their existence only by happenstance, through chance information filtered through conversations or news stories, and haphazard referrals by the police or Victim Support. Little is known about the 'representativeness' of their membership although it may be presumed that quite a few bereaved people choose not to join, and certainly not in the very first stages of grief when, quite characteristically, they are not only incapacitated by shock but also, for a while, more actively supported by those around them. The groups are not sizeable and they lack money. But they *are* beginning to play an increasingly visible role at the margins of the politics of criminal justice. Their members have spoken with ministers,[6] policy officials, Members of Parliament, and the officers of voluntary and statutory criminal justice agencies; and the incommensurability of the two discursive schemes—that of the survivors and that of the experts—is beginning to show. Their connections with one another may frequently be described as tenuous, ambiguous and loosely coupled. They lack certain steps and clear progression, and participants tend to come away from meetings bemused at how little they have achieved.

The Criminology of Homicide

Despite some variation in their theoretical frames, preoccupations and local particulars, there is a striking accord between broad criminological descriptions of homicide in Britain, North America, Australia and elsewhere (Daly and Wilson 1990: 81). First, there is an agreement that a sharp divide must be traced between the 'extraordinary' and the 'ordinary' murder. The study of the exceptional murder centres on homicides committed by people deemed variously to be 'mentally disordered', insane or of unsound mind. It also, more frequently, centres on analyses which

[4] Experiments with victim impact statements under the 1996 Victim's Charter, for example, exclude the 'survivors' of homicide because, despite their remonstrations, Home Office lawyers did not (for the time being) accept them as legitimate victims in any conventional sense. See *The Sunday Times*, 23 June 1996. Victim Support observed that 'Families of homicide victims are specifically excluded in spite of Victim Support's experience that they are the group who would most like to make such a statement' (1996: 2).

[5] SAMM claims some 1,000 members, but counting is very inexact because, like the other organizations, it estimates membership by the circulation of its newsletter.

[6] Indeed, when the former Home Secretary, Michael Howard, talks of 'victims', it appears that he tended to have the secondary victims of homicide in mind as much as any other group.

encapsulate press, police and, in particular, FBI classifications of mass and serial killings, and it typically consists of lengthy, annotated case histories in which the killer is represented as a fantasist, misogynist or socially marginal male who objectifies and dehumanizes his victims (Fox and Levin 1994). Writing on mass killings is inclined to be detailed, dramatic and prurient as authors try to reproduce and sometimes even to celebrate (Leyton 1995: 23) the working logic of a mind that is capable of such egregious acts.

By contrast, the analysis of 'ordinary' murder characteristically emphasizes just how very ordinary it is. It hinges on a demographic demonstration of who does what to whom. Murder and manslaughter are depicted as intra-class and intra-racial offences overwhelmingly committed by young, working-class, often unemployed, frequently non-white males against other young, working-class, often unemployed, frequently non-white males and against young, working-class women and children in areas rife with violence (Wolfgang 1983: 851; Leyton 1986: 9). They are rarely the outcome of chance meetings between strangers. To the contrary, they are almost always the culmination of a 'situated transaction' (Luckenbill 1977: 177) between people who know one another intimately (Getzel and Masters 1984: 138) and who may well have been members of the same family (Gelles 1972: 21; Duncan *et al.* 1978: 172). In England and Wales in 1991, for instance, 41 per cent of female victims were killed by their partners and 20 per cent by other members of the family; and 8 per cent of male victims were killed by their partners, 20 per cent by members of their family and 36 per cent by associates (Home Office 1993: 15). In the United States in the early 1990s, some 47 per cent of victims of homicide were related to their assailants (Bureau of Justice Statistics 1993), 28 per cent of women victims (but only 3 per cent of men victims) having been killed by their partner in 1992 (Bureau of Justice Statistics 1995).

Victims and offenders are aligned demographically and socially; they will have had long-standing and often acrimonious relationships; and in some places, and in America particularly, they are also both likely to possess appreciable histories of violent offending. Who finally becomes the victim and who the offender can then turn on little more than contingency in a perilous 'social act' or 'duet' (Polk 1994: 2–3) played out between violence-prone people who may well be in drink or on drugs (Polk 1994: 67). Moral character and causal primacy become blurred in such argument. Citing Wolfgang, Avison observed that only infrequently will an '"innocent" victim' be killed, and that, even in child killings, there is clear evidence of victim participation (Avison 1973: 58, 60). 'It is difficult', Avison concluded, 'to discern groups of homicides in which there are no circumstances of victim participation' (1973: 60). Indeed, it has been contended, victims may actually bring about their own deaths by acting provocatively, violently or suicidally (Wolfgang 1967*a*: 24). Their role is 'important and active' (Gelles 1987: 155). They are 'rarely struck down out of the blue' (Morris and Blom-Cooper 1967: 70). And they may have been drawn into homicidal situations as a result of problems of personality or adjustment (Morris and Blom-Cooper 1967: 322–3).

Murder, in short, arises wherever there are concentrations of poor, volatile young men for whom violence is a way of life (Wolfgang 1967*b*; Prothrow-Stith 1991: xii). Although it is expressly treated in law as the most heinous of all crimes, utterly different from the rest, criminologists would hold that much killing is actually fairly prosaic and many murderers are quite undistinguished sociologically. Some description even verges on portraying homicide as if it were, in effect, the property of enclosed, semi-private groupings that do not really implicate the wider, public world at all. Consider Hugh Klare's observation that 'An analysis of all victims between 1955 and 1960 shows that murder continues to be largely a family affair' (1963: 13–14). In place of the popular stereotype of homicide as a shocking encounter between a wholly unprovocative and innocent victim, on the one hand, and a malicious and premeditating perpetrator, on the other, many criminologists and practitioners would therefore choose to furnish a picture of shared moral and social complicity. So it was that, in their evidence to the Committee on the Penalty for Homicide, the Prison Governors Association argued that the image of a murderer as a dark, evil character was a misleading feature of a media-fostered mythology which needed to be challenged by campaigns of public education.

The word *murder* itself, declared the Committee on the Penalty for Homicide (1993: 6), is unduly emotive: public attitudes are shaped by media reports of the extraordinary and atypical offence which should really create 'no stir at all', and the Committee quoted with approval Morris and Blom-Cooper's remark (1964: 277) that murder can hardly be considered a serious social problem but a domestic crime in which men kill their wives, mistresses and children (1993: 22). Even in America, some criminologists emphasize the analytic inconsequentiality of much homicide. Interesting homicides, observed Felson, form only a very small proportion of the whole (Felson 1994: 3).

There are inevitable problems in counting murders, problems that flow from changing laws and categorizations, shifts in medical diagnoses of the causes of death, and improvements in the procedures that can keep victims alive. Murder rates per million of population in England and Wales have fluctuated, but they have also tended generally to increase since the Second World War. They have varied, for instance, between 8.1 per million in 1946 (House of Commons Library Research Division 1990: 9), 7.3 in 1968 (Gibson and Klein 1969: 3), 12.7 in 1989, and 11.8 (amounting to 689 homicides) in 1993 (Home Office 1993: 9). Yet, absolutely and relatively, those frequencies are small indeed. The rate in England and Wales in the early 1990s was equivalent to half that of Canada, one twentieth that of the United States, one fortieth that of Russia, and one fiftieth that of Mexico (Leyton 1994: 22).

Being at once analytically mundane, socially contained and statistically uncommon in England and Wales, murder does not appear to have been regarded as very problematic by British criminologists (Mitchell 1990: xii; Young 1987: 5). It tends to become contentious only when arguments are revived every so often at the prospect of restoring the death penalty. Little scholarly work has been undertaken, and some surprising lacunae have arisen in consequence. The first edition of the authoritative and encyclopaedic *Oxford Handbook of Criminology* contained no separate chapter or index entry on murder and homicide (Maguire, Morgan and Reiner 1994). The Home Office library, presumably the main repository of published materials for those who formulate policy and conduct research in the department, contained only 40 items on murder in the mid-1990s, and most of those were journalistic accounts of sensational crimes and criminals centred on such subjects as Jack the Ripper and the Evans-Christie case. The British Library Document Supply Centre, describing itself on the web as the 'most comprehensive document delivery service in the world', with a serial database that listed 54,000 titles in 1996, had 'no match' at all on the words 'murder' and 'homicide'. Part of that apparent bibliographic scarcity must be explained as little more than an artifact of categorization and retrieval procedures, but it is a revealing artifact none the less.

The demographic data on murderers and victims are stark and their concomitant criminology is simple and plausible. But it should also be noted that there is a striking absence or silence at the heart of expert knowledge about homicide: the 'primary' victims of homicide can only very rarely speak for themselves,[7] no relevant research has been undertaken on the survivors of attempted murder, and the 'secondary' victims have not been heeded. What might otherwise have formed the substance of the victims' own accounts must either be ignored altogether, pieced together inferentially or supplied at second hand in newspaper reports, trial transcripts and witness statements in police files. Practical narratives employed in the service of an adversarial system necessarily furnish a major portion of the available analytic data on homicide.

Take the key idea of victim-precipitated homicide. There are few legal defences to murder: it may be argued that there was no criminal intent because the defendant was not of sound mind; that the defendant was not there at the material time; that there was a mistake in identification and someone other than the defendant committed the crime; or that the killing was done in lawful self-defence, called 'justifiable homicide' in America, that is, that the defendant used appropriate force in response to a personal threat or provocation which would have been sufficient to make a 'reasonable man' lose his self-control. In Britain and America, legal doctrine holds, in the words of Judge Bazelon in the *Durham* case, that 'Our collective conscience does not allow punishment where it cannot impose blame' (quoted in Morris 1992: 126).

Self-defence stories are one-sided narratives that strive for attention in the police interview room, the courtroom (Bennett and Feldman 1981; Ewick and Silbey 1995: 207) and the public domain. They are routinely argued by advocates and just as routinely reported in the press and other media. Perhaps the most transparent example of that transmission of partisan rhetoric was the publication in the September 1992 issue of the magazine, *Marie Claire*, of an account of the murder of a young woman in a Glasgow school playground, an account that borrowed exclusively and uncritically from allegations made by the defendant after her trial and conviction. Whilst the victim was said to have been a school bully who had goaded the defendant beyond endurance, the defendant was more sinned against sinning, one who should not have been punished as she had. Only after frequent and anguished remonstrations by the victim's family that there was another story to be told was the account eventually retracted by *Marie Claire* in April 1993.

Now, it is undoubtedly the case that many homicides are indeed committed lawfully and in self-defence (or so the verdicts run), or, at least, they are committed unlawfully and in the midst of a confused situation in which the moral identities of the protagonists are far from resolved. But the defence is obliged professionally to deliver its client's version of what happened, however fanciful it may be, and the victims cannot answer back and give their own account unless they do so vicariously, suppositionally, and in the austere arguments of a prosecution that delivers what lawyers construe as 'the facts of the case'.

7 'Very rarely' because, under the 'year and a day rule', death does not have to be immediate to be prosecuted as murder or manslaughter.

Self-defence is often identical to what Lamb called the self-serving, *ex post facto* mitigation of the survivor (Lamb 1996: 80); the mitigation that trial lawyers sometimes describe as 'malicious'; and which a number of feminists and others prefer to define as 'victim-blaming' (Clark 1977). In the guise of victim-precipitation, it is also a central theme in the criminology of homicide that Wolfgang inaugurated in 1958 and others then pursued under the influence of von Hentig's victimology. In a chapter entitled the 'Victim's Contribution to the Genesis of Crime', and using police data from New York City between 1936 and 1940, von Hentig had argued that 'about 85 per cent of the murder and manslaughter cases [entail] . . . [a] motive of killing [that] indicates the operation of a partnership. The murderous act is a more or less adequate response to stimuli and irritating agents . . . (1948: 397). Overall, von Hentig concluded, 'Among common situations . . . We do not find the evildoer/evil-sufferer group . . . There is a definite mutuality of some sort' (p. 384).

In Britain, victim-precipitation has certainly been incorporated in standard criminological accounts of murder. And, coupled with arguments about the socially enclosed, transactionally specific, emotionally volatile and commonplace character of most homicides, it is a theme that gives plausibility to minor, supporting arguments against capital punishment.

The Howard League, the chief campaigning organization against the death penalty, has always derived its authority from claims to mastery over penological and criminological research supplied by experts (Rose 1961: 278), and those experts, in turn, have largely been moved by their antipathy to the death penalty. To be sure, the case advanced by abolitionists in England and Wales does focus principally on the immorality of state executions, the problematic efficacy of deterrence, and the dangers of unsafe convictions. But it does no damage to that case to belittle the significance of homicide, that is, to say, as the National Campaign for the Abolition of Capital Punishment and the Howard League jointly argued in 1974, that 'most murder is a matter of emotion and impulse, very largely within the family or among close associates, and therefore not subject to deterrence by calculation of the penalty' (National Campaign for the Abolition of Capital Punishment 1974: 3); with a former Permanent Under-Secretary of State at the Home Office, that deterrence is ineffective, given 'the circumstances in which so many murders are committed—family quarrels, panic in an unexpected situation, drunken or sexual frenzies. The carefully planned and calculated murder . . . is—happily—relatively rare' (Cunningham 1969: 109); or, with Barbara Wootton, that 'not all murderers are horrible characters through and through. Many a murder is an action quite out of keeping with the normal character of a man or woman who commits it. Sometimes the crime is the result of a long period of domestic stress in which one party suddenly reaches breaking point . . . ' (Wootton 1969: 18).

Wootton and Cunningham (and those who advised him) may well have been perfectly sound in their judgement; it would be sociologically myopic, indeed quite contrary to the thrust of this paper, not to treat crime, including murder, as a transaction to which the principal participants contribute; but it is impossible not to wonder just how much the motivated accounts of defendants, defence witnesses and defence lawyers, reported at first and second hand, have tinged what now passes for standard expert argument.

Murder and the Secondary Victims of Homicide

The survivors discussed here are people who have lost family members, often children, through homicide and who have been moved to play a prominent part in founding or maintaining the organizations which support and campaign for themselves and others like themselves. They are not necessarily 'typical' of the bereaved, but I have spoken to those who represent in their entirety the people who have been active in the new politics of secondary victims, and it is their world-view that I wish to reconstruct.

Secondary victims also share a striking accord about the character of murder, murderers and victims, but theirs is an existentially validated set of beliefs quite different in kind from the expertise of the criminologist. Whilst criminologists found their truth claims on secondary data sets, analytic distance, scholarly knowledge and specialist methodologies, secondary victims talk about a devastating symbolic passage that forces an understanding that can never be quite intelligible to the outsider. Theirs is the authority of profound personal experience. Secondary victims may try to capture and reproduce that understanding through different discursive techniques, through personal narratives and testimonies, shrines and memorials, poems and newsletters, but it defies complete translation (see Langer 1991: 7). They will say that it is quite impossible to understand what they feel unless one has suffered as they have done (Walter 1994: 5). A former coordinator of Parents of Murdered Children said to me, 'There is no way, however compassionate and kind you are as a person, there is no way you can understand or feel the pain that other people feel unless they are in a similar position. You cannot learn that from a book, you cannot learn it from a person, you cannot learn from me how if it was one of your children. You can't envisage it.' And they also remain adamant that they know about murder as others can not. One cried out on *Kilroy*, a television talk show, 'I'm the *expert*. I *know*.' For them, too, the victim is an absence or silence which must be filled, but their personal need is the greater and their knowledge more complicated and intimate. Let me offer a simplified and accentuated ideal type to reconstitute some elements of that knowledge.

Bereavement after homicide is described at first and second hand as quite different from mundane grief.[8] It follows a loss that was often violent and ugly, wanton or premeditated (Harris Hendriks *et al.* 1993: 9). One woman said to me, 'it's the fact that someone else has done that to you . . . Somebody chose to do that to you. It's not an accident. How dare they!' The loss was frequently ahead of its time and in seeming defiance of the natural order, upsetting the proper succession of generations (Raphael

[8] Much of what survivors describe can be captured by the clinical phrase 'post-traumatic stress disorder', although the resemblance is not identical in every particular. For example, there are no problems of repressed memory. To the contrary, memories and flashbacks are only too vivid. Post-traumatic stress disorder is supposed to ensue when a person encounters a frightening situation which he or she can neither flee nor master, symbolic defences are overwhelmed, and the outcome is a compound of anxiety, vulnerability, fearfulness, meaninglessness, bodily disorder, depression, guilt and much else. Those who have survived other shocking experiences—rape, incest, holocaust, combat, disaster and the like—report very similar reactions to those of homicide survivors, but survivors themselves may display a great resistance to that contention. Each survivor or group of survivors tends to claim to be beset in his or her own very distinctive way, and there are instances of what one survivor called 'competitive grief'. If the *forms* of distress are similar, the *content* is not, and the colouring and iconography of specific griefs do take specific guises. At the same time, it must be noted that it is part of the character of such griefs that content is largely ineffable, and it cannot but be expressed in a conventional form that is alien to it, reinforcing an appearance of similarity. At bottom, perhaps, it is not very helpful to inquire whether homicide survivors' grief is the 'same' as that of other groups. Each group would certainly argue for the uniqueness of its suffering, and that argument is part of the phenomenology of that suffering.

1984: 229), and little corresponding to any culturally framed conception of the 'good death' (Spierenburg 1984: 45). Secondary victims will typically have had little time to prepare or collect themselves, and no time to make a peaceful composition with the dead, and their immediate reactions invariably fuse disbelief and shock (Straebe and Straebe 1987: 204). One said 'it was just like a stroke'.

The aftermath of homicide is experienced on one level as a continuing and profound problem of powerlessness, vulnerability and guilt. Secondary victims were unable successfully to prevent the death and its attendant distress. They have survived and the victim has not (Murray-Parkes 1993: 49), and they are often beset by recurrent, frightening images of the terror and helplessness which the victim may have suffered and they might have averted (Rynearson 1984: 1453). Ineffective before, they can now do little that is purposeful because others, the police, coroner and lawyers, will have assumed control over almost all the events that follow. They may be denied access to the home if it is a 'crime scene', access to the victim until after the inquest, and access to his or her possessions until after the trial. Their child or relation is no longer practically or symbolically theirs at all. One woman said at a support meeting in California, 'we spent so much time in control, looking after our children, taking them to hospital. So . . . totally responsible for twenty years and then when this horror comes along we can't do anything.' Indeed, matters can become worse still because the body need never be recovered (Littlewood 1992: 55–8) and, in place of a funeral, there may simply be unchecked imaginings about how it was treated.

That loss of control can be conveyed and amplified repeatedly in the months that follow a homicide. Secondary victims are not left alone to recover or reconstruct their lives. Murder is an event that is of interest as public news, but they have neither the power nor the ability effectively to regulate what is reported about them, the murder or the victim—all matters that may be profoundly imbued with feeling, deeply sensitive to slight and in urgent need of interpretation. And the outcome can be a sense of forcible alienation from their own experience, others' more forceful definitions threatening to displace their own, 'their' loss no longer wholly theirs at all.

Alienation will be reanimated at every stage of the natural history of the formal management of a homicide, at the inquest, public appeals for information, reports of arrests, arraignments, trials, acts of sentencing, appeals and parole hearings (Amick-McMullan *et al.* 1989: 75). Poignantly, the trial itself (if there is a trial) will probably be listed on or about the anniversary of the death. One survivor said at a local meeting of SAMM, 'we're victimized first by the crime, and then victimized again and again and again afterwards.'

Getzel and Masters say that the depth of secondary victims' reactions cannot be overstated: grief is a compound of deep shock, helplessness, terror, guilt and yearnings (1984: 139). Above all, it is compounded out of confusing and intense emotional sensations that swamp the body as well as the mind, sensations most commonly, but perhaps only approximately, described as rage or anger (Peach and Klass 1987: 82). It is turbulent, chaotic (Murray-Parkes 1972: 77) and incoherent, characterized by 'wave after wave of violently contradictory emotions' (Littlewood 1993: 73). One survivor, Pat Green, likened it to 'being plunged into a deep, dark chasm of evil, violence and horror' (in *The Guardian*, 8 November 1994). It is often so overwhelming, unintelligible and confusing that there can be no learned responses to it, no recipe knowledge for managing it, no language with which to describe it, and normal structures of meaning collapse in consequence. If culture works to edit reality and make it manageable, the effect of such disaster is to endanger cultural pattern and meaning (Erikson 1994: 152–3). Ruggiero once said that 'on the threshold of being we encounter the gaping abyss of nothingness' (1946: 31) and so it is with survivors' reports of homicide.

One powerful purpose in the aftermath of homicide, then, is to shed turmoil, reassert control, and make some moral and cognitive sense of what has happened. Ann Robinson, co-founder of POMC, reflected that 'relatives of murder victims ask repeatedly *why* did it happen' (Robinson nd). Centrally important to that project will be a search for moral meaning, for a practical theodicy, which will enable the survivor to understand how things could have been allowed to happen as they did and how it might be possible to continue making intelligent choices and plans in the face of an apparent ethical and causal nihilism (Terr 1990: 116). One man said at a support meeting, 'you all start questioning some of your values. Is there a God? Isn't there a God? Why me?' It is as if the victim and survivors have been punished, and it is not always certain why. One source of moral justification, of course, is victim-precipitation, von Hentig's argument that the victim, in effect, earned his or her death (NOVA 1985: 2). Another is to blame oneself. The leader of an American chapter of POMC said at a meeting, 'we all play the stupid game of "what if?" . . . ' People ask themselves 'what if I had not let my child out that evening?', 'what if I had driven him (or her) rather than allowed him to make his own way to a meeting?', 'what if I had known more about what he (or she) was getting up to?', or 'what if I had known more about his (or her) friends?'

Much more common is the emergence of a distinctively new, simplified and more resilient symbolic structure that bears the marks of the urgency and narrow focus of the quest for certainty in a world turned upside down. It is as if the harrowing experiences and strong emotions through which they have passed induce survivors to reach for the reassurances of a more elemental and utilitarian system, a system which is shorn of distracting and irrelevant nuances, ambiguities and complexities.

Stark experiences lead to stark interpretations. There is little room for greyness in the moral world of many survivors. To the contrary, theirs is a symbolic system stripped down to basic classifications. The most fundamental of all classifications (Pagels 1995: 37; Mukerji and Schudson 1991: 19), binary oppositions, are repeatedly invoked (Lamb 1996: 5) to expose the raw polarities of the new world-view. Recounted in meetings of support groups, transformed into strong narratives, embedded in the here-and-now, familiar world of survivors, a firm line is traced between the victim and the offender, innocence and guilt, the good and the bad, us and them, the feeling and the unfeeling, the understanding and those who lack understanding, the interested and the uninterested, particularism and universalism. Positive and negative archetypes (Lévi-Strauss 1968: 35) are there matched to give dimension and structure to experience. More, those archetypes are linked together by an analogical reasoning that aids survivors as they attempt to understand and gauge the functioning of the social and moral order. At its very core, there is the homology of the victim and the murderer. Without an offender, it runs, there would be no murder and no victim. One constitutes the others. One is the necessary precondition of the others. They are yoked together in an indissoluble dialectic, the very word 'victim' predicating its own differentiation and its own antithesis (Merleau-Ponty 1973: 31).

That analogical reasoning would hold that what is done to the offender is a good enough measure of how the victim, and the victim's surrogates, the family, are thought to be seen, judged and respected by significant others in the wider world. A member of Justice for Victims, a small campaigning group, declared at a meeting in the Home Office in October 1993 that 'offenders receive everything, victims nothing'. And other members said at a reconvened meeting seven months later, 'we want as many rights as criminals, more', and, of the sentencing tariff, 'if prisoners have a right to know, why not me?' In their draft submission of February 1995 to the Home Affairs Select Committee, the group talked of the need to balance the human rights of the offender with those of the victim's family. Point by point, contrasts are thereby repeatedly drawn between the treatment and fate of the offender and the treatment and fate of the bereaved. A reiterated cry of SAMM is 'we are all aware of organizations who offer help to offenders, ex-offenders and their families. How many organizations can you think of who offer help to the families of murder victims?' NEVA claims that 'huge sums of money are spent trying to rehabilitate criminals but very little seems to go to those [survivors] who need help' (*Shield Gazette*, 23 July 1993). It is claimed that a prison ombudsman should be balanced by a victim's ombudsman, and that a 'victim justice system' should take the place of a criminal justice system.

As polarities emerge out of chaos, as ambiguities are dispelled and good and evil are separated (Ricoeur 1967: 207), therefore, so the victim and offender tend themselves to be firmly redefined, differentiated and retained in the survivors' consciousness (Burgess 1975: 395; Lamb 1996: 88–89). To do otherwise, to forget, would be one more betrayal of the victim and another collusion in his or her obliteration (Hass 1995: 46). One mother said 'you want them to understand how good this child was and they didn't deserve to die the way they did. Because when I think of —— she was a kind person, she would help the neighbours in the road. She was always doing something. She didn't deserve to die in that way.'

Victims become beatified and idealized in death (Murray Parkes 1972: 70), routinely described as 'selfless', 'bright', 'shining', 'special', 'beautiful', 'important' and 'good'. They become memorialized in pilgrimages (see *New York Times*, 19 August 1996), and eulogized in testimonies, poems, books and walls of remembrance, obituaries and special services, and the very organizations that so often bear their names as living monuments. Bedrooms and possessions may be left untouched (Marris 1986: 28). Domestic shrines may be created in the home. Candles may be left burning in front of photographs. One father said at a support meeting, 'When you lose your natural child, it's a broken love. The love's still there and you can't get rid of it. I kiss my daughter's photo every night.'

An article on 'griefwork' in an American group's newsletter put it that it was imperative 'To convert your relationship with the person who died from one of co-presence to memory. *The relationship you have with the person you have lost is now about memories*' (emphasis in original) (Edmonds-Norris 1996: 5). If all that remains is a memory of the other, it becomes imperative to work symbolically to edit and reshape recollection lest there be yet another wounding revictimization, an additional loss of innocence, a collusion with the idea of a victim's moral complicity, and a return to confusion. Moral distances must be enforced and slights rebuffed (see *The Guardian*, 15 October 1988). Victims cannot and must not be muddled with the offender, their very antithesis. The intensity of grief cannot manage too much ambivalence and contradiction, and symbolic proximity between the two archetypes would only be defined by many as a form of moral contamination, another infliction of violence. A mother said to me, 'I just felt that we have led good, clean honest lives and I just couldn't wash this filth and scum away... These people [the murderers of her son] are the dregs of society... They're just nobodies, nothing, there's just nothing decent about them at all, and I just felt that their indecency had washed into my family, and I just couldn't wash it away.'

Conclusion

The phenomenology of murder evidently produces very different narratives in different audiences. In the first instance, and for most sociological purposes, it is not always necessary to try to determine which narrative is 'correct' or which should be preferred. Judgements of that sort do not serve much purpose in phenomenological analysis. Rather, the point is to ascertain and set in place people's responses to their own and others' definitions as they jointly formulate lines of conduct. The sociologists' job is then, secondly, to describe how those different forms of life are configured in ways that may sometimes be apparent to the principals, sometimes less than visible, treating structures of common-sense reasoning simultaneously as topic and resource. That description should transcend and complement those structures, but it is not necessary to contradict them outright. The two forms of knowledge are not competitive in that way.

If people interact by 'adjusting what they do in the light of what others do, so that each individual's line of action "fits" into what the others do. [And if this] can only happen if human beings... construct a line of action by taking account of the meaning of what others do in response to their earlier actions' (Becker 1988: 18), it may be recognized how very fraught the politics of murder can become on occasion.

To be sure, in constructing strong ideal-types it would not do to underscore difference so emphatically that points of contact and commonality are wholly overlooked. Survivors, experts and professionals can work reflectively to distance themselves from their own life-worlds; they can listen to one another at first or second hand; they can change selves and attitudes as the politics of homicide unwind; they are not uniform in the positions they take; and their experiences can overlap existentially. Social groups are certainly not exclusive: experts may become bereaved and the bereaved may be experts. For example, the senior official of one civil libertarian organization had marked fellow feelings with the members of a survivors' group because he was mourning the death of his mother when they first approached him. *Pari passu*, some members of survivors' groups will be perfectly familiar with the work of formal organizations. Paul Lamplugh, the co-founder of the Suzie Lamplugh Trust, was a lawyer, and Frank Green, a former chairman of SAMM, had been a trade union negotiator who imported the practical recipe knowledge of the trade union committee into the dealings of SAMM itself.

But phenomenological tensions do nevertheless run through the politics and practices centred on homicide. Quite distinct systems of representation meet head on. In play are the two ideal-typical narratives which I have contrasted in this paper, but there are also others, including those of the police officer, the trial lawyer, the policy official in the Home Office and the Crown Prosecution Service, the coroner, and the staff of Victim Support. Each will bring his or her situated, occupationally framed and personally driven perspectives to train on murder, and possibilities of misunderstanding, incomplete alignment of viewpoints, and subsequent accusations of insensitivity, irrelevance and incomprehension are not uncommon. At the very forefront is the gap that can yawn between the rational, reasoned, universalistic, precedent-driven and cool talk of the professional and the impassioned, particularistic and hot talk of some survivors' representatives, two kinds of talk that cannot sustain a coherent conversation for very long.

If the very distinct world-view of the survivor is ignored analytically or dismissed merely as an angry show of unreason, it becomes quite impossible for the criminologist to produce an informed explanation of many of the practical and political consequences of homicide. It becomes all too easy to brush remonstrations away as 'meaningless', on the one hand, or to make simple *a priori* assumptions about the kind of people who are presumed to bear the subculture of violence or who are exposed to domestic stress, on the other.

References

AMICK-MCMULLAN, A. *et al.* (1989), 'Family Survivors of Homicide Victims', *The Behavior Therapist*, 12: 75–79.

AMIR, M. (1971), *Patterns in Forcible Rape*. Chicago: University of Chicago Press.

AVISON, N. (1973), 'Victims of Homicide', in I. Drapkin and E. Viano, eds., *Victimology: A New Focus*. Lexington, MA: Lexington Books.

BECKER, H. (1963), *Outsiders*. London: Free Press of Glencoe.

——(1988), 'Herbert Blumer's Conceptual Impact', *Symbolic Interaction*, 11.

BENNETT, W. and FELDMAN, M. (1981), *Reconstructing Reality in the Courtroom: Justice and Judgement in American Culture*. New Brunswick, NJ: Rutgers University Press.

BROWNMILLER, S. (1975), *Against Our Will: Men, Women, and Rape*. New York: Bantam.

BUREAU OF JUSTICE STATISTICS (1981), *National Crime Surveys: National Sample, 1973–1979*. Washington: US Department of Justice.

——(1993), *Criminal Victimization 1993*. Washington: U.S. Department of Justice.

——(1995), Special Report: National Criminal Victimization Survey, August 1995. Washington: U.S. Department of Justice.

BURGESS, A. (1975), 'Family Reaction to Homicide', *American Journal of Orthopsychiatry*, 45.

CAFFELL, C. (1994), *In Search of the Rainbow's End*. London: Hodder and Stoughton.

CASEY, S. (1995), 'Victims' rights', *Oxford Magazine*, 7.

CICOUREL, A. (1968), *The Social Organization of Juvenile Justice*. New York: Wiley.

CLARK, L. (1977), *Rape the Price of Coercive Sexuality*. Toronto: Women's Press.

COMMITTEE ON THE PENALTY FOR HOMICIDE (1993), *Report*. London: Prison Reform Trust.

CUNNINGHAM, C. (1969), 'Some practical considerations', in L. Blom-Cooper, ed., *The Hanging Question*. Duckworth: London.

DALY, M. and WILSON, M. (1990), 'Killing the Competition', *Human Nature*, 1: 81–107.

DUNCAN, J. *et al.* (1978), 'Murder in the Family', in I. Kutash *et al.*, eds., *Violence: Perspectives on Murder and Aggression*. San Francisco: Jossey-Bass.

EDMONDS-NORRIS, R. (1996), 'Griefwork. . . .', *Families and Friends of Murder Victims Newsletter*, 1, October.

EISNER, M. (1994), 'The effects of economic structures and phases of development', in *Criminological Research*. Strasbourg: Council of Europe.

ERIKSON, K. (1994), *A New Species of Trouble*. New York: W. W. Norton.

EWICK, P. and SILBEY, S. (1995), 'Subversive Stories and Hegemonic Tales: Towards a Sociology of Narrative', *Law and Society Review*, 29.

FELSON, M. (1994), *Crime and Everyday Life*. Thousand Oaks: Pine Forge.

FOX, J. and LEVIN, J. (1994), *Overkill*. New York: Plenum.

GELLES, R. (1972), *The Violent Home*. Beverly Hills: Sage Publications.

GETZEL, G. and MASTERS, R. (1984), 'Serving Families who Survive Homicide Victims', *Social Casework*, 65.

GIBSON, E. and KLEIN, S. (1969), *Murder: 1957 to 1968*. London: HMSO.

GRIFFIN, S. (1986), *Rape, the Politics of Consciousness*. San Francisco: Harper and Row.

HARRIS HENDRICKS, J., BLACK, D. and KAPLAN, T. (1993), *When Father Kills Mother*. London: Routledge.

HASS, A. (1995), *The Aftermath*. Cambridge: Cambridge University Press.

HOME OFFICE (1993), Information on the Criminal Justice System in England and Wales. London: Home Office.

HOUSE OF COMMONS LIBRARY RESEARCH DIVISION (1990), *Background Paper: Homicide Statistics*.

KATZ, J. (1996), 'The social psychology of Adam and Eve', *Theory and Society*, 25.

KLARE, H. (1963), *Notes on Capital Punishment*. London: Howard League.

LAMB, S. (1996), *The Trouble with Blaming*. Cambridge, MA: Harvard University Press.

LANGER, L. (1991), *Holocaust Testimonies*. New Haven: Yale University Press.

LÉVI-STRAUSS, C. (1968), *Structural Anthropology*. New York: Basic Books.

LEYTON, E. (1986), *Compulsive Killers*. New York: Washington Mews Books.

——(1995), *Men of Blood*. London: Constable.

LITTLEWOOD, J. (1992), *Aspects of Grief*. London: Routledge.

——(1993), 'The denial of death and rites of passage in contemporary societies', in D. Clark., ed., *The Sociology of Death*. Oxford: Blackwell.

LUCKENBILL, D. (1977), 'Criminal Homicide as a Situated Transaction', *Social Problems*, 25.

MAGUIRE, M., MORGAN, R. and REINER, R., eds. (1994), *The Oxford Handbook of Criminology*, Oxford: Clarendon Press.

MANNING, P. (1992), *Organizational Communication*. New York: A. de Gruyter.

MARRIS, P. (1986), *Loss and Change*. London: Routledge and Kegan Paul.

MATZA, D. (1969), *Becoming Deviant*, Englewood Cliffs, NJ: Prentice-Hall.

McCALL, M. and WITTNER, J. (1990), 'The Good News about Life History', in H. Becker and M. McCall, eds., *Symbolic Interaction and Cultural Studies*. Chicago: University of Chicago Press.

MERLEAU-PONTY, M. (1973), *The Prose of the World*. Evanston: Northwestern University Press.

MILLER, P. (1976), Blaming the Victim of Child Molestation: An Empirical Analysis. Ph.D. Dissertation, Northwestern University.

MITCHELL, B. (1990), *Murder and Penal Policy*. New York: St. Martin's Press.

MORGAN, J. and ZEDNER, L. (1992), *Child Victims*. Oxford: Clarendon Press.

MORRIS, N. (1992), *The Brothel Boy and Other Parables of Law*. New York, Oxford University Press.

MORRIS, T. and BLOM-COOPER, L. (1967), 'The victim's contribution', in M. Wolfgang, ed., *Studies in Homicide*. New York: Harper and Row.

——(1964), *A Calendar of Murder*. London: Michael Joseph.

MUKERJI, C. and SCHUDSON, M., eds. (1991), *Rethinking Popular Culture*. Berkeley: University of California Press.

MURRAY-PARKES, C. (1972), *Bereavement*. New York: International Universities Press.

——(1993), 'Psychiatric Problems Following Bereavement', *British Journal of Psychiatry*, 162.

NATIONAL CAMPAIGN FOR THE ABOLITION OF CAPITAL PUNISHMENT (1974), *Murder and Capital Punishment in England and Wales*. London: The National Campaign and the Howard League for Penal Reform.

NOVA (1985), *Survivors of Homicide Victims*. Washington: National Organization for Victim Assistance.

PAGELS, E. (1995), *The Origin of Satan*. New York: Random House.

PEACH, M. and KLASS, D. (1987), 'Special Issues in the Grief of Parents of Murdered Children', *Death Studies*, 11.

POLK, K. (1994), *When Men Kill: Scenarios of Masculine Violence*. Cambridge: Cambridge University Press,

PROTHROW-STITH, D. (1991), *Deadly Consequences*. New York: Harper-Collins.

RAPHAEL, B. (1984), *The Anatomy of Bereavement*. New York: Basic Books.

REISS, A. (1972), *The Police and the Public*. New Haven: Yale University Press.

RICOEUR, P. (1967), *The Symbolism of Evil*. New York: Harper and Row.

ROBINSON, A. (nd), 'The effects of murder on the family/relatives', unpublished.

ROSE, G. (1961), *The Struggle for Penal Reform*. London: Stevens.

RUGGIERO, G. (1946), *Existentialism*. London: Secker and Warburg.

RYNEARSON, E. (1984), 'Bereavement after Homicide', *American Journal of Psychiatry*, 141.

SPIERENBURG, P. (1984), *The Spectacle of Suffering*. Cambridge: Cambridge University Press.

STRAEBE, W. and STRAEBE, M. (1987), *Bereavement and Health*. Cambridge: Cambridge University Press.

TERR, L. (1990), *Too Scared to Cry*. New York: Harper and Row.

VICTIM SUPPORT (1996), 'The Victim's Charter 1996: A Briefing Paper by Victim Support'. London: Victim Support.

VON HENTIG, H (1948), *The Criminal and His Victim; Studies in the Sociobiology of Crime*. Hamden, CT: Archon Books.

WADDINGTON, P. (1993), *Calling the Police*. Aldershot: Avebury.

WALTER, T. (1994), *The Revival of Death*. London: Routledge.

WEST, A. (1989, *For the Love of Lesley*. London: Warner.

WOLFGANG, M. (1958), *Patterns in Criminal Homicide*, Philadelphia: University of Pennsylvania Press.

——, ed. (1967*a*), *Studies in Homicide*. New York: Harper and Row.

——(1967*b*), *The Subculture of Violence*. London: Tavistock.

——(1983), 'Homicide: Behavioral Aspects', in *Encyclopedia of Crime and Justice*. New York: Free Press.

WOOTTON, B. (1969), 'Morality and Mistakes', in L. Blom-Cooper, ed., *The Hanging Question*. Duckworth: London.

YOUNG, J. (1987), 'Murder Most English', *Time Out*, 14–21 January.

[12]
Victims, Prosecutors and the State in Nineteenth Century England and Wales

Abstract

Despite substantial misgivings about the activities and character of private prosecutors in England and Wales, the office of Director of Public Prosecutions was established only reluctantly and hesitantly in 1879. Tracing the history and aftermath of the decision to create that office reveals something of the manner in which victims and the state were represented officially throughout much of the nineteenth century, and it may help to explain why there is such a continuing reluctance to cede the victim a greater role in criminal procedure.

Key Words

Crown Prosecution Service • Director of Public Prosecutions • policy-making • private prosecution • victim

Introduction

Criminologists and others in the 1970s and 1980s occasionally remarked upon the invisibility of the personal victim as a protagonist in the Anglo-American criminal justice system (Bureau of Justice Statistics, 1981). He or she was defined as one who was quite overshadowed, the 'forgotten party' or 'non-person in the eyes of the professional participants' (Shapland, 1983: 8)—the person who had lost property in his or her conflict (Christie, 1977) and was reduced procedurally to the standing of a mere claimant, witness or recipient of compensation. There has been no formal history of victims of crime, and references to changes in the way in which they have been represented have largely been made *en passant*, but something can be pieced together, and it appears that their demise in England and Wales was not as simple or as remote in time as some have supposed. Neither was the heyday of the victim perhaps quite as unsullied as some of its admirers imagined (Schafer, 1968; Wright, 1991). In this article, I shall consider one strand of the symbolic work that was done during the first half of the nineteenth century to begin to bring the victim's prominence in criminal procedure to a close.

The consolidation of royal power through the courts and the establishment of the police as investigators, thief-takers and prosecutors undoubtedly shaped what eventually was to become the marginalization of the English and Welsh victim. But there was a third, complementary theme, which has received rather less scholarly attention: the creation in 1879 and subsequent development of the office of Director of Public Prosecutions. No claim can be made that it was any more influential than the others, but it is plausible that the personal victim's eventual eclipse must in some fashion be linked to the establishment of a public office that came in time to reinforce the transfer of the bulk of the formal responsibility for bringing prosecutions to an organization quite expressly and almost exclusively representing the Crown.[1]

It is not a connection easily made. The first half of the nineteenth century may have been portrayed as an era of extensive criminal justice reform, but, despite numerous attempts, the reforms barely touched the prosecutorial system and some contemporaries believed that the reform process had stagnated altogether in the latter half.[2] So very protracted was that evolution, so uncertain was its course, so confounded by developments in other institutions such as the courts and the police, that it is difficult to discern a clear-cut turning point or a clear-cut transformation of the public representations of victims and crime (Plucknett, 1956: 422) that accompanied it. Indeed, those public representations were themselves seldom objectified and discussed,[3] glimpsed, as it were, only out of the corner of the official eye when there were more important administrative questions of efficiency, effectiveness, cost, procedure, patronage and corruption to discuss. But a change in the iconography of crime and victimization most certainly did occur and it is a change that I intend to discuss.

Victims and prosecutions

Legal historians remind us that, at the very beginning, before the emergence of proper legal process in England and Wales, responses to injury and loss could not but be a matter of what they sometimes described as private vengeance (a term that reveals something important about their stance towards the victim). With the emergence of criminal procedure, however, that so-called vengeance came to be mediated by institutions and rules, and trial proceedings were brought formally by the victim, identified as the prosecutor, who had a stake in the wrong and was responsible for its redress. Plucknett remarked of its origins that 'First, it is in the hands of the injured party and his opponent' (Plucknett, 1956: 424). Disputes were palpably confrontational and immediate, and they remained so for centuries. Until the early modern period, there was what has been termed a 'lawyer-free' procedure in which private individuals joined their conflict in an altercation trial under the authority of an examining judge and without the intervention of counsel (Langbein, 2003: 2). Personal victims could not but bulk large in such dealings for there were no lawyers or other intermediaries to obscure them.

Practical and ideological remnants of that early state of affairs remained substantially in place throughout most of the nineteenth and twentieth centuries. Although there was a rise of the centralized State in England and Wales, which began with the Norman Conquest (Klerman, 2001) and was accelerated by the Reformation (Tallack, 1900),[4] a consolidation and professionalization of the magistrates' courts in the nineteenth century; and the establishment of police forces in the Metropolis and the provinces from the 1820s onwards; although the Attorney General could exceptionally prosecute cases of State importance, and coroners could inquire into cases and examine witnesses; although there was a growth from the beginning of the eighteenth century in the use of lawyers in the criminal courts who acted for private persons and for prosecuting associations (Hay and Snyder, 1985: 384), and of government-appointed solicitors instructed by the Bank, the Mint and the Treasury;[5] although grand juries stood in some fashion for the public; and the police came to bring an increasing number of charges throughout the period, prosecutions still remained largely private in law and in practice, and the police officer or infrequently appearing State official was himself held in doctrine to be acting only as a private individual. In Staffordshire, for instance, no more than 13 per cent of prosecutions were brought by anyone in public office in the second half of the eighteenth century (Hay and Snyder 1985: 21). For much of this time it was the victim who had to identify and perhaps apprehend an offender, lay a charge, find witnesses, collect depositions, and initiate and conduct proceedings. Cornish and Clark said of the 1700s and early 1800s that prosecution was chiefly 'a matter for the victims themselves or other private individuals who could be persuaded to take a sufficient interest in the matter' (Cornish and Clark, 1989: 552). To be sure, the individual prosecutor might well take the form of an association of private persons gathered together to share the costs and labour of prosecutions, but the origins and much of the conduct of action remained outside the control of the State. Such was the ideological and constitutional pre-eminence given to prosecution as a private act,[6] so important was its role considered to be in checking the powers of a potentially oppressive State and in preventing official indolence (Royal Commission on Criminal Procedure, 1981: 61), that it was effectively to dwindle (but not disappear) only in the latter half of the twentieth century.

During all of this time, images of the victim that were on offer seem inescapably to have been something of a composite or hybrid, part pragmatic and part ideological, part corporeal, part incorporeal; showing the personal victim serving both as an embodied individual and as a cipher for the suprapersonal many. I will show that, although their images are seldom explicit, personal victims did not disappear practically or symbolically. They could not have done so for how else could much crime have become manifest and actionable? But they had to co-exist inextricably with another kind of entity altogether—society, the Crown, the community or the State conceived as a metaphysical victim.[7]

Thus, it was Holdsworth who talked of how the origins of criminal law resided in the 'idea that wrong is not simply the affair of the injured individual. . . A wrong is regarded as the breach of the "*grith*" or "*frith*" or "*mund*" of the king'. (Holdsworth, 1903: 47) The very idea of *crime* presupposed that the sovereign had come to acquire an independent and increasingly monopolistic interest in the maintenance of peace; the promotion of morality; the ending of *vendetta*; the protection of the community, victim, witness and offender, especially where no one else could offer protection; the collection of fines and forfeitures; and the redress of offences that could not be remedied by monetary compensation alone. And, beyond that, there was an idea that was more transcendental still. It was pivotal to understanding the character of crime that what affected the individual also affected the sovereign allegorically. In Blackstone's early, still cited, formulation of 1769, crime was critically considered an affront to the Crown 'because the sovereign, in whom centres the majesty of the whole community, is supposed by the law to be the person injured by every infraction of the public rights belonging to that community' (Blackstone, 1769: 12). In 1875, over a century later, Lord Cockburn, the Chief Justice of the Queen's Bench, argued that 'every act which the law constitutes a crime is, as such, an offence, not against the individual who may have been injured by it, but against the Community or State' (submission to the Fifth Report of the Judicature Commission, 1875: xix).

Crime in the nineteenth century was an attack on a person and on a community, and, to make matters yet more complex, in Platonic fashion both the person and the community took what might be described as ideal and material forms. There were public images, open to elaboration and dissemination in moral stories, that fed the iconography of the ideal victim (Christie, 1986), the innocent and pitiable child, woman or underling perhaps, whose undeserved suffering invited compassion, justified trial and punishment and legitimized the politics of reform. Take the notorious Road Murder of June 1860, a murder that long 'filled' the columns of *The Times* (*The Times,* 10 October 1860), in which a 'gentleman's child [was] found with its throat cut on its father's own premises' (*The Times,* 10 November 1860) and whose murderer, his step-sister, was not apprehended until her confession in 1865 (*The Times*, 26 April 1865). 'The blood of the victim [had been] crying from the ground' (*The Times*, 10 October 1860), prompting harshly critical and widespread reflections about innocence unprotected and justice denied; the poverty of prevailing methods of investigation, case management and witness interrogation; and the need for a scheme of public prosecution based tacitly on the model of the French *juge d'instruction*. *The Times* was stirred to reflect in 1867 that 'the want of a State prosecutor has long been recognised. The Road Murder would not have been a mystery so long if there had been one.' (*The Times*, 18 April 1867) On the other hand, and in crude contrast, there was, as it were, the material victim in his or her more commonplace guise as prosecutor and we shall see that such a one was considered far from ideal. *Pari passu*, the idealizing rhetoric of the symbolic collectivity, sovereign or State in whose name trials were fought was obliged to contend with the messier, sometimes tarnished politics and practice of criminal justice in everyday life.

Those private and public, ideal and mundane, facets of the victim hybrid combined in varying and sometimes confusing ways, for where the empirical and private person not only implicated the ideal victim but also stood, in some fashion, for the abstract public, where private initiative was mediated by public institutions, what was one sometimes looked very much like the other, the boundaries could become blurred,[8] and images of crime and victimization became correspondingly murky.[9] For instance, Blackstone said before the founding of the office of public prosecutor that 'indictments. . . are preferred in the name of the King, but at the suit of any private prosecutor' (1769: 303). After the founding of that office in 1879, Maitland could still write that 'In this country any person can prosecute any person for any crime. But prosecution is theoretically a proceeding on the part of the Queen' (1885: 14) and, he could note, 'To speak of the English system as one of *private* prosecutions is misleading. It is we who have *public* prosecutions, for any of the public may prosecute.' (1885: 141; and see Stephen, 1883: 493) Legal scholars, lawyers (Devlin, 1960: 16) and Directors of Public Prosecutions themselves continued for a while thereafter to define criminal prosecution as a private act (Edwards, 1964: 335) conducted in some fashion in the name of the public. Indeed, as late as 1976, Sir Norman Skelhorn, the then Director of Public Prosecutions, could maintain that in law all criminal prosecutions remained strictly private in England and Wales (1981: 65). And commenting generally on the complexities and contradictions of the theme, Philip Rawlings said that the position was to emerge where

> the State defined through the courts and legislation both what a crime was and what was an appropriate response to a crime. So private prosecution almost seems a misnomer in that it was prosecution that took a particular form . . . which was controlled by the State. . . . I'm not convinced that [private prosecution] was seen in c18th as a form of justice that was

> controlled by the victim even if in reality this was the case (because, of course, they need do nothing in response to an offence): criminal law was after all written about in books called 'Pleas of the Crown'. (private communication)

The case for the Crown

Although lawyers, politicians, officials and others observed throughout the century before the 1879 Act that reform was necessary, the Government was tardy and hesitant in establishing the germ of a state-administered system of prosecutions. There were proposals to emulate practice in Scotland (Colquhoun, 1798),[10] France (Bentham, 1791), Ireland, India, the USA, South Australia (letter to *The Times*, 5 September 1874) and elsewhere that appeared to have welled up out of the general rationalizing impulse[11] that characterized other changes in the criminal justice system, an impulse particularly associated with an impatience with seeming inefficiency[12] and inconsistency;[13] a frustration at the difficulty of mounting successful prosecutions; a consciousness of how much better other States managed their affairs; and a sensitivity alerted by newspaper and other reports and the new official statistics after 1810 to apparent increases[14] in recorded crime that accompanied the ending of the Napoleonic wars (Radzinowicz, 1956: 67), the economic depression of 1837–44 and its successors, the establishment of police forces; the urbanization and displacement of population (Gurr et al., 1977), and much else, including the need to control a potentially unruly people that was beginning to organize itself politically.

'We are,' reflected a Metropolitan magistrate in 1845, 'the only country where no one takes care of the interests of the Crown in prosecutions' (letter published in Commissioners, 1845: 237). And his was not a lone voice. Public prosecution had been mooted for decades. Pioneering schemes had already been introduced *extempore* in the first half of the nineteenth century by benches of magistrates working with locally-appointed public prosecutors in the West Riding, Durham and Northumberland (see Commissioners, 1845: 233; and Select Committee, 1855: 3). Proposals for a new system were developed by a House of Commons committee in 1833, although its papers have apparently not survived (Bentley, 1998: 85), by Lord Brougham in 1834[15] and by the Criminal Law Commissioners in 1845.[16] In 1854, the Lord Chief Justice publicly upbraided the Attorney-General for his inactivity in bringing about change, and a private member's bill was subsequently introduced and then failed for want of Parliamentary time. The Select Committee on Public Prosecutors, a weighty body that included a former Attorney-General of Ireland and the Lord Advocate of Scotland, considered the matter in 1855 and reported in 1856, recommending reform, but the Bills that followed after a long lapse of 14 years in 1870, 1871 and 1872 failed, as did another such Bill in 1873,[17] despite a

Government promise to legislate that was made in the previous year. In 1874, the *Fifth Report of the Judicature Commission* again proposed a national system of prosecutors under a Director of Public Prosecutions and extending over the whole country, and another private Bill was again introduced in 1877, but without result (again, it was said, for lack of Parliamentary time [see *The Times*, 14 April 1877]). According to a leader in *The Times* of 17 March 1879, floating a Public Prosecutor's Bill had become a 'Wednesday afternoon annual'. But, the leader continued, the measure was necessary because 'under the prevailing system it was everybody's business and nobody's business to prosecute'.

Those delays, restraints and hesitations are informative because they show that, whereas there was a long-standing accord amongst professional lawyers and others that the system of private prosecutions was flawed (and they were flawed, I shall argue, because of a radical mistrust of the personal victim and the arrangements under which he or she was obliged to proceed), there was also for a long while a companion mistrust of almost all the institutions which might be enlisted to superintend an alternative system, and the powers and responsibilities of the new Director were to be cramped in proportion.

The same arguments were to be rehearsed over and over, the observations of one committee or authority drawing on those of another down the decades:[18] if personal victims were unreliable and inept protagonists, it was held, so were many of the candidates who might replace them. The assertions surviving in print were not always based on what would now pass as sound criminological or socio-legal evidence. Rather they quite characteristically drew on the practical experience of practitioners, legislators and lawyers rehearsed in anecdotes and impressions and unsubstantiated by survey, statistics or independent inquiry. They were motivated, reflecting always the view of the professionals, and never, except at a remote distance, that of the victim or lay prosecutor. But they were virtually unanimous, they were real enough in their consequences, and they survive unchallenged as the commanding representations of their time. It is those representations, and particularly the arguments marshalled by the critically important 1855 Select Committee, that I shall now consider, and this article could be read as an essay in mapping change that was as much symbolic as administrative.

The alleged failings of private prosecutors and private prosecutions

The existence of ideal victims may at some level have been acknowledged, but those victims who actually presented themselves as private prosecutors were very rarely publicly typified by practitioners and politicians as sympathetic, heroic, capable or admirable. They were not the creatures of any sort of Golden Age. Instead, their actions were frequently seen to be vengeful,[19] 'frivolous and groundless' (Select Committee, 1855: 98), and motivated by private interest (see Hay, 1985: 345). The future Lord Chief Justice, Lord Denman, said in 1824 that prosecutors tended to be helpless, ignorant, interested, corrupt and irresponsible, and his observations were to be reiterated approvingly in reports for years thereafter (in, for example, Commissioners, 1845: 211). His successor then continued in the same vein when he talked in 1855 of the 'shameful perversion of the criminal law for private ends' (Select Committee, 1855: 62).

Victims were represented as neither dependable nor disinterested. They could be intimidated (Select Committee, 1855: 12). They could be venal. They might be bought off by defendants and, indeed, it was alleged that they sometimes mounted prosecutions precisely to *be* bought off (Select Committee, 1855: 37) or pre-emptively to forestall charges that might be brought by the defendant. Private prosecution was said to often be deployed in the service of malice,[20] harassment, blackmail (Skelhorn, 1981: 66), extortion (Select Committee, 1855: 81, 107, 155, 162, 207), or what was, in effect, the pursuit of a civil claim through the criminal courts (Select Committee, 1855: 8, 50), opening the 'door to bribery, collusion and illegal compromises' (Commissioners, 1845: 14). Allegations were made that cases could be brought merely to earn the costs (see Hay and Snyder, 1985: 37). Overall, claimed Lord Brougham, the system was a 'perversion of the criminal law for personal and guilty purposes' (Select Committee, 1855: iii). A matter affecting the public good had been entrusted to those moved by private passion.[21]

A scheme of private prosecution required an individual or association with an interest and capacity to bring charges. It was 'irksome, expensive and inconvenient' (Commissioners, 1845: 14) and it could collapse, say, in cases of murder where the injured party had been killed and no one was prepared to act for them,[22] or in cases of domestic violence, child abuse (see the evidence of the Treasury Solicitor, Select Committee, 1855: 127) and the maltreatment of servants (Select Committee, 1855: 3) or the occupants of workhouses where the injured party was not powerful, wealthy or independent enough to go to law (Commissioners on Criminal Law, 1845: 252). A Queen's Counsel and magistrate observed in 1855, 'as a general rule nobody takes up murder prosecutions in the lower ranks of society' (Select Committee, 1855: 37).

Although from the late eighteenth century onwards, some of the expenses incurred by victims and prosecution witnesses began to be paid by local bodies, prosecuting associations (Schubert, 1981) and the State,[23] the system of financial assistance could be haphazard,[24] incomplete and uncertain (Commissioners, 1845: 305). It did not allow, for example, expenses before commitment (Commissioners, 1845: 265), and none at all if there was no committal (Select Committee, 1855: 233). Poor prosecutors were frequently obliged to rely on lawyers advancing them money for their witnesses' expenses but not all lawyers were willing to help[25] and cases would collapse for lack of funds.[26] For much of the opening years of the nineteenth century, prosecutions were being increasingly supervised by the police clerks to magistrates or borough solicitors and paid for out of public funds, there was still in many areas no one willing to venture on the trouble and expense of a prosecution (letter to *The Times*, 19 December 1850) or competent to take statements, investigate alibis or peruse a case or evidence (Select Committee, 1855: 11). Cases failed because they were too insubstantial or wanted proper preparation (see Langbein, 2003: 123). The poor, concluded the Under Secretary of State at the Home Office in 1855, might not get justice (Select Committee, 1855: 162, 167). And there was no effective regulation even where attorneys did prosecute on their behalf. Some prosecuting lawyers were said to be 'very improper people'[27] who 'scrambled' for cases, sought unnecessarily to multiply the number of trials they conducted in order to make money (Select Committee 1855: 117), skimped on case preparation, embezzled costs,[28] and might even be retained by the defendant or the defendant's family quite deliberately to abort the prosecution (Select Committee, 1855: iv, 49).

The State as the proper prosecuting authority

If the private individual was not always an appropriate person symbolically, politically and practically to prosecute, if the existing system was flawed, what of the State, the other, more metaphorical constituent of the victim-hybrid, the entity that had been damaged as if by sympathetic magic? It appears that English and Welsh legislators, officials and lawyers from the 1790s onwards acknowledged generally that almost all other States managed their affairs better—crime affected the collectivity and, they said, it followed that it was incumbent on public officials formally to prosecute in its name. Example after example was held up before the 1855 Select Committee. The Scottish Lord-Advocate stated that

> the system [in Scotland] proceeds upon the principle that it is the duty of the State to detect crime, apprehend offenders, and punish them, and that independently of the interests of a private party. The Scotch system acknowledges the right of a private party to prosecute; but the duty of the public prosecutor is altogether irrespective of that. (Select Committee, 1855: 17)

In India, said Charles Hay Cameron, a former member of the Legislative Council of that country, 'the business of criminal prosecution is one in which the public are so deeply interested that it is very wrong to entrust it to the feelings and caprices of individuals. . . it is the proper business of a government officer' (Select Committee, 1855: 95). Joseph Napier, the former Attorney-General for Ireland, claimed that prosecution in that country was

> founded on the principle. . . that the Executive Government is properly, and I would say primarily charged, with the security of society: that the security of life and property belongs peculiarly to the Executive Government, and

that all prosecutions ought to be conducted by responsible public officers. (Select Committee, 1855: 141).

And so it went on. The Select Committee's 1856 draft report quoted the Attorney-General of England as saying that in every other well-constituted country there was a minister of justice (Select Committee, 1855: xvii). It was a marked anomaly that England and Wales were the only developed nations to lack such provision, and inefficiency, waste and injustice were the result.

The alleged failings of alternative institutions

Yet there was a difficulty. If it was admitted that prosecutions should be brought publicly in the name of an ideal community or Sovereign, they had never the less practically to be organized by an officer or agency that was anything but abstract, and there was in the first 70 or so years of the nineteenth century a thoroughgoing distrust in many quarters of the State and all its agencies.

England and Wales were administered largely in the name of a laissez-faire politics. It was for the most part presumed that the role of the State was to intervene minimally,[29] cautiously and at the least expense,[30] and any significant increase in its powers was to be managed most gingerly lest personal freedoms suffer. John Stuart Mill, for instance, said in 1838 that 'when any power has been made the strongest power, enough has been done for it; care is thenceforth wanted rather to prevent that strongest power from swallowing up all others. Wherever all the forces of society act in one single direction, the just claims of the individual human being are in extreme peril' (reprinted as Mill, 1950: 88).

If the State was not to become over-mighty, there was a trepidation that, whereas the interests of the collectivity must be upheld, there was an attendant risk that organizations charged with their enforcement could prove in practice to be oppressive, inept, costly and corrupt. Removing the checks notionally built into the public's diffuse and autonomous right to prosecute, and diminishing the independence of the Bar to represent private individuals (see Select Committee, 1855: 62; Edwards, 1964: 349) could well introduce a new, arbitrary, politicized and despotic system. It must be recollected that debate about establishing public prosecutors came to a head at the very time of the Northcote-Trevelyan Report of 1854 and criticisms of the organization of the British army made during and immediately after the Crimean War (see Russell, 1856; Sweetman, 1984; Mandler, 1990) when the probity and competence of the State were not taken on trust, and when patronage and corruption were still endemic and feared.

To be sure, there was something of a shift already in progress. The new police, covering half the country when the 1855 Select Committee reported, were undertaking a growing volume of prosecutions (Select Committee,

1855: 123), and would later dominate proceedings, although they did so again as notionally private individuals, and their actions were not at first well received. The then Home Secretary, Robert Peel, had tried to ensure that they were not drawn from the ranks of professional men, saying 'I have refused to employ gentlemen as superintendents and inspectors, because I am certain they would be above their work' (in Smith, 1985: 44), and, not being gentlemen, they were not necessarily deemed intelligent (in the view of the Attorney-General [in Select Committee, 1855: 187]), honourable or competent[31] enough to be relied on, not, that is, 'proper people to mount prosecutions'.[32] The police in London were said to be promoted and rewarded on results. They were prone as prosecutors to excessive zeal and partiality,[33] and that was quite wrong—as 'mere turnkeys' they should never be involved in something like prosecutions or 'have an interest in the outcome' said the Attorney-General (Select Committee, 1855: 186). They were 'proper people to collect evidence, improper people to deliver instructions to counsel or prepare written statements for the court' said the clerk of indictments to the Home Circuit (Select Committee, 1855: 177). They did not themselves receive adequate legal advice except in the most serious cases.[34] They were occasionally corrupt, being said to bring charges for 'a market rate' (Select Committee, 1855: 77, 98, 100) or a share of the lawyer's fee and costs (Select Committee, 1855: 52). In Stafford, for instance, they had a 'tendency. . . to get up frivolous cases, forge connexions with low attorneys, and receive payment from them' (Select Committee, 1855: 105). That hostile stance was to change somewhat by the 1880s and after the founding of a Director of Public Prosecutions (Hay and Snyder, 1985: 45, 50) but, for a while, it seemed to lawyers and legislators that it was perhaps preferable not to resort to the police.

Reformers appeared to have had as little confidence that other practitioners[35] or State officials would be significantly more competent or honest, and it was no small thing to propose concentrating so much power to prosecute and deny liberty in a new office (Select Committee, 1855: 21). The appointment of dedicated State prosecutors might lead, it was said, to bribery,[36] nepotism, action in the interest of political faction, and the protection of the powerful from charges (Hay and Snyder, 1985: 44) and there were doubts about whether their selection and supervision could be entrusted to the Judges (they were venal, observed the Attorney-General in 1855 [Select Committee, 1855: 16, 194, 196]), local authorities (Commissioners, 1845: 295), the Crown or Government (Select Committee, 1855: 15). Prosecutors should be independent of party,[37] interest and influence. Said Lord Campbell, the Lord Chief Justice in 1855, 'another objection, which I was always afraid of, is as to the patronage; that it would be most alarming to vest such a patronage in the Crown, and I do not know in what other hands it could be safely vested' (Select Committee, 1855: 62), and the former Attorney-General of Ireland concurred (Select Committee, 1855: 202). It was precisely that anxiety about the enlargement of Government power and sponsorship that led to the demise of a number of the Bills that followed the report of the 1855 Select Committee.[38] Maitland concluded:

> It has very generally been believed that to put the control of the criminal law into the hands of state officials is not the way to make that law respected. It is better that some rogues should go quit, and some guiltless men be vexed by false charges, than that there should be any room for even a groundless suspicion that party politics have or can have anything to do with criminal law (1885: 148–9).

The 1879 Act and beyond

After 'half a century of controversy' (Skelhorn, 1981: 65), 'an Act for more effectually providing for the Prosecution of Offences in England and for other purposes' was finally approved embodying all that nervousness. It was 'a very small measure' (Maitland, 1885: 149), passed unopposed precisely because it *was* so small, providing for the appointment of a Director of Public Prosecutions, a solicitor or barrister of at least 10 years standing, who would work with up to six assistants[39] and under the Attorney-General to 'initiate, undertake and carry on criminal proceedings and give advice and assistance to chiefs of police, clerks to justice' (Prosecution of Offences Act, ch. 22, 3 July 1879). The Home Secretary had 'not wish[ed] to push his plans forward unduly' (*The Times,* 17 March 1879), and the result was an office that was modest by design, its powers reined in by parsimony and Liberal fears about what were seen to be the risks of giving excessive influence to ministers. The new director was to undertake cases of importance or difficulty referred to him; 'where refusal or failure of a person to proceed appear to make intervention necessary' (*The Times,* 17 November 1978) to secure the prosecution of an offender. It was not clear at first what his precise powers would be, the matter having been simply entrusted to regulations that would be drafted from time to time later, and it took decades to elucidate just what he could and should do.

It was apparent from the outset that his was to be a minor role. The very first director, Sir John Maule, said that he had 'no legal right to interfere or interpose, and it is only when [others] apply to me and I learn in that way what they wish for my interposition, that the interposition is well-founded or warrantable' (Rozenberg, 1987: 19). He was, said a later director, Sir Thomas Hetherington, 'in a sense the central controller but concerned only with a small number of cases of particular difficulty' (1989: 1). His work was to complement rather than replace the older system, the right to bring private prosecutions being substantially unaffected, and, during the first three years of his appointment, he took up only 809 out of 2324 cases (Bentley, 1998: 86–7).[40] Within five years, the report of a departmental committee[41] on his duties concluded not only that the new system was 'tentative and in need of modification' (*The Times,* 7 June 1884) but that the director was little more than a 'fifth wheel on the coach', and it recommended that legislation should be brought in both to increase the number of cases referred to him by the police and to strengthen his role by combining it with that of the Treasury Solicitor.[42] There was yet further debate in 1886 when a new set of regulations made it uncertain when it was his duty to intervene in the public interest. In 1892, *The Times* again complained that the director had very limited powers and few resources, spending only £15,000 per annum. His title did him an injustice, it said, because he actually directed only a very few prosecutions (*The Times*, 14 April 1892). The government was censured in 1924 when it intervened in his absence to withdraw the prosecution of Campbell, a communist, who had published an article advocating that workers should not fight fellow workers (see, for example, *The Times*, 16 December 1924). Controversy over the Savidge case in 1928 resolved that he was no *judge d'instruction* and was not to be closely involved with criminal investigation and interrogation.[43] By the 1950s, said Sir Thomas Hetherington, the director's duties had become better defined: he was not an investigator or examiner of witnesses, he was to be independent of government, his role was not to control but to advise the police, he should take decisions in cases referred to him, and the right of private prosecution was to be preserved. The director could 'direct no one and there [were] no public prosecutions in the ordinary sense of that term' (Edwards, 1964: 335). An increasingly professionalized police force had in any event effectively taken over the bulk of prosecutions, the director concentrating only on cases of difficulty and importance, and the police exercised control until the early 1980s.

What then came to precipitate significant structural change after a long period of inactivity was a succession of scandals centred on deaths in custody and allegations of police impropriety, most particularly in the case of the investigation of the murder of Maxwell Confait, involving a confession improperly elicited from a vulnerable suspect (*The Times*, 14 December 1977) and a successful appeal against conviction (*The Times*, 8 November 1974). A review of the conduct of the case was ordered in October 1975, and that, in its turn, contributed in 1978 to arguments leading to the establishment of the Royal Commission on Criminal Procedure with its brief to consider the extent of police powers in investigating crime, the rights of suspects and the procedure by which people were brought to trial. The Home Secretary of the time, Merlyn Rees, observed that some parts of that procedure had not been exposed to formal scrutiny for 50 years (*The Times*, 20 February 1978). And the arguments that came to be rehearsed about prosecutions were to be almost identical to those that had been paraded over the previous century.

In an increasingly volatile politics of crime and criminal justice (see Downes and Morgan, 1994: 188), where 'anxiety ha[d] been manifestly growing about the continuing rise in the level of crime. . . and [t]here were ignorance and confusion. . . about the ways in which crime was investigated and prosecuted' (Royal Commission 1981: 2), the question of the legitimacy and limits of the policing role was ever more contested.[44] Sir David McNee, the commissioner of Metropolitan Police, and the Police Superintendents' Association advised the Royal Commission that the police were unduly handicapped in the war against crime and that greater powers were required to interrogate and detain suspects. The president of the association submitted that the Royal Commission should 'resist efforts by the do-gooders and reformers to handicap our efforts even further. Anything which makes it more difficult for the police officer helps the criminal and harms the public'. (*The Times*, 27 September 1978) The police criticized defence lawyers for manipulating the system and chasing fees, but lawyers retorted by accusing the police of bringing insubstantial cases that should never have reached the courts, and legal commentators observed that the role of the English and Welsh police was anomalous and indefensible because, alone in western Europe, a single body was empowered not only to investigate but also to prosecute cases (*The Times*, 9 November 1982).

The Prosecuting Solicitors' Association of England and Wales resuscitated proposals to institute a nation-wide system of locally based prosecutors independent of the police, declaring that existing practice was inconsistent, ineffective and haphazard, distorted by the police propensity to make cases to secure convictions (*The Times*, 17 November 1978). It was joined by judges, including Lord Gardiner and Lord Devlin, and Members of Parliament who maintained that the prevailing system was inconsistent and defective in its 'fairness, openness, accountability and efficiency'. It also asserted that the police should not have responsibility for both investigation and prosecution, largely because the police had different standards about when to prosecute and they allowed too many weak cases to come to court. The Home Office at first claimed that the prevailing procedures were working well enough, and that establishing a system on Scottish lines was not only unnecessary but also likely to prove expensive (*The Times*, 15 November 1978), but the Royal Commission was unmoved, and proceeded to recommend its introduction. The government eventually acquiesced 'in principle' and re-convened a Home Office working party on an independent prosecution service (*The Times*, 27 July 1982), and that working party in its turn recommended the institution of a national system of local prosecutors working under a Director of Public Prosecutions (*The Times*, 9 December 1982). Moving the second reading of the Prosecution of Offences Bill on the 16 April 1985, Leon Brittan, the Home Secretary, supposed that the new system would 'improve openness and accountability, to increase consistency in prosecution policy, and... contribute to the timely and effective prosecution of offences'.

Only with the founding of the Crown Prosecution Service in 1986 was it perhaps possible to say at last that prosecutions are public acts formally undertaken independently of sectional interest[45] and expressly in defence of the public good.[46] Alex Lyon of the Home Office observed to the Home Affairs Committee on the eve of that final transition that the 'present prosecuting solicitor regards the police as his client and he takes his instructions from the police. The whole object of the public prosecutor is that he would be totally independent to form his own conclusions.' (Home Affairs Committee, 1982: 2) The Solicitor-General talked in the debate on the bill on 16 April 1985 about 'a wide degree of support for the proposition that the client should be the community and not the chief constable'. Sir Thomas Hetherington, the first head of the new Crown Prosecution Service, declared at the very onset that 'I would want to see the Crown Prosecutor a very powerful and strong figure, the holder of an office of great independence' (Home Affairs Committee, 1982: 6). Henceforth his policy would be 'to continue prosecutions while, and only while, they are in the public interest' (Rozenberg, 1987: 14). The impact was felt. By 1989, the Director of Victim Support, Helen Reeves, could inform the Home Affairs Committee in its inquiry into the workings of the new Crown Prosecution Service that 'we do have a very large number of complaints from victims who feel that they themselves were not understood and that the case had become so remote from their experience that they could barely recognize it in court' (Home Affairs Committee, 1990: vol. 2, para 316). To be sure, her observation could equally well have been made before 1986, but it does mark the transformation that had been accomplished.

Conclusion

My prime focus has been on the 1879 Act, an unquestionable turning point in the evolution of the public standing of the personal victim. It was certainly not the most important turning point (the establishment and extension of the police were probably far more significant) and it was not identified at the time as the beginning of the near-exclusion of the private prosecutor, but it did mark the birth of an interesting symbolic and administrative change. It ratified a principle and created a public office, however feeble it may have been in its infancy. It had within it the potential to discipline and circumscribe the role of the victim. It prepared a trajectory for the growth of an organization that was to culminate in the recommendations of the 1981 Royal Commission, the establishment of the Crown Prosecution Service in 1985,[47] and the final displacement of the individual as the party in conflict with the defendant.

What is especially notable for those interested in the iconography of the victim was the longevity and resilience of its negative imagery. The victim was for a long while regarded with unease, not least because at the typification's core there is a rogue element, the lay person who is defined as professionally uncontrolled, capricious and capable of all kinds of mischief, and there has been continual disquiet about awarding him or her too much influence in criminal proceedings (see Garland, 2001: 143). Legal and legislative fears about the personal victim are old, but what is comparatively new is the power administratively to deny him/her a substantial place in procedure. The new arrangements made possible by a system of public prosecution were in the long run finally to complete the virtual removal of private victims from participating in tribunals, and they are unlikely to return in force. The prospect of allowing victims to re-enter their role as a party with discrete interests in prosecution and sentencing is certainly now held by many English and Welsh lawyers and judges to be fraught with risk.[48] Victims, they argue, are undisciplined, self-interested, unschooled and potentially volatile non-professional persons who might disclose emotional or legally compromising matters to the jury and wield a prejudicial influence over legislators and members of the public. A nervous Howard League recently pronounced, for example, that 'victims of crime may be little more than a political tool. Indeed it may be that some of the measures taken in the name of enhancing the victims' position simply justify a more punitive criminal justice response' (1997: 11).

Embodied victims are emphatically not now and are unlikely again in the foreseeable future to become full-blown participants in criminal procedure in England and Wales. They will not be allowed to decide whether a prosecution should take place or what charges should be brought. They cannot speak freely at trial. They are not supposed to have a say in sentencing matters. They have been virtually squeezed out of the practical work of preparing for and conducting trials. They do not have justiciable rights. Trials now join conflicts between two recognized parties only, the defendant and State, and the personal victim is at most an 'alleged victim' or complainant until after a verdict or a guilty plea has been entered. From a defendant's committal to his or her release, the *sequelae* of crime lie almost wholly outside the victim's control. They are not the victim's business in any real sense (Fenwick, 1997) and some victims or their families profess surprise that it is not their name that appears in the title of proceedings. The Crown Prosecution Service put it thus in 1995:

> Prosecution and punishment by the Crown for criminal offences is recognition of the principle that crimes are offences against society as a whole, and not only against the individual victim. To return the decision to prosecute to the victim, would break that link. (Crown Prosecution Service, n.d.: 4)

But if there is a machinery devised substantially to corral victims and replace them by the State, it has not yet proved possible to expunge them and their claims altogether. Much crime still entails an incarnate person who has been assaulted, raped, defrauded, robbed or otherwise harmed, and it is he or she who typically reports the crime, makes a statement, and very occasionally testifies. Moreover, to strip the victim of an entitlement, say, privately to prosecute is still seen by lawyers as an excessive step capable of conferring too much power on the State and its agencies.[49] Victims are now treated by State agencies working under the new managerialism both as the 'consumers' of 'services' delivered by criminal justice agencies and as a check on their performance. It is conceded that they must be supported, protected and mollified because to alienate them would be to risk undermining their willingness to report crime and testify in court (Home Office, 1998). They have also recently been given a modest presence in the English and Welsh criminal justice system by acquiring minor rights of a sort for the first time in the Criminal Justice and Court Services Act 2000, quasi-rights (oscillating as 'service standards') in the Victim's Charters of 1990 and 1996, and the prospect of further indirect rights through the European Framework Decision of 2001 (European Community, 2001), and a Parliamentary Commissioner and a statutory code for criminal justice agencies in the current Domestic Violence, Crime and Victims Bill (Home Office, 2003). If the State has displaced the private individual as prosecutor, it has not been a complete eclipse, and contradictions and tensions still remain embedded in the procedures by which the victim role is activated by crime and criminal justice.

Notes

I am grateful to Nicky Lacey, Phillip Rawlings, Declan Roche and an anonymous reader for their helpful comments and advice.

1 By March 1995, nine years after the founding of the Crown Prosecution Service, the chairman of an area committee of the Criminal Justice Consultative Council, could state quite firmly that 'The Crown acted for the State. Many victims were under the misapprehension that the Crown was acting for them.' (Home Office, 1995: 6) I qualify that statement because the right to mount private prosecutions was retained in the 1879 Prosecution of Offences Act and subsequent legislation.

2 A *Times* leader of 4 December 1872 complained about 'the apathy which prevails about Law Reform in the country at large. . .The interest felt by the general public in re-organizing the Judicature and reconstructing the whole system of Courts is as nothing compared with the interest felt by a compact and powerful class in keeping things as they are.'

3 For example, debates in the House of Commons in April and May 1879 on the Prosecution of Offences Bill, the bill that was to lead to the establishment of a Director of Public Prosecutions, were brief and apparently poorly attended, touching only on such matters as the number of assistants the director would have, and the salaries they would be paid, rather than what was, in effect, the beginnings of a very major transformation of the relations between the State, the defendant and the victim. One exception, occurring at a time when such exceptions were to be expected, was Sir Thomas Hetherington's *Prosecution and the Public Interest.* Sir Thomas was the first Director of Public Prosecutions to administer the new Crown Prosecution Service under the 1985 Prosecution of Offences Act and he introduced his reflections about his role as a typical piece of stocktaking at a point of transition. He writes on the opening page:

> Naturally, I became deeply involved in the process of change. I had a unique and most interesting opportunity to ponder during that period on the whys and wherefores of public prosecution . . . What we were aiming to achieve, and why, and whether we were going about it the right way were questions which frequently occupied my mind. (Hetherington, 1989)

4 Sir Thomas Hetherington cites research prepared for the 1981 Royal Commission on Criminal Procedure, which claimed that the first proposal for a state prosecutor was made in 1534 (Hetherington, 1989: 4).

5 Langbein remarked that 'when the central authorities wanted to strengthen a criminal prosecution, they did it by sending in the lawyers' (Langbein, 2003: 121).

6 Rooted in the seventeenth and eighteenth centuries, argue Hay and Snyder, in memories of State prosecutions conducted by the Stuarts and the Commonwealth, and leading to a celebration of private prosecution as an exercise of constitutional freedom (Hay and Snyder, 1985: 34). The new police constituted in 1829 were accordingly at first denied a power to prosecute.

7 One of those scholars, Schafer, observed that 'generally speaking . . . the conventional view is that a crime is an offense against the state, while a tort is an offense only against individual rights . . . crime means only the offender and his offense; the victim's relationship to the crime is viewed in a civil rather than in a criminal light' (Schafer, 1968: 22).

8 Blackstone elsewhere argued that 'ordinarily a crime is a wrong which affects the security or well-being of the public generally so that the crime has an interest in its suppression . . . In all cases the crime includes an injury: every public offence is also a private wrong, and somewhat more; it affects the individual and it likewise affects the community . . . In . . . gross and atrocious injuries the private wrong is swallowed up in the public.' (1769: 5–7)

10 Colquhoun proposed public prosecutors to bring forward prosecutions that might not otherwise take place or which might fail because of some trifling technical difficulty. His proposals were based on his acquaintance with practice in his native Scotland (see Radzinowicz, vol. 3, 1956: 259).

11 Thus the Commissioners on Criminal Law, whose report on prosecutions was published in 1845, had been established to 'rationalise and consolidate the criminal law'.

12 The Attorney-General informed the 1855 Select Committee on Public Prosecutors that the want of a presiding authority led to repeated failures in the administration of criminal justice (Select Committee, 1855: xiv).

13 The Under Secretary of State at the Home Office told the 1855 Select Committee on Public Prosecutors that it was not right that there should be so much local variation in the administration of justice. There was an absence of system that he deplored (Select Committee, 1855: 159).

14 'Apparent' because there was great uncertainty about reporting and recording procedures at the time (see Commissioners, 1839: 6–16, esp. 15).

15 It was his suggestion that Treasury Counsel should be appointed to prepare and superintend all prosecutions at the Central Criminal Court.

16 They concluded on p. 15 and, somewhat gingerly, that the 'obvious answer' to the defects of the existing system was to appoint public prosecutors, but that that measure would require such a massive change that the Commissioners could not prescribe it at that point.

17 The proposal was that a director should be able to investigate crimes as well as prosecute but, according to Sir Thomas Hetherington, the bill contained no provision for circuit counsel or for standing advisory counsel to the Attorney-General for fear of patronage (Hetherington, 1989: 9).

18 For example, Lord Brougham, the first witness appearing before the 1855 Select Committee, alluded to the conclusion of the *Eighth Report of Her Majesty's Commissioners on Criminal Law* of 1845 that private prosecutions were 'irksome, inconvenient and burthensome' (Select Committee, 1855: 10).

19 The Attorney General, a member of the 1855 Select Committee, reflected that the injured party 'is one who is smarting under a sense of injury, smarting with a sense of wrong, and desirous of bringing the vengeance of law on the person who has injured him' (Select Committee, 1855: 186).

20 Leading to the passing of the Vexatious Indictments Act 1859, 22 & 23 Vict. c. 17, s. l.

21 The Chairman of the 1855 Select Committee, questioning H. Ellis, a barrister and the recorder of Leeds, remarked 'you have no doubt that the system which you have described to us is a remnant of the barbarous custom that an offence committed against an individual was an offence against him' (Select Committee, 1855: 25). It was a great anomaly, remarked *The Times* of 24 December 1879, that 'the State regards the prosecution of crime with something like unconcern and that private individuals are free to gratify their passions in a field where those passions should be excluded'.

22 There was, said *Report from the Select Committee on Public Prosecutors*, a 'great evil that flows from the fact that there may be no one with a personal interest to prosecute cases' (Select Committee, 1855: iv).

23 Thus, 25 Geo II, c. 36 accepted the principle that the system of private prosecution could not work unless some of the costs were paid—the bench was empowered to order the treasurer of the county to pay the prosecutor his charges including 'a reasonable allowance for his time and trouble therein'; 18 Geo III c. 19 allowed courts to pay any prosecutor and his or her witnesses their expenses and an allowance to those in poor circumstances; Benet's Act of 1818 enlarged the terms under which costs were awarded and, in 1826, expenses were allowed for attendance before committing magistrates. By 1836, 50 per cent of the costs of prosecution were said to fall on the national exchequer (see Maitland, 1885: 141).

24 A letter from a barrister in 1845 pointed out that costs were not, for instance, allowed for personal injury cases (Commissioners, 1845: 230).

25 It was said by a clerk of Assize in 1855 that lawyers could be out of pocket even in murder cases (Select Committee, 1855: 51).

26 Beattie lists amongst the expenses of a prosecution the costs of a *subpoena* and a warrant; fees for recognizances; fees for drawing up the indictment;

payment of the officer swearing in the witnesses; payment of doorkeeper, cryer and bailiff who took the prosecutor to the grand jury room; the costs of attending the court and compensating witnesses for their time and trouble; and, increasingly, of engaging a solicitor to prepare a case and of counsel to present it to court (Beattie, 1986: 41). See also the Select Committee (1855: 13, 36), and Select Committee (1817).

27 Evidence of the stipendiary magistrate for Manchester and Salford to the Select Committee on Public Prosecutors (1855: 88).

28 Evidence of the stipendiary magistrate for Manchester and Salford to the Select Committee on Public Prosecutors (1855: 89).

29 Colin Matthew remarked that 'no industrial economy can have existed in which the State played a smaller role than that of the United Kingdom in the 1860s' (in Wilson, 2002: 354).

30 A national system of local public prosecutors might, it was thought, be administratively massive and expensive, although the 1855 Select Committee consistently received reassuring replies to questions about its financial implications (see Select Committee, 1855: 6, 184, 203, 205).

31 The view of the taxing officer of the Northern Circuit in Select Committee (1855: 232).

32 See the letter from the Recorder of Warwick in *The Times,* 26 February 1872.

33 Joseph Napier, the former Attorney-General for Ireland, said that the 'police become zealous for convictions rather than for ascertaining the truth' (Select Committee, 1855: 139). That state of affairs came to an end only in 1986. See the report of the Home Affairs Committee (1990: i).

34 An observation repeated 53 years later. See Royal Commission (1908: vol. 1, 155).

35 There were numerous charges levelled against lawyers. Criminal advocates, it was said in evidence, brought cases for the fees rather than because they had a prospect of success (Select Committee, 1855: 117); were 'a very low class of practitioner' (p. 211); and, it was concluded in the 1855 Report, brought it about that the administration of justice had been 'flung into the hands of inferior and unscrupulous practitioners, allowing the guilty to escape and the innocent to be harassed' (p. xii).

36 See the evidence of a QC and magistrate (Select Committee, 1855: 46) and, more generally, see Edwards (1964: 347).

37 Reflecting on the Jamaica Committee and the prosecution of General Eyre, a *Times* leader of 18 April 1867 observed that 'a power of this kind is safer in the in the hands of a Grand Jury with all its faults, than of a lawyer dependent for his place and promotion on the Ministry of the day'.

38 See, for example, the letter from the Recorder of Warwick to *The Times,* 26 February 1872, touching on a Bill proposing a system of local prosecutors (the chief objection raised in Parliament against the Bill, reported *The Times* of 21 June 1872, was 'that it would place very large and novel powers in the hands of the Home Secretary') and the leader in *The Times* of 17 March 1879.

39 There were to be no staff working outside London until the 1985 Act.

40 That position changed little until the founding of the Crown Prosecution Service in 1986. In 1960, for example, the director prosecuted 525 of the 1,044,833 summary cases tried in the magistrates' courts (Edwards, 1964: 336).

41 The report was prompted by a controversial case when the director refused to prosecute two alleged blackmailers who were then successfully prosecuted privately.

42 Prosecution of Offences Act, 1884, ch. 58, a measure subsequently repealed by the Prosecution of Offences Act, 1908, ch. 3.

43 See the report of the Savidge Tribunal (1928). *Inter alia*, the tribunal investigated an allegation that the director had acted improperly in instructing the Commissioner of Metropolitan Police to establish what the evidence of two principal witnesses would be in a trial of police officers for perjury. If those witnesses were not called, it was probable that the prosecution would have failed. The allegation was not upheld but it reinforced the principle that there should be a firm division of labour between the police and the director.

44 For example, the Police Federation published an advertisement before the 1979 general election in which it claimed that 'there is no excuse for crime. Our laws and courts must reflect that concept. Crimes of violence must be met with the severest penalties.' (*The Times*, 3 December 1979)

45 John Morris, replying to the Home Secretary in the debate on the second reading of the Prosecution of Offences Bill, 16 April 1985, talked about the Labour Party welcoming 'the main thrust of the Bill to set up a prosecution service which is independent of those responsible for investigating offences —the police'.

46 An advertisement for Chief Crown Prosecutors placed in *The Times* of 30 December 2003 said that 'as an integral part of the criminal justice system, the CPS stands between the public and some of the most serious threats to its safety' (House of Commons debates, 16 April 1985).

47 Under the Prosecution of Offences Act 1985, C 23 that created the Crown Prosecution Service, consisting of the Director of Public Prosecutions, appointed by the Attorney-General, and Chief Crown Prosecutors responsible for the service in their areas; who would undertake all criminal proceedings other than specified proceedings instituted on behalf of a police force.

48 Consider the remarks of Geoffrey Bindman, a prominent solicitor associated with the law and practice of human rights legislation, in response to a Government proposal to introduce victim statements:

> Mr Straw is right to try to improve remedies for victims but, other than as a witness of fact, the victim has no proper voice at the trial of the alleged perpetrator. To give the victim a role in deciding innocence or guilt would flout our notion of impartial and independent justice . . . Within the criminal process itself the victim or the family may be able to contribute something to the sentencing process by providing information which will assist the judge. To this

> extent, a 'victim personal statement' may be of value. Beyond that, sympathy for the victim cannot in modern days detract from the state's responsibility to ensure the independence and impartiality of the justice system.
>
> ('Remedies for the Victim', *The Guardian*, 13 September 2000)

49 The 1981 Royal Commission supported the right of private prosecution as 'a preventative against partiality and inertia' (1981: 61). So did the government in its ensuing proposals. See Home Office Law Officers' Department (1983: 9). So did the Macpherson Report (Macpherson, 1999).

References

Beattie, J. (1986) *Crime and the Courts in England 1660–1800*. Oxford: Clarendon Press.

Bentham, J. (1791) *Draught of a Code for the Organization of the Judicial Establishment in France*. London.

Bentley, D. (1998) *English Criminal Justice in the Nineteenth Century*. London: The Hambledon Press.

Blackstone, W. (1769) *Commentaries on the Laws of England*, Book 4. Oxford: Clarendon Press.

Bureau of Justice Statistics, (1981) *Victims*. Washington: US Department of Justice.

Christie, N. (1977) 'Conflicts as Property', *The British Journal of Criminology* 17(1): 1–15.

Christie, N. (1986) 'The Ideal Victim', in E. Fattah (ed.) *From Crime Policy to Victim Policy*, pp.17–30. Basingstoke: Macmillan.

Colquhoun, P. (1798) *Treatise on the Police of the Metropolis*. London: C. Dilly.

Commissioners (1839) *First Report of the Commissioners Appointed as to the Best Means of Establishing an Efficient Constabulary Force in the Counties of England and Wales*. London: HMSO.

Commissioners (1845) *Eighth Report of Her Majesty's Commissioners on Criminal Law*. London: HMSO.

Cornish, W. and G. Clark (1989) *Law and Society in England: 1750–1950*. London: Sweet and Maxwell.

Crown Prosecution Service (n.d.) 'The Role of the Victim in the Criminal Justice Process', submitted as evidence to the 'Justice' Committee. London.

Devlin, P. (1960) *The Criminal Prosecution in England*. London: Oxford University Press.

Downes, D. and R. Morgan (1994) 'The Politics of Law and Order', in M. Maguire, R. Morgan and R. Reiner (eds) *The Oxford Handbook of Criminology*, pp.87–134. Oxford: Clarendon Press.

Edwards, J. (1964) *The Law Officers of the Crown*. London: Sweet and Maxwell.

European Community (2001) *Council Framework Decision of 15 March 2001 on the Standing of Victims in Criminal Proceedings (2001/220/JHA)*. Brussels.

Fenwick, H. (1997) 'Procedural "Rights" of Victims of Crime', *Modern Law Review* 60(3): 3.

Garland, D. (2001) *The Culture of Control: Crime and Social Order in Contemporary Society*. Oxford: Oxford University Press.

Gurr, T., P. Grabosky and R. Hula (1977) *The Politics of Crime and Conflict: A Comparative History of Four Cities*. Beverly Hills, CA: Sage.

Hay, D. (1985) 'Prosecution and Power: Malicious Prosecution in the English Courts, 1750–1850', in D. Hay and F. Snyder (eds) *Policing and Prosecution in Britain 1750–1850*. Oxford: Clarendon Press.

Hay, D. and F. Snyder (1985) *Policing and Prosecution in Britain 1750–1850*. Oxford: Clarendon Press.

Hetherington, T. (1989) *Prosecution and the Public Interest*. London: Waterlow Publishers.

Holdsworth, W. (1903) *A History of English Law*. London: Methuen and Co.

Home Affairs Committee (1982) *Prosecution Arrangements, Minutes of Evidence*. London: House of Commons

Home Affairs Committee (1990) *Fourth Report: Crown Prosecution Service*, Volume 1. London: House of Commons.

Home Office (1995) *The Work of the Criminal Justice System*. London: Home Office.

Home Office (1998) *Speaking up for Justice*. London: Home Office.

Home Office (2003) *A New Deal for Victims and Witnesses: National Strategy to Deliver Improved Services*. London: Home Office.

Home Office Law Officers' Department (1983) 'An Independent Prosecution Service for England and Wales'. Cmnd. 9074. London: HMSO.

Howard League (1997) *Information: Victims of Crime*. London.

Judicature Commission (1875) *Fifth and Final Report. C.1090*. London: HMSO.

Klerman, D. (2001) 'Settlement and the Decline of Private Prosecution in Thirteenth-Century England', Law and History Review, 19(1): 1.

Langbein, J. (2003) *The Origins of Adversary Criminal Trial*. Oxford: Oxford University Press.

Macpherson, W. (1999) *The Stephen Lawrence Inquiry: Report of an Inquiry by Sir William Macpherson of Cluny*. Cmnd. 4262. London: HMSO.

Maitland, F. (1885) *Justice and Police*. London: Macmillan.

Mandler, P. (1990) *Aristocratic Government in the Age of Reform, Whigs and Liberals 1830–1852*. Oxford: Clarendon Press.

Mill, J.S. (1950) *Mill on Bentham and Coleridge*. London: Chatto and Windus.

Plucknett, T. (1956) *A Concise History of the Common Law*. London: Butterworth.

Radzinowicz, L. (1956) *A History of English Criminal Law and its Administration from 1750*. London: Stevens and Sons.

Royal Commission (1908) *Report of the Royal Commission upon the Duties of the Metropolitan Police*, Cd. 4156. London: HMSO.

Royal Commission on Criminal Procedure (1981) *The Investigation and Prosecution of Criminal Offences in England and Wales: The Law and Procedure*. Cmnd. 8092. London: HMSO.
Rozenberg, J. (1987) *The Case for the Crown*. Wellinborough: Equation.
Russell, W. (1856) *The War*. London: Routledge.
Saunders, J. (ed.) (1988) *Words and Phrases Legally Defined*. London: Butterworth.
Savidge Tribunal (1928) *Inquiry in Regard to the Interrogation by the Police of Miss Savidge: Report of the Tribunal Appointed under the Tribunals of Inquiry (Evidence) Act, 1921*. Cmnd. 3147. London: HMSO.
Schafer, S. (1968) *The Victim and his Criminal*. New York: Random House.
Schubert, A. (1981) 'Private Initiatives in Law Enforcement: Associations for the Prosecution of Felons, 1744–1856', in V. Bailey (ed.) *Policing and Punishment in Nineteenth Century Britain*. London: Croom Helm.
Select Committee (1817) *First Report from the Select Committee on the State of the Police of the Metropolis*. London: House of Commons.
Select Committee (1855) *Report*. London: House of Commons.
Shapland, J. (1983) 'Victim Assistance and the Criminal Justice System', paper delivered to the 33rd International Course in Criminology, Vancouver, British Columbia.
Skelhorn, N. (1981) *Public Prosecutor*. London: Harrap.
Smith, P. (1985) *Policing Victorian London*. Westport, CT: Greenwood Press.
Stephen, J.F. (1883) *A History of the Criminal Law of England*. London: Macmillan.
Sweetman, J. (1984) *War and Administration: The Significance of the Crimean War for the British Army*. Edinburgh: Scottish Academic Press.
Tallack, W. (1900) 'Reparation to the Injured, and the Rights of the Victim of Crime to Compensation', a paper prepared for the Quinquennial International Prison Congress, Brussels.
Wilson, A. (2002) *The Victorians*. London: Arrow Books.
Wright, M. (1991) *Justice for Victims and Offenders*. Milton Keynes: Open University Press.

PAUL ROCK is Professor of Social Institutions at the London School of Economics. He has written a number of books and articles on policy-making for victims of crime in Canada, England and Wales. His most recent book, *Constructing Victims' Rights,* was published by Oxford University Press in September 2004.

---

[13]
Chronocentrism and British Criminology

Abstract

Criminologists display a largely unexamined propensity to ignore writings that are more than fifteen or so years old, with evident consequences for the public presentation and validation of expert knowledge. A citation study was combined with detailed observations from British criminologists to ascertain quite how that disavowal of the past was accomplished.

Keywords: Citation research; sociology of knowledge; chronocentrism

Introduction

This article is both something of a *jeu d'ésprit* and a serious attempt to bring to prominence an important but neglected feature of intellectual practice in criminology. It was prompted by reflections that arose over the years as I listened to papers at academic conferences and read books and articles. I was struck not only by how temporal *lacunae* seem to permeate what passes for warranted scholarly knowledge, but also by how successive generations of thinkers have for no apparent reason been anathematized. Redolent of a process described by Sorokin as the workings of 'amnesia and discoverer's complex', a process that contributed to 'an extreme scarcity of references to the basic works of . . . predecessors' in sociology at large, including, he noted, himself (Sorokin 1956: 7, 18), many authors who published their work in the 1950s, 1960s, 1970s and 1980s seem simply to have disappeared from contemporary intellectual consciousness, sometimes to be displaced by others, more recent and not always of equal merit, who have been credited with originating their ideas. Criminology has proceeded in a series of fits, being marked by radical discontinuities; a recurrence of new beginnings; and a quest for the seemingly distinctive, influenced, perhaps, by what the himself now-neglected

Jack Douglas once called 'simplificationism': 'the modern scientists' self-imposed professional myopia, the insistence of each specialist on seeing everything as caused by the few particular variables he happens to 'own' professionally. . . .' (Douglas, Rasmussen and Flan 1977: 51). Sorokin's and Douglas' claim that disciplines tend to forget their past was later to be given a title by Saul Morson – *chronocentrism* – the unsubstantiated, often uninspected, almost certainly untenable but powerful doctrine that what is current must somehow be superior to what went before, that ideas, scholars and scholarship inevitably become stale and discredited over time, and that, by implication, those who invoke older work must themselves become contaminated by the taint of staleness (Morson 1996: 278–82). 'Chronocentrism', he wrote, comes 'most readily to groups that imagine they possess wisdom . . . superior to that of their own predecessors' (Morson 1995: 9).

Morson did not expand his concept at all fully, and this paper should be read as an attempt to develop it empirically. I shall employ it to describe the state of criminology in Britain – and sociological criminology in particular, the branch of the discipline with which I am most familiar – although what follows may well be true of other disciplines elsewhere. The paper proceeds by citation research and by interview and email correspondence with practising criminologists in England and Wales, all of whom agreed to be quoted either by name or anonymously, and I shall make use of those interviews and emails as the argument unfolds.[1]

Chronocentric criminology

In an email, Adam Crawford observed of chronocentrism that there is

> a (rather sloppy) theoretical assumption that underpins some criminological and social science research that we live in 'new times' (be it post-modernity, post-Fordism or whatever) that demand new concepts, ideas, understandings. This tends to suggest a rupture with the past and hence effaces historic continuities.

Durkheim, Merton and the Matza of 'Techniques of Neutralization' and *Delinquency and Drift* (but not the Matza of *Becoming Deviant*) may have survived as ancestral figures, but few now seem to talk of Harold Garfinkel[2] or Joseph Gusfield.[3] Alfred Lindesmith, Hermann Mannheim, Walter Reckless, Thomas Scheff, Robert Scott, James Short, Paul Tappan and others have been obscured. Work on the social production of official crime statistics now returns to Michel Foucault and blots out what might well have been defined as the earlier and more pivotal work of Aaron Cicourel, John Kitsuse, David Sudnow and Jack Douglas.[4] The ethnomethodology and phenomenology of crime, deviance and control have apparently been expunged. Symbolic interactionism has been over-shadowed, but an odd entity called 'social constructionism' has appeared in its stead.[5] Many of those identified by Hermann Mannheim (1960b), Piers Beirne (1993, 1994) and David Garland (2002) as the 'founding fathers' of the discipline have been disowned (no doubt, it must be said, perfectly justly in many cases) and they include André-Michel Guerry, Adolphe Quetelet and Gabriel Tarde.

To be sure, there is not much of a case to be made for sociological criminology becoming akin to the Royal College of Heralds, ceaselessly poring over its pedigrees. Neither is it feasible or necessary always to give full acknowledgement to every precedent and ancestor. Like Funes (Borges 1998: 96), any discipline that retained too perfect a memory of its past would become mired in a chronicling of the particular, working in an eternal present, never able to rise to a plane of useful reflection, abstraction and synthesis. David Downes observed of that tension in referencing between the incomplete and the too-complete that

> it's a very difficult balance to achieve between neglecting what's important in previous work . . . and going in for a kind of monumental attempt to recall, total recall, citing everything that's ever been written about a particular subject and . . . having some kind of encyclopaedic set of references.

The literature of criminology has now grown so elephantine that there may have been an increasing and necessary resort to the lexical short cut or bibliographic shorthand, to what Declan Roche, also in an interview, called 'finding a good, recent article in a good journal'. Some pieces of writing may indeed be so original or novel in their ideas or empirical content that they really do have few precursors. Ideas shift. Data lose relevance.[6] Technical methods are superseded. Writers may wish to engage with policy issues of the moment. Lines of argument fork or become sterile (Nigel Fielding remarked, for instance, that it is no bad thing that the search for a monocausal explanation of crime has been abandoned, unlikely ever to be resuscitated[7]). Bibliographic data bases have their temporal limitations (the electronic catalogues of the library of the Cambridge Institute of Criminology and the British Library of Political and Economic Science do not extend back beyond 1973,[8] for instance, although the patterns I describe were apparent before they came into use). And works may be credited with their date of re-publication or translation rather than their original date of issue (Durkheim, for example, appeared five times in the citation survey prepared for this paper, and only once was the original publication dates of his books in France given).

But that is not elucidation enough. Amnesia does seem to be such a real force, leading as it does to the methodical extinction of many ideas and authors beyond a certain age, that I was moved to explore the matter empirically, and what I offer now is an attempt as much to expose questions as to resolve them.

A citation survey

The obvious area to begin the exploration of such matters was citation practices, 'criminology in general lives on journal articles' (Katz and Jackson-Jacobs 2004: 114), and the obvious journal to explore for a criminologist working in the UK is the *British Journal of Criminology*,[9] an international journal with what has been called a 'strong UK component.'[10] Citation research has in the past been geared conventionally to ranking scholars and journals in hierarchies of esteem and influence for purposes of comparison and assessment.[11] One early piece of research (that did not touch on criminology) noted without comment the tendency for the age-distribution of citations to be arrayed in a pattern that conforms to a J-shaped curve (Nicholas, Ritchie and Ritchie 1978: 46–7). However I know of no extended link that has yet been made between that pattern and the shaping of what is accepted as memorable scholarship in criminology or any other discipline.

The dates of all citations were plotted for the first volume of the *British Journal of Criminology*, issued in 1960, and for subsequent volumes at ten-yearly intervals thereafter until 2000.[12] Citations were also charted for the inaugural 1951 volume of the *Journal's* forerunner, *The British Journal of Delinquency*. And the ensuing patterns are revealing. They suggest that, although there may have been an ever-growing universe of works published in criminology, and although the number of citations may have increased and the content of papers may have changed over time, the *formal* character of the age distribution of publications cited was remarkably stable. It too followed a pronounced J-shaped curve. There is a relatively invariant pattern: the J-shaped insignia was quite as strong in the 1951 volume with its mere 195 references as in the 2000 volume with its 1873 references. Criminological citation practices are not new and they cannot be explained, say, merely by the expansion of the discipline. They seem instead to reflect a fixed form, habit or cast of the academic mind.

An examination of who and what were most commonly cited over the decades prompts an obvious explanation of part of that configuration: the paradigmatic revolutions to which criminology is so prone induce rapid jumps and discontinuities in referencing patterns. Hans Eysenck was one of the two equally most frequently cited authors of all across the entire period, attracting 28 references, but the citations referring to his work were clumped together in the 1960 (6) and 1970 (22) volumes and none appeared in the volumes sampled thereafter. The other most frequently cited author, David Garland, accumulated 6 references in 1990 and 22 in 2000, but none before (and his first published book, a co-edited volume, appeared in 1983 (Garland and Young 1983)). The next most often cited author, John Braithwaite, received 1 reference in 1980, 9 in 1990 and 17 in 2000, and the work that won him the widest criminological acclaim was published in 1989 (Braithwaite 1989). Authors and

Figure I: *Citations in the British Journal of Delinquency 1951 (n-195)*

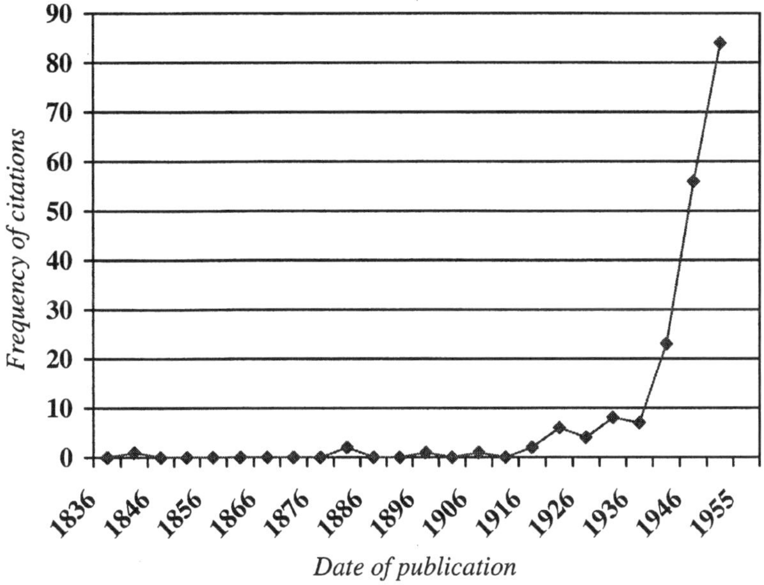

Figure II: *Citations in the British Journal of Criminology 1960 (n-131)*

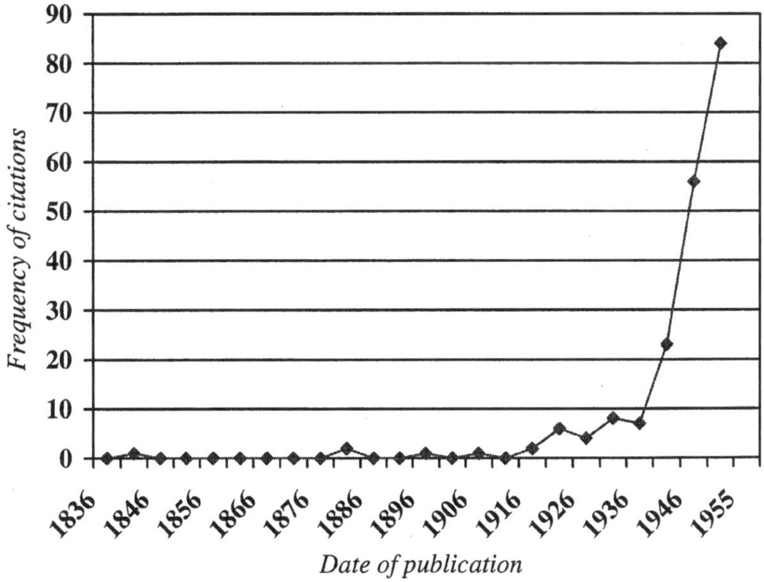

Figure III: *Citations in the British Journal of Criminology 1970 (n-320)*

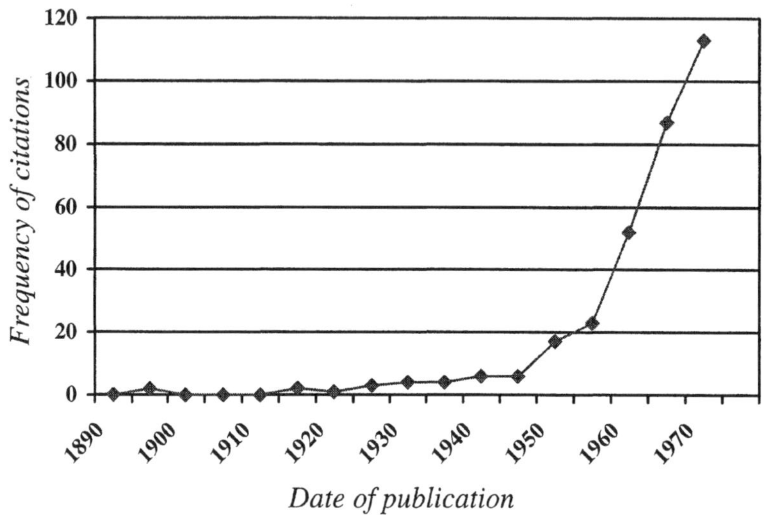

Figure IV: *Citations in the British Journal of Criminology 1980 (n-619)*

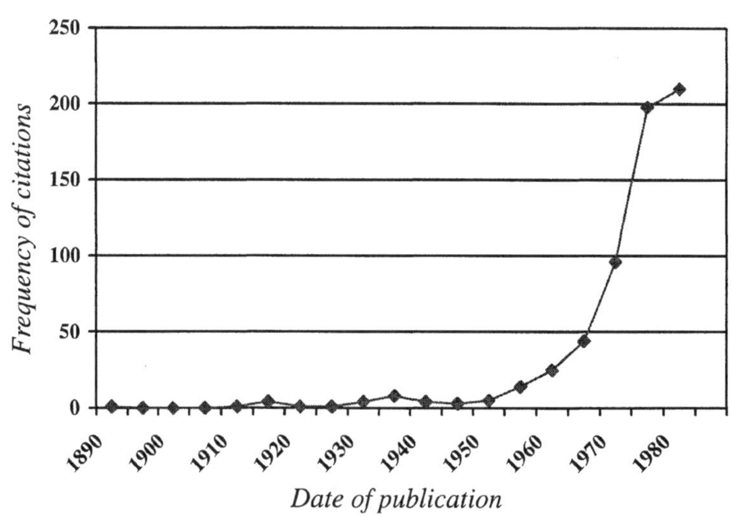

their books will have their day, and the former stars of citation reviews can wane: John Bowlby (esp. 1946 and 1951), cited seven times, but not later than 1970; Cyril Burt (esp. 1944) cited six times, twice in 1951, thrice in 1970, and once in 1980, but not thereafter; W.N. East (for example, 1939), cited three times but not later than 1960; and Trevor Gibbens (e.g. 1963), cited four times

Figure V: *Citations in the British Journal of Criminology 1990 (n-892)*

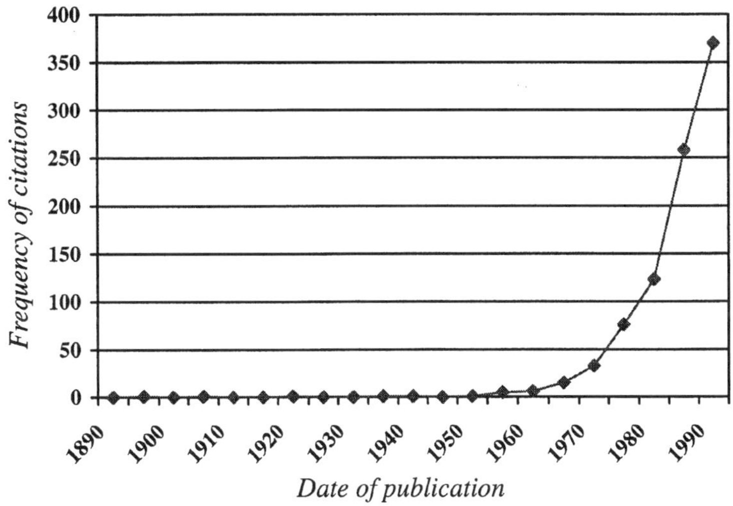

Figure VI: *Citations in the British Journal of Criminology 2000 (n-1873)*

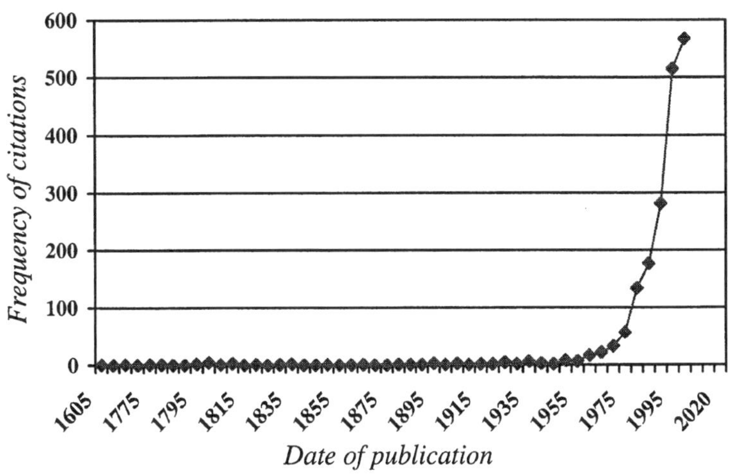

*1605–1760 is not grouped by 5 years-only one frequency

but not after 1980, are clear instances. They once helped to define the field in England and Wales and are now no more. Although a few defied that trend,[13] the age distribution of citations inevitably reflects the timing of when ideas entered the stream of thought, influenced writing and were then abandoned in tandem with the discipline's changing preoccupations.

No doubt, too, older books and journals may have become less accessible over time,[14] and there will be a tendency for authors to turn to what is at hand. Yet fluctuations in research *foci*, theoretical trend, empirical relevance and the accessibility of materials do not wholly explain the pronounced emphasis on the new. Neither does the sheer expansion of criminology, because the curves are invariant over time, irrespective of the mass of writings in the field at any one moment. If the raw shape of those curves does not speak for itself, I concluded that it would be profitable first to turn to indicative interviews with a sample of criminological colleagues (three women and four men, four of whom were relatively junior, three relatively senior) in the LSE to establish what personal gloss they would themselves place upon their own and others' citation practices, and then to consult more broadly by email with ten criminologists at different universities across the UK.[15] Their replies revealed that citation practices could be complex, personal and idiosyncratic, partly because the practices do not seem always to be reflexive; partly because there is an unresolved ambivalence about how evidence should best be deployed; partly because, as a result, citation appears to be an *ad hoc* procedure; and partly because there appears to be no formal schooling in the art and etiquette of referencing procedure other than, say, in the use of the Harvard system or its competitors. One of those former colleagues, Declan Roche, said 'it's made me think about something that I've done probably quite subconsciously, unconsciously, in that you just gravitate towards the recent stuff'. Stephanie Hayman, experienced in the field but only recently awarded a doctorate, observed that amongst her fellow research students citation procedure 'was never discussed. . . . I think there's a very good case [that] could be made for making students much more aware of how they use citations, good practice, etc. etc.' And Coretta Phillips said 'I've never talked to anybody about it . . . explicitly.'

Colleagues tended to maintain that they themselves were not prey to neophilia and that the practice lay elsewhere. One younger criminologist said

> I tend to . . . read too much perhaps and try and select too much when I'm referring to something, to show that . . . I've covered all of the bases. . . . I still feel like I'm learning in a sense and I think probably what I've tended to do is . . . assume that I need to try almost every source, basic, historical and contemporary, and really to . . . over-reference probably.

And another claimed that she wished to show in her citations that 'I'm not guilty of plagiarism', that others concurred with her arguments, and that, 'aware of the historic literature', she had returned to the oldest original sources and the more important writings that peppered the development of an idea. She was in a 'small [research] pond' and was 'in a much stronger position to make judgments about utility than if you're swimming in a much larger volume of water and you may choose more superficial criteria . . . Recency,' she said, did not imply 'anything to me. Recency implies that I'm trying to keep abreast of what is being said but it doesn't mean that it's any more important than what has gone before.' Robert Reiner too talked of his having been steeped in the Talmudic tradition in which one should never

> fail to attribute ideas to where you first came across them and, since in fact there is virtually nothing, probably nothing new under the sun, the truth is that all of us are constantly repackaging . . . and thinking again . . . ideas that we actually came across in a different context. I'm driven more by the fear that I won't attribute, that I'll appear to be plagiarising, stealing ideas and so on . . .[16]

If their professed practice had been widespread, one might have expected the spread of citations over time to be relatively flat; gradually declining with age; or bi-polar, with a disproportion of references to foundational works, on the one hand, and to recent works, on the other (leading to what might crudely be represented as '—', '/', 'V', 'W' or 'U'-shaped curves over time), but it was not, and their scholarly procedures, whilst admirable, do not seem to have been commonly emulated in the discipline (a criminologist at another university *did* conjecture that 'I can't help thinking that some of what some of your interviewees articulate is what we 'should do', not what we 'actually do!'') Rather, there was a pervasive ambivalence that was a contradictory meld of a respect for scholarly tradition (and, with it, a sense of the defining articles that give an agreed structure, sometimes almost irrespective of content, to the history of ideas[17]) and an apprehension that the new has its own self-conferring legitimacy. A colleague said for instance:

> Would I be worried if I didn't [cite] anything over the last decade? I'd only be worried about it if I felt that there was literature that I'd ignored that was important. . . . I mean I don't . . . look at material on the basis of when it was published. It has to be on . . . the merit . . . of the material. However, I think it's also true to say that if I can find up-to-date and contemporary things, . . . I would always . . . go to what's recently been written . . .

Although the criminologists interviewed claimed always to search the past of an academic problem quite extensively – and wished to be seen to have searched the past – there was also a concern about not appearing to have neglected what was current and relevant. The new was deemed generally to supersede the old, and especially where work was embedded in the empirical, as so much criminology tends to be. The repeated phrase was 'not missing out'. One said 'I wouldn't necessarily say that the more recent is the superior. . . . but . . . you always feel that you've missed something or that you're not as well read as you should be' if you do not allude to it. Another said 'I don't preference things on the basis of the timing when they're published but I would seek to make sure that I was up to speed with what was out there at this moment in time.' And yet another remarked:

> I think as a young, or younger [scholar], you worry that you'll leave something out or get something wrong. Reading the latest stuff helps reassure yourself that you're getting the up-to-date view of the world that you're writing about. And also the second . . . reason why you might use references is that if you're trying to show that you are writing something that's credible and authoritative, . . . including new references suggests to the reader you're keeping on top of your field. So I suppose it's partly about reassuring yourself and partly about reassuring your reader.

Tim Newburn reflected that the new:

> supersedes some of the things that will have gone before. There may be some sort of foundational pieces which one would refer back to but in relation to empirical research, one would hope, it isn't always borne out, but that the newer pieces will supersede the earlier ones in a number of ways, bigger samples, better research or simply more recent research that's the qualitative equivalent of its predecessor that happens to be of or in a generation that is current, and is indeed what one is talking about generally.

And David Downes said:

> I suppose recency is the attempt to show that you're being up to date, you know, you haven't missed anything. . . . I suppose it means that you are aware of the latest thinking, as far as you can be, about this particular question.

It was quite conceivable that there may actually be no recent work in a particular area but, without current citation, there was the possible risk that 'you had missed something significant . . . you always want to be seen as at the cutting edge.' He acknowledged the assumption held by some that the new envelopes the old, that the 'new has the edge on the old because it's got all the advantages of the old incorporated in it.' And, he continued, extraordinary reasons may have to be tendered to defend a use of old sources:

> the other day, I said to a student, you ought to go back to [a book published in 1938] . . . and I felt I had to give a great justification for that, you know, why should he want to go back that far? Well, it seems to me, what [the author] has to say there still has enormous relevance to where we are today.

Students, officers regulating what is called 'teaching quality assurance' (or TQA),[18] external examiners[19] and others were sensed as policing research and teaching and placing some pressure on criminologists to 'keep up to date'. Nigel Fielding said:

> Most students still just pester me to tell them which single book to buy so they could pass the course. . . . I would suggest that students have an important and generally negative influence in making lecturers feel guilty about

> citing 'old' contributions. Behind them stand external examiners and TQA hacks, for whom the most facile piece of 'advice' they can impose is to 'bring your reading lists up to date'. This will be exacerbated by the new pressure to put most of one's course materials 'on the web'. One has to be quite senior, or seriously stubborn, to resist the steady drip of such external impositions.

It is also perhaps conceivable that such a preoccupation with the recent marks the relative absence of a single, collective scholarly tradition in criminology which all novices are obliged to master. There is no formal accrediting body which controls who can call himself or herself a criminologist. Criminologists tend to stem from an abundance of scholarly disciplines, occupy what Alison Liebling called ever more 'differentiated/dispersed networks', are less and less frequently members of distinct, and well-defined intellectual lineages 'taught/supervised by chiefs in the field', and use different methods to pursue diverse problems.[20] And the outcome, Simon Holdaway said, is that

> They do not identify their research as standing within a disciplinary, theoretical tradition that seeks to refine its ideas, has a historical legacy of direct relevance to present work, and understand ideas as part of a body of scholarly knowledge. The phenomenon of the 'jobbing criminologist', moving from project to project, with no understanding that their research is rooted in fertile theoretical ground, is not new.

The more empiricist strands of an empiricist discipline are not necessarily held to need justification in social theory but in 'positivist research methods'.[21]

In an occupational setting increasingly governed by performance indicators, the exigencies of funding deadlines, and what Alison Liebling called the growing 'influence of modernization, and the infiltration of business thinking/management styles into academic life', many criminologists claim to find it hard to be as leisurely, contemplative or conventionally scholarly as they imagined their precursors to have been in some golden age before the imperatives of research contracts and the Research Assessment Exercise.[22] Theirs is a world of tight timetables, pressing demands and continual haste. Alison Liebling continued:

> . . . the mid-career turn to my elders is also happening now because I am 'getting round to it' after decades of full-on empirical work with less time for reading than some of my older colleagues may have had in the utopian academic past I never experienced. I feel it is a luxury to be reading e.g. Bowlby or Ericson in the original because their ideas are relevant to a report I might be writing (but that is already overdue). I manage a little more of this these days, but it has taken a long time to reach this point. We seem to have made academic life so strenuous (in the name of efficiency and 'bringing in money') that everything is done against the clock. This may be an

> important structural reason for the general tendency to concentrate on 'the apparently essential.

More graphic still was Dick Hobbs. In common with some others of his generation, he held to a Platonic history of ideas in which a prelapsarian age of British criminology appears to have been rudely abandoned by scholars who are less than scholarly:

> The sudden growth in British criminology seems to have caught sociology unawares . . . it seems to have given up [the] sociology of deviance, sociology of crime and control etc. Consequently what has replaced it is a bastardized concept of indeterminate lineage based upon populism, pragmatism, and a commodified notion of knowledge production increasingly driven by an unholy alliance of policy makers, publishers and entrepreneurial university administrators. British criminological forebears stressed the sociological underpinnings of the study of crime and control e.g. positivism, interactionism, phenomenology, ethnomethodology etc. Crime/deviance/control/ was part of a wider intellectual project. Increasingly criminology is taught as a discrete discipline bereft of epistemological considerations. If it is the second week in February it must be left realism. A hangover and the funeral of a cherished grandparent and both Lombroso and the Chicago School disappear up the Swanee. 1973 becomes year zero. Given that criminology degrees are increasingly influenced by policy considerations e.g. 'what works', forensics, criminal psychology etc., it is little wonder that what were once thought of as the foundations are increasingly ignored in citations. This is reinforced by the availability of expertly produced handbooks and textbooks. It is no longer necessary or indeed practical to go trawling through a library to dissect a 1938 text, a one liner in the reference book will suffice before confronting the more immediate concerns of crime surveys, or administrative evaluations. This can lead to an easily learnt citation shorthand. So stigma (Goffman), moral panic (Cohen). Criminology is no longer a branch of sociology, it's karaoke.

The phenomenology of citation practices

Strongly supporting these workings of chronocentrism, it might be supposed, is a more or less tacit phenomenology of time, fashion and the half-life of ideas. Those who write now or in the very recent past may well be seen by the criminologist to have an affinity, accessibility, immediacy, vivacity and openness of thought which cannot be so readily attached to the relatively closed life-world of his or her predecessors (Schutz and Luckmann 1974: 88). At a distance or immediately, they may be biographically, intellectually and socially engaged with the author, and what he or she writes and reads may be read by them and *vice versa*. They are in that sense part of an assumed and living community of the mind, a current intellectual generation or a working counterpart of a generation, a school or a politics, sharing a *Weltanschauung* or collective experience (Mannheim 1960a: 242), and having 'in common a sector of time which makes it possible for me to act upon them as they may act upon me within a communicative environment . . . ' (Schutz 1967: 318). Reference to them can signal that one is an informed and knowing associate of that which is fresh, timely and pressing, not at all lagging behind the movement of ideas, a privileged participant in a social process in which, as Tarde put it, 'the march of imitation from top to bottom . . . goes on' (Tarde 1969: 190). Robert Reiner reflected that

> academic life is riddled [by] . . . a love of the new and a wish to show that you're new. . . . there is this constant wish to show that you're [at] the frontiers of knowledge, you're absolutely up to date with current thinking and so on.

To be in or near a top or a centre where intellectual innovation is still taking place confers a sense of a closeness to events, of being an insider, of experiencing the still fermenting and the personal before it becomes fusty, formalized, alien, unremarkable, commonplace (see Simmel 1971: 363), scholastic or even, perhaps, antiquarian. David Downes remarked that 'I have a great fear of antiquarianism and I think maybe that our generation [of the] 1960s, we were frightened of being just antiquarians. . . .' And Tim Newburn agreed:

> References have a symbolic function as well, which is to say that they indicate that one is, in theory, up to date, reading broadly, aware of the latest theoretical ideas and so on and so forth. So I think there's a, without wanting to make it sound overly cynical, there is obviously a game being played as well with readers and I certainly have an eye to what I think is going to be considered to be, others will see as relevant, important, necessary in some way. . . . I would always include more recent citations [to show that I'm] up to speed, aware of current debates in the same way as we, using . . . the Goffmanesque dramaturgical analogy of acting on the stage and so forth, that, as in other areas of our life, we're aware of expectations and the need to try and meet those. And one of the ways we meet the expectations of scholarship apparently, is, I think is to show . . . that we're not just dinosaurs who happen [have] to read things in the [19]80s or the [19]70s or whatever and haven't kept abreast of developments.

By extension, and as the editor of a journal himself and a reader of submissions for other journals, he would scrutinize the impressions constructed by others in their deployment of references:[23]

> [I] always look at the citations to get a quick sense of who I think's written this or in what style it is and where it sits in relation to other things. So that

> citations would affect my . . . first reaction to a piece quite strongly. So that if they were all . . . reasonably ancient, then I would wonder where this person had been and what they were doing and why it was that there was apparently nothing relevant in the last 10 or 20 years, whatever the period may be.

Citations may not in that sense simply be technical or utilitarian devices but signifiers that bear a substantial iconic, existential and social load, signalling something about one's competence; who one is; whom one admires; what intellectual groups one claims as one's own, and how one defines their membership and boundaries.[24] They are attempts, in other words, symbolically to affirm the importance of people,[25] ideas and social worlds. They convey how one aspires publicly to be defined and placed as an alert and wide-awake person at the core of the academy. They create a self and its future trajectory, flagging what, as one colleague said, 'your life project is . . . it's a way of signifying that'. Adam Crawford remarked:

> References are signifiers of identity and belonging, they suggest who we reflect, who we are and the reference group to which we consider ourselves to belong in our intellectual endeavours. These are more likely to be (but not always) the living and our contemporaries.

It is perhaps but a step for citations to become features of a social engineering process in which criminologists individually or in combination more or less deliberately exercise patronage[26] or promote one another in what Nikolas Rose informally called 'citation rings or citation cabals.'[27] Very much to the point, Frances Heidensohn remembered a conversation at one of the meetings of the National Deviancy Symposium at the University of York in the early 1970s – the meetings which were to shape so many criminological life-chances. In that conversation, one sociologist of deviancy was overheard promising another 'I'll quote you if you quote me'.[28] Scholars may even refer heavily to themselves as they clamber up the ranks of citation indices.[29] Nikolas Rose remembered:

> I recall some years ago – when I was at a conference on the history of the human sciences – being amused by a Spanish psychologist and historian of psychology who used citation indices to study the relative importance of different Spanish psychologists. He cited his own work copiously in his published pieces, and was surrounded by a strangely large group of acolytes all of whom also cited him and one another profusely and exclusively – which of course meant that pretty soon he was far up the citation list of the most influential Spanish psychologists.

Conclusion

Chronocentrism and its allied beliefs must account in part for the pronounced custom in criminology and other disciplines to cite what is recent and neglect what is old. The matter is important because what is named and what overlooked mould what passes for authoritative learning; the phrasing of problems and the identification of answers; the selection and marshalling of evidence and argument; literary etiquette; the approved history of ideas; and, most central to the scholarly project of criminology, the accumulation of knowledge over time.[30] If Max Steuer was right when he said that 'science is a structure that is worked on for many, many generations';[31] if Nigel Fielding was right when he said that 'the most damaging thing is that this works against cumulative knowledge, which latter is the mark of a mature science;'[32] there may be grounds for concern about the enterprise of criminology.

(Date accepted: June 2005)

Notes

* I am grateful to Adam Crawford, David Downes, Nigel Fielding, Janet Foster, Stephanie Hayman, Dick Hobbs, Simon Holdaway, Jenny Law, Alison Liebling, Joyce Lorinstein, Tim Newburn, Coretta Phillips, Michael Prachar, Robert Reiner, Declan Roche, Nikolas Rose, Lucia Zedner and the anonymous reviewers of the *British Journal of Sociology* for their help in preparing this article. I am also grateful for the comments of the PhD students of the Cambridge Institute of Criminology to whom I gave this article as a paper in October 2004.

1. All quotations lacking reference to textual sources should be assumed to stem from those interviews or that correspondence.

2. Garfinkel baptized ethnomethodology and used it to effect in developing a methodology to explore or create marginal situations in which commonplace meanings became anthropologically strange.

3. Gusfield analysed deviance, and particularly drinking, as a cultural construction fabricated in the status politics of America. It would be possible to catalogue the equally valuable contributions made by the other anathematized authors to criminology and the sociology of deviance, but I wished only to provide illustrations of what has been lost.

4. In a survey conducted of all citations in the 1951, 1960, 1970, 1980, 1990 and 2000 volumes of *The British Journal of Delinquency* and the *British Journal of Criminology*, a survey which we describe at greater length below and which yielded a total sample of 4030 references, there was one reference to Matza's *Becoming Deviant;* 1 to Aaron Cicourel in 1970; none to Jack Douglas or Harold Garfinkel; 2 (one in 1980 and one in 1990) to the works of Joseph Gusfield; 1 to John Kitsuse in 1970; none to Alfred Lindesmith; 9 to the works of Hermann Mannheim, but none more recent than 1980; three to Walter Reckless, but none more recent than 1960; none to Robert Scott; none to Thomas Scheff; 2 to James Short, both in the 1970 volume; and four to Paul Tappan, none later than 1970.

5. Nigel Fielding remarked that 'The new label is about careers and the need to look like one's found something new. The new term lacks the virtue of precision, too. "Constructionism" is latched onto by students because they have heard the word

"de-construct", and find the approach appealing because it seems to involve playing with words in the kind of non-validate-able "analysis" that marks cultural and media studies. Students do not like to be told to look instead at SI, because there they find systematic procedures, formal validation criteria, and in some branches, quantification.'

6. Adam Crawford observed that 'There is a presumed "shelf-life" to empirical research, which suggests that "things change", people's attitudes and behaviour as well as professional practice. In some circumstances this may be true. But I also think there is an element of self-selection. If in doubt the more recent (so long as it is methodologically robust) may be the more empirically relevant, and therefore defendable.'

7. Although he may have been a little too sanguine. Some do still search for the single variable that will explain crime. See Gottfredson and Hirschi 1990.

8. But the electronic data base of the new Social Science Library of the University of Oxford does reach back to the 1920s.

9. It is, of course, possible that citation practices in journal articles are *sui generis*, and that books would disclose different patterns, but I can think of no good reason why this should be so.

10. Anonymous referee of an earlier draft of this article.

11. See, for example, the journals that are devoted in metaphysical fashion to citation research itself, including criminological citation: *Journal Citation Reports* and *Journal Performance Indicators*. Criminologists have themselves explored how often and where they and their colleagues have been cited (for instance, Cohn and Farrington 1998). And the *British Journal of Criminology*'s own web-site contains information about how it is ranked in citation studies.

12. The tabulations were done by Michael Prachar to whom I am grateful.

13. Edwin Sutherland was cited in the 1951 volume and in all other volumes except that of 1960, and Howard Becker began to make his mark in the 1960 volume and has been steadily cited thereafter.

14. Nicky Rafter, for example, found it difficult to come across a copy of the first edition of the English translation of Lombroso's *Donna Delinquante*, published by T. Fisher Unwin in London in 1895 as *The Female Offender*. See her introduction to the new version of the work which she herself edited (Lombroso 2004).

15. I was struck not only by the feeling that permeated many of their answers – it is clear that colleagues sense that all is not right with the discipline's management of its past – but also by their candour. People expressed themselves with admirable frankness. All quotations unaccompanied by documentary citation should be assumed to stem from interview or email correspondence.

16. But he added, and in illustration of the ambivalence we all tend to share in selecting authorities, that 'I also feel that you have to deal with arguments in terms of their strongest possible presentation and therefore if I know there's a kind of new book or article to be written on a particular line, then I'd probably want to tackle that rather than an earlier version of the same argument.'

17. Lucia Zedner observed 'for all the reasons your respondents set out, it is not so surprising that there is a strong tendency to quote the latest author. What intrigues me is why and how the 'classic' works, still cited decades hence, achieve this status. Presumably it is largely a result of their outstanding calibre, but I suspect it is not only that. Take the example example of Herbert Packer's *The Limits of the Criminal Sanction* [1969], a work still widely cited thirty years on but judging from the references probably scarcely ever read, it might be that some works gain a citation history that is almost independent of the original work.'

18. 'Teaching quality assurance' is part of the new battery of regulatory mechanisms imposed internally and externally on British universities under the new managerialism introduced in the 1980s and 1990s.

19. External examiners in the UK are recruited as a matter of course from other universities to inspect assessed work, advise on procedures and otherwise ensure that the

standards applied in examinations in one university are comparable in quality with those maintained elsewhere.

20. Adam Crawford said 'Criminology as many people have noted is a 'rendez-vous' discipline, and not everyone comes to the discipline with the same background rooted in traditional social/criminological texts.... [Some] have their backgrounds in philosophy, law, policy studies, politics etc. We should not expect all those that engage with criminology to be aficionados in the discipline.'

21. Yet I am still not sure that the fragmentation of an eclectic and pragmatic discipline wholly explains why the past should be so decisively obliterated within each of its strands.

22. The Research Assessment Exercise is a periodic review of the quantity, quality and environment of research in all university departments that is conducted for the purpose of apportioning State funds.

23. Another colleague remarked that, when reviewing articles for journals, she might in appropriate cases 'ask . . . why doesn't it have references beyond 1985? . . . I would certainly in referee's comments say 'why hasn't this person referred to a broader and more up-to-date literature?"

24. Tim Newburn said: 'I think in any of the fields we might work within, I suspect lots of people will have in their minds some sort of picture of who are the people who . . . for whatever reason, are closest to the centre of things, intellectually, scholarly, empirically or otherwise. And there becomes a kind of informal league table I suspect, one which we might not necessarily agree upon, but we probably all guess we might share to some extent. And I suspect . . . network analysis would find . . . first division folk citing first division folk more than . . . citing people they consider to be third division folk.' Robert Reiner said more simply, 'citing people you know is not just a question of being friendly, it's just that they are the first names that come to mind as it were.' Curiously enough, only one of the criminologists interviewed said that he circulated or received off-prints as a matter of course ('I realize now that even if [an article is] in a good journal, there's absolutely no guarantee [that people would see it]. And if you want someone to rate it, you probably need to send it to them. And so I've now started . . . ') It might have been supposed not only that off-prints would also act as boundary-markers but would contribute to the propensity to cite the current work of those regarded as fellow insiders.

25. Declan Roche said 'I think you probably do look to find opportunities to cite your friends if you can. I mean if it's a choice between two books and one was by a friend, you'd certainly put the one in by a friend or at least put it in as well.'

26. David Downes observed 'I don't think there's anything too wrong with that because there's a great danger that, in the huge wealth of work that's done, that people get overlooked and neglected even though their work is invaluable.' Coretta Phillips remarked 'I suppose what I've done sometimes is . . . cite Masters' dissertations or . . . things where somebody's done what I think is some really interesting work, and I . . . see that as a way of promoting them . . . [where] perhaps they're not exposed or well known about.' And Robert Reiner said very much the same.

27. In a rather different sense, Nigel Fielding commented that 'Catching these citation circles is a major objection of citation analysis. It involves some complex programming and is an established sub-field of science policy studies. A contemporary application is coming under the aegis of e-Science (Grid and High Performance computing for scientific applications), where citation analysis is used in fields like biology to deal with the overload in numbers of scientific papers; cross-citation is used to establish promising lines of research and the technique is of particular importance in human medicine. The key point about citation analysis is not to focus on individuals but on aggregates such as research groups connected with other research groups.'

28. That practice seems to have been rife in criminological folk-lore. Robert Reiner could also remember how 'I was once at a

National Deviancy Group symposium in the early '[19]70s and I was on the disco floor when one famous new criminologist kind of danced by, and there's another one, and they tapped each other on the shoulder and said, "right, it's agreed then, I'll cite you on page 7 if you cite me on page 14." ' It is not clear whether Frances Heidensohn was on that disco floor at the same time or whether it was another conversation she heard.

29. Nigel Fielding again remarked that 'The current equivalent of this includes practices that manipulate online search engines. There are several practices. One anonymously 'reviews' one's own book for Amazon, asks everyone with whom one is friendly to cite your review in an online message, and the compiler devices that look for 'hits' to identify publications about which 'everyone is talking' will elevate your item. . . . I am aware that there are several Masters programmes that have engaged in these practices so that if one types in a search for 'criminology and criminal justice' given courses come up receiving more mentions. It strikes me as pretty shoddy.'

30. I am grateful to Nigel Dodd for this point.

31. M. Steuer, seminar on *The Scientific Study of Society*, London School of Economics, 4 February 2004.

32. He went on to say that this affects 'patterns of adoption in new techniques and technologies for social research, such as secondary analysis of qualitative datasets.' Advancement in academic disciplines is associated with the 'new' and kudos comes from conducting 'original' empirical studies, preferably of some wholly new phenomenon, rather than from re-working data collected previously.

Bibliography

Beirne, P. 1993 *Inventing Criminology; The Rise of 'Homo Criminalis'*, Albany: State University of New York Press.

Beirne, P. (ed.) 1994 *The Origins and Growth of Criminology*, Aldershot: Dartmouth.

Borges, J. 1998 'Funes, His Memory', in *Fictions*, London: Penguin Books.

Bowlby, J. 1946 *Forty-four Juvenile Thieves*, London: Ballière.

Bowlby, J. 1951 *Maternal Care and Mental Health*, Geneva: World Health Organization.

Braithwaite, J. 1989 *Crime, Shame and Reintegration*, Cambridge: Cambridge University Press.

Burt, C. 1944 *The Young Delinquent*, London: Bickley.

Cohn, E. and Farrington, D. 1998 'Changes In The Most-Cited Scholars In Major International Journals Between 1986–90 and 1991–95', *British Journal of Criminology:* 38(2): 156–70.

Douglas, J., Rasmussen, P. and Flan, C. 1977 *The Nude Beach*, Beverly Hills: Sage.

East, W. 1939 *Report on the Psychological Treatment of Crime*, London: Home Office.

Garland, D. 2002 'Of Crimes and Criminals: The Development of Criminology in Britain', in M. Maguire, R. Morgan and R. Reiner (eds.), *The Oxford Handbook of Criminology*, Oxford: Oxford University Press.

Garland, D. and Young, P. 1983 *The Power to Punish*, London: Heinemann Educational.

Gibbens, T. 1963 *Psychiatric Studies of Borstal Lads*, London: Oxford University Press.

Gottfredson, M. and Hirschi, T. 1990 *A General Theory of Crime*, Stanford: Stanford University Press.

Katz, J. and Jackson-Jacobs, C. 2004 'The Criminologists' Gang' in C. Sumner (ed.) *The Blackwell Companion to Criminology*, Oxford: Blackwell.

Lombroso, C. 2004 *Criminal Woman, the Prostitute, and the Normal Woman*, Durham, NC: Duke University Press.

Mannheim, K. 1960a 'The Sociology of Knowledge' in *Ideology and Utopia*, London: Routledge.

Mannheim, H. (ed.) 1960b *Pioneers in Criminology*, London: Stevens.

Morson, G. 1995 'Opinion and the World of Possibilities', *Academic Questions* 8(1): 1–18.

Morson, G. 1996 *Narrative and Freedom: The Shadows of Time*, New Haven: Yale University Press.

Nicholas, D., Ritchie, M. and Ritchie, A. 1978 *Literature Usage and Interrelationships in the Social Sciences as Shown by Citations in Monographs*, London: Polytechnic of North London and Bath University.

Packer, H. 1969 *The Limits of the Criminal Sanction*, Stanford: Stanford University Press.

Schutz, A. 1967 'Symbol, Reality, and Society' in *Collected Papers*, Vol. 1, The Hague: Martinus Nijhoff.

Schutz, A. and Luckmann, T. 1974 *The Structures of the Life-World*, London: Heinemann.

Simmel, G. 1971 'The Transcendent Character of Life' in D. Levine (ed.) *Georg Simmel on Individuality and Social Forms*, Chicago: University of Chicago Press.

Sorokin, P. 1956 'Amnesia and New Columbuses' in *Fads and Foibles in Modern Sociology*, Chicago: Henry Regnery Company.

Tarde, G. 1969 'Processes of Imitation' in *Gabriel Tarde on Communication and Social Influence*, Chicago: University of Chicago Press.

[14]
Aspects of the Social Construction of Victims in Australia

Abstract: Representations of victims embody the distinctive practices of organizations in and around criminal justice systems. In Australia, the origins of victims' services are chiefly to be found in the activities of groups established to assist the families of homicide victims and the women victims of domestic violence and rape. The images of victimization engendered by those groups place a heavy emphasis on trauma, and the appropriate response is held to be counseling offered by specially trained practitioners. The outcome has been that the victims of volume crime such as theft, burglary, and malicious damage have been somewhat overlooked, blotted out, and left without substantial relief. To underscore the mediated nature of those representations, I shall conclude by describing a very different set of representations and attendant practices to be found in England and Wales, where victims are generally portrayed as those who have been affected by volume crime, and where services are provided by volunteers deemed not to require expert training in therapeutic support. The outcome should illuminate how very contingent are the policies, politics, and images of victimization.

Keywords: victim support, victims' policies, representations

INTRODUCTION

Institutional practices shape the public representations and private understandings of victims of crime. How victimization is framed formally can differ

---

I am grateful to Regnet (the Regulatory Institutions Network) of the Australian National University for the opportunity which the fellowship afforded to carry out this work. Ten interviews were undertaken with the staff of victims' support services and others and I am also grateful to them for discussing their work and supplying me with information and to Joyce Lorinstein who transcribed the interview disks. I would like finally to thank Ann Barrie, Marianne Curtis, Robyn Holder, Mike Shiner, and Lee Purches for their helpful comments on early drafts of this paper. Advance drafts of this paper were sent to the principals several weeks before submission to this journal with an invitation to suggest amendments, corrections, and deletions. Where such suggestions were made, they were invariably heeded.

markedly from jurisdiction to jurisdiction, with consequences in any society for the delineation of who its prototypical victims are, how its members are invited to experience the process of becoming a victim, and the formulation of wider public interpretations of crime and social order. This paper will focus on some features of that framing work in Australia and, in particular, the activities of the loosely coordinated web of interlocking voluntary and government victims' services that have been established under various names in its six component states and two principal territories, the Australian Capital Territory (ACT) and the Northern Territory. Those services were generally founded in the 1980s and 1990s and, in time, it was to them that victims in need would initially be referred (or would refer themselves) for information, advice, support, and counseling. They act as one of the first tiers of the criminal justice system encountered by victims, and it is of critical importance how they go about the task of defining, diagnosing, and prescribing remedies for harms suffered or imagined. Other agencies offering more or less complementary assistance may also come into play at some point—those involved with restorative justice, criminal injuries compensation, victims' rights, victims' impact statements, and the like—and it is to be expected that an analysis of their work would add complexity and detail to what I am about to describe. But here I shall apply Occam's razor and concentrate solely on victims' services, holding that they exercise one of the most important and interesting formal influences in the shaping of images of victimization. I shall accentuate certain traits for analytic purposes. And I will attempt not to judge arrangements but to explain, in Miller and Holstein's phrase (1997), victims' policies as an instance of social-problems-as-work, charting the origins and consequences of a particular configuration of ideas and practices that arose in one country.

The product of that work was to be a series of representations of crime victims as people suffering from trauma and requiring the services of specialist counselors, the representations and the services acting to support one another; and its unintended consequence was to exclude the mass of victims of mundane crime who are relatively little discussed and poorly tended to.

There is only a limited literature on which one might draw to build such an analysis. Most of the Australian material is primary, consisting of reports by the government and nongovernmental organizations affected or of survivors' and participants' accounts. The research reported here was conducted during my tenure of a visiting fellowship at the Australian National University in 2005, and it is based on primary and secondary accounts and on interviews with principals in and around the victims' and witnesses' services in the southeastern quadrant of Australia. I focused particularly on practices in Canberra and the ACT because that is where the Australian National University is set and they were to hand. The research on England and Wales is based more generally on studies of policy making conducted over the years and most recently between 1998 and 2002 (Rock, 2004).

THE PREVALENT IDEAL TYPES OF CRIME VICTIMS IN AUSTRALIA

Any reading of firsthand or secondhand accounts of the plight of victimization in Australia makes it clear that they resort almost as a matter of course to a stock terminology of trauma and counseling[1] on the one hand, and on the other to an accompanying (rather abbreviated) list of illustrative victims from cases involving death and dangerous driving; rape; child abuse; sexual and serious physical assault; "home invasion"; and kidnapping.[2] In the case of the New South Wales Witness Assistance Service (WAS), whose list I have just reproduced, a member of the organization explained to me in an e-mail that "all victims of crime under the definition of the NSW Charter of Victims Rights [Victims Rights Act, 1996] are entitled to services of WAS," but for "resources reasons WAS has to prioritise the services it provides. Priorities are determined on the basis of type of crime and on the basis of victims and witnesses with particular needs such as children, people with a range of disabilities, Indigenous people, and older people. These priorities are used by WAS for early referral and proactive contact." I shall show how it came about that certain victims of particularly devastating offences are now given prominence in this fashion—referred early and proactively contacted and, in so doing, how they act to underpin the validity of that terminology and those typifications and tend to overshadow the rest.

---

[1]Take one source (others will be cited in due course). There are relatively few Australian textbooks on criminology and criminal justice, but such textbooks are especially revealing because they represent learned and authoritative commentaries on the commentaries of others actually engaged in the work of criminal justice. They not only condense first-order constructs but also review them critically. If any source is to be reflective, it should be them. The Australian textbooks that have been published do tend to allude to victims of crime in the manner I shall describe in this paper. Consider the argument of Findlay and colleagues: "Nearly all victims of crime, irrespective of the type of the offence, experience some trauma." It follows, they argue, that "The concern is with providing services which will assist them in their recovery from the traumas resulting from the criminal incident" (Findlay, Odgers, & Yeo, 1994, pp. 303, 306). Cook and colleagues stated that "In the aftermath of traumatic experience, the degree and quality of social support received by the victim is of particular importance to their subsequent adjustment.... The experience of being victimised leads victims to question their positive perceptions of themselves. The trauma of victimization activates negative self-images in the victim.... What the responding patrol officer can do in a brief time to restore a sense of order and security to the victim, a detective or investigator can do at a slower pace, and a crisis counselor can do over as much time as is needed" (Cook, David, & Grant, 1999, pp. 18, 23, 50). Mukherjee and colleagues state that "The effects of a crime upon its victim naturally vary according to the type of crime. Property losses and physical injuries can be readily identified. Other effects such as psychological trauma and inconvenience are undoubtedly common but not readily measured" (Mukherjee, Neuhaus, & Walker, 1990, p. 16). Other, similar instances could also have been cited.

[2]Those items have been taken from Office of the Director of Public Prosecutions New South Wales (2005).

There is in Australia something of a sealed process which, despite occasional protests to the contrary and sporadic arguments that services do or should cater for *all* victims,[3] has brought it about that victims and witnesses of mundane crime have substantially removed themselves (and have been substantially removed) from the reach of official support and official consciousness. The chair of Victim Support Australasia, the umbrella organization for schemes in Australia and New Zealand, said simply in interview that "general victims don't fit anywhere." A member of the ACT Superior Court witness service, orientated principally toward the support of women testifying in domestic violence cases, said in similar fashion of witnesses in trials for mundane cases that "it's still a huge gap... in the service, whether you call it a service, but in the outreach that we have to victims. That is a very big gap and unless a victim is proactive about saying, "I need assistance" one would not know about him or her." (Such domestic violence cases amounted to 89 percent of the work undertaken although 78 percent of charges brought in the courts were for property offences (Director of Public Prosecutions, 2004, pp. 28, 32).

So it was that although 31 percent of burglary victims in a survey conducted in ACT said that the most recent incident had left them feeling unsettled or invaded, and another 30 percent were fearful of future burglary or personal safety, a government report concluded rather baldly that "victims of crime services are not generally regarded as necessary by victims of burglary and are therefore not commonly accessed by them" (ACT Burglary Victims Response Project, 2004, p. 2). It was only 1 percent of those burglary victims who were reported to have sought counseling, the distinguishing resource of the victims' services. In South Australia, a government review of services recorded that "not all victims require emotional support or counselling. . . . While nearly all victim support services focused on counselling. . . victims wanted practical advice on how to avoid becoming a victim again." (Justice Strategy Unit, 1999, p. 84). The chair of Victim Support Australasia commented more generally in interview:

> Victim support. . . has actually constrained that idea of support and advocacy . . . to counseling . . . . In terms of . . . the clinical disciplines, it's soundly based in terms of short interventions with a relatively small [number]—10% about—[where] you've got ongoing trauma impacts and so forth. But what it doesn't acknowledge is the extent to which victims require practical assistance, different things.

[3] "Jurisdictions should ensure that victim support services exist both for 'generic' crime victims and for specialised crime victims such as sexual assault and domestic violence" said Victim Support Australasia, for instance (1998b).

How that general situation arose and is now maintained will be the theme of this paper and, to demonstrate that the informing principles and procedures of victim support are structurally contingent rather than somehow given in the nature of victimization and the needs of victims, I shall end by briefly contrasting what is done in Australia with the current practices and equivalent sealed system of victim support in England and Wales. In that latter case (and although the position seems currently to be shifting fast) the language of trauma and counseling is virtually inaudible, the standard typification of a victim is that of everyman or everywoman afflicted by the lesser offences constituting "volume crime," and the population of victims who are supported is correspondingly diffuse and large.

THE ROOTS OF VICTIMS' SERVICES IN AUSTRALIA

Present practice has a clear genealogy. Australian victims' services schemes emerged very largely out of the work of women's groups supporting the victims or survivors of rape and domestic violence (Law Reform Commission New South Wales, 1996, p. 1) and, more substantially and saliently for the purposes of this paper, the work of groups of bereaved families who came together across the country for solace in the aftermath of murder and manslaughter.[4] There is Enough Is Enough—a New South Wales advocacy, support, and counseling group—established (as its Web site puts it) when "Michael Marslew, an 18 year old University student, an innocent employee, was shot dead during the execution of an armed robbery. This single senseless act, horrible and unacceptable as it was, had a profound effect upon the boy's father. Somehow through the devastation of the loss, Ken Marslew saw a serious community need that was not being addressed and Enough is Enough Anti-Violence Movement Inc. was founded." There are homicide victims' support groups established in Victoria, New South Wales, South Australia, and Queensland where, in 1995, "Two newspaper articles on separate families living in the aftermath of murder united a group of five families living in the North Queensland region. The bond they shared was the devastating isolation surrounding each family since the homicide of their loved one and the lack of support services available to assist them through the horrific trauma' (http://qhvsg.org.au/history.html). There is VOCAL ACT (the Victims of Crime Assistance League) founded "after several murders were committed in and around the surrounding districts. Families began making phone contact with each other and then decided to get together because they had all experienced the

[4]So it was that New South Wales established a dedicated program of Sexual Assault Services in the mid-1970s and, in response to the 1996 Victims Rights Act, a Victims of Crime Bureau.

aftermath of a violent death. Some of the members had their loved ones taken from them as far back as twenty years ago and yet for the first time they found they were able to speak out about their feelings to people who fully understood and cared. On the 15th of November 1988, the group met for the first time" (VOCAL (ACT) Inc., 2005, p. 1). "I think that they all started in a similar way," said the coordinator of the league in interview, "the New South Wales and Victoria, they all had the same history whereby people who had become victims met in somebody's lounge room at one time and then lobbied the government. The role was to lobby the government, to get the government to recognize the needs of victims, because at the time the government simply had no idea that victims needed services."

The earliest, eventually the largest, and perhaps the most frequently emulated scheme is the Victims of Crime Service founded in Adelaide, South Australia, in 1979 in the wake of a succession of murders in Truro and elsewhere[5] (Pinto & Wilson, 1990; Robinson, 2004, p. 1). The service started "as a self-help group for the families and friends of homicide victims. It was a small voluntary body of (primarily) crime victims helping each other by sharing experiences and providing friendship or support to each other" (Dawson, 2000, p. 1). And it became the acknowledged (and sometimes unacknowledged) template for groups inaugurated elsewhere (Cook, David, & Grant, 1999, p. 85; Victim Support Australasia, 2005). For simplicity's sake, it will be to the nongovernmental organizations—the Victims of Crime Service and VOCAL ACT—and the government-sited ACT Victims Services Scheme that I shall turn for the bulk of my illustrations.

Victims of serious crime such as rape, sexual abuse, and domestic violence claim a unique experiential authority peculiar to their offence. The homicide survivor too has been blooded, scoured, and tested to understand at least one form of crime and its effects as no one else can. In matters of victimization, he or she can also assert an existential knowledge, expertise, and moral standing alleged to be greater than any possessed by politician, official, scholar, or layperson (Rock, 1998). Said the then executive director of the umbrella organization Homicide Victims' Support Group (Australia) Inc., "Whilst Governments

[5]Michael Dawson, the chief executive officer of the Victims Services Scheme, told a conference in 2000, "Our state has the dubious distinction, if that is the right word, of being the scene of some very well known serial murders including:

- the recent so called "Snowtown" or "bodies in the bank" murders
- the "Family" murders of several young men in the late 1970s
- the Truro murders of several teenage girls
- the disappearance of the Beaumont children and of two girls from the Adelaide oval" (Dawson, 2000, p. 2).

legislate and academics attempt to define what 'a victim' really is—it is only through the victims, and the telling of their stories, that we can gain a greater understanding of the shock, trauma, devastation, grief and despair that victims experience" (Jabour, 1997, p. 1). And politicians and officials may concur.[6] The attorney general of South Australia remarked that "the physical and emotional impact of crime can be devastating both for those who are harmed and for their families and friends . . . . Those not directly affected by the crime often can't understand how difficult the recovery can be' (Victims of Crime Coordinator, 2005). The founder members possessed an authority which could not be easily be gainsaid, an authority which was yoked to a passion and anger, a desire to reconstruct moral meaning by coaxing good out of evil, a quest to prevent a like fate happening to others, and a wish to bear witness and memorialize the dead, and it fuelled a vigorous and unremitting activism that was eagerly reported and politically heeded (a member of the Victims Services of New South Wales affirmed in an e-mail that victims' issues are highly sensitive both in the social and political arenas and often attract a high level of media interest). It was an activism that gave birth to an archipelago of new organizations.

Over time, the groups' practices came to be expanded, incorporated, adopted, and routinized in a network of government and nongovernmental organizations offering succor to an increasingly generalized population of victims (Department of Justice, 2002, p. 2) and prosecution witnesses. The chief executive officer of the Victims Support Service of South Australia reported that "from this focus primarily on homicide victims families, the organization did begin to take on a listening ear role and support for victims of other crimes" (Dawson, 2003, p. 3) And the coordinator of VOCAL (ACT) said in interview of her members that "eventually they extended their compassion to people who had domestic violence or any other forms of trauma." Of course, as Robyn Holder, the ACT Victims of Crime coordinator and chair of Victim Support Australasia pointed out to me in an e-mail, the influence of homicide was at its strongest in the early days of the victims' movement, and once governments began to work on victims' services, they started to impart their own conceptions of needs and their own iconography. But what was extended was still inevitably something of an extrapolation of the familiar and tried, an instance of what John van Maanen (1984) once called "doing new things in old ways."

Consider the Web site of VOCAL New South Wales which recorded in November 2005 that "Christmas can be a difficult time for those whose lives

[6]Thus the government of South Australia promulgated a Declaration of Rights for Victims of Crime in 1985, a declaration consisting of administrative guidelines designed to "alleviate the trauma suffered by victims" (Justice Strategy Unit, 1999, p. 19).

have been tragically altered. VOCAL provides support to victims of crime and others affected by similar tragedy. We offer family and friends of those harmed or killed by crime and similar trauma the opportunity to be with others like them, and to hang a personal angel ornament on our special Christmas tree during an inspiring service at Christ Church Cathedral, in Newcastle." It is evident that the archetypal victim at the heart of that group's worldview appears still to be the homicide survivor, and it was not remarkable that the distinctive diagnoses and remedies propounded to contend with his or her suffering came to be embodied in the more general pattern of help that was emerging. If the survivor-families were anguished, benighted, confused, and distressed—if their world had been turned upside down—so, in turn, victims at large were held typically to be beset by physiological, psychic, and emotional disorder. Strong traces of the homicide survivor have come in effect to color the physiognomy of all Australian victims, and when victims and victimization are discussed generically it is that iconography which appears still to be influential. In that sense, the word *victim* condenses a very special history that must be invoked in its deconstruction. How else can one read the observations of one of the South Australian Victims Support Service's founders when she remarked "The physical and psychological reactions to becoming a victim are well documented as responses to severe stress. They include headaches, shaking, crying, sadness and feelings of isolation. In addition, there may be a loss of trust, flashbacks, panic attacks, nightmares and sleeping problems" (Robinson, 2004, p. 30)? And how else should one read the statement that "what crime victims in general cry out for are recognition, acknowledgement and meaningful participation within the criminal justice system. What they have experienced is exclusion, alienation and a lack of understanding" (Victim Support Service [South Australia], 2005, p. 3)? It may be victims as a genus broadly conceived who are being described, but the etiology of that description is quite specific. It was established in the wake of sudden death.

TRAUMA

Within the world of victims' services (and its linked worlds of criminal justice and criminology) the ideal type of Australian victim or prosecution witness bears the genetic marks of the homicide survivor, and his or her experience is defined significantly by the harrowing aftermath of traumatic crime. "Events which include victimization," remarked experts at the Australian Institute of Criminology, "produce tremendous stress and anxiety as the victim's experience cannot be readily assimilated . . . assumptions and theories are shattered, producing psychological upheaval . . . . Much of the psychological trauma produced by victimization derives from the shattering of very basic assumptions that victims have held about the operation of the world" (Cook, David, & Grant, 1999, pp. 20, 21).

That idea of *trauma* has come diffusely to order narratives of victimization. Thus the government-administered Victims of Crime Bureau of New

South Wales issued leaflets entitled *Helping Children Cope with Trauma* ("Children who have experienced trauma, especially very young children, express their feelings about a frightening event by means of behavioural changes . . . a list of symptoms that children may display after traumatic events: fear; anger and hostility; nightmares; physical symptoms such as tummy aches; regression; changes in eating habits; reluctance to go to school . . ."). The bureau issued leaflets entitled *Coping with Witnessing a Traumatic Event* ("Being a witness to a traumatic or violent event can have a very deep impact on people, especially children. The impact of this experience is often referred to as 'vicarious trauma' meaning that even if you were not physically hurt on actually involved in the event you can be affected psychologically by what you have seen or heard or experienced").

Crime can evidently be traumatic.[7] Being a bystander can be traumatic. Talking about crime with others can be traumatic ("Victims often have to suffer the additional trauma of re-telling their story too many times to different components of the [ACT Victims Services] scheme," reported VOCAL ACT to a government review of the provision of services [ACT Department of Justice & Community Safety, 2005, p. 7]). Testifying at trial can be traumatic. "We recognise," said a leaflet issued by the Witness Assistance Service of the Office of the Director of Public Prosecutions of New South Wales, "that victims have not only been traumatised by the crimes committed against them, but also sometimes by the prolonged nature of criminal proceedings. Reliving these events in court can also be a stressful experience." Instructions issued for the completion of Victim Impact Statements for use in the courts of Victoria and elsewhere suggest that victims should report their "emotional trauma" and "psychological harm" (also see Australian Federal Police, n.d.). Victims were invited to contact the Victims of Crime Helpline established by the state government of Victoria to acquaint themselves better with the "grief and trauma process" (Department of Justice, 2004). They may come to learn that "while every person's reaction to crime is unique, it is not unusual for people who have experienced serious crimes to immediately feel shocked, fearful or angry.

---

[7]VOCAL (ACT) issued a leaflet in which the question "Why Seek Help?" was asked. It proceeded to state that "You might have a person in you[r] home, a friend or a work colleague who has, at one time in their life, experienced being traumatized by the socially unacceptable behavior of another person . . . . Being a victim of crime . . . has serious effects on a person. The damage can sometimes take years before it is apparent to the victim. When a person faces a situation in which they sense danger, their body immediately switches on the inbuilt mechanism to help them either run away or put up a fight/defense. This is called the flight or fight reaction. But when the situation is so bad, often the victim can neither defend him/herself or run away. Their natural responses and production of body substances such as adrenaline, and mechanical motion in the body is frustrated and becomes distorted. These powerful emotions continue to seek an outlet just like flood waters do" (VOCAL (ACT) Inc., (n.d.(c))

It is quite normal for some victims to experience depression or anxiety. These reactions are natural and part of the process of dealing with a traumatic event" (Victims Support Agency, n.d.).

The police are encouraged to be mindful of trauma in their dealings with victims. Those who provide criminal injuries compensation to victims are encouraged to be mindful of the possible impact of trauma and traumatization ("The effects of crime can be profound and may impact in all areas of the victim's life. After experiencing a traumatic event a wide range of reactions can occur including: *Physical*—Nausea, headaches, sweating, tiredness, shaking, sleep difficulties, changes in appetite; *Emotional*—Tearful, depressed, scared, anxious, anger" [emphasis in original] [Dawson & Zada, 1999, p. 2]). Experimentation with service provision should be conducted with caution lest it exacerbate trauma. In reply to a consultant's report, the government of the ACT stated that "it would not be appropriate for VSS [Victims Services Scheme] resources to be used on experimental procedures, particularly where there is a risk of further traumatising the victim or delaying his or her recovery" (ACT Department of Justice & Community Safety, 2003a, p. 11). Trauma may not be the sole recognized interpretation of the aftermath of crime, but it does riddle talk about crime victims in Australia, and victims are invited to be alert to its risks. VOCAL ACT's *Useful Information for Dealing with the After-effects of a Crime* reminded victims and their intimates:

> *Important*: ... Remember, you are not "going crazy". You are having a normal reaction to an abnormal event. There is a wide range of after-effects—you may experience many or few. Not everyone has the same reaction, and in some people it can be delayed for years. Getting back to normal can be a difficult process after a personal traumatic experience . . . . *Some of the Aftereffects of Traumatic Experiences* ... *For Family Members and Friends* ... Spend some quiet time with the traumatised person, don't feel like you have to find clever things to say . . .. Don't tell them that they are "lucky it wasn't worse"—traumatised people are not consoled by those statements. (emphasis in original) (VOCAL (ACT) Inc., (n.d.(b))

Who then are the victims and prosecution witnesses occupying prominent positions in the figurative and practical world of support services in Australia? Other ideal types and other diagnoses are from time to time identified, but it is principally "stressed and traumatised" people (VOCAL (ACT) Inc., 2003a) who have been mustered as the recipients of services provided by the agencies, and it is with them that the staff of those agencies are primed to deal. Thus the training program of VOCAL ACT included sessions on "understanding grief and loss, categories of loss, losses during life, victims specific types of crime experiences ... sex and violence—male rape and female rape" but none on burglary, theft, petty assault, malicious damage, fraud, and other instances of volume crime. And between July 2003 and June 2004 members of VOCAL ACT's partner organization in the Victims Services Scheme, ACT Health, attended an "international conference on trauma, attachment and dissociation, 'Transforming Trauma', Melbourne, 12–14 September 2003; [and a] 3-day workshop 22–24 October . . . on practical skills for the assessment and treatment of PTSD auspiced by The Australian Centre for Post-traumatic Mental Health" (ACT Department of Justice & Community Safety, 2004, p. 32.) They were expected to do so because, as a member of the scheme explained in an e-mail, the contract that ACT Health had with the ACT Department of Justice and Community Safety to provide the Victims Services Scheme was "strictly defined by Legislation and Regulations that ask[ed] for a rehabilitation and counseling service with access to volunteers for practical support . . . . That was in our brief and those issues [at the conferences] were coming up with the clients we were seeing. This is how policy makers and legislators have defined the needs of crime victims—the ACT service was created in response to a call for tenders following the passing of the Act which said that such a service would begin."

COUNSELING

Trauma has the makings of a clinical or quasi-clinical condition which warrants the ministrations of appropriately qualified therapeutic experts—counselors—and intense counseling delivered freelance under contract or crisis counseling delivered by an agency's own staff has become a defining response to victims presenting themselves to victims service organizations in Australia. Helplines and volunteers providing information may also be on offer, but services do veer toward therapy. The Witness Assistance Service of New South Wales declared, for example, that it has "developed a range of services to meet the broader needs of victims and witnesses of crime." It "recognises that victims have not only been traumatised by the crimes committed against them, but also sometimes by the prolonged nature of criminal proceedings. Reliving these events in court can also be a stressful experience." Its aim accordingly was to "reduce the trauma to the crime victim" who "may benefit greatly from involvement with counselors and support groups. Our staff are trained counselors and we offer support throughout the court process. For ongoing counseling and therapy we are able to make referrals to . . . various organizations and professionals" (Office of the Director of Public Prosecutions, n.d.).[8] Similarly,

[8]It is not, however, a counseling service itself and has never run support groups. One of its members said in an e-mail that "The staff at WAS have relevant tertiary qualifications in social work, psychology or social science and have counseling experience in related areas, we do not ask in the selection criteria for them to be or to be in the role of 'trained counselors'. The services offered by WAS include: information and referral; court preparation; court familiarisation; and court support throughout the court process. Close liaison with ODPP lawyers and Crown Prosecutors and external agencies is a vital function of the service. For ongoing counseling and therapy the service can refer victims and witnesses to a wide range of organizations and professionals."

victims of crime in South Australia are told in a pamphlet that "victims can get help. Being a victim of crime can be a life-changing event, therefore, you are entitled to be told about the health and welfare services available for victims of crime. This book offers advice on coping with the impact of crime, and directs you to services that provide counseling, legal advice and practical information" (Attorney-General's Department, Government of South Australia, 2004, p. 5).

Access to counseling is one of the near-rights urged by Victim Support Australasia (1997, p. 2) and embodied in victims' charters enacted by New South Wales and South Australia. In many schemes, victims and vulnerable prosecution witnesses are now routinely entitled to a fixed diet of counseling (Cook, David, & Grant, 1999; Dawson, 2000, p. 1) that is rationed not only because crimes differ in their effects but also because expert personnel are expensive and few in number. It is a diet based on a tripartite classification ordered by seriousness and involvement, each part being allocated an appropriate number of hours of therapy, rising in the typical instance from a maximum of two hours on the first level to twenty or more on the third, and supplied by approved social workers and psychologist counselors.

So indissoluble have the apparent connections between victimization, trauma, and counseling become that any attempt to dismantle them may be taken as a sign of neglectfulness and incompetence. They are connections which impart a special gloss to diagnostics. If there is a tendency to channel victims of crime toward therapists who are sometimes contracted or funded by Departments of Health rather than Departments of Justice (therapists who may, moreover, be supervised by boards staffed in part by health professionals), it is perhaps inevitable that their problems have become increasingly (and sometimes resentfully) defined within a framework set by the preoccupations of the mental health occupations rather than those of criminal justice (Dare commented of the ACT Victims Service Scheme that his impression was that it "finds it a struggle to go beyond the client-therapist paradigm" [Dare, 2002, p. 46]. (It should be noted that the scheme was constrained by contract and its members took issue with that observation. One said in an e-mail that "ACT Health was contracted to provide a rehabilitation and counseling service—assistance other than counseling is offered but most people contacting us are asking for this form of intervention—of course this becomes a self-fulfilling process, as people are then told this is our area of expertise.")

Clients may then not be so much taken critically to be victims of *crime* but as people suffering emotional distress after a *traumatic* event (86 percent of clients of the Victims Services Scheme were said to have "presented with psychological and emotional injuries" in 2002–3 [ACT Department of Justice & Community Safety, 2003b, p. 16]). A social worker employed in that scheme by ACT Health, a government department, remarked in interview that "our service is specifically to provide the counseling and rehabilitation side of things to victims of crimes. So we're separate to the criminal justice system."

It was certainly the view of ACT Health that its limited funds would be better spent on "in-depth therapy" provided by counselors than on "providing a physical support presence, albeit with a therapeutic element in the immediate crisis hours following the offence" (ACT Department of Justice & Community Safety, 2005, p. 4). It would, after all, as a member of the scheme remarked in an e-mail, have been inefficient and inappropriate to commit a counselor earning some $A60,000 a year to "cooling their heels outside a courtroom with a client or escorting them to multiple appointments, this is what we hoped a competent volunteer service would offer; there is no documented evidence that . . . providing a physical support presence in the immediate aftermath of an offence occurring is of benefit to the affected person—information is of more help. ACT VSS [Victims Services Scheme] is not a crisis service.'

If victimization in Australia is a traumatic condition all too easily exacerbated by maladroit handling, if many victims can be safely approached only by those with a dedicated and proven therapeutic competence, it may be concluded that it is only professional counselors who can be entrusted with the provision of protracted psychological and emotional support. Counselors now make strong proprietorial claims to the management of the effects of victimization, and their claims are vested in their professional expertise in the workings of trauma. The importance of *professionalism* is thus repeatedly underscored to register the gravity of the victims' condition, the responsible fashion in which that condition is approached by service organizations, and the assertions of those organizations to be mature and accountable bodies eligible for state funding. Service agreements have come to stipulate that the release of public money should be contingent on proper management, and it is taken as virtually axiomatic in claims to ownership, answerability, and authority that a creditable service is supplied by professional people. Of the New South Wales Victims of Crime Bureau, a bureau that funded 33,000 counseling hours supplied by some 400 approved counselors in 2004–5, a member of staff said in interview: "Here at the bureau, we put the difference between providing information, referral, and support as compared to therapeutic counseling. And if you're going to offer therapy to a victim, we expect that to be done by a fully qualified person, a psychologist, a social worker, or a psychiatrist . . . . Support is different because support requires the listening ear, the normalizing . . . which is also a part of the process but . . . we very much recognize that if clients actually need therapy, then it's got to be provided by qualified people 'cause we don't want to risk re-traumatizing them by giving them . . . a dodgy counseling service.' In South Australia, the chief executive officer of the Victim Support Service recalled in a talk to students how the organization had "moved away from being a passionate lobby group to something more mature, more objective, more professional" (transcription of tape of a meeting of August 18, 2005).

Professionalism has thus come to delineate who is to be acknowledged as a proper and competent person in victim support, and it has tended to bring about not only a tightening of the boundaries around those eligible for care, but also around those deemed suitable to provide care, and it has been accompanied by a greater marginality of the unreconstructed homicide survivors' groups and their lay founders and volunteer successors. "Volunteers are a crucial component of victim support," noted Victim Support Australasia, "but should *never* be relied upon as the sole or even primary deliverers of service" (emphasis in original) (Victim Support Australasia, 1999, p. 1). It was said of VOCAL ACT in a government review that there was "significant disquiet" expressed by "at least four stakeholder agencies" that "some volunteers, while well meaning, are not skilled at supporting victims experiencing trauma resulting from crime" (ACT Department of Justice & Community Safety, 2005, p. 5). A contractually defined bifurcation between service organizations in a number of Australian jurisdictions has tended to amplify and reify such distinctions between the professional and the lay, leading one Australian official to remark of ACT in an e-mail that "this contract has been fraught. In an effort to distinguish between what each is supposed to do . . . , each has been forced to define and refine (very unhelpfully to my mind) what is 'professional' support and what is 'practical' support. This is local politics at its worst. And it helps the current 'senior' partner—ACT Health—to define itself so strongly as a health service."

Ironically, then, and in a way that has characterized the evolution of other "community"-based organizations such as self-help groups for the families of serious offenders (Condry, 2003) and drug counseling centers in England (Shiner, Thom, & McGregor, 2004), the logic which the founder-survivors first animated came in a number of schemes to resolve itself in their sometimes acrimonious loss of control. In ACT, there was what a member of a body appointed by the government to review the workings of the Victim Support Service and VOCAL ACT called in interview "a turf—well, turf war is probably putting it a bit strongly—but, you know, I suppose a turf conflict to some extent, that's probably more right. There's . . . a philosophical difference about what is appropriate for victims because I mean [in] one, the government provider, I suppose . . . a therapeutic model is given priority . . . and VOCAL has a different model entirely." (Yet VOCAL ACT itself, as I have shown, also talks about trauma and the need for counseling. At a forum on December 6, 2005, the first line of information that it provided about itself was that it offers "free professional counseling.") In South Australia, Ray Whitrod—one of the founders of the Victim Support Service and a former police commissioner—fought to retain its original character as a support group based on the mutual aid of bereaved people, but Harold Weir—a psychologist member of its board—eventually succeeded in replacing self-help by professional counseling as the staple method of service delivery. "An ongoing problem for some of those around Ray, and constantly referred to in his writing," reported a fellow founder, "was his passionate belief in the value of volunteers above paid staff.

He could be quite outspoken in his views . . . Harold Weir's view that volunteers are essential to VSS [Victim Support Service] but they must have professional guidance, counseling if necessary, and the ability to refer complicated cases, has prevailed" (Robinson, 2004, p. 34). The Victim Support Service is somewhat guarded about the general usefulness of volunteers and their enthusiasms as it is now, as its chief executive officer said in interview, "almost entirely reliant on professionals," has secured state funding, and has prospered:

> There is still passion and overwhelming commitment from all parts of the organization. It is however seen more as a service agency rather than a community group. Rather than emphasising the charitable nature of the organization we emphasise victims right to services, right to funding to provide those services, and that victims, like other disadvantaged groups in the community, have a right to high quality services delivered by well trained and well qualified professionals . . . . We deliberately set about being positive, constructive and balanced. We wanted to be reasonable and be seen to be reasonable rather than critical, radical or biased. (Dawson, 2003, pp. 5, 11)

Volunteers in that organization (and other similar nongovernmental organizations) may be helping with "court preparation" and act as "court companions," providing information and support to victims or prosecution witnesses in court; giving "information and advice" ("the Victim Support Service has a great deal of information which volunteers can share with victims of crime"); assisting victims who wish to make a victim impact statement; talking to community groups and organizations to "raise public awareness"; helping with office administration by producing a quarterly newsletter; "helping develop and update our resource folder"; engaging in general office and reception duties; assisting in "updating our website"; and offering "a crime scene cleanup service to clean up blood and guts for victims who are not covered by insurance or are traumatized by having to do that" (transcription of meeting of August 18, 2005).

But there are volunteers and volunteer-based organizations who protest that they can and should be allowed to do more, that they have been dispossessed and that their work has been devalued. VOCAL ACT, one such nongovernmental organization, was said publicly to have asserted that:

> volunteers can contribute a very valuable component of service provision. Whereas service staff need to maintain a certain professional distance from clients, volunteers, who are generally survivors of crime themselves, can offer a unique kind of empathy and support. VOCAL finds that volunteers have a high level of commitment . . . . They offer a broad range of skills and experience that agencies have difficulty in matching, and have a strong connection to community. VOCAL existed before the establishment of the VSS [Victim Support Service] and some VOCAL members may have hoped that the VSS would be established

> using VOCAL as a base. With the VSS being awarded to ACT Community Care and operating independent of VOCAL, some VOCAL members feel that the organization has been relegated and no longer is able to make the contribution it made prior to the establishment of the victims service scheme. (Dare, 2002, p. 31)

There is a sensitivity that the volunteer and the survivor may have been discredited by the twin stigmata of amateurishness and the low status of the victims they support and from whose ranks they may have emerged.. The coordinator of VOCAL ACT said in interview, for instance, "Why is it with ACT Health? We have lobbied the government to stop that but they, when, you see it's like working with people disability, those who work with people with disability, do not have a huge amount of fame and fortune and credibility because somehow you're thought to be like your clients. Well, we here work with volunteers, so we bear the label volunteers. Volunteers are not supposed to be very clever, professional." A member of the ACT Witness Service, heavily involved as a result of a political initiative in supporting victims of domestic violence—victims who were known to the service as a result of an offender having been charged by the police or a victim having sought help from a crisis service or refuge—gave in interview a complementary view about those bodies to whom she could responsibly refer witnesses: "Not to volunteers. I would very infrequently refer to volunteers, particularly for family violence . . . . I have a very strong belief that we need a specialized service to be responding to that."

THE RECRUITMENT OF VICTIM-CLIENTS

Rates of criminal victimization in Australia are high by international standards (Ministry of Justice, 2000). In 2004, the total population of the country was 20,431,000; 1.5 million lived in the illustrative state of South Australia and 324,000 lived in the illustrative territory of ACT. In 2002, victimization surveys reported that just under 9 percent of households (1 million) had been victims of crime; 4.7 percent being victims of a break-in (290,000 the victims of a single break-in, and 63,000 of two or more break-ins); 3.4 percent the victim of an attempted break-in (the figures for break-ins and attempted break-ins in South Australia being 6,700 and in ACT 7,400); and 1.8 percent (or 135,000 households) the victim of a motor vehicle theft (1,800 in South Australia and 2,300 in ACT). About 5.3 percent (or 2.8 million members) of the adult population were victims of personal crimes (4,900 in South Australia and 5,900 in ACT); 350,000 being victims of a single assault and 365,000 reporting two or more assaults (amounting to 5.3 percent of the total population, 4,500 in South Australia and 5,800 in ACT); 0.6 percent (or 96,000 people) were victims of a robbery (500 in South Australia and 200 in ACT); and 0.2 percent were the victims of sexual assault. There were 300 reported homicides in 2001, an incidence of 1.5 per 100,000 people (1.9 in South Australia but none

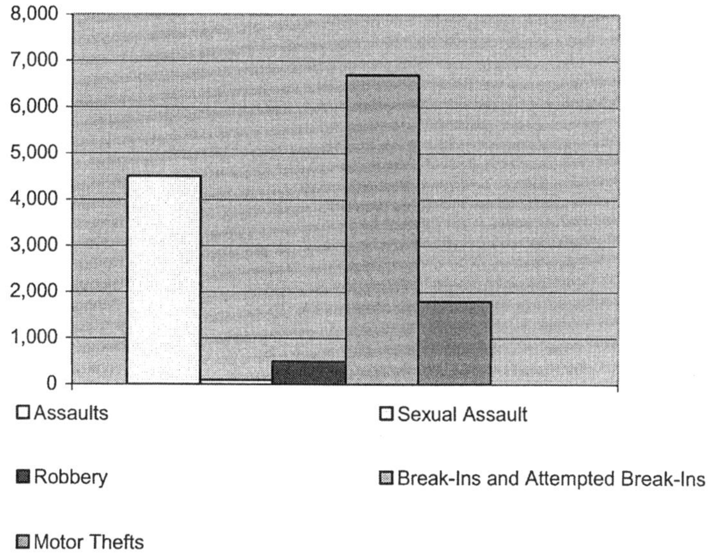

Figure 1: Victims per 100,000 population in South Australia, 2002.

in ACT) (Australian Bureau of Statistics, 2005). Those figures are echoed by the later 2004 International Crime Victimization Survey's findings for Australia (Johnson, 2005): 5 percent of Australians questioned in that survey reported that they had been the victims of completed and attempted burglaries, and 6 percent of thefts of and from motor vehicles. Another 5 percent had been the victims of assaults, 1 percent of robberies, and 4 percent of personal theft.

Recorded crimes (of interest in establishing the universe of victims who might more readily be referred or be persuaded by the police and other agencies to refer themselves to victims schemes) show that in 2004 there were 80 cases of murder, attempted murder, and manslaughter in South Australia, and 3 attempted murders in ACT; 36 cases of kidnapping and abduction in South Australia, and 6 in ACT; and 1,239 robberies in South Australia and 218 in ACT. There were, further, 26,728 cases of "unlawful entry with intent" in South Australia, and 5,202 in ACT; 10,511 motor thefts in South Australia and 1,746 in ACT; and 52,500 "other thefts" in South Australia, and 8,340 in ACT. The statistically preponderant crimes in Australia are burglaries and assaults.

The larger clusters of crimes recorded by the police may be presented graphically. Although there are a significant number of crimes against the person, they are recorded almost entirely as "assaults," particularly serious offences such as murder and kidnapping and abduction being too few to register in the graphs.

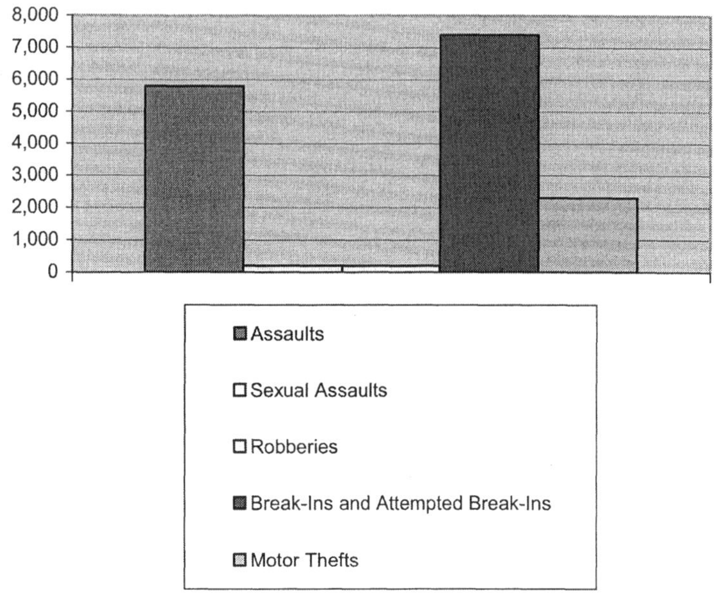

Figure 2: Victims per 100,000 population in ACT, 2002.

With the exception of assaults, it is clear that services focused on particular, grave, and statistically uncommon crimes against the person; they were expensive and proportionately modest in scale. Very rarely would property crimes or frauds figure (although the Australian Institute of Criminology claimed that consumer fraud was the most common offence in Australia in 2001 [2005, p. 2]). Thus the most frequent crimes coming before the Victims Service Scheme of South Australia between 2001 and 2003 were assault, child sexual abuse, home invasion, sexual assault (adult), murder, and family violence (Victim Support Service, 2004a, p. 3). Indeed, between 2002 and 2003 the service dealt with more secondary victims of murder than victims of property offences (Victim Support Service, 2004b, p. 11). "'High need trauma victims' cases have built up," it reported in 2004, "and staff have been less able to take on new clients. This became a problem from April and remained so for 4 months" (Victim Support Service [South Australia] 2004, p. 8). In the same year in ACT, the Victim Support Service "has become more involved in major and serious crime matters such as murder, attempted murder, and very serious assaults. These types of matters necessarily impact very heavily on the immediate family of the primary victim" (ACT Department of Justice & Community Safety, 2004, p. 12). About 79 percent of its clients in 2004–5 "sought assistance as a result of a violent crime (other than sexual assault), with 15 percent seeking assistance for crimes of sexual assault" (ACT Department of Justice & Community Safety, 2005). The clients had largely referred themselves (or had

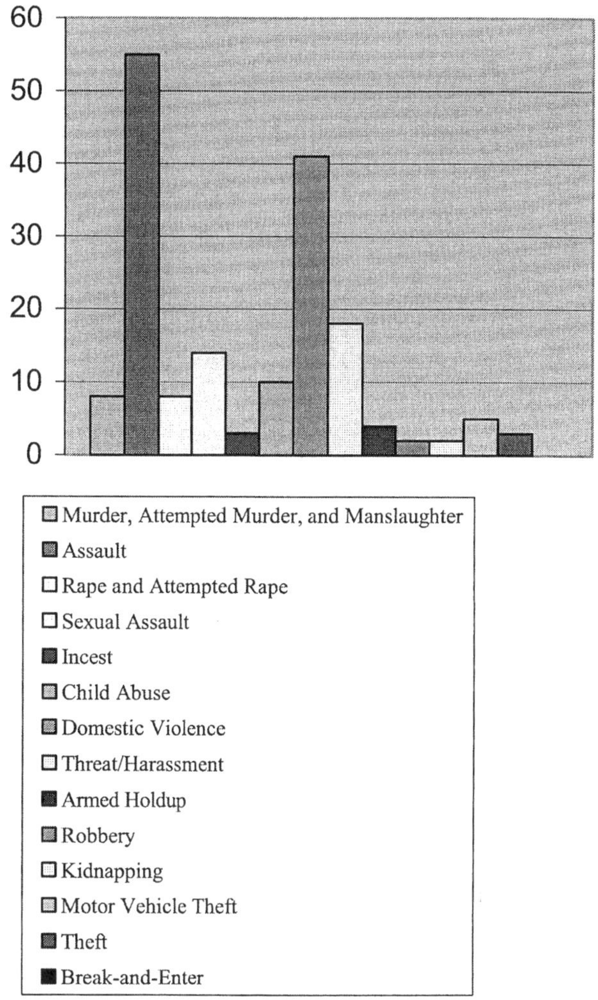

Figure 3: New clients at VOCAL ACT, July 2002–June 2003.

been referred by specialist agencies), they sought counseling, and they followed the forms of help on offer—a pattern to be expected of varieties of secondary victimization in which people respond to a transformative event by redefining themselves and assuming an identity as victims *für sich*, a response amplified by the politics of gender and age where (for instance) special attention has been paid to problems of domestic violence, sexual assault, and child abuse. So it was that the principal referring agencies to ACT Victim Support Service between July 2004 and June 2005 were the "child, youth and women's health program" (21); child and youth services (25); government-administered

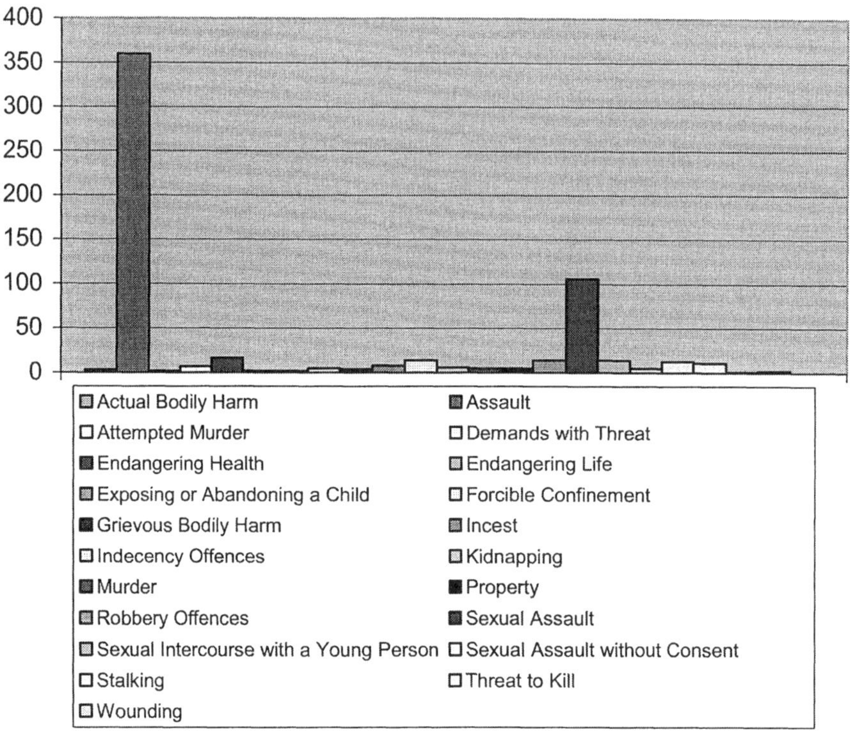

Figure 4: Clients received at Victims' Services Scheme ACT, July 2004–June 2005.

community welfare services (18); nongovernment administered community welfare services (26); the Domestic Violence Crisis Service (14); the police (93); an approved counselor (152); private counselor (19); "relative/friend/neighbour" (113); and VOCAL ACT (26) (ACT Department of Justice & Community Safety, 2005, p. 29). In South Australia, according to the Web site of the victims of crime coordinator, there were (apart from the Victim Support Service and the Director of Public Prosecution's Witness Assistance Service) a number of dedicated support schemes for victims: the Aged Rights Advocacy Service, the Child Abuse Report Line, Child Protection Services, Compassionate Friends (a self-help group for those whose children have died), the Coroners Court Social Worker, the Domestic Violence Helpline, the Domestic Violence Crisis Service, the Homicide Victims Support Group, and the Yarrow Place Rape and Sexual Assault Service. The government of Victoria, in its own review of victims' services, acknowledged a similar selective pattern: "Centres Against Sexual Assault, for example, were established in response to concerns in society about the appropriateness of contemporary responses to victims of rape and sexual assault. Their establishment was a response to a specific need

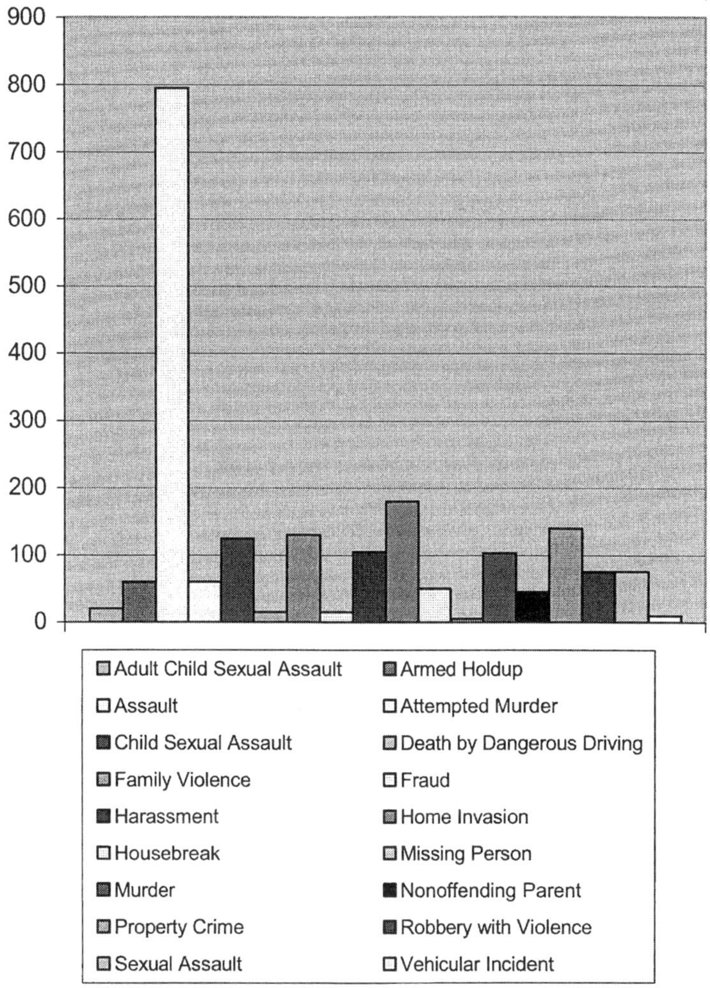

Figure 5: Client referrals to the Victim Support Service, South Australia, July 2002–June 2003.

rather than part of a coherent strategy to respond to the needs of victims of crime overall" (Department of Justice, 2002, p. 3).

But burglary victims and other victims *an sich* do not tend to take crime to be a pivotal signifier; their identities are not built around victimization; they have no attentive politics of their own, no committed agencies and organizations, and no one articulating their plight; and, although they may be troubled (and although they may receive information about services) they are less likely to seek or be extended help. A member of the New South Wales Victims of Crime Bureau said in an interview: "Our service is extremely minimalist in relation to property damage. It's very much injury focused." The result is the self-reinforcing system to which I alluded in the introduction to this paper. A lawyer serving on a review of victims services in ACT remarked:

> The VSS [Victim Support Service] . . . and the Victims Assistance Board . . . dispute the finding [of the Dare report] that the VSS services are provided only in a therapist/client paradigm. They say, "well, it's a responsive paradigm and if therapy is the asked-for response, then that's what's provided. If practical assistance is the asked-for response, then that's what's provided." So they would deny that suggestion that we are therapy only, I suppose . . . . VSS [would say] "we are responsive to what's requested." If therapy's requested, and it says the only reason the VSS has provided a high proportion of counseling services is that these are the services that most clients have sought. And if there is an aspect of this service that is, can be volunteer provided, then that is hived off to the volunteer, the volunteer providers.

The general point is made forcefully in figures 6 and 7 where I compare the numbers of crimes recorded by the police with those referred to the two main illustrative victim support agencies. It becomes clear that the absolute numbers of referrals are small, that they form a modest proportion of the victims eligible, and that only in a few cases (such as murder and attempted murder) is there anything like a parity of number. It will be instructive later to contrast that pattern with that prevailing in England and Wales.

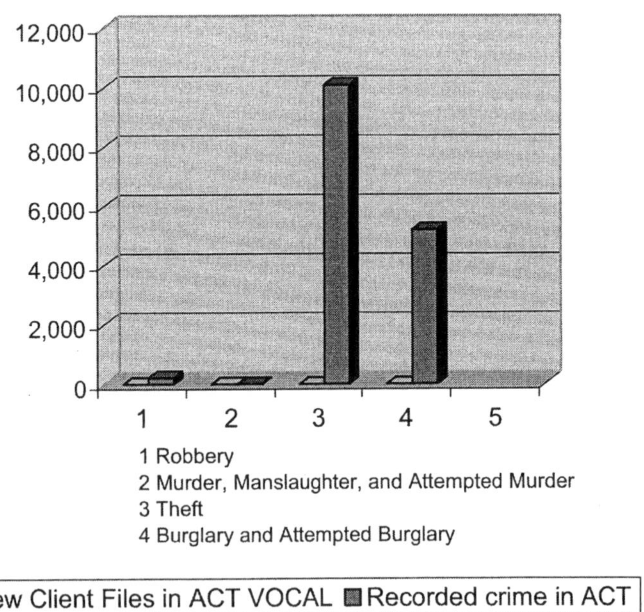

Figure 6: New VOCAL clients and recorded crime in ACT, 2003.

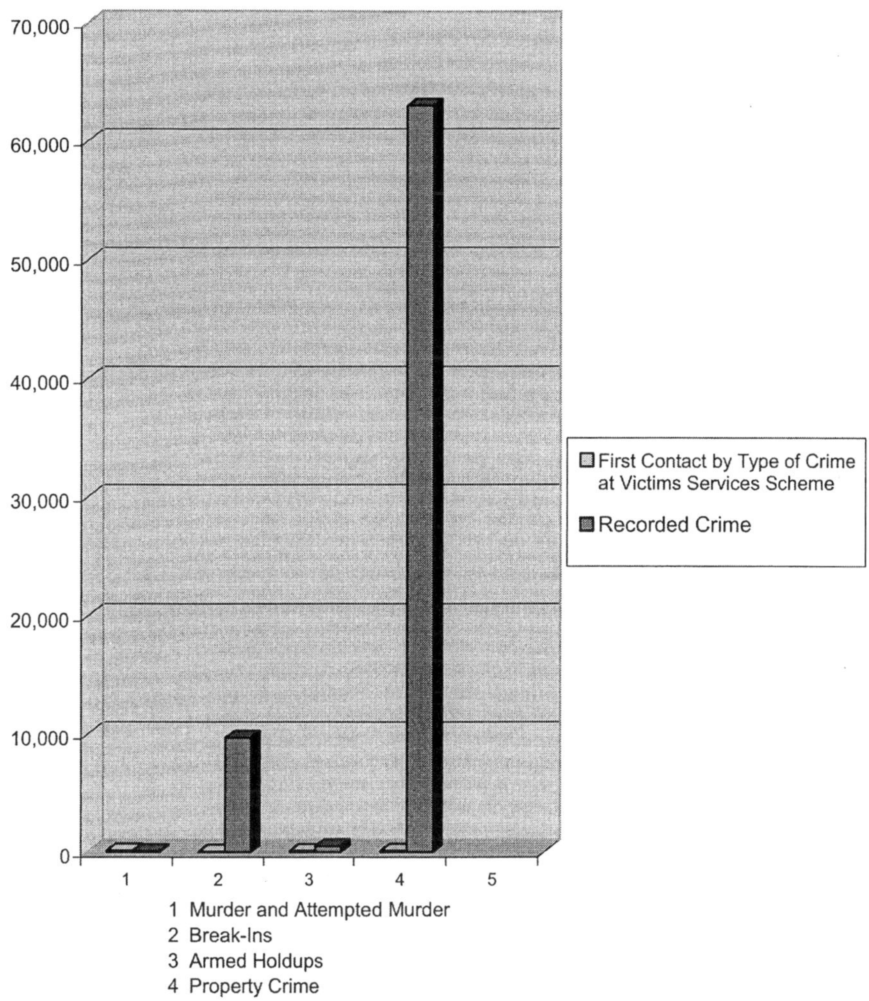

Figure 7: Instances of recorded crime and first contact by type of crime, Victims Services Schemes, South Australia (SA), 2004–5.

Commentaries may recognize that certain groups of potential clients have been systematically overlooked, but those who compose the populations singled out as so neglected are defined chiefly by a politics more diffuse and general than that of the simple demographics of criminal victimization—a politics not only responsive to conventional policy preoccupations with age, gender, and disability but also sensitive to the peculiarly Australian needs of non-English-speaking immigrants, indigenous people, vulnerable witnesses with special needs, and rural populations in a massive geographical country where people may be difficult to reach (Cook, David, & Grant, 1999, p. 94 *et seq.*; Victim Support Australasia, 1997, 2002, 2003). What stands out is that there is almost no talk about the neglected victims of volume crime or the less well-favored victims of violence, such as homosexual men and women (Mason, 1993, pp. 3–4).

The ideal type of Australian victim flows from all that figurative work. When the Victims Support Agency of Victoria described victims' needs, it stated that they "vary with the type of crime they experience. Children, for example, who experience physical or sexual abuse by members of their own families require different kinds of responses from adults who are victims of random assault. Women and men who are raped or sexually assaulted will require specialist support tailored to their particular needs. Primary victims, those who are the direct victims of assault, rape or other violent crime have different needs from secondary victims" (Department of Justice, 2002, p. 1). The accent and focus are there firm and unambiguous, and they expunge the vast majority of Australian victims.

A CONTRAST

I have argued that Australia's victims' services have largely turned away from the use of volunteers to devote their funds to the employment of specialist counselors catering for a small population of victims of the most severely disturbing offences, victims who came to the fore originally as a result of the work of activist survivors. It is otherwise in England and Wales, where a great mass of volunteers support through nontherapeutic means a larger proportion of victims—the victims of commonplace crime as much as any—and I present the case of Victim Support England and Wales for the interesting comparison it presents.

The first victim support scheme was founded in Bristol in 1974 as the progeny of the National Association for the Care and Resettlement of Offenders (NACRO), a penal reform and rehabilitative organization adamantly opposed to campaigns waged against offenders' rights and which fostered Victim Support's engrained commitment not to engage in advocacy or make public pronouncements about specific cases, specific offenders, or sentencing issues (Rock, 1986). Other like groups were formed, and they came together formally as a federation—the National Association of Victim Support Schemes (NAVSS)—in 1979. None had been established by survivors or victims *für sich*, none was dedicated to particular classes of victims, none was set up to be an advocacy organization, and none talked about trauma. They sought to "avoid more sensational publicity which could add to the distress of individuals or increase anxiety amongst vulnerable people" (NAVSS, n.d. (a)). They were part of no "victims' movement." They were no campaigning organization (Helen Reeves, its first and long-time director, argued at a formative stage

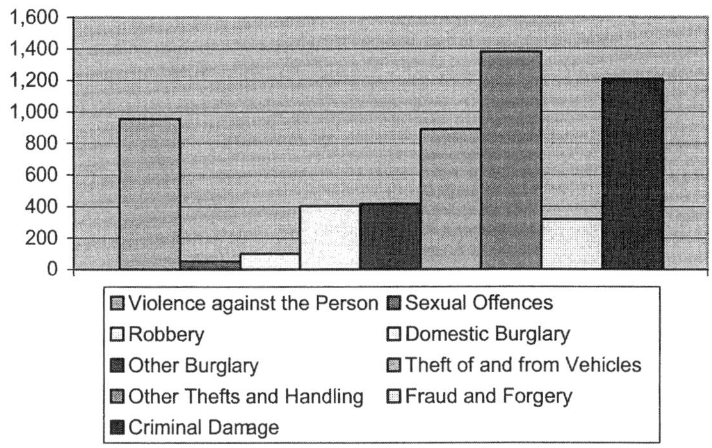

Figure 8: Number of crimes recorded by the police in England and Wales, 2003–4 (hundreds).

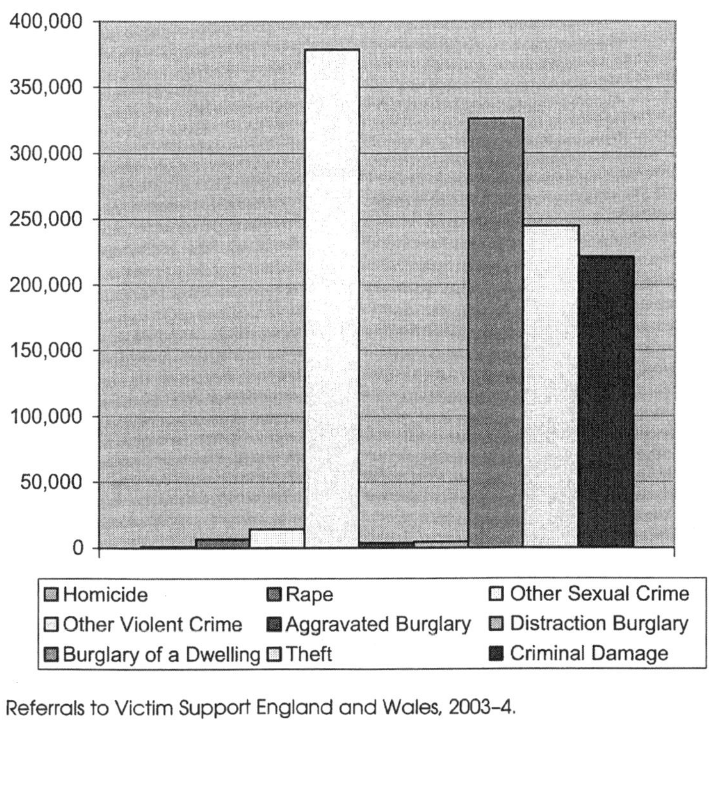

Figure 9: Referrals to Victim Support England and Wales, 2003–4.

that a "campaigning stance ... [is] unlikely to find favour in the U.K." [1984, p. 2]). In the mid-1980s, at a time of a highly contested politics of crime and criminal justice—when there was a mushrooming of police monitoring groups and other critical and radical organizations—it came to win the trust and patronage first of the police, then of the Home Office, the central criminal justice department of state, and lastly of the courts as a responsible organization that would not embarrass politicians or jeopardize the delicate balances of the criminal justice system. It came to be comparatively well funded, receiving £29 million from the Home Office in 2004–5, and being encouraged step by step by criminal justice agencies and successive governments to extend itself umbrella-like over all forms of victim—including distinctively gendered victims, such as the victims of rape, and homicide survivors. In the mid-1980s, it secured the agreement of police forces to introduce "automatic referrals" whereby almost all crimes reported were referred to schemes (although Figure 10 does suggest that there are still significant gaps and lapses in the practical implementation of that policy). Despite some upset induced by the New Labour government's brief flirtation with the introduction of competition and markets in "service-delivery," and despite a flurry of anxiety about the implications of data protection directives that appeared to protect the anonymity of victims and undermine automatic referrals, it still occupies a near-monopolistic position as an authority in its field and as a provider of support—its 10,000 volunteers from 375 local community support schemes and parallel witness service having dealings with 1,750,000 victims annually.

Until very recently, the concomitant archetype of the victim in the criminal justice politics of England and Wales has not been so much a victim of violence or domestic violence or a raped woman but a victim of everyday volume crime, the everyman or everywoman of the criminal justice system, who is framed by representations flowing from the practical work of Victim Support and the criminal justice agencies. "Anyone can be a victim of crime," an early handbook for Victim Support was to say, "and victims should not be regarded as a new 'problem group' . . . . People should not be encouraged to be 'victims' for longer than necessary" (NAVSS, n.d. (b)).

Although it is now at some risk, that typification is still generally reproduced in the sayings of civil servants and politicians. Take official definitions of who the victims of England and Wales are for the working purposes of criminal justice. Victims have been covered by the government's 1990 and 1996 *Victim's Charters*, which effectively laid out what people were supposed to expect from the criminal justice agencies with whom they have dealings, and victims were there described as "all individual victims of theft, burglary, criminal damage, arson, assault, domestic assault, racial harassment, sexual crimes and homicide' (Home Office, 2001, p. 4). Observe the order and composition of that list: it is the victims of commonplace, volume crime who loom large and appear first. Similarly, *A New Deal for Victims and Witnesses*, published by

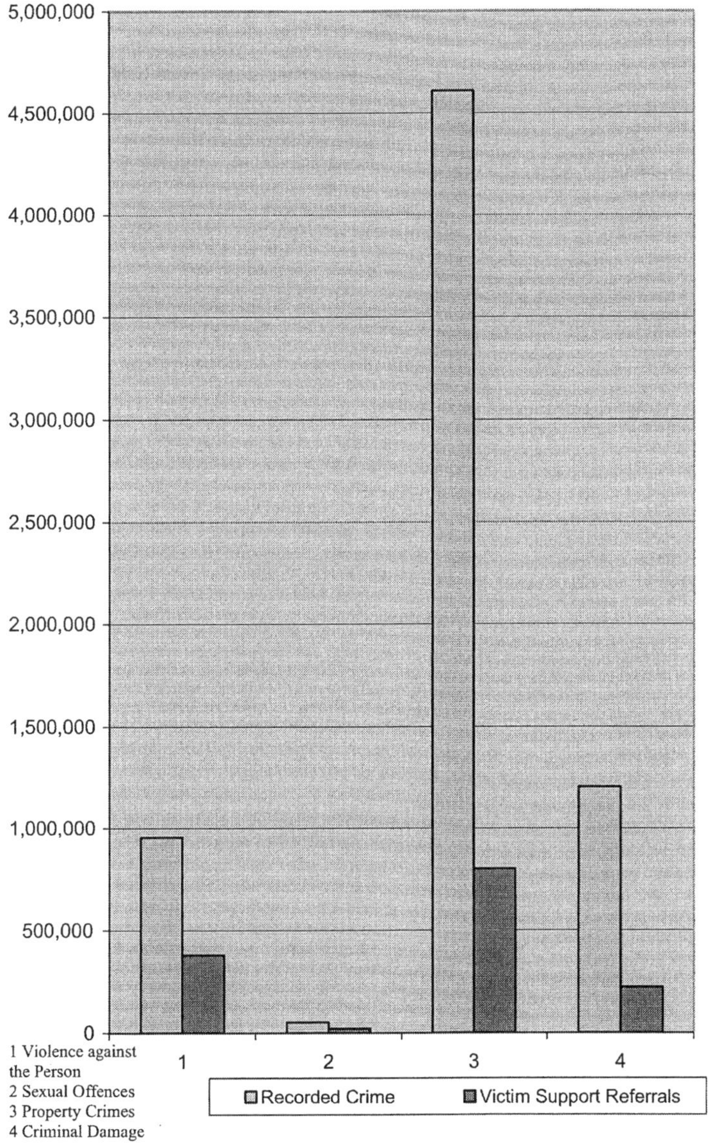

Figure 10: Recorded crime and Victim Support referrals in illustrative categories of victimization in England and Wales, 2003–4.

the Home Office in July 2003 as a "national strategy to deliver improved services," opened by stating in the names of the home secretary, the secretary of state for constitutional affairs, and the attorney general that "last year one in four people was a victim of crime . . . . Victims of crime are our families, our friends, our neighbours, our workmates. Ourselves . . . " (Home Office, 2003, p. 3). The victims there are not those who suffer from exceptional distress, alienation, and disturbance, and the volunteers who support them are not schooled in trauma management. Ideas of trauma are not discernible even in materials touching on the more extreme cases of rape victims, the victims of racist and homophobic attacks, and those bereaved by homicide (see www.vslondon.org). Trauma is not emphasized as a constitutive condition. And, in most instances, counseling is taken to be a less than wholly appropriate response. Volunteers are held to be fit, indeed ideal, people for the work of support—supposedly representing, as they do, the community whose symbolic integrity has been ruptured by crime. In discussing the rights of victims to proper health care, Victim Support declared:

> Our experience suggests that most people find it extremely helpful to talk about feelings arising as a result of crime. Victim Support volunteers are trained to listen in a constructive way and to provide reassurance that these feelings are normal, and even healthy. This emotional support is coupled with information and practical assistance. But Victim Support does not describe its services as counselling. One reason is that the word may suggest that the problem lies with the victim's personality, lifestyle, etc. rather than the fact that they need help and support to deal with understandable reactions to an external situation . . .' (www.victimsupport.org.uk).

CONCLUSION

Australia and England/Wales thus offer two contrasting but largely internally consistent models of practical and typifying work: the one taking its organizing imagery from the suffering of bereaved people, deploying it to construct an ideal type of victim at large as one who is bereft and traumatized, and devising suitable but expensive therapeutic remedies—no doubt significantly to the benefit of many of the clients who present themselves to schemes, but defining out the great mass of victims of mundane crime. The other did not arise from the ranks of victims themselves, is still diffuse in its definitions of types and conditions of victimization, and organizes a more catholic and massive response. In the one country, volunteering is a prevalent and legitimate mode of action in the criminal justice system, in the other it is not. Robyn Holder, who has worked in the area in both countries, observed in an e-mail that there is a "hugely different orientation to and culture of 'volunteerism' between Aust[ralia] and the UK. I noticed it very much on my return to Australia. In all offence areas in the UK, the use of volunteers has been pronounced even if in the rape crisis and refuge movements they might talk about them being 'activists' or 'survivors'. But in Australia these latter two movements very strongly abjured the use of volunteers from the early 80s."

Each model of action is self-reinforcing, producing and being justified by the iconography and clienteles it produces, and each generating work that is proper for the workforce that sustains it, the trained counselors and the citizen-volunteers. Above all, perhaps, it has been the effect of automatic referrals delivering victims to Victim Support in England and Wales that has been pivotal. Automatic referrals necessarily furnish the victims of volume, mundane crime. Selective referrals do not. Robyn Holder reflected in an e-mail that "aside from WA [Western Australia], no Australian jurisdiction has been able to get that referral process from police. Though now the NT [Northern Territories] has developed it, and ACT has commenced it this year "with consent". In the UK (at least when I was there) it was automatic except in certain offence areas where consent and/or choice of service then intervened. If there was not this referral mechanism, then I would lay bets that that the 'high end' victims would dominate the VS [victim support] stats."

The workings of victim support in two jurisdictions that are not unlike in many other respects invite consideration of how representations of crime and victimization are engendered and sustained, and (perhaps) further exploration of how the politics of criminal justice might themselves be affected by popular and expert constructions of those who chiefly sustain the impact of the crime problem.

A Caveat

I said at the outset that I would accentuate certain traits for analytic purposes. It would be proper at the end of the paper to restore balance and introduce some qualifications to emphasize that the contrasts I have traced are actually far from absolute. First, many of the referrals to Victim Support for property crime in England and Wales are followed only by the sending of letters and no contact of any substance may take place. A referral may then actually prove to be without obvious moment for the victim, and the coverage of victim populations may be quite token. Second, we know little about the conduct and content of encounters between victims and service providers in any of the three countries, although some English and Welsh volunteers are reported to look upon their work as an unpaid apprenticeship which could advance a later career in counseling. What is done, what typifications emerge, how they are applied, and their impact on victims' subjectivities must then remain moot. There is, third, a small growth in volunteer services such as Mission Australia and the Criminal Justice Support Network in Australia, on the one hand, and a plethora of activist and self-help organizations in England and Wales (Rock, 1998) on the other, and those English and Welsh organizations are very similar in origin and ideology to their counterparts in Australia, whose members claim (as they say) respect and recognition. They tend to be ambivalent about counseling, holding (on the one hand) that the attention of a paid specialist in trauma and bereavement offers an appropriately weighty acknowledgement of their plight, but (on the other) that it is only the really exceptional clinician or therapist who is capable of appreciating the existential transformation, the *rite de passage*, which they have undergone. Once placed quite firmly on the periphery of the politics of criminal justice, moreover, those survivors have been imported into the heart of the system as members of a relatively newly established National Victims Advisory Panel, founded in 2003 in anticipation of the Domestic Violence, Crime, and Victims Act of 2004 (c. 28), with a broad mandate to advise and pronounce on victims' policies. Victim Support may have fielded a member of the original panel, but the other members were mostly victims *für sich*, recruited quite expressly as experts whose knowledge was existentially grounded. So it was that public advertisements called for "victim[s] of crime or [those who] have a good understanding of the needs of victims of crime ... to share their experiences and to generate ideas and practical proposals for improving services to victims and witnesses." Of the initial 12 members—representing such organizations as Support After Murder and Manslaughter (SAMM), the North of England Victims Association (NEVA), the Zito Trust, Victims Voice, and other survivors' groups—6 were homicide survivors, 1 a victim of a stalker, 1 a victim of an aggravated burglary, 1 a victim of sexual assault, and another a victim of rape. The matters they discussed were, by extension, largely of significance to the traumatized victim, touching on the obtaining of trial transcripts (although some 3 percent of crimes in England and Wales go to trial, and even fewer to courts of record); a review of the Coroner Service; and on one occasion, and significantly, support in the management of Post-Traumatic Stress Disorder (PTSD) (Home Office, 2005). Chaired by a sympathetic minister of state, the panel has been heeded and it has come to serve as something of a counterweight to the once sovereign position of Victim Support. Its work may well blur a number of the distinctions I have mapped in this paper, but its consequences are as yet uncertain and narrow in scope, and Victim Support still retains its position as the dominant institution in the sector.

And last, just as I write and with characteristic perversity, the development of victims' services in the United Kingdom may well be about to undergo a marked shift which will make them more akin to the Australian organizations. The government of England and Wales is undertaking yet another review of its criminal injuries compensation scheme, a scheme deeply unpopular with ministers because it is demand-led and only marginally under financial control. In a consultation paper issued in December 2005 (Criminal Justice System, 2005), there is a new talk about the trauma of violent crime; the diverting of money from the compensation scheme into counseling, physiotherapy, and other supportive work for serious victims; and a creation of Victim Care Units which would commission services from a variety of bodies, including Victim Support. It was summarized thus on the Home Office Web site: "Even relatively minor crimes can be traumatic, but the most serious crimes cause enormous emotional and physical harm. That is why better support for victims is at the heart of our vision for improving the criminal justice system." The parallel, earlier case in Australia was described by one official there thus: "The growth in gov[ernment] provided or funded counseling support isn't so much about a direct linking to dealing with 'trauma', but rather gov[ernment's] finding a way that was acceptable to the public to cut a legal entitlement." In all this, a new (albeit limited) convergence may there be in prospect.

REFERENCES

ACT Burglary Victims Response Project. (2004). *Crime victims and the prevention of residential burglary*. Canberra, ACT: Department of Justice & Community Safety.

ACT Department of Justice & Community Safety. (2003a). *Government response to the report by Dr. Anthony Dare on* Assistance for victims of crime in the ACT: A review of the operation of the Victims of Crime (Financial Assistance) Act 1983 and the victims services scheme. Canberra, ACT: Author.

ACT Department of Justice & Community Safety. (2003b). *Victims of crime support program annual report 2002–2003*. Canberra, ACT: Author.

ACT Department of Justice & Community Safety. (2005). *Review of the victim services scheme issues paper*. Canberra, ACT: Author.

Attorney-General's Department, Government of South Australia. (2004). *Information for victims of crime*. Adelaide: Author.

Australian Bureau of Statistics. (2005). Retrieved from http://www.abs.gov.au/Ausstats/abs@nsf

Australian Federal Police, ACT. (n.d.). *How to prepare a victim impact statement*. Canberra, ACT: Author.

Australian Institute of Criminology, (2005). *Australian crime: Facts and figures 2001*. Canberra, ACT: Author.

Condry, R. (2003). *After the offence: The construction of crime and its consequences by families of serious offenders*. Unpublished doctoral dissertation, London School of Economics.

Cook, B., David, F., & Grant, A. (1999). *Victims' needs, victims' rights: Policies and programs for victims of crime in Australia*. Canberra, ACT: Australian Institute of Criminology.

Criminal Justice System. (2005). *Rebuilding lives—Supporting victims of crime*. London: Her Majesty's Stationary Office (HMSO).

Dare, A. (2002). *Assistance for victims of crime in the ACT: A review of the operation of the Victims of Crime (Financial Assistance) Act 1983 and the victims services scheme*. Melbourne, Victoria: Anthony Dare Consulting.

Dawson, M. (2000, August). *The changing face of victims' services*. Paper presented at the Tenth International Symposium on Victimology, Montreal, Canada.

Dawson, M. (2003, July). *Victims' rights—Fighting the fight*. Stellenbosch, Unpublished Paper.

Dawson, M., & Zada, J. (1999, May). *Victims of crime: The therapeutic benefit of receiving compensation*. Paper presented at the annual Australian and New Zealand Association of Psychiatry, Psychology, and the Law (ANZAPPL) Congress.

Department of Justice. (2002). *Report: Review of services to victims of crime*. Melbourne, Victoria: Author.

Department of Justice. (2004). *Victim impact statement*. Melbourne, Victoria: Author.

Director of Public Prosecutions, ACT. (2004). *Annual report 2003–2004*. Canberra, ACT: Author.

Findlay, M., Odgers, S., & Yeo, S. (1994). *Australian criminal justice*. Oxford: Oxford University Press.

Home Office. (2001). *A review of the victim's charter*. London: Author.

Home Office. (2003). *A new deal for victims and witnesses—National strategy*. London: Author.

Home Office. (2005). *Listening to victims: The first year of the Victims' Advisory Panel*. London: Author.

Jabour, M. (1997). Foreword. In B. Giuliano (Ed.), *Survival and beyond: An anthology of stories by victims of crime and a victims' resource guide* (pp. 1–3). Curtin, ACT: National Association for Loss and Grief.

Johnson, H. (2005). *Crime victimization in Australia*. Canberra, ACT: Australian Institute of Criminology.

Justice Strategy Unit. (1999). *Review of* Victims of crime report one. Adelaide: Government of South Australia.

Law Reform Commission New South Wales. (1996). *Discussion paper 33—Sentencing 11: Victims of crime*. Sydney: Author.

Mason, G. (1993). *Violence against lesbians and gay men: Trends and issues*. Canberra, ACT: Australian Institute of Criminology.

Miller, G., & Holstein, J. (Eds.). (1997). *Social problems in everyday life*. Greenwich, CT: JAI Press.

Ministry of Justice. (2000). *International crime survey*. The Hague: Author.

Mukherjee, S., Neuhaus, D., & Walker, J. (1990). *Crime and justice in Australia*. Canberra, ACT: Australian Institute of Criminology.

NAVSS. (n.d.(a)). *What is the NAVSS?* London: Author.

NAVSS. (n.d.(b)). *NAVSS members handbook*. London: Author.

Office of the Director of Public Prosecutions. (n.d.). *Witness assistance service*. Sydney: Author.

Office of the Director of Public Prosecutions New South Wales. (2005). *Services for victims of violent crime and vulnerable witnesses*. Sydney: Author.

Pinto, S., & Wilson, P. (1990). *Serial murder*. Canberra, ACT: Australian Institute of Criminology.

Reeves, H. (1984). *Towards a British policy for victims*. London: NAVSS.

Robinson, J. (2004). *Crime: It can happen to you*. Kent Town, South Australia: Wakefield Press.

Rock, P. (1986). *Helping victims of crime: The Home Office and the rise of victim support in England and Wales*. Oxford: Clarendon Press.

Rock, P. (1998). *After homicide: Practical and political responses to bereavement*. Oxford: Clarendon Press.

Rock, P. (2004). *Constructing victims' rights*. Oxford: Clarendon Press.

Shiner, M., Thom, B., & McGregor, S. (2004). *Exploring community responses to drugs*. York, UK: Joseph Rowntree Foundation.

Van Maanen, J. (1984). Doing new things in old ways: The chains of socialization. In J. Bess (Ed.), *College and university organization: Insights from the behavior sciences* (pp. 211–247). New York: New York University Press.

Victim Support Australasia. (1997). *Position paper no 1*. Canberra, ACT: Author.

Victim Support Australasia. (1998a). *Position paper no 3: A partnership with police services*. Canberra, ACT: Author.

Victim Support Australasia. (1999). *Position paper no 4: The role of volunteers in victim support*. Canberra, ACT: Author.

Victim Support Australasia. (2002). *Position paper no 5: Minimum standards for crime victims' services*. Canberra, ACT: Author.

Victim Support Australasia. (2003). *Position paper no 6: The role of crime victims in the criminal justice system*. Canberra, ACT: Author.

Victim Support Australasia. (2005). *Services and rights for crime victims in Australasia: A brief profile*. Canberra, ACT: Author.

Victim Support Service. (2004a). 23,000 Crime victims. *Victims' Voice, 25*(1), 3.

Victim Support Service. (2004b). More crime victims seek help. *Victims' Voice, 25*(3), 11.

Victim Support Service [South Australia]. (2004). *Annual report and accounts 2003–2004*. Adelaide, South Australia: Author.

Victim Support Service [South Australia]. (2005). Sentencing: Where we stand. *Victims' Voice,* 25(2).

Victims of Crime Coordinator. (2005). *Read a message from the attorney-general*. Retrieved from http://www.voc.sa.gov.au

VOCAL (ACT) Inc. (n.d.(a)). *Have you ever been through a crime or witnessed one?* Narrabundah, ACT: Author.

VOCAL (ACT) Inc. (n.d.(b)). *Useful information for dealing with the aftereffects of a crime*. Narrabundah, ACT: Author.

VOCAL (ACT) Inc. (n.d.(c)). *Why Seek Help?* Narrabundah, ACT: Author.

VOCAL (ACT) Inc. (2005, Autumn). About vocal. *Newsletter*, 1.

[15]
Urban Homelessness, Crime and Victimisation in England

ABSTRACT

A survey of homeless people carried out in the centres of three English cities in 2004 revealed unusually high levels of victimisation and offending, an engrained mistrust of the police and other formal institutions, and an ensuing recourse to informal justice which exacerbated insecurity and raised levels of crime and victimisation yet further.

Key words: crime survey, homelessness, victimisation

INTRODUCTION

Often unprotected by walls, doors and other physical shields; frequently overlooked and devalued; on the boundaries of society and not always fully acknowledged as public citizens or members of the community;[1] beset by problems of trauma[2] and depression,[3] mental and physical ill-health;[4] socially isolated;[5] representing as much a problem of crime and public incivility as a problem of victimisation,[6] the homeless form a vulnerable population whose difficulties are exacerbated by ignorance and neglect. Of all groups in English and Welsh society, they are probably most at risk from crime although their marginality renders much of their experience quite invisible.[7]

The homeless tend not to report crime in any numbers (Ballintyne, 1999).[8] They make very modest direct use of Victim Support, general practitioners (Shiner, 1995), and other caring agencies (Danczuk, 2000: p. 14); 'self-referrals' to Victim Support from *all* victims, including homeless victims, being less than 2% of the whole, a minute proportion (Victim Support, 2003: p. 20), and it is significant that Victim Support keeps no record of the residential status of those who *do* come before it.[9] The police are more likely to encounter the homeless as offenders than as victims (Ballintyne, 1999: p. 44), and, in any event, the official crime statistics do not record how victims and offenders are housed. The British Crime Survey, which measures people's exposure to crime, is a household survey which does not capture those who are sleeping rough (Simmons and

Dodd, 2003).[10] And survey and other reports about homelessness do not in the main touch on offending and victimisation (Crane and Warnes, 2001; Westminster City Council, 2002; St Mungo's, 2004), in some cases perhaps because of trepidation about stigmatising further an already stigmatised population, in others because competing problems (such as those of health) are thought to loom larger, and in others still because the practical and analytic insulation of policy areas can lead to homelessness being treated as an issue quite separate from crime. It was instructive that one of us was informed in the summer of 2004 that the management committee of a central London Victim Support scheme had never formally considered the problem of homeless victims (the numbers were not considered sufficient to warrant it) and that homelessness was thought to be a matter discussed only by the homelessness charities.[11] There is, in short, a lack of knowledge about offending by and against an intensively victimised population[12] and, according to an official of Westminster City Council, it is a lack remedied by anecdote and speculation. The one major English exception is Ballintyne's (1999) *Unsafe Streets*, based on a survey of 120 people and published in 1999, and we shall draw on it as this paper proceeds.

To compound matters, homelessness is and has long been a form of status deviance – rough sleeping, aggressive begging[13] and drinking in public being frequently censured and controlled (Danczuk, 2000: p. 9) as social problems in their own right, an example of broken windows that need fixing. In January 1997, for example, Tony Blair made a major and controversial speech in which he outlined his view of 'zero tolerance'. Asked by the editor of the *Big Issue* whether he supported the policy, he replied: 'Yes I do. It is important that you say we don't tolerate the small crimes. It says you don't tolerate the graffiti on the wall.'[14] He went on: 'Obviously, some people will interpret this in a way which is harsh and unpleasant, but I think the basic principle is here to say: yes it is right to be intolerant of people homeless on the streets'. Begging has been said to support drug-taking,[15] and those who give money to beggars are held by some – in what has become an acrimonious dispute – to be 'killing with kindness'.[16] Policies are confused,[17] but many are not now intended to equip rough sleepers to cope better *in situ as* homeless people but to move them away from the streets and into another status altogether, no longer homeless. They have become a problem of social exclusion, and a target was set in 1998 by the New Labour Government to reduce their numbers by two thirds by 2002.

METHODOLOGY

Crisis, the charity for the homeless, believed it important to throw more light on the problem of criminal victimisation, and we were approached to carry out a survey and produce a report. This paper is one of the outcomes. The research was undertaken relatively speedily and with limited resources. The nature of the methodology reflects some of these limitations. In August and September 2004,

336 people were interviewed, principally by graduate students of the London School of Economics.[18] Three hundred and five of those interviews were structured and they form the basis of the quantitative analysis. A further 31 unstructured, taped interviews were conducted, and these were used to explore questions in a more searching and flexible fashion, and they have been used to illustrate and extend some of the points which we shall make.[19] All the quotations from numbered respondents belong to that latter group.

Two hundred and five interviews were conducted in central London, the country's capital city where the bulk of homeless people are to be found;[20] but 50 were held in Oxford and 50 in Cambridge, other cities with concentrations of homeless people; not only to prevent the survey from reporting conditions in just one place but also for purposes of possible contrast. In the event, however, the differences between the homeless populations for the three cities were so very slight that they did not warrant detailed discussion, and that is itself an important finding. For practical purposes the length of the interviews was kept to 30–40 minutes and it was for that reason that we confined ourselves to a set of core issues. At the outset, our chief foci were the extent to which homeless people are victimised; the circumstances and nature of that victimisation; their assessment of the risks presented by different places and people; the measures which they took to protect themselves; their judgement of the extent and quality of the use, if any, which they made of statutory agencies and voluntary associations; their experiences and views of the police; and the level of their own offending. Other issues emerged in the course of the unstructured interviews, and we shall introduce them where appropriate.

We encountered some unexpected difficulty in securing permission to conduct the research in hostels, and interviewing was consequently confined to day centres in the three cities. Considerable discussion was undertaken with service providers about the process of approaching potential respondents. In the event, interviewers spent between four and eight hours per day in day centres where we had secured permission for interviews to take place. Their presence soon became known and interviews were conducted with all interviewees who made themselves available. Interviews were not conducted when it appeared that the respondent was clearly affected by recent alcohol or other substance use. Respondents were paid £10 for each interview – a sum agreed with service providers as an appropriate amount for a half-hour interview. The structured interview schedule comprised a series of questions about experience of victimisation. These questions were based in significant measure on cognate British Crime Survey questions for purposes of comparison. Other questions, about contact with the criminal justice system for example, arose out of discussion with officials of Crisis, the St Mungo's Trust, Thames Reach Bondway, Victim Support Westminster, Westminster City Council and Westminster City Guardians.

The circumstances of the population we were seeking to reach, and the circumstances under which interviewing took place, made it effectively im-

TABLE 1
Age of Respondents

Age	Number	%
Under 20	10	3
20–29	69	23
30–39	116	38
40–49	64	21
50–59	34	11
60–69	9	3
70 and above	2	1

possible to construct anything other than an opportunity sample. Interviewers were instructed to aim to interview as broad a range of people in the day centres as possible in order to attempt to ensure that the eventual sample included female and minority ethnic respondents as well as the white males that were expected to predominate. In the event, interviewers reported that the homeless in the day centres in which the research was conducted were eager to co-operate. No doubt the small fee that was paid played some part in this. However, it also appears that there were many respondents who felt that the survey gave them a voice. They were keen to talk and to have their stories heard. The unstructured interview sample was also an opportunity sample, constructed to reflect a range of demographic characteristics and experiences of homelessness. Of the 305 people interviewed for the survey, 256 (84%) were male and 49 (16%) female. Thames Reach Bondway's (2003) analysis of the 4,000 homeless people it worked with in London in 2003, was not dissimilar although its categories did not always correspond precisely to our own: 86% were male, 14% female; and 8% were aged 18–24, 30% 25–35; 49% 36–60, and 13% 60+; 7% were African, 2% Asian, 5% Caribbean, 68% 'British', 9% Irish and 9% 'other'. Another survey of the London homeless conducted for the then Bondway, Thames Reach and St Mungo's in 2000 showed that men outnumbered women by 4:1, and that 87% of rough sleepers were British (Crane and Warnes, 2001). The 2004 survey of homeless people conducted by St Mungo's reported that some 34% were aged 30–39, 22% 40–49, and 24% 50+. Comparisons between the four sets of figures do allow us to conclude that those we interviewed were not unrepresentative of the larger homeless population. The youngest (four in total) were aged 17, the oldest 79 and the mean age was 37. The overall age breakdown is shown in Table 1.

Data were collected on the respondents' self-reported ethnicity. Of the 304 for whom data were available, 255 (83%) described themselves as 'White British', 'Irish' or 'Other White'. Fuller details are contained in Tables 2 and 3.

TABLE 2
Respondents' Self-reported Ethnicity

Ethnicity	Number	%
White		
British	196	65
Irish	25	8
Other White	34	11
Asian or Asian British		
Indian	2	1
Pakistani	1	<1
Other Asian	3	1
Mixed		
White and Black Caribbean	1	<1
White and Black African	4	1
White and Asian	2	1
Any other mixed background	3	1
Black or Black British		
Caribbean	17	6
African	11	4
Other Bl;ack background	3	1
Chinese or other ethnic group		
Other ethnic group	2	1

More summarily, the composition of the group showed that the homeless preponderantly defined themselves as 'White'.

Respondents were asked about their current living situation and, in particular, whether they were sleeping rough, living in their own home, with family or friends or in bed and breakfast accommodation or a hostel. Perhaps predictably, given the nature of the survey, almost half (45%) said that they were currently

TABLE 3
Respondents' Self-Reported Ethnicity

	Number	%
White	255	84
Black	31	10
Mixed	10	3
Asian	6	2
Other	2	<1

TABLE 4
Number of Occasions of Rough Sleeping

Frequency	Number	%
Once	28	9
2–5 times	42	14
6–10 times	13	4
More than 10 times	211	72

TABLE 5
Length of Time Sleeping Rough (on Last Occasion)

Length of time	Number	%
Less than one month	73	26
1–3 months	59	21
4–6 months	44	16
7–12 months	36	13
Over a year	63	24

'sleeping rough' and over a quarter (27.5%) said they were living in a hostel. Only 26 respondents (8.5%) said they were living in their own home. Of those sleeping rough, slightly under half (47%) said that they had been doing so for over a year, with a not insubstantial minority (28%) saying they had done so for over four years.[21]

All respondents were asked when they had last slept rough. Over two fifths (41%) said 'last night' or 'currently' and a further 9% said they had done so within the last week. Only eight respondents (3%) said they had never slept rough. Respondents were also asked on how many occasions they had slept rough and what was the longest period they had done so. The answers are summarised in Tables 4 and 5.

It is apparent that there is a fairly high representation of current rough sleepers amongst our sample, arising, perhaps, from their recruitment in this survey through day centres and, more indirectly, through street recruitment by 'word of mouth'.

TABLE 6
Experience of Victimisation in the Past Year

Nature of victimisation	Number	%
Burglary	62	20
Theft	206	67
Damage to the place you live	85	28
Damage to something else belonging to you	45	15
Violence	157	52
Threats	152	50
Sexual assault	24	8

VICTIMISATION

Respondents were asked a series of questions about whether they had experienced various forms of criminal victimisation during the course of the past year. The results are displayed in Table 6, and they show very high levels of reported victimisation with, for example, two thirds of respondents saying that they had experienced theft in the past year and approximately half having experienced threats and/or violence. Compared to the much larger and more general 2003–4 British Crime Survey (BCS), a survey of 20,000 households in England and Wales (Dodd *et al.*2004) – and to its twin survey of 5,000 households in Scotland (McVie *et al.*, 2004) – the vulnerability of homeless people is revealed quite graphically.

One fifth (20%) of respondents suffered a burglary, whilst the British Crime Survey reported that 3.2% of all households in England and Wales and 2.1% of all Londoners and 5.3% of inner city households had done so in the comparable period. Two thirds (67%) of the homeless had suffered a theft, whilst 1.4% of all adults and 1% of all men in England and Wales had done so. Over two fifths (43%) of the homeless had experienced damage to property, whilst 7% of all households in England and Wales, and 9.6% of all households in Scotland, had done so. Over half the homeless had been subject to violence, in contrast to 4% of the general population of England and Wales and 5.8% of that of Scotland, 7.7% of Londoners at large, 7.7% of those living in a 'high physical disorder area' and 9.7% of the unemployed. Almost one tenth (8%) of the homeless had been sexually assaulted, whereas the British Crime Survey encountered too few cases 'to count.'

In short, the homeless suffer levels of crime against property and the person so very different from those faced by other groups that they may be said to live in a quite distinct world[22] – a dangerous world whose lack of predictability was repeatedly condensed in the phrase 'you never know what's around the corner.'

Respondent 23 talked about how 'I suppose you feel vulnerable unless you've got your own sort of like house, flat, bed-sit, whatever thing. You always feel vulnerable no matter where you are because you never know what's round the corner.' It was impossible, said Respondent 11, to convey the qualities of that world to outsiders:

> 'Describing it to people that don't, the general public, it's ... completely [different] ... it's a rite of passage, it's a very, very extremely intense period of one's life that can either destroy you or make you. It is very, very hard and it changes you immensely ... if you're a decent person or if you've got, if you're not built for this sort of lifestyle, I mean you have to sort of like toughen up very, very quickly because it's very, very physical, very, very rough, very, very difficult. And if you don't fit in, you'll just go under.'

Sexual assault was not uncommon, and it was not confined to attacks on women. Eleven of the 24 respondents reporting having been sexually assaulted were men and 13 women. In ten cases the attacker was reported to have been a member of the public, in six cases a friend, in four cases another rough sleeper and in one case each a family member or someone where they were living (no details were available for the other cases).

Just over half of the sample (157 or 52%) had experienced violence in the past year and a significant proportion of these had clearly been subject to serious levels of violence. In all, 68 of those having experienced violence in the past year (or 43% of those experiencing violence – 23% of the total sample) received injuries that required hospital treatment. Of the 68, 60 were men and eight women.

In relation to each form of victimisation, respondents were asked on how many occasions they had experienced each type of crime, whether they had reported it to the police and, if not, why not. If they did report a matter, they were asked about their experience of the police, their satisfaction with the treatment they received and whether or not they reported the matter to anyone else. Overall levels of reporting were not high. They ranged from under 10% (7% damage to property; 9% threats) to between one quarter (23% theft; 24% violence; 24% sexual assault) and one third (33% burglary; 33% damage to the 'place you live'). By contrast, those living in households and interviewed for the British and Scottish Crime Surveys declared much higher levels of reporting: 78% for burglary in England and Wales, and 66% in Scotland (presumably linked to the requirements of insurance claims); vandalism (31% in England and Wales, and 42.6% in Scotland); and violence (62% in England and Wales, and 46% in Scotland).

Expectations of the results of reporting were mixed[23] but they were generally low, relayed in the reiterated phrases 'they never do anything'[24] and 'they don't bother', and suggesting that the homeless did not in the main believe that they counted as valid victims or complainants in the eyes of the police. Respondent

TABLE 7
Satisfaction with the Police (Among those Reporting Crimes)*

Type of crime reported	% satisfied**	% dissatisfied
Burglary	44	56
Theft	50	50
Damage to property	30	70
Violence	50	50
Threat	43	57
Sexual assault	75	25

* Although percentages are given, the total numbers are so small that great care should be taken when referring to this table.
** This was originally a 5-point scale (very satisfied, satisfied, neither satisfied nor dissatisfied, dissatisfied, very dissatisfied). The categories 'very satisfied' or 'satisfied' and 'dissatisfied'/'very dissatisfied' were collapsed for the purposes of the table.

19 said, for instance, 'I wouldn't [report a crime to the police] because as they see it, we're homeless and they're not really bothered about us getting beaten or anything else, or if stuff is stolen. All they're bothered about is, right, 'we'll write it down' and that's it and nothing gets dealt with.' Respondent 8 asked rhetorically 'What they gonna do? They won't do nothing. They will not and honestly they will not do anything, honestly they won't.' And Respondent 9 said:

> 'The police, the police, the police don't care about homeless people fighting. They let them carry on unless a knife comes out, then they do look into it. But apart from that, 'oh, it's only a few homeless people, let them carry on.' The police don't give a ... you know what I'm saying? The police don't care if you're homeless and you're fighting. They don't give a shit . ... They ain't going to waste their time. ... as far as they can see, we're just a nuisance. They'll tell us to get up and run.'

It is evident that the higher levels of victimisation experienced by the homeless are not mirrored in the numbers of crimes made known to the police. Some part of that lower propensity to report is undoubtedly linked to fear of intimidation[25] (Respondent 26 said, 'there's a lot of people too scared to say anything'), a trepidation about the consequences of making oneself known to the police,[26] and a general proscription on informing[27] (there is, said an official of St Mungo's, a 'culture of not grassing on anybody'). But it is also linked to a relatively greater dissatisfaction with the police response where a report *is* made. Almost three fifths (58%) of the respondents in the British Crime Survey declared themselves satisfied with the way in which the police handled incidents that they had come to know about, whilst the homeless in our survey reported the following somewhat lower rates (though it is important to recognise that Table 7 probably overestimates satisfaction with the police given the very low numbers in the sample reporting crimes compared with the public more generally):

The dissatisfaction revealed in the Table was given flesh by Respondent 24. The police are rather generally believed to be indifferent to the homeless:

> '... the police don't like homeless people, it's as simple as that. They'd rather we'd not be there, full stop. You know to the police we're more of a burden and a nuisance than we are anything else you know. Like I told you that time about when we was begging and I got a good kicking and the police come along like within a minute of it happening and their response was, well you shouldn't be sat there like should ya, d'ya know what I mean? You know that sort of thing, you know, not like, oh right, let's get their names, let's get their descriptions down ... you know there's me stood there with a split lip and a bloody nose and they're like, 'well move on then, d'ya know what I mean? Don't cause trouble and if you're not there in the first place then nothing will happen will it, you know.' They don't care. Even it's not so much that they don't care, it's just they see it as not their problem you know. They're there to police normal people as they say, you know, people that pay their taxes. I think that's part of the big problem that people see it as if you don't go to work and you don't pay taxes, if you don't pay taxes then you don't deserve the treatment that everybody else gets. You don't deserve to have security and you don't deserve to have protection because you don't pay for it, because you're a lazy, no good thug, d'ya know what I mean?'

In relation to reporting offences to others, the general results are as follows. Burglary: of the 50 people giving details, 41 said they had reported it to a friend, five to a housing worker and four to a social worker. Theft: of the 72 reporting it, the bulk, (42) did so to friends. The next largest groups were housing workers (5), social workers (7) and outreach workers (2). Damage: very few reported damage to anyone else: two to a housing worker, and individuals to social worker, centre staff, hostel or housing worker, and individuals to social, centre staff, hostel or housing worker. Violence: about 18 people reported having told someone else – two to a housing worker or social worker and then single numbers to others such as Citizens Advice Bureaux, staff at Crisis or a day centre worker. Sexual assault: four respondents said they had reported their sexual assault to another professional but not to the police. Two reported it to a doctor, and one each to the management of a day centre and to a social worker.

CONTACT WITH THE POLICE

Homeless people can enjoy a fraught relation with the police. At stake, it may be supposed, can be a contest about who controls (Herbert, 1997) and wields authority (Werthman and Piliavin, 1967; Piliavin and Briar, 1964) in the streets and public spaces where both groups spend so much of their time (Stinchcombe, 1968; Reiss, 1971). But there is more. So crime-ridden is the world in which the homeless live that they may take it that the police view them almost wholly as offenders rather than as victims: they may wish as a result to have no dealings with the police for fear of attracting unwelcome attention;[28] or they may believe simply that the police have little interest in their plight. Respondent 15 said 'you do get the odd copper like who [is] ... really understanding and all that. And then you'll get another one, just like he doesn't want to know, it's like homeless people don't exist to some of them. It's one of those things unfortunately. Being on the streets, you just have to learn to live with it, don't you?' And they can be sceptical about the general police capacity to improve their security. Respondent 4 said:

> 'I think it makes a difference if you're ... homeless and you're approaching them with an attitude or if you're off your face ... but if you're homeless and you're straight off and ... report a crime then they will treat you in the same way as they'll treat anybody off the street but it's still, you know it's not a big deal to them because it just happens all the time. What can you do about it?'

But the police *can* exceptionally act to effect. Respondent 25 talked of how two officers prevented him from being seriously hurt by passers-by: 'I'd just received a couple of kicks to the side of my legs ... and just as the two chaps in question grabbed me and dragged me up to my feet, two coppers come round the corner which was perfect timing. It's the only time they'll ever have perfect timing in my life. ... [They] threatened the blokes with being arrested if they didn't basically piss off into the clubs and behave themselves.' Note however that in this episode the police had observed the incident whilst on foot patrol rather than being summoned by the homeless victim himself.

Of all the formal and voluntary agencies, the homeless have the most frequent dealing with police officers (Ballintyne, 1999), and respondents were asked a number of questions about their occurrence and character. The frequency of 'proactive' contact by respondents is very low,[29] although, by contrast, contact initiated by the police via stops and questioning appears common, reflecting in some measure their relatively pronounced presence on the street (Waddington *et al.*, 2004). A little under a quarter of respondents (22%) had contacted the police to report a crime in the past year, whereas under 10% had done so to report a disturbance (9%) a traffic accident (6%) or an alarm going off (2%). By contrast, over four fifths (83%) of respondents had been stopped and questioned by the

TABLE 8
Number of Times Arrested in the Last Year

How often	Number	%
None	159	52
Once	68	22
2–5 times	51	17
6–10 times	14	5
Over 10 times	11	4

police in the past year. Of these, just under one quarter (24%) had been stopped once or twice and just under one half (48%) had been stopped between 1–9 times. Over half of all respondents (52%) that had been stopped (or 46% of all respondents including those that had never been stopped) had been stopped more than 10 times in the past year. Some respondents said they had been stopped '100 or more times', 'almost every other night', 'daily, sometimes three or four times a day' or 'so many I've lost count'. In most cases, nothing had happened as a result of the stop (74%). In a minority of cases, respondents had either been moved on (33%), arrested (28%) or warned or cautioned (18%). Overall, just under half of all respondents (48%) had been arrested at some point in the past year (see Table 8). By comparison a recent national self-report study conducted by the Home Office found that 3% of males and 1% of females had been arrested in the past year and, indeed, only one quarter of males (24%) and 6% of females had ever been arrested (Budd *et al.*, 2005).

If one were to sum up, it would be in David Downes' phrase that the homeless took it that they were over-controlled and under-protected by the police, and it could rankle. Reactions could be heated. Respondent 11 said 'I rate the police, I rate social workers, quangos, all these pseudo-intellectual power is out there, I rate them just below Islamic terrorists. And I avoid them like the plague.' Respondent 20 said 'I avoid the police like the plague you know. I really, I see them coming, I'll get up and go. If I'm sitting with a group of people and I see them coming in the distance, just because I'm sick of talking to them, you just need to, don't want to be known to them, don't want to, and I think pretty much everyone's like that.'[30] Very similarly, Respondent 2, an erstwhile self-confessed anarchist, said the '... things I've seen police do. I can't stand them. I really can't stand them. I just think they're another army and they're thugs.' He continued, 'people deal with [crime] themselves. I don't know many people that would go to the police if they were assaulted or abused in any way. I don't think they would go to the police, not any of my friends anyway.'

It is a mark of their social exclusion that there is a gulf between the homeless, on the one hand, and civil society and its established institutions (including the police), on the other. Respondent 25, who professed to 'get on well with all the police officers' in Cambridge, also said 'It's hard for homeless people to break the barrier, break down the barriers and talk to the police ...' Just as had been the case in the isolated and self-regulating hobohemias adjoining the Chicago railroads in the 1920s (Anderson, 1965), so the homeless of early 21st century England are obliged to make out in a relatively feral world in which they depend principally on themselves for a kind of rough justice and rudimentary social order. Respondent 22 reflected: 'I wouldn't rely on the police, mate. They'd be the last people I'd ask. You just have to rely on yourself and your own wits, you know. ... If I had to fight, then I'd fight, simple as that. Got no choice have you? 'cause on the street it's just the same as it is in the real world, mate, it's dog eat dog. Alright, there is comradeship, there's friendship but you don't trust everybody. In fact, you hardly ever trust anybody if the truth be known, you know.' And Respondent 24 said:

> 'Nobody will grass someone up no matter what. Like with me being head-butted and I know that it's something I didn't do, I still won't go to the police because if you get known as a grass, that's a lot worse and you're in for an even bigger kicking, you know, so nothing with the police will ever help. It's like ... security itself, there's nothing that can be done really because at the end of the day it's a fact, you know you're on the streets and unfortunately people on the streets are more arsehole like than normal people you know. Perhaps they've had a hard upbringing. I mean we all have, that's why we're here in the first place but I suppose some people don't handle it as well as others. You know like we've all had like pretty rough time of it but some of us handle it better than the others and those of us that can't handle it bully instead you know.'

ANTI-SOCIAL BEHAVIOUR

Respondents were asked about their experiences of what in policy circles is conventionally called anti-social behaviour, including harassment on the street, and during their time staying in hostels. Significant proportions had experienced each of the main examples suggested to them. Respondent 18, a woman, reported 'I just get frightened, I suppose, 'cause you see the gangs hanging around, you know, the young children hanging around the streets and some of the stories that you hear from the past of that sort of area, you start thinking and seeing issues yourself, seeing other people being victimised. I've seen a lot of that.' Another woman, a young American squatter, said 'the only time I've ever felt really, really like upset about, about the way people treat me on the street is like kids like that who just scream horrible things at you and you don't even know them and they just want to bother you.' Almost two-thirds reported having been insulted publicly whilst sleeping rough and one tenth said that someone had

TABLE 9
Experiemce of Anti-social Behaviour

Type of behaviour	Number	%
Harassed by others at a hostel	128	45
People throwing things at you	125	42
People insulting you publicly	192	64
Intimidated/harassed by drug dealers	114	38
Someone urinating on you	30	10

urinated on them. The answers are reported in Table 9, and they are illustrated by Respondent 12 who talked about how:

> 'Basically you get more problems from members of the public. The police don't bother you ... one guy was about to spit on me, ... and I had another guy, I think he was going to vomit on me. It's like two o'clock in the morning and I woke up and this guy, he was like retching you know, and I woke up and he just again, turned around and walked away. I was almost mugged once with these two guys, they woke me up cause I've sleep on my bag. I used the bag as a pillow and they woke me up, they were trying to pull the bag and I woke up and they said "where's the money, where's the money?"'

It is not possible to find comparable figures of how often the wider population experienced anti-social behaviour in the British Crime Survey. Perhaps because householders are not so often and directly exposed to incivilities, that survey measures people's *perceptions* of anti-social behaviour in 'their area' instead. One of its key indicators is 'People being drunk or rowdy in public places' – presumably an instance of the homeless being held to be more sinning than sinned against – and there was also a question about 'People using or dealing drugs', and 25% of the BCS interviewees defined their presence as a local problem.

Two matters should be particularly observed about such a marked exposure to insult and incivility. There is an inevitable aggravation of the homeless person's sense of fear (Cohen and Sokolowsky; Jackson, 2004), danger and powerlessness (Shiner, 1995). People in hostels and on the street experience the world as an insecure, uncertain and troubled place where they are obliged continually to be wary. Respondent 16 said for example that:

> 'Rough sleeping is quite tough stuff. It is rough. I mean it's quite hard because you get moved from the police, you're not allowed to sleep in one place. Then you get waked up at night time. But cold weather, if it's not summer, it's quite hard to sleep outside actually. You can't even sleep

sometimes. Sometimes you got to make sure that you don't fall in deep sleep because some people can come and put the fire on you. I've never seen but I heard someone saying that.'

Fear could weigh especially heavy on women (D'Ercole and Struening, 1990) where harassment[31] and the risk of attack tend often to be linked to anxieties about rape and sexual assault (Ferraro, 1995). Respondent 19 talked about how frightening hostels could be: 'they have separate like doors, say like women's on one side and blokes on the other. But it's still scary being on your own as a woman. Even in a couple really, it's still scary because ... for women they can still get you at night, so it's scary really.' And Respondent 6, a homeless woman living in Oxford, powerfully conveyed how alarming victims' stories could circulate amongst the homeless to give meaning to the dangers of the street:

> 'There have been some cases where girls have been taken advantage of. There's also been cases where guys have been abused. I mean have you heard about this woman ... who got stabbed to death ... Jack the Ripper and the guy had only been out of prison about, he'd been in for eleven years for murder and he come out. The thing was, I'm not gonna say what happened ... but she was stabbed to death and chucked in the river. ... She was a very nice lady. I only met her one time and she got stabbed to death and chucked in the river.'

And, second, insult and incivility may be construed as yet further attacks on whatever conception of dignity and worth the homeless may retain. One of the major, recurrent themes that permeated the open interviews was an emphasis on the importance of *respect*. Richard Sennett has talked about that 'peculiar lack of respect which consists of not being seen, not being accounted as full human beings' (Sennett, 2003: p. 13). Many of those living rough share that social invisibility[32] and they wished strenuously to convey that they too were entitled to some esteem. The attitude of many, Respondent 11 said:

> 'certainly winds people up who are intelligent and have had a life before. You know, that used to have a family, that used to earn 30 grand a year. You know, I mean I used to do a lot and I'm a capable talented guy and you know, I just treated like some sort of like ... and when I was in hospital, I mean I was called severely mentally ill and made to feel like a criminal retard. Just I mean I just couldn't do anything, just sort of like you know, justified that I was more than that. And much more than that.'

The homeless persons' marginality; their fall from the respectable world; their constant and often unwelcome association with stigmatised companions who are drunks, drug-abusers and beggars,[33] their shameful exposure to the gaze of bystanders; and continual abuse (which Respondent 23 called the 'verbal diarrhoea'); underscored a pervasive feeling of moral, physical and social degradation that was reinforced and objectified by the presence of others who were degraded. Just as the inmate in Sykes' (1958: p. 77) study of the New Jersey State Prison remarked, 'The worst thing about prison is you have to live with other prisoners,' so the homeless could find the company of other homeless people symbolically disquieting.

It was a consequence that different homeless people tried often to distance themselves from one another, advertising their decency and, one may suppose, attempting to preserve some standing, by comparing themselves favourably with those lower in the moral ranks, just as poor Black men did in Elijah Anderson's (1978) study of 'a place on the corner' or poor whites once did in the southern states of the USA. Public humiliation inevitably framed and magnified the significance of what were already oppressively high levels of criminal victimisation. It was challenged repeatedly as those who were interviewed protested that they did actually have a legitimate claim to social merit, underscoring Dillon's (1995: p. 1) observation that 'Self-respect is undoubtedly something of great value. Perhaps those who lack it know this best ... '.

Take Respondent 5 who said of his time in London, 'they don't care d'ya know what I mean, they see you as a scumbag. ... They walk around as if you own something d'ya know what I mean? Do this, do that and they try and kick you out, d'ya know what I mean? Make sarky comments and that. They think you're a bum. "Why don't you go and get a job if you don't like it" and all this.' Respondent 9 said 'They shouldn't look at a person 'cause they're homeless. A homeless person has as much need as a person who's living in a house. This is what the police don't seem to understand. Don't look at me 'cause I'm homeless and think oh, and I'm dirty, I'm a nobody. I'm a human being same as you, so why should you look down on me and say, "oh he's homeless, fuck 'em." This is what they do.' Respondent 26 said 'I mean the older [police officers], some of them are okay. Yeah, they know, do you know what I mean? But the young ones, they can cause you so much hassle at night, they treat you like dirt 'cause you're on the street anyway, you know, they treat you like shit, they really do.' And Respondent 7 said simply it is 'like I'm on show, like a dummy in a shop ... so you're not like ... one of society'. The risk, of course, is that those who are so classified and treated may well become transformed in the process. As Rhodes (2004: p. 179) argued, 'Through a mutually reinforcing circuit, the available opportunities for how to be a person at a given historical moment interact with that moment's available practices for naming and interpreting human behaviour.' Some part of the public and private character of homeless people may be presumed to arise out of such self-fulfilling prophecies.

If only there could be greater understanding, a lessening of social distance, many homeless people said. Respondent 20, for instance, reflected of the defects in the training of the police and community support officers:

'I know it's hard 'cause [the police] got to be trained in the law and all that sort of stuff but yeah, maybe some sort of, some maybe a little bit of psychology with it you know, like ... a bit of a humanitarian teaching, to sort of understand. ... I don't know what training [the Community Support Officers] are given but maybe them especially, 'cause they seem to have a bit more time and a lot of them are moving into the police force, maybe while they're doing that, they do some sort of, I don't know some sort of work that involves working with the homeless like ... finding out what makes people tick.'

Part of the symbolic work done by some homeless people on the street took the form of trying to effect a distance from their publicly-devalued selves and the selves of stigmatised others. Respondent 3 certainly did so: 'the young people are mainly the ones using the drugs and they have very poor standards of personal hygiene because they don't care about it ... I try to keep myself tidy so that people don't look at me because ... when I've been a little more unkempt myself, people do notice it. You do alienate them and that's what puts me off. I try to dress tidily and keep myself clean because it do alienate, definitely, it's hurtful ... when people look down on you. I hate that.' Respondent 4 echoed him: 'I do my best to keep myself clean and normally I've got bits and piece of jobs so I've got friends where I can go and wash and shower. My clothes are dirty but nobody can ever guess that I'm homeless usually because I'm a student or whatever. So I do my best to look like a student or do my best, I've got a big backpack, I'm travelling, so I just look like a tourist, it's as simple as that.'

Respondent 8 wished that he could change some of the ways in which homeless people were defined: 'if every town only listened to us, well people like myself. I'm not being big-headed but I mean, listen to people like us, there's so much information we can give and help with. I'd love to do it, I really, really would. ... Now that I've been homeless myself and seen it as it really is ... now my eyes are open and I'd say good 70% of them are genuinely, there's so much talent there, untapped talent. I reckon 90% of all heroin users have got hidden talents, amazing hidden talents as well. Lot of them have got bloody degrees and you know are either artists or poets or song writers or, there's just so much untapped talent.' Respondent 9 said: '[the police and authorities] need to be taken out for a month and spend a month on the streets for a month. No food, no mobile phones, no nothing. ... all I want you to tell them [is] to go out there and experience homelessness. ... People sitting down and saying it's like "I've done and lived it," it's not the same unless you go out there and let them experience it for their self. That's what they need to do and then find out how hard it is when you're homeless to get things that you can't get.' The search for respect and a valued identity is perhaps one of the starkest and most poignant findings of our survey, and it should be borne in mind as the separate Tables in this report are studied.

TABLE 10
Worry in Different Locations

Worried about	Sleeping rough % (n = 295)	'Where you live' % (n = 77)	In a hostel % (n = 203)
Being assaulted	46	14	16
Being robbed	42	19	33
Being sexually assaulted	15	5	7
Being harassed	36	21	17
Being threatened	33	18	17
Being arrested	33	6	10
Mistreated by police	36	10	13

SAFETY AND SECURITY

Respondents were then asked a series of questions about safety and security, beginning with some questions about the extent to which they worried about particular circumstances such as being assaulted, robbed, and arrested. They were asked to compare their experiences and fears whilst sleeping rough, whilst in the place where they live (where relevant) and whilst in a hostel. The answers to questions about safety are reported in Table 10, and they may be compared with the worries expressed by the wider population: the 2003/4 BCS showed that 16% of those interviewed had a high level of worry about violent crime, and 13% about burglary. The homeless were often much more worried about safety, and they were worried for good reason.

It is evident that the homeless are obliged incessantly to be vigilant and 'streetwise'. Respondent 4 said: 'I think part of the reason why I've been successful in not being assaulted is, you're completely aware of it, you're completely aware, you know what time [it is], what kind of people to avoid, or how to deal with people who are aggressive towards you, like ... how to deal with them and that.'

When asked directly to compare their sense of security in hostels and on the streets, a little over one half of respondents (55%) said that they felt hostels were safer than sleeping rough. After all, public space can be dangerous. Respondent 22 talked, for instance, of his experience of living in central Birmingham: 'I was sleeping in the Bull Ring, people throwing bottles, glass bottles. One hit me on the head, one hit me on the elbow from you know, quite high up 'cause he had a stairwell coming down, like that. They were thrown from the stairwell. ... Just drunk office workers, had too much to drink, thought they'd take it out on the homeless people, you know?' And Respondent 25 spoke of how he had had 'several occasions where some drunks or alkies out on a Friday night [were] either throwing bottles or went over and started kicking or punching or pulling me to my feet.'

Small numbers of our respondents said that levels of safety on the street and hostel were the same (3%) or 'it depends on the type of hostel' (2%), and just under two fifths of respondents (39%) said that they felt safer sleeping rough than in a hostel. It is noteworthy that one of the chief sources of insecurity on the streets was said to be zealous regulation and mistreatment by the police, and there were frequent but not wholly consistent complaints about petty police harassment in public places[34] and squats. Respondent 8 complained of 'just moving you on, just hassle, hassle and you don't need it'. And he gave an illustration:

> 'So two weeks someone, three weeks ago somebody was asleep, ... [the police officer's] been looking for this one, asleep in a doorway, right? Trying to wake up, wouldn't wake up, so he's kicked him in his foot to wake him up right? 'What you're kicking him for?' He said, 'I'm not kicking you, I'm tapping you with my foot', so ______ gone mad and been nicked [and now] he's in court for it. Now he's gonna get found guilty because he's up against the police's word. They kicked him, they kicked him, d'ya know what I mean? How can you kick someone awake? How can you tap someone with your foot? You know, if I wanted to wake up, there's ways to wake you up. You know, I'd stand and call you or something, d'ya know what I mean? Or I'd get somebody, a witness or what have you. It's wrong what they're doing, some of these people and as I say you can't, not all of them. ... There are lots of good ones there, you know lots of good ones but ... the young ones should be able to come and talk to people like us and find out what we're about because we're not scary. We don't hurt nobody. Alright, there's one or two loud mouths, alkies, junkies, [but they should] come and talk to us, come and talk to us, don't, you know, wait until you're gonna nick or something ... we're human d'ya know what I mean? I mean, I've got to be honest, there's a good eight or nine stop and chat to me like, d'ya know what I mean, fair play, but no if only they stopped, took the time out, or had little courses even about us. D'ya know what I mean, we're not hostile or nuffin' or come into the shelter and have little meetings once a week or something just to get us not to be scared. You know 'cos people are so scared of them.'

Hostels at least provided protection from the police and from members of the public who were wont to attack and humiliate them, especially when bars, clubs and pubs closed. They were relatively private institutions that shielded the homeless from such interference by outsiders. Respondent 5 said that his present hostel was 'not too bad. You have to be out early in the morning but you do feel safe, yeah, a lot safer than when you're out there 'cos you never know what's round the corner. You're likely to get a load of drunks come back from a club and they can see you, d'ya know what I mean?'

But hostels could offer only limited security against the *insider*. It was Respondent 5 again who said of his earlier experience of hostels: 'You'd have to sleep with your clothes on because you'd wake up in the morning and then your trainers and all that would be gone.' Hostels were said often to be awash with drugs,[35] unsafe internally, lacking walls to shield, doors to close and cupboards and lockers to secure; they could be unwholesome[36] and hazardous to health;[37] they housed untrustworthy and possibly dangerous people,[38] dismissed characteristically by one, Respondent 20, as 'just too many loonies,' and by another, Respondent 25, as 'junkies, thieves, people constantly harassing you about this, that or the other ... people overdosing right outside my room'; and they were marked by frequent bickering about claims to beds, possessions and space. Respondent 7 remarked 'people can argue over chairs and which dorm they're in or somebody's got, somebody's going into their bed or someone's taken their bed. Clothes go missing and things like that.'

Although those who were interviewed were not always in agreement, many respondents tended to see their fellow hostel occupants as threatening, disagreeable and untrustworthy (Camden and Islington Council, 2004: p. 25). Respondent 1 said, for example, 'you get any Tom, Dick or Harry coming in the dorm ... and they're fucking disgusting, man.' Respondent 7 said 'There's always problems 'cos people have got problems there. They sort of like put their problems on you kind of thing. ... If ... say someone doesn't like some way the way you dress, your hair's cut or whatever, someone might, d'ya understand what I mean, they might verbally abuse, but that can get out of hand, so you've gotta [protect] yourself and when you [protect] yourself you get thrown out because the staff never intervene. ...' And others said pictorially:

> 'You've got one room, you've got thirty people in this one room. A third of them are smack heads, a third of them at least are alcoholics and the other third just don't want to be involved, yeah? And you've got the alcoholics and the smack heads that don't often get on together. So you've got all the atmosphere there, d'ya know what I mean, and you walk in and you can feel the atmosphere straight away ...' (Respondent 21).

> 'You've never seen a place like it in your life. I was shocked. I thought I was back in the 19th century. I was in this bed, they put me in this thing with all these, I mean I have nothing against anyone, but I mean they're not right in the head. And I tell you, they frightened the life out of me. I never went back there again. They closed it down in the end, it was because it was, it was disgraceful. You had people wandering around in a daze all night long, standing over you as you were sleeping and things like that, frightening place. Terrified, yeah I was, and I wasn't scared of much then, do you know what I mean? But I mean you've got a seven foot six geezer standing

TABLE 11
Do the Following Make You Feel Safer or Less Safe? %

	Safer	Less safe
CCTV	48	23
Bright lighting	48	30
Visible policing	47	31
Other rough sleepers close by	58	21
Being visible to the public	29	53
Being near pubs and clubs	12	76

over the top of you, bending down over you, you're wondering like it's three o'clock in the morning.' (Respondent 22).

' The trouble is, 'cos of the way things are, that a lot of homeless people don't want to go to [hostels] because there are things that have happened, you know ... they're not interested in going to a hostel, they'd rather live on the street, you know because you could meet someone, say, in a hostel, you know, who makes out to be your friend and all that and the next thing they could stab ya. You get your giro or something one day, or whatever, it's money, they could stab you to death. I've heard of it you know.' (Respondent 26).

Again, like the prisoners with whom they share so much in common, including lives continually oscillating between incarceration and homelessness,[39] those residing in hostels had always to be alert to challenge and provocation lest they appear weak and vulnerable before their fellow residents. After all, where other homeless people are seen as potential predators or potential prey, and where trust in the police and authorities is fragile, the homeless have to rely on their own rough presence to deter aggression, and such a reliance could itself amplify violence. Respondent 4, living in an Oxford hostel, said 'if there's a potential for me to argue with somebody, everyone else is also there watching ... if there was like a potential for violence between you and another person, and you're both trying to avoid losing like psychological ground ... you're careful about how you carry [yourself] so that person doesn't get the idea that you're an easy target ...[or] you're in any way intimidated by him. ...'

Respondents were shown a list containing a series of items, including CCTV (closed circuit television),[40] bright lighting and the presence of others sleeping rough, and asked whether each made them feel safer or less safe. Their answers, summarised in Table 11, indicate somewhat mixed feelings in relation to a number of factors, though there are others such as proximity to licensed premises that appear to be experienced largely negatively. Reinforcing what we shall have to say later about the perpetrators of crimes against the homeless, respondents were also generally negative about the consequences of being visible to the public – being almost twice as likely to say that they felt less safe as a consequence.

One difficulty emerged: crime prevention devices and stratagems can have a contradictory impact and significance for those who are at once frequent victims, frequent offenders and frequently 'moved on'. Respondent 25, for instance, viewed CCTV as a 'a double-edged sword. On the one hand, if you're in the view of the CCTV, if you get beaten, they can try and trace them, but on the other hand, a lot of people say that CCTV is used directly sort of to inform the police where people are and then they get moved on ... ' And an increased police presence:

> 'would obviously make it safer but because of the barrier between the police and the homeless, would make the homeless feel less safe because of constant police presence you know. But the majority of them will probably have some sort of substance they shouldn't have somewhere and will be constantly scared of having it taken off them. 'Cos a lot of them need something just to be able to cope with being on the streets ...'

The homeless must be particularly mindful of how physical space affects risk. Four fifths (80%) of respondents said that they attempted to avoid rough sleeping as a means of increasing their safety. Three fifths (60%) said they used hostels in the same way, though just under a third (30%) said they avoided hostels in order to increase their safety. Over half (54%) stayed in squats and a little under half (45%) in derelict buildings.

There is a tendency to seek safety, on the one hand, in places where the public are to be found, and where what Jane Jacobs (1961) once called 'eyes on the street' offer a limited reassurance that attacks will be witnessed, reported and perhaps curtailed. Respondent 18, a woman, said 'I would try to make my way to where there's lots of people, lots and lots and lots of people. That's what I done when I was on the streets. ... Like Victoria Station, somewhere like that or maybe Trafalgar Square 'cause I used to sleep up on St Martin-in-the-Fields steps, by there sometimes. So yeah, I'd probably try to find crowds of people or go where it's really, really busy, you know, somewhere like Leicester Square, places like that.' Yet Table 12 shows that the homeless are actually most at risk of burglary and offences of violence from the general public. Take Respondent 13's account of the hazards presented by the public to those who sleep rough:

> 'Sleeping outside the church, someone'd come up and kick you in the back, could be a kid you know, you know, he thinks you're an old tramp ... Someone'd come up and kick you in the back or – an example in Peckham, in Burgess Park – fella was killed in his tent. They set his tent alight. He

TABLE 12
The Perpetrators of Crime Against Homeless People**

Offence	Member of the public		Family		Friend		Someone where you live		A rough sleeper		Police	
	No.	%	No.	%	No.	%	No.	%	No.	%	No.	%
Burglary	30	42	0	0	7	10	14	20	12	17	8	11
Theft	72	32	1	<1	30	13	32	14	90	40	2	<1
Criminal damage – property	36	40	1	<1	15	17	15	17	19	21	4	4
Damage – other	22	47	0	0	10	21	4	8	9	19	2	4
Violence	98	48	3	1	19	9	17	8	52	26	13	6
Threats	100	49	0	0	22	11	20	10	52	25	10	5
Sexual assault	10	45	1	4	6	27	1	4	4	18	0	0

** The % figures in each table are of the sub-sample in each category that reported experiencing each particular form of victimisation. In some cses the overall numbers are very small and the % figures should therefore be treated with caution. The figures relating to the police as perpetrators probably referred to actions taken in searching premises, removing items of evidence and making arrests.

> was in his tent, he got a tent. ... Set it alight, boom, things like that. And that's what you have to watch where you go because people come down.'

The homeless may as an alternative go to secluded places where few people visit (Warnes *et al.*, 2003: p. 75) and where they will be less exposed to danger from the public.[41] Respondent 12 said 'What I like to do is get into a place, a doorway where it wouldn't be accessible in front of the public which are very few places there are. That's a case of finding them but other than that, there's not an awful lot you can do.' Respondent 22 said 'it could be a car park, could be a rubbish tip like where you've got to step in the rubbish, sleep on the step, you close the doors, it keeps out the wind. You could be living in a park, round the back of a fence, under the bushes, put a cardboard down and sleep there. As long as you're dry and you're out of the wind, yeah. ... If tell you there's security, there is no security. The only security you got is where you live, used to live should I say. Best places is out of the way, that's the way to get secure otherwise, there is no security.' And Respondent 5, living in Oxford, said 'I'll go like a college somewhere like that, where the gates are locked, d'ya know what I mean? I mean I can go somewhere which is sheltered and I know no one's gonna be there for the whole night. And then I'll leave there say seven in the morning and then just come straight down to here.'

There is however a companion possibility of being moved on by the police or others from public places, and they must be selected with care – harassment, risk and shelter having to be weighed against one another. Respondent 9 said of London:

> 'Some ... go down Oxford Street [to sleep in] shop doorways. I wouldn't do this. Shop doorways I don't sleep in. I always find somewhere in a park or back of a shop. I would never sleep in a park, on a bench, or in any park, because number one, the park keepers you can't do this, you got to get up, you got to go. It's the police or it's the security. So "no", do you know what I mean? You find somewhere, back of church, anything, church, front of church but not in Oxford Street ... you don't do that, you don't do that.'

What appears to work for many is avoidance behaviour. Respondent 18, a woman, said 'a lot of the time – I mean even when I was younger – I spent a lot of time on my own, loads and loads of time on my own. I used to try and steer away from all these people'. Respondent 26 said 'I always make sure that nobody knows where I am ... Most places I used to sleep is like you know, the tall wheelie bins? Like you can lock them from the inside, so I used to get in them, do you know what I mean? A lot of me other mates like sleep in doorways and that. I found that the times I done that, you've got people who are drunk on the streets and that and hey just come and they give you a kick ...' And safety may be found where one is ringed by a few trusted companions: 'As far as safety's concerned,' Respondent 15 said, 'like the only thing I'd say is ... try and find somewhere out of the way so you're not on any main streets. Always make sure you're never by yourself 'cause you never know what's around the next [corner].' One woman, Respondent 19, would not venture out without her partners; 'Yeah, my partner looks after me and makes sure that nothing happens to me ... [We're] always together, yeah.' Respondent 21 recalled how his allies had repelled an attack: 'I've been close to being a victim of crime [but] ... there was about eight of us in the one place and the people realised there was quite a few of us there, otherwise they would have come and caused trouble with us, d'ya know what I mean?' And Respondent 9 said:

> 'There was three of us and we live in a park and then we go into a library in Holborn and we was all like, we was alright. But they'll say, you got, you got, a lot of these, they sleep in groups of ten and ... they're protecting each other. This is how homelessness is out there. If you're vulnerable, then people will come and take. I'm seen it. But if you're streetwise, they can't do it. They can't take liberties, so to speak. I won't accept that. ... That's why they sleep in their gangs of six and seven because they feel safe in them. ... boys like to attack the homeless people. It's been done. Kick them ... I've seen it. ... to the police you're nobody, so where you going to get help from? There's no safety out there. The police don't give a shit cause you're homeless, so where you going to get help from? There's nobody to help you.'

But the presence of other homeless people was certainly not a safeguard. Table 12 shows that the second largest group of perpetrators of offences against the homeless are the homeless themselves, and the homeless do not necessarily trust one another. An outreach worker remarked that clusters of people can lead to 'a rough sleeping scene with lots of alcohol and drugs' and violence. One instance given by respondent 20 was that of a car park in Cambridge: 'there's a car park a lot of people go to, Level D, but I've never been there myself. But there's usually a fair few of them there and I think they get pretty much left alone there. 'Cause there's a hot air thing there that keeps them warm and stuff. I think they pretty much leave them alone there but sometimes there's trouble. Whenever you get a large group of people who are homeless, there's always a lot a drinking and drugs and whatever for various reasons. And that tends to instigate trouble and so on.' Respondent 16 remarked where 'you get, well a lot of mental and drug people on the streets and drinking people ... sometimes you get attacked as well. But it's more dangerous when you sleep at night, probably may get killed as well, never know.' Respondent 22 described the scene at the former Bull Ring in Birmingham: 'you could trust the alcoholics cause they ain't gonna ... the drug addicts, you could never turn your back on 'em, mate, cause it was too dangerous. 'Cause like at the end of the day, all they want to get is the next hit. Don't worry about who they hurt to get it, you know. That's the truth mate, that's the truth. In the Bull Ring, it was, you've never been in a place like it in your life, mate, never seen a place like it. So, the lowest form of humanity.' Respondent 11 added, 'people get very aggressive and occasionally your best mates can turn against you and you know, because if you're drinking yourself, you get, you turn into an asshole.' It is a scene where forms of criminal exploitation such as 'taxing' (stronger beggars extorting money and social security from those who are weaker) can abound. Respondent 9 remarked:

> 'Most of the fighting down here is done amongst their own self because someone's got money, someone needs a drink. Or someone's got drugs and someone wants them and this is where the fighting comes from all the time. It's not nobody coming outside and doing it. It's amongst their self. I ain't got no money, I want a can of beer yesterday, so what? You can fight over a can of beer. This is where the trouble comes from or over a bag of heroin. That's where the trouble, it doesn't come from outside, it comes from amongst their own – homeless are fighting each other over drugs and drink. That's what it's all 'oh, you stole my clothes, you stole my sandals.' This is there it's all coming from.'

Especially exposed are naive newcomers who are vulnerable to theft and assault and may be at risk of losing even their shoes and coats. Numbers thus provide scant security, but they do tend never the less to swell because they attract and are attracted by the provision of special services,[42] hostels, soup runs and the like in particular districts. The City of Westminster is one such especially dense area,[43] attractive because it is heavily policed and relatively secure, known by reputation to those who are not native Londoners, a sanctuary for those who have been displaced by violent attacks elsewhere,[44] and a place abounding in tourists and others from whom one can beg.[45] for rather different reasons, other attractive areas are Camden (because of its intermittently lively drugs market and the tourists visiting the Camden Lock market) and the City of London (which is quieter, especially appealing to older rough sleepers, and, like the City of Westminster, subject to intense security within the socalled 'ring of steel'[46]

SELF-REPORTED OFFENDING

Finally, respondents were asked about their own offending. They were provided with a list of possible offences and asked to report whether they had ever done any of them and, if so, whether they had done so in the past year. The results are summarised in Table 13.

A national self-report study of offending by adults in the United Kingdom allows for some comparison with the figures in Table 13 (Budd *et al.*, 2005) though the offence categories are not precisely comparable with our survey. However, where fairly direct comparison is possible, as expected, the national self-report survey generally shows lower levels of lifetime and recent offending.

TABLE 13
Self-Reported Offending

Offence	% Ever	% In last year
Taken car/motormike without permission	25	4
Drunk driving	27	4
Criminal damage	25	8
Theft from a shop	55	30
Theft from someone's house	13	2
Snatched purse/bag etc	4	<1
Burglary	19	4
Use stolen credit/debit card	21	10
Bought/sold stolen goods	47	27
Threatened someone with a weapon	19	10
Carried a weapon	35	21
Got into a fight in public	53	34
Bought drugs	63	52
Sold drugs	20	10
Beat up or hurt someone	29	14

Thus, within the national sample lifetime self-reported burglary was four percent for males and one percent for females, compared with 19% overall in our sample. Similarly, where only four percent of males in the national sample said they had ever sold drugs and one and a half percent said they had done so in the past year, the respective proportions in the homeless survey were 20% and 10%[47]. This general picture is reinforced by other, small surveys which have reported even higher rates of offending and repeat offending by the homeless, albeit mostly of minor crimes (Ballintyne, 1994, pp. iv and v; City of Westminster, 2002). After all, homelessness can be a major catalyst and amplifier of offending: homeless people are often thrust out of troubled homes,[48] care institutions, mental hospitals or prisons[49] into areas of high crime[50] where they are highly visible to the police, passers-by and community support officers. They are less tightly regulated informally, more tightly regulated formally; more distressed; more exposed to drugs, drink and inducements to prostitution; sometimes more prone to violence (indeed sometimes being driven on to the street *because* of their violence (North *et al.*, 1994)); sometimes obliged to defend themselves or retaliate in the relatively unprotected world of the street and hostel;[51] and more needy than those who are securely housed and financed (Carlen, 1996; Hagan *et al.*, 1997). It is not perhaps remarkable that high figures of recorded offending are a result (Stinchcombe, 1968) and, as we have observed, the victims of that offending are often other homeless people who are conveniently within reach.[52]

CONCLUSION

We have reached a few broad conclusions. First, there are, as one might expect, high levels of victimisation among individuals who are homeless. Individuals who are homeless are often victims of anti-social behaviour and incivilities, and yet at the same time they feel under-protected and unduly harassed by the police. The data in this study show very high levels of violence and threats against the homeless, far in excess of the levels experienced in the general population. Thus, over half of our respondents reported having been a victim of violence in the past year compared with approximately four percent of the general population. In addition, eight percent had been a victim of a sexual assault whereas the prevalence of such offences in the general population is insufficient to register in the British Crime Survey. Other forms of criminal victimization are equally over-represented within this population.

What appears starkly is how ill-defended the homeless are, how little they believe any formal authority has treated them as a group which requires protection and support, and how some part of their high rate of offending must as a result be explained by a perceived need to resort to extra-legal violence. Levels of trust and confidence in the police are extremely low among the homeless population and the likelihood that victimization will be reported is much diminished – further exacerbating the absence of protection and trust as well as boosting levels of offending. If Mike Hough was right when he argued that the effectiveness of policing rests on legitimacy, and legitimacy on a perception of fair procedures; fair outcomes; helpfulness and concern for the policed; and civil and even-handed treatment (Hough, 2004), it is clear that the homeless believe that they are poorly served.

One very striking finding is the prominent position of the general public as perpetrators of crimes against homeless people. In most major categories of criminal victimization – burglary, violence, threats, sexual assault, and criminal damage – respondents reported that the perpetrator had been a member of the public. The exception was theft where other homeless people appear slightly more likely to have been the perpetrators than were members of the public. Violence, threats, intimidation and abuse from the public, particularly where the latter are intoxicated, appear to be an everyday reality for the homeless population. Not only are the homeless unprotected, but their very identity can make them a target of ill-treatment. In all this, they may be said loosely to resemble the victims of what the Americans would call hate crime: 'the violence of intolerance and bigotry, intended to hurt and intimidate someone because of their race, ethnicity, national origin, religious, sexual orientation, or disability (United States Department of Justice, 2001: p. 1). If there is a moral continuum of victimisation to be traced, with Christie's 'ideal victim' (Christie, 1986) at one pole, the homeless hover near the other end where their very legitimacy *as* victims is in doubt, undermined by spoiled identities and a primary public status as offenders. Victims, it has been observed repeatedly, are socially constructed

(Holstein and Miller, 1990), and part of that work of construction entails processes of symbolic categorisation, sifting and segregation. Representations of victims as victims are clearest when they are most uncluttered, challenged by little disconcerting moral information, and free of allegations of possible 'provocation' or 'precipitation'. The homeless are not so clearly defined and, in all this, there are resonances of the Charity Organisation Society's distinction between the deserving and undeserving poor. Homeless people may be 'seen less [by some] as victims and more as a nuisance,'[53] not as people with problems but as a social problem in themselves. In the City of Westminster, for instance, there is a commitment to balancing what is called the 'social care agenda' (directed at the vulnerable and the socially excluded) with an 'enforcement agenda' (aimed at aggressive begging, incivilities and public drinking.)[54]

A central theme of our analysis is the fact that the homeless in hostels and on the street experience the world as an insecure, unpredictable and troubled place where they are obliged continually to be guarded and suspicious. This, we argue, is the almost inevitable product of the fear, danger and powerlessness that is at the core of much of the experience of rough sleeping. Many of those living rough take themselves to be socially invisible. The homeless feel – or perhaps more accurately are made to feel – marginal, apart from the respectable world, and heavily stigmatised. Theirs is a world of exposure to frequent if not continual abuse, and one in which they are denied 'respect'. The extraordinarily high levels of victimization, and the failure of formal agencies, especially the police, to provide protection, are the clearest indication of this absence of respect and of the denial of the 'rights' usually associated with full citizenship.

No doubt our findings sometimes reproduce what Peter Manning once called 'the "under-dog's" narrow, often very simplistic view of large complex social segments. ...' (Manning, 1975). After all, the views of our subjects cannot be taken to represent a wholly informed commentary on the political economy of homelessness, risk and control. No doubt, too, parts of what we were told can be challenged by other evidence and by the perspectives of other principals, but the outcome is a glimpse of a remarkable world-view. It conveys something of how the homeless make sense of their interlocking experiences of control, safety, victimisation and offending, and it is very real in its consequences. We believe that it should add to public understanding of a largely concealed, distorted and unappreciated problem.

NOTES

1 It was illuminating, for instance, that the Westminster City Guardian to whom one of us spoke was uncertain whether they should be reckoned part of the community which his organisation protected.
2 Based on Hoyt *et al.* (2004).
3 Respondent 20 said poignantly about sleeping rough in Cambridge: 'I'd say the majority suffer from some form of depression continuously but because I don't know how much is drug-based

150

and how much you laugh and joke with your friends, you get drunk, you're still, at the end of the day, it's you that lies here in the bushes by yourself and you're still, and you wake up there the next morning or two hours later or whatever it might be and it's still you and at night. And it's got to get to everyone at some point.'

4 A large contemporaneous survey reported that 40% have a 'mental health problem', 37% alcohol 'problems' and a comparable number drugs 'problems' (St Mungo's, 2004).

5 The same survey showed that 44% of those who were parents had lost touch with their children, and 50% had 'no next of kin details'.

6 Although street drinking and begging are not co-extensive with rough sleeping, a survey of the London boroughs of Camden and Islington and published late 2000 of street drinking and begging is quite revealing. 'Beggars and street drinkers', it stated, 'express a strong desire not to be treated just as a problem. Sixteen per cent of them say there's nothing good at all about being on the streets ... 15% say the police, and 13% say the aggression and violence.' (Camden and Islington Council, 2000: p. 5).

7 And it is an invisibility which some homeless people themselves believe to be quite deliberately engineered. One who was interviewed for this survey [Respondent 22] said: 'I mean if you slept in the station, you're moved on because you're a nuisance, right? But see the public don't want to see this, see the people on the street. They don't want to see them sleeping in doorways or under cars and things like that. They don't want to see that. They want, you know, to 'put it away, ignore it'.'

8 According to a 1998 survey analysed in Ballintyne (1999: p. 17), 21% of homeless people reported crimes to the police compared with 44% of those interviewed for the British Crime Survey.

9 See Victim Support News Release, 'New rights for victims of crime in Europe – Homeless persons project', 2003: 'The Victim Support service based in Glasgow discovered that out of an estimated 6,500 homeless people in Glasgow (17), very few had accessed their service. Although a number of organisations in this area offered assistance to this client group, none dealt specifically with the problems affecting homeless victims of crime. ...' Victim Support Westminster has appointed two out-reach workers precisely to overcome the problems presented by low police referrals and self-referrals.

10 See Simmons and Dodd (2003: p. 11). For an essay reflecting on the effects of such omissions, see Young (2004: esp. p. 17).

11 Although, to be sure, the scheme did unusually make provision for two outreach workers.

12 As Meddings and Levey (2000) argue, 'despite violence being a serious side of homeless life, it has not generally been addressed in the literature.' The problem of neglect is not, of course, confined to England and Wales. A report to the California Legislature observed, for instance, 'The extent and nature of homeless victimization in California has not been systematically tracked and therefore quantified because of the lack of reporting by homeless victims and because there is no centralized data-collection system in place which identified victims as being homeless.' (California Department of Justice, 2002: p. vii).

13 Thus *The Observer* newspaper, 30 April 2000, claimed that hostility was amplified by reports about activities such as a spate of aggressive begging by Romanians in London.

14 Clear beggars from streets, says Blair, *The Times*, 7 January 1997.

15 See *The Times*, 5 August, 2004.

16 A poster issued by Thames Reach Bondway reads 'can you spare 20p for a cup of tea? How about £10 for a bag of heroin? Or £12 for a rock of crack? The money you give to those who beg may help keep them on the streets. It may even help to buy the drugs that kill them. Put your spare change where it counts instead. Thames Reach Bondway – Ending street homelessness.'

17 The homeless have their champions, sometimes so fervid that, in the United States, public policies towards them have even been described as pogroms (Amster, 2003). They are ambiguous – free and yet unfree, victims and offenders, defenceless and yet threatening – and they excite a mix of compassion, fear and hostility which is mirrored in central and local

government policy. The preamble to a report issued by Camden and Islington Councils declared that the homeless are 'the subject of ferocious newspaper headlines, and often face more vilification and abuse than any other section of the population has to endure ... they invariably attract strong feelings – for every group of people who would like to see them simply swept out of sight, there will be others who show them real compassion.' (Camden and Islington Council, 2000: p. 4). And a survey of 500 residents living in the City of Westminster reported in 2002 that 7% were angered by the presence of rough sleepers (the nature and focus of the anger were not explained), 14% felt uncomfortable, 50% felt compassion and 14% paid them little attention (Westminster City Council, 2002: p. 19). Policies have followed suit, some exclusionary, some exclusionary, and others a pragmatic compromise between the two. For instance, there was a report of special drinkers' benches 'complete with ashtrays, rubbish bins and a low wall for privacy' that were about to be installed around Old Street station in London (*Evening Standard*, 25 October 2004).

18 We are most grateful for the painstaking, helpful and enthusiastic way in which Nisrine Mansour, Anthony Morgan, Ubaid Rehman, Melony Sanders and Caroline Turley carried out those interviews.

19 We would like to thank Jenny Law and Joyce Lorinstein for their work in transcribing those tapes.

20 According to Thames Reach Bondway, some 320 people slept rough in London on any one night in August 2002, of which much the greatest proportion, some 50%, was to be found in Westminster (Thames Reach Bondway, 2003: p. 37). Of the estimated rough sleepers living in England and Wales in 1998, some 370 were to be found in central London (Warnes *et al.*, 2003: p. 19).

21 It is conventional to distinguish different subpopulations of the homeless, although there is not always accord about classification. St Mungo's, for instance, would differentiate between rough sleepers, and those in 'first' (impermanent) and 'second' stage (more permanent but not necessarily permanent) accommodation, including 'crack dens', which present a very particular problem. They would further discriminate between refugees, asylum-seekers and 'over-stays' (or rejected asylum seekers) and homeless families. Homeless people sometimes seem to shift erratically between different forms of living. Respondent 23, for example, living in a Cambridge night shelter at the time of his interview, said that over the last five years he had been in 'hostels, night shelters, squats, whatever like wherever you can lay your head really. It's sort of like where you can be.'

22 A feature characteristic of the homeless across the world. For a survey of the victimisation of the homeless in San Francisco, see M. Kushel *et al.*, 2003.

23 Even Respondent 10, who described in interview how he had 'sold weed' and spent many of his nights 'doing graffiti or something', did not condemn all police officers: 'It depends like you get some police that are alright, yeah. And like you get other police that are just assholes.'

24 Respondent 26 said after one incident, 'my mum and that said "well why didn't you go to the police and that?" Now I considered it as well and I thought well, "I don't do that, I don't grass people up." And I actually did and they said well, "there's nothing we can do about it," do you know what I mean? That was the police's attitude, "we can't do nothing about it."'

25 Respondent 13 said 'It really wouldn't help [to approach the police] because you get to know people and things like that and it's, you know, it's best, it's really best for the police not to know 'cause you can get over it better, get over it quicker. You know, I might meet that fella or he might meet me and I might meet him next week and he'd go, I remember you.'

26 Respondent 19 said, 'the police just see us all as drug addicts and alcoholics. We're just homeless because of the way we are, because we've been through drugs and everything else. They're not much fussed. All they're bothered about is arresting us.'

27 See 'Crack Dens', *Housing Today*, 30 April 2004: p. 26.

28 Respondent 10 said 'I'm not that kind of person that I prefer police out of, out of certain situations. But I'm, well I'm not really a law-abiding citizen.'

29 See *ibid* p. 11.

152

30 But, he added, 'saying that, I've seen some really good coppers you know, down in London I saw a couple of guys that were just great, you know. I saw one lady ... she was a right mess and they said, 'oh well', and they took her away and saw her a month later and she was 'oh yeah, they were really good to me, they put me in a hostel ...'

31 Respondent 18 talked about her initial experience of living rough on the streets of London as difficult: 'I wouldn't stay there because [in hostels] was so many different issues there. The places were very angry because you had drunks and the same with streets. The streets were exactly the same. There's a lot of issues of being a youngster, of being, trying, people trying to pick you up, you know, you had gentlemen coming to try and pick you up for sex or offer you money to go with them somewhere.'

32 Respondent 16 said 'You feel useless, you feel down completely from there on. You get abuse from the people, you get, people just look at you like a beggar or something, like even if you're not begging.'

33 Thus Respondent 9, who had had a long history of intermittent homelessness, distanced himself morally from other homeless people: 'Drugs is more important than rent. That's why they're on the streets. Half of them that come here used [were] smack heads. I don't like being around these people. I don't have time for these people. ... You can go buy a bag of heroin but you can't afford to buy cigarettes or you can buy a beer but you can't buy cigarettes. So why am I going to give you the money when you can buy beer? This is my attitude towards them. If I have no money, I have no money. I don't go around begging because I won't do it. This lot, they have no respect and I've known people have been in hostels, every hostel. Why are you back on the street? That's because you don't want to pay the rent, you prefer to live on the street. Well go on the street, that's how they want to be.'

34 Respondent 7 recalled, for instance, how he had slept in one of the doorways of the Army and Navy Stores in Victoria Street, London: 'it was strange, [the police] didn't move us on. It was not the front, the back part I think, they didn't move us on. They were quite good about it. I think it's only the morning ... when the staff are coming in and all that, they get, you have to go ...' but he also remembered being repeatedly asked to move on at other times, much as the sturdy beggars of medieval England had been driven from parish to parish. Respondent 13 echoed that theme: 'they just move you about. They just move you on and move you on. See, that's where the problem starts, someone goes, I want somewhere to sleep, I want to be warm. And they get somewhere and they're pretty warm, pretty settled. Police come along and move them off. Well, they start thinking, right, now I need something to eat now. I got no money, I want a drink. It's an unsecure thing. The police have put him under his problem. You know, the police don't care if they've lost their kids or they ain't got [money] or they got no clothes. You know, I'm saying it's not their problem. What they worry about is moving that person on because he don't fit and so that causes the trouble with that person moves onto another place where it goes with people, we've all been moved on, we've all been moved on.'

35 Respondent 26 said: 'I wanted to get off drugs and that and I found the most easiest place to find them was going to them sort of places.'

36 Respondent 24 talked angrily about his fellow-residents in one hostel: 'there's so many pissheads in ______ but I was in a room with four pissheads. I was the fifth person, and all night it was snoring and shouting in their sleep and general pissed-up things – what pissheads do you know, and I got about two hours sleep in total, yeah, you know. One of the blokes even pissed the bed and he was on the top bunk above me ... '

37 Respondent 10 talked about a hostel which 'was like proper scary in there, ... there was quite a lot of crack addicts and heroin addicts in there and that, and the toilets and stuff yeah, that they didn't really object to people talking drugs in the building. And that, in the toilet they had, oh cheers, yeah, in the toilet they sharps box ... the needles, but that the lid wasn't on top of the box so that then if you stumbled in there a bit drunk like you could have just put your hand on the needles or something.'

38 Respondent 9 said, for example, 'I can't have my children come visit me because it's not secure. So I was in one, they said, 'no, you can't bring your children in.' 'Why?' 'Because we don't

know what there might be perverts or child molesters.' And I said, 'you should know if there are any because you should know people's background.'

39 Sykes (1958) remarked that 'an important aspect of this disturbingly problematical world is the fact that the inmate is acutely aware that sooner or later he will be "tested" – that someone will "push" him to see how far they can go and that he must be prepared to fight for the safety of his person and possessions. If he should fail, he will thereafter be an object of contempt, constantly in danger of being attacked by other inmates who view him as an obvious victim ...' (pp. 77–78).

40 Closed circuit television and enhanced street lighting appear to have an uneven and unpredictable impact on levels of crime, but they do seem to allay the fear of crime. See, for example, Painter (1989) and Ditton (2000).

41 Respondent 20, a Cambridge homeless man, talked about 'Jesus Green ... which is quite a lot of people sleep there from time and time and someone came along and sprayed lighter fluid on ______'s sleeping bag while he was yeah, things like that ... do happen. I've seen other people have left, put up tents and sleeping bags and stuff and had them, had them slashed up while they're not around and things like that. Other people being kicked, beaten up while still in their sleeping bags. Doesn't tend to happen to me 'cause I avoid those places ...sleep in the bushes. ... [and the police] possibly come round and spoil the place where they're sleeping or whatever, move them on which constantly happens anyway – security guards and police.'

42 Thus the City of Westminster offers over 2000 hostel places in 45 hostels (Westminster City Council, 2002: p. 6).

43 Some 20% of the homeless population of England and Wales are believed to live in the City of Westminster (Westminster City Council, 2002: p. 3).

44 Respondent 4 had removed to Oxford, for instance, because Glasgow had been too dangerous for him: 'it wasn't safe for me in Glasgow 'cos Glasgow's very different. ... It's certainly not safe to be running around and having enemies in Glasgow.'

45 Thus the Westminster City Guardians, the local version of community support officers, were required to keep a log of observations made of the numbers and activities of homeless people. The log from the beginning of February to the end of April 2004 reported 82 sightings of rough sleepers, 42 of whom were seen in Leicester Square (51%); 7 in Chinatown (8.5%) 23 in Piccadilly Circus (28%); and 10 in Soho (12%). It also reported 206 instances of begging, 69 of which were in Piccadilly Circus (33.5%); 19 in Chinatown (9%); 101 in Leicester Square (49%); and 17 in Soho (8%). To be sure, those figures embody the working practices of the City Guardians, and are not an absolute tally, but they do convey something of the sheer density of homeless people and beggars in a few key locations in central London.

46 Respondent 15 added that the 'City police are like, you know, they've got a lot better things to do than chase beggars around all the time.'

47 Other figures include 0.2% of the general male population admitting to having committed burglary during the past year; 0.7% to robbery; 7% to assault; 1.5% to selling drugs; and 1.5% to criminal damage.

48 See Warner *et al.* (2003: pp. 5, 9) and, for a comparable study undertaken in the United States, Boris *et al.* (2002).

49 Warnes *et al* (2003: p. 53).

50 See Silver (2001: p. 403). London has the highest rates of offending in England and Wales, and the City of Westminster, where the largest concentration of homeless live, including those interviewed in this survey, has a higher rate of recorded crime still. No doubt some of the figures reflect heavier policing, and Westminster City Council has cavilled at census estimates of the area's population, but the contrasts are impressive. Between April and June 2002, for instance, there were 4.7 drug offences per 1,000 population in Westminster, 0.6 for England and Wales as a whole; 2.8 robberies per 1,000 in Westminster, 0.5 in England and Wales as a whole; 1.2 sexual offences compared with 0.2; and 14.1 offences of violence against the person compared with 4.0 (www.crimestatistics.org.uk).

154

51 There appear to be marked differences within the homeless populations of the developed world. It is the young who seem disproportionately disposed to inflicting and suffering violence in Britain and North America (Boris *et al.* 2002: pp. 359, 361).
52 See Ballintyne (1999: p. 15); and *California Department of Justice* , 2002: p. vi).
53 N. Hellen; 'Begging set to become crime in policy shift;, *The Sunday Times*, 26.1.2003.
54 That balance is not unknown to rough sleepers themselves, and it is believed to affect action. One respondent, [Respondent 11] said 'you try and stay away from the police as much as possible because there's a serious chance that they'll beat you up themselves. But which most people find out is that the best way of avoiding you know, getting a good kicking from the police, it to, is to inform them that you are mentally ill or something, cause they don't want to get involved with beating up mentally ill people 'cause they get in a lot of trouble.'

REFERENCES

Amster, R. (2003). Patterns of Exclusion: Sanitizing Space, Criminalizing Homelessness. *Social Justice*, 30, (1), 199.
Anderson, E. (1978). *A Place on the Corner.* University of Chicago Press; Chicago.
Anderson, N. (1965). *The Hobo: The Sociology of the Homeless Man.* University of Chicago Press; Chicago.
Ballintyne, S. (1999). *Unsafe Streets: Street Homelessness and Crime.* IPPR; London.
Boris, N. *et al.* (2002). Partner Violence among Homeless Young Adults. *Journal of Adolescent Health*, 30, 355–363.
Budd, T., Sharp, C. and Mayhew, P. (2005). *Offending in England and Wales: First Results from the 2003 Crime and Justice Survey.* Home Office; London.
Camden and Islington Council (2000). *Time for Change.* Camden and Islington Council; London.
California Department of Justice (2002). *Crimes Committed Against Homeless Persons. Special Report to the Legislature on Senate Resolution 18.* Criminal Justice Statistics Center, California Department of Justice; Sacramento, California.
Camden and Islington Council (2004). *Strategically Speaking: Homeless People's Experience of Camden's Homelessness Strategy.* Camden and Islington Council; London.
Carlen, P. (1996). *Jigsaw: a Political Criminology of Youth Homelessness.* Open University Press; Buckingham.
Christie, N. (1986). The Ideal Victim. In *From Crime Policy to Victim Policy* (E. Fattah, ed.) pp. 17–30. Macmillan; Basingstoke.
City of Westminster (2002). *Rough Sleepers and Street Culture Strategy.* City of Westminster; London.
Cohen, C. and Sokolovsky, J. (1989). *Old Men of the Bowery: Strategies for Survival Among the Homeless.* The Guilford Press; New York.
Crane, M. and Warnes, A. (2001). *Single Homeless People in London.* Sheffield Institute for Studies on Ageing; University of Sheffield, Sheffield.
Danczuk, S. (2000). *Begging, Street Drinking and the Giving Age.* Crisis; London.
D'Ercole, A. and Struening, E. (1990). Victimization Among Homeless Women. *Journal of Community Psychology*, 18, 141–152.
Dillon, R. (Ed.) (1995). Introduction to *Dignity, Character, and Self-Respect.* Routledge; New York.
Ditton, J. (2000). Crime and the City: Public Attitudes towards Open-Street CCTV in Glasgow. *British Journal of Criminology*, 40, 692–709 .
Dodd, T. *et al.* (2004). *Crime in England and Wales 2003/2004.* Home Office; London.
Ferraro, K. (1995). *Fear of Crime: Interpreting Victimization Risk.* State University of New York Press; Albany.

Hagan, J. and McCarthy, B. (1997). *Mean Streets, Youth Crime and Homelessness.* Cambridge University Press; Cambridge.

Herbert, S. (1997). *Policing Space: Territoriality and the Los Angeles Police Department.* University of Minneapolis Press; Minneapolis.

Holstein, J. and Miller, G. (1990). Rethinking Victimization: An Interactional Approach to Victimology. *Symbolic Interaction.* **13**, 103–122.

Hough, M. (2004). Modernisation, Scientific Rationalism and the Crime Reduction Programme. *Criminal Justice*, **4**, (3), 239–253.

Hoyt, D. *et al.* (2004). Victimization and Posttraumatic Stress Among Homeless and Runaway Adolescents. Paper delivered at the meetings of the American Society of Criminology, Nashville, Tennessee, November.

Jackson, J. (2004). Experience and Expression: Social and Cultural Significance in the Fear of Crime. *The British Journal of Criminology*, **44**, (6), 946–966.

Jacobs, J. (1961). *The Death and Life of Great American Cities.* Random House; New York.

Kushel, M., Evans, J.L., Perry, S., Robertson, M.J. and Moss, A.R. (2003). No Door to Lock: Victimization Among Homeless and Marginally Housed Persons. *Arch Intern. Med.*, 10 November, **163**, 2492.

Manning, P. (1975). Deviance and Dogma. *British Journal of Criminology*, **15**.

McVie, S. *et al.* (2004). *Scottish Crime Survey 2003.* Scottish Executive Social Research; Edinburgh.

Meddings, S. and Levey, S. (2000). Staff Attribution and Management of Violent Incidents in Hostels for Homeless People. *Journal of Mental Health*, **9**, (5), 481.

North, C.S., Smith, E.M. and Spitznagel, E.L. (1994). Violence and the Homeless. *Journal of Traumatic Stress*, **7**, (1), XXX.

Painter, K. (1989). *Lighting and Crime Prevention for Public Safety.* Middlesex University; Enfield.

Piliavin, I. and Briar, S. (1964). Police Encounters with Juveniles. *American Journal of Sociology*, **70**, 206–214.

Reiss, A. (1971). *The Police and the Public.* Yale University Press; New Haven.

Rhodes, L. (2004). *Total Confinement.* University of California Press; Berkeley.

Sennett, R. (2003). *Respect: The Formation of Character in a World of Inequality.* Allen Lane; London.

Shiner, M. (1995). Adding Insult to Injury: Homelessness and Health Service Use. *Sociology of Heaelth and Illness*, **17**, (4), 525–549.

Silver, E. (2001). Neighbourhood Social Disorganization as a Cofactor in Violence Among People with Mental Disorders. *International Journal of Offender Therapy and Comaprative Criminology*, **45**, 403.

Simmons, J. and Dodd, T. (2003). *Crime in England and Wales 2002/2003.* Home Office Statistical Bulletin, Home Office, 2003.

St Mungo's (2004). *50:50. The BIGStat.* St Mungo's; London.

Stinchcombe, A. (1968). The Behavior of the Police in Public and Private Places. In *Deviance* (E. Rubington and M. Weinberg, eds). Macmillan; New York.

Sykes, G. (1958). *The society of Captives.* Princeton University Press; Princeton.

United States Department of Justice (2001). *Hate Crime: The Violence of Intolerance.* Community Relations Service, United States Department of Justice; Washington DC.

Victim Support (2003). *Annual Report and Accounts 2003.* Victim Support; London.

Waddington, P.A.J., Stenson, K. and Don, D. (2004). In Proportion: Race and Police Stop and Search. *The British Journal of Criminology*, **44**, (6), 889–914.

Warnes, A., Crane, M., Whitehead, N. and Fu, R. (2003). *Homelessness Factfile.* Crisis; London.

Werthman, C. and Piliavin, I. (1967). Gang Members and the Police. In *The Police* (D. Bordua, ed.) pp. 56–98. Wiley; New york.

Westminster City Council (2002). *Streets of London: A Study of Street Culture in Westminster.* Westminster City Council; London.

156

Young, J. (2004). Voodoo Criminology and the Numbers Game. In *Cultural Criminology Unleashed* (J. Ferrell, K. Hayward, W. Morrison and M. Presdee, eds) pp. 13–27. Glasshouse Press; London.

[16]
The Treatment of Victims in England and Wales

Abstract This article examines the discredited attributes of the public persona of the victim of serious crime. The author considers the construction of the victim and the victim's role within the trial process, looking at arguments which claim that the role of the victim is consider to inject emotionality into the conflicts leading up to and culminating in the criminal trial.

Introduction

According to the 2005–2006 British Crime Survey, there were some 11 million crimes committed against adults living in private households in England and Wales—just under a quarter of the interviewees reported having been a victim. Had children aged under 16, the homeless, and other groups also been questioned, that figure would have been appreciably larger.

Most of the victims of those offences would have had little formal acquaintance with the criminal justice system. 42% of all crimes were said to have been reported in 2005–6. Only 70% of crimes reported were recorded by the police, and a quarter of that number were said to have been 'cleared up' (Walker *et al.*, 2006). Some 3% of all known crimes reach the courts. Only 2% result in a conviction although certain offences, such as murder and manslaughter, have a much higher rate of detection and conviction.[1] Crime remains a mass phenomenon that impinges little on the courts and prisons and, in most instances, only perfunctorily on the police. It is not that sense 'treated' formally at all.

The experience of volume crime can be disturbing. Even offences against property that used once to be regarded as minor irritants that could be alleviated by the provision of better insurance, target hardening, and crime prevention measures (Waller and Okihiro, 1978), have been shown capable of inducing feelings of defilement, loss, disorder, and personal invasion that verge at the extreme on traumatic stress (Maguire and Bennett, 1982). Yet most English and Welsh victims do not appear to translate their acquaintance with crime into the foundation of an enduring identity around which to organise themselves psychologically, socially, or politically. They do not importantly shape their lives with narratives of crime and victimisation. They have not mobilised.

*Professor of Social Institutions, London School of Economics, London, UK and University of Pennsylvania, PA, USA. E-mail: p.rock@lse.ac.uk

[1] There were, for instance, 765 homicides recorded in England and Wales in 2005–2006, 81% of which had a named suspect (Walker et al. 2006, p. 147). Court proceedings had concluded for 377 suspects and there were 590 proceedings pending for other suspects.

The principal body representing the victims of volume crime, Victim Support, was not an organisation self-consciously founded *by* victims. Neither has it been maintained by them (Rock, 1990). It was instead designed for what might be called victims *an sich*. Sired by NACRO, a penal reform association composed of criminal justice practitioners aligned professionally as much with the defendant and offender as with the victim, it sought from the first not to litigate, to campaign about specific cases, or, more generally, to make policy pronouncements about sentencing and penal policy.

The crimes experienced by most English and Welsh victims are not usually reported in the mass media (although local newspapers may be less discriminating in what they choose to relay – see Roshier, 1981). Crime news tends to be constructed around prepared press releases, the news round, and routine briefings (Fishman, 1980) that centre on the most morally transgressive (Ericson *et al.*, 1991) and dramatic offences. Newsworthy crimes are infused with images of violence and sex (Ditton and Duffy, 1983) and the more violent and sexual their character, the greater is the likelihood that they will be reported. There are gradations in the newsworthiness even of rape (Soothill and Walby, 1991) and of murder and manslaughter ('the circumstance of the killing plays a crucial role in whether a homicide is reported, with sexual homicides and motiveless acts being more likely to be reported', said Peelo *et al.* (2002, p. 1)). The study of media effects is notoriously fraught, but the landscapes of crime constructed in the popular imagination do seem to be marked out by the sensational and unusual offence (Roberts *et al.*, 2003). In Jock Young's (1971) words, they are given contour by representations of the overly atypical set against a backcloth of the overly typical.

Volume Crime

Criminologists and victimologists might point to 'hot spots' and to particularly heavily victimised sub-groups within the larger population, but volume crime now seems to be a ubiquitous, continuous, and unsettling background feature of what some call late modernity (Garland, 2001). It is accompanied by waves of apprehension about offences that are themselves subject to fashions in behaviour, control (Ditton, 1979), reporting (Innes, 2004), and victimisation, waves that have become 'institutionalized, transformed from *ad hoc*, episodic, and short-lived occurrences ... into a permanent condition of personal insecurity' (Feeley and Simon, 2007, pp. 39–40). It is not clear that the individual victims of volume crime stand out in such an environment. They are instead part of a relatively anonymous crowd made up of everyman and everywoman—of you, me, and everyone. It was in this vein that the white paper, *A New Deal for Victims and Witnesses*, published by the Home Office in 2003, stated: 'Last year one in four people was a victim of crime... Victims of crime are our families, our friends, our neighbours, our workmates. Ourselves...' And where such a mass is nameless, unorganised and without a powerful voice, it is all too easy for politicians and others to bestow features, wants, needs, and aspirations on it at will.[2]

If the victims of volume crime tend to be relatively featureless, devoid of personality, and readily caricatured for political purposes, there are other victims who do quite plainly stand out. They are those for whom victimisation has been translated into a master status; who are associated perhaps with notorious crimes; subject to reporting in the mass media; liable to a prolonged, extensive and intensive experience of

[2] Victim Support has long been a doughty representative of the victim of volume crime, but it is a minor institution easily overshadowed in the political world of the criminal justice system, with modest funding and a voluntary status. It did for a long while represent an accumulation of expertise that lent it authority, but even that modest influence is waning. Jane Furniss, then head of the Home Office Justice and Victims Unit, was blunt in a meeting held in October 2002, and what she said counted because what is real to a powerful official is real enough in its consequences: 'Victim Support has less status than the police or the CPS [Crown Prosecution Service], but they're strongly affected by the decisions those bodies take. Victim Support can't require action of others—it can make a lot of noise—but at the end of the day, they can't say "you will, you must." Their

the criminal justice system; and members possibly of the activist groups that sustain an identity, engender a culture and politics, and provide narratives of suffering and loss. They are above all the victims of rape, sexual abuse, incest, and violent assault, and the relatives of homicide victims. I do not wish to examine here the more practical responses that have been mustered to support them—they have been dealt with elsewhere (see Rock, 1990, 1998, 2004a). Rather, I shall focus on the way in which their treatment refracts some special interpretive practices.

Treatment of individual victims

Individual victims may well be regarded as objects of pity and indignation, particularly when they conform to conventional canons of innocence and blamelessness—approximating the 'ideal victims' of Nils Christie's essay (1986)—but that is not always the case, and there are darker traits lurking in the formal and informal responses meted out to them, some of which are quite primitive in character. Indeed, the relatives of murder victims talk about the burden of bad luck they are supposed to bear. They say that people sometimes attempt to avoid them lest they too should be contaminated.

Holstein and Miller once reflected that '"victim" is a categorization device... an interpretive framework... that provides a set of instructions for understanding social relations.... As an act of interpretive reality construction, victimization unobtrusively advises others in how they should understand persons, circumstances, and behaviors under consideration' (1990, pp. 105, 107). The converse also holds: 'persons, circumstances and behaviors' shape how victims and victimisation are categorised. I would argue that, although it is not the only process at work and that it may not be at work on every occasion, there is a prominent but largely unheeded facet of the treatment of the direct and indirect victims of serious crime in England and Wales that can contribute to an understanding of how their moral and institutional identity is routinely constructed.

Those victims are not neutral entities viewed with benevolence and equanimity. They have acquired an uncomfortable and contradictory identity in and around the adversarial trial, and the trial can cast a long shadow. They tend to be embroiled at first or second hand in the formidable conflicts of criminal procedure and may have to take their place amongst the ranks of adversaries as targets for assaults on moral character. It is their allegations that can lead to the arrest, conviction and punishment of another, and their very legitimacy as a victim may be aggressively contested. Much of what is done, say, by the police in investigating an offence and taking witness statements is accomplished in anticipation of how accounts and representations will be tested in examination and cross-examination in the courtroom (see McConville *et al.*, 1991). What officers seek is a serviceable and simplified figure to give animation to a stripped-down and robust prosecution recital of the 'facts of the case', and it is that simplification and those facts that will be attacked in reply. Indeed, the very status of victim will be at issue in any fought trial. Complainants will be treated as no more than *alleged* victims until a verdict or plea of guilt has been tendered. In a debate on proposed protections for rape complainants conducted in the House of

funding is insecure. They have amateur status. They may be seen as having a weak voice and a limited influence. They can challenge the State but they can't make us listen. Problem: are we giving victims a lesser status because they are not catered for by a state institution?' It has as a result been part of the political history of victims in England and Wales that they are more defined than defined. Helen Reeves, the then Chief Executive Officer of Victim Support, observed to me in interview in 1999: 'We've always had difficulty getting people to see what we regard as a very simple fact: ... that [the matter of victims] is actually a third strand. People even now will try to say "well, it's part of crime prevention or it's part of restorative justice" or whatever. Unless you can actually separate [it] away from those things and focus [on it] in its own right ... then you can come back together and say "yes, there's a lot of crime prevention in here as well and yes, of course, it's part of restorative justice", [but] unless you've actually focused on the need to reduce the harm done by crime ... you're not going to achieve anything. You're just going to become ... hi-jacked by other priorities'.

Lords in March 2001, the Lord Chief Justice said, 'the trial cannot be conducted on the assumption that [a defendant] is a rapist and the complainant a victim, since the whole purpose of the proceeding is to establish whether that is so or not.'

Counsel will routinely challenge the credit and credibility of witnesses appearing before them, applying identical techniques of interrogation, making the same or very similar charges day after day and in almost every case. Testimony will be confronted, truthfulness impugned, competence questioned. As a matter of course, it will be contended that victims and prosecution witnesses were too forgetful, too drunk, too drugged, too myopic, too vindictive, too self-interested, and too mendacious to recall faithfully what they say they have seen and heard. Victims will be said to have brought misfortune on their own heads by striking the first blow, or by appearing to be threatening or acting provocatively. They will often retire from the witness box asserting ruefully that they felt as if they had been treated not as an innocent but as a criminal, as if *they* had been on trial, and so, in effect, they had been.

That wilful confusion of identity and role may be lent support by a complementary, almost silently presupposed, common-sense theory of moral action that provides some of the darkest traits attached to victims. Counsel make use of a widespread tacit presumption that good people cannot and will not be harmed because they do not *deserve* to be hurt, that in a just world virtuous acts will be rewarded and bad deeds punished. Those who meet with evil, it is said, must somehow have merited their fate (Lerner, 1980).

Victim-precipitation

'Victim-precipitation' is one of the core ideas of victimology and the trial defence, and it alleges that, rather than being an encounter between a wholly blameless victim and a wholly blameworthy offender, crime should be more properly viewed as an interaction, a 'duet' or an exchange, in which the victim contributed to his or her own fate.

> Are we permitted, the early victimologist Hans von Hentig once asked, 'to say that in some cases criminality is a self-consuming process of anti-social elements in which criminals prey on criminaloids, killers on suicides or other killers, oversexed on oversexed, dishonest individuals on dishonest? (1940, p. 309).

Victim-precipitation is the great foundational idea of victimology and its origins are to be found in the criminal trial. It was propounded by one who claimed to be the father of victimology—Beniamin Mendelsohn, a Roumanian defence lawyer—who,

> while preparing for the trial of Stephan Codreanu arraigned in 1945 for a crime passionel, ... began to elaborate the doctrine of Victimology .... There can be no doubt that, had it not been for the perversity of his former wife, [Codreanu] would never have been guilty of two crimes .... (1963, p. 241).

The responsibility for the murder lay squarely with Codreanu's victim, and that is a common-enough defence argument. In murder trials, after all, the available defences are that the defendant was not there, the offence was committed by someone else, the defendant was provoked, or that he was acting in self-defence. 'Precipitation' flows from the rhetoric of defendant and defence lawyers, and it has been dismissed by victims' advocates as 'victim-blaming' (Clark and Lewis, 1977). 'At the root of all victim-blaming', Lamb remarked,

> are the perpetrator's own attempts to present the victim as the cause of his violence or abuse ... Perpetrators will ... claim that their victims are almost directly responsible for their fates, that the little girl wanted to be fondled, that the raped woman was asking for it, and that the abused wife provoked her beating ... (1996, pp. 78, 79).

But 'victim-precipitation' is not peculiar to the language of offenders, counsel, and victimologists. Victims may themselves subscribe to 'survivor guilt', self-blame and talk about what they call the 'if onlys'—if only they had been more prudent, better informed, more vigilant, more active in preventing an offence—if only, that is, they had not through omission or commission brought about their own or another's misfortune. They can be vulnerable in the witness box to charges of complicity because they may well have had doubts about what they did or did not do. They may even be under some duress to forgive or reconcile themselves with the offender who has wronged them.[3]

At the heart of criminal justice, then, are institutionalised exchanges of argument about the victim's merit, culpability, and veracity. Victims may protest that they are more sinned against than sinning—sometimes with less than complete assurance—but it is the professional business of the defence to turn any such claims on their head.

Victims have long been framed, and framed artfully, by that imagery of complicity, mendacity, anger, and revenge. Until the early 19th century, and before the construction of a formal State machinery of professional criminal investigation, courts, and prosecutions, they played a central and almost wholly disparaged role at trial. 'First,' said Plucknett, justice 'is in the hands of the injured party and his opponent' (1956, p. 424) and it stayed in those hands for centuries. In what has been called 'lawyer-free trials' (Langbein, 2003, p. 2), victims were themselves obliged to collect evidence, interview witnesses, lay charges, and appear as lay advocates in court. Their own accounts from that period are largely silent, but their critics were adamant that they were vengeful, corrupt, and incompetent, motivated by private interest, inadequate as the gatherers of evidence, and suspect as prosecutors (see Rock, 2004b). Although they brought indictments in the name of the Crown, and although it was the Crown, acting as a metaphor for society, which was said somehow to have been injured, they were cast as people who were serving their own selfish purposes. Speaking before a committee entrusted with a major review of the system of prosecutions, the Lord Chief Justice pronounced in 1855 that the victim was responsible for engineering a 'shameful perversion of the criminal law for private ends'.[4] The injured party, echoed the Attorney General, was 'one who is smarting under a sense of injury, smarting with a sense of wrong, and desirous of bringing the vengeance of law on the person who has injured him' (Select Committee on Public Prosecutors, 1855, p. 186).

After the policing reforms that began in the 1820s, the introduction of the office of Director of Public Prosecutions in 1879, and the establishment of the Crown Prosecution Service in 1986, victims may no longer play a prominent part. Their role may have shrunk into that of complainant, witness, and applicant for compensation. But vestiges of those stigmata remain quite visible and are frequently cited, despite contrary evidence from crime surveys (see Hough and Roberts, 1998) and other sources that victims are not especially punitive or vengeful.

Activist victims

It is as if victims are still sometimes thought to be held barely in check, near feral, angry creatures of a Hobbesian world, restrained only by the legal apparatus of the State whose failure would lead to a reversion to 'wild justice'. Recall the words of C.H. Rolph, uttered in 1958, and made influential by their role in shaping the iconography of victims of violent crime adopted by the campaign for criminal injuries compensation:

[3] There is in the West's imagery of victims, suggests Jan van Dijk (2006, p. 1), a marked legacy of well-established Christian ideas of self-election, sacrifice, meekness, submission, acceptance, and mercy. Some of the earlier versions of restorative justice seemed to have been founded on just such notions of the imperative to forgive (see Marshall and Walpole 1985, p. 4), and the conflict between a traumatised, raped woman, and her clergyman father who enjoined forgiveness is recounted poignantly in Jill Saward's autobiography (1990).

[4] Select Committee on Public Prosecutors (1855), p. 62.

> The law for centuries has required the citizen to smother his natural [*sic*] desire for revenge and leave it to the police and the courts to deal with the offender. The disabled man's injury is the State's injury. When he was coshed, the community was coshed. Vengeance is mine, saith the State; but it does not repay . . . . Last November, the Home Secretary was presented with a petition, organized by a former Lord Mayor of Birmingham and signed by 87,000 people asking for heavier sentences on violent criminals, the revival of flogging and 'adequate compensation for victims—as far as possible at the expense of their attackers'. (1958)

Here is the victim as *euminides*, the penal reformer's bane, and it has been given new flesh in a political movement of victims *für sich*. Only 14 years after the formal inauguration in 1979 of what was then the National Association of Victim Support Schemes, later re-named Victim Support, a new constellation of small activist victims' groups emerged, and they are an amalgam of self-help and campaigning associations founded largely by the families of murder and manslaughter victims and intended to memorialise the dead and crusade on behalf of the living (Rock, 1998). Their members claim a new identity, part domestic, part imported, that was founded in the throes of traumatic bereavement, and it is an identity that stresses themes of loss, mourning, alienation, abandonment, and marginality. They are, they say, the orphans of the criminal justice system, virtually unacknowledged, denied (in their own words) 'respect and recognition', and left to flounder in their grief and anger. In an early leaflet, Justice for Victims, one of the activist groups, stated:

> We have tried being polite, we have tried to be logical. We have tried to let justice take its course!! We have held our anger, our emotions in check—we have tried to see—what we are told we must see. We have tried above all to be the reasonable, tolerant, honest people we once were, we have tried so very hard to hold on to this. We have been tried too much!!!!!!

The activist victims were at first held at bay by politicians and officials because they were thought to be too volatile and emotional, too unreasonable, to be treated as sound people who could or should be recruited into the committees, conferences, and consultations supervising the business of criminal justice policy making.[5] But politicians, officials, procedures, and structures have changed, and activists have now acquired a political presence as a result of the introduction into government of a Victims Advisory Panel chaired by ministers. Half its 12 founding members were homicide survivors, and they have voiced the survivors' discontents. The creation of the panel seemed originally to be little more than one small, almost unnoticed, provision amongst many in the Domestic Violence, Crime and Victims Act of November 2004, but it has succeeded in transforming the language in which victims are discussed.

Activist victims are now members of 'insider' groups with a political legitimacy and influence derived from direct access to power (see Maloney

[5] Thus, Alun Michael, the Home Office minister initially responsible for criminal justice policy, including policies for victims, in the first New Labour administration, 1997–2001, said to me an interview: 'I think each of us have approaches from different groups. I mean there are a lot of groups that are set up by people who've been the victims of violent and horrific events, who sometimes set it up because they say "nobody should have to go through what I went through without support and help". And sometimes it's almost a way of working through themselves, and being able to handle the experience that they've gone through. And the fact that it's done for those sort of personal reasons doesn't always make it a bad thing. I'm not suggesting that. Certainly on a number of occasions, I met groups of people who are very damaged and angry and upset because they've been through traumatic events. And sometimes those groups would be more focused on a single solution . . . . That's why I think that it was signally important that Victim Support, as an organisation, both actually tried to work with some of those groups in a positive way and was trying to take, if you like, a more objective view of the things, which it's actually very difficult to do. [But it is Victim Support that] remain[s] both authoritative and persuasive and practical'.

et al., 1994; Savage *et al.*, 2007). One member of the new Panel was reported to have said:

> All . . . are passionate about being involved in improving services offered to victims of crime. In some cases we want to offer our experience to ensure that others do not go through what we have been through. In others we simply want to bring our expertise right to the heart of government. Too often the voice of the victim is not heard properly or not heard early enough. Through the Victims Advisory Panel we are looking forward to being the voice of victims of crime at a crucial stage—when policy is first being developed.[6]

Another, a member of SAMM (Support After Murder and Manslaughter), said that she had been able, 'with the other lay members, to raise the awareness of Ministers and Officials of the need for better services for victims and the gross inequalities in the law and legal rights, favouring the offender' (SAMM, 2005, p. 3). The activists have had meetings with ministers, the Bar Council, Crown Prosecution Service and judges to become a visible and audible presence in the criminal justice system. They are said now by a number of politicians to be the authentic voice of victim experience, more authoritative than Victim Support, a voice that must be heard in policy making and at trial. It is that decision to allow the relatives of murder and manslaughter victims to speak that has galvanised lawyers and judges.

Victims are no longer deemed for political purposes to be merely 'ourselves' but those who have suffered from the most appalling harms. There have been new conversations about trauma, violence, and bereavement. The 2005 white paper, *Rebuilding Lives*, said, for instance, 'Even relatively minor crimes can be traumatic, but the most serious cause enormous emotional and physical harm . . .. There is scope for more use of specialist staff in delivering services to victims with particular needs, for example in the most serious cases such as sexual offences, domestic violence, serious violent offences and racial offences.' And there have been new conversations based on the homicide survivor's moral economy of binary oppositions: an economy that maintains that a Ministry of Justice should be matched by a Ministry for Victims, a lost life by life imprisonment, legal advice to the defendant by advice to the victim, defence lawyers by lawyers assisting the victim, and mitigation statements by Victim Impact Statements. Part of that discourse has been heeded by the Ministers who chaired the Panel's meetings and it has been given form in a pilot experiment providing 15 hours, legal advice on personal and social matters, the introduction of victims' advocates, and the inauguration of Victim Impact Statements, re-labelled Family Impact Statements, in homicide trials in five Crown Court centres. Announcing what was to happen in a press statement of 1 September 2005, the Minister of State for Constitutional Affairs, Harriet Harman, said:

> Bereaved relatives sometimes feel they are completely excluded from the system. It seems ironic to me that the people for whom the case matters most are silent in court. We must ensure the court hears not just from the defendant, but also from the victim's family.

Impact statements

Delivered after conviction and before sentence, the Family Impact Statement allows the relatives of victims to speak about the effect that the crime has had upon them and other members of their family. It introduces a new presence into the courtroom, a presence that some fear is laden with emotionality, potentially uncontrolled, lacking in the calm and dispassionate tones of criminal procedure, liable

[6] http://www.cjsonline.gov.uk/the_cjs/whats_new/news-3459.html.

improperly to influence the sentencing process. Impact statements and victims' advocates are regarded by many lawyers as a rogue element; the entry of an outsider, a private person, into a bipartisan conflict waged formally by practitioners between the State and defendant; and a claim made by the public on the quasi-private, professional terrain of the courts. *Hearing the Relatives of Murder and Manslaughter Victims*, the September 2005 consultation paper that broached the initiative, met with a critical reply. On 24 December 2005, *The Times* reported, for example:

> ... judges, including Lord Woolf, the former Lord Chief Justice, and Sir Igor Judge, the Deputy Lord Chief Justice, have expressed concerns. They say that the courtroom would become an emotional arena; that it would falsely raise victims' expectations of being able to influence the sentence; and that it would extend rights of audience in the courts beyond the legal profession. They are concerned that the plan would alter the adversarial basis of the trial and potentially interfere with the outcome of the case, although the address would be after the verdict.

The Bar Council stated:

> If [relatives] do feel disempowered under the present system, this proposal is not the answer. It could make the situation worse.... The proposal risks putting pressure on judges with no compensating advantage.... The proposal that victims should have a say in decisions as to whether prosecutions are started, terminated, and what charges are brought is potentially inimical to justice.... We also see a possibility of victims in high profile cases being pressurised by other parties with an axe to grind. That could be pressure to tell a more lurid story or it might be pressure to back off. Victims by definition will be emotionally vulnerable. A proportion come from disadvantaged sections of society and will be of modest intellectual and educational attainment.

And the Legal Action Group said:

> While we accept that many relatives may 'feel passionately that they should have their say in court' (paragraph 44), this is itself is not sufficient reason for the proposals, which must be looked at in terms of the criminal justice system as a whole. The criminal justice system necessarily has the defendant rather than the victim, at the centre. The case is brought by the state on behalf of all society, not only the victims and their families. The state must ensure a fair trial, seek to convict the guilty and acquit the innocent. If convicted, the sentence should be proportionate and reasonable in all the circumstances, including the facts of the case and the application of appropriate sentencing criteria. To give victims' families a direct voice in open court at the sentencing stage, presents a risk of exacerbating their stress while also posing problems of consistency and fairness for the defendant.

Conclusion

Trials have for centuries been taken to centre on a dispute between the defendant and the Crown 'because the sovereign, in whom centres the majesty of the whole community, is supposed by the law to be the person injured by every infraction of the public rights belonging to that community...' (Blackstone, 1769, p. 12). Even where the prosecutor was a private individual bringing an action for an injury committed against his own person or property, injury was not properly conceived to be against him or her but the 'whole community'. The victims of serious crimes are the makers of allegations; aligned with the police and prosecution; not above, but deeply implicated in, the conflicts of the trial; at risk of injecting emotionality where none should exist; and, embedded in an agonistic process, their moral standing and social identity are never assured.

It is not evident how widely those pragmatically hostile typifications are spread. Nor is it evident how they travel and with what result. They are certainly in currency amongst lawyers and legal commentators.[7] Consider the tone of a piece on the new measures written by Marcel Berlins, a legal journalist, and published in *The Guardian* on 4 December 2006:

> Harriet Harman, the scheme's main architect, insists that allowing the victim's loved ones to express their feelings in court is not meant to influence the sentence of the judge. That is nonsense. Judges are human. To suggest that they will remain immune to a highly emotional account of the grief felt by the survivor—and of the wonderfulness of the victim—is unrealistic and absurd.

They certainly colour the experiences of victims themselves, being associated with the marginality and oppressiveness that they call the 'secondary victimisation' inflicted by the criminal justice system. And they seem to have given a strong tinge to many of the representations of the victim to be found in academic criminology, particularly in the United States (where, admittedly, the history of the victims' movement took a distinct turn). Barker states, for example, 'Driven by anger, resentment, and pain, victim advocacy has brought out what David Garland . . . and others refer to as anachronistic sources of vengeance embedded in our modern criminal justice system . . .' (2005, p. 5). Whatever substance there is in such charges—and there is, of course, substance—it is remarkable how common it is for the victims of serious crime and their representatives to be treated with opprobrium, and one wonders whether some of the sources of that disfavour do not stem as much from the formal alignments and theories of culpability that I have sketched in this paper, as from any of the more overt actions and utterances of victims themselves.

References

Arrigo, B. and Williams, C. (2003). "Victim Vices, Victim Voices, and Impact Statements: On the Place of Emotion and the Role of Restorative Justice in Capital Sentencing." *Crime & Delinquency* **49**(4): 603–626.

Barker, V. (2005). "The Politics of Pain: A Comparative Political Analysis of Crime Victims' Moral Protests." Paper presented at the *Meetings of the American Society of Criminology*, Toronto.

Blackstone, W. (1769). *Commentaries on the Laws of England.* Book 4. Oxford: Clarendon Press.

Christie, N. (1986). "The Ideal Victim." In Fattah, E. (ed.), *From Crime Policy to Victim Policy*. Basingstoke: Macmillan, pp. 17–30.

Clark, L. and Lewis, D. (1977). *Rape: The Price of Coercive Sexuality.* Toronto: The Women's Press.

Ditton, J. (1979). *Contrology: Beyond the New Criminology.* London: Macmillan.

Ditton, J. and Duffy, J. (1983). "Bias in the Newspaper Reporting of Crime News." *British Journal of Criminology* **23**(2): 159–165.

Ericson, R., Baranek, P. and Chan, J. (1991). *Representing Order: Crime, Law and Justice in the News Media.* Buckingham: Open University Press.

Feeley, M. and Simon, J. (2007). "*Folk Devils and Moral Panics*: An Appreciation from North America." In Chinkin, C., Downes, D., Gearty, C. and Rock P. (eds), *Crime, Social Control and Human Rights.* Cullompton, Devon: Willan Publishing.

Fishman, M. (1980). *Manufacturing the News.* Austin: University of Texas Press.

Garland, D. (2001). *The Culture of Control.* Oxford: Oxford University Press.

[7] Writing about impact statements in the United States, Arrigo and Williams (2003, p. 604) say, for example, 'undesirability is linked to the emotionally laden and mostly negative consequences that VIS evince from jurors (and other decision makers), undermining and undoing a defendant's right to a fair and impartial meting out of criminal punishment. By "negative" emotions, we refer specifically to the resentment, anger, and vengeance that often accompany (or follow) the experience of such intensely charged and deeply felt victim allocutions.'

von Hentig, H. (1940). "Remarks on the Interaction of Perpetrator and Victim." *Journal of Criminal Law and Criminology* **31**: 303–309.

Holstein, J. and Miller, G. (1990). "Rethinking Victimization: An Interactional Approach to Victimology." *Symbolic Interaction* **13**(1): 103–122.

Hough, M. and Roberts, J. (1998). *Attitudes to Punishment: Findings from the British Crime Survey*. Home Office Research Study No. 179. London: Home Office.

Innes, M. (2004). "Crime as a Signal, Crime as a Memory." *Journal for Crime, Conflict and the Media* **1**(2): 15–22.

Lamb, S. (1996). *The Trouble with Blaming*. Cambridge, Mass: Harvard University Press.

Langbein, J. (2003). *The Origins of Adversary Criminal Trial*. Oxford: Oxford University Press.

Lerner, M. (1980). *The Belief in a Just World*. New York: Plenum Press.

Maguire, M. and Bennett, T. (1982). *Burglary in a Dwelling: The Offence, the Offender and the Victim*. London: Heinemann.

Maloney, W., Jordan, G. and McLaughlin, A. (1994). "Interest Groups and Public Policy: The Insider/Outsider Model Revisited." *Journal of Public Policy* **14**(1): 17–36.

Marshall, T. and Walpole, M. (1985). *Bringing People Together: Mediation and Reparation Projects in Great Britain*. London: Home Office.

McConville, M., Sanders, A. and Leng, R. (1991). *The Case for the Prosecution*. London: Routledge.

Mendelsohn, B. (1963). "The Origin of the Doctrine of Victimology." *Excerpta Criminologica* **3**: 239–245.

Peelo, M. *et al.* (2002). "The Public Construction of Justice: Homicide Reporting in the Press." University of Lancaster (unpublished paper).

Plucknett, T. (1956). *A Concise History of the Common Law*. London: Butterworth.

Roberts, J., Stalans, L., Indermaur, D. and Hough, M. (2003). *Penal Populism and Public Opinion. Findings from Five Countries*. New York: Oxford University Press.

Rock, P. (1990). *Helping Victims of Crime: The Home Office and the Rise of Victim Support in England and Wales*. Oxford: Clarendon Press.

Rock, P. (1998). *After Homicide: Practical and Political Responses to Bereavement*. Oxford: Clarendon Press.

Rock, P. (2004a). *Constructing Victims' Rights: The Home Office, New Labour and Victims*. Oxford: Clarendon Press.

Rock, P. (2004b). "Victims, Prosecutors and the State in Nineteenth Century England and Wales." *Criminal Justice* **4**(4): 331–354.

Rolph, C. (1958). "Wild Justice." *New Statesman*, 18 January.

Roshier, R. (1981). "The Selection of Crime News by the Press." In Cohen, S. and Young, J. (eds), *The Manufacture of News: Deviance, Social Problems and the Mass Media*. London: Constable.

SAMM. (2005). *Report and Financial Statements*. London: SAMM.

Savage, S., Grieve, J. and Poyser. (2007). "Putting Wrongs to Right: Campaigns against Miscarriages of Justice." *Criminology & Criminal Justice* **7**(1): 83–105.

Saward, J. (1990). *Rape: My Story*. London: Bloomsbury.

Select Committee on Public Prosecutors. (1855). *Report*. London: House of Commons.

Soothill, K. and Walby, S. (1991). *Sex Crime in the News*. London: Routledge.

Van Dijk, J. (2006). "The Mark of Abel: Reflections on the Social Labelling of Victims of Crime." Unpublished Inaugural Lecture delivered at the University of Tilburg.

Walker, A., Kershaw, C. and Nicholas, S. (2006). *Crime in England and Wales 2005/06*. London: Home Office.

Waller, I. and Okihiro, N. (1978). *Burglary: The Victim and the Public*. Toronto: University of Toronto Press.

Young, J. (1971). *The Drugtakers*. London: MacGibbon and Kee.

Name Index